ACCELERATING **POVERTY REDUCTION** IN AFRICA

ACCELERATING **POVERTY REDUCTION** IN AFRICA

Kathleen Beegle
Luc Christiaensen
Editors

1 2 3 4 22 21 20 19

ISBN (paper): 978-1-4648-1232-3
ISBN (electronic): 978-1-4648-1233-0
DOI: 10.1596/978-1-4648-1232-3

Cover art: Courtesy of Leen Boon. Used with the permission of Leen Boon; further permission required for reuse.
Cover design: Bill Pragluski, Critical Stages, LLC.

Library of Congress Cataloging-in-Publication Data has been requested.

Contents

Boxes

Figures

Maps

Tables

Foreword

Our goal is a world free of poverty. To get there, we must accelerate poverty reduction in Africa. Although the share of Africa's population living in extreme poverty has come down substantially, from 54 percent in 1990 to 41 percent in 2015, more Africans are living in poverty today than in 1990, in part because of population growth. In fact, the world's poor are increasingly concentrated in Africa.

Tackling this challenge begins with being able to measure it robustly. Following *Poverty in a Rising Africa*—the precursor to this report, which mapped the data landscape—efforts to improve Africa's poverty data are starting to pay off. More and better household surveys are now available to track and analyze poverty. And Africa's Statistical Capacity Indicator—which grades country statistical systems on the quality, frequency, and timeliness of core economic and social data—has been improving.

The key features of Africa's poverty, and its causes, have been widely documented. But some of the challenges, such as climate change, fragility, and debt pressures, are gaining in importance. And although macroeconomic stability and growth are critical components for reducing poverty and improving well-being, they are not sufficient. Despite economic growth in Africa, the region's persistently rapid population growth, structural impediments (low human capital, persistent gender inequality, and large infrastructure deficits), and increasing reliance on natural resources continue to hold back poverty reduction.

This report revisits the challenges and opportunities to tackle Africa's poverty, drawing on the latest evidence. It focuses on the income opportunities of the poor, the policies needed to support these opportunities, and the resources needed to finance pro-poor investments. A pro-poor agenda means generating more formal jobs while working to increase the incomes of smallholder farmers and informal workers in secondary towns and strengthening their capacity to manage risks. This approach is how the poor will likely benefit the most.

The report advances a poverty-reduction agenda for Africa that rests on four pillars: accelerating Africa's fertility transition; leveraging the food system, both on and off the farm; mitigating fragility; and addressing the poverty financing gap. The report further calls for integrated approaches in these areas—simultaneously addressing supply- and demand-side constraints—and highlights the promise of technological leapfrogging for poverty reduction in Africa.

The World Bank is committed to helping Africa build a better future for its people and to alleviating poverty in all its forms. Through comprehensive data and analysis, we are able to paint a more accurate picture of both the complexity of the issue and how best to address it. Thanks to this report, we are one step closer to achieving our twin goals of eradicating extreme poverty and boosting shared prosperity.

Hafez Ghanem
Vice President, Africa Region
The World Bank

Acknowledgments

This report has been prepared by a team led by Kathleen Beegle and Luc Christiaensen, with a core team comprising Tom Bundervoet, Alejandro de la Fuente, Lionel Demery, Patrick Eozenou, Isis Gaddis, Ruth Hill, Siddhartha Raja, Joachim Vandercasteelen, Philip Verwimp, and Eleni Yitbarek. Georgina Maku Cobla, Moctar N'Diaye, and Kwame Twumasi-Ankrah served as research assistants. Thomas Sohnesen also contributed.

The team is grateful to Albert Zeufack for his overall guidance throughout the process. The team has also benefited greatly from extensive consultations, discussions, and suggestions involving many colleagues throughout the preparation of the report. These include the inputs and guidance on specific chapters from Javier Baez, Umberto Cattaneo, Nabil Chaherli, Daniel Clarke, David Coady, Aline Coudouel, Julie Dana, Chris Delgado, Sunita Dubey, Patrick Eozenou, Louise Fox, Ugo Gentilini, Stephane Hallegatte, Bernard Haven, Ruth Hill, Gabriela Inchauste, Jon Jellema, Nora Lustig, Rose Mungai, Nga Thi Viet Nguyen, Nadia Piffaretti, Marco Ranzani, Emmanuel Skoufias, Andre Marie Taptue, and Dominique van de Walle. And we thank Nga Thi Viet Nguyen for her analysis on direct dividend payments. The team received valuable cross-cutting advice and inputs from Andrew Dabalen, Markus Goldstein, and Johannes Hoogeveen.

The team benefited from feedback from participants at workshops and presentations at the African Center for Economic Transformation (ACET) in Accra, Ghana; the ACET African Transformation Forum in 2018; the Centre for Social Policy Studies (CSPS) Second International Conference at the University of Ghana in 2018; the Households in Conflict Network (HiCN) 13th Annual Workshop in 2017; the International Union for the Scientific Study of Population (IUSSP) International Population Conference in Cape Town in 2017; the United Nations University-World Institute for Development Economics Research (UNU-WIDER) Think Development Conference in 2018; and the University of Guelph, Ontario.

The thoughtful comments of the peer reviewers—Stephan Klasen, Peter Lanjouw, Jacques Morisset, and an anonymous reviewer—are greatly appreciated.

This task received financial support from the Office of the Chief Economist of the World Bank Group's Africa Region.

The findings, interpretations, and conclusions are those of the authors and do not necessarily reflect the views of management, the reviewers, and other colleagues consulted or engaged in the preparation of the report.

About the Editors and Contributors

Kathleen Beegle is a lead economist in the World Bank's Gender Group. She was previously a human development program leader based in Accra, Ghana, covering Ghana, Liberia, and Sierra Leone. She co-led the World Bank regional studies *Realizing the Full Potential of Social Safety Nets in Africa* (2018) and *Poverty in a Rising Africa* (2016) and was deputy director of *World Development Report 2013: Jobs*. As part of the World Bank's Research Group for more than a decade, Kathleen's research focused on poverty, labor, and economic shocks. She was also a lead member of the World Bank Living Standards Measurement Study team, where she led the design and implementation of national household surveys, as well as methodological studies on survey design. Before joining the World Bank, she worked at RAND Corporation. Kathleen holds a doctorate in economics from Michigan State University.

Tom Bundervoet is a senior economist in the World Bank's Poverty and Equity Global Practice, based in Addis Ababa, Ethiopia, and previously in Rwanda. His work focuses on policy analysis of poverty, employment, and human development. He also leads or co-leads several lending operations in statistical capacity building and urban social protection. Before joining the World Bank in 2012, Tom worked in humanitarian environments in Burundi and the Democratic Republic of Congo. Prior to that, he was engaged as an academic in Belgium. Tom has a doctorate in economics from the University of Brussels and has published his research in several peer-reviewed academic journals.

Luc Christiaensen is a lead agricultural economist in the World Bank's Jobs Group. He has written extensively on poverty, structural transformation, and secondary towns in Africa and East Asia. He led the team that produced *Agriculture in Africa: Telling Myths from Facts* and was a core member of the team for the *World Development Report 2008: Agriculture for Development*. He also co-led the World Bank regional study, *Poverty in a Rising Africa*, the precursor to this report. He was a Senior Research Fellow at UNU-WIDER in Helsinki, Finland, during 2009–10. He is an honorary research fellow at the Maastricht School of Management and the Catholic University of Leuven. Luc holds a PhD in agricultural economics from Cornell University.

Alejandro de la Fuente is a senior economist in the World Bank's Poverty and Equity Global Practice. His current work involves providing policy advice and operational and technical support on poverty analysis, food and nutrition security, and program evaluation to Liberia and Sierra Leone. Previously, he worked on similar issues in Malawi, Zambia, and Zimbabwe. He has also worked on and led projects on poverty, natural disasters, and weather insurance in countries in East Asia and Latin America and the Caribbean. Before joining the World Bank, Alejandro worked for the Human Development Report Office at the United Nations Development Programme, the International Strategy for Risk Reduction Secretariat of the United Nations Office for Disaster Risk Reduction, the Inter-American Development Bank, and in various positions at the Ministry of Social Development and the Office of the President in Mexico. He holds a doctorate in development studies and development economics from Oxford University.

Lionel Demery is an independent consultant, specializing in development economics. Previously, he was a lead economist in the Africa Region of the World Bank. He has taught in the economics departments of the University of Warwick and University College Cardiff. He has also worked for the International Labour Organization in Bangkok and the Overseas Development Institute in London. He has published widely, focusing recently on poverty in Africa. Lionel holds a master's degree from the London School of Economics.

Patrick Eozenou is a senior economist at the World Bank in the Health, Nutrition, and Population Global Practice. He has more than 10 years of experience in development economics, microeconomics, and health economics, with a strong focus on Sub-Saharan Africa. Before joining the World Bank, Patrick was a postdoctoral fellow at the International Food Policy Research Institute (IFPRI) in Washington, DC. His current work focuses on health equity and health financing. Patrick has published in the *British Journal of Nutrition*, *Health Affairs*, *Journal of Development Economics*, *Journal of Development Studies*, *The Lancet Global Health*, *Oxford Review of Economic Policy*, and *PLoS Medicine*. He holds a doctorate in economics from the European University Institute in Florence.

Isis Gaddis is a senior economist in the World Bank's Gender Group. She was previously based in Dar es Salaam, working as a poverty economist for Tanzania. Isis was a member of the core team for the *Poverty and Shared Prosperity* (World Bank 2018) report and coauthored the regional study, *Poverty in a Rising Africa* (World Bank 2016). Her main research interest is empirical microeconomics, with a focus on the measurement and analysis of poverty and inequality, gender, labor, and public service delivery. She holds a doctorate in economics from the University of Göttingen, where she was a member of the development economics research group from 2006 to 2012.

Ruth Hill is a lead economist and the global lead for the spatial and structural transformation global solutions group in the World Bank's Poverty & Equity Global Practice. Previously, she was a senior economist in the South Asia region working on Bangladesh and Nepal and, before that, Ethiopia, Somalia, and Uganda. In addition to conducting analytical work on poverty and labor markets, she co-led the World Bank's Systematic Country Diagnostics for Nepal and Ethiopia, as well as the Ethiopian Urban Productive Safety Net Program. Before joining the World Bank in 2013, she was a senior research fellow at IFPRI. Ruth has published in the *American Journal of Agricultural*

Economics, *Economic Development and Cultural Change*, *Experimental Economics*, *Journal of Development Economics*, *World Bank Economic Review*, and *World Development*. She received her doctorate in economics from the University of Oxford.

Siddhartha Raja is a senior digital development specialist with the World Bank Group. He works with governments across Asia and Europe to connect more people to information, markets, and public services. Siddhartha's work has led to the expansion of broadband connectivity, to people developing their digital skills and working online, to public agencies getting online to deliver services to more people, and to exponential improvements in international connectivity in countries across Europe and Asia. He has published regularly with the World Bank on telecommunications policy and the future of work. Siddhartha has a bachelor's degree in telecommunications engineering from the University of Bombay and a master's degree in infrastructure policy studies from Stanford University. He has studied media law and policy at the University of Oxford and has a doctorate in telecommunications policy from the University of Illinois.

Joachim Vandercasteelen is an independent consultant and a postdoctoral fellow at the LICOS Centre for Institutions and Economic Performance at the University of Leuven (KU Leuven), Belgium. Currently, he is working on the impact evaluation of different value chain interventions in the agricultural subsectors of Côte d'Ivoire, Ethiopia, and Tanzania. He is working as a consultant for the World Bank, the World Food Programme, IFPRI, and the Weather Index-Based Risk Services (WINnERS) project based at Imperial College London. His research interests include themes crossing rural development and agricultural economics. Joachim holds a doctorate in economics from KU Leuven.

Philip Verwimp is a professor of development economics at Université Libre de Bruxelles, where he teaches in the Solvay Brussels School of Economics and Management; he is also a fellow at the European Center for Advanced Research in Economics and Statistics (ECARES). Philip is cofounder and codirector of the Households in Conflict Network (HiCN), which undertakes collaborative research into the causes and effects of violent conflict at the household level. Between 1999 and 2017, he spent 30 months of field work in Burundi, Ethiopia, Morocco, Rwanda, and Tanzania. Philip has offered policy advice and worked on reports for the World Bank and the United Nations Children's Fund (UNICEF), as well as various countries' ministries of foreign affairs. He has 30 peer-reviewed publications on the economics of conflict, poverty and undernutrition, child health and education, political economy, and migration in leading journals, including the *American Economic Review*, *Economic Development and Cultural Change*, *Journal of Conflict Resolution*, *Journal of Development Economics*, *Journal of Human Resources*, and *World Bank Economic Review*. Philip's academic studies have encompassed economics, sociology, and political science at the University of Antwerp (bachelor's degree), KU Leuven (bachelor's and master's degrees), University of Göttingen (master's degree), and Yale University (predoctoral work). He was a postdoctoral fellow at Yale with a Fulbright Fellowship and a visiting researcher at the University of California, Berkeley. He obtained his doctorate in development economics at KU Leuven, with a dissertation on the political economy of development and genocide in Rwanda.

Eleni Yitbarek is a postdoctoral research fellow at the University of Pretoria and a fellow in applied development finance at the European Investment Bank and Global Development Network. Eleni's research focuses on applied research in poverty dynamics, the socioeconomic effects of idiosyncratic and transient shocks, and gender-based social mobility in Africa. Eleni was a World Bank Africa Fellow while in graduate school. Before pursuing her doctorate, Eleni worked for the National Bank of Ethiopia and the Netherlands Development Organisation (SNV). She has a master's degree from Maastricht University in public policy and human development, specializing in social policy financing, and earned her doctorate in economics from Maastricht University.

Abbreviations

AEP	agroecological potential
AGI	Adolescent Girls Initiative
APG	aggregate poverty gap
ARC	Africa Risk Capacity
ATAF	African Tax Administration Forum
BEPS	Base Erosion and Profit Shifting
BIG	basic income guarantee
CAADP	Comprehensive Africa Agriculture Development Programme
Cat DDO	Catastrophe Deferred Drawdown Option
CEQ	Commitment to Equity
CO_2	carbon dioxide
DAC	Development Assistance Committee (of the OECD)
DC	direct current
DDP	direct dividend payment
DDR	disarmament, demobilization, and reintegration
DHS	Demographic and Health Survey
EC	Establishment Census
ECOWAS	Economic Community of West African States
EFA	Education for All
EITI	Extractive Industries Transparency Initiative
EU	European Union
FDI	foreign direct investment
FGP	fiscal gains to the poor
FI	fiscal impoverishment
FIA	fiscal incidence analysis
FISP	Farm Input Subsidy Program
FIV	flexible input voucher
FMNR	farmer-managed natural regeneration
GDP	gross domestic product
GER	gross enrollment rate

GIS	geographic information system
GNI	gross national income
GSMA	Global System for Mobile Association
HIV/AIDS	human immunodeficiency virus/acquired immune deficiency syndrome
HSNP	Hunger Safety Net Program
ICT	information and communication technology
ICTD	International Centre for Tax and Development
IDA	International Development Association (of the World Bank Group)
IDP	internally displaced person
ILO	International Labour Organization
IMF	International Monetary Fund
IPCC	Intergovernmental Panel on Climate Change
IRS	indoor residual spraying
ITN	insecticide-treated bed net
LDCs	least developed countries
LED	light-emitting diode
LIC	low-income country
LSMS-ISA	Living Standards Measurement Study-Integrated Surveys on Agriculture
MA	market access
MDG	Millennium Development Goal
MIC	middle-income country
MSMEs	micro, small, and medium enterprises
MVP	Millennium Villages Project
NCD	noncommunicable disease
NEET	not in employment, education, or training
NFE	nonfarm enterprise
NGO	nongovernmental organization
NRA	nominal rate of assistance
NRP	nominal rate of protection
NSDS	National Strategies for the Development of Statistics
ODA	official development assistance
OECD	Organisation for Economic Co-operation and Development
PEF	Pandemic Emergency Fund
P4P	Purchase for Progress
PPP	purchasing power parity
PV	photovoltaic
R&D	research and development
RFID	radio frequency identification
RRA	relative rate of assistance
SARA	semiautonomous revenue authority
SCI	Statistical Capacity Indicator
SDG	Sustainable Development Goal
SDI	Service Delivery Indicators
SEZ	special economic zone
SIGI	Social Institutions and Gender Index
SMEs	small and medium enterprises
SMS	short message service
SPEED	Statistics on Public Expenditures for Economic Development
SPS	sanitary and phytosanitary
STEM	science, technology, engineering, and mathematics

TFP	total factor productivity
TFR	total fertility rate
UN	United Nations
UNCTAD	United Nations Conference on Trade and Development
UNU-WIDER	United Nations University-World Institute for Development Economics Research
VAT	value added tax
VCD	value chain development
WASH	water, sanitation, and hygiene
WFP	World Food Programme

Currencies

CFAF	CFA franc
R	South African rand
RF	Rwanda franc
U Sh	Uganda shilling

Key Messages

Poverty in Africa Today and Tomorrow

- Poverty in Africa has fallen substantially—from 54 percent in 1990 to 41 percent in 2015—but the number of poor has increased, from 278 million in 1990 to 413 million in 2015.
- Under a business-as-usual scenario, the poverty rate is expected to decline to 23 percent by 2030, rendering global poverty primarily an African phenomenon.

Main Features of African Poverty

- Most of the poor (82 percent) live in rural areas, earning their living primarily in farming. Nonwage microenterprises are the main source of nonagricultural employment and income for the poor and near poor. Strikingly, rural poverty is higher in areas with better agroecological potential.
- Poverty is a mix of chronic and transitory poverty. Fragile and conflict-affected states have notably higher poverty rates.
- Low human capital and high gender inequality impede poverty-reduction efforts.

Four Primary Areas for Policy Action

- *Accelerate the fertility transition.* Rapid population growth and high fertility are features of many countries on the continent. They hold back poverty reduction through multiple channels. Family planning programs will play an important, cost-effective role in accelerating the fertility transition, which will complement the effect of increasing female education, and empowering women (including by offering life skills, addressing social norms around gender, and reducing child marriage).
- *Leverage the food system.* Raising smallholder agricultural productivity, especially in staple crops, increases the incomes of the poor directly and addresses rising urban demand for higher-value agricultural products. Complementary public investment (in agricultural research and extension, irrigation, and rural infrastructure) remains key. Inclusive value chain development and technological leapfrogging can bring previously unattainable markets and production techniques (such as irrigation and mechanization) within reach of the poor.
- *Mitigate fragility.* Uninsured risks and conflict entrap people or push them back into poverty. Many risk management solutions already exist, with roles for both the private and public sectors, but an important hurdle remains incentivizing the public and private actors to act now, before the shocks and conflict occur.
- *Address the poverty financing gap.* More, and more efficient, public financing focused on the poor is needed to finance this poverty-reduction policy agenda. In addition to the continued need for official development assistance (ODA), domestic tax compliance and international tax avoidance need to be addressed, as well as making public spending more pro-poor and more efficient. This is especially important in resource-rich countries, where poverty reduction and human development indicators are often relatively worse.

Overview

Poverty Reduction in Africa: A Global Agenda

Africa's turnaround over the past couple of decades has been dramatic.[1] After many years in decline, the continent's economy picked up in the mid-1990s, expanding at a robust annual average of 4.5 percent into the early 2010s. People became healthier and better nourished, youngsters attended schools in much greater numbers, and the poverty rate declined from 54 percent in 1990 to 41 percent in 2015 (World Bank 2018c). The region has also benefited from decreased conflict (although simmering in some countries and notwithstanding pressing numbers of displaced persons), an expansion of political and social freedoms, and progress in the legal status of women (Hallward-Driemeier, Hasan, and Rusu 2013; World Bank 2019b). The availability and quality of poverty data to record this progress have also improved.

Despite these accomplishments—described in detail in the precursor to this report, *Poverty in a Rising Africa* (Beegle et al. 2016)—the poverty and shared prosperity challenges remain daunting: Poverty rates in many African countries are the highest in the world and are forecast to continue to be in double digits. Slowing economic growth in recent years has also slowed poverty reduction. And notably, the number of poor in Africa is rising (from 278 million in 1990 to 413 million in 2015), in part because of high population growth (World Bank 2018c). Africa will not reach the United Nations Sustainable Development Goal (SDG) of eradicating poverty by 2030.[2]

Globally, there is a shifting concentration of poverty from South Asia to Africa. Forecasts suggest that poverty will soon become a predominantly African phenomenon. The nonmonetary dimensions of poverty (nutritional and health status, literacy, personal security, empowerment), while improving, are still the lowest in the world in many countries (Beegle et al. 2016). The world's bifurcating demography, inequality and climate change, and the resulting migratory pressures, add further global interest to address poverty in Africa. But the rapid spread of digital technologies and solar power and increasing South-South trade also provide new opportunities to tackle this pressing challenge (Dixit, Gill, and Kumar 2018; Gill and Karakülah 2018; World Bank 2019a). How Africa can accelerate its poverty reduction is now a global preoccupation—and the focus of this report.

Of course, Africa comprises many countries with quite varying poverty rates and divergent socioeconomic and agroecological conditions. Half of Africa's poor live in 5 countries; 10 countries account for 75 percent of Africa's poor.[3] Yet the poorest countries, and regions within countries (those with the highest poverty rates), are not necessarily the same countries or regions housing most of the poor. This poses a challenge as to where to target the poverty-reduction efforts, at least from a global perspective.

Fragility and resource abundance are key country features to account for in the design of poverty-reduction policies. Historically, neglect of regions and countries with high poverty rates, even when not densely populated, has often bred conflict, which easily spreads to the surrounding areas. Fragile and conflict-affected states have notably higher poverty rates as well as the slowest poverty reduction, even long after the conflict ended. This pattern emphasizes the debilitating role that conflict plays in improving well-being as well as the critical importance of tackling poverty in fragile states to advance Africa's poverty agenda.

Many African countries depend heavily on natural resources. Resource dependence has only grown since the commodity boom of the 1990s and 2000s (figure O.1) and is increasingly the environment within which Africa's poverty reduction must take place. Yet, resource dependence often undermines institutional quality and erodes long-run growth potential and poverty reduction. Spending on human capital in these countries, and the efficiency of that spending, is systematically lower than in non-resource-dependent countries (de la Brière et al. 2017). In extreme cases, resource abundance may even lead to conflict (Collier and Hoffler 2004).

FIGURE O.1 Natural resource dependence has increased substantially in most African countries

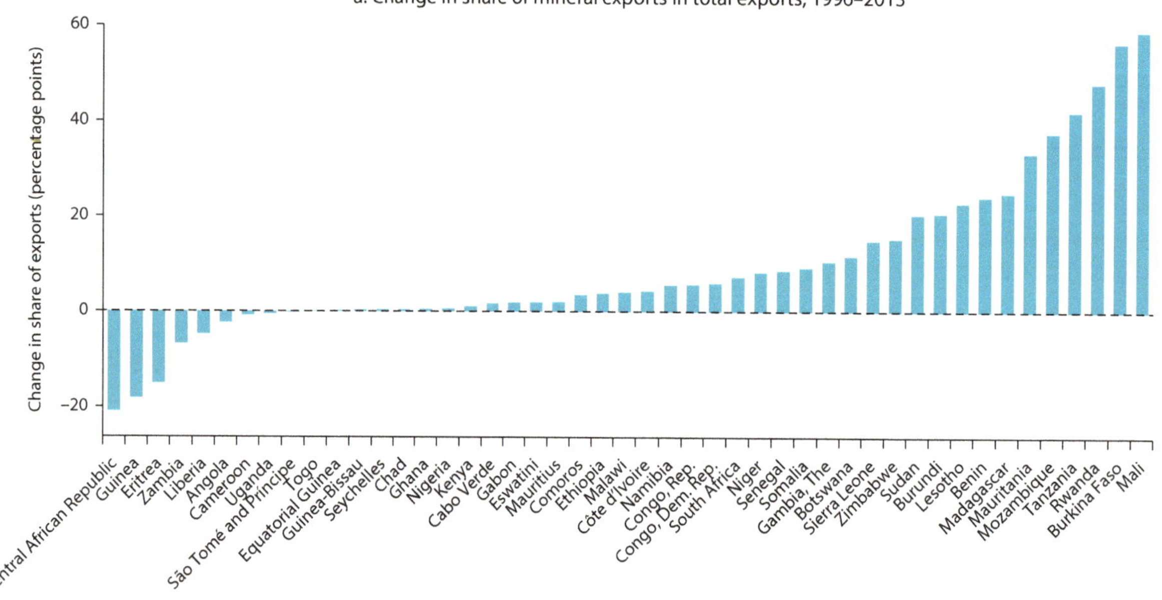

(Figure continues next page)

FIGURE O.1 Natural resource dependence has increased substantially in most African countries *(continued)*

b. Change in share of oil and gas exports in total exports, 1996–2013

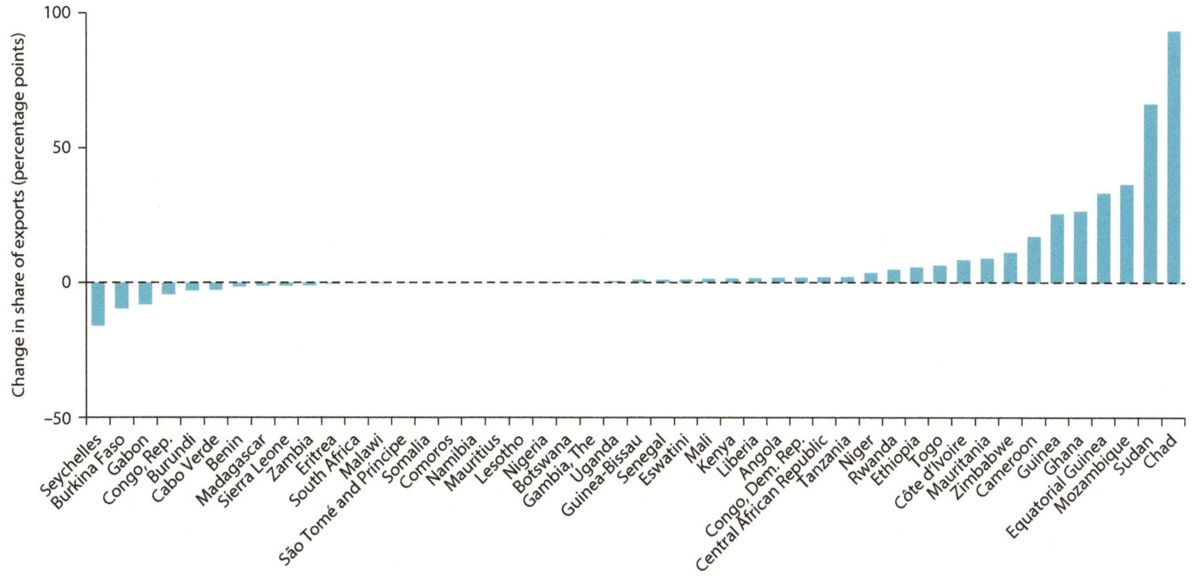

Source: Calculations based on United Nations Conference on Trade and Development (UNCTAD) data.
Note: There is a close correlation between the export and government revenue shares of natural resources. Data on the latter, although arguably the better indicator of resource dependence, are patchy.

Poverty in Africa: Stylized Facts

Across countries, poverty manifests itself also in many similar ways. First, poverty remains predominantly rural—82 percent of Africa's poor are rural—with the poor earning their living primarily in farming or, when working off the farm, in agriculture-related activities (Allen, Heinrigs, and Heo 2018; Beegle et al. 2016; Castañeda et al. 2018). Although this does not mean the solution lies automatically in agricultural or rural development, it does indicate a policy entry point—either to reinforce the income-earning opportunities of the poor in situ or to help them connect with income-earning opportunities elsewhere.

Second, poverty is a mix of chronic and transitory: about 60 percent of Africa's poor are chronically poor, and 40 percent are in transitory poverty. Therefore, asset building and the generation of income opportunities as well as effective risk management strategies are both important for poverty reduction. They often also interact with each other.

Third, about half of Africa's poor are younger than 15 years old, showing the need for greater attention to reach children. Measured gender gaps in monetary poverty are modest, though the data underpinning these numbers assume equal sharing in households. Numerous other nonmonetary indicators show large structural gender inequalities.

Fourth, the poor have weak links to the state. They have weak access to good-quality public goods (infrastructure) and services, and they have limited voice in public policy making.

Moreover, Africa's poverty rate has not only been higher than in most other low- and middle-income countries; it has also declined more slowly.

Africa's Slower Poverty Reduction

Three notable factors have contributed to Africa's slower poverty reduction:

- *Persistently high fertility and population growth.* Although Africa's gross domestic product (GDP) growth has been robust over the past couple of decades (except in recent years), economic output has grown more slowly in per capita terms than in other low- and middle-income countries. African countries' higher fertility and faster population growth have left their populations with much lower income per person.
- *Poor initial conditions.* Less of Africa's (rather modest) per capita household income growth has translated into poverty reduction than in other countries, simply because of the high initial poverty in the region. The lack of assets and access to public goods and services, as well as the limited availability of good income-earning opportunities for a large share of the population, limit the ability of many to contribute to and participate in economic growth. It is poverty, rather than inequality per se, that has been holding back poverty reduction in many African countries. When compared with other equally poor countries in other regions, African countries have not been less effective at converting per capita household income growth into poverty reduction.
- *The composition of Africa's growth.* Africa's poverty reduction has been slower because of the composition of Africa's growth—in particular, the increasing reliance on natural resources and the modest performance of its agriculture and manufacturing sectors.

Accelerating the fertility transition, addressing key facets of Africa's poor initial conditions, and shifting to a pro-poor growth and policy agenda will go a long way toward accelerating poverty reduction.

High Fertility, Slow Poverty Reduction

At 2.7 percent per year on average, rapid population growth remains a defining feature for many countries on the continent. It follows from continuing high fertility (5.1 children per woman in 2010–15 compared with 6.7 in 1950–55) despite a rapid decline in under-five child mortality (from 307 deaths per thousand in 1950–55 to 91 in 2010–15) (World Bank 2019c). High population growth poses a substantial burden on African governments, families, and especially women through several channels. It elevates the fiscal needs for social services, which only pay off much later. High fertility has also been an important direct contributor to Africa's explosive urban growth, not simply the result of rural-urban migration (Jedwab, Christiaensen, and Gindelsky 2017). Rapid urban growth makes it hard for urban centers to keep up the infrastructure base to remain productive, create employment, and be an effective force for poverty reduction (Lall, Henderson, and Venables 2017).

With rural populations often clustered on a small share of the arable rural land, high population growth is further increasing land pressures in several African countries, without concomitant agricultural intensification to compensate thus far (Jayne, Chamberlin, and Headey 2014). And, not least, the burden on women of care and domestic work increases with more children and reduces their income-earning opportunities. This is especially hard on poor women, who often begin childbearing at much younger ages and also have more children (on average at least twice as many [5–7] as women in wealthy households).

Fertility reduction, on the other hand, is associated with faster economic growth (the demographic dividend) and faster poverty reduction. A 1 percent fall in the dependency rate is associated with a 0.75 percentage point fall in headcount poverty (Cruz and Ahmed 2016). Accelerating fertility reduction is therefore an important entry point for accelerating Africa's poverty reduction. Africa's fertility rate per woman of childbearing age is, on average, one birth higher than in other least developed countries (LDCs), controlling for conventional demographic and socioeconomic factors (figure O.2) (Bongaarts 2017).

In addition to female education, much greater attention to family planning programming is needed. Outside Africa the average number of unwanted births per woman of childbearing age has decreased from one to zero over the past couple of decades. In Africa it has remained at two (Günther and Harttgen 2016), suggesting a large latent demand for contraception. Limited provision and poor implementation of family planning programs explains much of the delayed decline in Africa's fertility rate (de Silva and Tenreyro 2017). Other entry points to accelerate the demographic transition include empowering women, including providing life skills for women and girls, addressing social gender norms, and focusing on child marriage.

FIGURE O.2 In Africa, fertility is less responsive to conventional parameters of development than in other LDCs

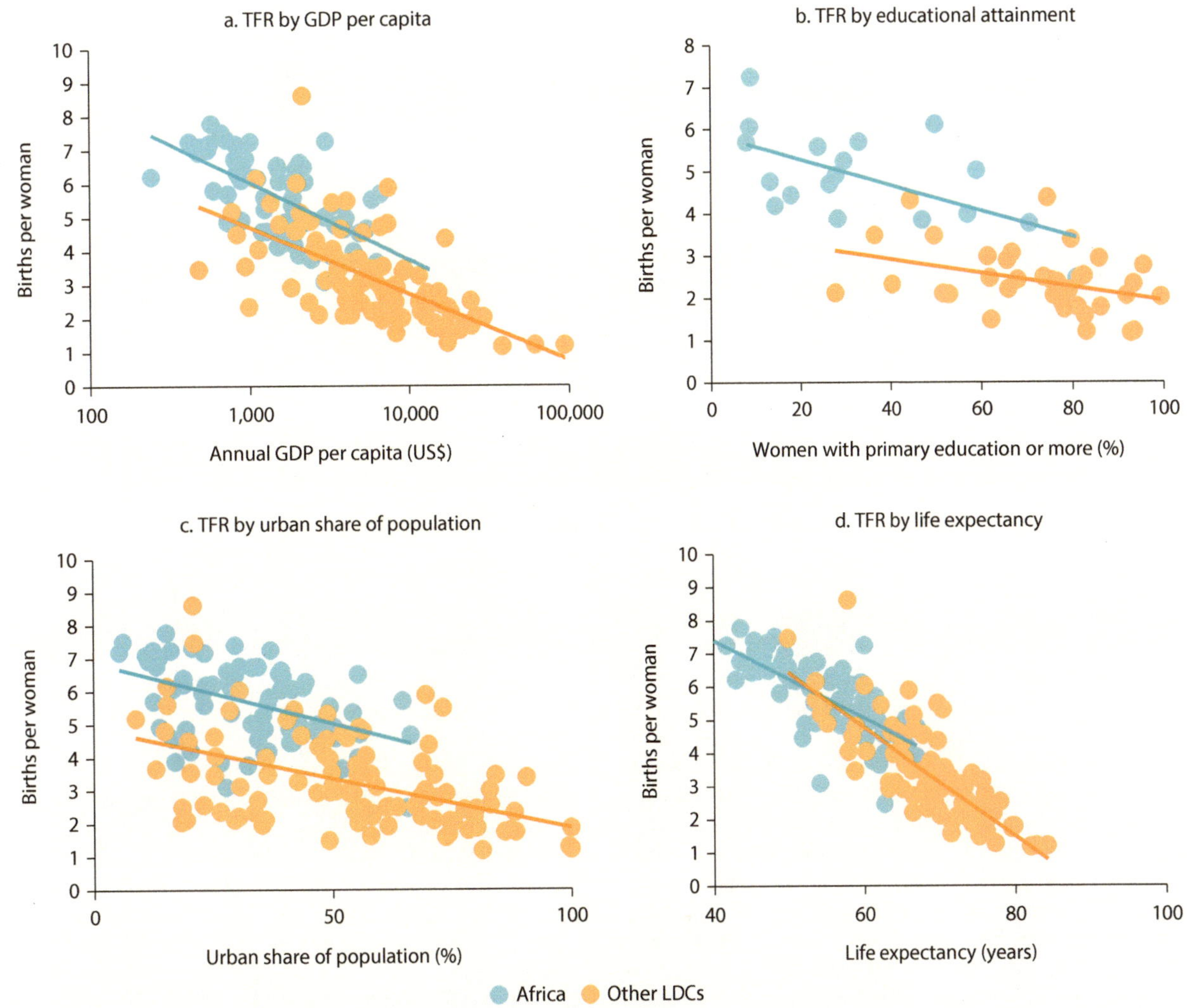

Source: World Bank calculations, adapted from Bongaarts (2017), using latest data from the World Development Indicators 2019 database.
Note: LDCs = least developed countries (as defined by the United Nations Committee for Development Policy); TFR = total fertility rate (total number of children born to a woman in her lifetime). Data used are for the years 1990 and 2018. Last available year chosen when data were missing.

Poor Initial Conditions

Poor initial conditions also hold Africa back in addressing poverty. These include not only the low levels of human capital and access to infrastructure but also the more deep-seated structural impediments such as natural resource dependence (discussed earlier), gender inequality, and social redistributive pressures.

At the individual level, poor educational attainment reduces the prospect of escaping poverty.[4] Where the gap in educational attainment is large, as in much of Africa, much growth and poverty reduction can already be expected from widespread, quality basic education (box O.1). A severe lack of infrastructure exacerbates things. The low returns to the poor's land, labor, and skills arise partly also from their inability to access and afford information and communication technology, energy, and transport services (Christiaensen, Demery, and Paternostro 2003; Grimm et al. 2017; James 2016). More recent insights on the psychology of poverty further show how the lack of human capital, physical assets, and access to basic infrastructure not only reduce the earning capacity of the poor but also tax their mental "bandwidth" and undermine their ability to plan, exercise self-control, and aspire—behaviors associated with escaping poverty (Haushofer and Fehr 2014; World Bank 2015).

Gender inequality also drives poorer economic growth outcomes by reducing total factor productivity—in addition to its influence on gender gaps in education, employment, and governance (Ferrant and Kolev 2016). This is particularly the case in low-income countries. Dismantling gender-based discrimination in social institutions could increase global growth by as much as 0.6 percentage points per year over the next 15 years (Branisa, Klasen, and Ziegler 2009, 2013, 2014; Yoon and Klasen 2018). Reducing gender gaps would also raise the growth prospects of African economies—and hence also reduce poverty (box O.2).

Finally, with poverty widespread, shocks frequent, and insurance absent, people often hold back from investing for fear of redistributive consequences (Platteau 2014).

More and Better Jobs for the Poor

Finally, the scope and need for pro-poor growth policies to accelerate poverty reduction in Africa is large. Although Africa will not be able to eradicate poverty by 2030,

BOX O.1 Investments in human capital are critical to alleviate poverty

Human capital investments yield substantial long-run benefits and are critical in the agenda to reduce poverty in Africa. A range of evidence shows that children who have a disadvantaged start in life face a greater lifelong risk of being trapped in poverty. A human development trap initiates a cycle of poverty that runs across generations and traps families in poverty (for example, low education and poor health result in low adult income, poor human development for children, and so on) (Bhalotra and Rawlings 2013; Bhutta et al. 2013; Victora et al. 2008). Because the economic benefits of public investments in human development are realized far into the future (a decade or longer), they may lack appeal to governments, given the many immediate demands on public finances.

Raising human capital in Africa is a pressing issue, and more so for the poorest. Children in poor households have worse childhood outcomes across many dimensions of well-being. The scale of undernutrition in Africa is staggering, with children in poor households having much higher rates (World Bank 2018b). And poor children (and poor parents) in Africa have starkly unequal access to critical services that influence children's health. Although universal education access has greatly shrunk the enrollment gap between poor and nonpoor children at least at the primary level, poor children are learning much less than their peers in nonpoor households (World Bank 2018d).

BOX O.2 Gender inequality is a hurdle to poverty reduction in Africa

African women continue to encounter disadvantages in education, health, empowerment, and income-generating activities. They tend to have significantly lower human capital endowments than men (although, among the youngest cohort, this gap has narrowed, with girls having caught up to boys in some countries); worse access to labor markets; lower wages; more limited access or title to productive assets (such as land, credit, and other inputs); fewer political and legal rights; and more stringent constraints on mobility and socially acceptable activities. As a result, gender inequality can trap women in poverty and generate a vicious cycle for their children.

Beyond the intrinsic value of equal opportunities, gender equality will bring with it economic growth and greater poverty reduction for countries. Four entry points to reap the economic returns from closing gender gaps include the following (Klasen 2006):

- A growth strategy that raises the demand for female labor (such as the export-led growth strategies of East Asia)
- Addressing gender gaps in education, especially in poorer households where school enrollment rates tend to be much lower than in the rest of the population
- Actions to improve women's access to productive assets—more secure property rights and access to land as well as better access to credit, modern inputs, and other means of production (including land)
- Policies that help poorer couples reduce their fertility.

the poverty projections show that 50 million more people could be lifted out of poverty by then if the incomes of the poor were to grow 2 percentage points faster annually (while keeping constant each country's historical per capita annual growth rate over the past 15 years) (Cattaneo 2017). Combined with lower population growth and addressing poor initial conditions, pro-poor growth—growth whereby the incomes of the poor also grow substantially as the economy develops—will go a long way in accelerating poverty reduction now and in the future.

A pro-poor policy agenda requires getting the growth fundamentals right as well as increasing growth where the poor work and live (so that they can contribute and benefit directly), while addressing the many risks to which households are exposed. With the scope for redistribution to solve Africa's poverty limited in most countries, the focus is squarely on the productivity and livelihoods of the poor and vulnerable—that is, what it will take to increase their earnings. As such, this report views its task through a "jobs" lens. This naturally focuses the report on the structural, spatial, and institutional transformations needed to raise the incomes of the poor and vulnerable, in particular, on sectoral and subsectoral policies and investments—on agriculture, on off-farm employment, and on managing risk and conflict—to broker these transformations. What these are is far from obvious, because just as not all growth policies are equally poverty reducing, neither are all agricultural growth or urbanization models equally good for the poor (Christiaensen and Kanbur 2017; Diao et al. 2012; Dorosh and Thurlow 2018; Pauw and Thurlow 2011).

Growth Fundamentals and Poverty Financing

Macroeconomic stability, regional integration and trade facilitation as well as a conducive business environment are fundamental for economic growth (Bah and Fang 2015; Sakyi et al. 2017). They also affect poverty (Antoine, Singh, and Wacker 2017; Dollar and Kraay 2002; Le Goff and Singh 2014; Rodrik 1998).

Particularly, three macroeconomic indicators have emerged as statistically important in the cross-country growth regressions:

- *The rate of price inflation*, reflecting monetary policy
- *The exchange rate*, reflecting openness to trade and other trade policies
- *The level of government consumption expenditure*, or the size of the fiscal deficit, reflecting fiscal policy.

When these indicators deteriorate, poverty is likely to rise (Antoine, Singh, and Wacker 2017; Christiaensen, Demery, and Paternostro 2003; Dollar and Kraay 2002; Rodrik 2016).

The evolution of inflation and exchange rates in Africa has been mostly favorable. Yet, rapidly rising fiscal deficits in many countries pose concern. Gross government debt in Africa increased from about 32 percent of GDP in 2012 to 56 percent of GDP in 2016. Fourteen countries were considered at high risk of debt distress at the end of 2017, compared with seven in 2012 (World Bank 2018a). Looking at debt dynamics—the growing difference between real interest and growth rates, and widening primary deficits—adds further urgency to reining in public debt (Gill and Karakülah 2018).

In addition to implementing the policy frameworks needed to broker pro-poor growth, financing the accompanying poverty-reducing investments—many of which only pay off over time, such as human capital—within a tightening fiscal space, is the other important challenge to tackle. More resource mobilization is needed as well as more, and more efficient, spending on areas important for the poor, such as health, education, agriculture (for example, extension and irrigation), and rural infrastructure. Here there is a considerable role for making maximum use of leapfrogging technologies to bring hitherto inaccessible (and traditionally expensive) communication, energy, and transport services within the reach of the poor (box O.3).

Earning More on the Farm

Leveraging Africa's food system, on and off the farm, is key to bringing poverty down and raising living standards. Agriculture has historically proven to be particularly poverty reducing, especially at low income levels (Christiaensen and Martin 2018). Rapid urbanization and income growth add opportunities for agribusiness development and employment generation in agriculture's value chains, off the farm. But not all agricultural growth is equally poverty reducing, with smallholder staple crop productivity and livestock development continuing to demand particular attention for poverty reduction. More integrated approaches are needed, leveraging the private sector through value chain development. But public investment focused on the provision of public goods (for example, irrigation) and services (for example, extension) remains equally vital, especially to boost smallholder staple crop and livestock productivity.

Favorable Conditions for Leveraging the Food System

The conditions for leveraging the food system for poverty reduction in Africa today are particularly favorable:

- Food demand is robust, though mainly driven by population growth.
- World food prices are still about 70 percent higher than before the 2008 world food crisis (40 percent in real terms).
- Urbanization and income growth add opportunities for product differentiation and value addition, and thus for off-farm employment opportunities in agribusiness.
- The domestic agricultural policy and trade environment (including intraregional) have improved.
- Political leadership remains largely supportive.

Against this background, supply has also responded. But not enough, and Africa's food import bill has still risen steeply,

BOX O.3 Leapfrogging technology holds promise for poverty reduction in Africa

Most of the poor in rural areas (and to a lesser extent in urban areas) remain deprived of access to affordable and reliable information and communication, energy, and transport infrastructure (and services). Without these, it is hard to access markets and public services, increase productivity, and raise income in either farm or off-farm activities. By reducing fixed costs and thus the traditional economies of scale in infrastructure provision, technology is helping Africa address this gap. Prepayment and per unit payment business models, facilitated by mobile-phone technology, are further bringing services within the reach of the poor. This holds great promise for poverty reduction.

Perhaps the most dramatic of these technological changes has been in telecommunication services, with 73 percent of Africa's population now having a mobile-phone subscription (World Bank 2018a). And the trend is not just about phone calls. The development of the M-Pesa mobile money application in Kenya ("M" for mobile, "pesa" for "money" in Swahili) put a rudimentary "bank account" in everyone's pocket. And Hello Tractor in Nigeria, an app for renting tractors, reduces search and matching costs, bringing the economies of scale of high-productivity, lumpy capital goods within the reach of smallholders (Jones 2018). The next frontier is widespread penetration of high-speed internet.

African rural towns and households might similarly leapfrog straight to cheap renewable electricity provided by solar panels and minigrids based on shared solar photovoltaic (PV) systems and direct current (DC) distribution lines. Tanzania has been a front-runner in the rollout of microgrid electrification programs; other countries have started to follow suit (including Kenya, Nigeria, Rwanda, and Uganda).

The poor can benefit from these leapfrogging technologies directly, as adopters, through greater access to productivity-enhancing capital goods (for example, solar power) as well as better market access to buy and sell their goods and services. But, more often than not, they mainly benefit indirectly, through the wider and cheaper availability of goods and services following adoption by others.

Importantly, however, these technologies will deliver on the promise of accelerating poverty reduction only when deliberate complementary public policies are taken in three areas: (a) the removal of barriers to the technologies' adaptation and diffusion to rural areas where the poor live and work; (b) investment in skill formation (foundational as well as digital); and (c) the creation of an appropriate enabling ecosystem to run and maintain the technologies.

by US$30 billion over the past 20 years (figure O.3). Many of these imports could be competitively produced domestically. Output growth in cassava and maize, and partly also in rice, including through yield growth, confirm the potential for a more robust supply response. Africa's rising food import bill poses a burden on the external balances and signifies an important missed opportunity. This holds even more in Africa's oil-rich countries, where public investment in agriculture is lower and poultry imports are higher.

Climate change and resurging conflict pose challenges to reap these opportunities. Yet, the expected climatic changes are not unequivocally detrimental. Maize yields, for example, are predicted to increase in the Sahel and many parts of eastern and central Africa (Jalloh et al. 2013; Waithaka et al. 2013). And agriculture also plays an important role in the prevention of conflict—which often finds its origins in climate-related agricultural shocks—as well as in the recovery of fragile states (Martin-Shields and Stojetz 2019). A climate-resilient and remunerative agriculture provides a viable alternative to illicit and mercenary activities for individuals who otherwise see a low opportunity cost to participating in conflict.

FIGURE O.3 Africa's food import bill has tripled since the mid-2000s

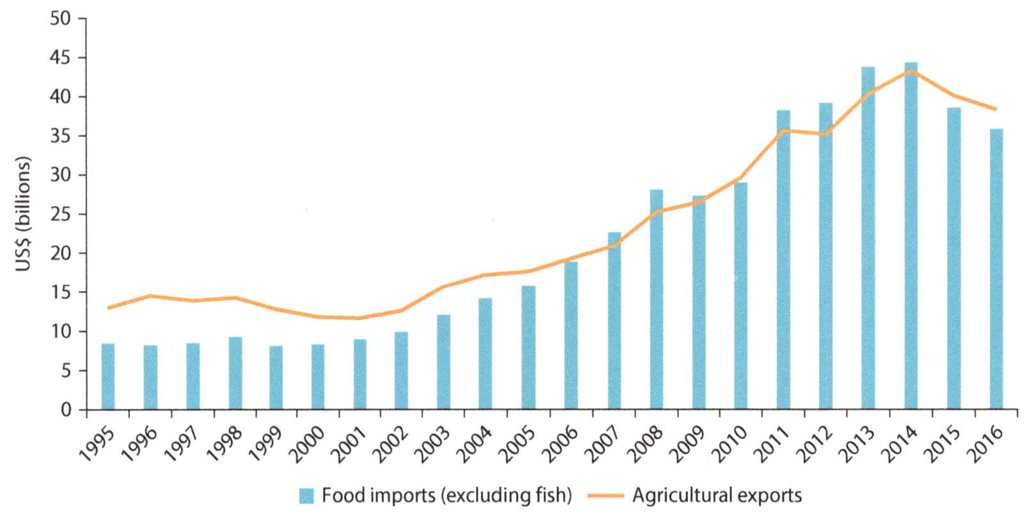

Source: FAOSTAT 2018 database, Food and Agriculture Organization (FAO), http://www.fao.org/faostat/.

Most important, brokering the supply response will require sustained political attention. The recent decline in the agricultural share of total spending to pre-2008 levels, despite declared political commitment, will need to be reversed.

Not All Agricultural Growth Is Equally Poverty Reducing

Raising smallholder staple crop productivity (the so-called Green Revolution) demands particular attention.[5] Low labor productivity in staple crops still locks many people into staple crop agriculture. Because of this, as well as more widespread income (including via the price channel) and linkage effects, raising staple crop productivity has larger growth multipliers and greater poverty-to-growth elasticities than an equal amount of productivity growth in cash crops (Diao et al. 2012).

Unfortunately, staple crops attract less public and private sector attention than cash crops, as does smallholder livestock holding, which is the second income source for many smallholders (Otte et al. 2012). Development of Africa's agricultural exports (old and new) complements the staple crop agenda. It also does not have to compete with public investment in staples, because private sector interests can be leveraged. The challenge is to balance policy attention.

Larger poverty-reducing effects come further from supporting slightly larger, commercially oriented smallholders, with the poorest and least productive farmers in the village (often also those with less land) benefiting primarily through lower food prices and the local labor markets (in and outside agriculture) (Hazell et al. 2010; Mellor 2017).

Poorer farmers may further benefit from better access to technology and inputs as well as markets. Such positive spillovers are less likely however when farms become large (more than 100 hectares) or even of medium scale (more than 10 hectares). These entities tend to use less agricultural wage labor and yield smaller local consumption linkages for the poor (that is, more of the revenues are spent on urban [and imported] goods and services) (Chamberlin and Jayne 2017;

Deininger and Xia 2016, 2018; Pauw and Thurlow 2011).

Larger ("estate") farm entities may however be needed for certain crops, to ensure consistent volumes of high-quality crops in compliance with standards to access the more-demanding export markets. Examples include labor-intensive exports of high-value fruits and vegetables, flowers, and fish. Less clear is the necessity of such an agrarian structure to supply the domestic urban markets.

An Integrated Approach Is Needed

So, what are the entry points to raise Africa's agricultural labor productivity? A myriad of input, factor, and product market constraints hold agricultural intensification back, with pockets of land scarcity emerging and the seasonality of agricultural labor calendars too often ignored. The latter often leads to underuse of agricultural labor and the perception of agriculture as an intrinsically less productive activity. This only holds, however, when agricultural labor productivity is expressed as agricultural output per worker, not when expressed per hour of work (McCullough 2017).

Mechanization and better water management can help. Less than 2 percent of the cultivated area and less than 5 percent of households in six African countries (which together cover 40 percent of Africa's population) use any form of water control (Sheahan and Barrett 2014). Small-scale, simple, affordable, self-managed irrigation systems that are rolled out at scale hold hope if access to complementary inputs and markets are developed simultaneously.

Yet, too often, singularly focused interventions are pursued, or interventions are poorly coordinated. Africa's Green Revolution, mechanization, and irrigation efforts each need an integrated approach that simultaneously addresses supply- and demand-side constraints to tackle poverty.

The experience of Ethiopia is illustrative. The government simultaneously and sustainably focused on

- *Increasing smallholder staple crop productivity* by deploying 45,000 extension agents (three per district), facilitating access to credit, and improving water and land management;
- *Improving market connectivity* through rural road investment; and
- *Providing a form of insurance* through the Productive Safety Net Program, one of the largest social protection programs in Africa.

Since the mid-1990s, smallholder cereal yields in Ethiopia have more than doubled; extreme poverty has more than halved.

Evidence from detailed microeconomic studies supports the existence of important synergies from integrated agricultural interventions (Ambler, de Brauw, and Godlonton 2018; Daidone et al. 2017; Pace et al. 2018). Yet, success of an integrated approach is not assured. With integration comes complexity, which challenges effective implementation, especially in low-capacity, poor-governance environments.

Inclusive Value Chain Development, but Also Public Goods

Value chain development (VCD), often facilitated by external agents such as governments as well as nongovernmental and international organizations, increasingly emerges as a market-based, institutional solution to simultaneously address the multiple market constraints (Swinnen and Kuijpers 2017). Smallholder farmers can be linked to higher-value domestic and export markets by (a) supplying raw agricultural products (gains stemming from reduced production and price risk, higher premium prices, and access to previously unattainable input and output markets and agronomic knowledge); or (b) indirectly through employment opportunities. Buyers gain by securing a consistent volume of high-quality crops as well as the standards compliance needed to access these markets. The poorest often benefit through localized spillovers. Horizontal coordination of smallholder farmers is often important to make value chains more inclusive. It reduces the transaction costs of involving small farmers and can increase bargaining power and thus their share of the value added.

Although VCD holds promise for traditional and new cash crops as well as for livestock and livestock products, contract enforcement is inherently more difficult in staple marketing because of the risk of either (opportunistic) side-selling by smallholders or strategic contract breach by buyers (Swinnen, Vandeplas, and Maertens 2010).[6] Experimentation with VCD for staples has begun, however, along with the growing demand for consistent volumes and quality as well as opportunities for value addition in Africa's domestic staple markets (rice and teff for urban markets, feedstock maize for livestock, barley for beer)—a space to be watched.

Nonetheless, to raise smallholder staple crop productivity, the need for public good provision remains undiminished. This requires increased public spending in agriculture, which has started to falter, as well as a shift in its composition away from private (input subsidies) to public goods, including (a) agricultural research and development (R&D) and extension for both staples and livestock, and (b) investment in irrigation and rural infrastructure. The latter also benefits the broader rural economy, and new technologies hold promise.

Moving Off the Farm: Household Enterprises

In addition to raising incomes on the farm, employment opportunities off the farm will become increasingly important as agricultural productivity and incomes rise, countries urbanize, and the demand for nonfood goods and services grows. About a third of this employment will still be linked to agriculture, up and down the value chain, in agricultural input production and provision as well as food processing, marketing, and services (Allen, Heinrigs, and Heo 2018; Tschirley et al. 2015).

Over the short to medium term, for many of Africa's poor, moving to work opportunities off the farm will largely mean moving into informal household enterprises (typically with no hired workers) but unlikely into wage employment (be it formal or informal wage work). Even in countries where wage employment is growing fast (for example, through increasingly challenged, labor-intensive exports), the low base of wage employment and the pace at which youth enter the labor force imply that wage employment will absorb only a small share of the job seekers over the coming 10–15 years.

Only a few household enterprises fall into the category of "opportunity" entrepreneurship, "constrained gazelles," or "transformational" entrepreneurs. Nonetheless, household enterprises are an important part of the broader economic transition—and a particularly important one at that for poverty reduction. They typically have low productivity, remain small and informal throughout their life cycle, are managed and operated by household members, and only a few create paid jobs for nonhousehold workers (Nagler and Naudé 2017).

These enterprises are often started from necessity. The lack of wage jobs and the absence of formal unemployment insurance push people to jump-start self-employment as a survival strategy. Therein also lies their strength for the poor. They are readily available, and with little skills and capital required, easy to enter and exit, and often critical in complementing the income, thus helping households cope and smooth consumption. They are often also an important source of cash for financing modern input purchases and thus for developing other activities (Adjognon, Liverpool-Tasie, and Reardon 2017).

The importance of the informal or semi-formal nonfarm sector as a provider of jobs and livelihoods for Africa's burgeoning labor force means it cannot be neglected by policy. The choice of focusing on the formal or informal sector or on small and medium enterprises (SMEs) and large firms or household enterprises is, however, not simply an "either-or" proposition. Investments in human capital, infrastructure, and a transparent regulatory framework will benefit the spectrum of enterprises. But not all investments cut across, and investments can also be made that more directly benefit nonfarm businesses run by poor households.

More Profitable Household Enterprises for the Poor

Because most household enterprises do not grow, they mainly create employment through entry. Available evidence suggests that job creation through entry can be achieved by relatively small amounts of financing, which can be combined with skills training, though the addition of training tends to make the interventions less cost-effective. As in agriculture, stand-alone interventions addressing one single constraint (such as skills or finance) tend to be less successful than interventions that target multiple constraints at the same time, highlighting the importance of packaging different interventions in one.

In many African countries, access to finance is difficult, especially for youth from less well-off families without collateral. Although several countries have attempted to improve access to finance, especially for the politically sensitive demographic segment of unemployed youth, financing modalities have not always been flexible enough to make a big impact (entailing short repayment periods without grace periods, high interest rates, requirements to borrow in groups, and so on). Creating jobs by facilitating entry of household enterprises will require the design of flexible and affordable financing mechanisms as part of a broader enabling environment.

To reach the poorest and most vulnerable, an emerging and promising approach is to combine safety net interventions with packages of support (including skills, finance, advisory services, working space, and so on) to facilitate entry into self-employment and raise the labor earnings of social protection beneficiaries (Banerjee et al. 2015). These combined "protection and promotion" interventions are currently being implemented on a large scale in several African countries, with ongoing impact evaluations examining their effects.

Much remains to be learned, including with respect to agricultural value chains linking SMEs with microenterprises. Few studies have focused specifically on poor or near-poor households, which may face different constraints than vocational or transformational entrepreneurs or may lack any ambition to grow their businesses in the first place. In addition, most studies have focused on urban settings, though most of Africa's poor live in rural areas.

Fostering Demand: The Roles of Towns, Regional Trading, and Digital Technology

Most interventions targeting the entry or growth of household enterprises focus on alleviating the supply-side constraints (such as finance or skills). Although these supply-side interventions can help entry into self-employment and, to some extent, increase earnings, the survival and growth of these small enterprises is ultimately determined by the demand for the goods and services they provide. Household enterprises are rarely a source of job creation beyond the household members, but data show that those better connected to markets (in urban areas and towns) and owned by a better-educated person nevertheless appear to have the ability to grow and hire workers (Nagler 2017; Nagler and Naudé 2017).

From this perspective, Africa's ongoing urbanization and the increasing education level of its youth could increase the potential for job creation in future household enterprises. In rural areas, improving connectivity with nearby markets and towns has the potential to improve earnings and spur welfare-enhancing diversification. Such an improvement entails not only investment in rural infrastructure but also policies to foster better transport services.[7]

Critical within this agenda is how governments manage their urban spaces. Not all urban development has shown equal poverty-reducing potential. Cross-country research and case country evidence from India, Mexico, and Tanzania suggest that, for poverty reduction, growing towns matters more than growing cities (Berdegué and Soloaga 2018; Christiaensen, De Weerdt, and Kanbur 2019; Christiaensen and Todo 2014; Gibson et al. 2017).[8] Secondary towns in rural areas provide local centers of economic activity and demand and are more accessible to the poor because of their proximity and the lower threshold for migration (Rondinelli and Ruddle 1983). This accessibility facilitates especially the first move, which is often the most difficult (Ingelaere et al. 2018), and their proximity makes it easier to return home, when things fail, which is especially important in the absence of formal safety nets. The type of employment available in towns (unskilled and semiskilled) also tends to be more compatible with the skill sets of the poor.

Public investments to help rural towns grow can increase demand for agricultural products produced in surrounding rural areas, thus increasing rural incomes, which in turn would increase demand for the nonfarm goods and services produced by household enterprises. Unfortunately, more often than not, governments view household enterprises, which are mostly informal, as a detriment to urban spaces rather than as a critical source of income for the poor and many nonpoor, especially in the larger urban centers. For example, efforts to "sanitize" city centers may well lead to impoverishment of vulnerable workers who depend on dense foot traffic for their livelihoods (Resnick 2017).

Integrating household enterprises or the informal economy in general into urban or national development plans would be a start toward leveraging their potential. It would provide a framework for the government and the informal sector to start discussing the design of supportive policies that facilitate the operation of household enterprises while still protecting the public interest.

The demand for the poor's goods and services often also finds itself just across the border. This is vividly illustrated by the concentration of (agriprocessing) enterprises along the eastern and northern borders of Zambia, catering to Lilongwe in Malawi and Lubumbashi in the Democratic Republic of Congo, respectively. Cross-border trade is often also an important driver of town development (the so-called border towns) (Eberhard-Ruiz and Moradi 2018).

Finally, digital technology holds promise to connect the enterprises of the poor with expanding urban and foreign demand for goods and services. Recent evidence from China shows the potential: e-commerce penetration (typically clustered in so-called Taobao villages) is associated with higher consumption growth, with the effects stronger for the rural sample, inland regions, and poorer households (Luo, Wang, and Zhang 2019). Capitalizing on this trend will require equipping youth from poor households with at least basic education and digital skills while also making internet connectivity affordable, reliable, and widely available (see box O.3 earlier in this overview).

Managing Risks and Conflict

Risk and conflict are higher in Africa than in other regions and exacerbate poverty challenges. Civil war is prevalent; the dominant livelihood, rainfed agriculture, is risky; markets are poorly integrated, making prices volatile; and health, water, and sanitation systems are weak. Price, weather, and health shocks have large impacts on welfare, especially given the inadequacy of financial markets, social protection, and humanitarian systems, as well as the continued reliance on costly coping mechanisms. Conflict has far-reaching consequences, including forced displacement and migration of those able to migrate.

The direct impact of a calamity on well-being is the visible, headline-grabbing way that conflict or poorly managed disasters set back progress. However, the persistent impact of uninsured risk on household behavior every year—regardless of whether the feared event occurs—is arguably the larger constraint to accelerating poverty reduction in Africa. Poor households choose safer, less remunerative activities that limit income growth and poverty reduction.

Addressing Risk and Conflict through Prevention

Much can be done to reduce risks and to help households manage risks ex post. The most prevalent shocks in Africa—relating to price, weather, health, and conflict—are slow in onset; affect incomes more than assets; and tend to be covariate, affecting many households in the same area at once. Risk is higher in poorer areas and in rural areas. The prevalence of different shocks varies across the continent (map O.1).

In many cases, the cost of prevention is lower than the cost of managing the event. Development of markets is the best way to reduce price risk in Africa, and this requires addressing tariff policies as well as investing in infrastructure and transport services. To reduce health risks and improve child health, improving water, sanitation, and hygiene (WASH); fighting malaria; and achieving mass immunizations are key. And targeted investments in irrigation, natural resource management, and improved seeds can reduce exposure to weather risks. In general, there is underinvestment in these cost-effective risk-reducing interventions.

As for conflict, a discussion on addressing the sources of fragility that underlie specific conflicts in Africa is beyond the scope of this report, but some emerging evidence has highlighted that well-targeted aid focused around job creation and support for disaffected youth and ex-combatants could help reduce the risk of conflict (Blattman and Annan 2016). More evidence is needed.

Better Insurance for the Poor

When prevention is not possible, a mix of safety nets and financial instruments can help households manage in the aftermath of a shock. Both are needed to manage shocks. Savings and regular safety net transfers help households manage small shocks, while larger shocks are better managed by insurance or by scaling up safety net support. Better-off households are more likely than poorer households to rely on financial markets to manage risk, but poor households still need access to financial markets to help them manage smaller shocks and to enable them to secure more "insurance" than could be provided through public safety nets alone.

Public finances spent on insurance subsidies and shock-responsive safety nets may target different households or different risks and may substitute for each other depending on the relative strength of public delivery and private markets in the local context. During conflict, financial market development that reduces the cost of sending and receiving remittances can also help, because private transfers and migration are predominant coping strategies.

However, financial markets are often weak, and safety net investments are too often made after shocks occur. Moreover, countries continue to rely on ex post humanitarian aid to help households, which by its nature is neither timely nor predictable. Reforming humanitarian financing—from reducing reliance on ex post appeals to using ex ante financing instruments with predictable and timely payout mechanisms (like the World Bank's Pandemic Emergency Financing Facility)—is essential. But it will not improve support to households on the ground unless it is combined with investments in contingency planning for support service delivery.

MAP O.1 Some parts of Africa are hit harder by risk

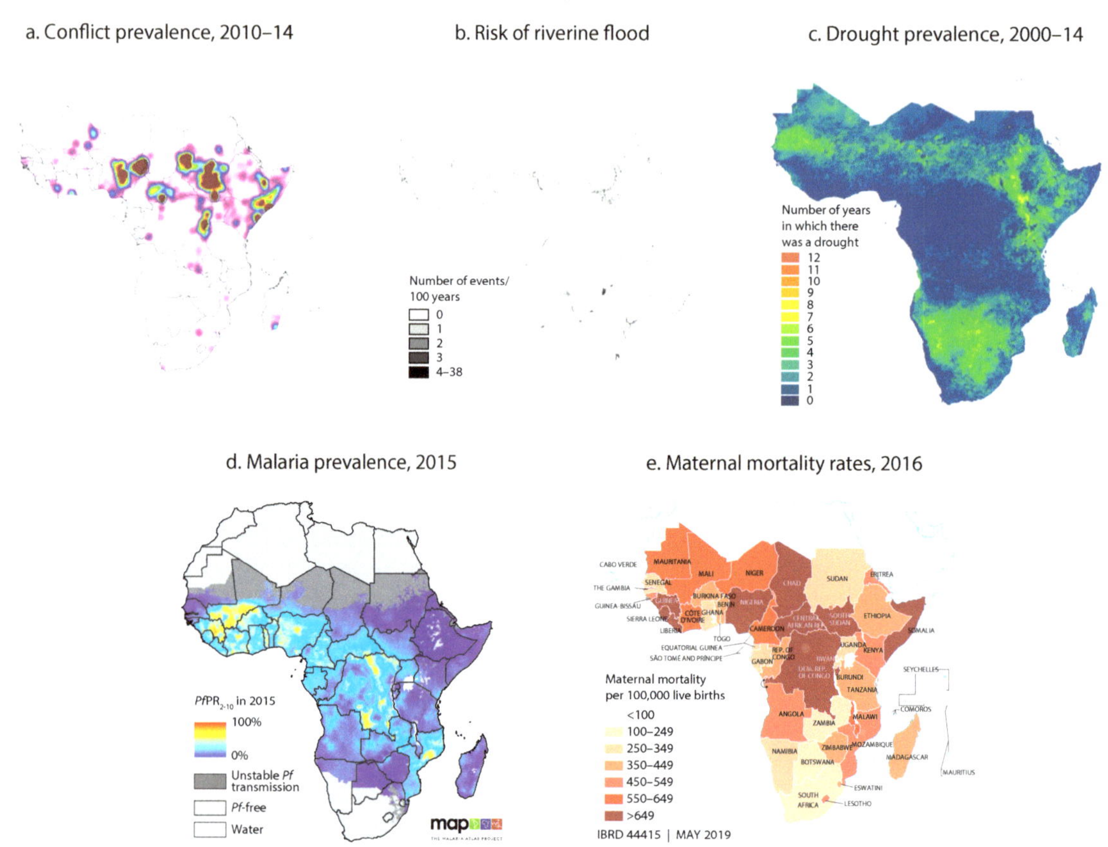

Sources: Panels a–c: Fisker and Hill 2018; panel d: the Malaria Atlas Project (https://map.ox.ac.uk/); panel e: World Development Indicators database, maternal mortality ratio.
Note: Panel c: A drought year is defined as a year in which at least half the growing period months are recorded to have a predicted greenness anomaly value below the 10th percentile of predicted greenness. Panel d: Each 5 km^2 pixel on the map shows the predicted *Plasmodium falciparum (Pf)* prevalence rate as a proportion of all children ages 2–10.

The Time to Act Is Now

Addressing risk and conflict—through either risk reduction or risk management—requires action before shocks occur. There is room for more technological innovation and better information systems, but fundamentally encouraging action before shocks occur will require addressing the incentives that currently keep postponing action until after shocks occur.

For governments, this requires addressing the perverse political incentives that reward them for big postdisaster gestures rather than for planning for a rainy day. Coping with disasters using humanitarian aid is much cheaper (that is, free) than predisaster investments in prevention and preparedness. Building capacity within governments to invest in risk reduction and risk management is also necessary.

For individuals, this will require inducing households to overcome behavior that limits household investment in risk reduction and management: a scarcity-induced focus on the present, resignation, and ambiguity aversion. This can be done by reducing the cost to households of investing in risk reduction and management while households learn about new strategies to reduce or manage risk. In addition, there is a need to expand mandates and regulations to address adverse selection in health insurance markets, to increase trust in financial institutions, and to reduce fixed-cost insurance markets.

And finally, as with many aspects of improving policies and programs, there is a data agenda. Better data on disasters as they unfold and on ex ante risk exposure will help improve financial market development and the design of shock-responsive safety nets.

Mobilizing Resources for the Poor

The agenda to address poverty in Africa extends beyond shifting programs and policies. It will also require a careful revisiting of a range of domestic revenue and spending patterns. Within the region, some countries have the means to address the poverty gap (the income needed for a poor household to just escape poverty), be it through theoretical tax rates on the nonpoor or through transfers of natural resource revenues directly to citizens, such as through "direct dividend payments" (DDPs).

For most African countries, however, closing the poverty gap (as a theoretical exercise) would mean implausibly high tax rates on the rich or implausible natural resource revenues. Current domestic revenues are not enough to tackle poverty in the short term, let alone to improve Africa's poor initial conditions in human capital—investments that only pay off a generation later. What is the path to tackle these challenges?

The Domestic Revenue Imperative

Several low-income African countries have tax revenues relative to GDP of under 13 percent (that is, revenues net of grants), which is often considered the "tipping point" necessary to execute basic state functions and to sustain development progress (Gaspar, Jaramillo, and Wingender 2016). The Organisation for Economic Co-operation and Development (OECD) average in 2015, for comparison, was 34.3 percent (OECD 2017).

While low on average, the level of revenue collection in Africa has shown improvement. The region experienced the largest increase in tax revenue across the globe since the turn of the century, albeit starting from a very low point (IMF 2015). But IMF projections find that the countries with the lowest domestic resource mobilization levels are also expected to grow at lower rates, further widening the gap. To turn this around, countries need to continue to improve tax compliance; start focusing more on local large taxpayers, corporate taxes, and transfer (mis)pricing (which has a global agenda); and expand excise and property tax collection.

Some countries in Africa also generate substantial revenues from natural resources. Out of 37 countries for which data are available, 22 are considered resource-rich—from oil-rich countries like Chad and the Democratic Republic of Congo to those with lucrative mining operations such as Botswana (diamonds) and Mauritania or Niger (minerals). In these countries, revenues make up 10–20 percent of GDP. Low- and middle-income countries with substantial natural resources also tend to have higher tax revenues than countries at the same income level that lack such resources.

Therefore, in principle, resource revenues can enhance spending on agriculture, rural infrastructure, and social sectors (for example, health and education as well as social protection programs) and thus contribute to poverty eradication. These revenues notwithstanding, poverty reduction is slower and multiple human development indicators are worse in resource-rich countries in Africa than in other African countries at the same income level—so this revenue is not resulting in greater pro-poor spending (Beegle et al. 2016; de la Brière et al. 2017).

Making Public Spending Go Further for the Poor

Turning from raising more money toward spending more effectively and with a pro-poor focus, there is a large unfinished agenda. A key area to make public spending more pro-poor is to address high subsidy expenditures (particularly fuel, energy, and fertilizer subsidies), which are often regressive with little impact on poverty. The lack of impact from agricultural input subsidies gets magnified when they crowd out other investments in the sector that could raise productivity. Cash transfers seem more effective and efficient than subsidies where evidence exists (Dabalen et al. 2017). But more research is needed to compare their performance relative to other competing needs like spending on education, health, WASH, public goods in agriculture (such as research and irrigation), rural infrastructure, and security.

Spending patterns from a "pro-poor" perspective have a mixed track record—with some sectors generally reaching international expenditure targets (like education) but others falling short for many countries (health, WASH, and agriculture). Although many countries are close to meeting or exceeding global targets for spending as a share of GDP or government expenditures, absolute spending levels are still very low.

And within-sector spending is often inefficient and sometimes regressive (such as spending more on services used disproportionately by the nonpoor than the poor). Inefficiency in spending on services manifests itself in several ways—for example, in high rates of absenteeism among teachers and supplies not reaching frontline providers. As a result of both limited spending on pro-poor sectors and inefficiency in the spending, many poor still pay for access to basic services critical for human development; out-of-pocket expenditures are high. Notably, resource-rich countries spend less on education and health than other African countries of similar income level (Cockx and Francken 2014, 2016).

Finally, combining the insights on taxation and spending practices, it emerges that many in the bottom 40 percent of income are often net taxpayers instead of net recipients. That is, in the aggregate, the total cash benefit transferred to the poorest 40 percent of the population through subsidies and direct transfers is smaller in absolute magnitude than the burden created by direct and indirect tax instruments (de la Fuente, Jellema, and Lustig 2018). Although these calculations refer only to the cash-based financial position purchasing power of individuals—excluding the value of in-kind benefits like education, health, or infrastructure services—they give cause for pause.

To accelerate poverty reduction in Africa, a careful reexamination of its fiscal systems from a pro-poor perspective is needed. It also requires a better understanding of the political dynamics of pro-poor policy making.

An Important Role Remains for Official Development Assistance

Taken together, the low base on which to tax, the low capacity to tax more, and the political inability (or lack of will) to channel revenues from natural resources into pro-poor social spending result in a large financing gap for critical spending. Although improving revenue and spending performance is important, even with improvements, official development assistance (ODA) will remain critical for the poorest countries.

Aid makes up more than 8 percent of gross national income (GNI) for half of low-income countries in Africa (figure O.4); ODA supports key sectors for reducing poverty, including health, agriculture, and education. But although global ODA has been increasing and reached an all-time high of US$140 billion in 2016 (at current prices), ODA to African countries increased from 2013 to 2017 (from US$45.8 billion to US$46.3 billion), after a dip to $42.5 billion in 2016. But in per capita terms, ODA declined from US$48.30 to US$42.60 because of the region's population growth.

FIGURE O.4 **ODA is a large share of GNI in low-income countries**

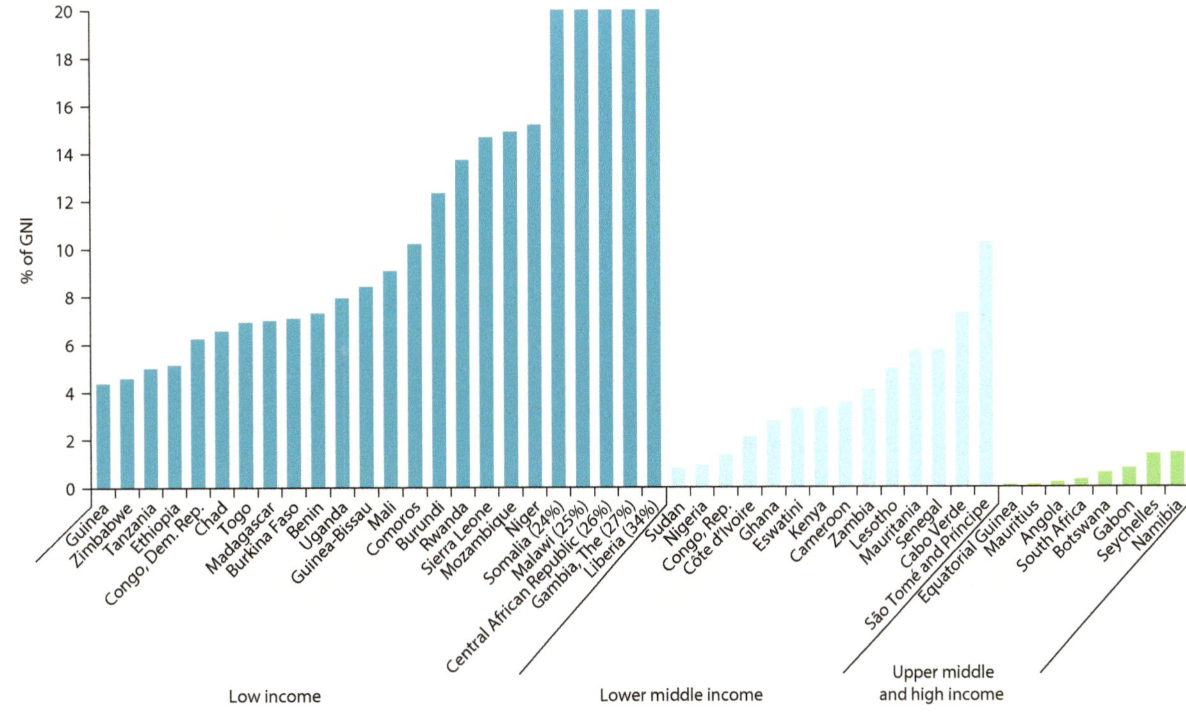

Source: Organisation for Economic Co-operation and Development (OECD) 2017 data, https://data.oecd.org/.
Note: GNI = gross national income; ODA = official development assistance. ODA data do not include aid inflows from international charities, international nongovernmental organizations, and private donations.

The proportion of aid going to African fragile and conflict-affected states also continued to decline. A total of 13 OECD Development Assistance Committee (DAC) donors, including the European Union (EU) institutions, reduced their contributions to African fragile and conflict-affected states between 2014 and 2015 (ONE 2017). The overall decline, at least in part, is because the donor countries were spending more in their own countries on refugees and asylum seekers.

The issuing of debt over the past decade in the face of macroeconomic slowdown over the past couple of years, combined with insufficient revenue and lagging ODA commitments, has put country debt concerns back on the radar. Although debt levels remain below those in the late 1990s—when several international debt relief initiatives were implemented—debt has been rising more rapidly in Africa than in other regions since 2009. So, while governments could borrow domestically and internationally to finance more spending on social sectors and WASH, many will find it difficult.

Way Forward: Four Primary Policy Areas

In conclusion, from the wide range of themes and issues discussed across the chapters of this report—focused on raising the incomes of Africa's poor and accelerating poverty reduction—four areas for primary policy attention are advanced.

Accelerate the Fertility Transition

Rapid population growth in Africa—averaging 2.7 percent per year—remains a defining feature that holds poverty reduction back for many countries and households on the continent. It elevates the fiscal needs for social services, which only pay off much later. High fertility has also been an important direct contributor to Africa's explosive urban growth, making it hard for urban centers to keep up the infrastructure base to remain productive and create employment. And high fertility limits women's income-earning opportunities.

Accelerating fertility reduction is therefore an important entry point for accelerating Africa's poverty reduction. A 1 percent fall in the dependency rate is associated with a 0.75 percentage point fall in headcount poverty (Cruz and Ahmed 2016). Investments in family planning programs can play an important cost-effective complementary role, in addition to female education, programs offering life skills for women and girls, addressing social norms around gender through social and behavior change communication, and reducing child marriage.

Leverage the Food System

Much poverty reduction remains to be gained from leveraging Africa's food system, on and off the farm. Raising smallholder agricultural labor productivity increases the income of the poor directly and reduces the price of food for the urban poor. Urbanization and economic growth are boosting domestic demand for higher-value agricultural products, also creating employment opportunities off the farm up and down the value chains, often particularly for women. Rising agricultural productivity will also increase demand for nonagricultural goods and services, facilitating intersectoral and rural-urban labor reallocation.

However, not all agricultural development and urbanization models are equally poverty reducing, with raising smallholder staple crop productivity and secondary town development particularly effective. More-integrated approaches—tackling both supply- and demand-side constraints at once—are needed, both to raise agricultural productivity and to increase the return to informal nonagricultural household enterprises, where most of the poor will find off-farm employment.

Inclusive value chain development provides a market-based solution to integrate, especially for nonstaple foods. But complementary public investment (in agricultural research and extension, irrigation, and rural infrastructure) remains key, especially for staple crop productivity.

Finally, technological leapfrogging and new business models bring previously unattainable markets and production techniques within reach of the poor (such as solar pump irrigation, and mechanization in agriculture, and e-commerce household enterprises). This, too, requires complementary public investments in ICT infrastructure and skills.

Mitigate Fragility

Risk and conflict have long permeated African livelihoods. This substantially complicates Africa's poverty-reduction efforts. Shocks are frequent, conflicts often cast a long shadow, coping capacity is mostly inadequate (especially for the poor and near-poor), and uninsured risks hold and push people back into poverty. Climatic change is making weather patterns even more erratic and extreme, and the upsurge in terror-related conflict adds further uncertainty.

Twenty-nine percent of Africa's poor live in fragile states, a share projected to increase to 50–80 percent by 2030. This trend puts fragile and conflict-affected states at the center of Africa's fight against poverty. Climate change and conflict may further interact to increase each other's occurrence and detrimental effects (Hsiang, Burke, and Miguel 2013).

Better risk and conflict management to address fragility is the third policy entry point for accelerating poverty reduction in Africa. Many of the solutions exist, with a role for both the private and public sectors, but the most important hurdle remains incentivizing public and private actors to act now, before the shocks and conflict occur. A more productive agriculture also helps.

Address the Poverty Financing Gap

Making progress in these three policy areas requires public financing focused on the poor, including to overcome Africa's poor initial conditions in human development. In Africa's few non-low-income countries, the challenge is not so much the amount of resources required to address poverty, but rather the decision and effort to redirect resources to policies and programs that benefit the poor. However, for most countries in Africa, which house most of the poor, current domestic resources are not nearly sufficient to address poverty—and insufficient domestic revenue mobilization, lagging ODA commitments, and rising debt levels following the macroeconomic slowdown further shrink their fiscal space.

In principle, the discovery of natural resources across Africa over the past two decades could help. Yet poverty reduction and multiple human development indicators are often worse in resource-rich countries in Africa than in other countries at the same level of income.

In addition to the continued need for ODA to address the fiscal gap, Africa's fiscal systems need to become more effective in raising incomes (including through addressing domestic tax compliance and international tax avoidance) as well as in making public spending more pro-poor and more efficient.

These four primary policy entry points are relevant across countries, albeit to different degrees. Fertility is, for example, already lower in southern Africa than in western and eastern Africa. Risks are pervasive everywhere but take on different forms. Finally, not all countries are struggling with fiscal deficits, but pro-poor spending and spending efficiency can be improved in most of them, and especially in the resource-rich countries.

Notes

1. Throughout this report, "Africa" refers to Sub-Saharan Africa.
2. This ambition is articulated in SDG 1, Target 1.1 (http://www.un.org/sustainable development/poverty/). It is tracked by measuring progress on the proportion of people living below the $1.90-a-day international poverty line (in 2011 purchasing power parity).
3. Ranking countries from those with the largest number of poor, Nigeria accounts for about one-quarter of Africa's poor (85.2 million); the next four (the Democratic Republic of Congo, Tanzania, Ethiopia, and Madagascar) for another quarter; and the next five (Mozambique, Uganda, Malawi, Kenya, and Zambia) for the following 25 percent.
4. In Africa, the likelihood of being poor is 3 percentage points lower on average when an individual has some primary education; 7 percentage points lower given completed primary or incomplete secondary education; 10 percentage points lower given completed secondary education; and 12 percentage points lower given tertiary education (controlling for the area of residence, household structure, and demographic characteristics) (Castañeda et al. 2018).
5. The increase in smallholder staple crop productivity is often referred to as the "Green Revolution," in reference to Asia's rapid increase in smallholder staple crop productivity in the 1960s and 1970s, through a package of modern inputs (seeds, fertilizer, and pesticides); water control; and reduction in price volatility.
6. Side-selling is a practice by which farmers divert part or most of their contracted production to other buyers. It is greater when limited value addition does not permit price premiums to make contracts more incentive-compatible. On the other hand, the wide availability of undifferentiated staples and the limited opportunity for value

addition also increases the opportunity for buyers to breach the contracts and reduces their incentives to engage in contracting to begin with.

7. The much wider availability of motorcycle and motorized tricycle taxi services able to navigate Africa's rugged rural roads, following the import of much cheaper models from China and India, is a good example of the importance of transport services for connectivity. The trend led the World Bank to raise its estimated distance of an all-season road providing rural connectivity from 2 kilometers to at least 5 kilometers, in constructing its 2016 Rural Access Index (https://datacatalog.worldbank.org/dataset/rural-access-index-rai).
8. Similarly, although there is a positive effect of city size and urban concentration on growth in high-income countries, no such effect has been found so far in low- and middle-income countries. If anything, the effect is likely negative (Frick and Rodríguez-Pose 2016, 2018).

References

Adjognon, S. G., L. S. O. Liverpool-Tasie, and T. A. Reardon. 2017. "Agricultural Input Credit in Sub-Saharan Africa: Telling Myth from Facts." *Food Policy* 67 (C): 93–105.

Allen, Thomas, Philipp Heinrigs, and Inhoi Heo. 2018. "Agriculture, Food and Jobs in West Africa." West African Papers No. 14, Organisation for Economic Co-operation and Development, Paris.

Ambler, Kate, Alan de Brauw, and Susan Godlonton. 2018. "Agriculture Support Services in Malawi: Direct Effects, Complementarities, and Time Dynamics." IFPRI Discussion Paper No. 01725, International Food Policy Research Institute, Washington, DC.

Antoine, Kassia, Raju Jan Singh, and Konstantin M. Wacker. 2017. "Poverty and Shared Prosperity: Let's Move the Discussion beyond Growth." *Forum for Social Economics* 46 (20): 192–205.

Bah, El-hadj, and Lei Fang. 2015. "Impact of the Business Environment on Output and Productivity in Africa." *Journal of Development Economics* 114: 159–71.

Banerjee, Abhijit, Esther Duflo, Nathanael Goldberg, Dean Karlan, Robert Osei, William Parienté, Jeremy Shapiro, Bram Thuysbaert, and Christopher Udry. 2015. "A Multifaceted Program Causes Lasting Progress for the Very Poor: Evidence from Six Countries." *Science* 348 (6236): 773–89.

Beegle, Kathleen, Luc Christiaensen, Andrew Dabalen, and Isis Gaddis. 2016. *Poverty in a Rising Africa*. Washington, DC: World Bank.

Berdegué, Julio, and Isidro Soloaga. 2018. "Small and Medium Cities and Development of Mexican Rural Areas." *World Development* 107: 277–88.

Bhalotra, Sonia, and Samantha Rawlings. 2013. "Gradients of the Intergenerational Transmission of Health in Developing Countries." *Review of Economics and Statistics* 95 (2): 660–72.

Bhutta, Zulfiqar A., Jai K. Das, Ajumand Rizvi, Michelle F. Gaffey, Neff Walker, Susan Horton, Patrick Webb, Anna Lartey, and Robert E. Black. 2013. "Evidence-Based Interventions for Improvement of Maternal and Child Nutrition: What Can Be Done and at What Cost?" *The Lancet* 382 (9890): 452–77.

Blattman, Christopher, and Jeannie Annan. 2016. "Can Employment Reduce Lawlessness and Rebellion? A Field Experiment with High-Risk Men in a Fragile State." *American Political Science Review* 110: 1–17.

Bongaarts, John. 2017. "Africa's Unique Fertility Transition." *Population and Development Review* 43 (Issue Supplement Fertility Transition in Sub-Saharan Africa): 39–58.

Branisa, Boris, Stephan Klasen, and Maria Ziegler. 2009. "Why We Should All Care about Social Institutions Related to Gender Inequality." Proceedings of the German Development Economics Conference, Hannover, No. 15, Verein für Socialpolitik, Ausschuss für Entwicklungsländer, Göttingen.

———. 2013. "Gender Inequality in Social Institutions and Gendered Development Outcomes." *World Development* 45: 252–68.

———. 2014. "The Institutional Basis of Gender Inequality: The Social Institutions and Gender Index (SIGI)." *Feminist Economics* 20 (2): 29–64.

Castañeda, Andrés, Dung Doan, David Newhouse, Minh Cong Nguyen, Hiroki Uematsu, and João Pedro Azevedo. 2018. "A New Profile of the Global Poor." *World Development* 101: 250–67.

Cattaneo, Umberto. 2017. "Poverty Headcount Projections in Sub-Saharan Africa."

Background note prepared for *Accelerating Poverty Reduction in Africa*, World Bank, Washington, DC.

Chamberlin, Jordan, and Thomas S. Jayne. 2017. "Does Farm Structure Matter? The Effects of Farmland Distribution Patterns on Rural Household Income in Tanzania." MSU International Development Working Paper 157, Michigan State University, East Lansing.

Christiaensen, Luc, Lionel Demery, and Stefano Paternostro. 2003. "Macro and Micro Perspectives of Growth and Poverty in Africa." *World Bank Economic Review* 17 (3): 317–47.

Christiaensen, Luc, Joachim De Weerdt, and Ravi Kanbur. 2019. "Decomposing the Contribution of Migration to Poverty Reduction: Methodology and Application to Tanzania." *Applied Economics Letters* 26 (12): 978–82.

Christiaensen, Luc, and Ravi Kanbur. 2017. "Secondary Towns and Poverty Reduction: Refocusing the Urbanization Agenda." *Annual Review of Resource Economics* 9: 405–19.

Christiaensen, Luc, and Will Martin. 2018. "Agriculture, Structural Transformation and Poverty Reduction: Eight New Insights." *World Development* 109 (September): 413–16.

Christiaensen, Luc, and Yasuyuki Todo. 2014. "Poverty Reduction during the Rural–Urban Transformation: The Role of the Missing Middle." *World Development* 63 (C): 43–58.

Cockx, Lara, and Nathalie Francken. 2014. "Extending the Concept of the Resource Curse: Natural Resources and Public Spending on Health." *Ecological Economics* 108: 136–49.

———. 2016. "Natural Resources: A Curse on Education Spending." *Energy Policy* 92: 394–408.

Collier, Paul, and Anke Hoffler. 2004. "Greed and Grievance in African Civil Wars." *Oxford Economic Papers* 56: 563–95.

Cruz, Marcio, and S. Amer Ahmed. 2016. "On the Impact of Demographic Change on Growth, Savings and Poverty." Policy Research Working Paper 7805, World Bank, Washington, DC.

Dabalen, Andrew, Alejandro de la Fuente, Aparajita Goyal, Wendy Karamba, Nga Thi Viet Nguyen, and Tomomi Tanaka. 2017. *Pathways to Prosperity in Rural Malawi*. Directions in Development Series. Washington, DC: World Bank.

Daidone, Silvio, Benjamin Davis, Joshua Dewbre, Borja Miguelez, Ousmane Niang, and Luca Pellerano. 2017. "Linking Agriculture and Social Protection for Food Security: The Case of Lesotho." *Global Food Security* 12 (March): 146–54.

de la Brière, Bénédicte, Deon Filmer, Dena Ringold, Dominic Rohner, Karelle Samuda, and Anastasiya Denisova. 2017. *From Mines and Wells to Well-Built Minds: Turning Sub-Saharan Africa's Natural Resource Wealth into Human Capital*. Directions in Development Series. Washington, DC: World Bank.

de la Fuente, Alejandro, Jon Jellema, and Nora Lustig. 2018. "Fiscal Policy in Africa: Welfare Impacts and Policy Effectiveness." Background paper prepared for *Accelerating Poverty Reduction in Africa*, World Bank, Washington, DC.

de Silva, Tiloka, and Silvana Tenreyro. 2017. "Population Control Policies and Fertility Convergence." *Journal of Economic Perspectives* 31 (4): 205–28.

Deininger, Klaus, and Fang Xia. 2016. "Quantifying Spillover Effects from Large Land-based Investment: The Case of Mozambique." *World Development* 87: 227–41.

———. 2018. "Assessing the Long-Term Performance of Large-Scale Land Transfers: Challenges and Opportunities in Malawi's Estate Sector." *World Development* 104: 281–96.

Diao, Xinshen, James Thurlow, Samuel Benin, and Shenggen Fan. 2012. *Strategies and Priorities for African Agriculture: Economywide Perspectives from Country Studies*. Washington, DC: International Food Policy Research Institute (IFPRI).

Dixit, Siddharth, Indermit Gill, and Chinmoy Kumar. 2018. "Are Economic Relations with India Helping Africa? Trade, Investment and Development in the Middle-Income South." Research paper, Duke Center for International Development, Duke University, Durham, NC.

Dollar, David, and Aart Kraay. 2002. "Growth Is Good for the Poor." *Journal of Economic Growth* 7 (3): 195–225.

Dorosh, Paul, and James Thurlow. 2018. "Beyond Agriculture versus Non-Agriculture: Decomposing Sectoral Growth-Poverty Linkages in Five African Countries." *World Development* 109: 440–51.

Eberhard-Ruiz, Andreas, and Alexander Moradi. 2018. "Regional Market Integration and City

Growth in East Africa: Local but No Regional Effects?" CSAE Working Paper Series 2018-09, Centre for the Study of African Economies, University of Oxford.

Ferrant, Gaëlle, and Alexandre Kolev. 2016. "Does Gender Discrimination in Social Institutions Matter for Long-Term Growth? Cross-Country Evidence." OECD Development Centre Working Paper No. 330, Organisation for Economic Co-operation and Development (OECD), Paris.

Fisker, Peter, and Ruth Hill. 2018. "Mapping the Nature of Risk in Sub-Saharan Africa." Background paper prepared for *Accelerating Poverty Reduction in Africa*, World Bank, Washington, DC.

Frick, Susanne, and Andrés Rodríguez-Pose. 2016. "Average City Size and Economic Growth." *Cambridge Journal of Regions, Economy and Society* 9 (2): 301–18.

———. 2018. "Change in Urban Concentration and Economic Growth." *World Development* 105: 156–70.

Gaspar, Vitor, Laura Jaramillo, and Philippe Wingender. 2016. "Tax Capacity and Growth: Is There a Tipping Point?" IMF Working Paper WP/16/234, International Monetary Fund, Washington, DC.

Gibson, John, Gaurav Datt, Rinku Murgai, and Martin Ravallion. 2017. "For India's Rural Poor, Growing Towns Matter More Than Growing Cities." *World Development* 87: 413–29.

Gill, Indermit, and Kenan Karakülah. 2018. "Is China Helping Africa? Growth and Public Debt Effects of the Subcontinent's Biggest Investor." Global Working Paper No. 3, Center for International and Global Studies, Duke University, Durham, NC.

Grimm, Michael, Anicet Munyehirwe, Jörg Peters, and Maximiliane Sievert. 2017. "A First Step Up the Energy Ladder? Low Cost Solar Kits and Household's Welfare in Rural Rwanda." *World Bank Economic Review* 31 (3): 631–49.

Günther, Isabel, and Kenneth Harttgen. 2016. "Desired Fertility and Number of Children Born across Time and Space." *Demography* 53: 55–83.

Hallward-Driemeier, Mary, Tazeen Hasan, and Anca Bogdana Rusu. 2013. "Women's Legal Rights over 50 Years: What Is the Impact of Reform?" Policy Research Working Paper 6617, World Bank, Washington, DC.

Haushofer, Johannes, and Ernst Fehr. 2014. "On the Psychology of Poverty." *Science* 344 (6186): 862–67.

Hazell, Peter, Colin Poulton, Steve Wiggins, and Andrew Dorward. 2010. "The Future of Small Farms: Trajectories and Policy Priorities." *World Development* 38: 1349–61.

Hsiang, Solomon, Marshall Burke, and Edward Miguel. 2013. "Quantifying the Influence of Climate on Human Conflict." *Science* 341 (6151): 1235367.

IMF (International Monetary Fund). 2015. *Regional Economic Outlook: Sub-Saharan Africa. Dealing with the Gathering Clouds.* Washington, DC: IMF.

Ingelaere, Bert, Luc Christiaensen, Joachim De Weerdt, and Ravi Kanbur. 2018. "Why Secondary Towns Can Be Important for Poverty Reduction: A Migrant Perspective." *World Development* 105: 273–82.

Jalloh, Abdulai, Gerald C. Nelson, Timothy S. Thomas, Robert Zougmoré, and Harold Roy-Macauley, eds. 2013. *West African Agriculture and Climate Change: A Comprehensive Analysis.* Washington, DC: International Food Policy Research Institute (IFPRI).

James, Jeffrey. 2016. *The Impact of Mobile Phones on Poverty and Inequality in Developing Countries.* Cham, Switzerland: Springer.

Jayne, Thomas S., Jordan Chamberlin, and Derek Headey. 2014. "Land Pressures, the Evolution of Farming Systems and Development Strategies in Africa: A Synthesis." *Food Policy* 48: 1–17.

Jedwab, Remi, Luc Christiaensen, and Marina Gindelsky. 2017. "Demography, Urbanization and Development: Rural Push, Urban Pull and...Urban Push?" *Journal of Urban Economics* 98 (C): 6–16.

Jones, Van. 2018. "How Hello Tractor's Digital Platform Is Enabling the Mechanization of African Farming." *AgFunder News*, July 4.

Klasen, Stephan. 2006. "Pro-Poor Growth and Gender Inequality." In *Pro-Poor Growth: Policy and Evidence*, edited by Lukas Menkhoff. Berlin: Duncker and Humblot.

Lall, Somik, J. Vernon Henderson, and Anthony J. Venables. 2017. *Africa's Cities: Opening Doors to the World.* Washington, DC: World Bank.

Le Goff, Maëlan, and Raju Jan Singh. 2014. "Does Trade Reduce Poverty? A View from Africa." *Journal of African Trade* 1: 5–14.

Luo, X., Y. Wang, and X. Zhang. 2019. "E-Commerce Development and Household Consumption Growth in China." Policy Research Working Paper 8810, World Bank, Washington, DC.

Martin-Shields, Charles P., and Wolfgang Stojetz. 2019. "Food Security and Conflict: Empirical Challenges and Future Opportunities for Research and Policy Making on Food Security and Conflict." *World Development* 119: 150–64.

McCullough, Ellen B. 2017. "Labor Productivity and Employment Gaps in Sub-Saharan Africa." *Food Policy* 67: 133–52.

Mellor, John Williams. 2017. *Agricultural Development and Economic Transformation.* Cham, Switzerland: Springer International Publishing.

Nagler, Paula. 2017. "A Profile of Non-Farm Household Enterprises in Sub-Saharan Africa." Background note prepared for *Accelerating Poverty Reduction in Africa*, World Bank, Washington, DC.

Nagler, Paula, and Wim Naudé. 2017. "Non-Farm Entrepreneurship in Rural Sub-Saharan Africa: New Empirical Evidence." *Food Policy* 67: 175–91.

OECD (Organisation for Economic Co-operation and Development). 2017. *Revenue Statistics in Africa 1990–2015.* Paris: OECD Publishing.

ONE. 2017. *The 2017 DATA Report: Financing for the African Century.* Annual statistical report, The ONE Campaign, Washington, DC.

Otte, J., A. Costales, J. Dijkman, U. Pica-Ciamarra, T. Robinson, V. Ahuja, C. Ly, and D. Roland-Holst, eds. 2012. *Livestock Sector Development for Poverty Reduction: An Economic and Policy Perspective—Livestock's Many Virtues.* Rome: Food and Agriculture Organization of the United Nations (FAO).

Pace, Noemi, Silvio Daidone, Benjamin Davis, Sudhanshu Handa, Marco Knowles, and Robert Pickmans. 2018. "One Plus One Can Be Greater than Two: Evaluating Synergies of Development Programmes in Malawi." *Journal of Development Studies* 54 (11): 2023–60.

Pauw, Karl, and James Thurlow. 2011. "Agricultural Growth, Poverty, and Nutrition in Tanzania." *Food Policy* 36: 795–804.

Platteau, Jean-Philippe. 2014. "Redistributive Pressures in Sub-Saharan Africa: Causes, Consequences, and Coping Strategies." In *African Development in Historical Perspective*, edited by E. Akyeampong, R. Bates, N. Nunn, and J. Robinson, 153–207. Cambridge, U.K.: Cambridge University Press.

Resnick, Danielle. 2017. "Governance: Informal Food Markets in Africa's Cities." In *IFPRI Global Food Policy Report*, 50–57. Washington, DC: International Food Policy Research Institute.

Rodrik, Dani. 1998. "Trade Policy and Economic Performance in Sub-Saharan Africa." NBER Working Paper 6562, National Bureau of Economic Research, Cambridge, MA.

———. 2016. "An African Growth Miracle?" *Journal of African Economies* 27 (1): 1–18.

Rondinelli, Dennis, and Kenneth Ruddle. 1983. *Urbanization and Rural Development: A Spatial Policy for Equitable Growth.* New York: Praeger.

Sakyi, Daniel, José Villaverde, Adolfo Maza, and Isaac Bonuedi. 2017. "The Effects of Trade and Trade Facilitation on Economic Growth in Africa." *African Development Review* 29 (2): 350–61.

Sheahan, Megan, and Christopher B. Barrett. 2014. "Understanding the Agricultural Input Landscape in Sub-Saharan Africa: Recent Plot, Household, and Community-Level Evidence." Policy Research Working Paper 7014, World Bank, Washington, DC.

Swinnen, Johan, and Rob Kuijpers. 2017. "Inclusive Value Chains to Accelerate Poverty Reduction in Africa." Background note prepared for *Accelerating Poverty Reduction in Africa*, World Bank, Washington, DC.

Swinnen, Johan F. M., Anneleen Vandeplas, and Miet Maertens. 2010. "Liberalization, Endogenous Institutions, and Growth: A Comparative Analysis of Agricultural Reforms in Africa, Asia, and Europe." *World Bank Economic Review* 24 (3): 412–45.

Tschirley, David, Thomas Reardon, Michael Dolislager, and Jason Snyder. 2015. "The Rise of a Middle Class in East and Southern Africa: Implications for Food System Transformation: The Middle Class and Food System Transformation in ESA." *Journal of International Development* 27 (5): 628–46.

Victora, Cesar G., Linda Adair, Caroline Fall, Pedro C. Hallal, Reynaldo Martorell, Linda Richter, Harshpal Singh Sachdev, and Maternal and Child Undernutrition Study Group. 2008. "Maternal and Child Undernutrition: Consequences for Adult Health and Human Capital." *The Lancet* 371 (9609): 340–57.

Waithaka, M., G. C. Nelson, T. S. Thomas, and M. Kyotalimye, eds. 2013. *East African Agriculture and Climate Change: A Comprehensive Analysis*. Washington, DC: International Food Policy Research Institute (IFPRI).

World Bank. 2015. *World Development Report 2015: Mind, Society, and Behavior.* Washington, DC: World Bank.

———. 2018a. *Africa's Pulse: An Analysis of Issues Shaping Africa's Economic Future*, vol. 17 (April). Washington, DC: World Bank.

———. 2018b. "All Hands on Deck: Reducing Stunting through Multisectoral Efforts in Sub-Saharan Africa." Report, World Bank, Washington, DC.

———. 2018c. *Poverty and Shared Prosperity 2018: Piecing Together the Poverty Puzzle.* Washington, DC: World Bank.

———. 2018d. *World Development Report 2018: Learning to Realize Education's Promise.* Washington, DC: World Bank.

———. 2019a. *Africa's Pulse: An Analysis of Issues Shaping Africa's Economic Future*, vol. 19 (April). Washington, DC: World Bank.

———. 2019b. *Women, Business, and the Law 2019: A Decade of Reform.* Washington, DC: World Bank.

———. 2019c. World Development Indicators (database). World Bank, Washington, DC.

Yoon, Jisu, and Stephan Klasen. 2018. "An Application of Partial Least Squares to the Construction of the Social Institutions and Gender Index (SIGI) and the Corruption Perception Index (CPI)." *Social Indicators Research* 138 (1): 61–88.

Introduction

Africa's turnaround over the past couple of decades has been dramatic.[1] After many years in decline, the continent's economy picked up in the mid-1990s, expanding annually at a robust annual average of 4.5 percent into the early 2010s. People became healthier and better nourished, youngsters attended schools in much greater numbers, and both men and women got greater control over their lives. There was also substantial poverty reduction, with the share of Africans living in extreme poverty—defined as living on less than US$1.90 per person per day—declining from 54 percent in 1990 to 41 percent by 2015 (World Bank 2018).

These improvements notwithstanding, progress on the nonmonetary dimensions of well-being was from very low levels. Many remain undernourished, illiterate, and unempowered, with gender gaps pronounced in all three of these dimensions (Beegle et al. 2016). Exposure to domestic violence remains high, and exposure to political violence has even increased since 2010. As Africa's population continued to expand rapidly (by 2.7 percent annually), the number of extreme poor in Africa also rose, from an estimated 278 million in 1990 to 413 million in 2015 (World Bank 2018).

And following the collapse in world commodity prices, economic progress slowed, as Africa's economic growth dropped substantially. In per capita terms, gross domestic product (GDP) turned even slightly negative during 2016–18. Without Nigeria, South Africa, and Angola—Africa's three largest economies, each highly dependent on commodities—the downfall was less severe, dropping to slightly below 2 percent growth per capita during 2016–18. More recently, along with the overall recovery of the world economy, Africa's growth prospects are improving again (World Bank 2019).

Africa's turnaround happened in the context of rapid poverty reduction across the world, especially in East and South Asia, which found themselves at similarly high poverty levels in the early 1990s. The share of the world's extreme poor is now reaching 10 percent (World Bank 2018), and a world free of extreme poverty has come increasingly into sight (Ravallion 2013).

With Africa's poverty rates still high and progress over the past couple of years stalling, the world's poor have become increasingly concentrated in Africa—from 15 percent of the world's poor in 1990 to 56 percent in 2015 (figure I.1). The ambition to eradicate poverty worldwide has now also formally

FIGURE I.1 More than half of the world's extreme poor live in Africa

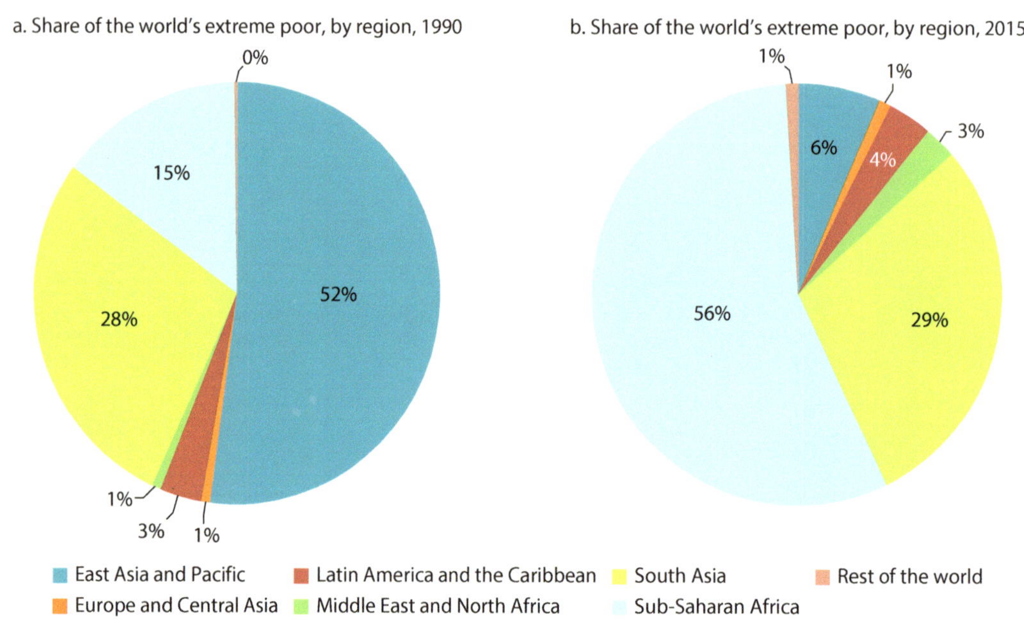

Source: World Bank 2018.
Note: "Extreme poor" refers to the percentage of the population living below US$1.90 per person per day.

been adopted as a global goal, and worldwide attention is increasingly turning toward accelerating poverty reduction in Africa. The 2015–16 migration crisis in Europe adds further political impetus.

This report examines policy entry points for accelerating poverty reduction in the region. It is the second of a two-part volume on poverty in Africa. The first report, *Poverty in a Rising Africa* (Beegle et al. 2016), reviewed Africa's poverty status in its monetary and nonmonetary dimensions and its evolution since the early 1990s. It focused specifically on data considerations.

This second report focuses on how to accelerate poverty reduction, with an eye on the United Nations Sustainable Development Goal (SDG) of eradicating poverty by 2030.[2] It draws on global historical experience in poverty reduction, as well as on recent successes in Africa, and accounts for Africa's specific conditions and overarching global trends in shaping Africa's poverty-reduction prospects. Its key entry point is increasing the earnings of the poor, and so it focuses on their livelihood strategies and increasing the productivity of their assets (labor and land).

The report proceeds as follows. Chapters 1 and 2 review the key features of Africa's poverty and the high-level impediments to accelerating poverty reduction: (a) persistently high fertility, (b) poor initial conditions, and (c) growth patterns that insufficiently (or unsustainably) benefit the poor. Natural-resource richness and fragility and conflict emerge as two further features that challenge poverty-reduction efforts. Chapters 3 and 4 explore how to increase earnings for the poor and near poor on and off the farm, within and outside the agriculture sector and rural areas, respectively. Chapter 5 examines the implications of risk and conflict on an agenda to alleviate poverty. Chapter 6 concludes by reviewing the poverty-reducing potential and performance of Africa's current fiscal systems and identifies options to increase poverty reduction by raising more resources, allocating them better, and improving the efficiency of countries' spending.

Chapters 1 and 2 raise the importance of four structural inequalities that hold poverty reduction back in Africa: the human development trap, deep-seated gender inequality, lack of infrastructure, and political realities. These are longstanding, entrenched issues, often requiring sustained efforts to address. As such, they are the topics of four "Fundamentals" sections, with inserted discussions on these areas between the chapters.

Notably, four critical areas emerge from the range of themes and issues that arise across the chapters of this report—fragility, fertility, food systems, and fiscal space—as outlined in more detail in the overview.

As an Africa-wide report, this volume does not aim to provide country-specific strategies but rather to identify broad common entry points to accelerate Africa's poverty reduction. Policy packages will need to be tailored to each setting. For example, conflict and high fertility are prominent challenges in the Sahel but arguably less so in southern Africa. Yet, in both cases, there is substantial scope for increasing agricultural productivity and leveraging the food system, for better risk management, and for more pro-poor and more efficient fiscal policy. Some eastern African countries have made some progress along each of the four paths identified, with some success in accelerating poverty reduction (such as Ethiopia and Rwanda), though not always on fertility reduction (for example, Uganda).

Notes

1. Throughout this report, "Africa" refers to Sub-Saharan Africa.
2. This ambition is articulated in SDG 1, Target 1.1 (http://www.un.org/sustainabledevelopment/poverty/). It is tracked by measuring progress on the proportion of people living below the $1.90-a-day international poverty line (in 2011 purchasing power parity).

References

Beegle, Kathleen, Luc Christiaensen, Andrew Dabalen, and Isis Gaddis. 2016. *Poverty in a Rising Africa*. Washington, DC: World Bank.

Ravallion, Martin. 2013. "How Long Will It Take to Lift One Billion People Out of Poverty?" *World Bank Research Observer* 28 (2): 139–58.

World Bank. 2018. *Poverty and Shared Prosperity 2018: Piecing Together the Poverty Puzzle*. Washington, DC: World Bank.

———. 2019. *Africa's Pulse: An Analysis of Issues Shaping Africa's Economic Future*, vol. 19 (April). Washington, DC: World Bank.

Poverty in Africa

1

Luc Christiaensen and Ruth Hill

In 2015, the world embraced the ambition to eradicate poverty by 2030. A review of Africa's poverty status today and its prospects for tomorrow show that, although the region has made substantial progress since the early 1990s, the number of poor has continued to increase. By 2030, Africa's poverty rate will still be around 20 percent, under most scenarios, and the world's poverty will become increasingly concentrated within Africa. How Africa can accelerate its poverty reduction is a global challenge.

Most of Africa's poor live concentrated in a limited number of countries: 5 countries account for more than 50 percent of Africa's poor; 10 countries account for 75 percent. Poverty rates are particularly high in fragile states, where poverty decline is also particularly slow. Four out of five of the poor live in rural areas, earning their living predominantly in farming. Both chronic and transitory poverty states persist, underscoring the importance of asset building as well as risk management. Measured gender gaps in poverty are small, though likely underestimating the pernicious consequences of structural gender inequalities. The poor also have weak links with the state—that is, weak access to good-quality public goods (infrastructure) and services as well as a limited voice in public policy. These stylized facts provide important entry points for poverty-reducing policy design, though caution remains warranted. They only indicate symptoms of poverty, not necessarily causes.

Africa's recent experience shows further that its poverty rate has not only been higher than in most other low- and middle-income countries; it has also declined more slowly. Three factors contribute to this:

- High population growth. *Per capita incomes have grown more slowly because a much larger share of gross domestic product (GDP) growth is eroded by faster population growth.*
- Poor initial conditions. *Although Africa's poverty-to-growth elasticity is lower than in other low- and middle-income countries, this is not the case in comparison with other, equally poor countries. Poverty itself is impeding the conversion of household income growth (not to be equated with GDP growth) in poverty reduction, just like in other poor countries.*

- Composition of Africa's growth. *Africa has been less efficient at converting (per capita) GDP growth into household income growth. This is plausibly linked to the composition of its growth process over the past couple of decades (more in capital-intensive natural resources, less in labor-intensive agriculture or manufacturing).*

The scope and need for more pro-poor growth policies in Africa is large. Fifty million more people could be lifted out of poverty by 2030 if the incomes of the poor were to grow 2 percentage points faster annually. Combined with lower population growth and better initial conditions, growth processes that foster growth in the places and sectors where the poor live and work, giving them a better chance of raising their incomes directly, could thus go a long way toward accelerating poverty reduction (now and in the future). These insights provide the overarching backdrop to the report.

Poverty Today and Tomorrow

Over the past decades, Africa has made substantial progress in reducing extreme poverty, with the share of Africans living on less than US$1.90 a day in 2011 purchasing power parity (PPP) terms declining by 13 percentage points, from 54 percent in 1990 to 41 percent in 2015 (figure 1.1).[1] Unfortunately, given high population growth (2.7 percent per year), the number of Africans living in poverty nonetheless rose, from an estimated 278 million in 1990 to 413 million in 2015.

In the rest of the low- and middle-income world, poverty reduction during 1990–2015 was faster—especially in East Asia but also in South Asia—and population growth lower. As a result, world poverty is increasingly concentrating in Africa. About three in five of the world's poor are now living in Africa—amounting to 57 percent in 2015, up from 15 percent in 1990.[2] Accelerating poverty reduction in Africa is central to the world's ambition of eradicating poverty by 2030—as expressed in United Nations (UN) Sustainable Development Goal 1 (SDG 1), Target 1.1, adopted in 2015.[3]

FIGURE 1.1 The poverty rate in Africa has gone down, but the number of African people living in poverty has increased

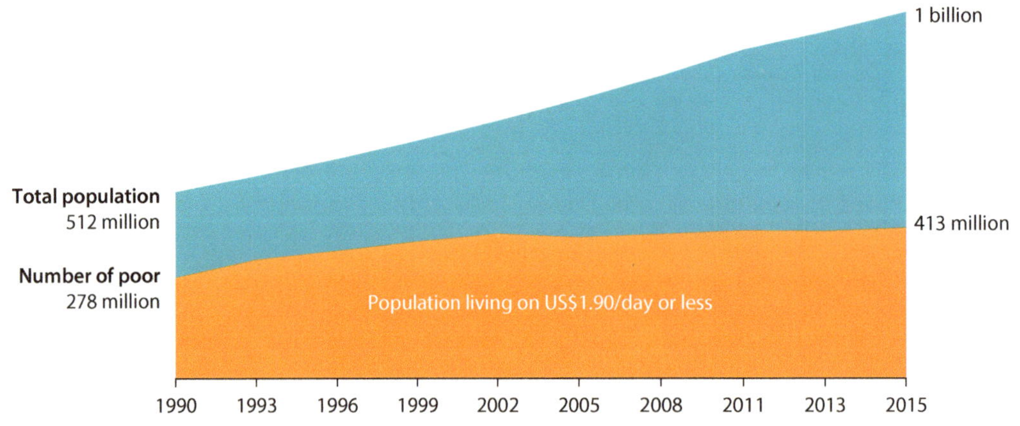

Source: World Bank PovcalNet data, http://iresearch.worldbank.org/PovcalNet.

Scenarios for Poverty Reduction in Africa

So, what are the prospects for Africa's poverty reduction in the future? In setting SDG 1, it was calculated that the world could eradicate poverty by 2030 if everyone's personal income in all low- and middle-income countries continued to expand by around 4.9 percent per year throughout 2008–30 (Ravallion 2013).[4] Under such a scenario, the poverty rate in Africa would decline to 19.2 percent. Further simulation studies, using different assumptions, all situated Africa's poverty rate in 2030 well above the eradication target of 3 percent (Cattaneo 2017).[5] So, when adopting SDG 1, it was already clear that eradicating Africa's poverty would not be feasible by 2030 and that the world's poverty would increasingly concentrate in Africa.

Which scenarios could bring Africa's poverty down faster? To address this question, a new baseline scenario is run first (figure 1.2). Each country's average annual per capita GDP growth rate during 1998–2013 is applied to the country's 2013 income distribution until 2030. This assumes distribution-neutral income growth of 2.8 percent a year on average[6] and would bring Africa's poverty rate down to 22.8 percent in 2030; the number of poor would decline to 323 million (figure 1.2, baseline scenario). Only if per

FIGURE 1.2 Africa cannot eradicate poverty by 2030 but can accelerate poverty reduction

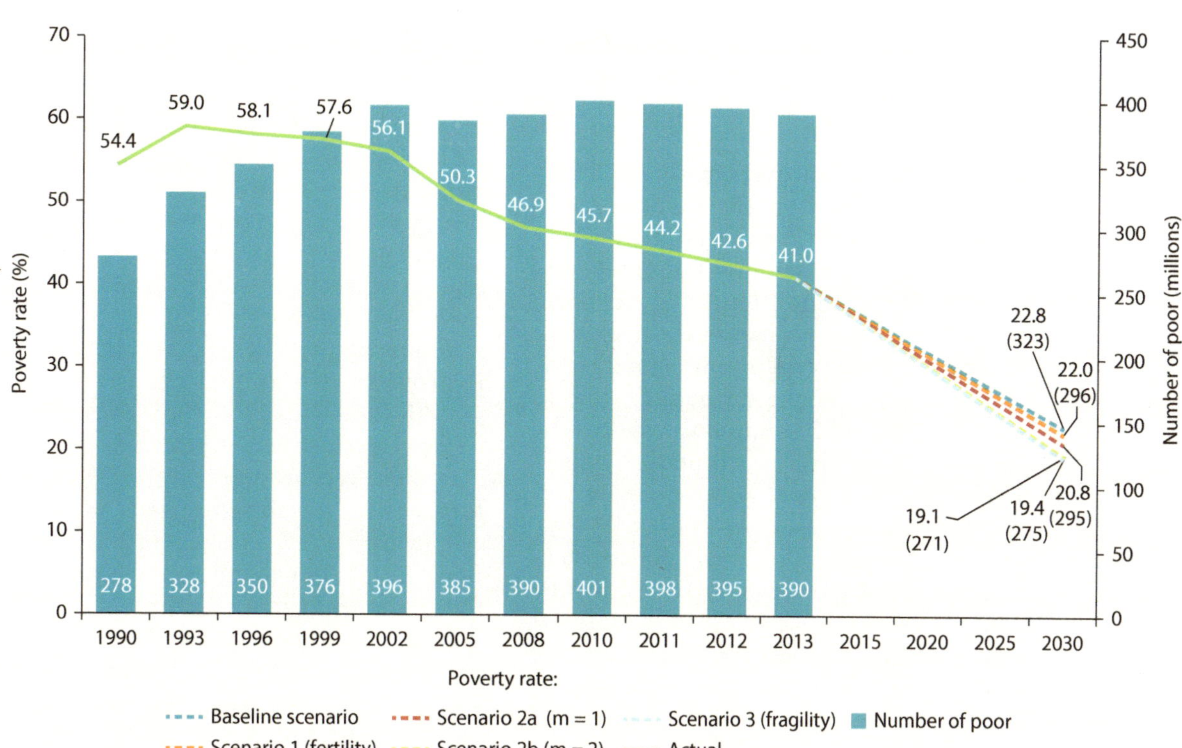

Source: World Bank calculations.

Note: The poverty rate is the percentage of the population living at or below US$1.90 per day. The *baseline scenario* assumes average distribution-neutral growth of 2.8 percent per year. *Scenario 1* assumes a low-fertility population growth scenario instead of the historical population growth rates. *Scenario 2a* assumes more pro-poor growth, with average GDP growth the same as in the baseline scenario but with the incomes of the poor growing 1 percentage point faster than the historical average. *Scenario 2b* also holds average GDP growth the same as in the baseline scenario, but assumes annual income growth among the poor that is 2 percentage points faster than the historical average. *Scenario 3* assumes that increased policy attention would make Africa's fragile states grow 3 percentage points faster than their historical average.

capita incomes grew about three times as fast (by 8 percent per year) would poverty come down to 3 percent (not shown). This is highly unlikely.

In a first alternative scenario (scenario 1), the slow downward trend in population growth is accelerated, using the UN's low-fertility population growth scenario during 2013–30 instead of the historical population growth rates. Doing so would bring poverty rates and numbers down to 22 percent and 296 million, respectively (figure 1.2, scenario 1). Given the multiple channels through which fertility affects growth and poverty, this likely underestimates the poverty-reducing effects of an accelerated fertility decline. Chapter 2 ("Africa's Demography and Socioeconomic Structure") elaborates on this in more depth.

In a second set of scenarios (scenarios 2a and 2b), average income growth stays the same, but the incomes of the poor in each country are now growing faster than the country's historical income growth.[7] If the incomes of the poor in each country were to grow 1 percentage point faster than their historical average, such redistribution of growth from the nonpoor to the poor would bring the poverty rate in 2030 down to 20.8 percent and the number of poor to 295 million (figure 1.2, scenario 2a: m = 1). If the incomes of the poor were to grow 2 percentage points faster, poverty rates and numbers would decline to 19.4 percent and 275 million, respectively. Almost 50 million more people would have been lifted out of poverty (figure 1.2, scenario 2b: m = 2).

Under scenario 3, increased policy attention to the challenges of Africa's fragile states is assumed to pay off in the form of faster (distribution-neutral) income growth in these states. An income increase of 1, 2, or 3 percentage points over their historical growth rates would reduce Africa's poverty rate to 22 percent, 20 percent, and 19.1 percent, respectively, compared with 22.8 percent in the baseline scenario (scenario 3, in figure 1.2).

Outlook from Recent Poverty Trends

How has Africa performed in the more recent past—that is, since the SDG 1 target was adopted? First, it is worth noting that it has become increasingly possible to track Africa's performance on meeting SDG 1 given the increasing availability of nationally representative surveys with which to monitor well-being and poverty (box 1.1). However, estimates of poverty for recent years always include some GDP growth-based poverty estimates for some countries that are in between survey years. Given the assumptions that go into GDP growth-based poverty estimates, these poverty estimates can only be an indication (Ferreira, Azevedo, and Lakner 2017).

Unfortunately, the drop in economic performance of African economies after 2013 has not been good for poverty reduction. The latest 2015 poverty numbers reflect this decline in economic performance, with the drop in Africa's poverty rate slowing to 0.72 percentage points per year. This contrasts with the 1 percentage point decline projected in the base-case scenario described earlier. Hence, based on the latest available poverty numbers, Africa's fight against poverty was already off track in 2015, even relative to the base-case scenario.

Since then, the situation has not improved, with annual per capita GDP growth for Africa as a whole even slightly negative each year (–0.3 percent in 2018). The most recent aggregate GDP growth forecasts suggest some recovery, to 2.8 percent in 2019 and 3.3 percent in 2020 (World Bank 2019). But this barely makes up for the decline in Africa's GDP during 2016–18. It also remains well below the 1998–2013 *per capita* average of 2.8 percent per year assumed in the base-case scenario. Over the past five years, progress in poverty reduction in Africa has in all likelihood been lagging well behind the base-case scenario.

In addition to accelerating growth across countries, the simulations also suggest that

BOX 1.1 Efforts to improve Africa's poverty data are starting to pay off

For a long time, knowledge of Africa's economic and social transformation has been compromised by weaknesses in the underlying data. Some of the key constraints to better statistical systems and data include infrequent surveys, low access to data produced, poor coordination and integration of statistical systems, minimal use of statistical evidence for decision making, and insufficient institutional capacity and political incentives, culminating in inadequate and unreliable financing.

These weaknesses were documented in the precursor report to this one, *Poverty in a Rising Africa* (Beegle et al. 2016). In 2015, and partly in response to the stark findings in that report, the World Bank committed to put more effort into strengthening the capacity of national statistical systems in low-income countries, including support for conducting at least one national household survey to measure well-being and poverty every three years.

There has been substantial progress since that report (figure B1.1.1). More than half of Africa's countries (26) had completed at least one such survey by the second quarter of 2018. For the period 2018–20, 34 countries (accounting for 76.4 percent of the population in Africa) have an ongoing or planned survey. Along with the effort to increase the frequency and quality of household surveys to measure poverty has come an expansion of other surveys such as agriculture production surveys and censuses, business registries, and population censuses.

Beyond improving data collection, the support to statistical capacity helped reform institutional incentives, turning statistical agencies into professional and functionally productive organizations. Africa's Statistical Capacity Indicator (SCI), which grades country statistical systems on the quality, frequency, and timeliness of core economic and social data, has now not only caught up with other low-income countries, but even looks already to be edging a bit higher. Sustaining this commitment will be essential to reliably track poverty.

Building on this experience, the World Bank is now working on a model that scales up capacity support for a core package (a "minimum data package") of economic and social statistics in all African countries. This regional approach aims to harmonize and benchmark country statistics, to facilitate peer learning, and to scale up innovations. These ongoing and planned efforts complement and build on country-developed and owned National Strategies for the Development of Statistics (NSDS). They also work with regional and global partners on the statistics agenda.

FIGURE B1.1.1 African countries' poverty status can now be estimated from recent household surveys

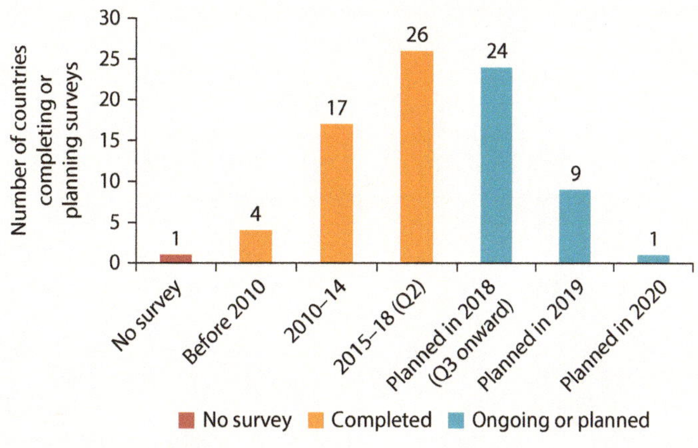

Number of countries completing or planning surveys
30
25
20
15
10
5
0
1
4
17
26
24
9
1
No survey
Before 2010
2010–14
2015–18 (Q2)
Planned in 2018 (Q3 onward)
Planned in 2019
Planned in 2020
No survey
Completed
Ongoing or planned

Source: World Bank.

work on different fronts will be needed to accelerate Africa's poverty reduction—that is, to accelerate the fertility transition (scenario 1), to make growth more inclusive (scenario 2), and to improve growth conditions in fragile states (scenario 3).

Africa's Poverty in Profile

Which groups are affected most by poverty? Where do the poor live, and what do they do for a living? How does their status evolve over time? And, how empowered are they to change their fate? Answers to these questions can provide useful entry points in designing poverty-reducing policies. Nonetheless, care must be taken not to overinterpret the findings. They indicate symptoms of poverty, not necessarily causes.

Which Individuals Are More Likely Poor?

Poverty, as currently assessed, is measured at the household level, because this is how consumption data are collected. It assumes that members in the same household share equally. This is clearly not always the case (box 1.2).

With this important caveat in mind, the available data indicate that child poverty is especially pervasive in Africa. Half of Africa's poor are below the age of 15. This should not surprise. At 2.7 percent per year, Africa's population growth is still high, and its population is predominantly young (43 percent are below 15 years old). Most children live in larger households, which tend to be poorer (Castañeda et al. 2018; Newhouse, Suarez-Becerra, and Evans 2016).[8] Childhood poverty affects malnutrition, school achievements, and thus the long-term earnings potential for the poor and the prospects of exiting poverty in adulthood (see Fundamentals 1, "Africa's Human Development Trap"). Greater focus on larger households in fighting poverty is thus called for, both to reduce poverty today and to build the capacity of poor children to exit poverty as adults (Watkins and Quattri 2016).

Contrary to expectations, the household-based consumption data further indicate that gender gaps in poverty are modest:

BOX 1.2 To measure gender and age gaps in poverty, you need to get into the household

Our current approach to measuring poverty falls far short when it comes to informing on age and gender gaps in poverty. Several recent papers use more-detailed consumption data from Africa to move away from assuming equal intrahousehold sharing and to better inform on gender and child poverty.

For example, the poverty headcount rate increased by 6–7 percentage points in Burundi when using declared food shares for each household member to correct for intrahousehold allocation patterns (Mercier and Verwimp 2017). This was mainly because a significant additional number of children were counted as poor who had been considered nonpoor under the standard calculations because they were living in nonpoor households. The substantial presence of poor children in nonpoor households in Africa is also underscored by Brown, Ravallion, and van de Walle (2017), in this case using nutritional status as a proxy for individual poverty.

Attempting to account for differences in consumption within households greatly increased poverty for women in Malawi (Dunbar, Lewbel, and Pendakur 2013) but not in Côte d'Ivoire (Bargain, Donni, and Kwenda 2014). In Senegal, there was inequality in nonfood consumption between men and women but not so much in food consumption (Lambert, Ravallion, and van de Walle 2014). Similarly, no appreciable gender difference in nutrient intake inadequacy was found when comparing *household*-based adult male equivalent estimates with those obtained from *individual* 24-hour recall measures in Ethiopia (Coates et al. 2017). When there were differences, it mainly concerned children under three years old.

Africa's female share of the poor is about the same as the male share (50.2 percent and 49.8 percent, respectively) (Munoz Boudet et al. 2018). When looking at the gender dimension of poverty by household type, female-headed households are not systematically poorer, either, and many have seen their poverty falling even faster than male-headed households (Castañeda et al. 2018; Milazzo and van de Walle 2017).[9]

Yet evidence also shows that multiple structural inequalities confront women relative to men (such as lower education levels, lower ownership and control over assets, less labor market engagement [linked to gendered time-use patterns], and lower social indicators), as further discussed in Fundamentals 2 ("The Nexus of Gender Inequality and Poverty"). A gendered lens in policy design aimed at reducing poverty is also needed. More broadly, an enhanced focus on intrahousehold allocation processes and on age- and gender-differentiated individual data collection is called for (Doss 2013) (box 1.2).

A third demographic trait of poverty, in addition to age and gender, is the education profile: poor people are considerably less educated. Among poor adults in Africa, two in five have no formal education, reflecting a legacy of poor educational outcomes (Castañeda et al. 2018). Gross primary school enrollment rates in Africa have increased substantially in the past two decades (from 73.4 percent in 1996 to 98.4 percent in 2014). Unfortunately, learning remains low (World Bank 2018) and secondary school enrollment limited (gross enrollment of 42.7 percent in 2014). Education, and human development more generally, are critical factors for the agenda to reduce poverty in Africa (as discussed further in Fundamentals 1).

Finally, other demographic and sociocultural traits frequently associated with higher poverty incidence include orphanhood, disability, displacement (internally or internationally), and ethnicity. The available evidence suggests, however, that orphanhood, for example, does not always confer a disadvantage, because it can be correlated with wealth and urban status (when deriving from the human immunodeficiency virus and the acquired immune deficiency syndrome [HIV/AIDS], for example). Similarly, the internally displaced are not necessarily always the poorest (Beegle et al. 2016). Despite these caveats, systematic, Africa-wide data about the size and poverty status of these groups are hard to come by. But they often also live geographically concentrated in certain regions (for example, ethnic groups or pastoralists) or at the outskirts of settlements, as in Ethiopia (World Bank, forthcoming). More specific studies are needed.

Where Do the Poor Live, and What Do They Do for a Living?

Most of Africa's poor live in a limited number of countries: 10 out of 48 countries house three-quarters of Africa's poor.[10] These are large countries in terms of overall population, but they are not always the poorest countries in terms of poverty rates.

Poverty rates are highest in the Sahel countries and the northern regions of the coastal West African countries, extending east into Ethiopia and southeast into the Congo Basin and its eastern surrounding regions in Burundi, Rwanda, Tanzania, and Uganda (map 1.1, panel a). These are mostly also landlocked regions. In some of these countries and regions, poverty numbers are also high (map 1.1, panel b). Poverty rates and numbers are also high in Madagascar and Mozambique. Rates and numbers are much lower in the higher-income countries of southern Africa, except for Lesotho, Eswatini, and Zambia, where poverty rates are high. The low poverty rate in the northern regions of the Sahel countries is likely linked to their high urbanization and the poor representation of pastoralists in household surveys.[11]

Beyond this broad-brush picture, the correspondence between poverty rates and the number of the poor is limited. This poses a policy challenge. The Central African

MAP 1.1 Africa's poverty and poor are concentrated in a limited number of (often landlocked) countries and regions within these countries

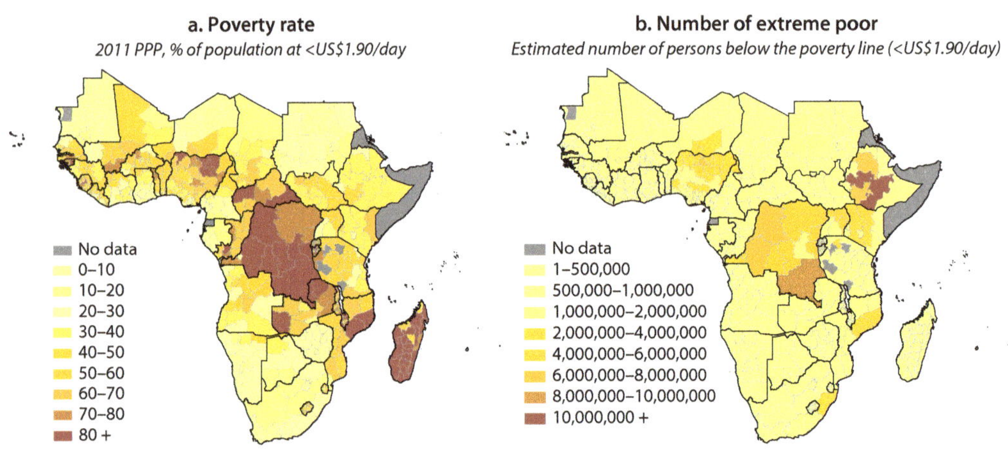

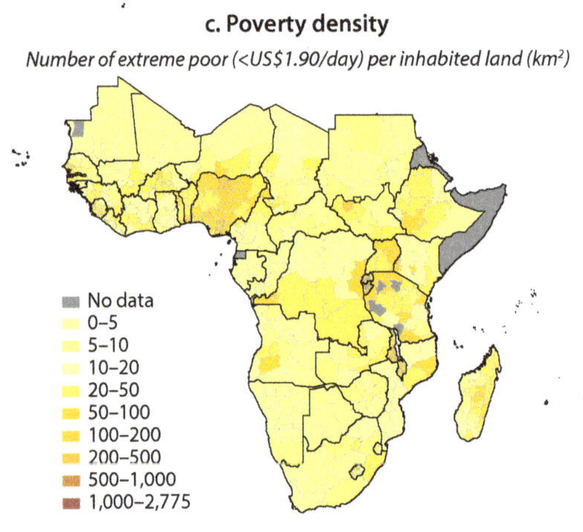

Source: World Bank's internal Global Monitoring Database.
Note: PPP = purchasing power parity. Poverty estimates are based on the latest available household survey.

Republic, for example, has a poverty rate of 79 percent. Compare this with Uganda, where an estimated 34.5 percent must live on less than US$1.90 a day. Yet, Uganda's poor are about 3.5 times as numerous as in the Central African Republic (13 million and 3.6 million, respectively).

Across countries, the correlation between the poverty rate and the number of poor people is 33 percent. Across subnational regions within countries, it is somewhat higher (57 percent on average). Countries with very low correspondence between the subnational poverty rates and the number of poor people within these regions include Côte d'Ivoire, Eswatini, Madagascar, and Malawi. In many countries, poorer regions (regions with higher poverty rates) also tend to have lower poverty density (fewer poor people per inhabited square kilometer), making it harder (or more expensive) to reach them (map 1.1, panel c).

From a utilitarian perspective, where the guiding principle is bringing the greatest happiness to the greatest number, the focus should be on reducing poverty in the countries and regions where most of the poor live. Yet, when most people in a region are poor (high rates), even if they are few in number, it can be particularly hard to escape from poverty. The clearest evidence for poverty traps emerges from geographic poverty traps, be they regions within a country or low-productivity countries altogether (Kraay and McKenzie 2014; also see chapter 2, "Africa's Demography and Socioeconomic Structure"). Geographic poverty traps can be fertile ground for conflict, especially when they coincide with ethnic, religious, or language divides;[12] repression; or economic shocks (Marks 2016). The long-lasting shadow that conflict frequently casts over development motivates a focus on regions and countries with higher poverty rates. Targeting countries, and regions within countries, that host the larger numbers of Africa's poor may yield faster poverty reduction, but the gains may be less sustainable.

Within countries and regions, as in the rest of the world, African poverty is predominantly rural, with farming dominating the livelihoods of the poor. About four out of five of Africa's poor (82 percent) live in rural areas,[13] and about three in four of Africa's poor working adults (76 percent) are engaged in agriculture (Beegle et al. 2016; Castañeda et al. 2018).[14]

Those engaged in agriculture (crops and livestock) work mostly for their own account (are smallholders rather than being wage workers on other farms) and tend to earn the bulk of their income in agriculture (Davis, Di Giuseppe, and Zezza 2017). Engagement in agricultural wage employment has so far been limited, and substantially less than in the rest of the world (except in Malawi).[15] With little or no land of their own, agricultural wage laborers worldwide are usually also among the poorest.

Once Poor, Forever Poor?

Poverty in Africa is both a chronic and a transitory condition.[16] Three in five of Africa's poor are chronically poor—that is, poor for several years in a row (Dang and Dabalen 2018). This suggests that poverty in Africa remains deeply structural, stemming from a lack of assets, weak access to public goods (infrastructure), and poor income-earning opportunities. This entrenched situation partly relates to the poor's location (the so-called geographic poverty trap) (Kraay and McKenzie 2014). But it can also reflect the costs of avoiding income shocks from occurring—the so-called risk-induced poverty trap (Dercon and Christiaensen 2011; Elbers, Gunning, and Kinsey 2007).

The remaining two in five of Africa's poor are in transitory poverty. This supports the notion that households (and firms) operate in highly risky environments, often with limited capacity to cope, as detailed in chapter 5 ("Managing Risks and Conflict"). African households experience a higher exposure to loss than other regions in nearly all risk factors. Poverty exits remain fragile, with many relapsing.

One particularly pernicious type of risk that many Africans face is the risk of physical insecurity and conflict. It pulls people back into poverty, also those who were substantially better off before, and once people are there, it tends to keep them there for a long time. Poverty is especially high in fragile states and poverty reduction in such states is much slower (Beegle et al. 2016). In 2013, 29 percent of Africa's poor lived in fragile and conflict-affected states, a number projected to increase to 43.6 percent under the business-as-usual scenario depicted in figure 1.2 (baseline scenario). Accelerating poverty reduction in fragile and conflict-affected states will have to be central to any poverty-reduction agenda for Africa.

Who Is in Charge?

The poor typically have a weak relationship with the state and are often disempowered. They have more limited access to public goods and services (typically those of poor quality) and have limited voice in public policy making (Beegle et al. 2016). This manifests in many ways, including in learning and health outcomes. Differences between the poorest and richest quintiles are often large. In Africa's oil-rich countries, they are usually even more stark (de la Brière et al. 2017). Fundamentals 1 provides further details.

To influence public policy and make demands upon the state, poor people in Africa rely substantially on electoral institutions.[17] Yet a sizable minority believes the elections to be unfairly counted or bought (World Bank 2016). Moreover, almost 40 percent of Africans do not regularly listen to the radio, watch television, or read a newspaper at least once a week. Lack of exposure to public information is even more pronounced among the poor (by 17 percentage points among poor versus nonpoor women) (Beegle et al. 2016), while the poor are particularly vulnerable to political clientelism.[18]

Community-driven development programs have often been used to counter national elite capture and increase public spending in favor of the poor. Thorough reviews of such participatory programs suggest that the poor often tend to benefit less than the better-off because the participants in civic activities tend to be wealthier, more educated, of higher social status, male, and more politically connected than nonparticipants (Mansuri and Rao 2013). This leaves the poor disempowered, on the receiving end of the policy-making process—with the result being less access to public goods and services, or only to public goods and services of poor quality.

Lessons from Recent Experience

Over the past couple of decades, Africa's poverty rate has not only been higher than in most other low- and middle-income countries; it also has declined more slowly. Three factors contribute to this (Christiaensen and Hill 2018).

Persistently high population growth. First, incomes have grown more slowly in per capita terms in Africa than in low- and middle-income countries of other regions because a much larger share of economic growth is eroded by faster population growth. When comparing *aggregate economic (GDP)* growth across African and non-African countries in the global database of poverty, there is no systematic difference in their growth performance, especially after 1995.[19] However, the estimated difference in annual *per capita GDP* growth after 1995 between African and similarly poor non-African countries is 1.2 percentage points on average. Although *aggregate* economic growth has been robust in Africa, especially during 1995–2013, a sizable part of growth in Africa is eroded by rapid population expansion.

Poor initial conditions. Second, less of Africa's (rather modest) *per capita household income* growth results in poverty reduction than in other countries, simply because the region *is* poor.[20] During 1981–2013, the average African country achieved a 1.9 percent reduction in the poverty rate for every 1 percentage point of household income growth. In other words, its poverty to household income growth elasticity was –1.9. Countries outside of Africa achieved a 3.3 percent reduction—1.7 times more. Yet these differences are largely mechanical; they disappear when controlling for differences in initial poverty (box 1.3). African countries are not worse (or better) at converting household income growth into poverty reduction than other similarly poor countries. Eighty-five percent of the explained difference in the elasticity of poverty to growth between African and non-African countries is explained by differences in initial poverty.[21]

Beyond a mechanical effect, the conditions of high poverty—the absolute lack of assets and access to public goods and services as well as limited income-earning opportunities for a large share of the population—limit the ability of many to contribute to and

BOX 1.3 Africa's poverty-to-growth elasticity is low because Africa is poor

The finding that African countries have a lower elasticity of poverty to growth is consistent with the finding in the literature that poorer countries achieve a lower percentage of poverty reduction from 1 percentage point of growth than richer countries (Ravallion 2012). Part of the reason could simply be mechanical: The elasticity is the percentage of poverty reduction from 1 percentage point of growth. Similar elasticities would thus imply a larger absolute reduction in poverty in countries that start with higher poverty rates. For example, a 10 percent reduction in poverty is a reduction from 5 percent to 4.5 percent but also a reduction from 50 percent to 45 percent (or of 0.5 percentage points compared with 5 percentage points, respectively) for a country starting with half of its population in poverty. This makes it harder for poorer countries to do as well as richer countries by this measure.

An alternative approach is to use semi-elasticities (Cuaresma, Klasen, and Wacker 2016). These measure the absolute percentage point change in poverty from 1 percentage point of growth. They do not depend on initial poverty, and countries with different initial poverty rates that record the same absolute decline in poverty per percentage point of growth would also record the same semi-elasticity.

On this measure, Africa has performed significantly better than the rest of the world. Growth of 1 percentage point has resulted in a poverty reduction of 0.37 percentage points in the rest of the world but an average reduction of 0.49 percentage points in Africa (table B1.3.1). The result should not surprise. With national income distributions often approximating the lognormal distribution, poorer countries tend to perform better on this measure for an equivalent (distribution-neutral) growth in income (and thus an equivalent shift in the income distribution).

So, the question is not so much how Africa has performed in converting its growth into poverty reduction relative to other countries but rather how it has performed on this measure relative to other *equally poor* countries. Matching each African country to a similarly poor non-African counterpart (using nearest-neighbor matching estimation) shows that countries in Africa are doing no better (and no worse) than similarly poor countries in other regions (neither on the elasticity nor on the semi-elasticity score). The differences are small and not statistically significant in either case (table B1.3.1, last row).

TABLE B1.3.1 Africa's elasticity and semi-elasticity of poverty to per capita income growth are not different from the rest of the world when controlling for initial poverty

Countries	Poverty-to-growth elasticity	Poverty-to-growth semi-elasticity
African average	−1.88	−0.49***
Global average excluding Africa	−3.33***	−0.37
Average treatment effect of being in Africa controlling for initial poverty (standard error)	−0.8 (1.4)	−0.002 (0.058)

Source: Christiaensen and Hill 2018.
Note: Available poverty spells during 1981–2013. Elasticities and semi-elasticities were calculated for each of the poverty spells with initial poverty rates of 5 percent or more, based on the percentage change in average per capita survey income and after omitting outlier values as well as the top and bottom 5 percent of the elasticity estimates themselves. Positive (semi-)elasticities (from negative growth spells) were further omitted to avoid artificially reducing the averages, though the order of magnitude of averages for the elasticities and semi-elasticities in both Africa and the rest of the world was very similar when expressed in absolute values. Average treatment effect calculated using nearest-neighbor matching on initial poverty.
Significance level: *** = 1 percent.

participate in growth. This is one mechanism by which inequality reduces the impact of growth on poverty. When inequality is high and average income low, a large share of the population is less likely to have what they need to take advantage of growth. From this perspective, it is not so much inequality per se that matters in low-income countries but rather initial poverty. When countries grow and average incomes rise—also increasing the scope for redistribution—inequality per se (the fact that some have more than others, as in South Africa) becomes more important for poverty reduction.[22]

Composition of Africa's growth. Third, Africa's poverty reduction has been slower because it has been less efficient than other regions in converting its aggregate economic growth (GDP per capita growth) into household income growth. Although Africa's poverty-to-growth elasticity has been like that of equally poor countries elsewhere, household incomes per capita (as captured in the surveys) have also been growing more slowly because less GDP growth is converted into private income growth (controlling for population growth).

Using a series of comparable household surveys from Africa during the 1990s and 2000s, annual per capita consumption growth was estimated to be 1.2 percentage points lower than the corresponding annual

BOX 1.4 High fertility and initial poverty reduce Africa's poverty-to-growth elasticity

High initial poverty is closely correlated with high fertility, poor human capital, and limited access to infrastructure. Several regression-based simulations (table B1.4.1) illustrate the detrimental effect on the conversion of growth in poverty reduction (as well as on the rate of poverty reduction directly, beyond the growth channel).

For example, were Africa to have the global median rates of child mortality and adult literacy, the average African country would realize an additional 1 percent and 1.3 percent of poverty reduction, respectively, for each 1 percent of growth. Together, this would be enough to bring the elasticity of poverty to growth to the global average. Closing the gap on rural electrification would result in an even larger gain: electrification rates at the global average are associated with an additional 1.6 percent of poverty reduction for every 1 percent of growth achieved.

The greatest gains, however, can be expected from reducing fertility. Bringing the number of children per woman to the global median of 2.5 would be associated with a lower poverty rate (of 7.3 percent), while also adding 1.8 percent of poverty reduction for every 1 percent of growth.

These results are illustrative. The regression results are not causal, in that they do not guarantee a decrease in poverty-to-growth elasticity were these specific health, education, or electricity outcomes to change. But they are indicative of the magnitude of the effect of Africa's poor initial conditions on its fight against poverty.

TABLE B1.4.1 Substantial poverty reduction could result from increasing Africa's human and physical capital indicators to the global median

	Fertility (births per woman)	Adult literacy (%)	Child mortality (per 1,000 births)	Access to electricity (%)
Average level (median)				
African median[a]	5.6	57.1	122.0	18.2
Global median[a]	2.5	87.3	22.6	97.2
Impact on poverty if African countries were to achieve the global median (from regression results)				
Poverty would fall by (%)	7.3*	1.6	5.4	6.6
Additional poverty reduction from each percent of growth (%)	1.8***	1.3***	1.0***	1.6***
Number of observations	456	439	456	456

Source: Christiaensen and Hill (2018), based on the World Bank's PovcalNet (http://iresearch.worldbank.org/PovcalNet) and the World Development Indicators database.

a. Figures are the averages for the initial survey year for the latest spell for which poverty reduction was measured. The regression analysis used a global dataset of poverty reduction, average income growth, and initial conditions for 85 countries with poverty rates higher than 5 percent from 1981 to 2013. Each observation is a country spell for which annual poverty reduction and income growth are recorded.

Significance level: * = 10 percent, *** = 1 percent.

growth in GDP per capita (Beegle et al. 2016). Not only does Africa's *aggregate* GDP growth not result in the same increase in *per capita* GDP (owing to high fertility and population growth), but the same GDP per capita increase also puts less income in the pockets of its people, including the poor.

This finding suggests that a focus on aggregate GDP growth alone may not be enough (even when also addressing population growth and poor initial conditions) and raises the question of the composition of Africa's GDP growth—in particular, the region's increasing reliance on natural resources and the associated governance challenges as well as the still rather modest performance of its agriculture and manufacturing sectors. The importance of the sources of growth for the elasticity of poverty to GDP growth has been documented widely, with growth being more poverty reducing when it occurs in sectors where the poor are working and when using production factors that the poor possess, such as labor and land. Growth in agriculture, for example, has been on average two to three times more poverty reducing than the same amount of GDP growth elsewhere in the economy, at least when land has not been distributed too unequally (Christiaensen, Demery, and Kuhl 2011; Ivanic and Martin 2018; Ligon and Sadoulet 2018; Loayza and Raddatz 2010; Ravallion and Chen 2003; Ravallion and Datt 2002).

So, what is the potential for a more pro-poor growth process, whereby the incomes of the poor also grow substantially as the economy develops? One view holds that governments should focus on policy packages that maximize growth (pro-growth), which are argued to be better understood and more effective, rather than on policy packages that focus on growing the incomes of the poor (pro-poor growth) (Dollar, Kleineberg, and Kraay 2015, 2016; Dollar and Kraay 2002). However, the distinction between pro-growth and distribution-oriented policies is less clear than is often purported. Many policies affect both, and often in opposite ways.[23] What ultimately matters is the joint effect of these policies on the income growth of the poor.[24] Also, as discussed, it is not clear that a pro-growth focus has worked for Africa.[25]

The scope and need for pro-poor growth policies in Africa is large. Although Africa will not be able to eradicate poverty by 2030, the poverty projections show that 50 million more people could be lifted out of poverty if the incomes of the poor were to grow 2 percentage points faster annually while keeping each country's historical per capita growth rate over the past 15 years constant (as indicated in figure 1.2, scenario 2b). Combined with lower population growth and better initial conditions, pro-poor growth could thus go a long way in accelerating poverty reduction (now and in the future). Naive cross-country regression analysis already provides a first (noncausal) indication of how Africa's high fertility, poor human capital, and low access to infrastructure impede poverty reduction (box 1.4). This is examined further in chapter 2 (on the demographic and socioeconomic determinants of poverty) and Fundamentals 1 ("Africa's Human Development Trap").

Notes

1. The focus in this report is on extreme poverty, defined as living below US$1.90 a day in 2011 purchasing power parity (PPP) terms. In the rest of the report, "poverty" will be used as shorthand. For an extensive discussion of Africa's poverty status, including the robustness of the underlying statistics, see Beegle et al. (2016).
2. Africa poverty data from the World Bank global poverty database, PovcalNet (accessed May 5, 2019): http://iresearch.worldbank.org/PovcalNet/povDuplicateWB.aspx.
3. This ambition is articulated in SDG 1, Target 1.1 (http://www.un.org/sustainabledevelopment/poverty/). It is tracked by measuring progress on the proportion of people living below the US$1.90 a day international poverty line (in 2011 PPP). The focus of this report—reduction of monetary poverty—aligns with this SDG target.
4. This corresponds to the average annual GDP per capita growth rate across the low- and

middle-income world during the first decade of 2000. The scenario assumes distribution-neutral growth in each country.

5. In practice, the objective of eradicating poverty was numerically translated as bringing the poverty rate to 3 percent or less. Given poverty churning, there will always be some people in poverty.
6. The 2.8 percent income growth is the population-weighted average of each country's 1998–2013 historical growth rate, which already signifies a high-growth period in Africa's recent history.
7. This is akin to the shared prosperity premium (m) developed by Lakner, Negre, and Prydz (2014). Yet instead of redistributing income growth from the top 60 percent to the bottom 40 percent, it is redistributed from the nonpoor in each country to the extreme poor in that country.
8. Worldwide, two out of three poor children live in households with six or more members. Sensitivity analysis suggests that these household consumption-based estimates are robust to sensible corrections for age-related differences in needs (using adult equivalence scales) and household economies of scale (Newhouse, Suarez-Becerra, and Evans 2016). Furthermore, households with more than two kids are 15 percent more likely to be poor, conditional on a number of characteristics of the household's residence and its demographics, as well as the age, educational attainment, and sector of work of the household head (Castañeda et al. 2018).
9. Castañeda et al. (2018) find that male-headed households across the world are, on average, 3.4 percentage points poorer than female-headed households. Female-headed households, though, make up a heterogeneous group, arising for a widely divergent number of reasons (such as divorce, widowhood, or seasonal migration of the adult male), each with different socioeconomic and cultural consequences. As such, they can only be a poor proxy of general poverty differences between men and women.
10. Ranking countries from those with the largest number of poor, Nigeria accounts for about one-quarter of Africa's poor (85.2 million); the next four (the Democratic Republic of Congo, Tanzania, Ethiopia, and Madagascar) for another one-quarter; and the next five (Mozambique, Uganda, Malawi, Kenya, and Zambia) for the following 25 percent.
11. Beyond pastoralism, there is typically not much activity outside the urban centers in these barren, arid regions (Allen, Heinrigs, and Heo 2018); see map 1.1. (Also see the Urban Population dataset of Harvest Choice and the International Food Policy Research Institute [IFPRI] at https://harvestchoice.org/data/pn00_urb.) Pastoralists are often poorer (Mburu et al. 2017), but they are poorly captured in the residence-based household surveys that form the basis for most poverty calculations.
12. Group-level inequalities can generate social and economic polarization that increases the risk of violent conflict (Kanbur 2006; Østby 2008, 2013; Stewart 2008).
13. These estimates are based on nominal per capita consumption data, which do not control for regional price differences. Given that the cost of living is typically lower in rural areas, they may overstate the share of poor who are rural. Evidence from seven South Asian countries for which spatially deflated data are available suggests that the overestimation is likely moderate (6–7 percentage points at most) (Castañeda et al. 2018). To the extent that these findings carry over to Africa, the core insight—that most of Africa's poor are rural—remains.
14. In the rest of the world, the share of the poor engaged in agriculture is about two in three (65 percent).
15. Among the 9 African countries studied by Davis, Di Giuseppe, and Zezza (2017), only 18 percent of rural households engage in agricultural wage labor, from which they obtain on average only 5 percent of their income. This compares with 27 percent and 13 percent, respectively, in the 13 non-African countries in their sample. A notable exception is Malawi. Here, 49 percent of the rural population reported engaging in agricultural wage labor in 2011. This is similar to what is observed in some countries in Latin America (such as Ecuador and Nicaragua) and South Asia (such as Bangladesh and Nepal). As in Malawi, inequality and landlessness are high. Recently, agricultural wage labor has also increased in Tanzania (Christiaensen et al. 2017).
16. Broadly speaking, people are considered chronically poor when they are poor for an

extended period, and in transitory poverty when they move in and out of poverty. For a more elaborate discussion on how to incorporate the time dimension in poverty measurement, see Christiaensen and Shorrocks (2012).

17. Self-reported voter rates in Africa have been around 70 percent and slightly higher among uneducated than among educated citizens (World Bank 2016). About 90 percent of African citizens further reported that honest elections could make a lot of difference in their and their families' lives, with little differentiation in responses between the more and less educated.
18. Clientelism is a political strategy characterized by an exchange of material goods in return for electoral support (World Bank 2017).
19. When controlling for initial poverty (comparing African countries with equally poor countries elsewhere), GDP growth rates in Africa are also only marginally lower.
20. Estimates are based on the World Bank's global dataset of poverty reduction, PovcalNet (http://iresearch.worldbank.org/PovcalNet). Elasticities were calculated for each poverty spell and based on the change in poverty reduction and the average survey-based household income growth. Note that in calculating the poverty-to-growth elasticity, per capita income growth can be captured through GDP growth per capita during the spell or, alternatively, through the average income growth per capita observed in the household surveys from which the poverty estimates are derived. Here, the latter approach is used, which implicitly assumes that GDP growth per capita translates one for one into household income growth. This is not automatic, because in addition to measurement issues, GDP comprises several elements other than private consumption, such as private investment as well as government consumption and investment, and these do not necessarily grow at the same rate (Beegle et al. 2016).
21. Controlling for initial poverty, no systematic difference in the Gini coefficient was observed across African and non-African countries.
22. In examining differences in poverty-to-growth elasticity, much of the literature has focused so far on the effect of initial inequality (possibly also controlling for initial mean income) without making this distinction, thereby conflating the initial poverty effect with that of initial inequality (López and Servén 2015; Perry et al. 2006; Ravallion 2012; Thorbecke and Ouyang 2018).
23. Macroeconomic, monetary, trade, financial, competition, and investment policies are typically considered to be generally growth-oriented (distribution-neutral). Policies fostering human capital formation, equal access to public goods and services and factor markets, and the rule of law, as well as tax, labor market, and social protection policies are typically considered to be more pro-poor growth-oriented (and, by implication, distribution-oriented and addressing inequality). In practice, the distinction is more blurred, rendering the heavy emphasis on growth and inequality as key policy entry points in the poverty-reduction debate less useful than commonly purported. Many of the growth-promoting policies are not distribution-neutral and, vice versa, distribution-related policies often also affect overall growth. Greater primary school enrollment, for example, may be growth enhancing and inequality reducing, while financial globalization may accelerate growth but at the expense of rising inequality (Jaumotte, Lall, and Papageorgiou 2013). From a poverty-reduction perspective, the "sweet spot" policies are those that increase growth while also disproportionately benefiting the poor. Policies that contain inflation may be one such candidate, as are those that foster primary school enrollment and quality education (Dollar, Kleineberg, and Kraay 2015, 2016; Dollar and Kraay 2002).
24. Examining this requires comparable information on the full income distribution for many countries and time periods, which has only become more widely available over the past decade. As a result, much of the poverty literature has focused on studying the links between the aggregate measures of growth, inequality, and poverty instead, drawing on the related growth and inequality literatures as well as the microeconometric evidence to assess qualitatively the joint effect on poverty of different policies through their effect on growth and distributional change. Given that policies typically affect both growth

and inequality, and that the effect of inequality and growth on poverty also depends on initial income, this accounting approach has tended to conflate initial poverty with initial inequality, and has also tended to objectify the poor as passive recipients undergoing the growth process ("participating in growth") rather than considering them as active agents ("contributing to growth"), shifting attention away from the importance of empowering poor people as a key policy entry point for poverty reduction.

25. Furthermore, the evidence that the incomes of the poor grow at the same rate as the average income of the country—the empirical finding that is at the heart of the pro-growth approach (Dollar, Kleineberg, and Kraay 2015)—assumed that positive and negative growth episodes have the same effect on the income growth (or decline) of the poor. Yet the poor may cope with shocks in ways that make subsequent recovery difficult (when they sell off assets to cope, for example). Given credit constraints and limited human capital, they may also be less able to benefit from growth spurts (Christiaensen, Demery, and Paternostro 2003). This is borne out by the data: a 1 percent *increase* in overall per capita income growth increases the income growth of the poor by 0.75 percent; a 1 percent *decline* reduces it by about 1.6 percent (Poll 2017).

References

Allen, Thomas, Philipp Heinrigs, and Inhoi Heo. 2018. "Agriculture, Food and Jobs in West Africa." West African Papers No. 14, Organisation for Economic Co-operation and Development (OECD), Paris.

Bargain, Olivier, Olivier Donni, and Prudence Kwenda. 2014. "Intrahousehold Distribution and Poverty: Evidence from Côte d'Ivoire." *Journal of Development Economics* 107 (C): 262–76.

Beegle, Kathleen, Luc Christiaensen, Andrew Dabalen, and Isis Gaddis. 2016. *Poverty in a Rising Africa.* Washington, DC: World Bank.

Brown, Caitlin, Martin Ravallion, and Dominique van de Walle. 2017. "Are Poor Individuals Mainly Found in Poor Households? Evidence Using Nutrition Data for Africa." Policy Research Working Paper 8001, World Bank, Washington, DC.

Castañeda, Andrés, Dung Doan, David Newhouse, Minh Cong Nguyen, Hiroki Uematsu, and João Pedro Azevedo. 2018. "A New Profile of the Global Poor." *World Development* 101: 250–67.

Cattaneo, Umberto. 2017. "Poverty Headcount Projections in Sub-Saharan Africa." Background note prepared for *Accelerating Poverty Reduction in Africa*, World Bank, Washington, DC.

Christiaensen, Luc, Lionel Demery, and Jesper Kuhl. 2011. "The (Evolving) Role of Agriculture in Poverty Reduction: An Empirical Perspective." *Journal of Development Economics* 96 (2): 239–54.

Christiaensen, Luc, Lionel Demery, and Stefano Paternostro. 2003. "Macro and Micro Perspectives of Growth and Poverty in Africa." *World Bank Economic Review* 17 (3): 317–47.

Christiaensen, Luc, and Ruth Hill. 2018. "Africa Is Not Poorer than Other Equally Poor Countries in Reducing Poverty." Background note prepared for *Accelerating Poverty Reduction in Africa*, World Bank, Washington, DC.

Christiaensen, Luc, Jonathan Kaminski, Armand Sim, and Yue Wang. 2017. "Poverty, Employment and Migration Patterns in Tanzania, 2008–2012: The Role of Secondary Towns." Unpublished manuscript, World Bank, Washington, DC.

Christiaensen, Luc, and Anthony Shorrocks. 2012. "Measuring Poverty over Time." *Journal of Economic Inequality* 10 (2): 137–43.

Coates, Jennifer, Beatrice Lorge Rogers, Alexander Blau, Jacqueline Lauer, and Alemzewed Roba. 2017. "Filling a Dietary Data Gap? Validation of the Adult Male Equivalent Method of Estimating Individual Nutrient Intake from Household-Level Data in Ethiopia and Bangladesh." *Food Policy* 72: 27–42.

Cuaresma, Jesús Crespo, Stephan Klasen, and Konstantin M. Wacker. 2016. "There Is Poverty Convergence." Department of Economics Working Paper 213, Vienna University.

Dang, Hai-Anh H., and Andrew L. Dabalen. 2018. "Is Poverty in Africa Mostly Chronic or Transient? Evidence from Synthetic Panel Data." *Journal of Development Studies* 55 (7): 1527–47.

Davis, Benjamin, Stefania Di Giuseppe, and Alberto Zezza. 2017. "Are African Households (Not) Leaving Agriculture? Patterns of

Household Income Sources in Rural Sub-Saharan Africa." *Food Policy* 67: 153–74.

de la Brière, Bénédicte, Deon Filmer, Dena Ringold, Dominic Rohner, Karelle Samuda, and Anastasiya Denisova. 2017. *From Mines and Wells to Well-Built Minds: Turning Sub-Saharan Africa's Natural Resource Wealth into Human Capital.* Directions in Development Series. Washington, DC: World Bank.

Dercon, Stefan, and Luc Christiaensen. 2011. "Consumption Risk, Technology Adoption and Poverty Traps: Evidence from Ethiopia." *Journal of Development Economics* 96 (2): 159–73.

Dollar, David, Tatjana Kleineberg, and Aart Kraay. 2015. "Growth, Inequality and Social Welfare: Cross-Country Evidence." *Economic Policy* 30 (82): 335–77.

———. 2016. "Growth Still Is Good for the Poor." *European Economic Review* 81: 68–85.

Dollar, David, and Aart Kraay. 2002. "Growth Is Good for the Poor." *Journal of Economic Growth* 7 (3): 195–225.

Doss, Cheryl. 2013. "Intrahousehold Bargaining and Resource Allocation in Developing Countries." *World Bank Research Observer* 28 (1): 52–78.

Dunbar, Geoffrey R., Arthur Lewbel, and Krishna Pendakur. 2013. "Children's Resources in Collective Households: Identification, Estimation and an Application to Child Poverty in Malawi." *American Economic Review* 103 (1): 438–71.

Elbers, Chris, Jan Willem Gunning, and Bill Kinsey. 2007. "Growth and Risk: Methodology and Micro Evidence." *World Bank Economic Review* 21: 1–20.

Ferreira, Francisco, Joao-Pedro Azevedo, and Christoph Lakner. 2017. "Feeding the Craving for Precision on Global Poverty." *Let's Talk Development* (blog), December 11. https://blogs.worldbank.org/developmenttalk/feeding-craving-precision-global-poverty.

Ivanic, Maros, and Will Martin. 2018. "Sectoral Productivity Growth and Poverty Reduction: National and Global Impacts." *World Development* 109: 429–39.

Jaumotte, Florence, Subir Lall, and Chris Papageorgiou. 2013. "Rising Income Inequality: Technology, or Trade and Financial Globalization?" *IMF Economic Review* 61 (2): 271–308.

Kanbur, Ravi. 2006. "The Policy Significance of Inequality Decompositions." *Journal of Economic Inequality* 4 (3): 367–74.

Kraay, Aart, and David McKenzie. 2014. "Do Poverty Traps Exist? Assessing the Evidence." *Journal of Economic Perspectives* 28 (3): 127–48.

Lakner, Christoph, Mario Negre, and Espen Prydz. 2014. "Twinning the Goals: How Can Promoting Shared Prosperity Help to Reduce Global Poverty?" Policy Research Working Paper 7106, World Bank, Washington, DC.

Lambert, Sylvie, Martin Ravallion, and Dominique van de Walle. 2014. "Intergenerational Mobility and Interpersonal Inequality in an African Economy." *Journal of Development Economics* 110: 327–44.

Ligon, Ethan, and Elisabeth Sadoulet. 2018. "Estimating the Relative Benefits of Agricultural Growth on the Distribution of Expenditures." *World Development* 109: 417–28.

Loayza, Norman V., and Claudio Raddatz. 2010. "The Composition of Growth Matters for Poverty Alleviation." *Journal of Development Economics* 93 (1): 137–51.

López, Humberto, and Luis Servén. 2015. "Too Poor to Grow." In *Economic Policies in Emerging-Market Economies: Festschrift in Honor of Vittorio Corbo*, edited by Ricardo J. Caballero and Klaus Schmidt-Hebbel, 309–50. Santiago: Central Bank of Chile.

Mansuri, Ghazala, and Vijayendra Rao. 2013. *Localizing Development: Does Participation Work?* Policy Research Report. Washington, DC: World Bank.

Marks, Zoe. 2016. "Poverty and Conflict." GSDRC Professional Development Reading Pack No. 52, University of Birmingham, U.K.

Mburu, Samuel, Steffen Otterbach, Alfonso Sousa-Poza, and Andrew Mude. 2017. "Income and Asset Poverty among Pastoralists in Northern Kenya." *Journal of Development Studies* 53 (6): 971–86.

Mercier, Marion, and Philip Verwimp. 2017. "Are We Counting All the Poor? Accounting for the Intra-Household Allocation of Consumption in Burundi." *Journal of Demographic Economics* 83 (3): 307–27.

Milazzo, Annamaria, and Dominique van de Walle. 2017. "Women Left Behind? Poverty and Headship in Africa." *Demography* 54 (3): 1119–45.

Munoz Boudet, Ana Maria, Paola Buitrago, Bénédicte Leroy de la Brière, David Newhouse, Eliana Rubiano Matulevich, Kinnon Scott, and Pablo Suarez-Becerra. 2018. "Gender Differences in Poverty and Household

Composition through the Life-Cycle: A Global Perspective." Policy Research Working Paper 8360, World Bank, Washington, DC.

Newhouse, David, Pablo Suarez-Becerra, and Martin C. Evans. 2016. "New Estimates of Extreme Poverty for Children." Policy Research Working Paper 7845, World Bank, Washington, DC.

Østby, Gudrun. 2008. "Polarization, Horizontal Inequalities and Violent Civil Conflict." *Journal of Peace Research* 45 (2): 143–62.

———. 2013. "Inequality and Political Violence: A Review of the Literature." *International Area Studies Review* 16 (2): 206–31.

Perry, Guillermo E., Omar S. Arias, J. Humberto López, William F. Maloney, and Luis Servén. 2006. *Poverty Reduction and Growth: Virtuous and Vicious Circles*. Washington, DC: World Bank.

Poll, Moritz. 2017. "Breaking Up the Relationship: Dichotomous Effects of Positive and Negative Growth on the Income of the Poor." CSAE Working Paper 2017–12, Centre for the Study of African Economies, University of Oxford.

Ravallion, Martin. 2012. "Why Don't We See Poverty Convergence?" *American Economic Review* 102 (1): 504–23.

———. 2013. "How Long Will It Take to Lift One Billion People Out of Poverty?" *World Bank Research Observer* 28 (2): 139–58.

Ravallion, Martin, and Shaohua Chen. 2003. "Measuring Pro-Poor Growth." *Economics Letters* 78: 93–99.

Ravallion, Martin, and Gaurav Datt. 2002. "Why Has Economic Growth Been More Pro-Poor in Some States of India than Others?" *Journal of Development Economics* 68 (2): 381–400.

Stewart, Frances, ed. 2008. *Horizontal Inequalities and Conflict: Understanding Group Violence in Multiethnic Societies*. New York and Basingstoke, U.K.: Palgrave McMillan.

Thorbecke, Erik, and Yusi Ouyang. 2018. "Is the Structure of Growth Different in Sub-Saharan Africa?" *Journal of African Economies* 27 (1): 66–91.

Watkins, Kevin, and Maria Quattri. 2016. "Child Poverty, Inequality and Demography: Why Sub-Saharan Africa Matters for the Sustainable Development Goals." Research report, Overseas Development Institute (ODI), London.

World Bank. 2016. *Making Politics Work for Development: Harnessing Transparency and Citizen Engagement*. Policy Research Report. Washington, DC: World Bank.

———. 2017. *World Development Report 2017: Governance and the Law*. Washington, DC: World Bank.

———. 2018. *World Development Report 2018: Learning to Realize Education's Promise*. Washington, DC: World Bank.

———. 2019. *Africa's Pulse: An Analysis of Issues Shaping Africa's Economic Future*, vol. 19 (April). Washington, DC: World Bank.

———. Forthcoming. *Diversity in Prosperity: Promoting Social Inclusion in Ethiopia*. Washington, DC: World Bank.

Africa's Demography and Socioeconomic Structure 2

Luc Christiaensen, Lionel Demery, and Ruth Hill

Analysis of the links between Africa's growth and poverty reduction points to high population growth, poor initial conditions, and the nature of Africa's growth process as three key factors in Africa's lesser performance in poverty reduction. Macro and micro evidence confirms the importance of brokering a fertility decline. At 4.8 births per woman, Africa's total fertility rate remains high and, after accounting for differences in conventional demographic and socioeconomic determinants, it is about 1 birth higher than in low- and middle-income countries outside Africa. Combined with a persistently high number of unwanted births, this points to the important complementary role that family planning programs can play in fostering the fertility transition, in addition to female education and greater economic returns to it.

Poor initial conditions further hold poverty reduction back. In addition to the widely documented lack of human capital and infrastructure—which further conspire to limit the poor's "mental bandwidth" and their capacity to aspire—Africa faces several other structural impediments. Natural resource dependence is now a defining feature of many African countries, undermining the quality of their institutions and governance. Gender inequality remains deep-seated, with a closure of gender gaps holding the prospect of raising Africa's growth. And, finally, social redistributive pressures are shown to discourage people from investing in their income activities.

Addressing these deep-seated structural impediments must begin today. It also takes time to pay off. With the scope for redistribution limited, the emphasis in this report is on policies to create better and more secure jobs in the sectors and places where the poor work and live—on the farm but increasingly also off the farm, especially in the secondary towns and their surrounding areas. These jobs are also more accessible and sustainable when the poor can better manage the multiple risks they face, whether natural or increasingly also political (conflict).

Accelerating the fertility transition, leveraging the food and urban system, addressing fragility, and mobilizing financing for the poor—to finance the associated investments and address the structural impediments—thus emerge as four overarching entry points to accelerate Africa's poverty reduction in the near future. This strategy is further predicated on maintaining a stable macroeconomic environment. The volume will elaborate on these points in this and subsequent chapters, while the policy challenge of improving Africa's initial conditions will be addressed in interspersing features, titled "Fundamentals."

High Fertility Holds Back Poverty Reduction

Despite substantial progress in reducing under-five child mortality (from 172.3 deaths per 1,000 live births in 1995 to 78.3 in 2016), Africa's total fertility rate (TFR) of 4.8 births per woman remains high. As a result, Africa's demographic transition is slow and its population growth still elevated (2.7 percent per year) (Canning, Raja, and Yazbeck 2015). Yet accelerating Africa's fertility reduction can play an important role in poverty reduction, both by influencing per capita gross domestic product (GDP) growth itself and by influencing the response of poverty to that growth.

The experiences of Botswana, and more recently Ethiopia, are illuminating even though not establishing causality. In Botswana, the TFR declined by 2.5 children per woman over a 24-year period (1985–2009), while the poverty rate dropped from 43 percent to 18 percent. More recently, Ethiopia equally experienced a rapid decline in its TFR (from 7.0 to 4.3 during 1995–2015) as well as a rapid decline in poverty (from 67 percent to 26 percent) through an approach combining education, health and family planning, and economic opportunity.

Potential for Fertility Decline to Raise Economic Growth and Reduce Poverty

A reduction in fertility can raise economic growth through several demographic changes:

- *Increased share of working-age population relative to younger and older people.* As the dependency ratio decreases, growth per person will be accelerated even without a productivity increase—that is, when output per person *of working age* (ages 15–65 years) remains constant (Bloom and Williamson 1998). Put simply, a larger share of the population can be at work.
- *Increased female labor force participation.* When women have fewer children, they may increase their participation in the labor market. Following a fertility decline, not only will the working-age share of the population increase, but a larger share of those of working age will also be economically active, raising the output per working-age person even further. These new economic opportunities are also critical for empowering women.
- *Increased workforce productivity.* With fewer children, families and governments will have the opportunity to invest more in each child's human capital. As these children with improved health and educational attainment come of working age and enter the workforce, the productivity of the workforce will increase.

Yet the gains from these changes are not automatic. Fertility reduction will result in accelerated growth only when the increasing number of working-age people can also find income-generating opportunities. The so-called demographic dividend "is not a given, it must be earned" (Groth and May 2017, 3). Macroeconomic stability and private sector fundamentals will be key (including the provision of infrastructure and an enabling business environment), as will be the education of the future workforce (as discussed later in this chapter). Beyond that, the sectoral and risk management policies that will enable such income-generating opportunities are discussed in chapters 3–5 with a focus on the poor.

The global evidence supports this link between the decline in fertility and the pace of economic growth. Cross-country estimates indicate that an increase of 1 percentage point in the share of the working-age population will boost economic growth by 1.1–2.0 percentage points (Ahmed and Cruz 2016; World Bank 2016a).[1] Using a more comprehensive empirical specification and more recent and robust data (especially education data), further research shows that the dividend may not be so much a demographic dividend (from an increase in the share of the working-age population) as an education dividend (from higher educational attainment of the new cohorts entering the labor force) (Cuaresma, Lutz, and Sanderson 2014). A better-educated population has a more productive labor force and is more likely to innovate (thus enhancing total factor productivity). This underscores the critical importance of educating the new cohorts to capture the demographic dividend.

But what about the effects of the demographic transition on poverty? The poor may not benefit (or may benefit less) from a broader fertility transition when fertility among poorer households remains high. Poverty affects fertility behavior, and poor households tend to have many more children (Schoumaker 2004).[2] They would then continue to face high dependency rates, even though dependency is declining among other households. The evidence from Demographic and Health Survey (DHS) data (at least for 2000–16) suggests that fertility rates have remained persistently high among the poorest wealth quintiles and continue to be about three births higher than among the richest quintiles.

Moreover, even when fertility declines across all households, if poorer households are less able to increase their access to income opportunities and raise the educational attainment of their children, the impact of declining fertility on poverty reduction will be weakened. Similarly, if the improved fiscal balance of the government following lower fertility and higher growth does not result in more and better social services for the poor, or in better access to infrastructure, the poor may not experience improved human development outcomes or employment opportunities. And if poor women have limited access to income opportunities, the reductions in their caregiving and domestic burdens through lower fertility may not yield as much empowerment.

Looking across countries and at poverty (rather than growth), a 1 percent fall in the dependency rate is associated with a 0.75 percentage point fall in the poverty rate (Ahmed and Cruz 2016). Although these results do not control for growth, and thus for the effect of fertility reduction via the growth channel, they confirm that the effects of a fertility transition extend to poverty reduction in sizable ways.

Africa's Prospects for a Demographic Dividend

Some African countries (Côte d'Ivoire, Ghana, Malawi, Mozambique, and Namibia) have had the prospect of a demographic dividend (Bloom et al. 2007). In others, the institutional settings have not been favorable. "Stalls" in fertility further indicate that the prospect of fertility reduction is always subject to change (Bongaarts 2008; Guengant 2017).

So, where are we today?

In the past 60 years, the under-five mortality rate has decreased rapidly in Africa—from 307 deaths per thousand in 1950–55 to just 91 deaths per thousand in 2010–15 (United Nations Population Division 2019). Given the limited economic growth over these decades, the improvements in child survival have come mainly from public health interventions rather than from rising household incomes.

Fertility in Africa has also declined, from 6.7 children per woman in 1950–55 to 5.1 in 2015. But this is a much slower decline than in other low- and middle-income regions. In East Asia, for example, the TFR declined from 5.6 to 1.8 over the same period (figure 2.1 gives trends for the main regions since 1960).

More than 50 percent of Africa's population live in countries where women on average still have five or more children (box 2.1). And of the three largest African countries (Nigeria, Ethiopia, and the Democratic Republic of Congo)—which together with Madagascar and Tanzania are home to 50 percent of Africa's poor—only Ethiopia appears to have embarked on a demographic transition. Because of the delayed reduction in fertility, Africa's dependency ratio is not expected to peak until 2080 (Canning, Raja, and Yazbeck 2015). The persistence of high fertility among the poorest households even when the demographic transition is occurring is a further concern. The demographic signal is too weak to be a decisive influence on socioeconomic progress (Cleland and Machiyama 2017).

FIGURE 2.1 Fertility has declined much more slowly in Africa than elsewhere

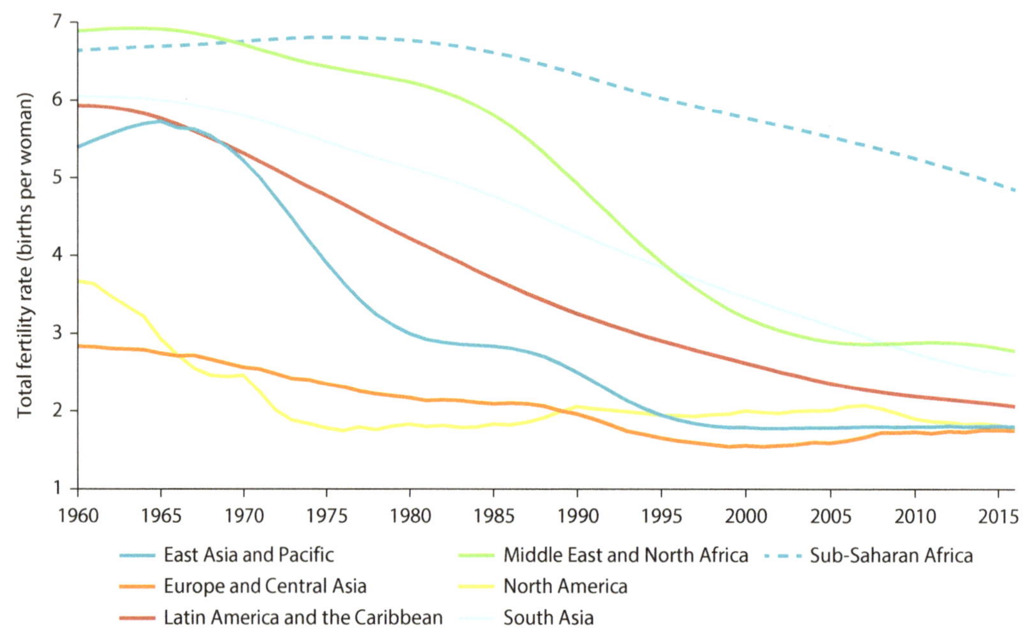

Source: World Development Indicators database.
Note: The total fertility rate is the average number of children born to a woman in her lifetime.

BOX 2.1 The fertility transition has not begun in much of Africa, and where it has, it bypasses the poorest

Based on the status of African countries in the fertility transition, Guengant (2017) identifies five groups:

- *Fertility transition complete (or close to completion):* In these countries, the TFR was less than three children per woman in 2010–15. Five countries are in this group: Botswana, Cabo Verde, Mauritius, the Seychelles, and South Africa. In 2015, these represented just 6 percent of the African population.
- *Fertility transitions under way:* In these countries, the TFR ranges from three to four. Four countries are in this group: Djibouti, Eswatini, Lesotho, and Namibia (representing 0.7 percent of the African population).
- *Fertility transitions initiated:* In these countries, the TFR ranges from four to five. This group consists of 20 countries: Benin, Cameroon, the Central African Republic, the Comoros, the Republic of Congo, Equatorial Guinea, Eritrea, Ethiopia, Gabon, Ghana, Guinea-Bissau, Kenya, Liberia, Madagascar, Mauritania, Rwanda, São Tomé and Príncipe, Sierra Leone, Togo, and Zimbabwe (representing 31 percent of Africa's population).
- *Slow and irregular transitions:* In these countries, the TFR ranges from five to six. These 12 countries are Burkina Faso, Côte d'Ivoire, The Gambia, Guinea, Malawi, Mozambique, Nigeria, Senegal, South Sudan, Tanzania, Uganda, and Zambia (representing 44 percent of the African population).
- *Very slow or incipient fertility transitions:* The seven countries in this group—Angola, Burundi, Chad, the Democratic Republic of Congo, Mali, Niger, and Somalia—have TFRs of more than six (representing 18.3 percent of the African population).

However, we should note that these TFRs are for each country's population as a whole. As mentioned earlier, fertility rates have been persistently high among the poorest wealth quintiles. The fertility transition appears to bypass the poorest so far.

Breaking the Fertility Barrier

Reducing fertility must surely be given a high priority if economic growth and poverty reduction are to be accelerated. But why has fertility remained so stubbornly high? Historically, fertility levels have declined in response to socioeconomic development. The decline in infant and child mortality associated with development typically leads households to revise their fertility preferences downward. The costs and benefits of having children will also change radically. As countries become more urbanized, the costs of children will increase and their benefits decrease. Similarly, the increase in the returns to education as development proceeds will encourage households to have fewer and better-educated children.

Female education is perhaps the most important single component: more-educated females will be more empowered, resulting in delayed first marriages and greater income opportunities. Both lead to lower fertility. With socioeconomic development, then, these factors combine to enhance the status of women and improve the health of women and children.

These fundamental drivers are all in evidence in Africa (figure 2.2). Yet having accounted for these conventional demographic and socioeconomic determinants of fertility, the TFR in African countries remains on average about one birth higher than in other least developed countries (LDCs). This has been labeled "the Africa Effect," and it has been suggested that African societies are "exceptionally" pro-natalist relative to other low- and middle-income countries (Bongaarts 2017; Bongaarts and Casterline 2013). This may partly reflect the lower empowerment of women in the region compared with peer countries in other contexts.

The pro-natalist culture may also explain why family planning interventions have not received sufficient policy priority despite the persistently large number of unwanted births. While the average level of unwanted births outside Africa has decreased from one to zero over the past couple of decades, in Africa it has remained at two (Casterline 2009; Casterline and El-Zeini 2014; Günther and Harttgen 2016). This suggests a large latent demand for contraception.

Nonetheless, fertility has been responsive to the implementation of family planning in the low- to middle-income world—measuring the family planning program effort either as the level of spending on family planning programs or through the index of family planning effort proposed by Ross and Stover (2001). There is a significant, negative association between fertility outcomes and exposure to family planning messages after controlling for other covariates.

The conclusion that emerges is that "the delay in the implementation of family planning programs in Sub-Saharan Africa explains the delayed decline in fertility in the region" (de Silva and Tenreyro 2017, 219). General equilibrium simulations grounded in empirically estimated parameters of fertility behavior and actual costing of family planning programs further show that an expansion of family planning services can also reduce poverty and do so cost-effectively (Christiaensen and May 2007).

Female education further plays a central role in reducing fertility. Better-educated women have preferences for fewer children, given their labor market opportunities and thus the higher opportunity costs of childcare. They are also likely to invest more in each child. They marry later and often delay childbearing compared with the uneducated. They experience lower infant and child mortality and are more likely to use modern contraception (Kim 2016).

Raising the economic returns to education would lead to quantity versus quality tradeoffs in fertility decision making. Declining child mortality reinforces this trade-off, because investment in children (focusing on quality) is more guaranteed to yield returns than in situations where children have a higher likelihood of dying. A key issue here is whether the recent recovery of growth in African countries will raise the returns to education, including in rural areas. Another critical question is whether African countries

FIGURE 2.2 In Africa, fertility is less responsive to conventional parameters of development than in other LDCs

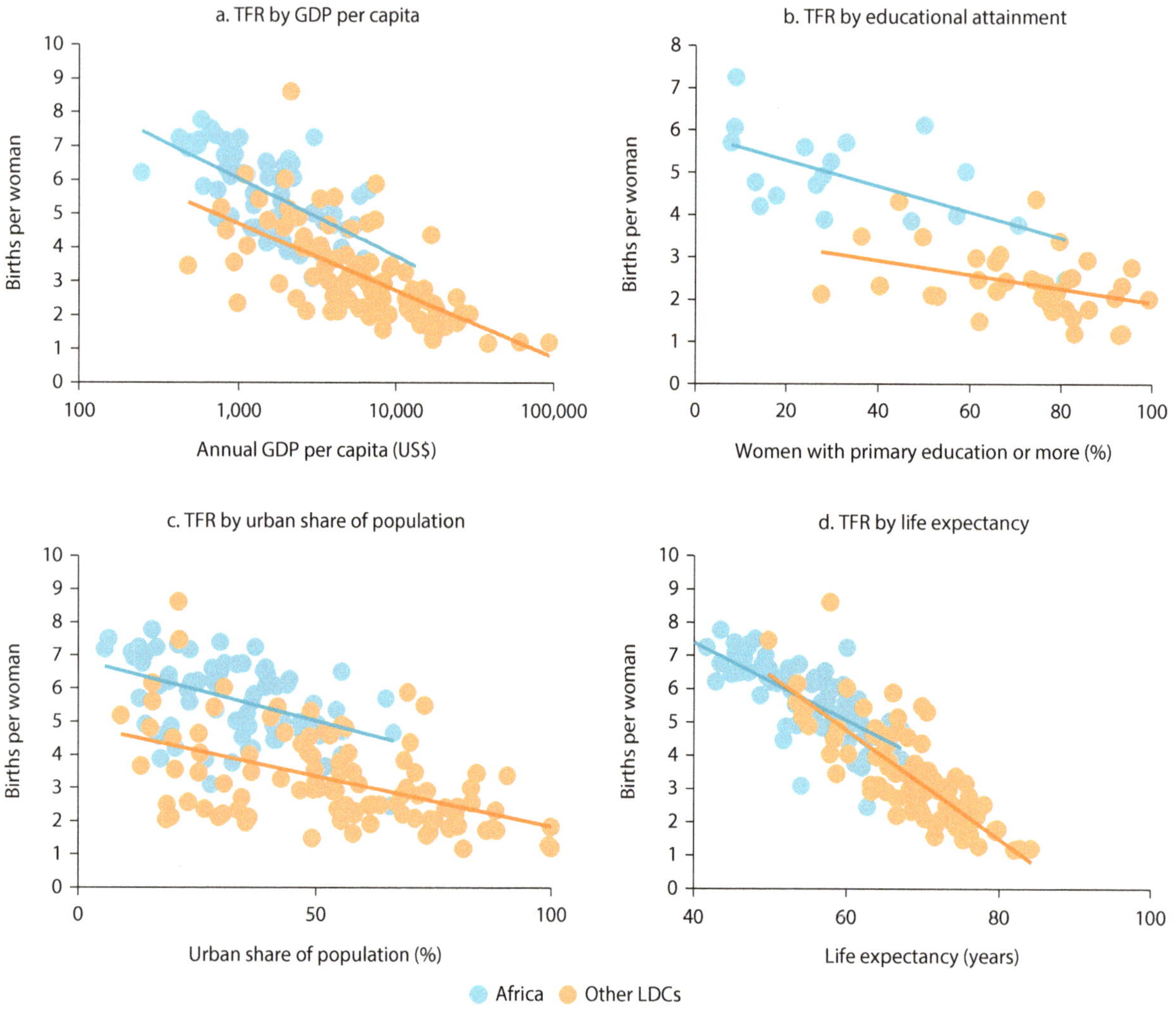

Source: World Bank calculations, adapted from Bongaarts (2017), using latest data from the World Development Indicators 2019 database.
Note: LDCs = least developed countries (as defined by the United Nations Committee for Development Policy); TFR = total fertility rate (total number of children born to a woman in her lifetime). Data used are for the years 1990 and 2018. Last available year chosen when data were missing.

can raise postprimary educational attainment and schooling quality—critical for both economic growth and poverty reduction, as further addressed in Fundamentals 1 ("Africa's Human Development Trap") and chapter 6 ("Mobilizing Resources for the Poor").

Finally, these efforts should be complemented with other entry points to empower women and accelerate the demographic transition, including programs that offer life skills for women and girls, address social gender norms, and reduce child marriage.

Poor Initial Conditions

The "demographic dividend" is therefore not automatic—certainly not in raising the living standards of poor households. It is conditional on a favorable growth environment for such households. The challenge of accelerating poverty reduction in Africa must also confront the initial conditions that determine and sometimes constrain the pro-growth environment.

As noted earlier, being poor itself influences how growth translates into poverty reduction. But a range of other, more deep-seated structural impediments related to the economic structure and sociocultural organization of African societies—such as natural resource dependence, gender inequality, and social redistributive pressures—matter as well.

Lack of Human Capital and Access to Infrastructure

When households have little education, poor access to health services, and limited access to good infrastructure, they are less able to contribute to and participate in economic growth. The importance of better educational attainment for poverty reduction has been widely documented (World Bank 2018b).

At the national level, quality education underpins growth by improving the productivity of the labor force; by increasing the capacity to absorb and adapt new technology, which will affect short- to medium-term growth; and by catalyzing the technological advances that drive long-term growth.[3] Growth regression and growth accounting analyses that account for differences in educational quality suggest that education can explain a significant share of growth (Bosworth and Collins 2003; Hanushek and Woessmann 2010; Jones 2014). Where the gap in educational attainment is large, as in much of Africa, and when there is learning, much growth can already be expected from widespread basic education. It facilitates the absorption and adaptation of technologies that are already available globally.

At the individual level, the likelihood of being poor is 3 percentage points lower on average when an individual has some primary education, 7 percentage points lower given completed primary or incomplete secondary education, 10 percentage points lower given completed secondary education, and 12 percentage points lower given tertiary education (controlling for the area of residence, household structure, and demographic characteristics) (Castañeda et al. 2018). Further analyses that also control for the possibility that the positive effects of education merely reflect greater innate capability confirm the sizable positive effects of education on income.[4] Although progress in educational outcomes has been slow, the slight increase in the share of households with secondary education can, for example, account for half of the household consumption growth at the bottom of the consumption distribution in Uganda (World Bank 2016c).

Yet Africa's human capital base remains largely underdeveloped, with especially the poor being less healthy and poorly educated (Beegle et al. 2016). More than two in five Africans cannot read a sentence, and life expectancy is only 57 years, well below the global average of 71 years. Nearly 1 in 10 children (9.2 percent) do not live to see their fifth birthday. Almost 4 out of 10 children under five years old are stunted.

These numbers mask substantial variation across countries: more than half of the population of seven countries (mostly in West Africa) is illiterate, while literacy rates exceed 80 percent in southern African countries. Controlling for national income per capita, human capital outcomes are also systematically lower in resource-rich countries, with the difference even more pronounced in Africa's oil-rich countries (de la Brière et al. 2017).

And although primary school enrollment rates are approaching 100 percent (and gender gaps in primary enrollment rates have greatly declined),[5] secondary school enrollment is still only 43 percent. More important, learning has often been limited. More than half of sixth-grade students in West and Central Africa are not sufficiently competent in reading and mathematics. Actual skills development in Africa remains largely lacking (World Bank 2018b).

Most human capital is acquired before adulthood, with children in poor households typically accumulating the least of it. As discussed in Fundamentals 1 ("Africa's Human Development Trap"), early learning deficits magnify over time, and there is limited scope for catch-up during adulthood. Similar observations hold for child malnutrition. This poses a policy conundrum, especially for countries and poor households. Investments today only pay off one generation later, locking poor households and countries in a vicious circle of poverty.

A second initial condition that impedes poverty reduction in Africa is the lack of access to infrastructure. The low returns to the poor's land, labor, and skills arise partly from their inability to access and afford information and communication technology, energy, and transport services (Christiaensen, Demery, and Paternostro 2003; Grimm et al. 2017; James 2016). There is clear evidence of a positive effect of infrastructure (of all three categories) on growth, but the positive effects on equity are more tentative (Calderón and Servén 2014).

Lack of access to infrastructure in rural areas, limited affordability of the related services, and the absence of the analog complements (no electricity or roads) frequently combine to exclude the poor from benefiting directly. But technological and institutional innovations are bringing down the economies of scale and costs of providing and operating infrastructure services. This trend will help the poor leapfrog the infrastructure gap. It will not occur automatically, however, and given the complementarity of the different services, the effects will be greater if the limited access to the different services is tackled jointly. These points are elaborated further in Fundamentals 3, "Leapfrogging with Technology (and Trade)."

Finally, and only more recently acknowledged, the lack of human capital, physical assets, and access to basic infrastructure do not only reduce the earning capacity of the poor but also conspire to limit their mental "bandwidth" and their capacity to aspire, making the escape from poverty an even bigger challenge (box 2.2).

BOX 2.2 New insights from the psychology of poverty can inform project design

Poverty entails making many difficult decisions daily to survive and try to prosper (World Bank 2015b). As such, poverty taxes the mental bandwidth of the poor (Mani et al. 2013) and can impede higher-level cognitive functioning. Whether it is called concentration, focus, or executive control, such higher-level cognitive functioning is needed to remember important tasks, to plan for the future, and to exercise self-control.

Poverty further induces stress that can compromise these traits (Chemin, De Laat, and Haushofer 2013; Spears 2011). As a result, poor people often face difficulty saving, investing, and planning for the future—including for investment in the education and health of their families—and may become highly risk-averse (Haushofer and Fehr 2014). Yet good financial management and calculated risk taking are key behaviors associated with escaping poverty. By crowding out mental bandwidth and inducing stress, poverty begets poverty (Ghatak 2015).

Poverty can furthermore affect the ability to aspire (Appadurai 2004; Dalton, Ghosal, and Mani 2016; Genicot and Ray 2017). Higher aspirations help a person achieve better outcomes—and better outcomes (gained through greater effort) can encourage individuals to have higher aspirations. These effects can be intergenerational (Bernard et al. 2014).

Aspirations respond to living conditions and social conditions. The policy of reserving seats for women leaders in West Bengal, India, changed the aspirations of girls and their parents and increased the educational attainment of girls despite the lack of direct investment in education facilities by women leaders (Beaman et al. 2012). Although less studied in low- and middle-income countries, membership theory and the psychological effects of one's social influences have been studied extensively in the United States in the context of racial inequality (Durlauf 2006).

Few interventions exist to date to tackle the "psychology" of poverty directly. Yet awareness of the mental constraints and aspiration failures the poor face can greatly help improve project design (World Bank 2015b).

Natural Resource Dependence and Governance

Following the commodity price boom of the 1990s and 2000s, natural resource dependence in Africa has dramatically increased and is now a defining feature of many African economies (figure 2.3).[6] Natural resources generate significant export earnings and fiscal revenues but have at times even been found to be a "curse" for economic growth.[7] More particularly, although exploiting natural resource abundance can

FIGURE 2.3 Natural resource dependence has increased substantially in most African countries

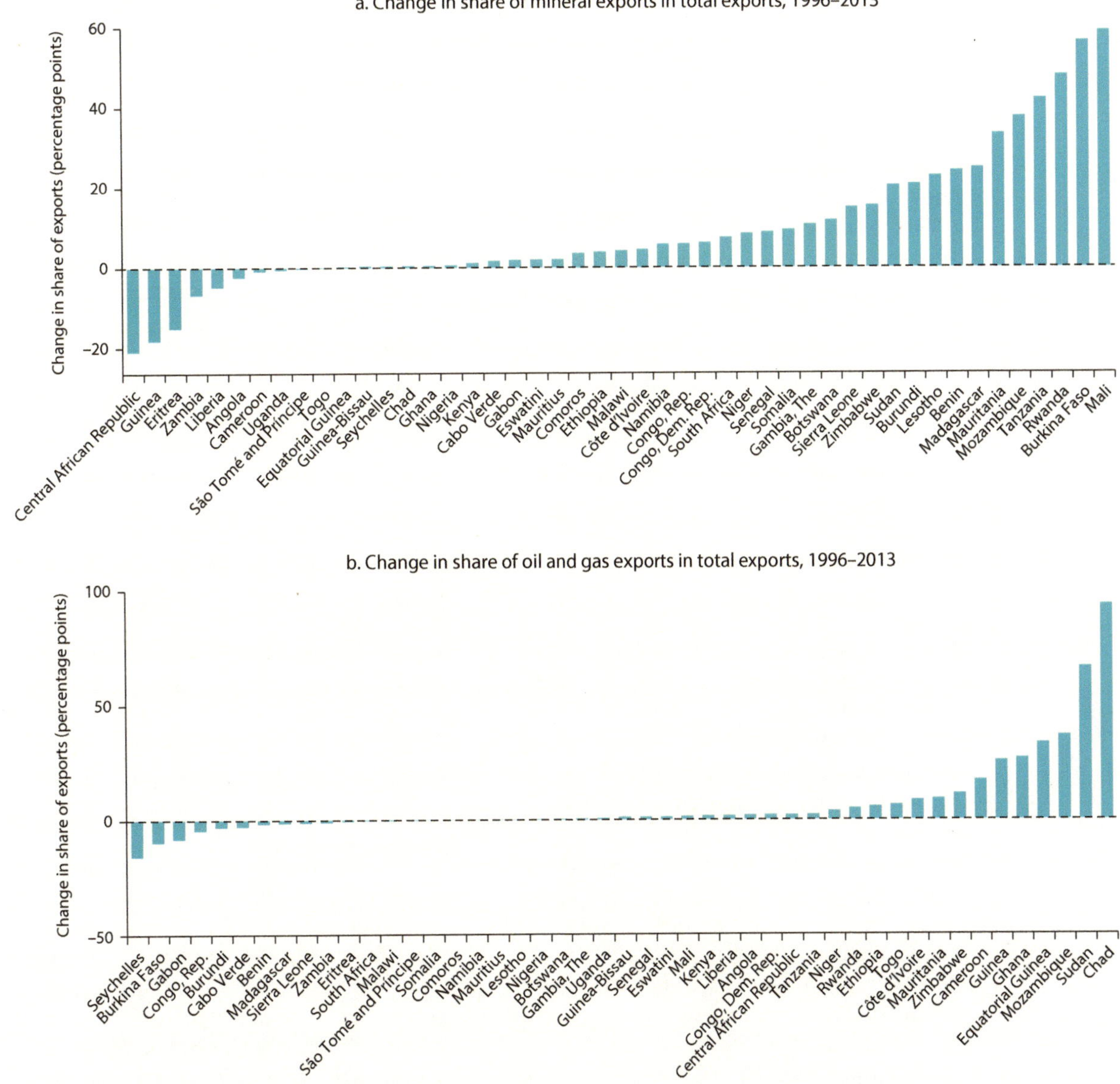

Source: Calculations based on United Nations Conference on Trade and Development (UNCTAD) data.
Note: There is a close correlation between the export and government revenue shares of natural resources. Data on the latter, although arguably the better indicator of resource dependence, are patchy.

improve growth prospects in the short run, countries with significant resources typically experience lower growth in the long run (Demery 2018).[8] An assessment of growth in the nonresource sector in 18 resource-rich countries during the 2000s resource boom suggests that resource abundance provides no positive (or negative) payoff for the rest of the economy, leaving these countries without the anticipated productivity transformation in their domestic economies (Warner 2015).

Among the different natural resources, oil produces the largest problem for the greatest number of countries (Ross 2012). For example, in Nigeria (where oil exports represent 34 percent of GDP), a 10 percent increase in the oil price is predicted to lead to a 5 percent lower long-run GDP per capita growth rate (Collier and Goderis 2012). In Angola (where oil exports are 64 percent of GDP), the same oil price increase would lead to a 9.9 percent lower long-run GDP per capita growth rate.

One oft-cited reason why resource abundance might undermine economic growth is its negative effect on institutions and governance.[9] Natural resources (especially oil) affect government functioning in profound ways: the revenues they yield are usually large, are subject to large fluctuations, are not dependent on the support of the taxpaying electorate, and can readily be hidden from public scrutiny (Ross 2012). These factors combine to undermine the "open" functioning of governments in society and distort government incentives. Governments that rely more heavily on revenue from natural resources are also less likely to be democratic and accountable to their citizens (Prichard, Salardi, and Segal 2018; Ross 2001). Once the negative impact of natural resources on long-run GDP growth (through their impact on governance and government institutions) is controlled for, the presence of oil and other mineral resources tends to benefit growth prospects (Isham et al. 2005; Sala-i-Martin and Subramanian 2008).[10]

The implication of these findings is that extractive resources are unlikely to benefit the population at large and thus are less likely to reduce poverty. Evidence from across countries confirms this, with the presence of extractive industries found to dampen the poverty-reducing effects of growth in the nonagricultural sectors (Christiaensen, Demery, and Kuhl 2011). Natural resource abundance induces the emergence of "consumption cities," where workers are engaged principally in nontraded sectors (personal services and commerce). Poverty is higher in such cities than in "production cities," those associated with urbanization in the absence of natural resources (Gollin, Jedwab, and Vollrath 2016).

Finally, what about the potentially beneficial impact on the fiscal resources available to governments to support those public goods and services that are especially important for the poor (Warner 2015)? Here, too, the evidence is that resource abundance has adversely influenced public spending on sectors that tend to benefit the poor such as agricultural research and development (R&D), education, and health (noted further in chapter 6).

Clearly, the increasing resource dependence of African countries poses a challenge. It threatens to reduce their growth and prospects for poverty reduction, mainly through governance channels. Yet this is increasingly also the context within which policies to accelerate poverty reduction in Africa must operate. Interventions to tackle the rent-seeking behavior and corrupt practices will need to be part and parcel of policy packages, both to increase the public finances available and to spend them more efficiently on the needs of the poor.

Gender Inequality

Gender inequalities are deep-seated in most African countries. They have persisted in access to health and education, to employment, and to resources more generally. At a deeper level, women generally have more limited political engagement and power than men and are treated differently from men in the legal system (including in rights to land tenure). And within the household, women have limited voice and power, being often subject to domestic violence. These areas are discussed further in Fundamentals 2 ("The Nexus of Gender Inequality and Poverty").

Gender equality as an intrinsic objective is enshrined in international conventions and is expressed in United Nations (UN) Sustainable Development Goal 5 (SDG 5): "Achieve gender equality and empower all women and girls." It is an objective in its own right (Duflo 2012; World Bank 2011). Here the focus is on how gender inequalities affect growth and poverty reduction. Conceptually, reducing gender gaps in access to schooling will raise the average level of human capital in the economy and increase the prospects for long-run growth—part and parcel of the broader argument that human capital is important for growth (as discussed earlier in this chapter as well as in Fundamentals 1, "Africa's Human Development Trap").

However, reducing gender gaps in education can also lead to externalities that further enhance economic performance. Promoting female education will reduce fertility, leading to the "demographic dividend" discussed earlier. Similarly, raising a mother's educational attainment is likely to reduce the mortality and morbidity of her children and to encourage their schooling. And there may be more profound indirect effects of reducing the gender gap in education. It could well raise the status of women in households, hence increasing their bargaining power at home, which could have far-reaching favorable growth effects (Doss 2013; King, Klasen, and Porter 2009). Women are likely to encourage higher savings and (although more speculatively) to be less prone to corruption and nepotism (Branisa, Klasen, and Ziegler 2013). And gender gaps in health care have been found to reduce the pace of long-run growth (Bloom, Kuhn, and Prettner 2015).

Some observers are cautious about the robustness of the evidence (Bandiera and Natraj 2012; Duflo 2012), while others are more convinced—especially about the impact on growth of gender gaps in education (Dollar and Gatti 1999; Klasen 2002, 2006, 2018; Knowles, Lorgelly, and Owen 2002). If African countries had started with more balanced educational attainments in 1960 and done more to promote gender-balanced education growth, their annual real GDP per capita growth rate could have been almost 1 percentage point higher (Klasen 2002). And the favorable indirect effect of female education in reducing fertility can lead to a demographic dividend that is even larger than this estimate (Klasen and Lamanna 2009). A wide-spanning review of 54 studies confirms that reducing the education gender gap improves economic growth and that in terms of its quantitative magnitude, the effects are quite large (Minasyan et al. 2017).[11]

Recent research further shows that social institutional gender inequality is not only an important driver of the gender gaps in education, employment, and governance (Branisa, Klasen, and Ziegler 2009, 2013, 2014; Yoon and Klasen 2018) but is also associated directly with poorer growth outcomes (Ferrant and Kolev 2016).[12] This is particularly the case in low-income countries. Dismantling gender-based discrimination in social institutions could increase global growth by as much as 0.6 percentage points per year over the next 15 years (Ferrant and Kolev 2016).

Reducing gender gaps in all likelihood will raise the growth prospects of African economies. In so doing, it is also likely to reduce poverty, though the evidence on how reducing gender gaps helps reduce poverty by increasing the effect of growth on poverty is not as clear. The closing of gender gaps to reap poverty and growth returns could happen through a focus on four broad areas (Klasen 2006):

- A growth strategy that raises the demand for female labor (such as the export-led growth strategies of East Asia)
- Policies that remove gender gaps in education, especially in poorer households where school enrollment rates tend to be much lower than in the rest of the population
- Actions to improve women's access to productive assets—more secure property

rights and access to land as well as better access to credit, modern inputs, and other means of production (including land)
- Policies that help poorer couples reduce their fertility.

In addition to documenting the gender gaps in more detail, Fundamentals 2 ("The Nexus of Gender Inequality and Poverty") explores these and other policy entry points to overcome gender inequality.

Social Dynamics and Investment Traps for the Poor

A more recently documented structural impediment to poverty reduction concerns the social dynamics that hold people back from investing in their income activities for fear of the redistributive consequences. Faced with the burden of having to bear the full cost of failure but only able to appropriate a limited part of the benefits of success, they may forgo saving and investment opportunities, leading to an investment trap.

Redistributive pressures from family and friends are strong in many parts of Africa. Strong social norms in West Africa dictate that an individual who has cash on hand supports friends and relatives who may need it (Platteau 2000). There are benefits to this system. In Benin, for example, having just one educated family member greatly improves educational outcomes in the extended family (Wantchekon, Klašnja, and Novta 2015). Also, assistance from family and friends is among the most important means households have to manage shocks—and *the* most important for households in the bottom 40 percent in Nigeria and Uganda (Nikoloski, Christiaensen, and Hill 2018), as also discussed in chapter 5 ("Managing Risks and Conflict").

At the same time, there is increasing discussion on how reliance on informal networks may have negative consequences (Platteau 2014). Avoiding redistributive pressures from family by hiding one's income, or tying it up in nonliquid forms, can result in suboptimal investment and savings decisions. The kin system can even be a poverty trap when it results in a "status quo bias" and collective opposition to individuals' efforts to pursue income opportunities (Hoff and Sen 2005).

The evidence (experimental and observational) that this matters is emerging along with the theory of the process. For example, when individuals in an economic experiment in Kenyan villages were given cash, they were found to invest less when the amount they invested was made public than when the amount they invested was kept private (Jakiela and Ozier 2016). In Malawi, redistributive pressures on lottery winners was varied by publicizing the results of some winners and not others. Those who were publicly announced spent 30 percent more than those whose identities were kept private in the period immediately following the lottery (Goldberg 2017). In Senegal, a field experiment elicited the "willingness to pay" to keep their income private, with two-thirds of the experiment participants forgoing up to 14 percent of income gains to hide these gains (Boltz, Marazyan, and Villar 2016). Evidence from real-world behavior drawing on survey data is more circumstantial[13] but points in the same direction.[14]

To be sure, many other constraints to investment may be more important, and not all studies that have looked at the impact of redistributive norms have found them to have an effect. For example, external pressure to share could not account for the inability of many small entrepreneurs in Ghana to invest in their businesses (Fafchamps et al. 2011). Nonetheless, the evidence above also suggests that redistributive pressures are a factor to consider.

In addition, not all individuals are affected equally. The evidence suggests that women and poor households are more susceptible to the social pressures. In Kenya, women were found to be less able to say no, as were people living in poorer villages (Jakiela and Ozier 2016; Schaner 2017). In Malawi, there is evidence that social pressures to share windfall income have a larger effect on poorer households (Goldberg 2017). That redistributive

BOX 2.3 Formal safety nets and commitment savings devices can help households overcome the investment trap

As with all poverty traps, income gains can help break the cycle. As households become richer, they need to rely less on redistribution and are less subject to redistributive pressures. Structural change that accompanies development may also lessen redistributive pressures. For example, when individuals migrate from rural to urban areas and become more distant from members of their informal network, they are less subject to the same redistributive pressure. On the other hand, this could also cause the informal network to prevent the more entrepreneurial from migrating (Hoff and Sen 2005). Formal safety nets as well as savings commitment devices may provide more immediate policy entry points to help households overcome the investment trap.

Redistributive pressures remain high in Africa in part because, for many households, informal transfers from friends and family are the main source of support in times of need. Formal safety nets, which could displace informal transfers, still cover only a small proportion of the population in most countries. Displacement of informal transfers through safety nets is usually seen as a negative side effect of safety nets: the household may be left more vulnerable than before. However, if it reduces the negative impacts of redistributive pressure, this could represent a positive change. A meta-analysis on safety nets in Africa concludes that the crowding-out impact of safety nets on other financial flows has been modest so far (Ralston, Andrews, and Hsiao 2017). It may take time for redistributive norms to change in response to the development of a social safety net.

Commitment savings devices also help individuals commit to savings goals, often with the aim of helping individuals protect savings from their own lack of self-control. Increasing evidence suggests that they can also help households protect their money from requests from friends and family, and without the transaction costs involved in tying up cash in illiquid forms. Commitment savings devices are popular with women in rural Kenya in part because they protect money from unplanned requests for transfers to families and friends (Dupas and Robinson 2013). In Malawi, households with more assets, presumably at higher risk of being taxed by family and friends, are more likely to benefit from a commitment savings device (Brune et al. 2015). The evidence is suggestive (Karlan, Ratan, and Zinman 2014), but more research is needed because redistributive pressures cannot easily be exogenously varied across households in real-world settings.

pressures bind more strongly on poor households is what makes this dynamic even more pernicious. Box 2.3 reviews entry points to overcome this investment trap for the poor. A comprehensive discussion of how to better manage risks is in chapter 5.

More and Better Income-Earning Opportunities for the Poor

High fertility and limiting initial conditions (poor human capital and infrastructure, resource dependence, and deep-seated gender inequalities) are key traits of the setting in Africa within which the poor (and near-poor) are organizing their economic activities to earn a living. Their main income activities are still largely confined to agriculture and rural areas, albeit with differentiation across countries, and regions within countries, though with income streams subject to high volatility everywhere.

With GDP per capita low in most countries, there is limited scope for redistribution to accelerate poverty reduction. Possible exceptions are Africa's middle-income and natural-resource-rich countries, as in southern Africa, where inequality (including of land) is also highest (see box 2.4 and chapter 6, "Mobilizing Resources for the Poor").

The main focus of this report is thus on how best to increase and secure the poor's income-earning capacity in the near and medium term, on and off the farm, through wage or self-employment—put differently, how best to generate better and more secure jobs that are accessible to the poor.

BOX 2.4 Should low- and middle-income countries go BIG?

In 2016, the Swiss rejected a proposal for a monthly income for all. Meanwhile, in 2017, Finland became the first European country to implement a two-year social experiment that provides a monthly stipend to unemployed citizens—not quite a monthly income for all but moving in that direction. The idea of a basic income guarantee (BIG)—also referred to as a guaranteed minimum income or universal basic income—is being discussed not only in high-income countries but also as a debated policy option for low- and middle-income countries (Devarajan 2017; Ravallion 2014).

The notion that low- and middle-income countries cannot possibly offer universal income is being challenged by new thinking and analysis, not least in the context of direct dividend payments (DDPs) in low-income countries with sizable natural resource revenue. However, it is discussed not only in these contexts. The government of India has done extensive calculations on the fiscal feasibility and studied the practical issues that introducing a universal basic income would entail (MoF GoI 2017).

The idea of guaranteed minimum income is not new. One of the U.S. Founding Fathers, Thomas Paine, argued that every person is entitled to share the state's resources, proposing that citizens be paid the equivalent of what was at the time more than half of a laborer's annual income, as a share of the national wealth (Paine 1797). In the 1960s, Nobelist and classical economist Milton Friedman proposed a negative income tax that included a transfer for those with no income. More recently, the International Labour Organization (ILO) proposed a Social Protection Floor that includes minimum income security through social assistance for those who cannot earn sufficient income.

Some regard a BIG as a "right of citizenship," while others emphasize that it can be an effective tool to alleviate poverty with modest distortionary impact on the economy. For the poorest households, it can potentially address constraints to livelihoods and result in an increase in labor supply, especially when much work is informal self-employment (Andrews, Hsiao, and Ralston 2018).

In practice, a BIG makes obsolete the complex issues and costs of targeting the poor in existing social assistance schemes. A universal approach may even outperform targeted programs in terms of reaching the poor (Brown, Ravallion, and van de Walle 2017). And with the advent of social registries and biometric systems, it may be less prone to corruption in the distribution of cash payments than other means of social assistance. The relatively new social protection systems in middle-income countries and the even smaller-scale systems in low-income countries limit such gains from a BIG in these contexts.

Although the tight fiscal space to provide programs for the poor may limit the scope for BIGs in low- and middle-income countries today, as experiences with them grow in other contexts, they may increasingly become part of the menu of social assistance options even in low-income settings. A number of factors will ultimately influence the take-up of universal basic income: the policy challenges to be addressed, existing safety net systems, administrative ability to do means-testing, the range of tax instruments available to raise revenue, and responsiveness of labor supply (IMF 2017).

Note: For more about universal basic income proposals, also see the discussions in Ferguson (2015), IMF (2017), and Ravallion (2016).

Unemployment is mostly less of an issue, because most of the poor are too poor to afford *not* to work except in countries like South Africa, which has much less informal employment and smallholder agriculture (Bigsten 2018). Underemployment or low-productivity employment with unreliable income streams, on the other hand, are widespread.

Maintaining Macroeconomic Stability

A large literature has documented the fundamental importance of macroeconomic stability, regional integration, and trade facilitation as well as a conducive business environment for economic growth. These factors also affect inequality and poverty (Antoine, Singh, and Wacker 2017; Bah and Fang 2015; Dollar and Kraay 2002;

Le Goff and Singh 2014; Rodrik 1998; Sakyi et al. 2017).[15]

Three macroeconomic indicators have particularly emerged as statistically important in the cross-country growth regressions: the rate of price inflation, reflecting monetary policy; the exchange rate, reflecting openness to trade and other trade policies; and the level of government consumption expenditure, or the size of the fiscal deficit (reflecting fiscal policy).

Improvements in these macroeconomic balances are also associated with reductions in poverty, and when the macro imbalances deteriorate, poverty is likely to rise as a result (Antoine, Singh, and Wacker 2017; Christiaensen, Demery, and Paternostro 2003; Dollar and Kraay 2002; Rodrik 2016).

Inflation indirectly increases poverty over time through its negative effect on the pace of economic growth. But it also harms the living standards of poor households directly. They are less able to protect their savings against the purchasing-power-eroding effects of inflation, and their incomes are often not fully indexed to the changes in the price level (Easterly and Fischer 2001). In other words, the "inflation tax" is generally considered to be regressive, its incidence being disproportionately on poorer households. Lowering inflation would thus reduce poverty, as evidenced by the econometric findings from Brazil and India (Ferreira, Leite, and Ravallion 2010; Ravallion and Datt 2002).[16]

Overall, headline inflation has declined across the region, reflecting the confluence of stable exchange rates and slowing food price inflation, with the median annual consumer price inflation just over 5 percent in 2016 and 2017. However, inflation has remained elevated in some countries (for example, Angola, Mozambique, and Nigeria). Overall, the indications are favorable: inflation will continue to moderate in the region as food prices stabilize and exchange rates equilibrate (World Bank 2018a).

Overvalued exchange rates tend to penalize traded-goods sectors and especially agriculture, on which most poor households in Africa rely for their livelihoods. They make food imports cheaper (such as rice and maize) and reduce agricultural export revenues (Benjamin, Devarajan, and Weiner 1989; Townsend 1999). Although there is little evidence linking overvalued exchange rates to the "Dutch disease" consequences of natural resource endowments (Collier and Goderis 2007, 2012; Sala-i-Martin and Subramanian 2008), where they have arisen, growth outcomes are harmed. Foreign exchange markets were often characterized in Africa by administrative controls, leading to foreign exchange overvaluation, exchange rationing, and the emergence of black-market premiums—with the familiar negative consequences for economic growth (Ndulu et al. 2007). Removing such distortions (when combined with other sound macroeconomic policies) has been associated with significant improvements in growth outcomes (Maehle, Teferra, and Khachatryan 2013; Stotsky et al. 2012).[17]

Great reliance on aid for financing public investment (as in Rwanda, for example) can also cause real exchange appreciation, favoring the more traditional, domestic-oriented nonagricultural sector over the more-productive, open modern sector, thereby slowing growth. The distributional and poverty effects are less clear, however (Diao and McMillan 2018). Overall, while in some countries (Angola and Nigeria) the spread between the official and the parallel markets has persisted, recent exchange rate trends have been favorable (World Bank 2017).

Finally, high fiscal deficits are also not conducive to economic growth, though the immediate effects on inequality and poverty are less clear (Dollar and Kraay 2002). Fiscal deficits are a rising concern in the region. The reasons for the negative effects of fiscal deficits on growth are complex, typically involving their adverse effects on other macroeconomic aggregates. If the deficit is financed through monetary financing, it leads to increased inflation. If governments borrow domestically, it raises interest rates, which discourages private investment. External borrowing leads to balance-of-payments challenges and exchange rate overvaluation. Borrowing also leads to increased external debt. Whichever macroeconomic balance gets disturbed, the effects on growth are negative.[18]

Africa used countercyclical fiscal policy (the use of fiscal deficits to prevent recession) to help deal with the economic downturn of 2008–09. This was an appropriate policy stance given the global crisis, and governments generally had fiscal space to do so. (On average, Africa was in primary fiscal *surplus*—at 0.6 percent of GDP in 2006–08—and it had access to global capital markets.) Primary fiscal *deficits* of around –2.2 percent of GDP were in operation in 2009–10 (World Bank 2017), as shown in figure 2.4, panel a. But with the economic recovery, African governments need to consolidate their fiscal accounts.

Unfortunately, they have been slow to do so (Gill and Karakülah 2019). World Bank (2018a) projected the median primary fiscal deficit to remain around –3.6 percent in 2018. As a consequence, gross government debt in Africa increased from about 32 percent of GDP in 2012 to 56 percent of GDP in 2016 (figure 2.4, panel b).

The growing debt burden means that African governments have less fiscal space to manage their economies and to invest in poverty reduction now and for the future. The number of tax years it will take to repay general government debt has increased from 2.7 in 2006–08 to 3.6 in 2015–16 (World Bank 2017). Fourteen countries were considered at high risk of debt distress at the end of 2017 compared with 7 in 2012 (World Bank 2018a). When fiscal tightening comes largely at the expense of spending on social sectors, as has often been the case in the past, the poor and their children stand to suffer most.

Leveraging the Food System

The focus thus far has been on the macroeconomic drivers of aggregate GDP growth in the neoclassical tradition. An important complementary perspective comes from the dual-economy growth models. These start

FIGURE 2.4 Fiscal accounts and government debt in Africa have deteriorated since the global crisis of 2008–09 and have yet to recover

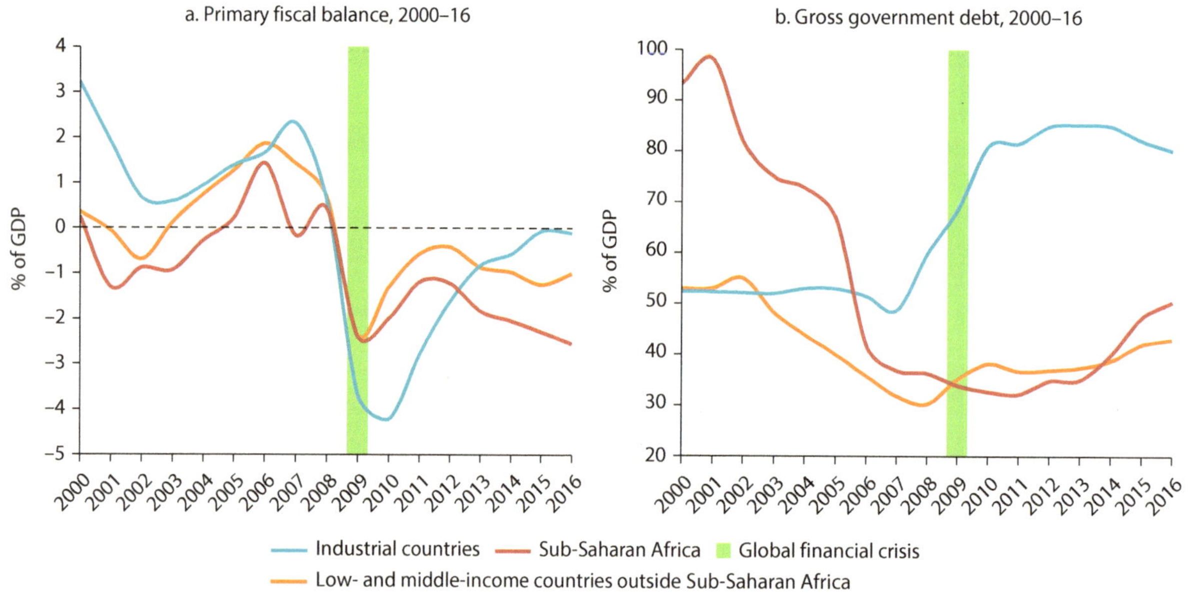

Source: World Bank, based on data in Kose et al. (2017).
Note: "Industrial countries" denotes Organisation for Economic Co-operation and Development (OECD) member countries.

from the observation that there is a wide dispersion in labor productivity across economic activities in low- and middle-income countries—modern versus traditional, formal versus informal, traded versus nontraded, cash crops versus staple crops, and so on. Mechanically, much is thus to be gained from moving people from traditional, backward sectors with (seemingly) low intrinsic productivity to more modern activities that exhibit higher returns to scale and produce tradable goods, that generate spillovers, and that have high productivity growth potential—the "structural transformation."

Traditionally, the low-productivity sector has come to be equated with agriculture and the high-productivity sector with nonagricultural activities, even though this was not the case in the original writings of Lewis (1954). He identified the low- and high-productivity sectors with informal and formal activities, respectively. The distinction is important because informal and formal modes of production are frequent in both agricultural and nonagricultural operations. From this perspective, increasing labor productivity is as much about increasing productivity *within* sectors as it is about reallocating labor *across* sectors (Barrett et al. 2017; Rodrik 2016). That agriculture is not intrinsically less productive (and thus not without important growth potential) is increasingly recognized (McCullough 2017), even though its productivity in Africa is still very low (ACET 2017).

Moreover, even if people working in agriculture earn less in practice (for example, because of the seasonal nature of agricultural production and resulting underemployment), the models do not tell one how to broker the move across sectors. Is it primarily a question of reducing frictions in labor movement, or does it depend critically on raising labor productivity in staple crop production first so that incomes rise, the demand for nonfood products grows, and labor can be released productively to meet this rising nonfood demand (while the demand for food, including more diversified food, continues to grow as well)? Although the conventional interpretation of the structural transformation premise—as moving people across sectors—sounds imminently sensible, its policy implications are far from straightforward in practice. How to move millions of people in smallholder farming and informal household enterprises into formal wage jobs outside agriculture? And how to especially target the poor?

A large body of evidence further shows that the effects of growth on poverty, not surprisingly, depend on the sector where the growth is generated. Multiple studies show growth in agriculture on average to be two to three times more effective at reducing poverty than an equivalent amount of growth outside agriculture.[19] African case country experience confirms the important (causal) role agricultural growth can play for poverty reduction. In Ethiopia, agricultural growth caused reductions of poverty by 1 percent per year between 2000 and 2005 and by 4 percent per year between 2005 and 2011, making it by far the largest contributor to Ethiopia's dramatic reduction in poverty during 2000–11 (from 55.6 percent in 2000 to 30.7 percent in 2011) (World Bank 2015a). Large contributions of agricultural growth to poverty reduction during the 2000s have also been observed in Rwanda (World Bank 2015c), Uganda (World Bank 2016c), and in more developed Ghana (Molini and Paci 2015).

The advantage of agriculture over nonagriculture in reducing poverty is greater for the poorest in society but ultimately disappears as countries become richer (Christiaensen, Demery, and Kuhl 2011; Ivanic and Martin 2018; Ligon and Sadoulet 2018), as shown in figure 2.5. After robust agricultural growth has been sustained for some time, and the sectoral economies and factor markets have integrated further (especially the labor markets), agriculture gradually loses its comparative advantage in reducing poverty.

The shift in diets and agricultural output from staples to protein-rich foods (meat and dairy), fruits, and vegetables as incomes rise (Bennett's Law) and the associated expansion of agribusiness (storage, transport, processing, wholesale, and retail of food) are part

FIGURE 2.5 The relative advantage of agricultural growth in reducing poverty declines with development

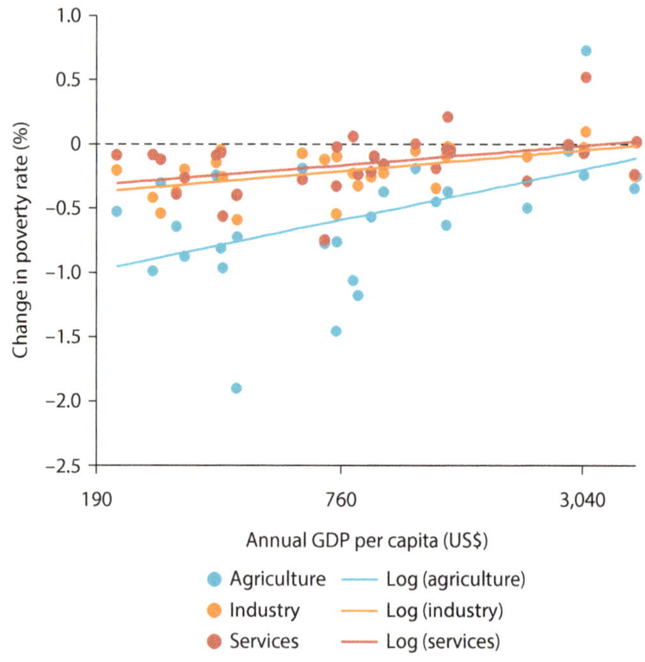

Source: Ivanic and Martin 2018.
Note: Figure shows single-country simulations of the poverty change from a sectoral productivity increase equal to 1 percent of GDP.

and parcel of this process. While agribusiness is recorded as nonagriculture in the national accounts, this extended agriculture typically is an important first source of off-farm employment. Today, it makes up about one-third of off-farm employment: 65–70 percent of that in food marketing, 20–25 percent in food processing, and 10 percent in food services (food away from home) (Allen, Heinrigs, and Heo 2018; Tschirley et al. 2015). The Asian experience suggests that poverty reduction is faster if this *agricultural* transformation (from staples to nonstaples) accompanies the *structural* transformation (from agriculture to industry) (Huang 2016).

The role of agriculture in an economy's structural transformation and poverty reduction described above depends on the extent of economic integration within the economy and with global markets. With full integration, food imports could in principle substitute for domestic food production; labor could then be absorbed directly by export-oriented industry and services, which would also provide the necessary foreign exchange to finance food imports (Dercon 2009; Dercon and Gollin 2014). Yet most African countries have large populations distant from ocean ports and rely for most of their food on domestic production. Computable general equilibrium simulations for 315,000 households from 31 countries indicate that agriculture's advantage in reducing poverty holds (a) under both open (food is tradable) and closed (food is nontradable) economy assumptions, and (b) whether productivity growth is confined to one country or is widespread (across all low- and middle-income countries or across all countries) (Ivanic and Martin 2018).[20] The priority of agricultural growth for poverty reduction extends well beyond Africa's landlocked countries.

Despite progress over the past decade, African staple crop yields (at 1.5 tons of cereals per hectare) remain extremely low, while within-country labor productivity differences in agriculture suggest substantial scope for gains. For example, bringing those households operating at the 25th percentile in the net agricultural labor productivity distribution to the 75th percentile would increase net agricultural labor productivity by 4.5 times in Uganda and by 7.8 times in Côte d'Ivoire (Christiaensen and Kaminski 2014; Christiaensen and Premand 2017).

Urbanization and GDP growth add further opportunities for agricultural transformation and value addition. Agriculture and agribusiness together are projected to be a US$1 trillion industry in Africa by 2030 compared with US$313 billion in 2010 (World Bank 2013a).

These theoretical and empirical findings indicate the substantial scope and critical importance of leveraging Africa's food system to accelerate its poverty reduction by increasing agricultural labor productivity both on the farm (in many instances still in staples, but increasingly also in other crops and livestock as well as agricultural exports) and off the farm along the agricultural chain. This holds across most African countries—in fragile and stable countries, in coastal and landlocked countries, and in resource-rich and resource-poor countries alike.

How to make best use of agriculture for accelerating Africa's poverty reduction is the topic of chapter 3 ("Earning More on the Farm"). The history of economic development in Europe and Southeast Asia further suggests that the agricultural growth and nongrowth processes should not be too much out of balance so that nonagricultural growth can provide the necessary incentives and assets for households that remain in agriculture, while also absorbing the labor released from agriculture, as agricultural growth takes off.

Moving Off the Farm

Labor productivity growth in agriculture is thus key for the poverty agenda, both because of its larger poverty-reducing powers, given the current level of development of most African countries, and because it helps create the demand for locally produced goods and services and thus increases employment off the farm. The latter happens not only, importantly, within extended agriculture (agribusiness) but also outside agriculture in the rural and urban economy (construction, manufacturing, transport, and trade). The mere existence of labor productivity differences across sectors typically does not suffice to trigger sustainable growth and poverty reduction through labor reallocation, even though it can reduce poverty in a first round.

The latter is what has been observed across much of Africa over the past two decades. There has been structural transformation. Agriculture's share of GDP declined from 22.6 percent in 1995 to 17.5 percent in 2016. The share of agricultural employment likewise fell during the 2000s by an estimated 10 percentage points or about 1 percentage point per year (Barrett et al. 2017), consistent with the pattern historically observed in other countries (Diao, McMillan, and Wangwe 2018).

Yet Africa's structural transformation has been mainly toward low-productivity, nontradable services in urban areas, and much less to tradable manufacturing (or services), as historically observed in other countries (Rodrik 2016). This partly links with Africa's commodity boom during the 2000s, which fueled economic growth and urbanization in many countries. Consumption cities arose, characterized by higher shares of imports (including of food) and higher shares of employment in nontradable services (Gollin, Jedwab, and Vollrath 2016).

The move to low-productivity, nontradable urban services has contributed to structural change and poverty reduction (McMillan, Rodrik, and Verduzco-Gallo 2014; World Bank 2014). But it has not put countries on a sustainable growth-increasing and poverty-reducing path. The emergence of a number of newly resource-rich countries (such as Ghana and Mozambique) does not bode well from this perspective (as discussed earlier), especially because many resource discoveries have happened in weak institutional environments. Then, countries have often found themselves with growth rates even lower than before the discoveries (Cust and Mihalyi 2017). Recent evidence from Africa confirms however that when structural change is induced by an increase in agricultural labor productivity, it also increases the employment share in manufacturing, often related to agriculture. The experiences of Ethiopia and Tanzania over the past decade are illustrative (Diao, McMillan, and Wangwe 2018).

Finally, off-farm employment generation does not happen in a spatial vacuum. Structural and spatial transformation, or urbanization, go hand in hand. There is growing evidence that it is especially secondary town development, as opposed to metropolitization, that may be more conducive to poverty reduction (Christiaensen and Kanbur 2017; Gibson et al. 2017). Africa's cities are often crowded, given rapid internal population growth (Jedwab, Christiaensen, and Gindelsky 2017; Lall, Henderson, and Venables 2017), and even when functional, they are much less accessible to the poor than secondary towns, which are physically and culturally more proximate. Proximity helps reduce transport, search, and settlement costs for prospective migrants and helps maintain access to the village as a safety net when things go wrong (Ingelaere et al. 2018).

From a poverty-reduction perspective, then, secondary towns and secondary cities emerge as an important, though in the past somewhat neglected, node in countries' urban systems. The *composition* of Africa's urbanization will be as important as the urbanization itself, which has so far not been associated with much poverty reduction. How the poor's off-farm earning opportunities can be improved is discussed in chapter 4 ("Moving to Jobs Off the Farm").

Addressing Fragility

After a relatively peaceful period in the 2000s, the incidence of conflict has again increased, putting a major burden on Africa's poverty-reduction efforts. Countries suffering more than 100 casualties in a year experience a 2.3 percent decline in economic growth (Beegle et al. 2016). Every year that a 1-degree grid cell experiences more than 50 conflict-related fatalities, that area has a 4.4 percentage point lower growth rate (Mueller 2016).

And the effects are often long-lasting (Minoiu and Shemyakina 2014; Moya 2018; Serneels and Verpoorten 2015). Households whose houses were destroyed or who lost land in Rwanda during the violent 1990s ran a higher risk of falling into poverty many years later (Justino and Verwimp 2013). Conflict also limits human capital acquisition (Blattman and Annan 2010). It is no wonder, then, that poverty levels are higher in fragile states that are ridden by conflict (Beegle et al. 2016). Neighboring regions and countries can be affected through the impact of internally displaced persons and refugees on labor markets and health systems. But forced migration does not always put a burden on the host economy (Maystadt et al. 2018).

Among the different natural disasters and economic shocks, ill health, drought, and price shocks pose the largest risks to welfare in Africa, primarily through their effects on income and not assets (as in the case of conflict). The effects can be significant. Malaria alone reduces income by 10 percent when it goes undetected and untreated (Dillon, Friedman, and Serneels 2014). A moderate drought of 30 percent yield loss is predicted to reduce consumption by 15 percent and 9 percent in Uganda and Ethiopia, respectively (World Bank 2015a, 2016c). Uneducated urban households in Ethiopia reduced their consumption by 10–13 percent because of higher food prices in urban markets at the end of 2010 (Hill and Porter 2016). But higher food prices can also be beneficial. In Uganda, they accounted for almost half of the crop income growth of the bottom 40 percent during 2006–12 (World Bank 2016c).

Shocks of these kinds often cast a long shadow—even more so when children are involved, as these examples illustrate:

- *Weather shocks* can have multiple impacts. For example, drought-induced consumption losses during childhood have caused losses of 2.3 centimeters and 3 centimeters in adult stature in Zimbabwe and Ethiopia, respectively (Alderman, Hoddinott, and Kinsey 2006; Dercon and Porter 2014). And in Ethiopia, 10 years after the drought, income was 16 percent lower than among counterpart households that had not suffered to the same degree, and cattle holdings had recovered to only two-thirds of their prefamine levels (Dercon 2004).
- *War* in Eritrea, Ethiopia, and Rwanda caused children to be shorter by 0.76–1.37 of a standard deviation of the height-for-age distribution (Akresh, Lucchetti, and Thirumurthy 2012; Akresh, Verwimp, and Bundervoet 2011).
- *Nutritional and educational shocks* have a substantial impact on adult incomes—from a 3 percent reduction in earnings per year in Ethiopia to 20 percent lower wages in Burundi and 14 percent lower lifetime earnings in Zimbabwe (Alderman, Hoddinott, and Kinsey 2006; Bundervoet, Verwimp, and Akresh 2009).

However, the more pernicious effect may not be when disasters actually occur but in the costly behavior that the anticipation of shocks (uninsured risk) causes year after year. When households cannot manage the risks in their environment, they eschew investments and livelihood strategies that offer great reward but that leave them too exposed. Although harder to prove empirically, a body of robust empirical evidence has emerged over the past decade supporting this theory. Recent randomized controlled trials have, for example, consistently documented that when farmers feel insured (as a result of holding an insurance policy), they increase their agricultural investments. In northern Ghana, investment in agricultural inputs increased by 88 percent, from US$375 to US$705 (Karlan et al. 2014). And in Mali, spending on cotton inputs increased by 14 percent (Elabed and Carter 2014).

Clearly, risks are omnipresent in African livelihoods, and the extent to which they can be managed is closely intertwined with Africa's poverty dynamics. In addition to generating income-earning opportunities on and off the farm that are accessible to the poor, accelerating Africa's poverty reduction thus also requires more cost-effective conflict and risk management tools—to help households reduce their exposure to shocks (such as with bed nets or irrigation) as well as to help them better manage shocks that cannot be avoided or that should be embraced given the opportunity they bring (such as through financial market development and adaptive safety nets).

In the case of conflict, lessons are emerging on the role of well-directed public programs to reduce conflict and on how financial inclusion can help households manage in the face of an increased risk of violence. Chapter 5, "Managing Risks and Conflict," reviews the challenges and options for better risk management for the poor, including in fragile, conflict-affected, and violent states.

Making Fiscal Systems Go Further for the Poor

The question remains of how to finance this agenda of more and better jobs for the poor on and off the farm; how to incentivize farmers and governments to invest in risk prevention in the face of many more-immediate needs; how to invest in improving the initial conditions, which often also only pays off later; and how to do all of this in a tightening fiscal environment and in different natural resource and governance settings.

Current levels of public spending that effectively reach and benefit the poor are not nearly sufficient. The issue is partly a lack of resources, especially in low-income countries. In two out of five African countries, simply filling the average poverty gap—that is, transferring the minimum amount of money so that nobody is any longer poor—would require 10 percent of GDP. With government tax revenues equivalent to only 9 percent of GDP on average in Africa's low-income countries, this would leave nothing for public investment.

Greater domestic resource mobilization can help, including through greater focus on large local taxpayers, corporate taxes, and transfer (mis)pricing as well as excise and property tax collection. Resource-rich countries could also generate much more government revenue from the extractive industries (APP 2013). But more international financial assistance will also be needed (Greenhill et al. 2015; Manuel et al. 2018), which could also go further by leveraging private sector finance (World Bank 2017) provided that care is taken that the financing is additional and that it leverages investments that disproportionately benefit the poor.[21]

But the available resources could also be targeted more in the sectors and subsectors (for example, staples, primary education, and safety nets) as well as the places (towns and rural areas) that improve the livelihoods of the poor more effectively. For example, at about 3 percent of government spending over the past two decades, Africa's spending on agriculture has been well below what East Asian governments spent when they embarked on their trajectory of rapid poverty reduction (8–10 percent during 1980–2000) (IFPRI 2018). And the amounts spent could often be spent more efficiently, not only by targeting public instead of private goods (such as input or fuel price subsidies) but also by improving the quality of services, such as through the reduction of absenteeism among teachers and health personnel.[22]

How to make public resources go further in reducing poverty—by mobilizing more resources, better allocating them to pro-poor public goods, and using the available resources more efficiently—is the topic of chapter 6, "Mobilizing Resources for the Poor."

A Way Forward

Generating more and better jobs for the poor requires a policy package that fosters pro-poor growth in an environment of greater natural resource dependence and increasingly strained globalization but also much faster technological advances. The remainder of this report goes beyond identifying the key sectors that need strengthening and elaborates on the subsectoral policies needed to broker Africa's structural and spatial transformation (chapters 3 and 4) and to equip the poor with better risk management tools (chapter 5).

Countries must simultaneously also begin to address the longer-run structural impediments to pro-poor growth: human development of the next generation, gender inequality, infrastructure gaps, and the politics of pro-poor policy making. In this, the report's focus is on the fiscal implications of addressing both these short- and long-run agendas—helping the poor earn more today and preparing them for the future—when budgets are becoming increasingly tight (as explored further in chapter 6).

The challenges and policy entry points that each of the structural constraints poses, pointing to policies and investments that only tend to pay off in the long-term future, are further reflected upon in the four "Fundamentals" interspersed between the chapters: "Africa's Human Development Trap"; "The Nexus of Gender Inequality and Poverty"; "Leapfrogging with Technology (and Trade)"; and "Politics and Pro-Poor Policies." Because these topics were also discussed in depth in four recent *World Development Reports*, they are not discussed in great detail here.[23]

Notes

1. These are like previous assessments (Bloom and Canning 2004; Eastwood and Lipton 2011; Kelley and Schmidt 2007). The dividend explained around a fifth of the growth acceleration in East Asia (Bloom and Williamson 1998).
2. After controlling for access to family planning and education, the economic status of the household influences fertility decisions (Schoumaker 2004).
3. Education was also found to be the key central element in gaining the demographic dividend (Cuaresma, Lutz, and Sanderson 2014).
4. Showing the causal impact of education is difficult. Some studies have tackled this. Secondary schooling in Kenya reduces the likelihood of low-skilled (and low-earning) self-employment (Ozier 2018). Education increases the probability of migration, growth in agricultural income, and diversification of income outside of agriculture in Uganda (Hill and Mejía-Mantilla 2017; Lekfuangfu, Machin, and Rasul 2012; Mensah and O'Sullivan 2017).
5. School enrollment or the gross enrollment ratio is the ratio of total enrollment, regardless of age, to the population of the age group that officially corresponds to the level of education shown.
6. Despite a substantial drop in commodity prices during the first half of the 2010s, there has been little evidence of a reversal in resource dependence (Roe and Dodd 2017).
7. Several studies have pointed to a negative effect of natural resources on GDP growth (Ross 2012; Sachs and Warner 1995, 1997). Others found that commodity price booms were favorable for growth; see Deaton and Miller (1996) for evidence of this in Africa.
8. When taking growth forecasts, as opposed to growth in nonresource countries, as counterfactual, higher short-run growth episodes in fact often do not materialize. Growth forecasts are arguably the closest counterfactual of what would have happened in the absence of a resource discovery/price boom. Cust and Mihalyi (2017) speak of a "pre-resource" or

"expectations" curse, whereby, following the discovery of new natural resources, economic growth already starts to wane long before production has started. Exuberant expectations lead to (over)optimistic growth forecasts and overspending. It has been observed in Ghana and Mozambique in the late 2000s, but is common across the world, especially in countries with weak political institutions.

9. Other reasons include the "Dutch disease" and increased price volatility. The boost in foreign exchange earnings leads to exchange rate overvaluation that adversely affects the other tradable sectors including agriculture (the Dutch disease). This could lead to lower overall growth, although studies of this phenomenon find little or no evidence (Collier and Goderis 2012; Sala-i-Martin and Subramanian 2008). Second, countries with resource abundance face more volatility, especially in prices, which harms investment and growth. Some evidence of this has been found (Collier and Goderis 2012; Sala-i-Martin and Subramanian 2008).
10. In extreme circumstances, the presence of natural resources can lead to civil conflict in a country. According to Collier and Hoeffler (2004), a country that has no natural resources faces a probability of civil conflict of 0.5 percent, whereas a country with a natural resources-to-GDP share of 26 percent faces a 23 percent probability of conflict. Civil conflict, of course, is an extreme manifestation of institutional collapse.
11. The empirical evidence linking gender gaps in the labor market to growth is not so well established as for education, mainly because of data limitations (Gaddis and Klasen 2014).
12. The Social Institutions and Gender Index (SIGI) was used to proxy these deep-seated gender inequalities (Jütting et al. 2008; Morrison and Jütting 2005). The SIGI seeks to assess the social *roots* of gender inequalities rather than their *outcomes*. Using the approach by Foster, Greer, and Thorbecke (1984), the index combines five (unweighted) subindexes, each measuring a different dimension of gender inequality: (a) *Family code* measures gender inequalities within the household (parental authority, inheritance rights, early marriage, and polygamy). (b) *Civil liberties* refers to the public sphere of life, covering freedom of movement and freedom of dress. (c) *Physical integrity* combines different indicators of violence against women (the existence of laws against domestic violence, rape, and sexual harassment, and the presence of female genital mutilation). (d) *Ownership rights* covers the economic dimensions of social institutions, including access to land, to bank loans, and to property other than land. (e) *Son preference* is a generic term referring to gender bias (or "missing women") in the demographic data.
13. The redistributive pressures can be controlled by the experiment to some extent, allowing the impact of redistributive pressure on behavior to be assessed.
14. In Cameroon, 20 percent of borrowers state that they would take on a costly loan to signal to others in their community that they do not have money available and could not be asked for financial help (Baland, Guirkinger, and Mali 2011). Investment decisions in business activity and productivity can also be negatively influenced by social pressure to redistribute earnings or income, as shown in seven West African cities (Grimm et al. 2013) and in Burkina Faso (Grimm, Hartwig, and Lay 2017; Hadnes, Vollan, and Kosfeld 2013). A study of 31 African countries found that "family taxation" discourages some talented individuals from entering entrepreneurship and results in fewer formal enterprises (Alby, Auriol, and Nguimkeu 2018). In KwaZulu-Natal, in South Africa, those with larger kinship networks are more likely to invest in durables that are nonsharable and less likely to save in liquid assets. This results in lower income for those with larger kinship networks (Di Falco and Bulte 2011). In Ethiopia, kinship networks reduce the incentive to invest in the reduction of exposure to weather shocks (Di Falco and Bulte 2013).
15. One key component of the business climate is access to finance. Others include infrastructure, crime, corruption, and regulation. Encouraging the development of the financial sector has been found to encourage economic growth, but its effect on poverty is uncertain. Beck, Demirgüç-Kunt, and Levine (2007) and Naceur and Zhang (2016) find that financial development is associated with reduced poverty. But Jaumotte, Lall, and Papageorgiou (2013) and Antoine, Singh, and Wacker (2017) find that financial sector deepening appears to be negatively associated

with income growth for the poorest two quintiles. Especially financial liberalization proves challenging for the poor (Jaumotte, Lall, and Papageorgiou 2013; Naceur and Zhang 2016).

16. Antoine, Singh, and Wacker (2017) suggest that it is especially unanticipated changes in inflation rather than the level of inflation that harm poorer households. In that view, poorer households have learned to cope with price increases as well as others, if those increases are steady. But poorer households cannot cope easily with sudden increases in prices.
17. These IMF studies cover several African countries: Ethiopia, Ghana, Kenya, Malawi, Mozambique, Tanzania, Uganda, and Zambia.
18. Adam, Bevan, and Gollin (2018) show empirically how the financing modalities of public investments affect their poverty-reducing effects. They compare the different effects of deficit financing (internal or external borrowing); domestic taxation (for example, value added taxes and sales taxes); trade taxation (tariff increases); and aid financing.
19. See Christiaensen and Martin (2018) for a recent review. Among the more recent studies are Christiaensen, Demery, and Kuhl (2011); Dorosh and Thurlow (2018); Ivanic and Martin (2018); and Ligon and Sadoulet (2018).
20. The source of the poverty-reducing benefits from agricultural productivity growth changes, however, as innovations are more widely adopted, from increases in producer returns (and wage labor opportunities) to reductions in consumer prices (Ivanic and Martin 2018).
21. See "Maximizing Finance for Development" on the World Bank website: http://www.worldbank.org/en/about/partners/maximizing-finance-for-development.
22. The Service Delivery Indicators (SDI) is an Africa-wide initiative that collects facility-based data to provide a set of metrics for benchmarking service delivery in education and health. It is a partnership of the World Bank, the African Economic Research Consortium, and the African Development Bank. For more information, see https://www.sdindicators.org. For the SDI databank, see https://databank.worldbank.org/data/source/service-delivery-indicators.
23. These include *World Development Report 2012: Gender Equality and Development; World Development Report 2016: Digital Dividends; World Development Report 2017: Governance and the Law;* and *World Development Report 2018: Learning to Realize Education's Promise.*

References

ACET (African Center for Economic Transformation). 2017. *African Transformation Report 2017: Agriculture Powering Africa's Economic Transformation.* Accra, Ghana: ACET.

Adam, Christopher, David Bevan, and Douglas Gollin. 2018. "Rural-Urban Linkages, Public Investment and Transport Costs: The Case of Tanzania." *World Development* 109: 497–510.

Ahmed, S. Amer, and Marcio Cruz. 2016. "On the Impact of Demographic Change on Growth, Savings and Poverty." Poverty Research Working Paper 7805, World Bank, Washington, DC.

Akresh, Richard, Leonardo Lucchetti, and Harsha Thirumurthy. 2012. "Wars and Child Health: Evidence from the Eritrean–Ethiopian Conflict." *Journal of Development Economics* 99 (2): 330–40.

Akresh, Richard, Philip Verwimp, and Tom Bundervoet. 2011. "Civil War, Crop Failure, and Child Stunting in Rwanda." *Economic Development and Cultural Change* 59 (4): 777–810.

Alby, Philippe, Emmanuelle Auriol, and Pierre Nguimkeu. 2018. "Does Social Pressure Hinder Entrepreneurship in Africa? The Forced Mutual Help Hypothesis." TSE Working Papers 18-956, Toulouse School of Economics (TSE).

Alderman, Harold, John Hoddinott, and Bill Kinsey. 2006. "Long-Term Consequences of Early Childhood Malnutrition." *Oxford Economic Papers* 58 (3): 450–74.

Allen, Thomas, Philipp Heinrigs, and Inhoi Heo. 2018. "Agriculture, Food and Jobs in West Africa." West African Papers No. 14, Organisation for Economic Co-operation and Development (OECD), Paris.

Andrews, Colin, Allan Hsiao, and Laura Ralston. 2018. "Social Safety Nets Promote Poverty Reduction, Increase Resilience, and Expand Opportunities." In *Realizing the Full Potential of Social Safety Nets in Sub-Saharan Africa*, edited by Kathleen Beegle,

Aline Coudouel, and Emma Monsalve, 87–138. Washington, DC: World Bank.

Antoine, Kassia, Raju Jan Singh, and Konstantin M. Wacker. 2017. "Poverty and Shared Prosperity: Let's Move the Discussion beyond Growth." *Forum for Social Economics* 46 (20): 192–205.

APP (Africa Progress Panel). 2013. *Africa Progress Report 2013. Equity in Extractives: Stewarding Africa's Natural Resources for All.* Geneva: APP.

Appadurai, Arjun. 2004. "The Capacity to Aspire: Culture and the Terms of Recognition." In *Culture and Public Action: A Cross-Disciplinary Dialogue on Development Policy*, edited by Vijayendra Rao and Michael Walton, 59–84. Stanford, CA: Stanford University Press.

Bah, El-hadj, and Lei Fang. 2015. "Impact of the Business Environment on Output and Productivity in Africa." *Journal of Development Economics* 114: 159–71.

Baland, Jean-Marie, Catherine Guirkinger, and Charlotte Mali. 2011. "Pretending to Be Poor: Borrowing to Escape Forced Solidarity in Cameroon." *Economic Development and Cultural Change* 60 (1): 1–16.

Bandiera, O., and A. Natraj. 2012. "Does Gender Inequality Hinder Development and Economic Growth? Evidence and Policy Implications." *World Bank Research Observer* 28 (1): 2–21.

Barrett, Christopher B., Luc Christiaensen, Megan Sheahan, and Abebe Shimeles. 2017. "On the Structural Transformation of Rural Africa." *Journal of African Economies* 26 (suppl. 1): i11–35.

Beaman, Lori, Esther Duflo, Rohini Pande, and Petia Topalova. 2012. "Female Leadership Raises Aspirations and Educational Attainment for Girls: A Policy Experiment in India." *Science* 335 (6068): 582–86.

Beck, Thorsten, Asli Demirgüç-Kunt, and Ross Levine. 2007. "Finance, Inequality, and the Poor." *Journal of Economic Growth* 12 (1): 27–49.

Beegle, Kathleen, Luc Christiaensen, Andrew Dabalen, and Isis Gaddis. 2016. *Poverty in a Rising Africa.* Washington, DC : World Bank.

Benjamin, Nancy C., Shantayanan Devarajan, and Robert J. Weiner. 1989. "The 'Dutch' Disease in a Developing Country: Oil Reserves in Cameroon." *Journal of Development Economics* 30 (1): 71–92.

Bernard, Tanguy, Stefan Dercon, Kate Orkin, and Alemayehu Seyoum Taffesse. 2014. "The Future in Mind: Aspirations and Forward-Looking Behavior in Rural Ethiopia." CSAE Working Paper 2014-16, Centre for the Study of African Economies, University of Oxford.

Bigsten, Arne. 2018. "Determinants of the Evolution of Inequality in Africa." *Journal of African Economies* 27 (1): 127–48.

Blattman, Christopher, and Jeannie Annan. 2010. "The Consequences of Child Soldiering." *Review of Economics and Statistics* 92 (4): 882–98.

Bloom, David E., and D. Canning. 2004. "Global Demographic Change: Dimensions and Economic Significance." In *Global Demographic Change: Economic Impacts and Policy Challenges*, symposium proceedings, 9–56. Jackson Hole, WY: Federal Reserve Bank of Kansas City.

Bloom, David E., David Canning, Günther Fink, and Jocelyn Finlay. 2007. "Realizing the Demographic Dividend: Is Africa Any Different?" PGDA Working Paper No. 23, Program on the Global Demography of Aging, Harvard University, Cambridge, MA.

Bloom, David E., Michael Kuhn, and Klaus Prettner. 2015. "The Contribution of Female Health to Economic Development." NBER Working Paper 21411, National Bureau of Economic Research, Cambridge, MA.

Bloom, David E., and J. G. Williamson. 1998. "Demographic Transitions and Economic Miracles in Emerging Asia." *World Bank Economic Review* 12 (3): 419–55.

Boltz, Marie, Karine Marazyan, and Paola Villar. 2016. "Income Hiding and Informal Redistribution: A Lab in the Field Experiment in Senegal." G-MonD Note No. 18, Paris School of Economics (PSE).

Bongaarts, John. 2008. "Fertility Transitions in Developing Countries: Progress or Stagnation?" *Studies in Family Planning* 39 (2): 105–10.

———. 2017. "Africa's Unique Fertility Transition." *Population and Development Review* 43 (Supplement): 39–58.

Bongaarts, John, and John Casterline. 2013. "Fertility Transition: Is Sub-Saharan Africa Different?" *Population and Development Review* 38 (Supplement): 153–68.

Bosworth, Barry P., and Susan M. Collins. 2003. "The Empirics of Growth: An Update." *Brookings Papers on Economic Activity* 34 (2): 113–79.

Branisa, Boris, Stephan Klasen, and Maria Ziegler. 2009. "Why We Should All Care about Social Institutions Related to Gender Inequality." Proceedings of the German Development Economics Conference, Hanover, No. 50, Association for Social Policy, Committee on Developing Countries, Göttingen, Germany.

———. 2013. "Gender Inequality in Social Institutions and Gendered Development Outcomes." *World Development* 45 (C): 252–68.

———. 2014. "The Institutional Basis of Gender Inequality: The Social Institutions and Gender Index (SIGI)." *Feminist Economics* 20 (2): 29–64.

Brown, Caitlin, Martin Ravallion, and Dominique van de Walle. 2017. "Are Poor Individuals Mainly Found in Poor Households? Evidence Using Nutrition Data for Africa." Policy Research Working Paper 8001, World Bank, Washington, DC.

Brune, Lasse, Xavier Giné, Jessica Goldberg, and Dean Yang. 2015. "Facilitating Savings for Agriculture: Field Experimental Evidence from Malawi." *Economic Development and Cultural Change* 64 (2): 187–220.

Bundervoet, Tom, Philip Verwimp, and Richard Akresh. 2009. "Health and Civil War in Rural Burundi." *Journal of Human Resources* 44 (2): 536–63.

Calderón, César, and Luis Servén. 2014. "Infrastructure, Growth, and Inequality: An Overview." Policy Research Working Paper 7034, World Bank, Washington, DC.

Canning, David, Sangeeta Raja, and Abdo S. Yazbeck. 2015. *Africa's Demographic Transition: Dividend or Disaster?* Africa Development Forum Series. Washington, DC: World Bank.

Castañeda, Andrés, Dung Doan, David Newhouse, Minh Cong Nguyen, Hiroki Uematsu, and João Pedro Azevedo. 2018. "A New Profile of the Global Poor." *World Development* 101 (C): 250–67.

Casterline, J. B. 2009. "Demographic Transition and Unwanted Fertility: A Fresh Assessment." *Pakistan Development Review* 48 (4): 387–421.

Casterline, J. B., and L. O. El-Zeini. 2014. "Unmet Need and Fertility Decline: A Comparative Perspective on Prospects in Sub-Saharan Africa." *Studies in Family Planning* 45 (2): 227–45.

Chemin, Matthieu, Joost De Laat, and Johannes Haushofer. 2013. "Negative Rainfall Shocks Increase Levels of the Stress Hormone Cortisol among Poor Farmers in Kenya." Unpublished manuscript. doi:10.2139/ssrn.2294171.

Christiaensen, Luc, Lionel Demery, and Jesper Kuhl. 2011. "The (Evolving) Role of Agriculture in Poverty Reduction: An Empirical Perspective." *Journal of Development Economics* 96 (2): 239–54.

Christiaensen, Luc, Lionel Demery, and Stefano Paternostro. 2003. "Macro and Micro Perspectives of Growth and Poverty in Africa." *World Bank Economic Review* 17 (3): 317–47.

Christiaensen, Luc, and Jonathan Kaminski. 2014. "Structural Change, Economic Growth and Poverty Reduction: Micro Evidence from Uganda." Working Paper No. 2322, African Development Bank, Abidjan, Côte d'Ivoire.

Christiaensen, Luc, and Ravi Kanbur. 2017. "Secondary Towns and Poverty Reduction: Refocusing the Urbanization Agenda." *Annual Review of Resource Economics* 9 (1): 405–19.

Christiaensen, Luc, and Will Martin. 2018. "Agriculture, Structural Transformation and Poverty Reduction: Eight New Insights." *World Development* 109: 413–16.

Christiaensen, Luc, and John May. 2007. "Ethiopia—Capturing the Demographic Bonus in Ethiopia: Gender, Development and Demographic Actions." Report No. 36434-ET. World Bank, Washington, DC.

Christiaensen, Luc, and Patrick Premand. 2017. "Jobs Diagnostic, Côte d'Ivoire: Employment, Productivity, and Inclusion for Poverty Reduction." Report No. AUS13233, World Bank, Washington, DC.

Cleland, John, and Kazuyo Machiyama. 2017. "The Challenges Posed by Demographic Change in Sub-Saharan Africa: A Concise Overview." *Population and Development Review* 43 (Supplement): 264–86.

Collier, Paul, and Benedikt Goderis. 2007. "Commodity Prices, Growth, and the Natural Resource Curse: Reconciling a Conundrum." CSAE Working Paper No. 274, Centre for the Study of African Economies, University of Oxford.

———. 2012. "Commodity Prices and Growth: An Empirical Investigation." *European Economic Review* 56 (6): 1241–60.

Collier, Paul, and Anke Hoeffler. 2004. "Greed and Grievance in Civil War." *Oxford Economic Papers* 56 (4): 563–95.

Cuaresma, J. C., W. Lutz, and W. Sanderson. 2014. "Is the Demographic Dividend an Education Dividend?" *Demography* 51 (1): 299–315.

Cust, James, and David Mihalyi. 2017. "The Presource Curse: Oil Discoveries Can Lead First to Jubilation Then to Economic Jeopardy." *Finance and Development* 54 (4): 36–40.

Dalton, Patricio S., Sayantan Ghosal, and Anandi Mani. 2016. "Poverty and Aspirations Failure." *Economic Journal* 126 (590): 165–88.

de la Brière, Bénédicte, Deon Filmer, Dena Ringold, Dominic Rohner, Karelle Samuda, and Anastasiya Denisova. 2017. *From Mines and Wells to Well-Built Minds: Turning Sub-Saharan Africa's Natural Resource Wealth into Human Capital.* Directions in Development Series. Washington, DC: World Bank.

de Silva, Tiloka, and Silvana Tenreyro. 2017. "Population Control Policies and Fertility Convergence." *Journal of Economic Perspectives* 31 (4): 205–28.

Deaton, A., and R. Miller. 1996. "International Commodity Prices, Macroeconomic Performance and Politics in Sub-Saharan Africa." *Journal of African Economies* 5 (3): 99–191.

Demery, Lionel. 2018. "Natural Resource Dependence." Background note prepared for *Accelerating Poverty Reduction in Africa*, World Bank, Washington, DC.

Dercon, Stefan. 2004. "Growth and Shocks: Evidence from Rural Ethiopia." *Journal of Development Economics* 74 (2): 309–29.

———. 2009. "Rural Poverty: Old Challenges in New Contexts." *World Bank Research Observer* 24 (1): 1–28.

Dercon, Stefan, and Dough Gollin. 2014. "Agriculture in African Development: Theories and Strategies." *Annual Review of Resource Economics* 6 (1): 471–92.

Dercon, Stefan, and Catherine Porter. 2014. "Live Aid Revisited: Long-Term Impacts of the 1984 Ethiopian Famine on Children." *Journal of the European Economic Association* 12 (4): 927–48.

Devarajan, Shantayanan. 2017. "Three Reasons for Universal Basic Income." *Future Development* (blog), The Brookings Institution, Washington, DC, February 15. https://www.brookings.edu/blog/future-development/2017/02/15/three-reasons-for-universal-basic-income/.

Di Falco, Salvatore, and Erwin Bulte. 2011. "A Dark Side of Social Capital? Kinship, Consumption, and Savings." *Journal of Development Studies* 47 (8): 1128–51.

———. 2013. "The Impact of Kinship Networks on the Adoption of Risk-Mitigating Strategies in Ethiopia." *World Development* 43: 100–10.

Diao, Xinshen, and Margaret McMillan. 2018. "Toward an Understanding of Economic Growth in Africa: A Reinterpretation of the Lewis Model." *World Development* 109: 511–22.

Diao, Xinshen, Margaret McMillan, and Samuel Wangwe. 2018. "Agricultural Labour Productivity and Industrialization: Lessons for Africa." *Journal of African Economies* 27 (1): 28–65.

Dillon, Andrew, Jed Friedman, and Pieter Serneels. 2014. "Health Information, Treatment, and Worker Productivity: Experimental Evidence from Malaria Testing and Treatment among Nigerian Sugarcane Cutters." Policy Research Working Paper 7120, World Bank, Washington, DC.

Dollar, David, and Roberta Gatti. 1999. "Gender Inequality, Income and Growth: Are Good Times Good for Women?" Working Paper No. 1, Policy Research Report on Gender and Development, World Bank, Washington, DC.

Dollar, David, and Aart Kraay. 2002. "Growth Is Good for the Poor." *Journal of Economic Growth* 7 (3): 195–225.

Dorosh, Paul, and James Thurlow. 2018. "Beyond Agriculture versus Non-Agriculture: Decomposing Sectoral Growth-Poverty Linkages in Five African Countries." *World Development* 109: 440–51.

Doss, Cheryl. 2013. "Intrahousehold Bargaining and Resource Allocation in Developing Countries." *World Bank Research Observer* 28 (1): 52–78.

Duflo, Esther. 2012. "Women's Empowerment and Economic Development." *Journal of Economic Literature* 50 (4): 1051–79.

Dupas, Pascaline, and Jonathan Robinson. 2013. "Savings Constraints and Microenterprise Development: Evidence from a Field Experiment in Kenya." *American Economic Journal: Applied Economics* 5 (1): 163–92.

Durlauf, Steven. 2006. "Groups, Social Influences, and Inequality." In *Poverty Traps*, edited by Samuel Bowles, Steven Durlauf, and Karla Hoff, 141–75. Princeton, NJ: Princeton University Press.

Easterly, William, and Stanley Fischer. 2001. "Inflation and the Poor." *Journal of Money, Credit and Banking* 33 (2): 160–78.

Eastwood, R., and M. Lipton. 2011. "Demographic Transition in Sub-Saharan Africa: How Big Will the Economic Dividend Be?" *Population Studies* 65 (1): 9–35.

Elabed, Ghada, and Michael Carter. 2014. "Ex-Ante Impacts of Agricultural Insurance: Evidence from a Field Experiment in Mali." Unpublished paper, University of California, Davis.

Fafchamps, Marcel, David McKenzie, Simon R. Quinn, and Christopher Woodruff. 2011. "When Is Capital Enough to Get Female Microenterprises Growing? Evidence from a Randomized Experiment in Ghana." NBER Working Paper 17207, National Bureau of Economic Research, Cambridge, MA.

Ferguson, James. 2015. *Give a Man a Fish: Reflections on the New Politics of Distribution.* Durham, NC: Duke University Press.

Ferrant, Gaëlle, and Alexandre Kolev. 2016. "Does Gender Discrimination in Social Institutions Matter for Long-Term Growth? Cross Country Evidence." OECD Development Centre Working Paper No. 330, Organisation for Economic Co-operation and Development, Paris.

Ferreira, Francisco H. G., Phillippe G. Leite, and Martin Ravallion. 2010. "Poverty Reduction without Economic Growth? Explaining Brazil's Poverty Dynamics, 1985–2004." *Journal of Development Economics* 93 (1): 20–36.

Foster, James E., Joel Greer, and Erik Thorbecke. 1984. "A Class of Decomposable Poverty Measures." *Econometrica* 52 (3): 761–66.

Gaddis, I., and S. Klasen. 2014. "Economic Development, Structural Change, and Women's Labor Force Participation Rate: A Re-Examination of the Feminization U-Hypothesis." *Journal of Population Economics* 27: 639–81.

Genicot, Garance, and Debraj Ray. 2017. "Aspirations and Inequality." *Econometrica* 85 (2): 489–519.

Ghatak, Maitreesh. 2015. "Theories of Poverty Traps and Anti-Poverty Policies." *World Bank Economic Review* 29 (suppl 1): S77–S105.

Gibson, John, Gaurav Datt, Rinku Murgai, and Martin Ravallion. 2017. "For India's Rural Poor, Growing Towns Matter More than Growing Cities." *World Development* 98 (C): 413–29.

Gill, Indermit S., and Kenan Karakülah. 2019. "Is Africa Headed for Another Debt Crisis? Assessing Solvency in a Sluggish Subcontinent." Working Paper No. 2, Center for International and Global Studies, Duke University, Durham, NC.

Goldberg, Jessica. 2017. "The Effect of Social Pressure on Expenditures in Malawi." *Journal of Economic Behavior and Organization* 143: 173–85.

Gollin, Douglas, Remi Jedwab, and Dietrich Vollrath. 2016. "Urbanization with and without Industrialization." *Journal of Economic Growth* 21 (1): 35–70.

Greenhill, Romilly, Paddy Carter, Chris Hoy, and Marcus Manuel. 2015. *Financing the Future.* London: Overseas Development Institute.

Grimm, Michael, Flore Gubert, Ousman Koriko, Jann Lay, and Christophe J. Nordman. 2013. "Kinship Ties and Entrepreneurship in Western Africa." *Journal of Small Business and Entrepreneurship* 26 (2): 125–50.

Grimm, Michael, Renate Hartwig, and Jann Lay. 2017. "Does Forced Solidarity Hamper Investment in Small and Micro Enterprises?" *Journal of Comparative Economics* 45 (4): 827–46.

Grimm, Michael, Anicet Munyehirwe, Jörg Peters, and Maximiliane Sievert. 2017. "A First Step Up the Energy Ladder? Low Cost Solar Kits and Household's Welfare in Rural Rwanda." *World Bank Economic Review* 31 (3): 631–649.

Groth, Hans, and John F. May, eds. 2017. *Africa's Population: In Search of a Demographic Dividend.* Cham, Switzerland: Springer International.

Guengant, Jean-Pierre. 2017. "Africa's Population: History, Current Status and Projections." In *Africa's Population: In Search of a Demographic Dividend,* edited by Hans Groth and John F. May, 11–32. Cham, Switzerland: Springer International.

Günther, Isabel, and Kenneth Harttgen. 2016. "Desired Fertility and Number of Children Born across Time and Space." *Demography* 53 (1): 55–83. doi:10.1007/s13524-015-0451-9.

Hadnes, Myriam, Björn Vollan, and Michael Kosfeld. 2013. "The Dark Side of Solidarity." Working paper, World Bank, Washington, DC.

Hanushek, Eric A., and Ludger Woessmann. 2010. "Education and Economic Growth."

In *International Encyclopedia of Education*, 3rd ed., edited by Penelope Peterson, Rob Tierney, Eva Baker, and Barry McGraw, Vol. 2: 245–52. Oxford, U.K.: Academic Press.

Haushofer, Johannes, and Ernst Fehr. 2014. "On the Psychology of Poverty." *Science* 344 (6186): 862–67.

Hill, Ruth, and Carolina Mejía-Mantilla. 2017. "With a Little Help: Shocks, Agricultural Income, and Welfare in Uganda." Policy Research Working Paper 7935, World Bank, Washington, DC.

Hill, Ruth, and Catherine Porter. 2016. "Vulnerability to Drought and Food Price Shocks: Evidence from Ethiopia." Policy Research Working Paper 7920, World Bank, Washington, DC.

Hoff, Karla, and Arijit Sen. 2005. "The Kin System as a Poverty Trap?" Policy Research Working Paper 3575, World Bank, Washington, DC.

Huang, Jikun. 2016. "Fostering Inclusive Rural Transformation in China and Other Developing Countries in Asia." Presentation at the Latin American Center for Rural Development (RIMISP) International Conference on Territorial Inequality and Development, Puebla, Mexico, January 25–27.

IFPRI (International Food Policy Research Institute). 2018. *Global Food Policy Report 2018*. Washington, DC: IFPRI.

IMF (International Monetary Fund). 2017. *Fiscal Monitor: Tackling Inequality*. Washington, DC: IMF.

Ingelaere, Bert, Luc Christiaensen, Joachim De Weerdt, and Ravi Kanbur. 2018. "Why Secondary Towns Can Be Important for Poverty Reduction: A Migrant Perspective." *World Development* 105: 273–82.

Isham, Jonathan, Lant Pritchett, Michael Woolcock, and Gwen Busby. 2005. "The Varieties of the Resource Experience: How Natural Resource Export Structures Affect the Political Economy of Economic Growth." *World Bank Economic Review* 19 (2): 141–74.

Ivanic, Maros, and Will Martin. 2018. "Sectoral Productivity Growth and Poverty Reduction: National and Global Impacts." *World Development* 109: 429–39.

Jakiela, Pamela, and Owen Ozier. 2016. "Does Africa Need a Rotten Kin Theorem? Experimental Evidence from Village Economies." *Review of Economic Studies* 83 (1): 231–68.

James, Jeffrey. 2016. *The Impact of Mobile Phones on Poverty and Inequality in Developing Countries*. Cham, Switzerland: Springer.

Jaumotte, Florence, Subir Lall, and Chris Papageorgiou. 2013. "Rising Income Inequality: Technology, or Trade and Financial Globalization?" *IMF Economic Review* 61 (2): 271–308.

Jedwab, Remi, Luc Christiaensen, and Marina Gindelsky. 2017. "Demography, Urbanization and Development: Rural Push, Urban Pull and ... Urban Push." *Journal of Urban Economics* 98: 6–16.

Jones, Benjamin F. 2014. "The Human Capital Stock: A Generalized Approach." *American Economic Review* 104 (11): 3752–77.

Justino, Patricia, and Philip Verwimp. 2013. "Poverty Dynamics, Violent Conflict, and Convergence in Rwanda." *Review of Income and Wealth* 59 (1): 66–90.

Jütting, Johannes, Christian Morrison, Jeff Dayton-Johnson, and Denis Drechsler. 2008. "Measuring Gender Inequality: The OECD Gender, Institutions and Development Data Base." *Journal of Human Development* 9 (1): 65–86.

Karlan, Dean, Aishwarya Lakshmi Ratan, and Jonathan Zinman. 2014. "Savings by and for the Poor: A Research Review and Agenda." *Review of Income and Wealth* 60 (1): 36–78.

Karlan, Dean, Robert Osei, Isaac Osei-Akoto, and Christopher Udry. 2014. "Agricultural Decisions after Relaxing Credit and Risk Constraints." *Quarterly Journal of Economics* 129 (2): 597–652.

Kelley, Allen, and Robert Schmidt. 2007. "A Century of Demographic Change and Economic Growth: The Asian Experience in Regional and Temporal Perspective." In *Population Change, Labor Markets and Sustainable Growth: Towards a New Economic Paradigm*, edited by A. Mason and M. Yamaguchi, 39–74. Amsterdam: Elsevier.

Kim, Jungho. 2016. "Female Education and Its Impact on Fertility." Article, IZA World of Labor online platform, Institute for the Study of Labor (IZA), Bonn. doi:10.15185/izawol.228.

King, Elizabeth, Stephan Klasen, and Maria Porter. 2009. "Women and Development." In *Global Crises, Global Solutions*, 2nd ed., edited by B. Lomborg, 585–656. Cambridge, U.K.: Cambridge University Press.

Klasen, Stephan. 2002. "Low Schooling for Girls, Slower Growth for All? Cross-Country Evidence on the Effect of Gender Inequality in Education on Economic Development." *World Bank Economic Review* 16 (3): 345–73.

———. 2006. "Pro-Poor Growth and Gender Inequality." In *Pro-Poor Growth: Policy and Evidence*, edited by L. Menkhoff, 151–79. Berlin: Duncker and Humblot.

———. 2018. "The Impact of Gender Inequality on Economic Performance in Developing Countries." Poverty, Equity and Growth Discussion Paper No. 244, Courant Research Centre on Poverty, Equity and Growth in Developing Countries, University of Göttingen, Germany.

Klasen, Stephan, and Francesca Lamanna. 2009. "The Impact of Gender Inequality in Education and Employment on Economic Growth: New Evidence for a Panel of Countries." *Feminist Economics* 15 (3): 91–132.

Knowles, Stephen, Paula K. Lorgelly, and P. Dorian Owen. 2002. "Are Educational Gender Gaps a Brake on Economic Development? Some Cross-Country Empirical Evidence." *Oxford Economic Papers* 54 (1): 118–49.

Kose, M. Ayhan, Sergio Kurlat, Franziska Ohnsorge, and Naotaka Sugawara. 2017. "A Cross-Country Database of Fiscal Space." Policy Research Working Paper 8157, World Bank, Washington, DC.

Lall, Somik Vinay, J. Vernon Henderson, and Anthony J. Venables. 2017. *Africa's Cities: Opening Doors to the World*. Washington, DC: World Bank.

Le Goff, M., and R. J. Singh. 2014. "Does Trade Reduce Poverty? A View from Africa." *Journal of African Trade* 1 (1): 5–14.

Lekfuangfu, Nuarpear Warn, Stephen Machin, and Imran Rasul. 2012. "Report on Uganda's Return to Schooling." Working Paper F-43007-UGA-1, International Growth Center, London School of Economic and Political Science, London.

Lewis, Arthur. 1954. "Economic Development with Unlimited Supplies of Labor." *Manchester School of Economic and Social Studies* 22 (2): 139–91.

Ligon, Ethan, and Elisabeth Sadoulet. 2018. "Estimating the Relative Benefits of Agricultural Growth on the Distribution of Expenditures." *World Development* 109: 417–28.

Maehle, Nils, Haimanot Teferra, and Armine Khachatryan. 2013. "Exchange Rate Liberalization in Selected Sub-Saharan African Countries: Successes, Failures, and Lessons." IMF Working Paper 13/32, International Monetary Fund, Washington, DC.

Mani, Anandi, Sendhil Mullainathan, Eldar Shafir, and Jiaying Zhao. 2013. "Poverty Impedes Cognitive Function." *Science* 341 (6149): 976–80.

Manuel, Marcus, Harsh Desai, Emma Samman, and Martin Evans. 2018. "Financing the End of Extreme Poverty." Report, Overseas Development Institute, London.

Maystadt, Jean-François, Kalle Hirvonen, Athur Mabiso, and Joachim Vandercasteelen. 2018. "Conflict, Migration and Food Security from the Host Perspective." Unpublished manuscript.

McCullough, Ellen. 2017. "Labor Productivity and Employment Gaps in Sub-Saharan Africa." *Food Policy* 67: 133–52.

McMillan, Margaret, Dani Rodrik, and Inigo Verduzco-Gallo. 2014. "Globalization, Structural Change, and Productivity Growth, with an Update on Africa." *World Development* 63: 11–32.

Mensah, Edouard, and Michael O'Sullivan. 2017. "Moving Out and Up: Panel Data Evidence on Migration and Poverty in Uganda." Policy Research Working Paper 8186, World Bank, Washington, DC.

Minasyan, Anna, Juliane Zenker, Stephan Klasen, and Sebastian Vollmer. 2017. "The Impact of Gender Inequality in Education on Economic Growth: A Systematic Review and Meta-Analysis." Unpublished manuscript, University of Göttingen, Germany.

Minoiu, Camelia, and Olga N. Shemyakina. 2014. "Armed Conflict, Household Victimization, and Child Health in Côte d'Ivoire." *Journal of Development Economics* 108: 237–55.

MoF, GoI (Ministry of Finance, Government of India). 2017. "Economic Survey 2016–17." Flagship annual document of the Department of Economic Affairs, Ministry of Finance, Government of India, New Delhi.

Molini, Vasco, and Pierella Paci. 2015. "Poverty Reduction in Ghana: Progress and Challenges, 2015." Report No. 101230, World Bank, Washington, DC.

Morrison, Christian, and Johannes P. Jütting. 2005. "Women's Discrimination in Developing Countries: A New Data Set for Better Policies." *World Development* 33 (7): 1065–81.

Moya, Andrés. 2018. "Violence, Psychological Trauma, and Risk Attitudes: Evidence from Victims of Violence in Colombia." *Journal of Development Economics* 131: 15–27.

Mueller, Hannes. 2016. "Growth and Violence: Argument for a Per Capita Measure of Civil War." *Economica* 83 (331): 473–97.

Naceur, Sami Ben, and RuiXin Zhang. 2016. "Financial Development, Inequality and Poverty: Some International Evidence." IMF Working Paper 16/32, International Monetary Fund, Washington, DC.

Ndulu, Benno J., Stephen A. O'Connell, Robert Bates, Paul Collier, and Chukwuma C. Soludo. 2007. *The Political Economy of Economic Growth in Africa, 1960–2000*. Vol. 1. Cambridge, U.K. Cambridge University Press.

Nikoloski, Zlatko, Luc Christiaensen, and Ruth Hill. 2018. "Coping with Shocks: The Realities of African Life." In *Agriculture in Africa: Telling Myths from Facts*, edited by Luc Christiaensen and Lionel Demery, 123–34. Directions in Development Series. Washington, DC: World Bank.

Ozier, Owen. 2018. "The Impact of Secondary Schooling in Kenya: A Regression Discontinuity Analysis." *Journal of Human Resources* 53 (1): 157–88.

Paine, Thomas. 1797. *Agrarian Justice, Opposed to Agrarian Law, and Agrarian Monopoly. Being a Plan for Ameliorating the Condition of Man, by Creating in Every Nation a National Fund*. Paris: W. Adlard.

Platteau, Jean-Philippe. 2000. *Institutions, Social Norms and Economic Development*. Amsterdam: Harwood.

———. 2014. "Redistributive Pressures in Sub-Saharan Africa: Causes, Consequences, and Coping Strategies." In *African Development in Historical Perspective*, edited by E. Akyeampong, R. Bates, N. Nunn, and J. Robinson, 153–207. Cambridge, U.K.: Cambridge University Press.

Prichard, Wilson, Paola Salardi, and Paul Segal. 2018. "Taxation, Non-Tax Revenue and Democracy: New Evidence Using New Cross-Country Data." *World Development* 109: 295–312.

Ralston, Laura, Colin Andrews, and Allan Hsiao. 2017. "The Impacts of Safety Nets in Africa: What Are We Learning?" Policy Research Working Paper 8255, World Bank, Washington, DC.

Ravallion, Martin. 2014. "Time for the BIG Idea in the Developing World." Center for Global Development Blog, December 12. https://www.cgdev.org/blog/time-big-idea-developing-world.

———. 2016. *The Economics of Poverty: History, Measurement, and Policy*. Oxford, U.K.: Oxford University Press.

Ravallion, Martin, and Gaurav Datt. 2002. "Why Has Economic Growth Been More Pro-Poor in Some States of India than Others?" *Journal of Development Economics* 68 (2): 381–400.

Rodrik, Dani. 1998. "Trade Policy and Economic Performance in Sub-Saharan Africa." NBER Working Paper 6562, National Bureau of Economic Research, Cambridge, MA.

———. 2016. "An African Growth Miracle?" *Journal of African Economies* 27 (1): 1–18.

Roe, Alan, and Samantha Dodd. 2017. "Dependence on Extractive Industries in Lower-Income Countries: The Statistical Tendencies." WIDER Working Paper 2017/98, United Nations University World Institute for Development Economics Research (UNU-WIDER), Helsinki.

Ross, John, and John Stover. 2001. "The Family Planning Program Effort Index: 1999 Cycle." *International Family Planning Perspectives* 27 (3): 119–29.

Ross, Michael L. 2001. "Does Oil Hinder Democracy?" *World Politics* 53 (3): 325–61.

Ross, Michael. 2012. *The Oil Curse: How Petroleum Wealth Shapes the Development of Nations*. Princeton, NJ: Princeton University Press.

Sachs, Jeffrey D., and Andrew M. Warner. 1995. "Natural Resource Abundance and Economic Growth." NBER Working Paper 5398, National Bureau of Economic Research, Cambridge, MA.

———. 1997. "Sources of Slow Growth in African Economies." *Journal of African Economies* 6 (3): 335–76.

Sakyi, Daniel, José Villaverde, Adolfo Maza, and Isaac Bonuedi. 2017. "The Effects of Trade and Trade Facilitation on Economic Growth in Africa." *African Development Review* 29 (2): 350–61.

Sala-i-Martin, Xavier, and Arvind Subramanian. 2008. "Addressing the Natural Resource Curse: An Illustration from Nigeria." In *Economic Policy Options for a Prosperous Nigeria*, edited by P. Collier, C. C. Soludo, and C. Pattillo, 61–92. London: Palgrave Macmillan.

Schaner, Simone. 2017. "The Cost of Convenience? Transaction Costs, Bargaining Power, and Savings Account Use in Kenya." *Journal of Human Resources* 52 (4): 919–45.

Schoumaker, Bruno. 2004. "Poverty and Fertility in Sub-Saharan Africa: Evidence from 25 Countries." Paper presented at the Population Association of America meeting, Boston, April 1–3.

Serneels, Pieter, and Marijke Verpoorten. 2015. "The Impact of Armed Conflict on Economic Performance: Evidence from Rwanda." *Journal of Conflict Resolution* 59 (4): 555–92.

Spears, Dean. 2011. "Economic Decision-Making in Poverty Depletes Behavioral Control." *B.E. Journal of Economic Analysis and Policy* 11 (1): 1–44.

Stotsky, Janet Gale, Manuk Ghazanchyan, Olumuyiwa S. Adedeji, and Nils O. Maehle. 2012. "The Relationship between the Foreign Exchange Regime and Macroeconomic Performance in Eastern Africa." IMF Working Paper 12/148, International Monetary Fund, Washington, DC.

Townsend, Robert. 1999. "Agricultural Incentives in Sub-Saharan Africa: Policy Challenges." World Bank Technical Paper No. 444, World Bank, Washington, DC.

Tschirley, David, Jason Synder, Michael Dolislager, Thomas Reardon, Steven Haggblade, Joseph Goeb, Lulama Traub, Francis Ejobi, and Ferdi Meyer. 2015. "Africa's Unfolding Diet Transformation: Implications for Agrifood System Employment." *Journal of Agribusiness in Developing and Emerging Economies* 5 (2): 102–36.

United Nations Population Division. 2019. World Population Prospects 2017. https://population.un.org/wpp/DataQuery/.

Wantchekon, Leonard, Marko Klašnja, and Natalija Novta. 2015. "Education and Human Capital Externalities: Evidence from Colonial Benin." *Quarterly Journal of Economics* 130 (2): 703–57.

Warner, Andrew. 2015. "Natural Resource Booms in the Modern Era: Is the Curse Still Alive?" IMF Working Paper 15/237, International Monetary Fund, Washington, DC.

World Bank. 2011. *World Development Report 2012: Gender Equality and Development.* Washington, DC: World Bank.

———. 2013a. "Growing Africa: Unlocking the Potential of Agribusiness." Working Paper No. 75663, World Bank, Washington, DC.

———. 2013b. *World Development Report 2014: Risk and Opportunity.* Washington, DC: World Bank.

———. 2014. *Africa's Pulse: An Analysis of Issues Shaping Africa's Economic Future,* vol. 10 (October). Washington, DC: World Bank.

———. 2015a. "Ethiopia Poverty Assessment 2014." Report No. AUS6744, World Bank, Washington, DC.

———. 2015b. *World Development Report 2015: Mind, Society, and Behavior.* Washington, DC: World Bank.

———. 2015c. *Rwanda Poverty Assessment.* Washington, DC: World Bank.

———. 2016a. *Global Monitoring Report 2015/2016: Development Goals in an Era of Demographic Change.* Washington, DC: World Bank.

———. 2016b. *Making Politics Work for Development: Harnessing Transparency and Citizen Engagement.* Policy Research Report. Washington, DC: World Bank.

———. 2016c. "The Uganda Poverty Assessment Report 2016. Farms, Cities and Good Fortune: Assessing Poverty Reduction in Uganda from 2006 to 2013." Report No. ACS18391, World Bank, Washington, DC.

———. 2017. *Africa's Pulse: An Analysis of Issues Shaping Africa's Economic Future*, vol. 16 (October). Washington, DC: World Bank.

———. 2018a. *Africa's Pulse: An Analysis of Issues Shaping Africa's Economic Future,* vol. 17 (April). Washington, DC: World Bank.

———. 2018b. *World Development Report 2018: Learning to Realize Education's Promise.* Washington, DC: World Bank.

Yoon, Jisu, and Stephan Klasen. 2018. "An Application of Partial Least Squares to the Construction of the Social Institutions and Gender Index (SIGI) and the Corruption Perception Index (CPI)." *Social Indicators Research* 138 (1): 61–88.

FUNDAMENTALS 1

Africa's Human Development Trap

Eleni Yitbarek and Kathleen Beegle

The circumstances into which children are born and raised will have enduring effects on their socioeconomic adulthood outcomes. Children who have a disadvantaged start in life face a greater risk of being trapped in poverty over the course of their lives. Less-healthy childhood is associated with poor adulthood outcomes, including lower income and poorer health (Barrett, Garg, and McBride 2016; Bhutta et al. 2013). And impeded cognitive and social-emotional development results in lifelong welfare and behavioral disadvantages (Conti, Heckman, and Urzua 2010; Heckman 2006).

Notably, there are limited ways to compensate adults for the consequences of poor childhood health and schooling outcomes. Although human development is a lifelong process, the social and individual returns on childhood investments specifically are high and, critically, the chances to catch up later in life are minimal (Cunha et al. 2006; Hoddinott et al. 2013). Low human development of children results in a poverty trap when remediation of these impacts is partly or mostly irreversible (Barrett, Garg, and McBride 2016; Cunha et al. 2006). This human development trap initiates a cycle of poverty—low education and poor health results in low adult income and poor human development for children and so on—that runs across generations and traps families in poverty (Bhalotra and Rawlings 2013; Bhutta et al. 2013; Victora et al. 2008). Child marriage is arguably one of the most visible signs of this intergenerational trap (box F1.1).

The macroeconomic returns to investing in the human development of children today are high: these investments contribute to stable economic growth tomorrow (Flabbi and Gatti 2018). Although human development is accepted as critical for economic growth, building human capital can also be important for stability and reduced conflict (World Bank 2018b). Education raises the opportunity cost of fighting: it is easier to recruit people who have poor job prospects. Also, education can promote tolerance and cooperation, thereby reducing the propensity to turn to violence to resolve conflicts.

In sum, human development is central to long-term poverty reduction in Africa. However, because the economic benefits of this investment are realized far into the future (a decade or longer), public investments in human development (by spending more or significantly improving efficiency) may lack appeal to governments and politicians looking for short-run wins for the economy.

It is difficult to improve human development outcomes quickly for two reasons: First, even among those countries that are making progress, progress is typically slow, meaning that it will take many years to reach the universal school enrollment or learning outcomes in Organisation for Economic Co-operation and Development (OECD) countries (Wild et al. 2015; World Bank 2018b). Second, changing the stock level of human development among the adult population takes a generation or more; one must wait for children to cycle into adulthood.

Poverty in Africa is a large obstacle in the way of improving human development. Almost 170 million children live in poverty in Africa. The region has the highest rate of children in poverty, about 49 percent, and the largest share of the world's poor children, more than 50 percent (Newhouse, Suarez-Becerra, and Evans 2016). Living in poor households has lifelong implications when it means less investment in childhood. And the evidence is strong indeed that children in

BOX F1.1 Child marriage and early childbearing trap girls in poverty

In Africa, 4 in 10 girls marry before their 18th birthdays (UNICEF 2016). In some countries, the rate is much higher. At least two-thirds of girls are married by age 18 in the Central African Republic, Chad, and Niger; about half of girls are married by 18 in Burkina Faso, Guinea, and Mali. Most child marriages occur between 15 and 18 years of age, but in Chad and Niger, more than a third of 20- to 24-year-olds were married before the age of 15. Although the prevalence of child marriage is declining, because of high population growth rates the number of girls who are married is increasing in some countries like Burkina Faso and Nigeria.

Several interacting factors result in child marriage, including poverty and poor education options including school fees. Domestic chores and early childbearing become a substitute for an education or apprenticeship to improve girls' livelihoods and lift themselves out of poverty. Notwithstanding the important point that child marriage is a violation of human rights, it also has significant economic costs such as population growth and earnings losses (Parsons et al. 2015; Wodon et al. 2017).

Child brides have more children in their lifetimes than women who marry later. These girls also get less schooling: each additional year of early marriage is associated with lower girls' schooling, resulting in literacy rates for girls that are lower by 5.7 percentage points and a 3.5-point lower probability of completing secondary school (Nguyen and Wodon 2014). Delaying child marriage by one year is associated with an extra half year of schooling (Delprato et al. 2015).

The future life of a married girl is also likely to be fraught with perpetual health consequences. The lack of power in the marriage is typically associated with greater risk of domestic violence, which in turn is strongly correlated with adverse physical and mental health outcomes (Kidman 2017). Marrying men with multiple sexual partners can also expose young married girls to sexually transmitted diseases including human immunodeficiency virus and acquired immune deficiency syndrome (HIV/AIDS) (Bingenheimer 2010; Nour 2006). Psychologically, child brides are much more likely to show symptoms of sexual abuse and post-traumatic stress such as feelings of despair and severe depression (Lal 2015).

Early childbearing not only puts the girl's health in jeopardy but also places her children at severe risk of under-five mortality and malnutrition compared with children born of older mothers. Part of the reason is that young mothers are socioeconomically and physically unready to undergo childbirth. Children born to women who were child brides also tend to receive less schooling, and these negative impacts are larger for daughters than for sons (Delprato, Akyeampong, and Dunne 2017).

The programs that have shown more success at addressing child marriage are those that work directly with girls and address multiple issues that underlie child marriage (Lee-Rife et al. 2012). In some cases, direct incentives have targeted families of underage girls in areas with high prevalence of child marriage. This strategy not only delays the age at which young girls marry but also increases the proportion of girls still in school at ages 22–25 as well as their total years of schooling (Buchmann et al. 2017). If contraceptives are widely used in countries where child marriage is high and widespread, then the impact of child marriage might be reduced because couples would have more control over their fertility (Wodon et al. 2017).

poor households have worse childhood outcomes across many dimensions. Poverty combined with vulnerability and lack of insurance mechanisms exacerbates these challenges. Climate, conflict, or other income shocks in utero and during early childhood—to which the poor are more exposed—significantly reduce parental investment in human capital accumulation, causing adverse long-term outcomes on adult educational attainment, health, and labor market participation (Baez and Santos 2007; Bharadwaj, Lundborg, and Rooth 2017; Maccini and Yang 2009). The impact of nutritional and educational shocks on adulthood income is substantial, ranging from 3 percent in Ethiopia to 20 percent in Burundi (for details, see chapter 5, "Managing Risks and Conflict").

The Health Poverty Trap

Poverty is one of the driving factors of malnutrition (Dasgupta 1997; Osmani 1992) and disease burden for children (Bond et al. 2009). Beyond physical health and schooling outcomes, childhood poverty is also related to poor mental health (Evans and Cassells 2014).

Poor health translates into future poverty through a number of pathways.[1] Poor health in early childhood is significantly correlated with suboptimal brain development that negatively affects children's cognitive development; educational attainment (in the broad sense, encompassing formal and informal schooling, skill training, and knowledge acquisition); and economic productivity later in life (Leroy et al. 2014).

The first 1,000 days of life are a critical phase of rapid physical and mental development (De Onis and Branca 2016; Mukhebi, Mbogoh, and Matungulu 2011). A shortfall in realizing cognitive developmental potential adversely affects school progress, in terms of both fewer years of schooling and less learning per year in school (Feinstein 2003). In particular, poor health in children due to worms has been shown to result in lower cognitive levels and poorer educational outcomes in the short and long run (Baird et al. 2016; Croke and Atun 2019; Ozier 2018).[2] In contrast, early cognitive development is positively associated with improved school outcomes (Grantham-McGregor et al. 2007).

Poor childhood health is a trap because those outcomes in childhood are difficult to compensate for later in life. Although some catch-up is possible (Mendez and Adair 1999), most of the effects of malnutrition persist into adulthood (Checkley et al. 2003; Martorell, Khan, and Schroeder 1994).

The Vicious Cycle of Undernutrition

The health-induced poverty trap is a pressing long-term development challenge in Africa, where 33.2 percent, 7.1 percent, and 16.3 percent of children under five years of age are stunted, wasted, or underweight, respectively (Akombi et al. 2017).[3] Stunted children have impaired cognitive development, delayed school starts, lower test scores, lower educational attainment, and higher class repetition and dropout rates (Galasso and Wagstaff 2018; Mendez and Adair 1999). Taller siblings from the same mothers perform better on cognitive tests, and height is positively correlated with better economic, health, and educational outcomes (Case and Paxson 2010; Glewwe and Jacoby 1995). In sum, the social and individual economic returns of reducing stunting are high (Galasso and Wagstaff 2018; Hoddinott et al. 2013).

Over the past two decades, the prevalence of stunting has been declining across Africa, from 45 percent in 1995 to 33 percent in 2016 (Akombi et al. 2017; Beegle et al. 2016). However, the region still has the highest rate of child stunting globally and is the only region where the *number* of stunted children is increasing (World Bank 2018a).[4] And being born in a fragile or resource-rich country increases one's chance of being malnourished despite the higher national income associated with resource wealth (APP 2013; Beegle et al. 2016; de la Brière et al. 2017).

The scale of undernutrition in Africa is "staggering" (World Bank 2018a). In addition to the overall high level of malnutrition in Africa, there is a notable poverty aspect. Children in poor households have much higher rates of stunting than their peers in wealthier households (figure F1.1). This positive correlation between parental socioeconomic status and child health is well documented in both high-income countries and low- and middle-income countries.

The influence of parental socioeconomic status on their children's health starts in utero (Almond 2006; Almond and Mazumder 2005; Harper, Marcus, and Moore 2003) or soon after birth, being highly pronounced in the first three years (Martorell 1995). This has long-term consequences into adulthood and even intergenerationally (Barham, Macours, and Maluccio 2013; Grantham-McGregor et al. 2007). Mothers born in poor areas—a proxy for low socioeconomic status—are likely to have been of low birth

FIGURE F1.1 **In Africa, poor children are much more likely to be stunted**

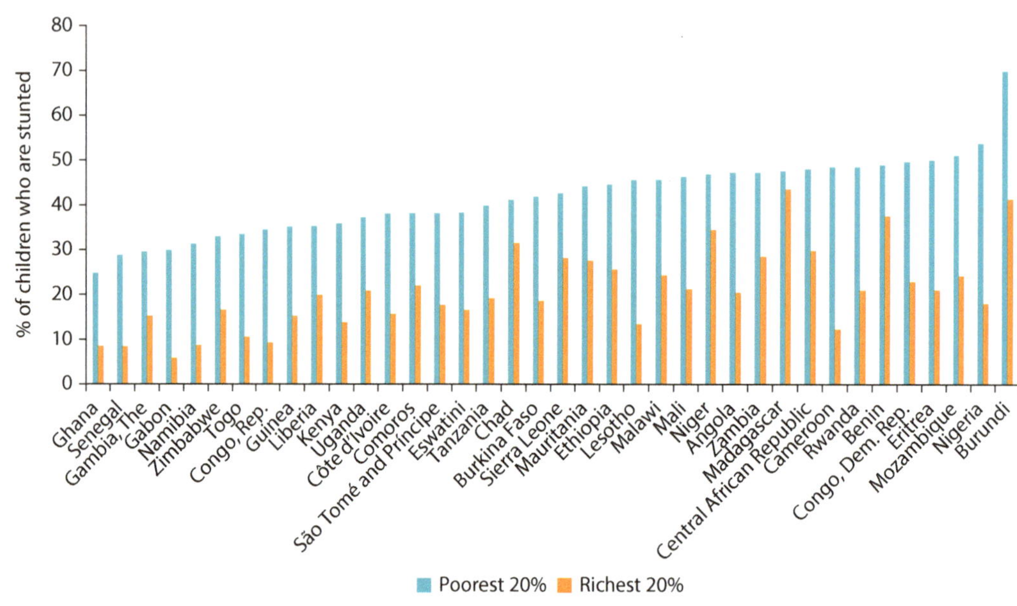

Sources: Countries' Demographic and Health Surveys, various years.
Note: Stunting is defined as low height-for-age among children under the age of five.

weight and to have low-birth-weight babies (Currie and Moretti 2007). Children born of fathers in higher-income occupations have higher birth weights than those born of fathers in the lower-income occupations (Currie and Hyson 1999). A significant difference in early childhood cognitive development by socioeconomic status persists once children enter school and beyond (Case, Lubotsky, and Paxson 2002; Schady et al. 2015).

The Battle to Increase Immunization

Poor children and poor parents in Africa have starkly unequal access to critical services that influence children's health (World Bank 2018a). For example, immunization is one of the most cost-effective policy interventions that can reduce the burden of infectious disease, illness, and disability among children. Over the past three decades, Africa has made huge improvements in childhood immunization against preventable diseases such as polio, pneumonia, diphtheria, measles, and tuberculosis. Despite the progress, many African children are not vaccinated and suffer from preventable diseases that have a decisive effect on their human development during childhood and later in life.

In 2014, of the 19 million children who did not receive basic vaccines (diphtheria, tetanus, and pertussis) globally, more than 40 percent—or more than 7.6 million—were from Sub-Saharan Africa (Machingaidze, Wiysonge, and Hussey 2013). There are considerable intercountry and intracountry differences in vaccination outreach. For instance, diphtheria, pertussis, and tetanus vaccination among children aged 12–23 months ranges from 56 percent in Nigeria to 97 percent in The Gambia (Kazungu and Adetifa 2017). Children from poor households, girls, children in rural areas, and children with lower parental education and income are more likely to remain unimmunized (Canavan et al. 2014; Wiysonge et al. 2012). Low-income, resource-rich, and fragile and conflict-affected countries in Africa have relatively lower vaccination rates.

The Education Poverty Trap

Low school attainment and poor educational quality among children are the main factors that perpetuate poverty over the life course and across generations. Ample evidence from low- and middle-income countries as well as high-income countries document the importance of education to raise incomes and promote social mobility (Deaton 2013; Fogel 2004). The effect is highest in Africa, where an additional year of schooling leads to an average 13 percent increase in earnings (Montenegro and Patrinos 2013). Education is consistently highly correlated with poverty status in every country. Education is also one of the strongest determinants of income inequality in Africa (Beegle et al. 2016).

Poor schooling is a trap because realistically catching up on schooling as a young adult is unlikely, not least because family formation starts young and inhibits a return to school. The size of adult literacy programs in the region has been historically quite limited (Blunch 2017).

Since the launch of the "universal basic education" movement, Africa's progress toward universal primary education has been tremendous. The average primary gross enrollment rate rose from 68 percent in 1995 to 106 percent in 2012 (Beegle et al. 2016).[5] Between 1990 and 2015, the total number of children enrolled in primary schools more than doubled, from 63 million in 1990 to 152 million in 2015.[6] Despite the impressive increase in the number of students enrolled in primary school, more than 50 million primary and lower-secondary school-age children are out of school, most of whom have never been enrolled. The three most populous countries—Nigeria, Ethiopia, and the Democratic Republic of Congo—together account for about 40 percent of the out-of-school children in the region (Bashir et al. 2018).

Improvements in primary school enrollment have not translated into improvements in learning. Many African students do not reach the minimum levels of learning, reading, or math. A staggering number of students in second grade, 50–80 percent, lack basic reading skills, and a large proportion of these children could not read even a single word in the language of instruction in their country (Bashir et al. 2018). The pattern of poor learning in primary and lower-secondary school across countries in Africa is quite consistent, and scores for numeracy and mathematics skills are equally poor, well below those of other low- and middle-income countries (Bashir et al. 2018; Beegle et al. 2016; World Bank 2018b).

This pattern is notably linked to children's poverty status: that is, poor children learn even less (figure F1.2). Of concern, as new technology requires a minimum set of "digital" skills, poor children will fall further behind as new opportunities to escape poverty are lost (see Fundamentals 3, "Leapfrogging with Technology (and Trade)").

In Sub-Saharan Africa, poor learning starts in the early years of a child's life: 61 percent of preschool children—children under five years old—experience cognitive delays (Grantham-McGregor et al. 2007). Recent evidence shows that preschool care of children (ages 0–4.5 years) is vital for cognitive development, and the effect persists throughout an individual's life (Heckman 2006, 2011; Shonkoff and Phillips 2000; Vandell et al. 2010). Preschool care has far-reaching effects on adulthood educational outcomes. This is particularly a huge challenge for disadvantaged children from poor households who have poor home learning environments and lower parenting quality, as measured by maternal responsiveness and language simulation (Berger, Paxson, and Waldfogel 2009).

Poor children also lack access to preschool relative to their wealthier peers. In South Africa, for instance, less than 30 percent of children in the poorest school have attended two years of preschool, compared with about

FIGURE F1.2 **In Africa, poor children learn less**

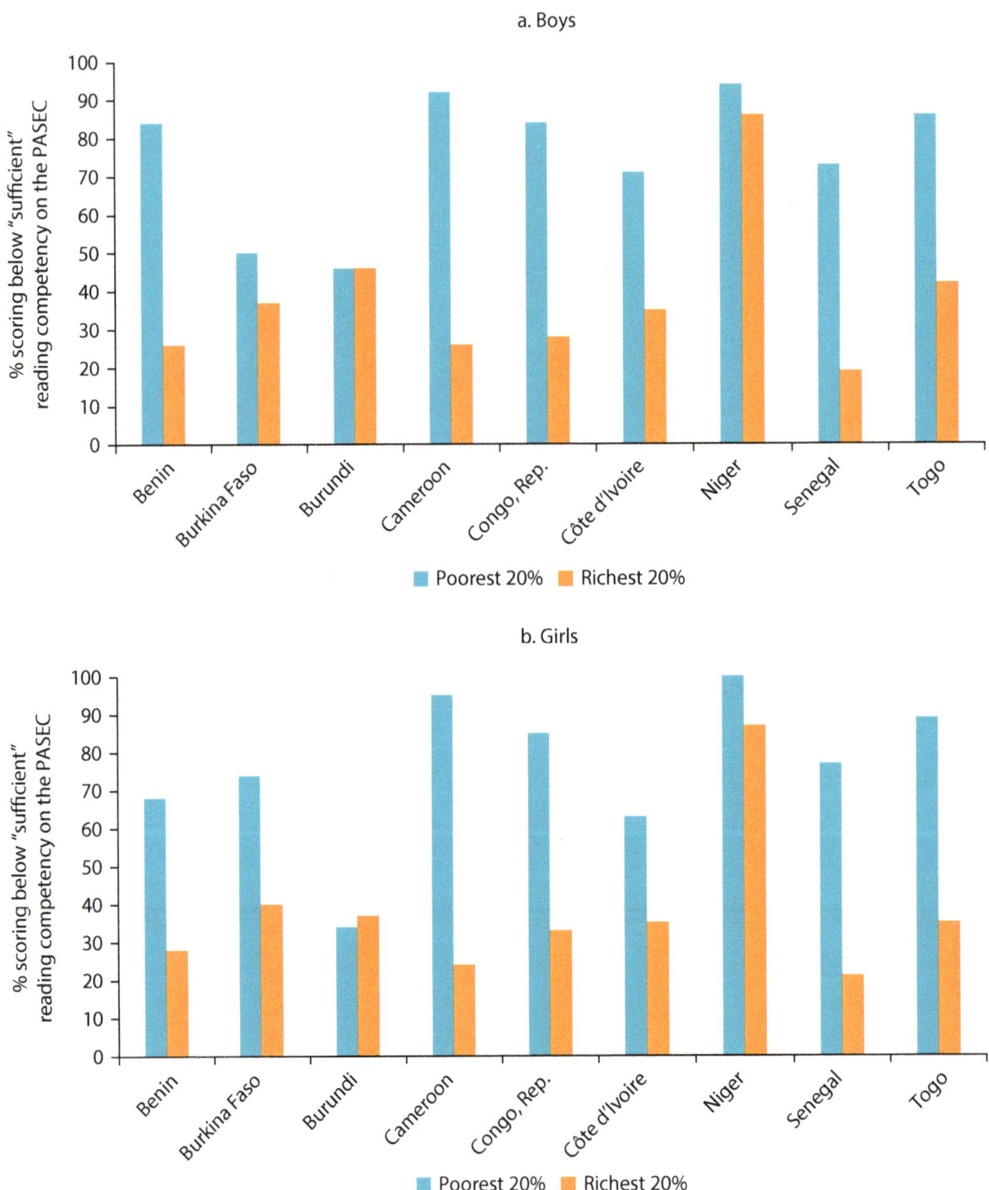

Source: World Bank 2018b.
Note: PASEC = Programme d'analyse des systèmes éducatifs de la CONFEMEN, a regional assessment survey across the African francophone countries. The figure shows the percentage of sixth-grade PASEC test takers in 2014, from the poorest and richest quintiles by gender, who scored below the sufficiency level on reading achievement.

60 percent of children in richer schools (Spaull 2013). In Madagascar, there are substantial wealth gradients among young children in multiple domains (receptive vocabulary, cognition, sustained attention, and working memory). And these gaps in cognitive outcomes translate into gaps in learning outcomes between children from poor and rich households (Galasso, Weber, and Fernald 2019).

When it comes to delays in cognitive development, emerging empirical evidence from Africa shows that socioeconomic gradients accumulate over time. The education story is not one of only the primary school years. In most African countries, few children from poor households reach tertiary education. In addition, parents' education remains a strong determinant of their children's educational outcomes in the region. Intergenerational education persistence is strong from mothers to children, and the persistence is more pronounced among daughters than sons (Azomahou and Yitbarek 2016; Branson et al. 2012; Kwenda, Ntuli, and Gwatidzo 2015; Lambert, Ravallion, and van de Walle 2014; Ranasinghe 2015; Thomas 1996).

Escaping the Human Development Poverty Trap

Across a range of indicators, the main takeaway is that progress in Africa is happening but at a slow pace and especially for poor households (Wild et al. 2015). Speeding up the improvements in human development is critical to addressing poverty in the region over the long run.

More money is part of the solution but with two caveats: First, in terms of the national income available, the source and type of economic growth matters, as evidenced by the poor performance of resource-rich economies regarding human development (de la Brière et al. 2017).[7] Second, within-sector spending matters for it to reach the poor. Chapter 6 ("Mobilizing Resources for the Poor") discusses various aspects of fiscal investments in human capital, emphasizing the level of spending, within-sector spending, and the efficiency of spending.

Technology will also be part of the solution, bringing greater efficiency to spending and improving services (see Fundamentals 3, "Leapfrogging with Technology (and Trade)"). As with the story of employment (chapters 3 and 4), an integrated approach is needed to improve human development outcomes for the next generation.

Notes

1. The combined effect of health on income today and income tomorrow (next generation having worse human capital and lower income) means that health matters for development overall. The historical contribution of health to economic development ranges from 30 percent to 40 percent of today's economic wealth (IMF 2004). Longer life expectancy is also associated with increased gross domestic product (GDP) (Biciunaite and Gordon 2014; Cervellati and Sunde 2011). On the other hand, higher GDP does not necessarily resolve the problems of poor health (Harttgen, Klasen, and Vollmer 2013).
2. Even in adulthood, poor health has poverty impacts. Individuals with poor health are either excluded from rewarding labor markets or earn less. Malaria, which is quite prevalent in Africa, has been shown to reduce farm work and productivity (Alaba and Alaba 2009; Cropper et al. 2004; Dillon, Friedman, and Serneels 2014). Health shocks also reduce savings and investment as well as current income. (See the discussion in chapter 5 of this report.)
3. Stunting (low height-for-age) is an indicator of chronic malnutrition reflecting linear and cumulative growth deficits in children. Wasting (low weight-for-height) is an indicator of acute child malnutrition. Underweight (low weight-for-age) is a composite index of stunting and wasting without distinguishing between the two.
4. Before the battle against malnutrition has been won, overnutrition is also emerging in the region. Many countries in Africa are experiencing an increase in overweight and obesity, and a quarter of the world's obese and overweight preschool-age children live in the region. The estimated prevalence of childhood overweight and obesity in Africa was 8.5 percent in 2010 and is expected to reach 13 percent in 2020. Overweight and obesity prevalence rates in Africa were higher than in Asia (4.9 percent) in 2010 (De Onis, Blössner, and Borghi 2010).
5. The gross enrollment rate (GER) is the percentage of total enrollment, including grade repeaters, compared with the population of the official primary-school age range. Hence, GERs exceeding 100 percent

represent students not of primary school age but who are enrolled in primary school.

6. African primary enrollment totals from United Nations Educational, Scientific, and Cultural Organization (UNESCO) Institute for Statistics (UIS) data: http://uis.unesco.org/.
7. The limits of economic growth as a swift driver of improvements in core public services (including education and health) are strikingly apparent in extrapolation of trends in outcomes from 3 of the 10 strongest economies in the region: Ghana, Rwanda, and Tanzania (Wild et al. 2015). For example, it took an estimated 200 years to achieve full coverage of skilled birth attendants in Tanzania.

References

Akombi, Blessing J., Kingsley E. Agho, Dafna Merom, Andre M. Renzaho, and John J. Hall. 2017. "Child Malnutrition in Sub-Saharan Africa: A Meta-Analysis of Demographic and Health Surveys (2006–2016)." *PLoS One* 12 (5): e0177338.

Alaba, Olufunke A., and Olumuyiwa Alaba. 2009. "Malaria in Rural Nigeria: Implications for the Millennium Development Goals." *African Development Review* 21 (1): 73–85.

Almond, Douglas. 2006. "Is the 1918 Influenza Pandemic Over? Long-Term Effects of In Utero Influenza Exposure in the Post-1940 US Population." *Journal of Political Economy* 114 (4): 672–712.

Almond, Douglas, and Bhashkar Mazumder. 2005. "The 1918 Influenza Pandemic and Subsequent Health Outcomes: An Analysis of SIPP Data." *American Economic Review* 95 (2): 258–62.

APP (Africa Progress Panel). 2013. *Africa Progress Report 2013. Equity in Extractives: Stewarding Africa's Natural Resources for All.* Geneva: APP.

Azomahou, Theophile T., and Eleni Abraham Yitbarek. 2016. "Intergenerational Education Mobility in Africa: Has Progress Been Inclusive?" Policy Research Working Paper 7843, World Bank, Washington, DC.

Baez, Javier Eduardo, and Indhira Vanessa Santos. 2007. "Children's Vulnerability to Weather Shocks: A Natural Disaster as a Natural Experiment." Research report, Social Science Research Network, New York.

Baird, Sarah, Joan Hamory Hicks, Michael Kremer, and Edward Miguel. 2016. "Worms at Work: Long-Run Impacts of a Child Health Investment." *Quarterly Journal of Economics* 131 (4): 1637–80.

Barham, Tania, Karen Macours, and John A. Maluccio. 2013. "Boys' Cognitive Skill Formation and Physical Growth: Long-Term Experimental Evidence on Critical Ages for Early Childhood Interventions." *American Economic Review* 103 (3): 467–71.

Barrett, Christopher B., Teevrat Garg, and Linden McBride. 2016. "Well-Being Dynamics and Poverty Traps." *Annual Review of Resource Economics* 8: 303–27.

Bashir, Sajitha, Marlaine Lockheed, Elizabeth Ninan, and Jee-Peng Tan. 2018. *Facing Forward: Schooling for Learning in Africa.* Washington, DC: World Bank.

Beegle, Kathleen, Luc Christiaensen, Andrew Dabalen, and Isis Gaddis. 2016. *Poverty in a Rising Africa.* Washington, DC: World Bank.

Berger, Lawrence M., Christina Paxson, and Jane Waldfogel. 2009. "Income and Child Development." *Children and Youth Services Review* 31 (9): 978–89.

Bhalotra, Sonia, and Samantha Rawlings. 2013. "Gradients of the Intergenerational Transmission of Health in Developing Countries." *Review of Economics and Statistics* 95 (2): 660–72.

Bharadwaj, P., Petter Lundborg, and Dan-Olof Rooth. 2017. "Birth Weight in the Long Run." *Journal of Human Resources* 53 (1): 189–231.

Bhutta, Zulfiqar A., Jai K. Das, Ajumand Rizvi, Michelle F. Gaffey, Walker Neff, Susan Horton, Patrick Webb, Anna Lartey, and Robert E. Black. 2013. "Evidence-Based Interventions for Improvement of Maternal and Child Nutrition: What Can Be Done and at What Cost?" *The Lancet* 382 (9890): 452–77.

Biciunaite, Audre, and Lydia Gordon. 2014. "Economic Growth and Life Expectancy: Do Wealthier Countries Live Longer?" Market Research Blog, Euromonitor International, March 14. https://blog.euromonitor.com/economic-growth-and-life-expectancy-do-wealthier-countries-live-longer/.

Bingenheimer, Jeffrey B. 2010. "Men's Multiple Sexual Partnerships in 15 Sub-Saharan African Countries: Sociodemographic Patterns and Implications." *Studies in Family Planning* 41 (1): 1–17.

Blunch, Niels-Hugo. 2017. "Adult Literacy Programs in Developing Countries." Article, IZA World of Labor online platform, Institute for the Study of Labor (IZA), Bonn.

Bond, Matthew, Donald C. Kennan, Pejman Rohani, and Jeffrey D. Sachs. 2009. "Poverty Trap Formed by the Ecology of Infectious Diseases." *Proceedings of the Royale Society B* 277 (1685): 1185–92.

Branson, Nicola, Julia Garlick, David Lam, and Murray Leibbrandt. 2012. "Education and Inequality: The South African Case." SALDRU Working Paper 75, Southern Africa Labour and Development Research Unit, University of Cape Town, South Africa.

Buchmann, Nina, Erica Field, Rachel Glennerster, Shahana Nazneen, Svetlana Pimkina, and Iman Sen. 2017. "Power vs Money: Alternative Approaches to Reducing Child Marriage in Bangladesh, a Randomized Control Trial." Unpublished manuscript, Abdul Latif Jameel Poverty Action Lab (J-PAL), Cambridge, MA.

Canavan, M. E., H. L. Sipsma, G. M. Kassie, and E. H. Bradley. 2014. "Correlates of Complete Childhood Vaccination in East African Countries." *PLoS One* 9 (4): e95709.

Case, Anne, Darren Lubotsky, and Christina Paxson. 2002. "Economic Status and Health in Childhood: The Origins of the Gradient." *American Economic Review* 92 (5): 1308–34.

Case, Anne, and Christina Paxson. 2010. "Causes and Consequences of Early-Life Health." *Demography* 47 (1): S65–S85.

Cervellati, Matteo, and Uwe Sunde. 2011. "Life Expectancy and Economic Growth: The Role of the Demographic Transition." *Journal of Economic Growth* 16 (2): 99–133.

Checkley, William, Leonardo D. Epstein, Robert Gilman, Lilia Cabrera, and Robert E. Black. 2003. "Effects of Acute Diarrhea on Linear Growth in Peruvian Children." *American Journal of Epidemiology* 157 (2): 166–75.

Conti, Gabriella, James Heckman, and Sergio Urzua. 2010. "The Education-Health Gradient." *American Economic Review* 100 (2): 234.

Croke, Kevin, and Rifat Atun. 2019. "The Long Run Impact of Early Childhood Deworming on Numeracy and Literacy: Evidence from Uganda." *PLOS Neglected Tropical Diseases* 13 (1): e0007085.

Cropper, Maureen L., Mitiku Haile, Julian Lampietti, Christine Poulos, and Dale Whittington. 2004. "The Demand for a Malaria Vaccine: Evidence from Ethiopia." *Journal of Development Economics* 75 (1): 303–18.

Cunha, Flavio, James J. Heckman, Lancer Lochner, and Dimitriy V. Masterov. 2006. "Interpreting the Evidence on Life Cycle Skill Formation." *Handbook of the Economics of Education* 1: 697–812.

Currie, Janet, and Rosemary Hyson. 1999. "Is the Impact of Health Shocks Cushioned by Socioeconomic Status? The Case of Low Birth Weight." *American Economic Review* 89 (2): 245–50.

Currie, Janet, and Enrico Moretti. 2007. "Biology as Destiny? Short- and Long-Run Determinants of Intergenerational Transmission of Birth Weight." *Journal of Labor Economics* 25 (2): 231–64.

Dasgupta, Partha. 1997. "Nutritional Status, the Capacity for Work, and Poverty Traps." *Journal of Econometrics* 77 (1): 5–37.

de la Brière, Bénédicte, Deon Filmer, Dena Ringold, Dominic Rohner, Karelle Samuda, and Anastasiya Denisova. 2017. *From Mines and Wells to Well-Built Minds: Turning Sub-Saharan Africa's Natural Resource Wealth into Human Capital.* Directions in Development Series. Washington, DC: World Bank.

De Onis, Mercedes, Monika Blössner, and Elaine Borghi. 2010. "Global Prevalence and Trends of Overweight and Obesity among Preschool Children." *American Journal of Clinical Nutrition* 92 (5): 1257–64.

De Onis, Mercedes, and Francesco Branca. 2016. "Childhood Stunting: A Global Perspective." *Maternal and Child Nutrition* 12 (S1): 12–26.

Deaton, Angus. 2013. *The Great Escape: Health, Wealth, and the Origins of Inequality.* Princeton, NJ: Princeton University Press.

Delprato, Marcos, Kwame Akyeampong, and Mairead Dunne. 2017. "Intergenerational Education Effects of Early Marriage in Sub-Saharan Africa." *World Development* 91: 173–92.

Delprato, Marcos, Kwame Akyeampong, Ricardo Sabates, and Jimena Hernandez-Fernandez. 2015. "On the Impact of Early Marriage on Schooling Outcomes in Sub-Saharan Africa and South West Asia." *International Journal of Educational Development* 44: 42–55

Dillon, Andrew, Jed Friedman, and Pieter Serneels. 2014. "Health Information, Treatment, and Worker Productivity: Experimental Evidence from Malaria Testing and Treatment among Nigerian Sugarcane Cutters." Policy

Research Working Paper 7120, World Bank, Washington, DC.

Evans, Gary W., and Rochelle C. Cassells. 2014. "Childhood Poverty, Cumulative Risk Exposure, and Mental Health in Emerging Adults." *Clinical Psychological Science* 2 (3): 287–96.

Feinstein, Leon. 2003. "Inequality in the Early Cognitive Development of British Children in the 1970 Cohort." *Economica* 70 (277): 73–97.

Flabbi, Luca, and Roberta Gatti. 2018. "A Primer on Human Capital." Policy Research Working Paper 8309, World Bank, Washington, DC.

Fogel, Robert W. 2004. *The Escape from Hunger and Premature Death, 1700–2100: Europe, America, and the Third World*. Cambridge, U.K.: Cambridge University Press.

Galasso, Emanuela, and Adam Wagstaff. 2018. "The Aggregate Income Losses from Childhood Stunting and the Returns to a Nutrition Intervention Aimed at Reducing Stunting." Policy Research Working Paper 8536, World Bank, Washington, DC.

Galasso, Emanuela, Ann Weber, and Lia C. H. Fernald. 2019. "Dynamics of Child Development: Analysis of a Longitudinal Cohort in a Very Low Income Country." *World Bank Economic Review* 33 (1): 140–59.

Glewwe, Paul, and Hanan G. Jacoby. 1995. "An Economic Analysis of Delayed Primary School Enrolment in a Low Income Country: The Role of Early Childhood Nutrition." *Review of Economics and Statistics* 77: 156–69.

Grantham-McGregor, Sally, Yin Bun Cheung, Santiago Cueto, Paul Glewwe, Linda Richter, Barbara Strupp, and International Child Development Steering Group. 2007. "Developmental Potential in the First 5 Years for Children in Developing Countries." *The Lancet* 369 (9555): 60–70.

Harper, Caroline, Rachel Marcus, and Karen Moore. 2003. "Enduring Poverty and the Conditions of Childhood: Lifecourse and Intergenerational Poverty Transmissions." *World Development* 31 (3): 535–54.

Harttgen, Kenneth, Stephan Klasen, and Sebastian Vollmer. 2013. "Economic Growth and Child Under-Nutrition in Sub-Saharan Africa." *Population and Development Review* 39 (3): 397–412.

Heckman, James J. 2006. "Skill Formation and the Economics of Investing in Disadvantaged Children." *Science* 312 (5782): 1900–02.

———. 2011. "The Economics of Inequality: The Value of Early Childhood Education." *American Educator* 35 (1): 31–35, 47.

Hoddinott, John, Harold Alderman, Jere R. Behrman, Lawrence Haddad, and Susan Horton. 2013. "The Economic Rationale for Investing in Stunting Reduction." *Maternal and Child Nutrition* 9 (S2): 69–82.

IMF (International Monetary Fund). 2004. *Health and Development: Why Investing in Health Is Critical for Achieving Economic Developmental Goals*. Washington, DC: IMF.

Kazungu, Jacob S., and Ifedayo M. Adetifa. 2017. "Crude Childhood Vaccination Coverage in West Africa: Trends and Predictors of Completeness." *Wellcome Open Research* 2: 12.

Kidman, R. 2017. "Child Marriage and Intimate Partner Violence: A Comparative Study of 34 Countries." *International Journal of Epidemiology* 46 (2): 662–75.

Kwenda, Prudence, Miracle Ntuli, and Tendai Gwatidzo. 2015. "Temporal Developments in Intergenerational Transmission of Education: Case for Black South Africans." *Research in Social Stratification and Mobility* 42: 96–113.

Lal, Suresh B. 2015. "Child Marriage in India: Factors and Problems." *International Journal of Science and Research* 4 (4): 2993–98.

Lambert, Sylvie, Martin Ravallion, and Dominique van de Walle. 2014. "Intergenerational Mobility and Interpersonal Inequality in an African Economy." *Journal of Development Economics* 110: 327–44.

Lee-Rife, Susan, Anju Malhotra, Ann Warner, and Allison McGonagle Glinski. 2012. "What Works to Prevent Child Marriage: A Review of the Evidence." *Studies in Family Planning* 43 (4): 287–303.

Leroy, Jeff L., Marie Ruel, Jean-Pierre Habicht, and Edward A. Frongillo. 2014. "Linear Growth Deficit Continues to Accumulate beyond the First 1,000 Days in Low- and Middle-Income Countries: Global Evidence from 51 National Surveys." *Journal of Nutrition* 144 (9): 1460–66.

Maccini, Sharon, and Dean Yang. 2009. "Under the Weather: Health, Schooling, and Economic Consequences of Early-Life Rainfall." *American Economic Review* 99 (3): 1006–26.

Machingaidze, Shingai, Charles S. Wiysonge, and Gregory D. Hussey. 2013. "Strengthening the Expanded Programme on Immunization in Africa: Looking beyond 2015." *PLoS Med* 10 (3): e1001405.

Martorell, Reynaldo. 1995. "Results and Implications of the INCAP Follow-Up Study." *Journal of Nutrition* 125 (4): 1127S–1138S.

Martorell, Reynaldo, Kettel L. Khan, and Dirk G. Schroeder. 1994. "Reversibility of Stunting: Epidemiological Findings in Children from Developing Countries." *European Journal of Clinical Nutrition* 48: S45–S57.

Mendez, Michelle A., and Linda S. Adair. 1999. "Severity and Timing of Stunting in the First Two Years of Life Affect Performance on Cognitive Tests in Late Childhood." *Journal of Nutrition* 129 (8): 1555–62.

Montenegro, Claudio E., and Harry Anthony Patrinos. 2013. "Returns to Schooling around the World." Background paper for *World Development Report 2013: Jobs*, World Bank, Washington, DC.

Mukhebi, Adrian, Stephen Mbogoh, and K. Matungulu. 2011. "An Overview of the Food Security Situation in Eastern Africa." Study commissioned by the United Nations Economic Commission for Africa (UNECA) Sub-Regional Office for Eastern Africa, Addis Ababa, Ethiopia.

Newhouse, David, Pablo Suarez-Becerra, and Martin C. Evans. 2016. "New Estimates of Extreme Poverty for Children." Policy Research Working Paper 7845, World Bank, Washington, DC.

Nguyen, Minh Cong, and Quentin Wodon. 2014. "Impact of Child Marriage on Literacy and Education Attainment in Africa." Background paper for *Fixing the Broken Promise of Education for All*, UNESCO, Paris.

Nour, N. M. 2006. "Health Consequences of Child Marriage in Africa." *Emerging Infectious Diseases* 12 (11): 1644–49.

Osmani, Siddiqur Rahman, ed. 1992. *Nutrition and Poverty*. Oxford U.K.: Oxford University Press.

Ozier, Owen. 2018. "Exploiting Externalities to Estimate the Long-Term Effects of Early Childhood Deworming." *American Economic Journal: Applied Economics* 10 (3): 235–62.

Parsons, Jennifer, Jeffrey Edmeades, Aslihan Kes, Suzanne Petroni, Maggie Sexton, and Quentin Wodon. 2015. "Economic Impacts of Child Marriage: A Review of the Literature." *Review of Faith and International Affairs* 13 (3): 12–22.

Ranasinghe, Rasika. 2015. "The Transmission of Education across Generations: Evidence from Australia." *B.E. Journal of Economic Analysis and Policy* 15: 1893–1917.

Schady, Norbert, Jere Behrman, Maria Caridad Araujo, Rodrigo Azuero, Raquel Bernal, David Bravo, Florencia Lopez-Boo, et al. 2015. "Wealth Gradients in Early Childhood Cognitive Development in Five Latin American Countries." *Journal of Human Resources* 50 (2): 446–63.

Shonkoff, Jack P., and Deborah A. Phillips, eds. 2000. *From Neurons to Neighborhoods: The Science of Early Childhood Development*. Washington, DC: National Academies Press.

Spaull, Nicholas. 2013. "Poverty and Privilege: Primary School Inequality in South Africa." *International Journal of Educational Development* 33 (5): 436–47.

Thomas, Duncan. 1996. "Education across Generations in South Africa." *American Economic Review* 86: 330–34.

UNICEF (United Nations Children's Fund). 2016. *State of the World's Children: A Fair Chance for Every Child*. New York: UNICEF.

Vandell, Deborah Lowe, Jay Belsky, Margaret Burchinal, Laurence Steinberg, and Nathan Vandergrift. 2010. "Do Effects of Early Child Care Extend to Age 15 Years? Results from the NICHD Study of Early Child Care and Youth Development." *Child Development* 81 (3): 737–56.

Victora, Cesar G., Linda Adair, Caroline Fall, Pedro C. Hallal, Reynaldo Martorell, Linda Richter, Harshpal Singh Sachdev, and Maternal and Child Undernutrition Study Group. 2008. "Maternal and Child Undernutrition: Consequences for Adult Health and Human Capital." *The Lancet* 371 (9609): 340–57.

Wild, Leni, David Booth, Clare Cummings, Marta Foresti, and Joseph Wales. 2015. "Adapting Development: Improving Services to the Poor." Report, Overseas Development Institute (ODI), London.

Wiysonge, Charles, Olalekan A. Uthman, Peter M. Ndumbe, and Gregory D. Hussey. 2012. "Individual and Contextual Factors Associated with Low Childhood Immunization Coverage in Sub-Saharan Africa: A Multilevel Analysis." *PLoS One* 7 (5): e37905.

Wodon, Quentin, Chata Male, Ada Nayihouba, Adenike Onagoruwa, Aboudrahyme Savadogo, Ali Yedan, Jeff Edmeades, et al. 2017. "Economic Impacts of Child Marriage: Global Synthesis Report." Paper prepared for the Economic Impacts of Child Marriage project, World Bank and International Centre for Research on Women (ICRW), Washington, DC.

World Bank. 2018a. "All Hands on Deck: Reducing Stunting through Efforts in Sub-Saharan Africa." Working Paper No. 127344, World Bank, Washington, DC.

———. 2018b. *World Development Report 2018: Learning to Realize Education's Promise.* Washington, DC: World Bank.

Earning More on the Farm

3

Luc Christiaensen and Joachim Vandercasteelen

Africa's agriculture is well positioned to help accelerate its poverty reduction. Food demand is robust, the agricultural policy and trade environment supportive, and many of the poor are in good agroecological potential areas. But food consumption is increasingly met by imports, for cereals—which are both produced and consumed by the poor—as well as for higher-value products.

This chapter shows that to maximize the poverty-reducing effect of Africa's agricultural supply response, three pathways will need to be developed: (a) raising smallholder staple crop productivity; (b) developing higher-value products for domestic (urban) markets; and (c) expanding agricultural exports. In this, public investment to raise staple crop productivity on smallholder farms remains a first-order public policy issue.

Myriad input, factor, and product market constraints hold agricultural intensification back. Pockets of land scarcity are emerging, and the seasonality of agricultural labor calendars remains too often ignored. Mechanization and better water management can help. Yet, too often, singular focused interventions are pursued, or interventions are poorly coordinated. Africa's Green Revolution, mechanization, and irrigation efforts need an integrated approach that simultaneously addresses supply- and demand-side constraints to tackle poverty.

Inclusive value chain development (VCD) provides a market-based, organizational solution to do so. Smallholder farmers can be linked to higher-value domestic and export markets either directly as producers (by supplying raw agricultural products) or indirectly as laborers (through employment opportunities). Buyers gain by securing the consistency in product volume and quality that is needed to access these markets. Larger smallholders are more frequently contracted; the poorest often benefit through localized spillovers. Producer organization support can help make value chains more inclusive.

Contract enforcement is more difficult in staple production. But the demand for consistent volumes and quality as well as opportunities for value addition are also growing in Africa's domestic staple markets (rice and teff for urban markets, feedstock maize for livestock, and barley for beer). This increases the scope for experimentation with VCD for staples, often facilitated by third-party intermediaries to overcome trust and coordination issues.

Nonetheless, the need very much remains to provide complementary public goods to help poor smallholders raise their staple crop and livestock productivity, given limited private sector interest and the importance for poverty reduction. This requires increased public spending in agriculture, which has started to falter, as well as a shift in its composition to supporting mostly public goods (as opposed to private) including agricultural research and development (R&D) and extension for not only staples but also livestock, as well as investment in irrigation and rural infrastructure. Inclusive agricultural VCD further requires the establishment of a conducive business environment, including to enable cost-effective contract enforcement, and a lowering of transaction costs to facilitate coordination among the actors in the chains.

Largely Favorable Conditions for Agricultural Development

Growing Domestic Food Markets but Lagging Supply

Africa's demand for food has been growing rapidly. It will continue to do so in the foreseeable future, exceeding 3 percent per year in volume through 2025 (OECD and FAO 2016). This continues to be largely driven by Africa's high population growth (2.7 percent per year).

Income growth and urbanization add further impetus, including to add more value.[1] They induce a dietary shift to agricultural products that are richer in proteins (meat and dairy, eggs, and pulses); richer in nutrients (fruits and vegetables); and richer in calories (oils and fats and sugars). They also further increase the demand for processed, packaged, and prepared foods (Cockx, Colen, and De Weerdt 2018).

Africa's agriculture and agribusiness are projected to be a US$1 trillion industry by 2030 (compared with US$313 billion in 2010) (World Bank 2013). Following urbanization and rural income diversification, more people will also be buying rather than producing their food (Davis, Di Giuseppe, and Zezza 2017).

Together these trends signal favorable domestic market conditions to exploit agriculture and agribusiness to create better and more jobs and accelerate poverty reduction. In this, unprocessed staples will continue to be important (box 3.1).

So far, especially the production of maize and cassava (two dominant staples) has been growing in response. The region remains largely self-sufficient in maize (except in drought years) as well as in roots and tubers (though, unlike maize, with little yield increase). Maize is also actively traded within the region,[2] underscoring the opportunities offered by intraregional trade for securing Africa's food supplies (World Bank 2012). Growth in domestic rice production (especially in western Africa) met about half of the growing demand. Wheat production has not grown much. The poultry and dairy sectors remain also largely underdeveloped.

As a result, Africa's food import bill has risen by about US$30 billion over the past two decades (from US$8 billion during 1995–97 to US$37.9 billion during 2014–16) (figure 3.1). Growing imports of cereals make up a third of this increase (ACET 2017).[3] Africa's cereal import dependency ratio increased from 10 percent in 1994–96 to 23 percent in 2016–18. The growing demand for vegetable oils and poultry has also been largely met by imports.

Rising food imports do not have to pose an issue if they can be financed by other exports (Collier and Dercon 2014; Rakotoarisoa, Iafrate, and Paschali 2011). For Africa, such exports have traditionally been other agricultural products (such as coffee, cocoa, cotton, fruits, and vegetables) as well as other primary natural resources (minerals, oil, and gas). On both accounts, Africa has done well. Growth in the value of agricultural exports (which includes nonfood products) has broadly kept pace with the growing food import bill, with some deterioration in the aftermath of the 2008 world food crisis, and natural resource

BOX 3.1 Unprocessed staples make up much of Africa's rapidly growing food demand

Despite faster growth in the demand for higher-value, processed, and convenient foods, demand for unprocessed staples will continue to drive a significant part of Africa's overall food demand. Unprocessed staples (cereals, roots, and tubers) still make up 80 percent of total food intake in volume (kilograms) and 50–67 percent of total caloric intake, depending on the region (less in central and southern Africa, more in western and eastern Africa) (OECD and FAO 2016). Smaller increments (in volume and value) of higher-value agricultural products than those of staples result.

In particular, the consumption of cereals and roots and tubers in Africa is predicted to increase by 52.2 million and 25 million tons, respectively, by 2025, up by about a third from the 160 million and 73.3 million tons consumed per year during 2013–15 (OECD and FAO 2016). Most of the increase is for human consumption (90 percent for cereals, 72 percent for roots and tubers). The demand for meat is also expected to grow by about a third, but from a much lower base.[a] For poultry, where the predicted demand increase is most pronounced, this results in an additional demand of 1.6 million tons; for beef, an additional 1.5 million tons; for lamb and mutton, 0.9 million tons; and for pork, 0.6 million tons. This pales in comparison to the increase in cereal demand (also in value).

Overall, income per capita growth has remained relatively modest, and urbanization (controlling for income) is mainly shifting preferences toward more conveniently consumed foods such as bread (wheat) and high-sugar and prepared foods rather than to animal-source foods and fats (Cockx, Colen, and De Weerdt 2018). The demand for sweeteners and vegetable oil is expected to grow fastest in per capita terms (OECD and FAO 2016).

The particular demand patterns vary across Africa's geographic regions. Demand growth for rice is projected to be highest in West Africa; for maize, it is highest in eastern and southern Africa. Demand growth for roots and tubers is concentrated in western and eastern Africa. These trends are consistent with the historical dietary preference patterns. Given the prevalence of conflict, little growth in caloric intake is predicted for central Africa.

a. During 2013–15, average per capita consumption of cereals and roots and tubers in Africa amounted to 128 kilograms and 53 kilograms, respectively, out of a total per capita food consumption of 227 kilograms. Average consumption per capita of meat, fish, dairy (dry equivalent), sweeteners, and vegetable oils were 11, 9, 4, 12, and 11 kilograms, respectively (OECD and FAO 2016).

FIGURE 3.1 Africa's food import bill has tripled since the mid-2000s

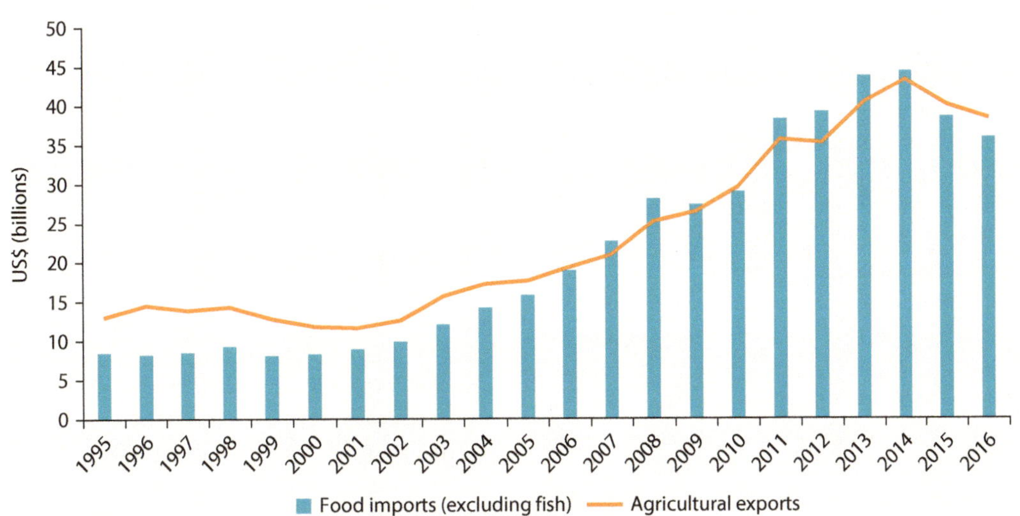

Source: FAOSTAT 2018 database, Food and Agriculture Organization (FAO), http://www.fao.org/faostat/.

revenues have grown rapidly in many countries following the commodity supercycle of the 1990s and 2000s.

Nonetheless, in a number of mainly smaller, non-resource-rich countries and some of the islands, food imports have been taking more than 50 percent out of total merchandise export revenues (in 10 countries during 2011–13). This puts pressure on the external macroeconomic balances and diverts precious foreign exchange away from the much-needed imports of capital goods and technologies. In another 9 countries, food imports have equated to 25–50 percent of total merchandise exports.[4]

But Africa's rising food import bill signifies especially a missed opportunity for accelerating poverty reduction through food import substitution. While not all African countries should become self-sufficient in staples (especially not when needed as feed grains), much scope remains for improving food security and reducing poverty by raising staple crop productivity as a first step. Agriculture has greater poverty-reducing powers, especially in low-income countries (Christiaensen and Martin 2018). Africa also has a comparative advantage in land and labor. And Africa's recent output growth in maize, cassava, and rice, including through better yields, confirms the potential for a more robust supply response.[5] This holds even more in Africa's oil-rich countries, where public investment in agriculture is systematically lower and imports of poultry are systematically higher—associations that aren't observed in oil-rich countries in other parts of the world (N'diaye and Christiaensen 2017).

The comparative advantage of many African countries in production of staple crops, but also of nonstaples and processed foods, can be further exploited for poverty reduction through improved intraregional agricultural trade (World Bank 2012). The potential for increased soybean trade as animal feed for poultry production between Zambia and South Africa is just one example (Ncube 2018).

Improved Price and Policy Environment

Poor price incentives following a declining trend in world food prices, as well as a lack of public investment, held Africa's agriculture back during the 1990s and early 2000s (World Bank 2007). Much has changed since then: World food prices are about 70 percent higher today than before the 2008 world food crisis (or 40–50 percent higher in real terms). And they are expected to remain at these levels through 2025 (FAO 2017; World Bank 2018).[6] Higher world food prices have so far positively affected food security (except for urban consumers and short-run effects) and reduced poverty on aggregate (Headey and Martin 2016).

The domestic agricultural trade and policy environments are also more favorable. Africa's relative rate of assistance (RRA) to agriculture—a comprehensive measure of domestic policy bias against agriculture over nonagriculture—steadily increased from between –40 percent and –50 percent (indicating strong bias against agriculture) in the early 1980s, to between –5 percent and –10 percent in the late 2000s (Janssen and Swinnen 2016).[7] This dramatic improvement is largely on account of the substantial decline in export taxes on industrial crops (cocoa, coffee, cotton, tea, and rubber) and fruits and vegetables. Cash crop producers are now getting a much larger share of the world price. This helped reduce poverty (Breisinger et al. 2008; Deininger and Okidi 2003; Molini and Paci 2015) and holds promise for greater poverty reduction from further productivity gains in these commodities.

More recently, the nominal rate of protection (NRP) for staples—a measure indicating domestic output price support—has also been edging up across countries in response to the world food crisis and to stimulate import substitution. It rose from virtually no protection over the past decades to around 10 percent during 2014–16 (Pernechele, Balié, and Ghins 2018).[8]

It is typically higher in East African countries than in West African countries. Domestic production of cereals increased.[9] The supply response was further aided by the rapid expansion of input subsidy programs (Jayne and Rashid 2013). Regional trade agreements are also deepening. This holds good prospects for expanding market opportunities for farmers in food surplus countries, even though substantial nontariff barriers remain (Asenso-Okyere and Jemaneh 2012; Geda and Seid 2015; Hoekman and Njinkeu 2017; Janssen and Swinnen 2016; OECD and FAO 2016).[10]

Since 2003, African governments have committed to pursue annual agricultural sector growth of 6 percent and to increase agriculture's share in public spending to 10 percent.[11] Relative to the 1990s and early 2000s, this signifies a fundamental shift in perspective and political support toward agriculture as an entry point for growth and poverty reduction. Noticeable progress toward achieving these targets has been recorded in some countries (for example, Burkina Faso, Ethiopia, and Rwanda). Nonetheless, until today, still only a few countries have reached these targets. In several countries, the share of agricultural expenditure in total government spending has in fact dropped over the past couple of years. On average, it is back at the pre-2008 level of 3 percent (De Pinto and Ulimwengu 2017).

As the latest price elasticity estimates of staple crop production for Africa confirm, these price and policy developments have provided a broadly favorable environment for African agriculture to respond (box 3.2).

New Challenges of Climate Change and Resurging Conflict

Africa's food supply response needs to happen in a changing climatic environment. Mean surface temperatures are rising, rainfall patterns are changing, and agricultural seasons are shifting. In addition, weather patterns are becoming more variable and

BOX 3.2 African staple crop supply responds to price incentives and reductions in transaction costs

African farmers respond to price changes. A 10 percent increase in the own-price of a staple food crop triggers a 6 percent increase in production in the next year (based on the experience from 10 African countries during 2005–13) (Magrini, Balié, and Morales-Opazo 2018). Slightly more than half of this increase (55 percent) follows from area expansion, and the remainder (45 percent) from intensification (yield increase). The effects are larger when the price increase follows from an increase in the border or world price (elasticity = 0.87) but are also significant when it follows from an increase in the exchange rate (elasticity = 0.59) or an increase in nominal protection (elasticity = 0.44).

The results further confirm the importance of transaction or marketing costs for boosting supply: a 10 percent increase in transaction (marketing) costs reduces staple crop production by 2.9 percent (Magrini, Balié, and Morales-Opazo 2018). This is about half the positive supply response from an output price increase. African agriculture can, and has, responded to better prices, but high transaction costs can rapidly stand in the way.

Input prices also matter. A 10 percent increase in real fertilizer and oil prices reduces annual staple production in the next year by 1.9 percent and 4.9 percent, respectively (Magrini, Balié, and Morales-Opazo 2018). The effects are relatively small for fertilizer, at least for now, given the still limited use of fertilizer. Oil prices are especially influential through their effect on transport (and thus marketing) costs, outweighing the positive effect they may have on production by increasing global food prices (Dillon and Barrett 2016).

extreme (Jalloh et al. 2013; Niang et al. 2014; OECD and FAO 2016; Waithaka et al. 2013). Much evidence suggests that crop production in Africa stands to suffer significantly (Hallegatte et al. 2016; Lesk, Rowhani, and Ramankutty 2016; Niang et al. 2014). Yet there is substantial variation across regions.

Temperatures are on the rise continent-wide, but the expected increase is larger in West Africa than in East Africa (Jalloh et al. 2013; Niang et al. 2014; Waithaka et al. 2013). Rainfall is expected to decline in southern Africa and along the coast of several western African countries. It will increase in East Africa and the Sahelian countries but become more unpredictable and extreme everywhere (Serdeczny et al. 2017). The productivity and welfare effects of these changing weather patterns further differ by the crops grown. Maize and wheat are, for example, very sensitive to exceeding tolerance thresholds of the maximum daytime temperature, while cassava tends to be more resilient to higher temperatures (Niang et al. 2014; Serdeczny et al. 2017; Ward, Florax, and Flores-Lagunes 2014).

Taking these and related climatic and agronomic factors into account, the climate models predict that maize yields will decrease in most countries of western Africa but will increase in the Sahel. Similarly, the models predict an increase in maize yields in most parts of eastern and central Africa but a decline in large parts of the Democratic Republic of Congo, Ethiopia, Tanzania, and northern Uganda (Jalloh et al. 2013; Waithaka et al. 2013). In southern African countries, maize production and yields are expected to increase (Hachigonta et al. 2013). Moreover, crops that are less efficient in transforming carbon dioxide (CO_2) into energy (the so-called C_3 plants like rice and wheat) could potentially benefit from increased CO_2 concentrations, although faster plant growth may also render them less nutritious.[12] At the same time, higher temperatures and unreliable water sources are likely to put pressure on livestock production in arid and semiarid areas (Jalloh et al. 2013; Niang et al. 2014).

Although the expected climatic changes are not unequivocally detrimental to Africa's crops or agricultural incomes, their exact contours at the micro level remain largely unknown. This makes it difficult to adapt and cope, especially for the poorer and more vulnerable populations, who often earn the bulk of their incomes in rainfed agriculture. Accounting for the effects of changing temperatures and rainfall patterns on local crop and farming systems will need to be part and parcel of any policy design to boost labor productivity in agriculture. It makes exploiting agriculture for poverty reduction more challenging.

Intrastate conflicts, which are often fought in the countryside and affect a growing number of countries, provide another challenge (Arias, Ibáñez, and Zambrano 2019; FAO 2017; Goyal and Nash 2017; Martin-Shields and Stojetz 2019; Sanch-Maritan and Vedrine 2018). Conflict can directly reduce agricultural production through confiscation, destruction, or abandonment of crops and animals.[13] It reduces access to land, labor, and credit and disrupts trade of agricultural products and food between areas of surplus and deficit. Labor-intensive export crops and capital-intensive production systems that rely on mechanized power and seasonal migrant labor are especially vulnerable. They are more sensitive to exchange rate effects; the potential for looting; and disruptions in public infrastructure, services, and seasonal labor flows.

Production is also affected indirectly—and often long after conflicts have been ended. The perceived risk or prevalence of unrest or conflict induces farmers to switch to low-risk, low-return investment strategies and discourages public investment. Cross-country estimates suggest that agricultural total factor productivity (TFP) declines by 1 percent for each year a country has been in armed conflict (Fuglie and Rada 2013). This is close to Africa's average annual growth in agricultural TFP. Nonetheless, it likely only presents a lower bound of the overall effect of conflict on agricultural production, because it abstracts from the resources withdrawn from production (land, labor, and capital).

Agriculture also plays an important role in the *prevention* of conflict (which often finds its origins in climate-related agricultural shocks) as well as in the recovery of fragile states (Martin-Shields and Stojetz 2019). First, a remunerative agriculture provides a viable alternative to illicit and mercenary activities for individuals with otherwise low opportunity cost to participate in conflict.[14] More generally, decreases in agricultural productivity, often because of drought, may directly activate societal grievances because of increasing destitution, famine, and distress migration as in the Syrian Arab Republic (Kelley et al. 2015).[15]

Second, because agricultural production factors can be more rapidly mobilized, the agriculture sector is often the first sector to recover from crisis and hence plays an important role in reconstructing conflict-ridden areas.[16] It is often also well placed to absorb demobilized combatants (Blattman and Annan 2016).

Not All Agricultural Growth Is Equally Poverty Reducing

Unpacking the Food System

Chapter 2 showed that not all growth is equally poverty reducing, but that it is especially growth in agriculture that is poverty reducing, especially during the earlier stages of development. Similarly, not all agricultural growth is equally poverty reducing. And early on, it is smallholder staple crop productivity growth that is particularly important.

As countries develop and household incomes rise, household food expenditure shares decline (Engel's Law) and the demand for dietary diversification and convenience increases (Bennett's Law). This micro behavior is mirrored at the macro level in a growing share of nonstaples in agriculture and an expanding share of agribusiness in the food system (box 3.3). Importantly, this happens while each of these subsectors also expands in absolute numbers, value added, and employment (Yeboah and Jayne 2018). Further in the development process, employment in agriculture and the food system will also decline, but no African country has reached this stage yet (Christiaensen and Brooks 2018).

BOX 3.3 Shifts in agriculture bring new terminology

The increase in smallholder staple crop productivity is often referred to as the "Green Revolution," in reference to Asia's rapid increase in smallholder staple crop productivity in the 1960s and 1970s through a package of modern inputs (seeds, fertilizer, and pesticides); water control; and reduction in price volatility. The shift in agriculture to nonstaple crops is also known as the "agricultural transformation"; the shift in rural areas to off-farm work as the "rural transformation"; and, finally, the shift from rural to urban off-farm work as the "structural transformation" (De Janvry and Sadoulet 2018).

With about one-third of rural and urban off-farm work initially closely related to agribusiness, one often also considers "extended agriculture" or the "food system." This includes both employment and value added on the farm as well as the agriculture- and food-related employment and value added off the farm, up and down the value chain—that is, in agricultural input production and provision, food assembly and storage, processing, trading (wholesale and retail), and preparation of food for consumption outside the home (Allen, Heinrigs, and Heo 2018; Tschirley et al. 2015; Tschirley et al. 2017).

The development of the different subsectors in this food system is intricately dynamic and interlinked, with the subsectors feeding off each other (as well as off the urban, nonfood economy). Increases in staple crop productivity may, for example, generate demand for products produced in the other agriculture subsectors and elsewhere in the food system (eggs, meat, dairy, and prepared foods) and release labor to produce them. With the exception of some large farms in southern Africa, most livestock production in Sub-Saharan Africa is small in scale and mixed with crop production. Hence, because of several back-and-forth production links at the farm level (for example, demand for animal feed), productivity growth in one subsector could enhance the productivity of the other sector as well as the development of processing and value addition opportunities further down the chain (Otte et al. 2012).[17] Development of agribusiness further down the chain, on the other hand, may be needed to open up markets, especially those—such as the urban and export markets—that need consistent supplies of large quantity and high quality (Swinnen, Vandeplas, and Maertens 2010).

The export of traditional (coffee, cocoa, and rubber) and new (fruits, vegetables, and flowers) agricultural exports complements and interacts with these developments in the food system. At the micro level, income from cash crop production can assist farmers to overcome credit constraints to purchasing modern inputs for their staple crops. Well-functioning and reliable staple crop markets may, on the other hand, enable farmers to specialize in export crop production.[18]

At the macro level, export crops generate foreign exchange and tax income. They can also be a source of knowledge transfer and learning, and depending on the labor intensity of the production process, they generate a lot of rural employment (Stiglitz 2018). In this, they act like normal export-oriented industries, without smokestacks (Newfarmer, Page, and Tarp 2018). Although export crop growers are not subject to the challenge of a local price treadmill—whereby the income gains from technological advances need to outpace the losses from price declines given inelastic demand—they face their own fluctuations in demand and prices, derived from the international commodity price cycles. They also compete for land and policy attention.

The effectiveness of growth in the different agriculture subsectors to reduce poverty depends on the size of these subsectors, their growth potential, and the scope for adding value in the chain. The poverty reduction per producer from the expansion of small subsectors (such as fruits and vegetables) can, for example, be larger given higher labor productivity. Yet the total number of people lifted out of poverty from productivity improvements in large but less productive sectors (for example, staples) can nonetheless be much larger. This happens when the size effect (the number of poor affected) outweighs the poverty reduction per grower.[19] It also explains why broad-based staple crop productivity growth is favored to reduce poverty in the early stages of development.

How Agricultural Gains Can Benefit the Poor

The poor can benefit from agricultural productivity gains and market expansion through three channels. First, through the *income channel*, they can benefit either directly as producers or indirectly through the labor market as wage laborers.

Second, through the *price channel*, they can also benefit as consumers when food prices decline. The extent to which prices respond to productivity increases, thereby eroding some of the income gains for net sellers, will depend on their tradability: sensitive if not tradable, less sensitive if tradable. This price response will also affect who benefits most—the net food sellers[20] or the net food buyers—with the ultimate poverty effects depending on the shares of both groups among the poor (Ivanic and Martin 2018).

Third, the poor can benefit through the *linkage channel*. New off-the-farm employment opportunities emerge when increased agricultural incomes raise demand for agricultural inputs and production services; agribusiness development (backward and forward production linkages); and locally produced goods and services (consumption linkages). These indirect linkage effects are often the most important, especially the consumption linkages. They crucially depend on the number of people who benefit from the productivity increase (that is, how broadly based the agricultural growth is) as well as on their propensity to consume locally produced goods and services (Delgado et al. 1998).

How Best to Broker the Agricultural Transition?

In most African countries, the agrarian structure is still dominated by low-productivity smallholders focused on staples, often mixed with some livestock holding (Otte et al. 2012).[21] The end point is a commercial agriculture on larger farms integrated into a well-functioning food system, with high-value agricultural products making up the bulk of value added and employment. Much debate remains on how best to broker this transition while maximizing poverty reduction (ACET 2017; Collier and Dercon 2014; De Janvry and Sadoulet 2010; Diao et al. 2012; Hall, Scoones, and Tsikata 2017; Mellor 2017).

There are two salient aspects to this debate. First, what is the appropriate sequencing and distribution of relative policy attention and public investment to the different subsectors? Should more attention go to (a) productivity growth and commercialization of staples for the domestic market (the Green Revolution); (b) the transition to nonstaple crops and agribusiness development to feed the cities and the new rural consumers (agrarian and rural transformation); or (c) productivity growth and value addition in both traditional and new export crops (akin to the structural transformation)? Furthermore, how do the answers differ depending on the state of development and trade openness?

Second, how is production best organized: on large-scale or on small-scale entities (or a mixture of both), and should it be labor-intensive or capital-intensive? Should the transition to larger-scale farming be accelerated, or is organic farm growth more desirable and feasible? How do countries' land endowments (land abundance or scarcity) and agrarian structures as well as the characteristics of the crops and market structure of the subsectors affect the answer?

The Continuing Importance of Staple Crop Productivity Growth

Two factors explain why brokering Africa's Green Revolution remains a first-order public policy issue for accelerating poverty reduction: First, low labor productivity in staple crops still locks too many people into staple crop agriculture. Second, because of this as well as greater income (including via the price channel) and linkage effects, raising staple crop productivity has larger growth multipliers and greater poverty-to-growth elasticities than an equal amount of productivity growth in cash crops.[22]

Recent household survey evidence from Tanzania vividly illustrates the continuing pertinence of staples in food demand and employment (Tschirley et al. 2017), as shown in table 3.1. The income elasticities for staples are still high among the rural and the poorer segments of the urban population (close to 1 or above), and their food expenditure share is still large. As a result, the bulk of the additional agricultural labor (person-days) needed to meet the additional food demand from income growth remains concentrated in staples.[23] Growing demand for vegetables offers new employment opportunities and the highest returns per grower, but few growers benefit.

The additional staple demand could be met by imports. This comes at the expense of raising trade imbalances. With an increase in productivity, it could also be grown domestically.[24] Wheat, and especially rice, hold growth and poverty-reduction potential. They generate the most employment and, after

TABLE 3.1 In Tanzania, there are larger income gains per grower in fruits and vegetables but much larger employment gains in staples, especially rice

		Landholding size class				
Type of annual projected increase	**Total**	**< 1 ha**	**1–2 ha**	**2–5 ha**	**5–10 ha**	**> 10 ha**
US$ output (gross) per day of labor						
Wheat and rice	7.1	5.6	6.7	7.1	16.7	12.5
Other grains	3.6	2.9	3.2	3.6	8.3	3.2
Roots and tubers	3.3	2.6	5.0	3.4	4.0	2.5
Pulses	3.1	2.3	2.9	3.6	5.9	4.8
Oilseeds	6.7	3.4	4.5	6.3	14.3	—
Vegetables	11.1	9.1	12.5	12.5	7.7	—
Expected change in labor (person-days, thousands) from dietary change following income growth						
Wheat and rice	5,471	1,904	1,456	1,573	240	299
Other grains	3,413	920	1,049	1,031	259	155
Roots and tubers	3,547	1,606	808	871	137	125
Pulses	4,246	1,266	1,323	1,169	240	248
Oilseeds	708	109	247	231	122	—
Vegetables	1,654	564	484	497	109	—
Total	19,040	6,368	5,367	5,371	1,106	828
Gross income per grower (US$ per year)						
Wheat and rice	31	18	31	39	80	98
Other grains	2	1	2	3	7	4
Roots and tubers	11	7	15	13	11	10
Pulses	3	2	3	5	7	11
Oilseeds	10	4	6	10	48	—
Vegetables	50	32	48	93	83	—

Source: Tschirley et al. 2017.
Note: ha = hectares; — = not available. Table shows projected changes in labor needs, by crop, following rising demand from increased income and dietary change one year ahead. Imports are netted out (assuming constant import shares); prices, investments or technology, and the structure of landholdings and labor productivity are held constant. The projections represent the distribution of short-run employment and income opportunities at the farm level from rising food demand engendered by one year's income growth.

vegetables, offer the highest income growth per grower, including on small farm units (table 3.1). Similar observations hold for other countries, as in Côte d'Ivoire (Christiaensen and Premand 2017). Incidentally, rice and wheat are also an important share of Africa's food imports, as noted earlier,[25] which makes rice and wheat particularly important for poverty reduction (as well as for the external macroeconomic balance) in the Tanzanian example and elsewhere.

The estimated demand for other grains, pulses, and roots and tubers equally requires much additional labor but generates little income growth. However, if the labor productivity of poorer farmers in these subsectors could be raised cost-effectively, it would substantially improve food security and over time also free up much labor for other activities. Poor rural farmers still consume large portions of their staple crop production.[26] Alternative income opportunities remain absent, and food markets to buy and sell their food are often insufficiently reliable.

These findings highlight the continuing dominance of staples in food demand, the sheer amount of labor required to meet this demand, and thus the opportunities for direct income gains and poverty reduction. When the effects of price and intersectoral linkages are further considered, productivity growth in the food staple sector proves more effective than export crops in increasing national income and reducing poverty (Diao et al. 2012). This happens because of its larger growth multipliers and the higher poverty elasticities of growth relative to growth in the nonstaple sector: 1 percent growth in agriculture driven by cereal or root and tuber productivity growth generates a larger decline in national poverty than does 1 percent growth in agriculture driven by growth in export crops (table 3.2). When smallholders are engaged in growing export crops (such as cotton in Zambia and tobacco in Malawi), the gaps in poverty gains between staple and export crops are usually smaller.

Because of the concentration of Africa's livestock holdings among poorer smallholders (often women) in mixed crop-livestock farming systems[27] and its strong links with staple crops, productivity growth in the livestock sector often comes in second (after productivity growth in staples) in terms of growth multipliers and impact on poverty reduction, as in Ethiopia, southern Africa, and Uganda (Diao and Nin-Pratt 2007; Nin-Pratt and Diao 2006; Benin et al. 2008, respectively). This results from the strong direct income gains among rural households and the production links to the staple crop sector as supplier of livestock feed (including through its byproducts) as well as the consumption linkages (Otte et al. 2012).

Unfortunately, staple crops (and smallholder livestock holdings) tend to attract relatively less public and private attention. Cash crops—whether traditional (such as cotton, coffee, and cocoa) or new ones (fruits, vegetables, and flowers)—are an important source of foreign exchange and taxation. They are also needed as primary materials for processing firms in western countries. Staple crops generally do not command such interest, despite their larger poverty-reducing effects and the importance of food security for sociopolitical stability (Barrett 2013).

TABLE 3.2 Staple crop productivity growth is more poverty reducing than export crop productivity growth

	Staple foods			Export crops		
Country	Growth multiplier	Poverty-growth elasticity	Lead sector	Growth multiplier	Poverty-growth elasticity	Lead sector
Ethiopia	1.13	−1.40	All cereals	1.04	−1.16	All export crops
Kenya	—	−2.13	All food crops	2.62	−1.90	All export crops
Malawi	1.11	−0.74	Maize	1.05	−0.62	Tobacco
	—	−0.85	Horticulture	1.06	−0.57	Other export crops
Mozambique	1.42	−0.73	Maize	1.48	−0.29	Traditional exports
	—	−0.65	All cereals	0.83	−0.43	Biofuel crops
Nigeria	—	−1.02	All cereals	0.70	−0.81	All export crops
	—	−0.92	Roots	—	—	—
Rwanda	—	−2.39	Maize	—	−1.81	Coffee
	—	−2.59	Pulses	—	−1.63	Tea
	—	—	—	—	−2.27	Other export crops
Tanzania	—	−1.09	Maize	1.15	−1.00	All export crops
Uganda	—	−1.07	Roots	0.62	−0.64	All export crops
	1.39	−1.38	Horticulture	—	—	—
Zambia	1.63	−0.27	All cereals	0.30	−0.25	All export crops
	1.88	−0.33	Roots	—	—	—

Source: Diao et al. 2012.
Note: — = not available.

International food crises can be a powerful trigger to shift political attention to food crops, as observed in the aftermath of the 1973, 1978, and 2008 crises. Yet, this typically fades away rapidly as international prices come down (Timmer 2010). Specific public policy attention and investment is especially important when subsector-specific public investments are needed (for example, for R&D, extension, and infrastructure) or when institutional innovations such as inclusive value chain development (VCD)—successful in overcoming input, factor, and product market constraints in cash crops—do not carry over easily to staple crops, as elaborated further below (Swinnen, Vandeplas, and Maertens 2010).

In sum, African cereal yields are still only 1.5 tons per hectare (about half of those in India and a quarter of those in China). Most of the poor still rely on their own staple production to meet their food needs and have no obvious sustainable alternative to gain a living outside agriculture and buy food, at least not at scale. Staple crop productivity growth generates greater multiplier effects. And there is less political incentive, but greater need, for public sector engagement.

Clearly, specific policy attention to and investment in raising staple crop productivity is warranted. In China and Vietnam, cereal yields were already at 2.7 tons per hectare when those countries introduced their Household Responsibility System and Doi Moi programs, respectively. These programs boosted staple productivity further and drove much of their poverty reduction in the early and late 1980s (Ravallion and Chen 2007). Similar arguments hold for smallholder livestock promotion, albeit to a lesser extent, given the greater potential for inclusive VCD (for example, in the dairy subsector), as discussed further later in this chapter.

Development of Africa's agro-exports (old and new) importantly complements the staple crop agenda. In addition to foreign exchange and tax revenues, it provides important additional employment and poverty-reducing opportunities, including to absorb surplus labor or labor released from staple crop productivity growth, as in Ethiopia (Suzuki, Mano, and Abebe 2018) and Senegal (Van den Broeck, Swinnen, and Maertens 2017). Spillovers from cash crop production (such as the relaxation of liquidity constraints and improved market access to inputs) may also benefit staple crop productivity (Govereh and Jayne 2003).

Yet the numbers will be too small for agro-export development to broker a structural transformation on its own.[28] Furthermore, export crop development does not have to compete with public investment in staples, because private sector interests can further be leveraged. The challenge is to balance policy attention. The importance of staples also holds in coastal countries, which are arguably more exposed to external markets and agricultural trading opportunities, as well as in mineral-rich countries (see table 3.2, Mozambique and Zambia, respectively).

The Promise of the Larger Smallholder

Greater capacity to learn and innovate, better access to finance, and greater ability to facilitate returns to scale in the organization of the downstream market (storage, processing, and wholesale and retail trading) arguably favor a food system organized around large farming units. In this view, the main cause for Africa's low agricultural labor productivity lies in the concentration (and misallocation) of land and production on smallholder farms with poor farming skills.

If so, the apparent policy solution is to remove agriculture policy distortions that favor smallholder farming and to foster land tenure security to enable farm consolidation so that the best farmers can eventually buy out those who lack the skill to farm productively.[29] After all, most African smallholders have not chosen to be farmers; they were born into it (Adamopoulos and Restuccia 2014, 2015; Collier and Dercon 2014; Restuccia and Santaeulalia-Llopis 2017).

But the evidence on this is quite nuanced. To begin with, the widely documented inverse farm size-to-productivity relationship would suggest otherwise (Carletto, Savastano, and Zezza 2013; Larson, Muraoka, and Otsuka

2016).[30] Also, evidence from Ghana and Uganda suggests that much of the variance in productivity can be explained by (unobserved) measurement error, idiosyncratic shocks, and heterogeneity in land quality (Gollin and Udry 2019). As such, gains from reallocation to the more productive farmers may be substantially more modest than current distributions of farm size and labor productivity would suggest.

Much of this evidence comes from household surveys. They often do not capture many large farms (Jayne et al. 2016). More direct evidence shows the following:

- *In Malawi,* large agricultural estates have underperformed small ones (yield, productivity, and intensity of land use are below those of small farms) and failed to generate positive spillovers (Deininger and Xia 2018).[31]
- *In Mozambique,* private sector, large-scale farm expansion had some positive spillovers: agricultural practices and input use by small farms within 50 kilometers from the newly established large operations improved, and there were also some signs of job creation. However, it did not lead to greater participation in output markets, cultivated area expansion, or better yields, and it decreased perceived well-being among the farmers around these large farms (Deininger and Xia 2016).
- *In Ethiopia,* large farm establishment did not lead to job creation and provided only modest benefits in terms of technology, input market access, or greater resilience to crop shocks for neighboring smallholders (Ali, Deininger, and Harris 2019).

These more recent experiences suggest that large-scale agricultural estates are, in practice, not necessarily more productive and that the benefits for smallholders are typically too small to justify large unconditional subsidies.

The empirical evidence is much clearer that increasing smallholder productivity is particularly effective at reducing poverty (as opposed to fostering efficiency and growth) (Christiaensen, Demery, and Kuhl 2011; Ivanic and Martin 2018; Ligon and Sadoulet 2018; Mellor and Malik 2017). It raises the income of the poor directly and, by reaching many with a higher propensity to consume locally produced goods and services, it also creates more important demand effects (or consumption linkages) for the other sectors.

Several countries have also successfully developed by increasing smallholder productivity in the initial stages, such as China and Vietnam (Vietnam is now the second-largest exporter of rice and coffee).[32] Conversely, in Tanzania, rapid economic growth did not significantly improve poverty during the 2000s, partly because of the structure of agricultural growth, which favored larger-scale production of rice, wheat, and traditional export crops in specific geographic regions. Accelerating growth in a wider range of subsectors (especially maize) grown extensively by subsistence smallholders, but also livestock, would have strengthened the growth-poverty relationship while also contributing significantly to growth itself (Pauw and Thurlow 2011).

These historical experiences suggest that rapid concentration of agriculture on large landholdings is neither necessary nor sufficient for rapid growth or poverty reduction. This is not to be confused with the observation that farm sizes consolidate as countries develop and urbanize (the agricultural transformation). In this, the process is arguably more important than the actual end points. So, what is the appropriate way forward?

The starting point remains a predominantly smallholder family farming structure.[33] But not everyone should stay in farming. Nor should efforts to increase labor productivity (in crop as well as livestock production) necessarily focus mainly on the poorest and smallest farmers. Rather, it is the slightly larger, dynamic, and commercially oriented smallholders who hold the most promise to act as catalysts, with the poorest benefiting through lower food prices and the local labor markets (Hazell et al. 2010; Mellor 2017). Furthermore, institutional innovations such as machinery services (tractor rental), contract farming, and VCD—more recently fueled by the information and communication technology (ICT) revolution (noted in Fundamentals 3, "Leapfrogging with Technology (and Trade)")—can help smallholders capture economies of scale in mechanization and in trading, processing, and marketing further down the chain.

The rise of medium-scale farmers in Africa (farms of 5–100 hectares) is adding a new element to the farm-size debate (Jayne, Chamberlin, and Headey 2014; Jayne et al. 2016). They now control roughly 20 percent of total farmland in Kenya, 32 percent in Ghana, 39 percent in Tanzania, and slightly more than 50 percent in Zambia (Jayne et al. 2016). Their number, average size, and share of land cultivated has been expanding rapidly over the past decade, especially in the more land-abundant African countries.[34] This expansion has been largely driven by relatively wealthy urban investors, many of them former or current government employees, and much less through organic growth of smallholder farms.

Will medium-size farms be more effective than large-scale farms at reducing poverty? Indications from Kenya, Tanzania, and Zambia are that medium-scale farms are attracting new investments in the chain by large trading companies, suppliers of mechanization equipment, and other agribusinesses. Smallholders have benefited through slightly higher output prices—for example, 3.6 percent and 4.9 percent higher for maize in Kenya and Zambia, respectively (Sitko, Burke, and Jayne 2017)—and better access to mechanization services (Van der Westhuizen, Jayne, and Meyer 2018).

Incipient evidence from Tanzania further suggests that the concentration of land among farms of 5–10 hectares comes along with an increase in labor income among smallholders in that district (Chamberlin and Jayne 2017). This also holds for the poorer households because of an increase in their off-farm incomes, which more than offsets the decline in their incomes from farming and agricultural wages on which they now spend less time. This positive spillover no longer holds, however, when land in the district is more concentrated on larger farms (larger than 10 hectares); if anything, it may even negatively affect the incomes of the poor.

The emerging picture suggests that poor smallholders can benefit from some farm consolidation, albeit less likely from large-scale farms (more than 100 hectares) and even from the larger medium-scale farms (more than 10 hectares)—and mainly through the generation of rural off-farm employment opportunities nearby. Possible reasons for this are that the larger medium-scale farms are more capital-intensive and use less agricultural wage labor. More of these farms also result from acquisition by outsiders rather than organic growth, with the owners often urban-based (Jayne et al. 2016). More of the revenues are likely spent on urban (and imported) goods and services with few local, rural multipliers. This leads to smaller local consumption linkages for the poor.

The findings suggest a focus on the slightly larger, more innovative smallholder farmers as entry points to raise agricultural productivity—an approach also advocated by Mellor (2017) and Otte et al. (2012) in the case of livestock. They also suggest an emphasis on farm consolidation through organic productivity growth and farm expansion rather than external acquisition. The optimal farm size for this "larger smallholder" will differ across countries—larger in land-abundant countries, smaller in land-scarce countries, and depending on the crop (larger for land-intensive cereals, smaller for labor-intensive fruits and vegetables). Yet with many of Africa's countries no longer land-abundant, it could in many cases already occur with farms from 2 hectares onward.

Because of lower transaction costs, much larger ("estate") farm entities may still be needed to ensure consistent volumes, quality, and standards to enable access to more-demanding markets. This has, for example, been the case in the labor-intensive export niche markets for high-value agricultural products such as fruits and vegetables, flowers, and fish (Van den Broeck, Swinnen, and Maertens 2017). The poor (often especially poor women) can then benefit through the labor markets as agricultural wage laborers. Whether such estate farming is also necessary to ensure the standards and volumes required to supply the domestic urban markets is not clear. The feasibility of alternative models, including producer alliances and contract farming, is explored further in the VCD section later in this chapter.

Poverty Highest in Remote, High-Potential Areas

So, where should efforts focus to increase smallholder staple crop productivity and agricultural labor productivity more broadly? It is commonly assumed that poverty is worst in remote settings with poor agroecological potential (Barbier 2016; Jalan and Ravallion 2002; Kraay and McKenzie 2014). Incipient evidence suggests, however, that in Africa, it is areas with more fertile soils that have the higher poverty rates, with the negative effect exacerbated when these regions are poorly connected to markets (Wantchekon and Stanig 2016). Further analysis using alternative measures of poverty, agroecological potential, and rural market access also points in this direction (Vandercasteelen and Christiaensen 2018), as figure 3.2 indicates.

Poverty rates are higher in areas with better agroecological potential, and they increase the farther these higher-potential areas are from the nearest urban agglomeration of 50,000 or more inhabitants. After three hours of travel time, the negative effect of distance levels off. Poverty density (number of poor per square kilometer), on the other hand, drops dramatically as one moves away from urban agglomerations. The drop is most dramatic during the first two hours of travel time, from 77 to 24 people per square kilometer (in high-potential areas). The higher poverty rates as one moves away from urban agglomerations are offset by much lower population density. Interestingly, poverty rates and poverty density in low-potential areas are not only lower but also decline with distance.

The mechanism behind these findings remains poorly understood. High-potential areas may attract more people, inducing higher population density. If not followed by

FIGURE 3.2 Poverty rates in Africa are highest in more-remote areas with better agroecological potential

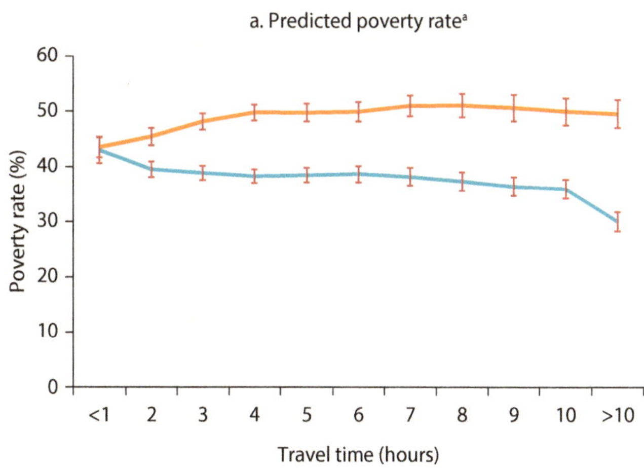

Source: Vandercasteelen and Christiaensen 2018.
Note: km^2 = square kilometer. Travel time is the time needed to travel to the nearest urban agglomeration of at least 50,000 inhabitants using the most convenient mode of transport, distance being corrected for terrain and road conditions. Poverty is defined as living on less than US$1.90 per person per day. Agroecological potential is assessed as either high or low based on a combination of a soil suitability index and the length of growing period.
a. The predicted values of the poverty rate by travel time are obtained as the margins after the regression of the poverty rate on an indicator variable taking the value 1 if agroecological potential is high, the one-hour intervals of travel time, their interactions, and a set of control variables. Bars indicate the 95 percent confidence intervals.
b. The number of poor per square kilometer is obtained by multiplying the population density in each 10-square-kilometer pixel by the predicted poverty rate for that pixel.

commensurate agricultural intensification, agricultural involution and stagnation or impoverishment ensues. Africa's rural population does live spatially clustered in areas with high soil quality (Jayne, Chamberlin, and Headey 2014). Agricultural intensification in Africa has remained much below what would have been expected given current population densities (Binswanger-Mkhize and Savastano 2017). Although the practice of fallow has virtually disappeared, it has not been compensated by a commensurate increase in the use of soil fertility-enhancing inputs (organic or inorganic). Widespread soil and environmental degradation are now commonly observed (Jayne, Chamberlin, and Headey 2014).

Remoteness exacerbates this situation, making it harder for people to commercialize their production, diversify their activities, or move (Davis, Di Giuseppe, and Zezza 2017; Deichmann, Shilpi, and Vakis 2009). This fosters even greater reliance on agriculture and becomes especially challenging in the areas whose greater agroecological potential attracted larger populations to begin with. Fertile land may also have fostered larger family sizes (to work the land), with isolation further reducing households' investment in human capital given the fewer off-farm opportunities and thus the lower returns to education (Wantchekon and Stanig 2016).

Poorly connected areas with good agroecological potential are not uncommon. Historically, much of Africa's road infrastructure has been constructed to connect mining areas to cities and seaports, thereby bypassing some of the areas with the greatest agroecological potential. Rapid population expansion in the face of limited alternatives may have trapped people in isolated fertile areas into low-productivity subsistence agriculture and poverty (Wantchekon and Stanig 2016).

The findings draw attention to areas of high agroecological potential as key action entry points for accelerating poverty reduction (map 3.1), with an emphasis on rural infrastructure and transport services (as well as schooling) to better connect them to markets. In 2013, an estimated 51 million poor people lived in high-potential areas that were three or more hours away from an urban agglomeration of at least 50,000 people; another 201 million were in high-potential areas within three hours from the nearest urban center of 50,000. This compares with 142 million poor people (or about a third of Africa's 396 million poor in 2013) who lived in areas with low agroecological potential, of whom 119 million were within three hours of the nearest urban center and 22 million were more than three hours from an urban center (Vandercasteelen and Christiaensen 2018).

Although this does not exclude the need for attention to areas with lower agroecological potential—including to prevent rising interregional inequality and conflict—it does highlight the potential for accelerating poverty reduction through in situ investments, especially in the more remote fertile areas with greater population densities, which in the classifications used here also include much of the African savanna.[35] Similar observations hold in the context of smallholder livestock promotion (Otte et al. 2012).

An Integrated Approach Is Needed

Persistently Low Agricultural Labor Productivity

Growth in Africa's agricultural labor productivity has picked up somewhat since 2000, to 3.3 percent per year on average during 2001–12 (Benin and Nin-Pratt 2016). This is consistent with the favorable change in Africa's agriculture policy environment since the 2008 world food crisis. It plausibly also reflects urban distress migration of surplus labor, reducing land pressure. Yet there are sizable differences across countries, and following decades of sluggish growth,[36] Africa's agricultural labor productivity is still extremely low,[37] especially in the countries where most of Africa's poor live and where poverty rates are high.[38]

In an accounting sense, agricultural labor productivity can be seen as the product of two components: the amount of land per agricultural worker and the output per unit of land. But given the seasonal nature of rainfed agricultural production, farm labor goes often underused outside the agricultural seasons.

MAP 3.1 **Remote, high-potential areas are concentrated in central Africa, eastern Ethiopia, and Madagascar**

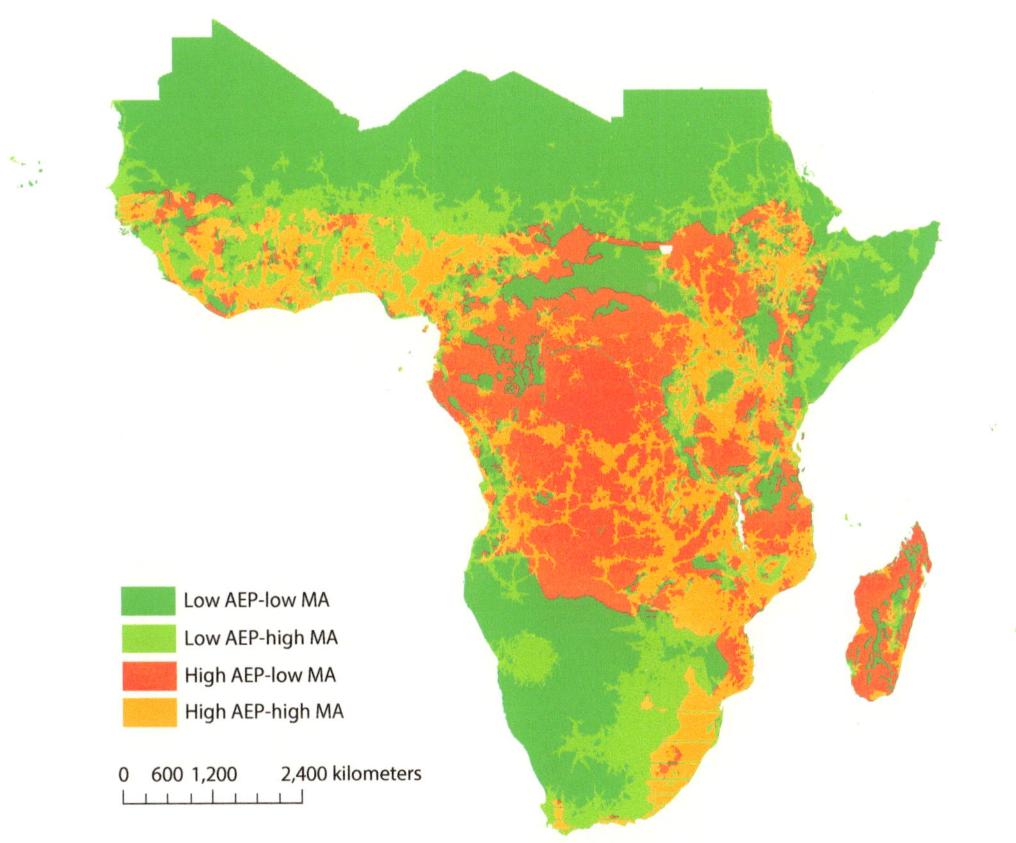

Source: Vandercasteelen and Christiaensen 2018. © World Bank. Used with permission; further permission required for reuse.
Note: The presentation is based on 100-square-kilometer pixels. In pixels with high market access (MA), travel times to the nearest urban agglomeration of at least 50,000 inhabitants are less than three hours. In pixels with high agroecological potential (AEP), the average length of a growing period is at least 120 days, and the value of the soil-crop suitability index is at least 25. Travel time data come from Weiss et al. (2018), the length of growing-period data are derived from the "Global Agro-Ecological Zones Assessment for Agriculture" (Fischer et al. 2008), and the Soil Production Index is derived from the "Digital Soil Map of the World" (Sanchez et al. 2009).

To account for this, it is useful to also consider the intensity of farm labor use.

This analysis suggests three entry points to raise agricultural labor productivity through actions on the farm:[39]

- *Increase the intensity of labor use in farming per farm laborer:* that is, the number of hours worked in agriculture per farm laborer, holding the amount of land constant.
- *Increase the farm size:* that is, the amount of cultivated land per full-time equivalent worker.
- *Increase land productivity:* that is, the agricultural value added per unit of land.

Underuse of Agricultural Labor Given Seasonality

A widely shared observation is that labor productivity in agriculture is lower than in other sectors, even after accounting for differences in human capital (Gollin, Lagakos, and Waugh 2014). Yet when expressed in full-time labor equivalents—accounting for the differences in actual hours worked in the sector per sectoral worker—the gap in productivity largely disappears.[40] It suggests that agriculture is not intrinsically less productive. Analysis further shows that labor among agricultural workers is underused: workers primarily engaged in agriculture work fewer hours than those primarily engaged in other sectors (McCullough 2017). This appears closely tied to the seasonal nature of agricultural production (figure 3.3) (De Janvry, Duquennois, and Sadoulet 2018).

Seasonality in production, especially when it is rainfed as in most of Africa, implies cyclical labor calendars in agriculture. Demand for farm labor peaks during the planting and harvesting seasons but remains underused on the farm during the rest of the year. Irrigation investment can increase the number of crops grown per year (such as an early and late crop, either the same, such as rice, or another one, such as vegetables). Another possibility is diversification into livestock, such as poultry for egg production or dairy cows for milk production, with a more continuous labor demand throughout the year. The potential of both strategies depends on market demand and is likely more viable near urban centers. Their development also requires complementary measures such as extension, access to credit and inputs, a cold storage chain, standards, and certification.

Alternatively, farm household members may seek off-farm employment through rural–urban migration during the lean season (Bryan, Chowdhury, and Mobarak 2014) or permanent migration. Yet remunerative countercyclical off-farm employment is not always available. Urban employment opportunities for the unskilled are mainly low-paying and in the informal sector, while the few labor-intensive export manufacturers available that pay a wage premium do so exactly to avoid worker turnover (Blattman and Dercon 2016; Suzuki, Mano, and Abebe 2018), as discussed further in chapter 4 ("Moving to Jobs Off the Farm").

FIGURE 3.3 Rural individuals in Malawi work less, and more seasonally, than urban residents

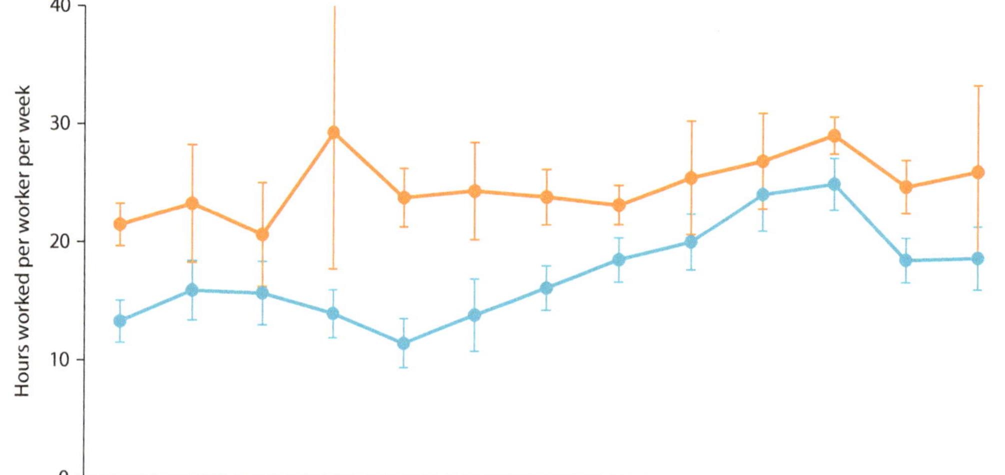

Source: De Janvry, Duquennois, and Sadoulet (2018), based on Malawi's 2010–11 Integrated Household Survey.
Note: Bars indicate the 95 percent confidence intervals.

Moreover, seasonal migration may be detrimental to the agricultural practices on the home plot. Experiments from Zambia show, for example, that smallholder households in villages randomly selected for a loan program worked on average 25 percent less as laborers off the farm (than they had in the past) and opted to work more on their own farms instead. They saw their consumption rise and even started to hire local agricultural wage laborers themselves, pushing up local farming wages (Fink, Jack, and Masiye 2014). Mechanization can help overcome seasonal labor bottlenecks on the farm—for example, when the harvesting windows are too short. This can facilitate the uptake of full-time off-farm employment elsewhere (as further discussed below).

Seasonality in agricultural income and labor is especially problematic for poor farmers, who have limited access and face large transaction costs to participate in credit and labor markets to smooth consumption (Dercon and Krishnan 2000; Khandker 2012). Filling and smoothing the rural labor calendars (by intensifying labor use on the farm as well as in the rural off-farm economy) is thus key to raising labor productivity and reducing poverty. More broadly, the interaction between seasonality in production, agricultural labor supply, off-farm employment, and poverty needs more attention from researchers and policy makers. The precise dynamics of agricultural labor underuse in Africa remain poorly understood.

Limited Scope for Farm Size Expansion

Over the past decades, much of Africa's agricultural output growth has come from the expansion of cultivated land, which has been especially fast since the 1990s.[41] This has been driven by population growth and the increase in domestic food prices and has been concentrated in land-abundant countries. As a result, average farm sizes in these countries have remained largely constant (around 3 hectares). In land-constrained countries, on the other hand, strong population growth has come along with a substantial drop in farm size—from 2.3 hectares to 1.2 hectares, on average (Headey 2016).[42]

The scope for further agricultural labor productivity growth through farm-size expansion as a way out of poverty appears limited. Africa still has surplus farmland, but it is concentrated within relatively few (eight or so) land-abundant countries, some of which are fragile and conflict-affected states.[43] Much of the land is also not readily available or economically viable for smallholders, given poor infrastructure and the presence of human (malaria) and zoonotic diseases (Jayne, Chamberlin, and Headey 2014). It might be more suitable for large-scale, capital-intensive farming. However, the poverty-reducing effects remain to be established, as noted earlier.

What about most of the remaining countries in the region (about 40), where also most of the poor reside? Not only have average farm sizes been declining in many of these countries, but their land distribution has also been bifurcating: a much larger number of smallholders live on even smaller farms than the averages would suggest. A class of land-poor (or even landless) individuals is emerging, especially in the most land-constrained countries.[44] For example, owned land per adult in the bottom quartile of households (ranked by land ownership) in Nigeria, Malawi, and Uganda amounts to 0.02, 0.08, and 0.09 hectares per adult, respectively. The share of landless rural households in these three countries is 8 percent, 5 percent, and 5 percent, respectively—compared with about 2 percent in Ethiopia, Niger, and Tanzania, where the land-to-labor ratio is still somewhat larger (Deininger, Savastano, and Xia 2017, table 3).

Especially women and unemployed youth tend to lack the social connections and the necessary resources to access new land (ACET 2017). Well-functioning land rental markets can lower their barriers to accessing land, and these markets have indeed emerged in response. Land rental markets are more active than commonly assumed, especially in countries where land constraints are more binding.[45] This has helped transfer land to land-poor, labor-rich households, thus helping to equalize land endowments, but it has not yet resulted in a reallocation of farmland to larger or more productive farmers (Deininger, Savastano, and Xia 2017; Muraoka, Jin, and Jayne 2018).

Land market performance is lower where land tenure security (real or perceived) is lower as well (Deininger, Savastano, and Xia 2017). Improving land tenure security is a high-priority policy area to help farmers sort themselves by comparative advantage and to facilitate farm consolidation. Despite earlier evidence to the contrary (Jacoby and Minten 2007), recent experience from Ethiopia and Rwanda suggests that land title registration may be one cost-effective way to improve land tenure security, with the effects largest among those groups with weaker initial levels of tenure—notably women (Ali et al. 2015; Deininger, Ali, and Alemu 2011). Greater land tenure security can also foster long-term investment in land productivity (Ali, Deininger, and Goldstein 2014; Goldstein et al. 2018).

Myriad Constraints on Land Productivity

To overcome shrinking farm size, land productivity must be increased. African countries have started to do so, with the land-constrained countries and those with less-favorable agricultural conditions most recently more successful than the others (Benin and Nin-Pratt 2016), as figure 3.4 illustrates.

Increasing land productivity requires modern inputs and farming techniques—in other words, the Green Revolution package. Yet the prevalence and amount of modern input adoption (improved seeds, fertilizer, and agrochemicals) has been mixed and the adoption of mechanization and irrigation especially low (Sheahan and Barrett 2017). The profitability of modern inputs appears far from assured and highly variable across time and space, causing some farmers to opt out and others to apply inputs at rates that are not yet economically rewarding.[46] Some studies in eastern and western Africa show, for example, that the adoption of inorganic fertilizer in maize production is, on average, profitable (Duflo, Kremer, and Robinson 2008; Harou et al. 2017; Ragasa and Chapoto 2017). Yet several other studies show that fertilizer uptake is not, or is only marginally, profitable (Beaman et al. 2013; Darko et al. 2016; Liverpool-Tasie et al. 2017) or is profitable only when subsidized (Koussoubé and Nauges 2017) or used within a limited range of rainfall distributions (Rosenzweig and Udry 2016).

Heterogeneity in the profitability of technologies comes partly from differences in the physical environment (Otsuka and Muraoka 2017). Soil quality, for example, can vary substantially across villages but also across plots within the village. Yet in the absence of the right soil chemistry and physical conditions, crop yield response to inorganic fertilizer is often limited and the use of inorganic fertilizer no longer pays (Burke et al. 2016; Carter, Lybbert, and Tjernström 2015; Harou et al. 2017; Koussoubé and Nauges 2017; Marenya and Barrett 2009; Morris et al. 2007). Poorer farmers may be especially susceptible because they tend to cultivate the more-degraded lands, trapping them in a vicious circle of low soil quality and low yield response to modern inputs (Tittonell and Giller 2013). So far, the role of soil fertility and soil organic carbon has not been incorporated sufficiently as a primary determinant of technology use and its profitability in Africa (Bhargava, Vagen, and Gassner 2018).

Timely availability, good quality, and proper application of inputs (seeds, fertilizers, and pesticides or fungicides) are also critical for a proper yield response and profitable adoption (Burke et al. 2016; Darko et al. 2016). Yet inputs are not always available in a timely manner, also not when provided through government programs (Morris et al. 2007). Moreover, inputs on the market are at times adulterated (with nutrient contents well below the labeled content), rendering input adoption unprofitable

FIGURE 3.4 Land productivity in Africa grows faster in countries with lower agricultural endowments

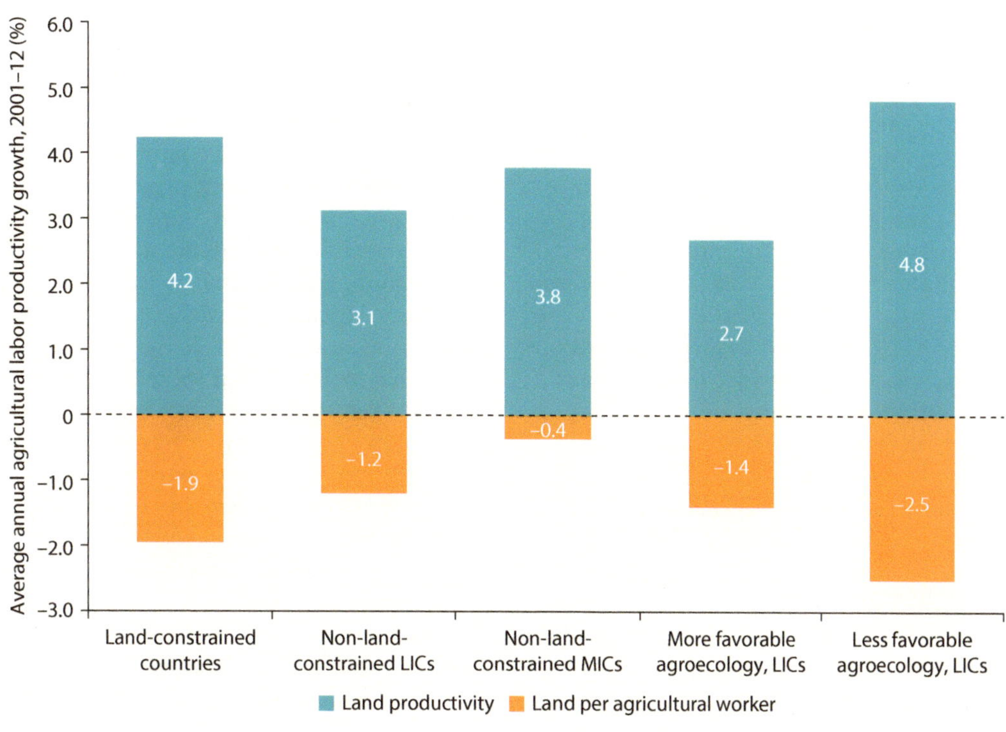

Sources: Calculations based on Benin and Nin-Pratt (2016) and Jayne, Chamberlin, and Headey (2014).
Note: LICs = low-income countries; MICs = middle-income countries. Land-constrained countries are those with a rural population density of more than 100 rural people per square kilometer of arable land. In the sample underlying the numbers shown, those countries include Burundi, Malawi, Nigeria, and Rwanda. Non-land-constrained MICs include Angola, Botswana, Cameroon, Gabon, Namibia, and South Africa. *Land productivity* is defined as the value of gross crop and livestock production in constant 2004–06 international dollars per hectare of cultivated land.

(Bold et al. 2015; Carter, Lybbert, and Tjernström 2015; Michelson et al. 2018; Ragasa and Chapoto 2017).

Finally, even if technologies are locally available and of good quality, farmers might not know how to use them well. Extension systems have been only partially successful in promoting the adoption of new agricultural technologies. Farmers can also self-experiment and learn by doing as well as observe, replicate, and learn from other farmers in their social networks (Bandiera and Rasul 2006; Krishnan and Patnam 2014). Yet this is no full substitute for good extension services.

Input-output price ratios further determine the profitability of input use. Transaction costs to obtain modern inputs can make them too expensive to be profitable (De Janvry, Sadoulet, and Suri 2017; Suri 2011). This sometimes even relates to relatively exorbitant costs to overcome the "last mile."[47] Institutional and regulatory failures in the distribution and supply of agricultural inputs (and other services) add further to the price (Goyal and Nash 2017; Kydd et al. 2004; Poulton, Dorward, and Kydd 2010).

Moreover, most agrochemical inputs in Africa are imported by only a few companies. Their oligopolistic market power allows them to impose artificially high markups in retail prices (ACET 2017; Ncube, Roberts, and Vilakazi 2015), as further discussed in chapter 6 ("Mobilizing Resources for the Poor"). The formation of rent-seeking cartels in the trucking and transport industry, given the lack of competition and regulation, further inflates transport prices (Teravaninthorn and Raballand 2008). Similar forces depress output prices with growing distance to the market, disincentivizing technology adoption and market participation (Damania et al. 2017; Vandercasteelen et al. 2018).

But even if the economics of input use are favorable and farmers understand how to optimize input application, some are locked out because of financial market failures. Cross-country evidence from Africa shows that the use of credit to purchase agricultural inputs is extremely low—across credit type (formal and informal), country, crop, and farm size category. The vast majority of farmers rely on self-finance (cash from nonfarm activities and crop sales) (Adjognon, Liverpool-Tasie, and Reardon 2017). Access to formal credit markets is limited (if they exist) because of limited collateral and high transaction costs to lenders (high screening costs and covariate risk) (Poulton, Dorward, and Kydd 2010).

Finally, risk plays a role. Input use is often not profitable under several states of nature. For example, rainfall variability explains half of the variability in the returns to fertilizer in northern Ghana (Rosenzweig and Udry 2016). Farmers who are risk-averse or lack the financial capacity to buffer consumption against income volatility might be reluctant to adopt agricultural technologies or services because of the risk of losing the investment or collateral in case of an adverse shock (Carter, Laajaj, and Yang 2016; Dercon and Christiaensen 2011). Hence, risk-averse farmers need a higher return on investment than risk-neutral farmers (Goyal and Nash 2017; Liverpool-Tasie et al. 2017). Price risks, even though negatively correlated with production, further compound the challenge. The importance and consequences of uninsured risk in agricultural production are further discussed in chapter 5 ("Managing Risks and Conflict").

In addition to the adoption of modern inputs, land productivity can also be increased by shifting to higher-value crops (such as fruits and vegetables) or to smallholder animal husbandry. Yet access to quality inputs and proper husbandry is even more problematic for smallholder livestock-rearing farmers, resulting in low and stagnating livestock productivity levels; for example, current yields of milk, beef, and poultry stay well below their potential (IFAD 2016; OECD and FAO 2016). Although the use of veterinary services, artificial insemination, and commercial feed are strong drivers of livestock productivity, these inputs are of low quality and often unavailable, especially for the most remote rural households (ACET 2017). In eastern and southern Africa, the East Coast fever, a tick-borne infectious disease, is the leading cause of animal mortality, but vaccination is rarely applied (Perry 2016). Moreover, complementarities in the application of modern inputs are even stronger in livestock production but only rarely applied in combination.[48] And the cost of modern livestock inputs is high because most veterinary and health services need to be imported (from abroad or urban areas), and there exist important scale economies in livestock rearing, making the small-scale production of livestock often unprofitable (for example, in dairy production [Gehrke and Grimm 2018]).

Need for Mechanization and Irrigation, along with a Support Ecosystem

Mechanization

Mechanization can help overcome several of the constraints to increasing agricultural labor productivity discussed thus far, as follows:

- It helps farmers to cultivate more land and expand their farm size where land is available, thereby complementing as opposed to substituting labor (ACET 2017; FAO 2017).[49]
- It permits greater intensification in the more-land-constrained systems. For example, plowing typically does not increase yields directly but enables timely cultivation of the land, which is especially important for crop productivity under rainfed conditions with short planting windows (Diao, Silver, and Takeshima 2016).

- It can also increase the profitability of adopting modern inputs and labor-intensive practices (Ragasa and Chapoto 2017), thereby increasing labor use and further improving land productivity as observed in the rice farming systems in Côte d'Ivoire (Mano, Takahashi, and Otsuka 2017).
- It overcomes seasonal labor constraints, freeing up labor for other agricultural tasks or even for off-farm income generation (part-time farming). But it may also increase the seasonal labor bottlenecks, for example, when more land is plowed but not enough labor is available for harvesting the sown crops.

Yet, until recently, farm mechanization in Africa has been limited. A recent survey of the uptake of mechanized farm equipment in six African countries shows that only 1 percent of farmers own a tractor, and only 12 percent used machinery services (Sheahan and Barrett 2017). Part of the reason is the indivisibility of machines and thus the need for larger farming units to capture their economies of scale. The emergence of medium-size farms would be helpful in this regard, though, as indicated earlier, the poverty-reducing effects remain unclear. It is also not strictly necessary. Rural rental markets for machinery services can overcome problems with machinery indivisibility, with tractors rented out either by larger farmers or specialized private agents, as in China (Wang et al. 2016; Zhang, Yang, and Reardon 2017).[50] The transaction costs of participating in machine rental markets can be substantially reduced through mobile-phone applications such as "Trotro Tractor" in Ghana or "Hello Tractor" in Nigeria (AfDB et al. 2018). Joint ownership of farm machinery by farm organizations is another potential solution (ACET 2017).

Another reason for limited machine ownership is the challenge of financing. Historically, many African governments tried to overcome this through subsidization and state-run machinery parks. Yet the main focus was too often on importing tractors, neglecting the complementary training of machinery operators, the provision of adequate maintenance and repair services, and further development of new locally adapted appliances. The quality of plowing and the machinery services was often poor as a result, with the equipment grinding to a halt prematurely. In particular, a full ecosystem of support services—that is, a machinery value chain—is needed for agricultural mechanization to be able to take off and flourish (Diao et al., forthcoming).

Since the 2008 world food crisis, agricultural mechanization in Africa has gained renewed attention from governments as well as from the world's leading private sector agricultural machinery providers: they do not want to miss out on the world's last growth market for mechanized agricultural equipment. Yet these firms are now not only providing the machinery but also investing in after-purchase skill development and maintenance support. There are also indications that farming systems have evolved sufficiently for farmers to demand mechanization (Binswanger-Mkhize 2018; Diao, Silver, and Takeshima 2016; Mrema, Baker, and Kahan 2008). Rural wages are rising in a number of land-abundant countries or land-abundant regions within countries (for example, in Côte d'Ivoire, Ghana, and Tanzania), and some large and medium-scale farms have emerged. As a result, pockets of mechanization adoption have arisen.[51] Nonetheless, the spread of mechanization in Africa remains limited and has much lagged behind Asia.

An important lesson from Asian mechanization is that much mechanization happened without much direct government intervention. Where they intervened, governments addressed coordination failures so that private supply could meet existing farmer demand. A third party is often needed to overcome the coordination issues across the buyers and suppliers of machinery services (Zhang, Yang, and Reardon 2017). Governments further provided key public goods to overcome market failures.

African mechanization equally needs an integrated approach to address the different constraints focused on provision of public goods. It also needs the development of institutional mechanisms to foster public-private partnerships and local mechanization supply-chain development. Public-good provision includes, for example, the following (ACET 2017; Diao et al., forthcoming):

- *Supporting R&D* on better-adapted machines or on adjustments of imported models to the local context
- *Providing training and extension* to increase awareness about improved mechanized services for smallholder farmers
- *Setting up training centers and curricula* for machine operators as well as supporting small local manufacturing of spare parts
- *Reducing the administrative and import costs* on agricultural machinery (including parts).

Irrigation

Just like mechanization, irrigation is also back on the agenda to increase agricultural labor productivity, following a 20-year hiatus in the wake of disappointing performance during the 1970s and 1980s. Irrigation can intensify the use of farm labor by facilitating year-round cultivation. It also increases land productivity by fostering modern input adoption given lower variation in crop yields, by improving crop response to modern inputs such as improved seeds and fertilizer, by aiding in weed control, and by facilitating the adoption of higher-value crops such as fruits and vegetables (Jayne and Rashid 2013; Otsuka and Muraoka 2017; Tonitto and Ricker-Gilbert 2016).

However, only 7.3 million hectares of Africa's lands are irrigated, mostly concentrated in four countries (Madagascar, Nigeria, South Africa, and Sudan), while an estimated 40 million hectares are suitable for irrigation (Burney, Naylor, and Postel 2013). Adoption of any form of water control by smallholder farmers in Africa has been extremely low so far—less than 2 percent of the cultivated area and less than 5 percent of households in six African countries, which together cover 40 percent of Africa's population (Sheahan and Barrett 2017).

As with the adoption of other technologies, low adoption of irrigation is linked to myriad constraints, resulting in limited availability, poor operation, and low profitability of irrigation schemes in Africa (Schuenemann et al. 2018; You et al. 2011). On the supply side, irrigation development in Africa has been constrained by poor governance structures, limited participation by private operators, negative health and environment consequences, and high cost of irrigation financing. On the demand side, the major constraints are the lack of market access; the heterogeneity in easily accessing renewable freshwater resources; and the lack of technical knowledge, complementary inputs, and at times also labor or access to mechanized agricultural equipment to operate irrigation facilities efficiently (Barrett et al. 2017; Burney and Naylor 2012; Mashnik et al. 2017; Schuenemann et al. 2018).

Similarly, access to reliable and sustainable energy to fuel irrigation systems remains limited, and local banks remain hesitant to approve loans to farmers for the substantial up-front capital investments in irrigation (Mashnik et al. 2017). Finally, many rural areas lack adequate infrastructure to support large-scale irrigation infrastructure and drainage systems, or their maintenance has been proven too expensive (ACET 2017).

Limited Effect of Singular Focused Interventions

A common thread among the agricultural modernization efforts of the past is that an integrated approach has typically been lacking. From the discussion above, it also emerges that the different input, factor, and output market constraints often act like quasi-complements rather than quasi-substitutes. Following the release of one constraint, another one binds rapidly such that the technology is still not adopted or is disadopted rapidly thereafter because it is either not profitable or only profitable as long as the intervention (for example, subsidization) lasts. This lack of a more holistic approach to technology adoption is increasingly seen as a major impediment to Africa's agricultural modernization.

Africa's "smart" fertilizer subsidy program (Morris et al. 2007; World Bank 2007), for example, had limited productivity and poverty impacts because of the lack of complementary investments in agricultural extension, R&D, and soil fertility management (Goyal and Nash 2017; Jayne et al. 2018). Many interventions promoting improved irrigation facilities have also failed because they focused on one aspect of water management—for example, on either reliable access or equitable distribution of irrigated freshwater—without making complementary investments or paying sufficient attention to project implementation and market development (Burney and Naylor 2012; ECOWAS, UEMOA, and CILSS 2017). And for agricultural mechanization to take off and flourish, it is now emphasized that a full ecosystem of support services—a machinery value chain—is equally needed (Diao et al., forthcoming).

Detailed microeconomic studies increasingly support the potential of synergies.[52] For example, joint input application (such as combining inorganic fertilizer with improved seeds) has important synergistic effects on crop profitability (Carter, Lybbert, and Tjernström 2015; Dzanku, Jirström, and Marstorp 2015; Harou et al. 2017; Vanlauwe et al. 2011). However, because the use of inorganic fertilizer and improved seeds might make crops more susceptible to weed growth, pests, and diseases, the simultaneous application of herbicides, pesticides, or other pest control techniques is further required (Tonitto and Ricker-Gilbert 2016). It is exactly the jointness of modern input use combined with water control that has been at the heart of the Green Revolution.

Despite the agronomic synergies of joint input use, even having access to complementary inputs alone does not always suffice. Among those households using modern inputs, few apply more than one input, and when they do, they often do not use them on the same plot (Sheahan and Barrett 2017). This practice underscores the critical, complementary role of agronomic advice. Where extension systems have promoted joint input uptake, as in Ethiopia, the use of modern seeds and inorganic fertilizer is strongly correlated (Abay et al. 2016).

Programs that simultaneously relax agricultural credit and information constraints (for example, through cash transfers and extension services) frequently demonstrate synergistic effects (Ambler, de Brauw, and Godlonton 2018; Daidone et al. 2017; Pace et al. 2018).[53] And the take-up of credit is more successful when bundled with insurance (Carter, Cheng, and Sarris 2016). Outside of agriculture, supplementation of temporary cash transfers to poor and vulnerable people with a package of an asset grant, entrepreneurship training and support, life skills coaching, and access to savings accounts (known as BRAC's ultra-poor graduation approach, pioneered in Bangladesh) produced sustainable improvements in livelihoods (Banerjee et al. 2015).

Although conceptually and empirically appealing, an integrated approach is not guaranteed to succeed, however. With integration comes complexity, which challenges effective implementation especially in weak-capacity, poor institutional environments. Integrated rural development was popular in the 1970s but not successful. It was top-down and not sufficiently context-specific or locally owned. The Millennium Villages Project (MVP) provides a more recent variant of the integrated rural development approach with outcomes that were possibly more positive although still hard to prove in the absence of rigorous evaluation (Mitchell et al. 2018).

In the face of limited resources, integrated approaches often also entail thorny choices about which people, places, or crops or products to target first—with political dynamics often pressuring policy makers not to provide more than one program to the same beneficiaries, even when the complementarities are clear. Overall, more experimentation, learning, and evaluation of integrated approaches is needed. This is also the direction in which Africa's agriculture and food security policies and research have been moving.

Integration can happen around a *population group* such as the BRAC graduation approach; a *place or territory* such as the MVP and territorial development; or around a *product* such as value chain development (VCD). While not mutually exclusive, each entry point is different. In agriculture, a lot of attention goes to VCD. The next section explores the extent to which this can also help the poor. The first two integration channels are further elaborated in chapter 4 ("Moving to Jobs Off the Farm").

Inclusive Value Chain Development as Response

The Potential of VCD for the Poor

Value chains concern the organization of the flow of a product between producers and final consumers (from farm to fork). They range from full vertical integration of all steps in one firm (production, storage, processing, transport, and marketing) over either formal and hierarchical or more informal and hybrid contracting arrangements between the different actors, to fully atomistic chains with many agents at each stage. Value chains can be either long (stretching over long distances, with much value added in between) or short (for example, local farmers markets, often with little value added after production).

VCD interventions aim to reduce the transaction costs and upgrade the efficiency in the chain. They can focus on

- *Improving the overall business environment* in which the chain operates;[54]
- *Facilitating coordination between stakeholders* through multistakeholder platforms; and
- *Providing temporary support to different actors* (such as farmers, processors, input and service providers,[55] or marketing companies) or to groups of actors within an overall strategic framework of support to the chain.

Support to farmers can include training, activities to help farmers organize themselves in groups for collective exchange in input and output markets, and improvements in farmer links with other upstream and downstream actors in the chain (for example, by representing them in coordination and negotiation with these actors). Sustainability of such links once the third-party support phases out is often a challenge.

The essence is to start from consumer demand (expected volumes as well as quality and standard requirements), to involve all actors, and to consider their constraints to meet this demand. Coordination and integration can be initiated not only by the different actors in the chain, including producers, but also by agents external to the chain and governments as well as nongovernmental organizations (NGOs) and international organizations. External agents are in principle well placed to help overcome the coordination costs and broker an equitable distribution of the value added. They can also provide complementary public goods and services (Swinnen and Kuijpers 2017).

Integrated VCD models that "link" smallholder producers with input companies, processing factories, or marketing agents through contractual arrangements are increasingly advanced as a market-based, organizational solution to help smallholder farmers overcome the multiple constraints they face in accessing technology and (higher-value) markets. In these arrangements, a steady supply of higher volumes of more consistent quality can be assured by the stakeholders in the chain in return for access to credit, inputs and technology, agronomic knowledge, price premiums, and a reduction of production and market risks for the producers. Risks are shared, value can be added, and smallholder producers get access to both new (domestic and export) and higher-value markets.

Theoretical and empirical evidence suggests that integrated value chains are more likely to be effective for nonstaple crops (such as cash crops, fruits, and vegetables) and agricultural products with high potential for value addition (such as dairy and meat) than for staple crops (Swinnen, Vandeplas, and Maertens 2010). This is partly because higher value addition facilitates incentive-compatible contract design, with buyers (exporters, processors, or supermarkets) that are concerned about consistent supplies, quality attributes, and traceability more willing and able to pay price premiums to farmers, thereby increasing contract adherence. Also, when the specificity of the contract, technology, or product is higher (that is, if the specific value of the product is lower for alternative buyers or farmers are locked in through crop- or market-specific investments), the cost of contract breach is higher. Other factors, such as product characteristics (perishability and storage requirements) and economies of scale in processing, play as well (Swinnen and Kuijpers 2017).

VCD thus opens up opportunities, especially to connect smallholders to the increasing urban demand for nonstaple foods as well as to export markets (traditional and nontraditional). The poor can gain directly by participating as self-employed, smallholder (contract) producers. But they can also benefit indirectly by being employed as wage workers on larger farms or in the agro-food sector or through spillover effects in the local economy (Deininger and Xia 2018; Devaux et al. 2016; Swinnen and Kuijpers 2017).

Direct gains by the poor as smallholder producers are more likely when smallholder production is dominant in the region (that is, when larger farms are absent) and when sourcing from smallholders is not more expensive. The latter happens, for example, when production is more labor-intensive, as for some cash crops (for example, tobacco) that require care in handling and have fewer opportunities for substituting capital for labor (Devaux et al. 2016) or dairy (Janssen and Swinnen 2017). In Mozambique, South Africa, and Zambia, commercial poultry industries are also developing that use contract farming to buy broilers from smallholder farmers (Devaux et al. 2016; Otsuka, Nakano, and Takahashi 2016).

The size of gains to the poor further depends on their bargaining power in claiming their share of the value added. When there is significant demand for the produce, the farmer's holdup opportunities (side-selling or diversion of value-chain-provided inputs or technology) are larger and their bargaining powers bigger. Similarly, the buyer's holdup opportunities are lower when there are more alternative buyers, fewer alternative suppliers, few product-specific requirements (that is, the product's valuation by other buyers is higher), and the transferred technology has long-term effects.

Producer organizations can increase bargaining power. They can also help reduce transaction costs (searching, screening, contracting, and contract enforcement), which makes them more attractive parties to contract with. They can coordinate contractual arrangements, establish trust against contract breach, and facilitate aggregation and delivery to processors or buyers (IFC 2019). The need for farmer organizations to coordinate and provide input and service delivery is especially important when institutions and the public provision of rural services are weak, as in postconflict settings (Ragasa and Golan 2014). Given weak rural infrastructure and marketing systems, complementary public investments are often needed to further incentivize companies in the downstream supply systems, as documented in the dairy sector (Chagwiza, Muradian, and Ruben 2016; Janssen and Swinnen 2017; Kilelu, Klerkx, and Leeuwis 2017).

Numerous studies show positive effects of contract farming on farmgate prices, farm productivity, and farm household income (Otsuka, Nakano, and Takahashi 2016; Swinnen and Kuijpers 2017; Wang, Wang, and Delgado 2014). A review of 30 empirical studies situates income gains in the range of 25–75 percent (Minot and Sawyer 2016). Similar conclusions were reached by other review studies (Otsuka, Nakano, and Takahashi 2016; Swinnen and Kuijpers 2017; Wang, Wang, and Delgado 2014). This finding holds promise, but vexing methodological issues remain to establish causality (Bellemare and Bloem 2018).

At the same time, the evidence also suggests that it is typically the larger, more commercially oriented smallholders that participate in contract farming; the costs of transacting with them are smaller (Otsuka, Nakano, and Takahashi 2016; Ton et al. 2018). Similarly, evidence confirms that farm organizations (that is, horizontal coordination) can play a role in integrating smallholders in modern value chains and enhancing their incomes (Ito, Bao, and Su 2012; Ma and Abdulai 2016; Verhofstadt and Maertens 2015). Yet farm organizations often also struggle to function well and, like in contract farming, it is the relatively better-off farmers who tend to participate in producer organizations (Bernard and Spielman 2009; Fischer and Qaim 2012; Mojo, Fischer, and Degefa 2017).

That it is mainly the larger smallholders that benefit directly does not have to be a concern, because most of the benefits for the poorest are expected to happen through spillover effects in the local economy through increased demand for agricultural labor as well as consumption links, as documented earlier regarding Tanzania (Chamberlin and Jayne 2017). This is an area for further policy attention and empirical inquiry.

Similarly, if quality or volume requirements emanating from consumer demand (for example, for export vegetables), economies of scale in processing (for pork or beef), or timeliness of processing (sugarcane) necessitate a tight control over the production process, vertical integration into large companies is more likely to occur (Masters et al. 2013; Otsuka, Nakano, and Takahashi 2016; Swinnen and Kuijpers 2017). The poor can again benefit as wage workers or from spillovers in the local economy (off-farm employment, discussed in chapter 4), which is more likely if the employment is complementary to their small-farm activities and requires relatively low skills. Important poverty-reducing effects through wage employment on horticulture-exporting estate farms have been documented in Senegal, for example (Van den Broeck, Swinnen, and Maertens 2017).

Experimenting with VCD in Staples

As discussed, staple crops are typically less suitable for VCD. Homogeneous product dimensions leave little room for quality upgrading and value addition. This reduces buyers' capacity and incentives to provide a price premium to incentivize producers to ensure a consistent supply of high quality and volume to run their factories or cater to their urban markets (Devaux et al. 2016; Otsuka, Nakano, and Takahashi 2016; Ragasa, Lambrecht, and Kufoalor 2018). There are also many potential buyers, making contract enforcement much more difficult. It increases the risk of (opportunistic) side-selling as well as strategic contract breach by buyers, an equally frequent occurrence (Maertens and Vande Velde 2017; Swinnen and Kuijpers 2017).[56] Limited economies of scale in procurement, storage, processing, and marketing further provide few incentives for traders and processors to invest in coordinating the chain (Fischer and Qaim 2012; Poulton, Dorward, and Kydd 2010).

Income growth and urbanization, however, have added complexity to the quality and quantity requirements for staple foods. This has induced the need for better and more advanced forms of coordination to capture the new market opportunities and has increased interest in VCD and contract farming as market-driven organizational solutions for poorer smallholders to capture those opportunities. Staple crops with higher income elasticities (for example, teff in Ethiopia and rice in Côte d'Ivoire) are increasingly organized in short value chains (instead of atomistic markets) to meet the more-demanding domestic urban market.

Local procurement of basic staples by food relief institutions (for example, the World Food Programme [WFP]) and the expansion of regional supermarkets (Barrientos et al. 2016; IFAD 2016) add further demand for greater certainty in quantity and quality. Similarly, greater volumes of staples of higher and consistent quality are needed as feedstock for the growing beer and livestock sectors (Swinnen and Kuijpers 2017).

VCD initiatives in staple crops (especially rice and maize) are emerging in response. An evaluation from Benin shows how smallholder participants in rice contract farming, facilitated by a French research institute, sustainably increased the area cultivated, intensified their rice productions, commercialized more of their output, and eventually increased farm income (Maertens and Vande Velde 2017). However, this experience has not been shared in Ghana, where smallholder participants in maize contract farming, initiated by private sector input providers, saw their maize profits decline because elevated production costs were not sufficiently offset by higher productivity (Ragasa, Lambrecht, and Kufoalor 2018).

Rice contract farming also has arguably more scope for success than maize because greater potential for quality differentiation enables rice buyers to pay a price premium, hence reducing the risk of side-selling (Maertens and Vande Velde 2017; Ragasa, Lambrecht, and Kufoalor 2018). Neutral or third-party intermediaries coordinating the chain can further establish more trust and contract commitment between farmers and different stakeholders (Ashraf, Giné, and Karlan 2009; Poulton, Dorward, and Kydd 2010). In the Purchase for Progress (P4P) intervention, the WFP took the role of coordinating supply- and demand-side interventions by investing in warehouse facilities and warehouse receipt systems and training farmers on a host of topics, while ensuring demand through WFP-guaranteed purchasing contracts at a preset or minimum price. Smallholder farm participants in the P4P program in Tanzania intensified and commercialized more of their maize and bean production, though household incomes did not change (Lentz and Upton 2016).

Overall, much remains to be learned, and more experimentation and systematic learning with VCD in staples is needed. The margins of error are often not that large. Proper intervention design; effective, predictable implementation; and a stable policy environment are very much needed for the contracting schemes to be profitable and sustainable.

In Ghana, for example, lower implicit interest rates and the provision of better locally adapted technological packages (which are available) could already make the contracting schemes more profitable (Ragasa, Lambrecht, and Kufoalor 2018). The P4P purchases in Tanzania, on the other hand, were irregular across years. Regular communication between the scheme operators and the contracted farmers is also required to maintain the links and trust. Here, ICT tools can help. In Tanzania, export bans and other national initiatives have at times interfered with program implementation. Finally, clear exit strategies are needed when third-party funders are involved to ensure sustainability (Swinnen and Kuijpers 2017).

These considerations are particularly pertinent when it comes to VCD for smallholder staple crops, given the continuing challenges to access capital, technology, and markets and the generally lesser incentives for agribusiness firms up and down the chain to engage in contract farming to begin with.

The Need for Complementary Public Goods, Especially for Staples

An important public policy and investment agenda remains for African agriculture, particularly for staples, and to support VCD more generally. This agenda concerns not only an appropriate regulatory and institutional framework but also higher public spending and a more effective composition of that spending. Fundamentals 4 ("Politics and Pro-Poor Policies") and chapter 6 ("Mobilizing Resources for the Poor") review the political economy and fiscal space to increase pro-poor spending overall. Key agriculture-related items are highlighted here.

Throughout history, agriculture spending in Africa as a share of total public spending has been substantially smaller than in East Asia and the Pacific (figure 3.5). Hovering between 2 percent and 3 percent during most of the 1990s and 2000s (except in 1999), it increased slightly to almost 4 percent toward the end of the 2000s in response to the world food crisis. It has slowed down to pre-2008 levels since and has remained well below the Comprehensive Africa Agriculture Development Programme (CAADP) commitment of 10 percent.

Furthermore, long-term improvements in agricultural labor productivity and poverty reduction especially need investments in public goods that help to overcome market failures. For example, econometric analysis shows how, in Latin America, higher shares of public spending on *private* goods (relative to *public* goods) in governments' fiscal budgets even negatively affected rural incomes and poverty reduction (López and Galinato 2007).[57]

Recent country experience from Africa supports the importance of spending on rural public goods. Ethiopia and Rwanda, for example, have invested more intensively in the provision of rural public goods like extension and agricultural infrastructure as well as, in the case of Ethiopia, productive rural safety nets. Malawi and Zambia, on the other hand, have focused on private goods instead, most notably input subsidies (and maize floor prices above the market price in Zambia). Aggregate cereal output (and yields) increased substantially in all four countries. In Ethiopia and Rwanda, this increase has come along with a substantial

FIGURE 3.5 Agriculture spending in Africa substantially lags spending in East Asia and the Pacific

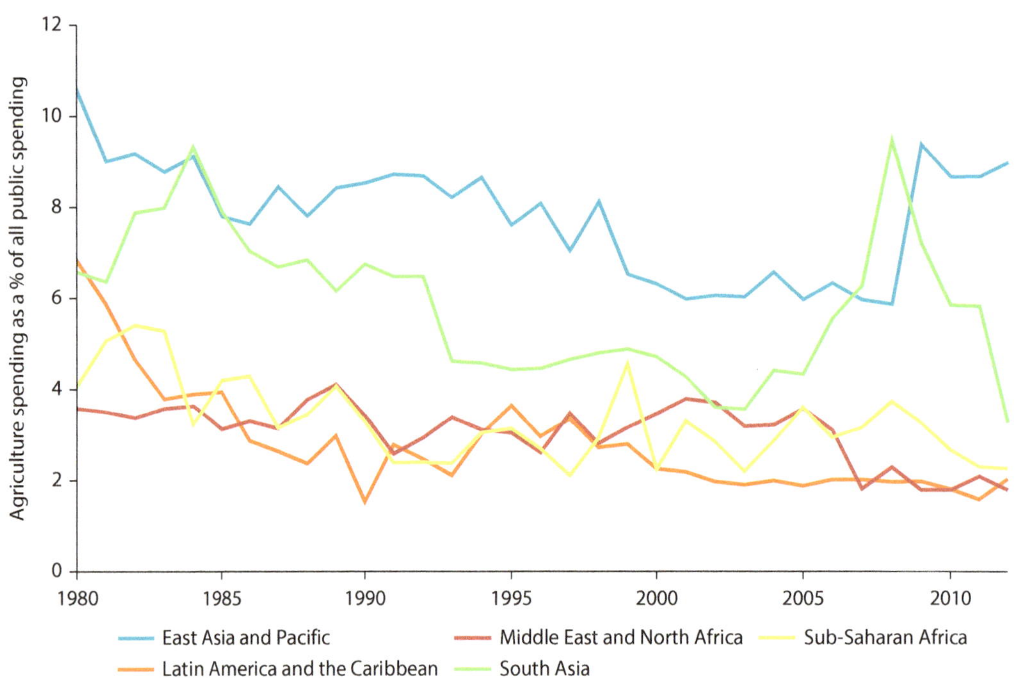

Source: Calculations based on 2015 Statistics on Public Expenditures for Economic Development (SPEED) country-level dataset, International Food Policy Research Institute (IFPRI).

decline in poverty, but not in Malawi and Zambia, where most of the subsidies are captured by the larger farmers. The policies are also fiscally unsustainable or only affordable during times of high commodity prices, as in Zambia (World Bank 2014).

A review of the evolution of public spending patterns in 13 African countries shows that input subsidies are still the most important public spending item (Pernechele, Balié, and Ghins 2018, figure 30)—higher than spending on knowledge dissemination, rural infrastructure (rural roads and irrigation), agricultural R&D, and market infrastructure. The reasons behind this are discussed further in chapter 6 ("Mobilizing Resources for the Poor").

From a poverty perspective, important areas for public spending and policy attention in Africa's agriculture include the several described below.

Agricultural research, development, and extension. Africa's agricultural scientific knowledge base remains largely insufficient and underfunded (Barrett et al. 2017). Less than 2 percent of agricultural gross domestic product (GDP) is spent on agricultural research. Priorities include the breeding of high-yielding, climate-robust staple crop varieties; development of more-productive animal breeds and feeds (regarding new poultry breeds, see Narrod, Pray, and Tiongco [2008]); access to small-scale, locally adapted agricultural equipment; and the development of rural financial products that are adapted to the seasonality in agricultural production.

More decentralized, demand-driven extension systems that improve the content and the speed of how agricultural information and technologies are transmitted to farmers are also needed. This is especially critical for increasing staple crop productivity, which typically does not benefit much from private investment in technology development or technology transfer. Mobile-phone-based extension and social media can help. They provide cost-effective ways to share agricultural knowledge and improve adoption rates that increase inclusion of youth as well as farmers who are poor, illiterate, or female (ACET 2017; Aker 2011; Cole and Fernando 2014; Fu and Akter 2016). However, greater use of these new digital technologies requires complementary public investment and adequate policies (see further below and in Fundamentals 3, "Leapfrogging with Technology (and Trade)").

Policy integration on input modernization and land and water management. Much is to be gained from combining policies that foster modern input adoption (such as seeds and inorganic fertilizer) with management techniques that improve land quality (such as improving organic-matter content from integrated soil fertility management or legume intercropping) as well as water availability (Jayne and Rashid 2013; Otsuka and Muraoka 2017; Tonitto and Ricker-Gilbert 2016).

Small-scale, participatory, local irrigation systems have been identified as the most cost-effective approach to expansion of irrigation systems in Africa, yielding higher rates of return than centrally organized, large-scale irrigation projects (Burney, Naylor, and Postel 2013; You et al. 2011). Democratization (or individualization) of water management (for example, through water user associations) is key to make smallholder-scale irrigation more attractive, and its importance is recently on the rise in Africa (De Fraiture and Giordano 2014). Experiments with low-cost, solar-powered pumps linked with small-scale and low-pressure drip irrigation show promising results while also limiting the environmental impact in light of climate change (Burney and Naylor 2012; Mashnik et al. 2017). These solutions need to be coupled with financial innovations (on-demand service payment), secure water and land rights, and proper training of farmers.

Complementary public investments in rural infrastructure, including ICT. Investments in rural roads, storage facilities, aggregation centers, and warehouses reduce transaction costs, allowing more value to be captured not only by smallholder farmers but also by small and medium-size agro-enterprises (Devaux et al. 2016). Such investment also promotes an enabling environment for "crowding in" private investment in processing and storage by midstream players (as observed in Ethiopia and India) and for VCD, generating off-farm employment (ACET 2017; Goyal and Nash 2017), as further discussed in chapter 4 ("Moving to Jobs Off the Farm").

Digital services can dramatically reduce transaction costs. Farmers and warehouses can be linked to electronic commodity exchange platforms via digital services. Electronic platforms can also increase the speed of transactions, thereby also reducing the strategic behavior of side-selling (ACET 2017). In addition, ICT can support smallholder livestock production in rural areas to satisfy quality requirements in export markets. Radio frequency identification (RFID) chips, for example, are being used in the beef sector in Botswana and Namibia to improve the ability to track and monitor animals' health status and movement (Deichmann, Goyal, and Mishra 2016; World Bank 2016). Yet the extent to which these services also benefit the poor directly will critically depend on whether they have access to the digital infrastructures (such as mobile money and the internet) and the human skills to operate them. Making these widely available is a high-priority public policy agenda (as covered in Fundamentals 3, "Leapfrogging with Technology (and Trade)").

Support for smallholder livestock production. Although increasing smallholder staple crop productivity remains a first-order priority, smallholder livestock production is also widespread among the poor, with productivity levels equally low. Much remains to be gained from public facilitation of access to improved breeds and animal feed, animal health service, access to water and insurance, and risk-coping mechanisms (as covered in chapter 5, "Managing Risks and Conflict"). VCD interventions can further facilitate access to feed and markets, including for large-scale livestock production.

Development of a supportive regulatory and institutional environment. In the absence of an effective legal system, alternative dispute settlement institutions can, for example, help address the challenge of contract enforcement (Swinnen and Kuijpers 2017). The liberalization of input markets (especially for seed) and the promotion of interregional trade (for example, for animal feed) by reducing the cost of trade and transport are important examples of how macroeconomic policies can contribute to VCD (Swinnen and Kuijpers 2017).[58]

Notes

1. Across Africa, the food demand for energy production remains limited, mainly concentrated in southern and western Africa and focused on sugar (ethanol) and vegetable oil (biodiesel) as feedstock. The use of food staple crops (such as maize) as feedstock for energy production is uncommon and in many cases prohibited (OECD and FAO 2016).
2. Ethiopia, South Africa, Uganda, and Zambia are traditional surplus producers of maize; Kenya and Zimbabwe represent the largest deficit markets (OECD and FAO 2016).
3. Net imports of maize, wheat, and rice have risen to about 20 million, 47 million, and 12 million tons a year, respectively, up from 7 million, 22 million, and 4 million tons in the mid-1990s (FAOSTAT database, http://www.fao.org/faostat/). This reflects the rising (urban) demand for more convenient staples (rice and wheat) and meat (maize being an important animal feed).
4. This includes revenues from agriculture as well as manufacturing and primary natural resources but not from services such as tourism. The latter is an important source of foreign exchange in some of the island countries. During 2011–13, the latest period for which the food import-to-merchandise export ratio is available, there were 10 countries for which the food import-to-merchandise export ratio exceeded 50 percent; only 2 of these were resource-rich: Liberia (61 percent) and Sierra Leone (76 percent), mainly because of rice imports for urban consumption. Data are from the World Development Indicators database.

5. The case for wheat is less clear. Wheat is a temperate climate crop and cannot be grown in many parts of Africa. Production has been mainly confined to the highlands in East Africa, which have cooler climates, and the temperate zones in southern Africa. These lands are not abundant, and expanding wheat production must largely come through an increase in yields. It is unlikely to suffice to meet the growing demand. Mixing cassava or sorghum with wheat flour (up to 30 percent can be substituted) provides one way to reduce growing wheat demand. This is now mandated in Nigeria (ACET 2017). Wheat is also almost exclusively grown by large-scale, commercial farmers except in Ethiopia (Mason, Jayne, and Shiferaw 2015).
6. Downward pressures on world food prices from Organisation for Economic Co-operation and Development (OECD) agricultural policies have been largely eliminated. OECD members have decoupled public support to farmers from their production decisions, most notably in the European Union (EU) (Brooks 2014; Bureau and Swinnen 2018; World Bank 2007). EU tariff and quota free market access granted to the 50 poorest countries following a series of agreements (including the "Everything But Arms" initiative) further facilitates the expansion of agricultural exports. In practice, only a narrow range of products have benefited so far, such as sugar, given the oft limited capacity to meet the sanitary and phytosanitary (SPS) regulations. This has been especially challenging for the exports of animal products that need to be free from contagious disease carriers (for example, foot-and-mouth disease, African swine fever, and so on). At the same time, EU imports from developing countries of several higher-value agricultural products with stringent SPS standards, such as fruits and vegetables, but also fish, have dramatically increased (Bureau and Swinnen 2018).
7. The RRA is a ratio of the nominal rate of assistance (NRA) to agriculture over nonagriculture. The NRA is a measure of output price deviations from those determined by the international markets through trade policies, existing market structures affecting the performance of the value chains, or budgetary allocations to a commodity (for example, input subsidies) (Anderson 2009; Pernechele, Balié, and Ghins 2018).
8. The NRP indicates whether the policy environment and market dynamics provide price incentives or disincentives to produce or commercialize, depending on whether the ratio is positive or negative, respectively. It excludes direct support to commodities. Staple crops have never been much taxed or protected except during short periods of price destabilization. The NRP average of 10 percent masks substantial differences in NRPs across the 14 African countries and commodities studied (Pernechele, Balié, and Ghins 2018). The overall average was 10 percent, but it was 20 percent for East African countries. This difference was mainly due to the high import tariff of 75 percent on rice following the recognition of rice as a sensitive product by the East African Community (OECD and FAO 2016). The rice import tariff rate in West Africa, on the other hand, has eventually been set at only 10 percent.
9. Per capita gross agricultural output for cereals expanded at 4.7 percent annually during 2007–12, compared with 0.4 percent before the world food crisis. After the food crisis, cereal per capita output also grew much faster than the output of the other crops, which did not benefit from the same improvement in price incentives and input subsidization. Gross annual output of roots and tubers, industrial crops, and fruits and vegetables grew by 2.2 percent, 1.6 percent, and 1.6 percent per capita, respectively (Janssen and Swinnen 2016).
10. Intraregional agricultural trade has so far been especially important in southern Africa. It is about three times as large as in the rest of Africa and accounted for the lion's share of the doubling of intra-African agricultural exports and imports between 2003 and 2016 (De Pinto and Ulimwengu 2017). There are also food trade flows (maize) between South Africa and western Africa through maritime routes and between larger and smaller western African countries. Recent analysis of Africa's maize markets concludes that although most local price series are more sensitive to price developments in regional neighbors than to global shocks, the integration of domestic maize markets within the continent (and with the global market) is generally still weak (Pierre and Kaminski 2019).

11. The agreement, the 2003 Maputo Declaration on Agriculture and Food Security, was reaffirmed in the 2013 Malabo Declaration on Accelerated Agricultural Growth. Progress toward achieving these targets is tracked under the Comprehensive Africa Agriculture Development Programme (CAADP): http://www.resakss.org/.
12. Field trials of wheat, rice, maize, and soybeans showed that higher CO_2 levels significantly reduced the levels of the essential nutrients iron and zinc while also cutting protein levels. In environments where meat consumption is still limited and C_3 grains and legumes are the primary dietary source of zinc and iron, this exacerbates the widespread challenge of zinc and iron deficiencies, which harm pregnant women and the development of babies and undermine learning (Luo et al. 2012; Myers et al. 2014).
13. The destruction of food crops ("scorched earth tactics") can be a military tactic applied by both sides of the conflict, but is often used by the government as a means of undermining support for insurgents. It has a long history, often with disastrous effects on the rural population.
14. The increase in conflict intensity outside the harvest season, when demand for agricultural labor is lower (as observed in Afghanistan, Iraq, and Pakistan), is just one example of this (Guardado and Pennings 2017). But the importance for conflict prevention of reduced incentives for individuals to engage in criminal activities has been observed more widely (Collier and Hoeffler 1998; Miguel, Satyanath, and Sergenti 2004).
15. Food prices are one obvious channel through which agriculture affects conflict. The effects, however, are difficult to establish clearly and vary widely depending on the marketing status of the populations and countries affected (net buyer or seller, net importer or exporter) and the nature of the change (permanent or transitory) (Martin-Shields and Stojetz 2019). Most evidence links food prices to urban unrest, for example, not so much to violent conflict, typically driven by prices of basic staples such as wheat and rice (Van Weezel 2016), with some arguing that it is food price levels that matter in this context more than food price volatility (Bellemare 2015). In food-producing areas, global food price shocks are found to reduce large-scale conflict over land and the control of territory, while they increase small-scale conflict over the appropriation of the surplus (McGuirk and Burke 2017). Food-exporting countries often also see a deterioration in the quality of their political institutions (away from democracy) as global food prices increase. An increase in average income growth following the food price increase in these exporting countries comes along with a widening gap between rich and poor, which induces the elites to suppress demonstrations and riots and reduce de jure political rights to protect their new economic surplus (Arezki and Brueckner 2014).
16. For lessons on how best to administer post-conflict agricultural programs to rekindle production, see Birner, Cohen, and Ilukor (2011) and Giordano (2011).
17. Whether the promotion of smallholder livestock production also leads to increased animal-sourced food consumption and better child nutrition is less clear. The higher-value livestock products are often also sold (Headey, Hirvonen, and Hoddinott 2018).
18. When food markets are incomplete or unreliable, farmers often diversify their cropping mix, allocating part of it to food crops for food security, even though the returns from export crop production may be higher (De Janvry, Fafchamps, and Sadoulet 1991).
19. For a more formal discussion, see Christiaensen, De Weerdt, and Kanbur (2018).
20. Net food sellers may even lose, if prices decline more rapidly than productivity increases.
21. Purely subsistence households are rare. In Côte d'Ivoire, for example, four out of five agricultural smallholders sell at least some of their output, with one in five reporting that they sell their complete harvest (Christiaensen and Premand 2017).
22. With an increasing share of food being purchased, also in rural areas, commercial biofortification of purchased staple flours and processed foods is arguably the more cost-effective way to address widespread micronutrient deficiency in the absence of dietary diversification. Nonetheless, several authors have also highlighted the potential of direct biofortification of staples through breeding or the application of micronutrient fertilizer, especially to address micronutrient deficiency among poor, remote populations that are often semisubsistence. Examples include

iron-biofortified beans and millet; Vitamin A-biofortified maize, sweet potato, and cassava (such as orange sweet potato, orange maize, and yellow cassava); and zinc-biofortified rice and wheat. HarvestPlus is the global program that leads the development of staple biofortification. But many challenges remain, including to reach scale (Bouis and Saltzman 2017; De Valença et al. 2017; Vasconcelos, Gruissem, and Bhullar 2017).

23. These simulations abstract from the effects of population growth, which, at current levels of income, would tie up even more labor in staple crop production. Given data constraints on labor input in livestock rearing and dairy production, the additional labor needs for meat and dairy production are not calculated.
24. The simulations assume constant labor-land ratios. With land increasingly scarce (and staples especially land-intensive), it is imperative to raise yields to meet the additional demand for staples.
25. Given growing domestic production, rice imports in Tanzania have remained limited to less than 1 percent of total food import (in value).
26. In Tanzania, elasticities for consumed own production of nonperishable foods (mostly maize and other grains as well as pulses) are still well above 1 (1.37) for the poorest tercile in rural areas. They are slightly negative for the middle (–0.01) and top tercile (–0.1), suggesting that market participation (sales of own staple crop production) occurs only after basic staple needs have been met (Tschirley et al. 2017).
27. Given the complexity of intrahousehold power dynamics, it is not straightforward, however, that promotion of livestock that involves women also effectively raises their hold over the additional income and improves their livelihoods and thus the welfare of their children (FAO 2013).
28. The export value of Ethiopia's flower industry increased from US$0.4 million in 2000 to US$245 in 2013/14 (Suzuki, Mano, and Abebe 2018), and 35,000 wage jobs were added, predominantly for poor women. During this period, Ethiopia's population continued to expand by 2 million a year.
29. This approach does not carry over to megafarms. These typically arise in noncompetitive fashion and follow a different rationale than improving efficiency, such as food security in the lease-holding country, even at the expense of efficiency (Collier and Dercon 2014).
30. Arguably, this may still reflect misallocation due to factor market imperfections, as observed in Pakistan (Heltberg 1998). In contrast, in Madagascar, only a small proportion of the inverse productivity-to-farm size relationship is explained by market imperfections, each time controlling for heterogeneity in soil quality (Barrett, Bellemare, and Hou 2010).
31. These estates have been an important part of Malawi's rural economy for a long time (covering 1.35 million hectares or about 25 percent of the country's arable area).
32. Farm consolidation only started to happen later in the development process, when yield increases (at first), and land value addition through crop and livestock diversification (thereafter), became too small to compensate for and compete with rising rural wages and earning opportunities off the farm (Christiaensen 2012).
33. Eighty percent of the farms cultivated are under 2 hectares, and the number of large commercial farmers is still low (Masters et al. 2013).
34. These include Angola, Chad, the Democratic Republic of Congo, Madagascar, Mozambique, Sudan, Tanzania, and Zambia (Deininger and Byerlee 2012). Indications are that a similar trend has happened in Malawi (Anseeuw et al. 2016), with roughly 300,000 hectares, or slightly more than 10 percent of the cultivated area, newly acquired by medium- to large-scale holders in Malawi. This is truly remarkable given that most of the people face acute land scarcity (Binswanger-Mkhize and Savastano 2017).
35. The savanna area of Africa is often considered an underdeveloped region with potential to bring uncultivated land into agricultural production. It has recently attracted investments—for example, the ProSavana project in Mozambique (ACET 2017). What is classified here as area with high agroecological potential includes almost two-thirds (62 percent) of Africa's savanna (using MODIS land cover classification: https://modis.gsfc.nasa.gov/data/dataprod/mod12.php).
36. Annual agricultural labor productivity growth in low-income countries with good agricultural potential was slightly negative

during 1961–2012 (–0.04 percent). This is consistent with the higher poverty rates and poverty density observed in Africa's more-fertile areas (figure 3.2). In low-income countries with less agricultural potential, annual agricultural labor productivity growth reached 0.32 percent (Benin and Nin-Pratt 2016). It was higher in Africa's middle-income countries (2.14 percent).

37. In Africa, agricultural value added per agricultural worker reached US$1,305 (2010 US$) during 2014–16 (or about US$3.57 a day), according to the World Development Indicators database (http://wdi.worldbank.org). This is about a third of the level in East Asia and the Pacific (US$3,867) and less than a fifth of the level in Latin America and the Caribbean (US$6,925).
38. Only a minority of African countries (14) have higher agricultural labor productivity than the African average (most notably, South Africa; other countries in southern Africa with high land inequality such as Lesotho and Namibia; and some oil-rich, middle-income countries with capital-intensive agriculture such as Gabon and Sudan). In 15 countries, agricultural labor productivity was even lower than US$730 (2010 US$), equating to US$2 a day per agricultural worker. These are also among Africa's poorest countries (among the 10 poorest in terms of either head counts or head count ratios). Nigeria, which more than doubled its agricultural labor productivity over the past 15 years to US$5,515 (2010 US$) is the main exception.
39. From a poverty perspective, as opposed to an aggregate sectoral or growth perspective, it is the return to labor and thus the partial measure of productivity (agricultural labor productivity) that is most of interest, as opposed to the more frequently reported total factor productivity, a summary measure of the joint return to all production factors. Labor is the main asset of the poor (together with land).
40. Across nine countries, farming takes up between 42.1 percent of all jobs in Nigeria and 67.4 percent in Rwanda. Using the full-time equivalent approach, this drops to between 33.7 percent in Nigeria and 54 percent in Rwanda (Yeboah and Jayne 2018).
41. Between 1985 and 2012, agricultural output in Africa grew 3.3 percent per year. Expansion of land under cultivation contributed the bulk, 2.1 percent; total factor productivity growth, 1 percent; and input intensification, only 0.2 percent (Goyal and Nash 2017). Cultivated land increased by 40.3 percent between 1990 and 2012, compared with 19.3 percent between 1961 and 1990 (Headey 2016).
42. Headey (2016, table 3) defines land-constrained countries as those with a rural population density of more than 100 persons per square kilometer of arable land. They include, among others, Rwanda (420 rural people per square kilometer), Burundi (339), the Comoros (309), Malawi (209), Uganda (201), Ethiopia (194), Benin (152), Kenya (113), The Gambia (108), Nigeria (106), and Sierra Leone (104).
43. Land-abundant countries include Angola, Chad, the Democratic Republic of Congo, Madagascar, Mozambique, Sudan, Tanzania, and Zambia (Deininger and Byerlee 2012).
44. Spatial clustering of the rural population exacerbates the challenge to farm expansion. Eighty-two percent of Africa's rural population resides on 20 percent of the arable rural land, resulting in an average population density of 197 rural people per square kilometer in these areas, compared with 50 rural people per square kilometer of arable land in the continent as a whole (Jayne, Chamberlin, and Headey 2014). This concentration also speaks to the limited ability or willingness of rural labor in densely populated areas to relocate to any of the country's land "surplus" areas.
45. Land rentals, rather than land sales, are typically the first line of response.
46. It is profitability that matters for the adoption of new technology, not just the more commonly studied effect on yields. The wide adoption of improved chickpea by smallholders in Ethiopia serves as an important reminder of this basic but oft-neglected insight (Michler et al. 2018). Adoption was widespread not because of higher yields—yield gains were limited—but because of higher profitability following reallocation away from crops that were costlier to produce (such as maize) as well as from crops that commanded lower prices when sold (such as local chickpea varieties or other staple crops). The dramatic increase in herbicide use in a number of countries also stands out. The production of generic variants of herbicides after the expiration of patent protection

for key herbicides such as glyphosate has substantially reduced the cost. At the same time, rural wages have been rising—partly because of increased school enrollment of children—making the use of herbicide more profitable (Haggblade et al. 2017).

47. In Ethiopia, transporting a bag of fertilizer from the local distribution center to the farm costs about as much as transporting it more than 1,000 kilometers from the international port to the local distribution center (Minten, Koru, and Stifel 2013). Similar observations about prohibitively high last-mile transportation costs have been made for Nigeria (Liverpool-Tasie et al. 2017).
48. The higher productivity of improved breeds, for example, is conditional on the use of quality feed and proper livestock-rearing knowledge and management (ACET 2017).
49. Mechanization in early stages of agricultural development often kicks off with mechanizing the labor-intensive preharvest activities, such as plowing the fields using tractors. The return to investments in mechanizing land preparation are large and hence warrant the initial high cost. As farming systems evolve, the mechanization of skill-intensive activities will take off more slowly because the large fixed costs make mechanized harvesting rarely profitable (Binswanger 1986; Pingali, Bigot, and Binswanger 1987).
50. Hiring services through private owner-operators are essential in overcoming failures of machinery equipment in the rural market (Diao et al., forthcoming). While hiring-in services might be the only access to mechanization for commercial smallholder farmers, hiring-out (outsourcing) services are essential to ensure the profitability of machine equipment owned by medium-size or large farmers.
51. Adoption of mechanization has increased, for example, in the Western Highlands of Ethiopia, the central and northern zones of Nigeria, the central and southern provinces of Zambia, the northern regions in Ghana, and the commercial farming sector in Zimbabwe (Diao, Silver, and Takeshima 2016).
52. In the past, economic policy research has also been preoccupied with the identification and quantification of the effects of one or two constraints, rather than with the conditions under which the constraints bind and the possible synergies from relieving several constraints simultaneously. In recent years, research interest in measuring the joint effect of interventions has been rising.
53. No complementarities were found between the public works programs and the Farm Input Subsidy Program in Malawi (Beegle, Galasso, and Goldberg 2017).
54. These interventions are typically not recognized as VCD interventions because their benefits—such as a more transparent regulatory environment and better-functioning judiciary systems—are not limited to the particular value chain. Yet they are an important tool in improving the functioning of value chains. They lower transaction costs and reduce holdup problems.
55. Popular in this regard is the use of public finance to leverage private sector investment, especially foreign direct investment (FDI) (by banks, fertilizer companies, or commodity companies) through de-risking. Risk guarantees or matching grants could, for example, be provided to banks, fertilizer companies, commodity traders (for example, Cargill), or commodity companies to extend input credit to smallholders or to invest in small and medium enterprises (SMEs) in agriprocessing, cold storage, or wholesaling and retailing. Concerns include the level of additionality, the creation of dependence, and whether the farmers are indeed best served this way.
56. Although most focus has been on side-selling when farmers face liquidity constraints or when spot market prices are higher, buyers sometimes do not honor the contract themselves by rejecting products on loose grounds of low quality or when spot market prices are lower (ACET 2017; Swinnen and Kuijpers 2017).
57. Public investment in private goods (such as price support or input subsidies) often has market-distorting effects. It crowds out private investments, has perverse distributional effects toward wealthier farmers, and threatens human capital accumulation (Brooks 2014; López and Galinato 2007).
58. An appealing example is the regional poultry value chain in southern Africa. The growing demand for feed used in poultry production (soybeans) in South Africa is increasingly sourced from neighboring Zambia, although the competitiveness of the value chain is undermined by high transportation costs and policy incongruence across countries (Ncube 2018; Ncube et al. 2017).

References

Abay, Kibrom A., Guush Berhane, Alemayehu Seyoum Taffesse, Bethlehem Koru, and Kibrewossen Abay. 2016. "Understanding Farmers' Technology Adoption Decisions: Input Complementarity and Heterogeneity." Ethiopia Strategy Support Program Working Paper No. 82, International Food Policy Research Institute (IFPRI), Washington, DC.

ACET (African Center for Economic Transformation), ed. 2017. *African Transformation Report 2017: Agriculture Powering Africa's Economic Transformation.* Accra, Ghana: ACET.

Adamopoulos, Tasso, and Diego Restuccia. 2014. "The Size Distribution of Farms and International Productivity Differences." *American Economic Review* 104 (6): 1667–97.

———. 2015. "Land Reform and Productivity: A Quantitative Analysis with Micro Data." Working Paper tecipa-540, Department of Economics, University of Toronto.

Adjognon, Serge G., Lenis Saweda O. Liverpool-Tasie, and Thomas A. Reardon. 2017. "Agricultural Input Credit in Sub-Saharan Africa: Telling Myth from Facts." *Food Policy* 67: 93–105.

AfDB, ADB, EBRD, and IDB (African Development Bank, Asian Development Bank, European Bank for Reconstruction and Development, and Inter-American Development Bank). 2018. "The Future of Work: Regional Perspectives." Joint study of the AfDB, ADB, EBRD, and IDB, Washington, DC.

Aker, Jenny C. 2011. "Dial 'A' for Agriculture: A Review of Information and Communication Technologies for Agricultural Extension in Developing Countries." *Agricultural Economics* 42 (6): 631–47.

Ali, Daniel Ayalew, Klaus Deininger, and Markus Goldstein. 2014. "Environmental and Gender Impacts of Land Tenure Regularization in Africa: Pilot Evidence from Rwanda." *Journal of Development Economics* 110: 262–75.

Ali, Daniel Ayalew, Klaus W. Deininger, Markus P. Goldstein, Eliana La Ferrara, and Marguerite Felicienne Duponchel. 2015. "Determinants of Participation and Transaction Costs in Rwanda's Land Markets." Case study, Report No. 99426, World Bank, Washington, DC.

Ali, Daniel, Klaus Deininger, and Anthony Harris. 2019. "Does Large Farm Establishment Create Benefits for Neighboring Smallholders? Evidence from Ethiopia." *Land Economics* 95 (1): 71–90.

Allen, Thomas, Philipp Heinrigs, and Inhoi Heo. 2018. "Agriculture, Food and Jobs in West Africa." West African Papers No. 14, Organisation for Economic Co-operation and Development (OECD), Paris.

Ambler, Kate, Alan de Brauw, and Susan Godlonton. 2018. "Agriculture Support Services in Malawi: Direct Effects, Complementarities, and Time Dynamics." IFPRI Discussion Paper 01725, International Food Policy Research Institute, Washington, DC.

Anderson, Kym, ed. 2009. *Distortions to Agricultural Incentives: A Global Perspective, 1955–2007.* Washington, DC: World Bank.

Anseeuw, Ward, Thomas Jayne, Richard Kachule, John Kotsopoulos, Ward Anseeuw, Thomas Jayne, Richard Kachule, and John Kotsopoulos. 2016. "The Quiet Rise of Medium-Scale Farms in Malawi." *Land* 5 (3): 19.

Arezki, Rabah, and Markus Brueckner. 2014. "Effects of International Food Price Shocks on Political Institutions in Low-Income Countries: Evidence from an International Food Net-Export Price Index." *World Development* 61: 142–53.

Arias, María Alejandra, Ana María Ibáñez, and Andrés Zambrano. 2019. "Agricultural Production amid Conflict: Separating the Effects of Conflict into Shocks and Uncertainty." *World Development* 119: 165–84

Asenso-Okyere, Kwadwo, and Samson Jemaneh. 2012. "Increasing Agricultural Productivity and Enhancing Food Security in Africa: New Challenges and Opportunities." Conference Concept Note, International Food Policy Research Institute (IFPRI), Washington, DC.

Ashraf, Nava, Xavier Giné, and Dean Karlan. 2009. "Finding Missing Markets (and a Disturbing Epilogue): Evidence from an Export Crop Adoption and Marketing Intervention in Kenya." *American Journal of Agricultural Economics* 91 (4): 973–90.

Bandiera, Oriana, and Imran Rasul. 2006. "Social Networks and Technology Adoption in Northern Mozambique." *Economic Journal* 116 (514): 869–902.

Banerjee, A., E. Duflo, N. Goldberg, D. Karlan, R. Osei, W. Pariente, J. Shapiro, B. Thuysbaert, and C. Udry. 2015. "A Multifaceted Program

Causes Lasting Progress for the Very Poor: Evidence from Six Countries." *Science* 348 (6236): 1260799.

Barbier, Edward B. 2016. "Is Green Growth Relevant for Poor Economies?" *Resource and Energy Economics* 45: 178–91.

Barrett, Christopher B., ed. 2013. *Food Security and Sociopolitical Stability*. Oxford, U.K., and New York: Oxford University Press.

Barrett, Christopher B., Marc F. Bellemare, and Janet Y. Hou. 2010. "Reconsidering Conventional Explanations of the Inverse Productivity–Size Relationship." *World Development* 38 (1): 88–97.

Barrett, Christopher B., Luc Christiaensen, Megan Sheahan, and Abebe Shimeles. 2017. "On the Structural Transformation of Rural Africa." *Journal of African Economies* 26 (suppl_1): i11–35.

Barrientos, Stephanie, Peter Knorringa, Barbara Evers, Margareet Visser, and Maggie Opondo. 2016. "Shifting Regional Dynamics of Global Value Chains: Implications for Economic and Social Upgrading in African Horticulture." *Environment and Planning A* 48 (7): 1266–83.

Beaman, Lori, Dean Karlan, Bram Thuysbaert, and Christopher Udry. 2013. "Profitability of Fertilizer: Experimental Evidence from Female Rice Farmers in Mali." *American Economic Review* 103 (3): 381–86.

Beegle, Kathleen, Emanuela Galasso, and Jessica Goldberg. 2017. "Direct and Indirect Effects of Malawi's Public Works Program on Food Security." *Journal of Development Economics* 128: 1–23.

Bellemare, Marc F. 2015. "Rising Food Prices, Food Price Volatility, and Social Unrest." *American Journal of Agricultural Economics* 97 (1): 1–21.

Bellemare, Marc F., and Jeffrey R. Bloem. 2018. "Does Contract Farming Improve Welfare? A Review." *World Development* 112: 259–71.

Benin, Samuel, and Alejandro Nin-Pratt. 2016. "Intertemporal Trends in Agricultural Productivity." In *Agricultural Productivity in Africa: Trends, Patterns and Determinants*, edited by Samuel Benin, 25–104. Washington, DC: International Food Policy Research Institute (IFPRI).

Benin, Samuel, James Thurlow, Xinshen Diao, Allen Kebba, and Nelson Ofwono. 2008. "Agricultural Growth and Investment Options for Poverty Reduction in Uganda." IFPRI Discussion Paper 00790, International Food Policy Research Institute, Washington, DC.

Bernard, Tanguy, and David J. Spielman. 2009. "Reaching the Rural Poor through Rural Producer Organizations? A Study of Agricultural Marketing Cooperatives in Ethiopia." *Food Policy* 34 (1): 60–69.

Bhargava, Anil K., Tor Vagen, and Anja Gassner. 2018. "Breaking Ground: Unearthing the Potential of High-Resolution, Remote-Sensing Soil Data in Understanding Agricultural Profits and Technology Use in Sub-Saharan Africa." *World Development* 105: 352–66.

Binswanger, Hans. 1986. "Agricultural Mechanization: A Comparative Historical Perspective." *World Bank Research Observer* 1 (1): 27–56.

Binswanger-Mkhize, Hans P. 2018. "Agricultural Mechanization in Sub-Saharan Africa: A Review." Background paper prepared for *Accelerating Poverty Reduction in Africa*, World Bank, Washington, DC.

Binswanger-Mkhize, Hans P., and Sara Savastano. 2017. "Agricultural Intensification: The Status in Six African Countries." *Food Policy* 67: 26–40.

Birner, Regina, Marc J. Cohen, and John Ilukor. 2011. "Rebuilding Agricultural Livelihoods in Post-Conflict Situations." Uganda Strategy Support Program Working Paper No. USSP 7, International Food Policy Research Institute (IFPRI), Washington, DC.

Blattman, Christopher, and Jeannie Annan. 2016. "Can Employment Reduce Lawlessness and Rebellion? A Field Experiment with High-Risk Men in a Fragile State." *American Political Science Review* 110 (1): 17.

Blattman, Christopher, and Stefan Dercon. 2016. "Occupational Choice in Early Industrializing Societies: Experimental Evidence on the Income and Health Effects of Industrial and Entrepreneurial Work." NBER Working Paper 22683, National Bureau of Economic Research, Cambridge, MA.

Bold, Tessa, Kayuki C. Kaizzi, Jakob Svensson, and David Yanagizawa-Drott. 2015. "Low Quality, Low Returns, Low Adoption: Evidence from the Market for Fertilizer and Hybrid Seed in Uganda." Faculty Research Working Paper Series RWP15-033, John F. Kennedy School of Government, Harvard University, Cambridge, MA.

Bouis, Howarth E., and Amy Saltzman. 2017. "Improving Nutrition through Biofortification: A Review of Evidence from HarvestPlus, 2003 through 2016." *Global Food Security* 12: 49–58.

Breisinger, Clemens, Xinshen Diao, Shashidhara Kolavalli, and James Thurlow. 2008. "The Role of Cocoa in Ghana's Future Development." Ghana Strategy Support Program Background Paper No. GSSP 11, International Food Policy Research Institute (IFPRI), Washington, DC.

Brooks, Jonathan. 2014. "Policy Coherence and Food Security: The Effects of OECD Countries' Agricultural Policies." *Food Policy* 44: 88–94.

Bryan, Gharad, Shyamal Chowdhury, and Ahmed Mushfiq Mobarak. 2014. "Underinvestment in a Profitable Technology: The Case of Seasonal Migration in Bangladesh." *Econometrica* 82 (5): 1671–748.

Bureau, Jean-Christophe, and Johan Swinnen. 2018. "EU Policies and Global Food Security." *Global Food Security* 16: 106–15.

Burke, William J., Emmanuel Frossard, Stephen Kabwe, and Thomas S. Jayne. 2016. "Understanding Fertilizer Effectiveness and Adoption on Maize in Zambia." Food Security International Development Working Paper 147, Michigan State University, East Lansing.

Burney, J. A., R. L. Naylor, and S. L. Postel. 2013. "The Case for Distributed Irrigation as a Development Priority in Sub-Saharan Africa." *Proceedings of the National Academy of Sciences* 110 (31): 12513–17.

Burney, Jennifer A., and Rosamond L. Naylor. 2012. "Smallholder Irrigation as a Poverty Alleviation Tool in Sub-Saharan Africa." *World Development* 40 (1): 110–23.

Carletto, Calogero, Sara Savastano, and Alberto Zezza. 2013. "Fact or Artifact: The Impact of Measurement Errors on the Farm Size–Productivity Relationship." *Journal of Development Economics* 103: 254–61.

Carter, Michael R., Lan Cheng, and Alexandros Sarris. 2016. "Where and How Index Insurance Can Boost the Adoption of Improved Agricultural Technologies." *Journal of Development Economics* 118: 59–71.

Carter, Michael R., Rachid Laajaj, and Dean Yang. 2016. "Subsidies, Savings and Sustainable Technology Adoption: Field Experimental Evidence from Mozambique." Working paper, Innovations for Poverty Action, New Haven, CT.

Carter, Michael R., Travis Lybbert, and Emilia Tjernström. 2015. "The Dirt on Dirt: Soil Characteristics and Variable Fertilizer Returns in Kenyan Maize Systems." Feed the Future Assets and Market Assets (AMA) Innovation Lab Working Paper, University of California, Davis.

Chagwiza, Clarietta, Roldan Muradian, and Ruerd Ruben. 2016. "Cooperative Membership and Dairy Performance among Smallholders in Ethiopia." *Food Policy* 59: 165–73.

Chamberlin, Jordan, and T. S. Jayne. 2017. "Does Farm Structure Matter? The Effects of Farmland Distribution Patterns on Rural Household Incomes." Feed the Future Innovation Lab for Food Security Policy Research Paper 77, Michigan State University, East Lansing.

Christiaensen, Luc. 2012. "The Role of Agriculture in a Modernizing Society: Food, Farms and Fields in China 2030." Discussion Papers, Report No. 77367, World Bank, Washington, DC.

Christiaensen, Luc, and Karen Brooks. 2018. "In Africa, More Not Fewer People Will Work in Agriculture." *Jobs and Development* (blog), World Bank, November 12. https://blogs.worldbank.org/jobs/edutech/water/ppps/africa-more-not-fewer-people-will-work-agriculture.

Christiaensen, Luc, Lionel Demery, and Jesper Kuhl. 2011. "The (Evolving) Role of Agriculture in Poverty Reduction: An Empirical Perspective." *Journal of Development Economics* 96 (2): 239–54.

Christiaensen, Luc, Joachim De Weerdt, and Ravi Kanbur. 2018. "Decomposing the Contribution of Migration to Poverty Reduction: Methodology and Application to Tanzania." *Applied Economics Letters* 26 (12): 978–82.

Christiaensen, Luc, and Will Martin. 2018. "Agriculture, Structural Transformation and Poverty Reduction: Eight New Insights." *World Development* 109: 413–16.

Christiaensen, Luc, and Patrick Premand. 2017. "Jobs Diagnostic, Côte d'Ivoire: Employment, Productivity, and Inclusion for Poverty Reduction." Report No. AUS13233, World Bank, Washington, DC.

Cockx, Lara, Liesbeth Colen, and Joachim De Weerdt. 2018. "From Corn to Popcorn? Urbanization and Dietary Change: Evidence from Rural-Urban Migrants in Tanzania." *World Development* 110: 140–59.

Cole, Shawn Allen, and A. Nilesh Fernando. 2014. "The Value of Advice: Evidence from the Adoption of Agricultural Practices." Harvard Business School Working Group Paper, Harvard University, Cambridge, MA.

Collier, Paul, and Stefan Dercon. 2014. "African Agriculture in 50 Years: Smallholders in a Rapidly Changing World?" *World Development* 63: 92–101.

Collier, Paul, and Anke Hoeffler. 1998. "On Economic Causes of Civil War." *Oxford Economic Papers* 50 (4): 563–73.

Daidone, Silvio, Benjamin Davis, Joshua Dewbre, Borja Miguelez, Ousmane Niang, and Luca Pellerano. 2017. "Linking Agriculture and Social Protection for Food Security: The Case of Lesotho." *Global Food Security* 12: 146–54.

Damania, Richard, Claudia Berg, Jason Russ, A. Federico Barra, John Nash, and Rubaba Ali. 2017. "Agricultural Technology Choice and Transport." *American Journal of Agricultural Economics* 99 (1): 265–84.

Darko, Francis Addeah, Jacob Ricker-Gilbert, Talip Kilic, Raymond Florax, and Gerald Shively. 2016. "Profitability of Fertilizer Use in SSA: Evidence from Rural Malawi." Paper presented at the Fifth International Conference of the African Association of Agricultural Economists (AAAE), Addis Ababa, September 23–26.

Davis, Benjamin, Stefania Di Giuseppe, and Alberto Zezza. 2017. "Are African Households (Not) Leaving Agriculture? Patterns of Households' Income Sources in Rural Sub-Saharan Africa." *Food Policy* 67: 153–74.

De Fraiture, Charlotte, and Meredith Giordano. 2014. "Small Private Irrigation: A Thriving but Overlooked Sector." *Agricultural Water Management* 131: 167–74.

De Janvry, Alain, Claire Duquennois, and Elisabeth Sadoulet. 2018. "Labor Calendars and Rural Poverty: A Case Study for Malawi." Working paper, University of California, Berkeley.

De Janvry, Alain, Marcel Fafchamps, and Elisabeth Sadoulet. 1991. "Peasant Household Behaviour with Missing Markets: Some Paradoxes Explained." *Economic Journal* 101 (409): 1400–17.

De Janvry, Alain, and Elisabeth Sadoulet. 2010. "Agriculture for Development in Africa: Business-as-Usual or New Departures?" *Journal of African Economies* 19 (Supplement 2): ii7–39.

———. 2018. "Agriculture for Development 10 Years Later." Presented at the ICABR-World Bank conference, Washington, D.C., June 13.

De Janvry, A., E. Sadoulet, and T. Suri. 2017. "Field Experiments in Developing Country Agriculture." In *Handbook of Economic Field Experiments,* vol. 2, edited by Abhijit Vinayak Banerjee and Esther Duflo, 427–66. Amsterdam: Elsevier.

De Pinto, Alessandro, and John Ulimwengu, eds. 2017. *A Thriving Agricultural Sector in a Changing Climate: Meeting Malabo Declaration Goals through Climate-Smart Agriculture.* ReSAKSS Annual Trends and Outlook Report 2016. Washington, DC: International Food Policy Research Institute (IFPRI).

De Valença, A. W., A. Bake, I. D. Brouwer, and K. E. Giller. 2017. "Agronomic Biofortification of Crops to Fight Hidden Hunger in Sub-Saharan Africa." *Global Food Security* 12: 8–14.

Deichmann, Uwe, Aparajita Goyal, and Deepak Mishra. 2016. "Will Digital Technologies Transform Agriculture in Developing Countries?" *Agricultural Economics* 47 (S1): 21–33.

Deichmann, Uwe, Forhad Shilpi, and Renos Vakis. 2009. "Urban Proximity, Agricultural Potential and Rural Non-Farm Employment: Evidence from Bangladesh." *World Development* 37 (3): 645–60.

Deininger, Klaus, Daniel Ayalew Ali, and Tekie Alemu. 2011. "Impacts of Land Certification on Tenure Security, Investment, and Land Market Participation: Evidence from Ethiopia." *Land Economics* 87 (2): 312–34.

Deininger, Klaus, and Derek Byerlee. 2012. "The Rise of Large Farms in Land Abundant Countries: Do They Have a Future?" *World Development* 40 (4): 701–14.

Deininger, Klaus, and John Okidi. 2003. "Growth and Poverty Reduction in Uganda, 1999–2000: Panel Data Evidence." *Development Policy Review* 21 (4): 481–509.

Deininger, Klaus, Sara Savastano, and Fang Xia. 2017. "Smallholders' Land Access in Sub-Saharan Africa: A New Landscape?" *Food Policy* 67: 78–92.

Deininger, Klaus, and Fang Xia. 2016. "Quantifying Spillover Effects from Large Land-Based Investment: The Case of Mozambique." *World Development* 87: 227–41.

———. 2018. "Assessing the Long-Term Performance of Large-Scale Land Transfers: Challenges and Opportunities in Malawi's Estate Sector." *World Development* 104: 281–96.

Delgado, Christopher L., Jane Hopkins, Valerie Kelly, P. B. R. Hazell, Anna A. McKenna, Peter Gruhn, Behjat Hojjati, Jayashree Sil, and

Claude Courbois. 1998. "Agricultural Growth Linkages in Sub-Saharan Africa." Research Report 107, International Food Policy Research Institute (IFPRI), Washington, DC.

Dercon, Stefan, and Luc Christiaensen. 2011. "Consumption Risk, Technology Adoption and Poverty Traps: Evidence from Ethiopia." *Journal of Development Economics* 96 (2): 159–73.

Dercon, Stefan, and Pramila Krishnan. 2000. "Vulnerability, Seasonality and Poverty in Ethiopia." *Journal of Development Studies* 36 (6): 25–53.

Devaux, André, Máximo Torero, Jason Donovan, and Douglas Horton, eds. 2016. *Innovation for Inclusive Value-Chain Development: Successes and Challenges.* Washington, DC: International Food Policy Research Institute (IFPRI).

Diao, Xinshen, and Alejandro Nin-Pratt. 2007. "Growth Options and Poverty Reduction in Ethiopia: An Economy-Wide Model Analysis." *Food Policy* 32 (2): 205–28.

Diao, Xinshen, Jed Silver, and Hiroyuki Takeshima. 2016. "Agricultural Mechanization and Agricultural Transformation." IFPRI Discussion Paper 1527, International Food Policy Research Institute, Washington, DC.

Diao, Xinshen, Jed Silver, Hiroyuki Takeshima, and Xiaobo Zhang. Forthcoming. "Introduction." In *A New Paradigm of Agricultural Mechanization Development: How Much Can Africa Learn from Asia?* edited by Xinshen Diao, Hiroyuki Takeshima, and Xiaobo Zhang.

Diao, Xinshen, James Thurlow, Samuel Benin, and Shenggen Fan, eds. 2012. *Strategies and Priorities for African Agriculture: Economywide Perspectives from Country Studies.* Washington, DC: International Food Policy Research Institute (IFPRI).

Dillon, Brian M., and Christopher B. Barrett. 2016. "Global Oil Prices and Local Food Prices: Evidence from East Africa." *American Journal of Agricultural Economics* 98 (1): 154–71.

Duflo, Esther, Michael Kremer, and Jonathan Robinson. 2008. "How High Are Rates of Return to Fertilizer? Evidence from Field Experiments in Kenya." *American Economic Review* 98 (2): 482–88.

Dzanku, Fred M., Magnus Jirström, and Håkan Marstorp. 2015. "Yield Gap-Based Poverty Gaps in Rural Sub-Saharan Africa." *World Development* 67: 336–62.

ECOWAS, UEMOA, and CILSS (Economic Community of West African States, West African Economic and Monetary Union, and Permanent Inter-State Committee for Drought Control in the Sahel). 2017. "Strategic Framework for Agricultural Water in the Sahel." Framework document for the Sahel Irrigation Initiative, Report No. 127722, World Bank, Washington, DC.

FAO (Food and Agriculture Organization of the United Nations). 2013. *Understanding and Integrating Gender Issues into Livestock Projects and Programmes: A Checklist for Practitioners.* Rome: FAO.

———. 2017. *The Future of Food and Agriculture: Trends and Challenges.* Rome: FAO.

Fink, Günther, B. Kelsey Jack, and Felix Masiye. 2014. "Seasonal Credit Constraints and Agricultural Labor Supply: Evidence from Zambia." NBER Working Paper 20218, National Bureau of Economic Research, Cambridge, MA.

Fischer, Elisabeth, and Matin Qaim. 2012. "Linking Smallholders to Markets: Determinants and Impacts of Farmer Collective Action in Kenya." *World Development* 40 (6): 1255–68.

Fischer, Guenther, Freddy Nachtergaele, Sylvia Prieler, Harrij van Velthuizen, Luc Verelst, and David Wiberg. 2008. "Global Agro-Ecological Zones Assessment for Agriculture (GAEZ 2008)." International Institute for Applied Systems Analysis (IIASA), Laxenburg, Austria; and Food and Agriculture Organization of the United Nations (FAO), Rome.

Fu, Xiaolan, and Shaheen Akter. 2016. "The Impact of Mobile Phone Technology on Agricultural Extension Services Delivery: Evidence from India." *Journal of Development Studies* 52 (11): 1561–76.

Fuglie, Keith, and Nicholas Rada. 2013. "Resources, Policies, and Agricultural Productivity in Sub-Saharan Africa." Economic Research Report No. 145, Economic Research Service, U.S. Department of Agriculture, Washington, DC.

Geda, Alemayehu, and Edris Hussein Seid. 2015. "The Potential for Internal Trade and Regional Integration in Africa." *Journal of African Trade* 2 (1–2): 19–50.

Gehrke, Esther, and Michael Grimm. 2018. "Do Cows Have Negative Returns? The Evidence Revisited." *Economic Development and Cultural Change* 66 (4): 673–707.

Giordano, Thierry. 2011. "Agriculture and Economic Recovery in Post-Conflict Countries: Lessons We Never Learnt." Development Planning Division Working Paper Series No. 22, Development Bank of Southern Africa, Johannesburg.

Goldstein, Markus, Kenneth Houngbedji, Florence Kondylis, Michael O'Sullivan, and Harris Selod. 2018. "Formalization without Certification? Experimental Evidence on Property Rights and Investment." *Journal of Development Economics* 132: 57–74.

Gollin, Douglas, David Lagakos, and Michael E. Waugh. 2014. "Agricultural Productivity Differences across Countries." *American Economic Review* 104 (5): 165–70.

Gollin, Douglas, and Christopher Udry. 2019. "Heterogeneity, Measurement Error, and Misallocation: Evidence from African Agriculture." NBER Working Paper 25440, National Bureau of Economic Research, Cambridge, MA.

Govereh, Jones, and T. S. Jayne. 2003. "Cash Cropping and Food Crop Productivity: Synergies or Trade-Offs?" *Agricultural Economics* 28 (1): 39–50.

Goyal, Aparajita, and John Nash. 2017. *Reaping Richer Returns: Public Spending Priorities for African Agriculture Productivity Growth.* Washington, DC: World Bank.

Guardado, Jenny, and Steven Pennings. 2017. "The Seasonality of Conflict." Unpublished manuscript, World Bank, Washington, DC.

Hachigonta, Sepo, Gerald C. Nelson, Timothy S. Thomas, and Linidiwe S. Sibanda, eds. 2013. *Southern African Agriculture and Climate Change: A Comprehensive Analysis.* Washington, DC: International Food Policy Research Institute (IFPRI).

Haggblade, Steven, Bart Minten, Carl Pray, Thomas Reardon, and David Zilberman. 2017. "The Herbicide Revolution in Developing Countries: Patterns, Causes, and Implications." *European Journal of Development Research* 29 (3): 533–59.

Hall, Ruth, Ian Scoones, and Dzodzi Tsikata. 2017. "Plantations, Outgrowers and Commercial Farming in Africa: Agricultural Commercialisation and Implications for Agrarian Change." *Journal of Peasant Studies* 44 (3): 515–37.

Hallegatte, Stephane, Mook Bangalore, Laura Bonzanigo, Marianne Fay, Tamaro Kane, Ulf Narloch, Julie Rozenberg, David Treguer, and Adrien Vogt-Schilb. 2016. *Shock Waves: Managing the Impacts of Climate Change on Poverty.* Climate Change and Development Series. Washington, DC: World Bank.

Harou, Aurélie P., Yanyan Liu, Christopher B. Barrett, and Liangzhi You. 2017. "Variable Returns to Fertiliser Use and the Geography of Poverty: Experimental and Simulation Evidence from Malawi." *Journal of African Economies* 26 (3): 342–71.

Hazell, Peter, Colin Poulton, Steve Wiggins, and Andrew Dorward. 2010. "The Future of Small Farms: Trajectories and Policy Priorities." *World Development* 38 (10): 1349–61.

Headey, Derek D. 2016. "The Evolution of Global Farming Land: Facts and Interpretations." *Agricultural Economics* 47 (S1): 185–96.

Headey, Derek, Kalle Hirvonen, and John Hoddinott. 2018. "Animal Sourced Foods and Child Stunting." *American Journal of Agricultural Economics* 100 (5): 1302–19.

Headey, Derek D., and William J. Martin. 2016. "The Impact of Food Prices on Poverty and Food Security." *Annual Review of Resource Economics* 8 (1): 329–51.

Heltberg, Rasmus. 1998. "Rural Market Imperfections and the Farm Size–Productivity Relationship: Evidence from Pakistan." *World Development* 26 (10): 1807–26.

Hoekman, Bernard, and Dominique Njinkeu. 2017. "Integrating Africa: Some Trade Policy Research Priorities and Challenges." *Journal of African Economies* 26 (suppl_2): ii12–39.

IFAD (International Fund for Agricultural Development). 2016. *Rural Development Report 2016: Fostering Inclusive Rural Transformation.* Rome: IFAD.

IFC (International Finance Corporation). 2019. *Working with Smallholders: A Handbook for Firms Building Sustainable Supply Chains.* Washington, DC: World Bank.

Ito, Junichi, Zongshun Bao, and Qun Su. 2012. "Distributional Effects of Agricultural Cooperatives in China: Exclusion of Smallholders and Potential Gains on Participation." *Food Policy* 37 (6): 700–09.

Ivanic, Maros, and Will Martin. 2018. "Sectoral Productivity Growth and Poverty Reduction: National and Global Impacts." *World Development* 109: 429–39.

Jacoby, Hanan G., and Bart Minten. 2007. "Is Land Titling in Sub-Saharan Africa

Cost-Effective? Evidence from Madagascar." *World Bank Economic Review* 21 (3): 461–85.

Jalan, Jyotsna, and Martin Ravallion. 2002. "Geographic Poverty Traps? A Micro Model of Consumption Growth in Rural China." *Journal of Applied Econometrics* 17 (4): 329–46.

Jalloh, Abdulai, Gerald C. Nelson, Timothy S. Thomas, Robert Bellarmin Zougmoré, and Harold Roy-Macauley. 2013. *West African Agriculture and Climate Change: A Comprehensive Analysis*. Washington, DC: International Food Policy Research Institute (IFPRI).

Janssen, Emma, and Johan Swinnen. 2016. "Political Economy of Agricultural and (Regional) Trade Policies and Value Chain Performances in Sub-Saharan Africa." In *Political Economy of Regional Integration in Sub-Saharan Africa*, edited by Paul Brenton and Barak Hoffmann, 13–48. Washington, DC: World Bank.

———. 2017. "Technology Adoption and Value Chains in Developing Countries: Evidence from Dairy in India." *Food Policy* 83: 327–36.

Jayne, T. S., Jordan Chamberlin, and Derek D. Headey. 2014. "Land Pressures, the Evolution of Farming Systems, and Development Strategies in Africa: A Synthesis." *Food Policy* 48: 1–17.

Jayne, T. S., Jordan Chamberlin, Lulama Traub, Nicholas Sitko, Milu Muyanga, Felix K. Yeboah, Ward Anseeuw, et al. 2016. "Africa's Changing Farm Size Distribution Patterns: The Rise of Medium-Scale Farms." *Agricultural Economics* 47 (S1): 197–214.

Jayne, Thomas S., Nicole M. Mason, William J. Burke, and Joshua Ariga. 2018. "Review: Taking Stock of Africa's Second-Generation Agricultural Input Subsidy Programs." *Food Policy* 75: 1–14.

Jayne, T. S., and Shahidur Rashid. 2013. "Input Subsidy Programs in Sub-Saharan Africa: A Synthesis of Recent Evidence." *Agricultural Economics* 44 (6): 547–62.

Kelley, Colin P., Shahrzad Mohtadi, Mark A. Cane, Richard Seager, and Yochanan Kushnir. 2015. "Climate Change in the Fertile Crescent and Implications of the Recent Syrian Drought." *Proceedings of the National Academy of Sciences* 112 (11): 3241–46.

Khandker, Shahidur R. 2012. "Seasonality of Income and Poverty in Bangladesh." *Journal of Development Economics* 97 (2): 244–56.

Kilelu, Catherine W., Laurens Klerkx, and Cees Leeuwis. 2017. "Supporting Smallholder Commercialisation by Enhancing Integrated Coordination in Agrifood Value Chains: Experiences with Dairy Hubs in Kenya." *Experimental Agriculture* 53 (02): 269–87.

Koussoubé, Estelle, and Céline Nauges. 2017. "Returns to Fertiliser Use: Does It Pay Enough? Some New Evidence from Sub-Saharan Africa." *European Review of Agricultural Economics* 44 (2): 183–210.

Kraay, Aart, and David McKenzie. 2014. "Do Poverty Traps Exist? Assessing the Evidence." *Journal of Economic Perspectives* 28 (3): 127–48.

Krishnan, Pramila, and Manasa Patnam. 2014. "Neighbors and Extension Agents in Ethiopia: Who Matters More for Technology Adoption?" *American Journal of Agricultural Economics* 96 (1): 308–27.

Kydd, Jonathan, Andrew Dorward, Jamie Morrison, and Georg Cadisch. 2004. "Agricultural Development and Pro-Poor Economic Growth in Sub-Saharan Africa: Potential and Policy." *Oxford Development Studies* 32 (1): 37–57.

Larson, Donald F., Rie Muraoka, and Keijiro Otsuka. 2016. "Why African Rural Development Strategies Must Depend on Small Farms." *Global Food Security* 10: 39–51.

Lentz, Erin, and Joanna Upton. 2016. "Benefits to Smallholders? Evaluating the World Food Programme's Purchase for Progress Pilot." *Global Food Security* 11: 54–63.

Lesk, Corey, Pedram Rowhani, and Navin Ramankutty. 2016. "Influence of Extreme Weather Disasters on Global Crop Production." *Nature* 529 (7584): 84–87.

Ligon, Ethan, and Elisabeth Sadoulet. 2018. "Estimating the Relative Benefits of Agricultural Growth on the Distribution of Expenditures." *World Development* 109: 417–28.

Liverpool-Tasie, Lenis Saweda O., Bolarin T. Omonona, Awa Sanou, and Wale O. Ogunleye. 2017. "Is Increasing Inorganic Fertilizer Use for Maize Production in SSA a Profitable Proposition? Evidence from Nigeria." *Food Policy* 67: 41–51.

López, Ramón, and Gregmar I. Galinato. 2007. "Should Governments Stop Subsidies to Private Goods? Evidence from Rural Latin America." *Journal of Public Economics* 91 (5–6): 1071–94.

Luo, Renfu, Yaojiang Shi, Linxiu Zhang, Chengfang Liu, Scott Rozelle, Brian Sharbono, Ai Yue, Qiran Zhao, and Reynaldo Martorell. 2012. "Nutrition and Educational Performance in Rural China's Elementary Schools: Results of a Randomized Control Trial in Shaanxi Province." *Economic Development and Cultural Change* 60 (4): 735–72.

Ma, Wanglin, and Awudu Abdulai. 2016. "Does Cooperative Membership Improve Household Welfare? Evidence from Apple Farmers in China." *Food Policy* 58: 94–102.

Maertens, Miet, and Katrien Vande Velde. 2017. "Contract-Farming in Staple Food Chains: The Case of Rice in Benin." *World Development* 95: 73–87.

Magrini, Emiliano, Jean Balié, and Cristian Morales-Opazo. 2018. "Price Signals and Supply Responses for Staple Food Crops in Sub-Saharan Africa." *Applied Economic Perspectives and Policy* 40 (2): 276–96.

Mano, Yukichi, Kazushi Takahashi, and Keijiro Otsuka. 2017. "Contract Farming, Farm Mechanization, and Agricultural Intensification: The Case of Rice Farming in Côte d'Ivoire." Working Paper No. 157, Japan International Cooperation Agency Research Institute (JICA-RI), Tokyo.

Marenya, Paswel P., and Christopher B. Barrett. 2009. "Soil Quality and Fertilizer Use Rates among Smallholder Farmers in Western Kenya." *Agricultural Economics* 40 (5): 561–72.

Martin-Shields, Charles P., and Wolfgang Stojetz. 2019. "Food Security and Conflict: Empirical Challenges and Future Opportunities for Research and Policy Making on Food Security and Conflict." *World Development* 119: 150–64.

Mashnik, Daria, Headley Jacobus, Amer Barghouth, Eva Jiayu Wang, Jeannelle Blanchard, and Ryan Shelby. 2017. "Increasing Productivity through Irrigation: Problems and Solutions Implemented in Africa and Asia." *Sustainable Energy Technologies and Assessments* 22: 220–27.

Mason, Nicole M., T. S. Jayne, and Bekele Shiferaw. 2015. "Africa's Rising Demand for Wheat: Trends, Drivers, and Policy Implications." *Development Policy Review* 33 (5): 581–613.

Masters, William A., Agnes Andersson Djurfeldt, Cornelis De Haan, Peter Hazell, Thomas Jayne, Magnus Jirström, and Thomas Reardon. 2013. "Urbanization and Farm Size in Asia and Africa: Implications for Food Security and Agricultural Research." *Global Food Security* 2 (3): 156–65.

McCullough, Ellen B. 2017. "Labor Productivity and Employment Gaps in Sub-Saharan Africa." *Food Policy* 67: 133–52.

McGuirk, Eoin, and Marshall Burke. 2017. "The Economic Origins of Conflict in Africa." NBER Working Paper 23056, National Bureau of Economic Research, Cambridge, MA.

Mellor, John W. 2017. *Agricultural Development and Economic Transformation*. Cham, Switzerland: Springer International Publishing.

Mellor, John W., and Sohail J. Malik. 2017. "The Impact of Growth in Small Commercial Farm Productivity on Rural Poverty Reduction." *World Development* 91: 1–10.

Michelson, Hope, Brenna Ellison, Anna Fairbairn, Annemie Maertens, and Victor Manyong. 2018. "Misperceived Quality: Fertilizer in Tanzania." Munich Personal RePEc Archive (MPRA) Paper No. 90798, University Library of Munich.

Michler, Jeffrey D., Emilia Tjernström, Simone Verkaart, and Kai Mausch. 2018. "Money Matters: The Role of Yields and Profits in Agricultural Technology Adoption." *American Journal of Agricultural Economics* 101 (3): 710–31.

Miguel, Edward, Shanker Satyanath, and Ernest Sergenti. 2004. "Economic Shocks and Civil Conflict: An Instrumental Variables Approach." *Journal of Political Economy* 112 (4): 725–53.

Minot, Nicholas, and Bradley Sawyer. 2016. "Contract Farming in Developing Countries: Theory, Practice, and Policy Implications." In *Innovation for Inclusive Value-Chain Development: Successes and Challenges*, edited by André Devaux, Maximo Torero, Jason Donovan, and Douglas Horton, 127–58. Washington, DC: International Food Policy Research Institute (IFPRI).

Minten, Bart, Bethlehem Koru, and David Stifel. 2013. "The Last Mile(s) in Modern Input Distribution: Pricing, Profitability, and Adoption." *Agricultural Economics* 44 (6): 629–46.

Mitchell, Shira, Andrew Gelman, Rebecca Ross, Joyce Chen, Sehrish Bari, Uyen Kim Huynh, Matthew W. Harris, et al. 2018. "The Millennium Villages Project: A Retrospective, Observational, Endline Evaluation." *The Lancet Global Health* 6 (5): e500–513.

Mojo, Dagne, Christian Fischer, and Terefe Degefa. 2017. "The Determinants and Economic Impacts of Membership in Coffee Farmer Cooperatives: Recent Evidence from Rural Ethiopia." *Journal of Rural Studies* 50: 84–94.

Molini, Vasco, and Pierella Paci. 2015. "Poverty Reduction in Ghana: Progress and Challenges 2015." Report No. 101230, World Bank, Washington, DC.

Morris, Michael L., Valerie Kelly, Ron Kopicki, and Derek Byerlee. 2007. *Fertilizer Use in African Agriculture: Lessons Learned and Good Practice Guidelines.* Directions in Development Series. Washington, DC: World Bank.

Mrema, Geoffrey C., Doyle C. Baker, and David Kahan. 2008. *Agricultural Mechanization in Sub-Saharan Africa: Time for a New Look.* Rome: Food and Agriculture Organization of the United Nations (FAO).

Muraoka, Rie, Songqing Jin, and T. S. Jayne. 2018. "Land Access, Land Rental and Food Security: Evidence from Kenya." *Land Use Policy* 70: 611–22.

Myers, Samuel S., Antonella Zanobetti, Itai Kloog, Peter Huybers, Andrew D. B. Leakey, Arnold J. Bloom, Eli Carlisle, et al. 2014. "Increasing CO_2 Threatens Human Nutrition." *Nature* 510 (7503): 139–42.

Narrod, Clare A., Carl Pray, and Marites Tiongco. 2008. "Technology Transfer, Policies, and the Role of the Private Sector in the Global Poultry Revolution." IFPRI Discussion Paper 841, International Food Policy Research Institute, Washington, DC.

Ncube, Phumzile. 2018. "The Southern African Poultry Value Chain: Corporate Strategies, Investments and Agro-Industrial Policies." *Development Southern Africa* 35 (3): 369–87.

Ncube, Phumzile, Simon Roberts, and Thando Vilakazi. 2015. "Study of Competition in the Road Freight Sector in the SADC Region: Case Study of Fertilizer Transport and Trading in Zambia, Tanzania and Malawi." CCRED Working Paper No. 3/2015, Centre for Competition, Regulation and Economic Development (CCRED), University of Johannesburg, South Africa.

Ncube, Phumzile, Simon Roberts, Tatenda Zengeni, and Paul Chimuka Samboko. 2017. "Identifying Growth Opportunities in the Southern African Development Community through Regional Value Chains: The Case of the Animal Feed to Poultry Value Chain." WIDER Working Paper No. 2017/4, United Nations University World Institute for Development Economics Research (UNU-WIDER), Helsinki.

N'diaye, Moctar, and Luc Christiaensen. 2017. "Natural Resource Endowment and Agricultural Development in Sub-Saharan Africa." Background paper prepared for *Accelerating Poverty Reduction in Africa*, World Bank, Washington, DC.

Newfarmer, Richard, John Page, and Finn Tarp, eds. 2018. *Industries without Smokestacks: Industrialization in Africa Reconsidered.* United Nations University World Institute for Development Economics Research (UNU-WIDER) Studies in Development Economics. Oxford, U.K., and New York: Oxford University Press.

Niang, I., O. C. Ruppel, M. A. Abdrabo, A. Essel, C. Lennard, J. Padgham, and P. Urquhart. 2014. "Africa, Climate Change 2014: Impacts, Adaptation and Vulnerability." In *Contributions of the Working Group II to the Fifth Assessment Report of the Intergovernmental Panel on Climate Change*, edited by V. R. Barros, C. B. Field, D. J. Dokken, M. D. Mastrandrea, and K. J. Mach, 1199–1265. New York: Cambridge University Press.

Nin-Pratt, Alejandro, and Xinshen Diao. 2006. "Exploring Growth Linkages and Market Opportunities for Agriculture in Southern Africa." Development Strategy and Governance (DSGD) Discussion Paper 42, International Food Policy Research Institute (IFPRI), Washington, DC.

OECD and FAO (Organisation for Economic Co-operation and Development and Food and Agriculture Organization of the United Nations). 2016. *OECD-FAO Agricultural Outlook 2016–2025—Special Focus: Sub-Saharan Africa.* Paris: OECD Publishing.

Otsuka, Keijiro, and Rie Muraoka. 2017. "A Green Revolution for Sub-Saharan Africa: Past Failures and Future Prospects." *Journal of African Economies* 26 (suppl_1): i73–98.

Otsuka, Keijiro, Yuko Nakano, and Kazushi Takahashi. 2016. "Contract Farming in Developed and Developing Countries." *Annual Review of Resource Economics* 8 (1): 353–76.

Otte, J., A. Costales, J. Dijkman, U. Pica-Camarra, T. Robinson, V. Ahuja, C. Ly, and D. Roland-Holst. 2012. *Livestock*

Sector Development for Poverty Reduction: An Economic and Policy Perspective—Livestock's Many Virtues. Pro-Poor Livestock Policy Initiative. Rome: Food and Agriculture Organization of the United Nations (FAO).

Pace, Noemi, Silvio Daidone, Benjamin Davis, Sudhanshu Handa, Marco Knowles, and Robert Pickmans. 2018. "One Plus One Can Be Greater than Two: Evaluating Synergies of Development Programmes in Malawi." *Journal of Development Studies* 54 (11): 2023–60.

Pauw, Karl, and James Thurlow. 2011. "Agricultural Growth, Poverty, and Nutrition in Tanzania." *Food Policy* 36 (6): 795–804.

Pernechele, Valentina, Jean Balié, and Léopold Ghins. 2018. *Agricultural Policy Incentives in Sub-Saharan Africa in the Last Decade (2005–2016)*. Rome: Food and Agriculture Organization of the United Nations (FAO)

Perry, Brian. 2016. "The Control of East Coast Fever of Cattle by Live Parasite Vaccination: A Science-to-Impact Narrative." *One Health* 2: 103–14.

Pierre, Guillaume, and Jonathan Kaminski. 2019. "Cross Country Maize Market Linkages in Africa: Integration and Price Transmission across Local and Global Markets." *Agricultural Economics* 50 (1): 79–90.

Pingali, Prabhu, Yves Bigot, and Hans P. Binswanger. 1987. *Agricultural Mechanization and the Evolution of Farming Systems in Sub-Saharan Africa*. Baltimore: Johns Hopkins University Press.

Poulton, Colin, Andrew Dorward, and Jonathan Kydd. 2010. "The Future of Small Farms: New Directions for Services, Institutions, and Intermediation." *World Development* 38 (10): 1413–28.

Ragasa, Catherine, and Antony Chapoto. 2017. "Moving in the Right Direction? The Role of Price Subsidies in Fertilizer Use and Maize Productivity in Ghana." *Food Security* 9 (2): 329–53.

Ragasa, Catherine, and Jennifer Golan. 2014. "The Role of Rural Producer Organizations for Agricultural Service Provision in Fragile States." *Agricultural Economics* 45 (5): 537–53.

Ragasa, Catherine, Isabel Lambrecht, and Doreen S. Kufoalor. 2018. "Limitations of Contract Farming as a Pro-Poor Strategy: The Case of Maize Outgrower Schemes in Upper West Ghana." *World Development* 102: 30–56.

Rakotoarisoa, Manitra A., Massimo Iafrate, and Marianna Paschali. 2011. *Why Has Africa Become a Net Food Importer? Explaining Africa Agricultural and Food Trade Deficits*. Rome: Food and Agriculture Organization of the United Nations (FAO).

Ravallion, Martin, and Shaohua Chen. 2007. "China's (Uneven) Progress against Poverty." *Journal of Development Economics* 82 (1): 1–42.

Restuccia, Diego, and Raul Santaeulalia-Llopis. 2017. "Land Misallocation and Productivity." NBER Working Paper 23128, National Bureau of Economic Research, Cambridge, MA.

Rosenzweig, Mark, and Christopher Udry. 2016. "External Validity in a Stochastic World." NBER Working Paper 22449, National Bureau of Economic Research, Cambridge, MA.

Sanch-Maritan, Mathieu, and Lionel Vedrine. 2018. "Forced Displacement and Technology Adoption: An Empirical Analysis Based on Agricultural Households in Bosnia and Herzegovina." *Journal of Development Studies* 55 (6): 1325–43.

Sanchez, Pedro A., Sonya Ahamed, Florence Carré, Alfred E. Hartemink, Jonathan Hempel, Jeroen Huising, Philippe Lagacherie, et al. 2009. "Digital Soil Map of the World." *Science* 325 (5941): 680–81.

Schuenemann, Franziska, James Thurlow, Stefan Meyer, and Richard Robertson. 2018. "Evaluating Irrigation Investments in Malawi: Economy-Wide Impacts under Uncertainty and Labor Constraints." *Agricultural Economics* 49 (2): 237–50.

Serdeczny, Olivia, Sophie Adams, Florent Baarsch, Dim Coumou, Alexander Robinson, William Hare, Michiel Schaeffer, Mahé Perrette, and Julia Reinhardt. 2017. "Climate Change Impacts in Sub-Saharan Africa: From Physical Changes to Their Social Repercussions." *Regional Environmental Change* 17 (6): 1585–600.

Sheahan, Megan, and Christopher B. Barrett. 2017. "Ten Striking Facts about Agricultural Input Use in Sub-Saharan Africa." *Food Policy* 67: 12–25.

Sitko, Nicholas J., William J. Burke, and Thomas Jayne. 2017. "Food System Transformation and Market Evolutions: An Analysis of the Rise of Large-Scale Grain Trading in Sub-Saharan Africa." Feed the Future Innovation Lab for Food Security Policy Research Paper 259554, Michigan State University, East Lansing.

Stiglitz, Joseph E. 2018. "From Manufacturing-Led Export Growth to a 21st-Century Inclusive Growth Strategy: Explaining the Demise of a Successful Growth Model and What to Do About It." Paper presented at the United Nations University World Institute for Development Economics Research (UNU-WIDER) "Think Development, Think WIDER" conference, Helsinki, Finland, September 13.

Suri, Tavneet. 2011. "Selection and Comparative Advantage in Technology Adoption." *Econometrica* 79 (1): 159–209.

Suzuki, Aya, Yukichi Mano, and Girum Abebe. 2018. "Earnings, Savings, and Job Satisfaction in a Labor-Intensive Export Sector: Evidence from the Cut Flower Industry in Ethiopia." *World Development* 110: 176–91.

Swinnen, Johan, and Rob Kuijpers. 2017. "Inclusive Value Chains to Accelerate Poverty Reduction in Africa." Background note prepared for *Accelerating Poverty Reduction in Africa*, World Bank, Washington, DC.

Swinnen, Johan F. M., Anneleen Vandeplas, and Miet Maertens. 2010. "Liberalization, Endogenous Institutions, and Growth: A Comparative Analysis of Agricultural Reforms in Africa, Asia, and Europe." *World Bank Economic Review* 24 (3): 412–45.

Teravaninthorn, Supee, and Gaël Raballand. 2008. *Transport Prices and Costs in Africa: A Review of the Main International Corridors.* Directions in Development Series. Washington, DC: World Bank.

Timmer, C. Peter. 2010. "Reflections on Food Crises Past." *Food Policy* 35 (1): 1–11.

Tittonell, Pablo, and Ken E. Giller. 2013. "When Yield Gaps Are Poverty Traps: The Paradigm of Ecological Intensification in African Smallholder Agriculture." *Field Crops Research* 143: 76–90.

Ton, Giel, Wytse Vellema, Sam Desiere, Sophia Weituschat, and Marijke D'Haese. 2018. "Contract Farming for Improving Smallholder Incomes: What Can We Learn from Effectiveness Studies?" *World Development* 104: 46–64.

Tonitto, Christina, and Jacob E. Ricker-Gilbert. 2016. "Nutrient Management in African Sorghum Cropping Systems: Applying Meta-Analysis to Assess Yield and Profitability." *Agronomy for Sustainable Development* 36 (10): 1–19.

Tschirley, David, Benedito Cunguara, Steven Haggblade, Thomas Reardon, and Mayuko Kondo. 2017. "Africa's Unfolding Diet Transformation and Farm Employment: Evidence from Tanzania." Feed the Future Innovation Lab for Food Security Policy Research Paper 43, Michigan State University, East Lansing.

Tschirley, David, Thomas Reardon, Michael Dolislager, and Jason Snyder. 2015. "The Rise of a Middle Class in East and Southern Africa: Implications for Food System Transformation: The Middle Class and Food System Transformation in ESA." *Journal of International Development* 27 (5): 628–46.

Van den Broeck, Goedele, Johan Swinnen, and Miet Maertens. 2017. "Global Value Chains, Large-Scale Farming, and Poverty: Long-Term Effects in Senegal." *Food Policy* 66: 97–107.

Vandercasteelen, Joachim, Seneshaw Tamru Beyene, Bart Minten, and Johan Swinnen. 2018. "Cities and Agricultural Transformation in Africa: Evidence from Ethiopia." *World Development* 105: 383–99.

Vandercasteelen, Joachim, and Luc Christiaensen. 2018. "The Geography of Africa's Poverty: Remoteness and Agro-Ecological Potential." Background note prepared for *Accelerating Poverty Reduction in Africa*, World Bank, Washington, DC.

Van der Westhuizen, D., Thomas S. Jayne, and Ferdi Meyer. 2018. "Rising Tractor Use in Sub-Saharan Africa: Evidence from Tanzania." Paper presented at the International Conference of Agricultural Economists, Vancouver, August 28.

Vanlauwe, Bernard, Job Kihara, Pauline Chivenge, Pieter Pypers, Ric Coe, and Johan Six. 2011. "Agronomic Use Efficiency of N Fertilizer in Maize-Based Systems in Sub-Saharan Africa within the Context of Integrated Soil Fertility Management." *Plant and Soil* 339 (1–2): 35–50.

Van Weezel, Stijn. 2016. "Food Imports, International Prices, and Violence in Africa." *Oxford Economic Papers* 68 (3): 758–81.

Vasconcelos, Marta W., Wilhelm Gruissem, and Navreet K. Bhullar. 2017. "Iron Biofortification in the 21st Century: Setting Realistic Targets, Overcoming Obstacles, and New Strategies for Healthy Nutrition." *Current Opinion in Biotechnology* 44: 8–15.

Verhofstadt, E., and M. Maertens. 2015. "Can Agricultural Cooperatives Reduce Poverty? Heterogeneous Impact of Cooperative Membership on Farmers' Welfare in Rwanda." *Applied Economic Perspectives and Policy* 37 (1): 86–106.

Waithaka, Michael, Nelson C. Gerald, Thomas S. Timothy, and Miriam Kyotalimye, eds. 2013. *East African Agriculture and Climate Change: A Comprehensive Analysis*. Washington, DC: International Food Policy Research Institute (IFPRI).

Wang, H. Holly, Yanbing Wang, and Michael S. Delgado. 2014. "The Transition to Modern Agriculture: Contract Farming in Developing Economies." *American Journal of Agricultural Economics* 96 (5): 1257–71.

Wang, Xiaobing, Futoshi Yamauchi, Keijiro Otsuka, and Jikun Huang. 2016. "Wage Growth, Landholding, and Mechanization in Chinese Agriculture." *World Development* 86: 30–45.

Wantchekon, Leonard, and Piero Stanig. 2016. "The Curse of Good Soil? Land Fertility, Roads, and Rural Poverty in Africa." Working paper, Princeton University, Princeton, NJ.

Ward, P. S., R. J. G. M. Florax, and A. Flores-Lagunes. 2014. "Climate Change and Agricultural Productivity in Sub-Saharan Africa: A Spatial Sample Selection Model." *European Review of Agricultural Economics* 41 (2): 199–226.

Weiss, D. J., A. Nelson, H. S. Gibson, W. Temperley, S. Peedell, A. Lieber, M. Hancher, et al. 2018. "A Global Map of Travel Time to Cities to Assess Inequalities in Accessibility in 2015." *Nature* 553 (7688): 333–36.

World Bank. 2007. *World Development Report 2008: Agriculture for Development*. Washington, DC: World Bank.

———. 2012. "Africa Can Help Feed Africa: Removing Barriers to Regional Trade in Food Staples." Report No. 73887, World Bank, Washington, DC.

———. 2013. "Growing Africa: Unlocking the Potential of Agribusiness." Working Paper No. 75663, World Bank, Washington, DC.

———. 2014. *Africa's Pulse: An Analysis of Issues Shaping Africa's Economic Future*, vol. 10 (October). Washington, DC: World Bank.

———. 2016. *World Development Report 2016: Digital Dividends*. Washington, DC: World Bank.

———. 2018. "Commodity Markets Outlook, April. Oil Exporters: Policies and Challenges." Biannual data report, World Bank, Washington, DC.

Yeboah, Felix Kwame, and Thomas S. Jayne. 2018. "Africa's Evolving Employment Trends: Implications for Economic Transformation." *Journal of Development Studies* 54 (5): 803–32.

You, Liangzhi, Claudia Ringler, Ulrike Wood-Sichra, Richard Robertson, Stanley Wood, Tingju Zhu, Gerald Nelson, Zhe Guo, and Yan Sun. 2011. "What Is the Irrigation Potential for Africa? A Combined Biophysical and Socioeconomic Approach." *Food Policy* 36 (6): 770–82.

Zhang, Xiaobo, Jin Yang, and Thomas Reardon. 2017. "Mechanization Outsourcing Clusters and Division of Labor in Chinese Agriculture." *China Economic Review* 43: 184–95.

FUNDAMENTALS 2

The Nexus of Gender Inequality and Poverty

Isis Gaddis

Gender inequality in Africa across many dimensions is well documented, as discussed in chapter 2. Women face disadvantages in education, health, empowerment, and income-generating activities. On average, women in the region are less productive than men as farmers, and their nonfarm business activities are less profitable. Gender inequality traps women in poverty and generates a vicious cycle for daughters. Poverty traps emerge when there is a minimum threshold for capital—whether human, physical, or financial—that is required for an individual to be productive and stay out of poverty. To be sure, poverty traps affect both men and women. However, because women face more-severe borrowing constraints and lower levels of human and physical capital, their trap is often deeper.

In many nonmonetary dimensions, girls and women suffer large inequalities in Africa and other regions (UNDP 2013; World Bank 2011, 2018). Much evidence shows that African women, relative to men, tend to have significantly inferior human capital endowments (though education gaps have closed in many countries in recent years); worse access to labor markets; lower wages; limited access or title to productive assets (most importantly to land, credit, and other inputs); fewer political and legal rights; and more-stringent constraints on mobility and socially acceptable activities. They face discrimination and higher burdens of childcare and eldercare. For all these reasons, returns to their investments can be expected to be inferior. And if a threshold effect also exists (as is likely), then the associated trap will be a bigger threat to women. For example, although both poor men and women face credit constraints, the constraint is often more severe for women, notably when they cannot borrow as much as men with the same initial collateral. Women will then be more vulnerable to being trapped in poverty or unable to recover from economic shocks without help, exacerbating the implications of risk for women.

Monetary measures of poverty (which are available only at the household level and hence cannot reveal inequalities within households) show that there is only a small difference between the poverty rates of men and women in Africa but that women are overrepresented in poor households during their peak productive and reproductive years (Munoz-Boudet et al. 2018; World Bank 2018).

These structural inequalities not only matter in their own right but also impede poverty-reduction efforts. Beyond the intrinsic value of equal opportunities, gender equality brings with it economic growth and poverty-reduction opportunities for countries. This discussion briefly touches on several domains related to critical gender gaps.

Gender Gaps in Human Endowments

Almost all countries in Africa have seen major increases in school enrollments of girls and boys over the past two decades. In many countries, gender disparities in primary and secondary enrollments have closed or, in a few, even reversed. Yet, the gender gap in current attendance or enrollment is especially pronounced in the Sahel region. (And in other countries, new challenges are on the horizon, such as boys lagging girls in school enrollments or learning, a pattern that is also increasingly common in other parts of the world.)

Although girls are enrolled in far greater numbers in African schools than ever before, education levels in the *adult* population are slow to change. Therefore, adult women continue to be significantly disadvantaged in educational attainment and literacy relative to adult men. The average gender literacy gap across African countries is 25 percentage points, reflecting historical gender inequalities in the education sector whose legacy will persist for years, even decades (Beegle et al. 2016). And although the gap is shrinking, some countries still have literacy gaps between young adult men and women (ages 15–24 years) of more than 30 percent (figure F2.1).

Beyond education, Africa continues to face a maternal mortality crisis. Although mortality rates have declined by about one-third between 2000 and 2015, still far too many women die from (often preventable) conditions during pregnancy and childbirth. In 2015, African women faced a staggeringly high lifetime maternal-death risk of 1 in 36, compared with, for example, 1 in 200 in South Asia and 1 in 6,000 in high-income countries.[1] Clearly, access to affordable reproductive health care is a first-order concern for poor African women and their families.

Women are also disproportionately affected by the human immunodeficiency virus and acquired immune deficiency syndrome (HIV/AIDS) epidemic, making up 59 percent of the African population (ages 15 years and up) living with the virus. Prevalence rates vary substantially across countries but, as might be expected, relative to married-once and single women, prevalence is considerably higher among women who have had a marriage dissolution (Djuikom and van de Walle 2018).

FIGURE F2.1 The literacy gap between men and women in Africa is shrinking but still large

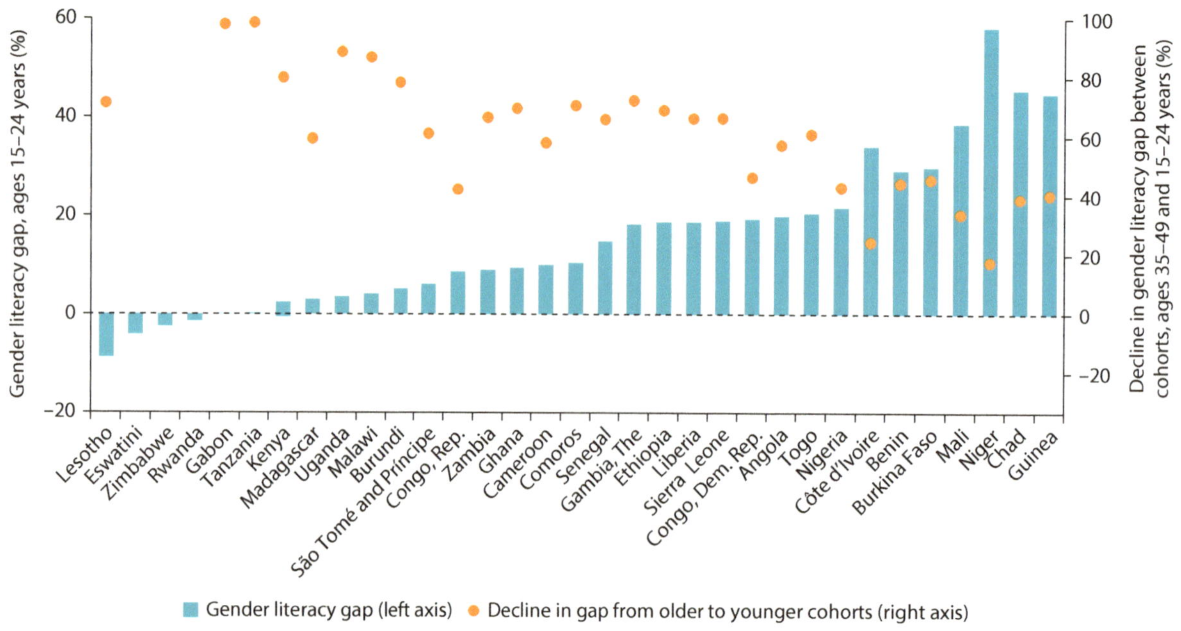

Source: Most recent country Demographic and Health Survey data.
Note: Changes that are off the scale of the figure include Eswatini (1,676%), Zimbabwe (189%), and Rwanda (111%).

Among them, widows tend to have the highest prevalence, followed by divorcées, and then by remarried widows and divorcées (ex-widows and ex-divorcées). For instance, in the low-prevalence country of Ethiopia, 0.9 percent of women in their first marriage tested positive versus 8.1 percent of widows; at the other extreme, the percentages for Zambia are 12.3 percent versus 57.2 percent, respectively.

Women who have suffered a marital dissolution and are HIV-positive are doubly disadvantaged. The virus may or may not have caused their widowhood, but having this often debilitating and life-threatening disease together with the accompanying stigma and ostracism exacerbates the negative welfare effects of marriage dissolution (Loomba Foundation 2015).

FIGURE F2.2 **Across African countries, women carry most of the burden of unpaid domestic and care work**

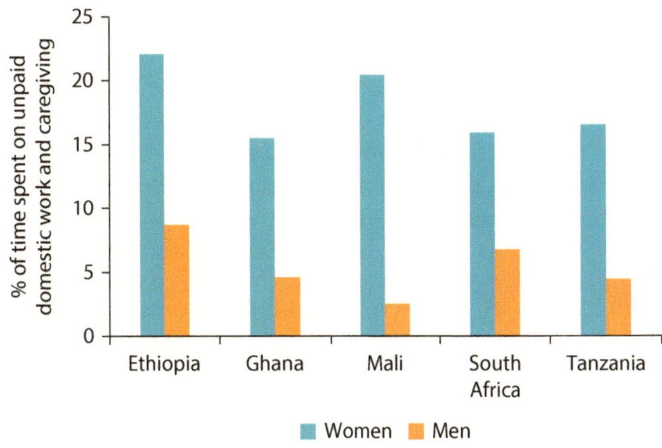

Source: World Bank Gender Data Portal: http://datatopics.worldbank.org/gender/.
Note: Figure shows the average percentage of time that men and women spend on household services according to surveys conducted from various years between 2008 and 2014.

Glaring Differences in the Time Use of Men and Women

Gender differences in time use over the life cycle are among the most pertinent factors that distinguish the lives of men and women in Africa. Although marriage is practically universal across the continent, women tend to form families earlier than men so that important decisions about marriage, childbearing, and labor market entry often fall together (Chakravarty, Das, and Vaillant 2017; Djuikom and van de Walle 2018). And while most African countries have seen a decline in fertility over the past decade, the pace of decline has been modest, and there is evidence that fertility transitions have stalled in some countries—a pattern not commonly observed in other parts of the world (Bongaarts 2017) (see the discussion in chapter 2).

As in other regions, African women spend a disproportionate amount of time on unpaid domestic and care services (figure F2.2). Although the availability and comparability of time-use data for African countries leave much to be desired, recent estimates from a handful of countries suggest that women spend on average 15–22 percent of their time on unpaid work, compared with only 2–9 percent among men. These differences are manifestations of cultural gender norms about the roles and responsibilities of men and women in society (Kevane and Wydick 2001). Empirical evidence suggests not only that domestic requirements negatively affect women's participation in paid employment outside the home (Ruiz Abril 2008) but also that the time and labor constraints on female farmers and entrepreneurs may be one of the most salient factors underlying gender gaps in productivity (Carranza et al. 2017; Nordman and Vaillant 2014; O'Sullivan et al. 2014; Palacios-López and López 2015).

Differences in Asset Ownership and Control between Women and Men

Across Africa, there are profound differences between men and women in ownership, use, and control over assets and wealth (Gaddis, Lahoti, and Li 2018). Gender gaps emerge prominently in ownership of land and housing property, which are important assets for the poor in Africa and the primary means to store wealth in rural communities.[2]

Just under 13 percent of African women (ages 20–49 years) claim sole ownership of land, compared with 36 percent of African men (figure F2.3, panel a). The gender gap is smaller if one considers joint ownership, but even then, it remains significant: 38 percent of African women report owning any land (alone or jointly), compared with 51 percent of African men. A similar picture emerges for housing ownership (figure F2.3, panel b).

Why is it important that in most African countries land and housing property and, by extension, overall wealth is disproportionately concentrated in the hands of men? First, women's ownership, use, and control over resources matter for their well-being and agency (Grown, Gupta, and Kes 2005).

Second, married women's rights to marital property and other assets can be linked to their bargaining position within the family (Fafchamps and Quisumbing 2005a; Manser and Brown 1980; McElroy and Horney 1981). Empirical studies from Africa show that a more egalitarian distribution of assets between husband and wife correlates with the wife's participation in decision making, such as in Ghana (Oduro, Boakye-Yiadom, and Baah-Boateng 2012). Studies from India show that legislative changes under the Hindu Succession Act, which strengthened women's inheritance rights, positively affected women's and girls' education and health outcomes. These effects were even larger for the "second generation," that is, daughters born to women themselves affected by the reforms (Deininger, Goyal, and Nagarajan 2013; Deininger et al. 2018).

Gender gaps extend beyond property to other forms of assets, including financial assets. Data for Africa collected under the 2017 Global Findex round show that 38 percent of men have a bank account at a financial institution, compared with only 27 percent of women (Demirgüç-Kunt et al. 2018). This hides some regional variation: in Chad, Liberia, Mali, and South Sudan, men are more than twice as likely as women to have an account, while there are no gender gaps in Lesotho, Namibia, and South Africa. The sweeping expansion of Kenya's mobile money service, M-Pesa, benefited women disproportionately, increasing the financial savings of female-headed households and enabling women to move out of agriculture into business (Suri and Jack 2016).

FIGURE F2.3 Far fewer African women than men own land or housing

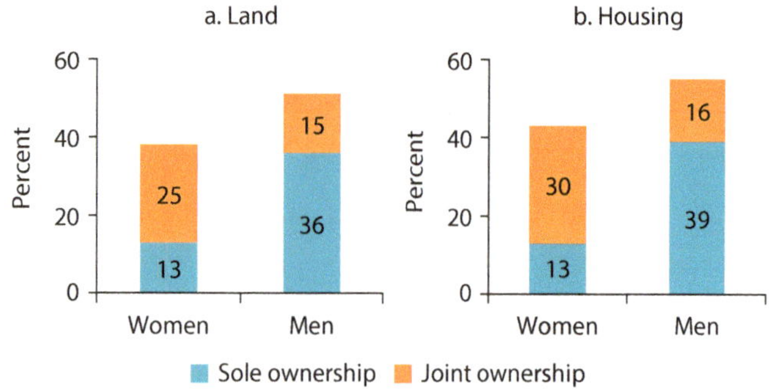

Source: Country Demographic and Health Survey data.
Note: Data are from 27 countries (panel a) and for 28 countries (panel b) from 2010 to 2016 for the population of ages 20–49 years.

Gender Gaps Exacerbated by Formal and Informal Institutions and Norms

Gender gaps in human endowments, time use, and property ownership often reflect gender biases in legal systems, social norms, and institutional structures. In terms of legal frameworks, many African countries have enacted progressive legislation in recent years, with the top reforming economies being in the region. Still, the average country gives women only half the legal rights of men in the areas measured in the Women, Business, and the Law database (World Bank 2019).

Gender biases often linger in statutes about marriage, divorce, land and property rights, and labor (Hallward-Driemeier and Hasan 2013; World Bank 2019). For example, married women do not have equal rights to their husbands in property ownership in 11 out of 47 African countries for which data are available. In 12 out of 47 countries, daughters do not have rights equal to sons to inherit assets from their parents.

Across Africa, women's rights are shaped by legal pluralism, which includes vestiges of colonial, modern constitutional, customary, and religious laws, often leading to conflicting legal provisions and overlapping jurisdictions (Deere and Doss 2006). Informal norms and institutions are arguably even more important than formal laws. Customary law often grants land ownership to men in their role as the head of the family, while married women receive only secondary rights through their husbands, fathers, or other male family members (Kes, Jacobs, and Namy 2011).

Juxtaposed with the many legal, social, and economic disadvantages faced by women together with underdeveloped safety net and insurance mechanisms, marital dissolution can be catastrophic (Djuikom and van de Walle 2018). For women, a marital rupture frequently entails a loss of economic means and support that are acquired through and conditional on marriage—including access to productive assets (such as land) and a home (Kevane 2004). Customary laws governing unions and their dissolution, child custody arrangements, property rights, and inheritance privilege men. Marriage remains the basis for production as well as women's avenue to social and economic rights (Fafchamps and Quisumbing 2005b). It is common for widows and divorcées to inherit little or nothing and, in some settings, to be expropriated of all possessions and ejected from the marital home (Cooper 2008; HRW 2017; Izumi 2007).

Polygyny—the practice of one man marrying multiple wives—may also undermine women's bargaining power and involvement in decisions affecting themselves and their families. This social institution is most prevalent across a wide belt that stretches from Senegal in West Africa to Tanzania in East Africa (Fenske 2015). Polygyny can alter power relations within the family and reduce wives' decision-making powers, as in Mali, Sierra Leone, and Tanzania (Anderson et al. 2016; Newbury 2017). Evidence suggests that polygyny negatively affects the agricultural productivity of female farmers because of less-intensive input use on the plots that they manage (McCarthy, Damon, and Seigerink 2016).

Mobility and Safety Challenges for Women

Norms for acceptable behavior and concerns about gender-based violence often constrain women's physical mobility, thus limiting their labor market opportunities and life choices. Norms differ across countries and even across communities. For example, in Guinea, a staggering 83 percent of women (ages 15–49) agree with the statement that a husband is justified in beating his wife if she goes out without telling him, compared with only 5 percent of women in Malawi who agree (from country Demographic and Health Surveys [DHS]).

Aside from the high levels of gender-based violence in some countries, two other salient points emerge from these data. First, there is a poverty dimension: poor women are much more likely than wealthier women to agree with that statement (figure F2.4). Second, women agree more often than men in most countries (not shown). However, norms are changing in most African countries, and sometimes rapidly so. In Zambia, for example, the share of women and men accepting this type of domestic violence fell from 79 percent and 58 percent, respectively, in the 2001/02 survey to 30 percent and 16 percent in the 2013/14 survey.

Mobility constraints can affect women's labor market participation in a variety of ways. These constraints can directly affect women's preferences for seeking work outside the home, but they also limit women's access to education, markets, banks, and social networks and thus affect their labor market behavior indirectly (as discussed in Chakravarty, Das, and Vaillant 2017). Mobility constraints may further increase the time women spend on domestic tasks—for example, when norms restrict women from

FIGURE F2.4 Norms constrain women's physical mobility, especially in western and central Africa

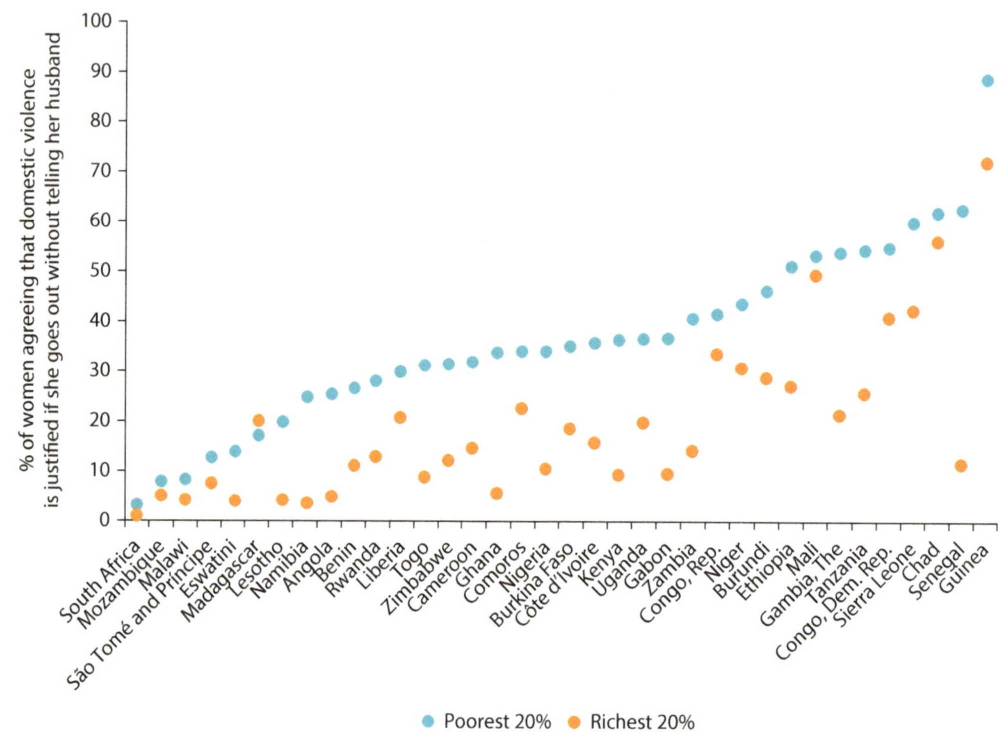

Source: DHS Program STATcompiler, U.S. Agency for International Development: https://www.statcompiler.com/en/.

using bicycles or other forms of transportation (Marcus 2018).

In addition, social norms combined with inadequate laws or weak law enforcement can create an environment where women are at high risk of sexual harassment and gender-based violence (Chakravarty, Das, and Vaillant 2017). Although representative data are difficult to come by, case studies suggest that concerns over harassment by employers and other figures of authority are an important factor in women's labor market decisions and economic opportunities. Female cross-border traders in the Great Lakes region in central Africa are often subjected to acts of violence, threats, and sexual harassment (Brenton et al. 2011). Concerns over sexual harassment from teachers and employers are factors that may limit adolescent girls' participation in training programs and school-to-work transition in Liberia (Ruiz Abril 2008).

Policy Levers to Address Gender Gaps and Reduce Poverty

Addressing the range of gender inequities in Africa is no small task. Development progress in general—such as increasing school enrollment rates through universal primary access or improving health services for all—will go a long way toward equalizing outcomes. However, in some spheres, directed efforts can help bring girls and women closer to escaping the gender poverty trap.

In education, for example, programs subsidizing the direct or indirect cost of education can be effective in increasing enrollments and the educational performance of girls and boys—as shown in Kenya (Duflo, Dupas, and Kremer 2015; Friedman et al. 2016)—and sometimes with a differential and greater impact on women even when not gender-targeted, as in Ghana (Duflo, Dupas, and Kremer 2017).

In the health sphere, most maternal deaths can be prevented by ensuring that pregnant women have access to prenatal care, skilled care during childbirth, and postpartum care following delivery—which requires tackling a range of demand and supply factors (Gordillo-Tobar, Quinlan-Davidson, and Mills 2017). Postnatal follow-ups and checklist approaches can lead to earlier use of postnatal care (McConnell et al. 2016). As for the disproportionate prevalence of HIV/AIDS among women, programs providing life skills and reproductive health knowledge to adolescent girls can improve knowledge about sexual and productive health and associated behaviors (Bandiera et al. 2017). And for those women going through a marital dissolution, which may make them vulnerable, there is need for better access to social protection and health programs for women who are widowed or divorced.

The domestic time-use burdens of women constrain them in terms of both leisure and time for income earning. Scaling up services for childcare (especially for preschool-age children) can be done through a range of policies and regulations that the public sector can put in place to support private childcare provision. And public infrastructure provision (water, sanitation, electricity, and roads) and labor-saving technologies can potentially ease women's time constraints, but more empirical evidence is needed to better understand how this would affect time constraints and the intrahousehold distribution of labor (see ADB [2015] for a desktop review from Asia).

Finally, greater financial inclusion is crucial. Women have lower savings and access to productive assets, which could be addressed through several mechanisms. Savings products with an element of illiquidity and soft commitment can increase women's savings (Dizon, Gong, and Jones 2017; O'Sullivan 2017) and improve the performance of woman-owned businesses (Dupas and Robinson 2013). Technology will also help to reach more rural women (Williams et al. 2018), as further discussed in Fundamentals 3, "Leapfrogging with Technology (and Trade)." And legislative reforms that strengthen women's inheritance rights can improve measures of female empowerment (Deininger, Goyal, and Nagarajan 2013; Deininger et al. 2018). Similarly, land formalization programs promoting joint registration of both spouses can improve outcomes for women and narrow gender gaps (Ali, Deininger, and Goldstein 2014; Goldstein et al. 2015; O'Sullivan 2017). Rwanda's land tenure regularization program, however, while improving documentation of informal land rights among married women, led to an erosion of rights among women who are not legally married (Ali, Deininger, and Goldstein 2014).

Addressing the limited mobility and vulnerability to violence of women is of critical importance to ensure basic human rights. Addressing the patriarchal institutional frameworks and cultural structures that discriminate against women and perpetuate limited mobility and violence against women requires long-term cultural change. Education should be part of the solution (as examined in Friedman et al. 2016) because it can change attitudes toward domestic violence.

Notes

1. Maternal mortality data are based on model estimates of the Maternal Mortality Inter-Agency Group (WHO, UNICEF, UNFPA, World Bank, and UN DESA 2015). Regional estimates are from the World Bank Gender Data Portal: http://datatopics.worldbank.org/gender/.
2. In addition to laws which disadvantage women in terms of property ownership and lower income, women's lower levels of productive assets and savings may be due to social pressures to share their income with family members and friends (Dupas and Robinson 2013; Jakiela and Ozier 2016; Schaner 2017).

References

ADB (Asian Development Bank). 2015. *Balancing the Burden? Desk Review of Women's Time Poverty and the Infrastructure in Asia and the Pacific*. Manila: ADB.

Ali, Daniel A., Klaus Deininger, and Markus Goldstein. 2014. "Environmental and Gender Impacts of Land Tenure Regularization in Africa: Pilot Evidence from Rwanda." *Journal of Development Economics* 110: 262–75.

Anderson, C. Leigh, Travis W. Reynolds, Pierre Biscaye, Melissa Greenaway, and Joshua Merfeld. 2016. "Polygamous Households and Intrahousehold Decision-Making: Evidence and Policy Implications from Mali and Tanzania." EPAR Technical Brief 330, Evans School Policy Analysis and Research Group, University of Washington, Seattle.

Bandiera, Oriana, Niklas Buehren, Robin Burgess, Markus Goldstein, Selim Gulesci, Imran Rasul, and Munshi Sulaiman. 2017. "Women's Empowerment in Action: Evidence from a Randomized Control Trial in Africa." Report No. 118203, World Bank, Washington, DC.

Beegle, Kathleen, Luc Christiaensen, Andrew Dabalen, and Isis Gaddis. 2016. *Poverty in a Rising Africa*. Washington, DC: World Bank.

Bongaarts, John. 2017. "Africa's Unique Fertility Transition." *Population and Development Review* 43 (S1): 39–58.

Brenton, Paul, Celestin Bashinge Bucekuderhwa, Caroline Hossein, Shiho Nagaki, and Jean Baptiste Ntagoma. 2011. "Risky Business: Poor Women Cross-Border Traders in the Great Lakes Region of Africa." *Africa Trade Policy Notes* Note 11, World Bank, Washington, DC.

Carranza, Eliana, Aletheia Donald, Rachel Jones, and Léa Rouanet. 2017. "Time and Money: A Study of Labor Constraints for Female Cotton Producers in Côte d'Ivoire." Gender Innovation Lab Policy Brief Issue 19, World Bank, Washington, DC.

Chakravarty, Shubha, Smita Das, and Julia Vaillant. 2017. "Gender and Youth Employment in Sub-Saharan Africa: A Review of Constraints and Effective Interventions." Policy Research Working Paper 8245, World Bank, Washington, DC.

Cooper, Elizabeth. 2008. "Inheritance Practices and the Intergenerational Transmission of Poverty in Africa: A Literature Review and Annotated Bibliography." CPRC Working Paper No. 116, Chronic Poverty Research Centre, Manchester, U.K.

Deere, Carmen D., and Cheryl R. Doss. 2006. "The Gender Asset Gap: What Do We Know and Why Does It Matter?" *Feminist Economics* 12 (1–2): 1–50.

Deininger, Klaus, Aparajita Goyal, and Hari Nagarajan. 2013. "Women's Inheritance Rights and Intergenerational Transmission of Resources in India." *Journal of Human Resources* 48 (1): 114–41.

Deininger, Klaus, Fang Xia, Songqinq Jin, and Hari Nagarajan. 2018. "Inheritance Law Reform, Empowerment, and Human Capital Accumulation: Second-Generation Effects from India." *Journal of Development Studies* (online): 1–23. doi:10.1080/00220388.2018.1520218.

Demirgüç-Kunt, Asli, Leora Klapper, Dorothe Singer, Saniya Ansar, and Jake Hess. 2018. *The Global Findex Database 2017: Measuring Financial Inclusion and the Fintech Revolution*. Washington, DC: World Bank.

Dizon, Felipe, Erick Gong, and Kelly Jones. 2017. "The Effect of Promoting Savings on Informal Risk-Sharing: Experimental Evidence from Vulnerable Women in Kenya." Unpublished paper, World Bank, Washington, DC.

Djuikom, Marie Albertine, and Dominique van de Walle. 2018. "Marital Shocks and Women's Welfare in Africa." Policy Research Working Paper 8306, World Bank, Washington, DC.

Duflo, Esther, Pascaline Dupas, and Michael Kremer. 2015. "Education, HIV, and Early Fertility: Experimental Evidence from Kenya." *American Economic Review* 105 (9): 2757–97.

———. 2017. The Impact of Free Secondary Education: Experimental Evidence from Ghana. Working paper, Stanford University, Stanford, CA.

Dupas, Pascaline, and Jonathan Robinson. 2013. "Savings Constraints and Microenterprise Development: Evidence from a Field Experiment in Kenya." *American Economic Journal: Applied Economics* 5 (1): 163–92.

Fafchamps, Marcel, and Agnes Quisumbing. 2005a. "Assets at Marriage in Rural Ethiopia." *Journal of Development Economics* 77 (1): 1–25.

———. 2005b. "Marriage, Bequest, and Assortative Matching in Rural Ethiopia." *Economic Development and Cultural Change* 53 (20): 347–80.

Fenske, James. 2015. "African Polygamy: Past and Present." *Journal of Development Economics* 117: 58–73.

Friedman, Willa, Michael Kremer, Edward Miguel, and Rebecca Thornton. 2016. "Education as Liberation?" *Economica* 83 (329): 1–30.

Gaddis, Isis, Rahul Lahoti, and Wenjie Li. 2018. "Gender Gaps in Property Ownership in Sub-Saharan Africa." Policy Research Working Paper 8573, World Bank, Washington, DC.

Goldstein, Markus, Kenneth Houngbedji, Florence Kondylis, Michael O'Sullivan, and Harris Selod. 2015. "Formalizing Rural Land Rights in West Africa: Early Evidence from a Randomized Impact Evaluation in Benin." Policy Research Working Paper 7435, World Bank, Washington, DC.

Gordillo-Tobar, Amparo, Meaghen Quinlan-Davidson, and Samuel Lantei Mills. 2017. "Maternal and Child Health: The World Bank Group's Response to Sustainable Development Goal 3: Target 3.1 and 3.2." Discussion paper, World Bank, Washington, DC.

Grown, Caren, Greeta Rao Gupta, and Aslihan Kes. 2005. *Taking Action: Achieving Gender Equality and Empowering Women.* London, U.K.; Sterling, VA: Earthscan for the United Nations Development Programme.

Hallward-Driemeier, Mary, and Tazeen Hasan. 2013. *Empowering Women: Legal Rights and Economic Opportunities in Africa.* Africa Development Forum Series. Washington, DC: World Bank.

HRW (Human Rights Watch). 2017. "You Will Get Nothing: Violations of Property and Inheritance Rights of Widows in Zimbabwe." Report, HRW, New York.

Izumi, Kaori. 2007. "Gender-Based Violence and Property Grabbing in Africa: A Denial of Women's Liberty and Security." *Gender and Development* 15 (1): 11–23.

Jakiela, Pamela, and Owen Ozier. 2016. "Does Africa Need a Rotten Kin Theorem? Experimental Evidence from Village Economies." *Review of Economic Studies* 83 (1): 231–68.

Kes, Aslihan, Krista Jacobs, and Sophie Namy. 2011. "Gender Differences in Asset Rights in Uganda." Gender Land and Asset Survey, International Center for Research on Women (ICRW), Washington, DC.

Kevane, Michael. 2004. *Women and Development in Africa: How Gender Works.* Boulder, CO: Lynne Rienner Publishers.

Kevane, Michael, and Bruce Wydick. 2001. "Social Norms and the Time Allocation of Women's Labor in Burkina Faso." *Review of Development Economics* 5 (1): 119–29.

Loomba Foundation. 2015. "The Global Widows Report 2015: A Global Overview of Deprivation Faced by Widows and Their Children." Study, Loomba Foundation, London.

Manser, Marilyn, and Murray Brown. 1980. "Marriage and Household Decision-Making: A Bargaining Analysis." *International Economic Review* 21 (1): 31–44.

Marcus, Rachel. 2018. "The Norms Factor: Recent Research on Gender, Social Norms, and Women's Economic Empowerment." Research paper of the Overseas Development Institute (ODI), London, for the International Development Research Centre (IDRC), Ottawa.

McCarthy, Aine Seitz, Amy L. Damon, and Vincent Seigerink. 2016. "Favoritism and Farming: Agricultural Productivity and Polygyny in Tanzania." Unpublished paper, University of Minnesota, St. Paul.

McConnell, Margaret, Allison Ettenger, Claire Watt Rothschild, Faith Muigai, and Jessica Cohen. 2016. "Can a Community Health Worker Administered Postnatal Checklist Increase Health-Seeking Behaviors and Knowledge? Evidence from a Randomized Trial with a Private Maternity Facility in Kiambu County, Kenya." *BMC Pregnancy and Childbirth* 16 (1): 136.

McElroy, Marjorie, and Mary Jean Horney. 1981. "Nash-Bargained Household Decisions: Toward a Generalization of the Theory of Demand." *International Economic Review* 22 (2): 333–49.

Munoz-Boudet, Ana Maria, Paola Buitrago, Bénédicte Leroy de la Brière, David Newhouse, Eliana Rubiano Matulevich, Kinnon Scott, and Pablo Suarez-Becerra. 2018. "Gender Differences in Poverty and Household Composition through the Life-cycle." Policy Research Working Paper 8306, World Bank, Washington, DC.

Newbury, Emma. 2017. "Understanding Women's Lives in Polygamous Marriages: Exploring Community Perspectives in Sierra Leone and DRC." Report, Trócaire, Maynooth, Ireland.

Nordman, Christophe J., and Julia Vaillant. 2014. "Inputs, Gender Roles and Sharing Norms? Assessing the Gender Performance Gap among Informal Entrepreneurs in

Madagascar." IZA Discussion Paper 8045, Institute for the Study of Labor, Bonn.

Oduro, Abena D., Louis Boakye-Yiadom, and William Baah-Boateng. 2012. "Asset Ownership and Egalitarian Decision-Making among Couples: Some Evidence from Ghana." Gender Asset Gap Project Working Paper No. 14, Indian Institute of Management, Bangalore, India.

O'Sullivan, Michael. 2017. "Gender and Property Rights in Sub-Saharan Africa: A Review of Constraints and Effective Interventions." Policy Research Working Paper 8250, World Bank, Washington, DC.

O'Sullivan, Michael, Arathi Rao, Raka Banerjee, Kajal Gulati, and Margaux Vinez. 2014. "Levelling the Field: Improving Opportunities for Women Farmers in Africa." Report No. 86039, World Bank and the ONE Campaign, Washington, DC.

Palacios-López, Amparo, and Ramón López. 2015. "The Gender Gap in Agricultural Productivity: The Role of Market Imperfections." *Journal of Development Studies* 51 (9): 1175–92.

Ruiz Abril, Maria Elena. 2008. "Girls' Vulnerability Assessment." Background study for the Economic Empowerment of Adolescent Girls in Liberia project, Government of Liberia, Nike Foundation, and World Bank, Washington, DC.

Schaner, Simone. 2017. "The Cost of Convenience? Transaction Costs, Bargaining Power, and Savings Account Use in Kenya." *Journal of Human Resources* 52 (4): 919–45.

Suri, Tavneet, and William Jack. 2016. "The Long-Run Poverty and Gender Impacts of Mobile Money." *Science* 354 (6317): 1288–92.

UNDP (United Nations Development Programme). 2013. *Humanity Divided: Confronting Inequality in Developing Countries*. New York: UNDP.

WHO, UNICEF, UNFPA, World Bank, and UN DESA (World Health Organization, United Nations Children's Fund, UN Population Fund, and UN Population Division of the UN Department of Economic and Social Affairs). 2015. *Trends in Maternal Mortality: 1990 to 2015*. WHO/RHR/15.23. Geneva: WHO.

Williams, Melissa, Narnia Bohler-Muller, Boris Branisa, Lynne Cadenhead, Carolyn Currie, Graciela Hijar, Sandhya Seshadri Iyer, Mariela Magnelli, Margo Thomas, and Helen Walbey. 2018. "Economic Empowerment of Rural Women." Gender Economic Equity Policy Brief for T20 (Think 20) Argentina 2018, Buenos Aires.

World Bank. 2011. *World Development Report 2012: Gender Equality and Development*. Washington, DC: World Bank.

———. 2018. *Poverty and Shared Prosperity 2018: Piecing Together the Poverty Puzzle*. Washington, DC: World Bank.

———. 2019. *Women, Business, and the Law 2019: A Decade of Reform*. Washington, DC: World Bank.

Moving to Jobs Off the Farm

4

Kathleen Beegle and Tom Bundervoet

Moving to jobs off the farm for Africa's poor will largely mean moving into informal employment, often into nearby towns. It typically concerns running household enterprises—small, unincorporated, and often informal nonfarm enterprises owned and managed by household members—either full- or part-time and sometimes done only during certain parts of the year. While wage employment is growing fast in some African countries, the low base of wage employment and the pace at which growing cohorts of young adults enter the labor force imply that wage employment will absorb only a small share of the job seekers over the coming 10–15 years. And private sector formal wage employment is even more limited.

The importance of the informal nonfarm sector as a provider of jobs and livelihoods for Africa's burgeoning labor force means it cannot be neglected by policy. From a policy perspective, the choice of focusing on the formal or informal sector, or on small and medium enterprises (SMEs) and large firms or household enterprises, is not an either-or proposition. Investments in human capital, infrastructure, and a transparent regulatory framework will benefit the spectrum of enterprises, from household enterprises to SMEs and large firms. Still, not all investments cut across. Investments can also be made that more directly benefit nonfarm businesses run by poor households, as discussed in this chapter.

The available evidence suggests that investments to benefit the enterprises of the poor require an integrated approach, jointly addressing skills and financing constraints. Although this will typically not suffice to help most household enterprises grow into firms that generate wage employment, it can help many of the poor diversify their incomes and secure and increase their income streams.

Second, the demand-side aspect requires much more attention—that is, how to foster demand for the goods and services produced by the informal sector. This has often been overlooked in the agenda to raise nonfarm incomes for the poor, especially the importance of the proximity of demand. Rural town development appears especially promising. It facilitates access to off-farm employment for the poor, pointing to the need to focus on what it takes to develop a town—such as rural road connectivity, electricity, and social services. As centers of agro-manufacturing and trade, secondary towns and cities are often also at the nexus of agro-value chain development, with extended agriculture accounting for one-third of off-farm employment in the early stages of development. But demand often also finds itself just across the border, underscoring the importance of deepening Africa's regional integration.

A Profile of Africa's Off-Farm Work

The employment structure in Sub-Saharan Africa is gradually changing for all, including the poor. Although agriculture will remain the main engine of poverty reduction in the near future, the growing share of individuals and households, including the poor, who are engaged in nonfarm activities highlights the need to raise nonfarm incomes.[1]

There are numerous ways to describe "off-farm" employment and income activities in Africa. This includes by broad sector classification (by industry or services, sometimes described as secondary and tertiary sectors) (World Bank, forthcoming[b]). Some characterize by the link with agriculture (agriprocessing, food retailing and services, or outside the agriculture system) (Yeboah and Jayne 2018). And other work emphasizes employment status (such as wage or nonwage work in a household enterprise) (Davis, Di Giuseppe, and Zezza 2017). And within these framings, one can further discuss concepts of formality and informality.

The decreasing employment share of agriculture is partly related to urbanization and partly to the growth of the rural nonfarm economy. The share of Africans living in urban areas increased from 27 percent in 1990 to 38 percent by 2016, which is associated with a relative decline in agricultural employment—few city dwellers are primarily employed in farming. At the same time, rural households also increasingly diversify their livelihoods or even transition completely to activities beyond the farm, typically called the rural nonfarm economy. Almost half of rural households have income from off-the-farm activities (Davis, Di Giuseppe, and Zezza 2017), which accounts for, on average, 23 percent of household income for rural households.

These averages hide considerable variation across countries in the region. Among the southern African countries, Botswana, Eswatini, Namibia, and South Africa have far lower shares of employment in agriculture than the rest of the region (World Bank, forthcoming[b]). As for the rural nonfarm economy, rural households in some countries (such as Ethiopia) have much lower percentages of nonfarm employment than the regional average, and others have higher percentages (such as Kenya, Niger, and Uganda). Participation in nonfarm activities and percentages of nonfarm income increase with gross domestic product (GDP), but they tend to be lower in rural Africa than in other low- and middle-income regions, even after controlling for differences in GDP (Davis, Di Giuseppe, and Zezza 2017).

What does moving off the farm in terms of work mean for African households? There is considerable heterogeneity within the nonfarm sector, often with notable dualism. It is characterized by low-productivity subsistence activities with few or no barriers to entry, at one end, but also a small segment which has high-productivity, high-earning activities with high entry barriers (in terms of physical and human capital) at the other end. The high-return subsector is largely the privilege of better-endowed households; the low-return subsector is usually dominated by casual labor and small household enterprises.[2]

Though nonfarm livelihood opportunities and their respective entry barriers are country- and context-specific, three broad observations emerge from surveying the literature[3] related to household enterprises, nonagricultural wage employment, and agro-food sector employment.

Household Enterprises

First, working "off the farm" usually means working without a salary or employer but rather in an informal household enterprise, especially for the poor and near poor. This broad group of activities, labeled "household enterprises," is profiled later in the chapter but is marked by often being solo activities (one or more household members) with no hired labor. The term "household enterprise" refers to a business activity owned and operated by one or more household members. This covers a wide array of business activities and occupations: petty trading, retail of prepared foods, street hawking, tailoring, beauty parlors, electricians, bricklayers, and so on.

Despite the label, household enterprises are not necessarily activities operated within the dwelling of the household. Although they are most often microenterprises without hired workers, they do sometimes employ hired workers, though typically only one or two. The vast majority of these enterprises are engaged in commerce—as street vendors and in petty trading (World Bank 2012). Those who work in household enterprises go by varying labels: self-employed, own-account worker, unpaid or contributing family worker, and less commonly, employers (if the business has hired workers—labor that is wage employed).[4] These businesses are typically unincorporated and not registered for social security, value added tax, or other registration processes involved in formalization. As such, they are considered informal (ILO 1993).

Nonagricultural Wage Employment

Those African households that have household members in nonagricultural wage employment tend to be wealthier than those with other types of employment (figure 4.1). The incidence of wage employment increases with wealth and shows a particularly large jump for the wealthiest 20 percent, who are more likely to be employed in public sector and formal private sector salaried jobs (jobs

FIGURE 4.1 Household enterprise work is far more common than wage employment for the poor in Africa

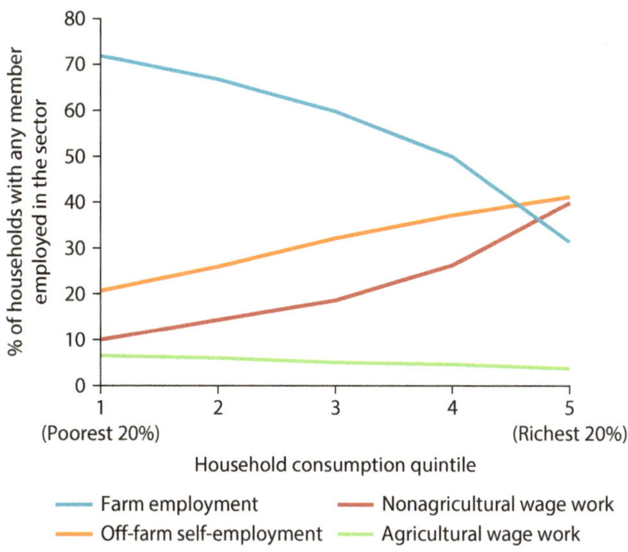

Sources: World Bank Africa Poverty database and International Income Distribution Database (I2D2).
Note: Figure represents data from 40 African countries. Informal "household enterprises"—a business activity owned and operated by one or more household members with no hired labor—are the most common form of off-the-farm self-employment in Africa.

that pay more and require higher education levels).[5] Exceptions include South Africa (a middle-income country), which has a very low level of nonfarm self-employment. This pattern—the income gradient with respect to employment type—is even starker when looking at rural areas with very low rates of wage employment.

Despite the dominance of agriculture, the share of agricultural wage work in the labor force is low in the region and lower than in other regions. Particularly in West Africa, only a small share of household income is derived from wage work in agriculture—for example, 3 percent of rural household income in Niger (Davis, Di Giuseppe, and Zezza 2017). Poorer households are more likely to be in agricultural wage employment, though participation rates are still low even for these households. Only the wealthiest 20 percent of households in urban areas are as likely to work for wages as to work in a household enterprise. In rural areas, self-employment dominates nonfarm work across the entire wealth distribution.

Household enterprises are often, though not always, a stepping-stone out of poverty. Strong poverty reduction in Rwanda between 2000 and 2010 was partly explained by the large increase in household enterprise employment, particularly in rural areas (World Bank 2015c). Welfare levels tend to be higher for households with a household enterprise than for households that are uniquely engaged in farming. Controlling for household human capital and location, household enterprise earnings have the same marginal effect on consumption as private wage employment (Fox and Sohnesen 2012). Even in countries such as Ethiopia, where the rural nonfarm economy is small and its contribution to poverty reduction limited, consumption levels are higher for households running a nonfarm enterprise (though not many poor households do so) (World Bank, forthcoming[a]).

Another key point is that, especially in rural areas, households diversify their income sources. They diversify not only by type of employment (farm, nonfarm business, or wage work) but also by sector. However, the poor are less likely to diversify their income sources, which is consistent with the notion that diversification is a pathway out of poverty.

Agro-Food Sector Employment

A quarter to one-third of off-farm employment is in the agro-food system. Including farmers, the food economy is Africa's biggest employer (Allen, Heinrigs, and Heo 2018; Yeboah and Jayne 2018).[6] This work is concentrated in downstream commerce, food transportation, and distribution rather than agriprocessing. It is expanding rapidly but from a low base.

Moreover, nonfarm employment in the "food economy" is predominately female. Youth are also disproportionately involved in the nonfarm food sector. And employment off the farm can bring demographic changes. In Senegal, for example, an expansion of nonfarm jobs for women leads to significantly higher average ages at marriage and first birth as well as fewer children born (Van den Broeck and Maertens 2015).

The Prospect of Formal Wage Jobs

At the country level, countries with higher national incomes have lower shares of workers in household enterprises; development and wage work go hand in hand. In Africa, as elsewhere, modern firms in the formal sector are of crucial importance. Large firms in Africa pay higher wages, even after controlling for all worker characteristics (Fafchamps and Söderbom 2006; Söderbom and Teal 2004; Söderbom, Teal, and Wambugu 2005). Formal firms (usually larger) are more productive than informal firms (La Porta and Shleifer 2014). Large informal firms in Africa have lower labor productivity than formal firms (Mohammad and Islam 2015). Hence a focus on improving the business and investment climate to facilitate the growth of private formal sector employment is among the main proximate goals of economic development.

Wage employment in Africa

Wage employment, especially in the formal sector, remains relatively rare and mostly inaccessible to Africa's poor and near poor.[7] The formal wage sector's share of employment in African economies is small, with a substantial share of it in the public sector, and is projected to remain so even under highly optimistic scenarios. Though wage employment expanded rapidly during Africa's 1995–2013 high-growth period, the low base of wage employment, combined with rapid growth of the labor force (driven by high fertility), means that the wage employment share increased only marginally, as the following examples illustrate:

- *In Rwanda*—a country lauded for its business-friendly environment and sharp improvements in investment climate—formal sector employment increased by two-thirds between 2006 and 2011.

Despite this, the formal private wage sector constituted a mere 4 percent of all employment in 2011 (World Bank 2016b).

- *In Côte d'Ivoire,* wage employment (both formal and informal) is projected to grow from 19 percent of employment to 23–26 percent, depending on the sector growth scenarios (Christiaensen and Premand 2017).
- *In Ghana,* a country that transitioned from low-income to low-middle-income status, private wage employment grew considerably from 1991 to 2012 but is still only 16 percent of employment (up from 6 percent), and not all is formal employment (Honorati and Johansson de Silva 2016).
- *In Nigeria,* the most populous country in the region, wage employment is projected to account for 20 percent of all work by 2025 (World Bank 2015b).

These specific examples reflect the regional pattern: even under a "game changer" scenario, marked by exceptionally strong industrial employment growth, the share of the African labor force in private wage employment will likely not exceed 20 percent by 2020 (Fox et al. 2013). At best, one in four of Africa's youth will find a wage job between 2010 and 2020, and only a small share of these jobs will be "formal" jobs in modern enterprises. Rather, it is projected that 37 percent of these new labor force entrants will work in household enterprises, putting the employment share of household enterprises at more than 25 percent by 2020 (up from about 16 percent in 2005–15).

Failure of Manufacturing Growth

Taking a sectoral approach, the changes taking place in the labor allocation in Africa are broadly described as a shift from agriculture to services and not to manufacturing. Modern manufacturing firms in the region account for about 3 percent of employment (Filmer and Fox 2014). And in some cases, the relative share of manufacturing in employment or GDP has been declining—described as premature deindustrialization (see case studies in Newman et al. [2016]).[8] Although the shift to services has so far enhanced productivity in Africa, such productivity increases through expansion of low-end services may be unsustainable because of limited demand beyond the domestic market (McMillan, Rodrik, and Sepulveda 2017).

The failure of manufacturing to grow in Africa is of pressing concern (as discussed by, among others, Bhorat, Steenkamp, and Rooney [2016]). Historically, manufacturing has led the way to higher income and greater poverty reduction. The manufacturing sector can be both labor-intensive and export-oriented, giving it advantages over other high-productivity sectors such as the mining or services sectors. Export orientation is critical, given that many countries in the region have small domestic markets and given the established link between exports and economic growth. Manufacturing firms in Africa, however, have among the lowest export rates in the world (Filmer and Fox 2014).

Manufacturing can also offer agglomeration effects derived from the clustering of firms (World Bank 2012), but the specific urbanization process in Africa has prevented firms from realizing these benefits (Lall, Henderson, and Venables 2017). And unit labor costs, a key attribute of the growth of labor-intensive manufacturing for exportation, appear to be higher in Africa than in other regions (Gelb et al. 2017; Golub et al. 2017). One notable exception to the decline in manufacturing as a share of GDP is food and beverage manufacturing, which typically expanded (Hallward-Driemeier and Nayyar 2018).

The projections for wage employment in the region may understate the potential for reducing poverty by growing firms and expanding wage employment opportunities from new, innovative industrial approaches (box 4.1) and new technology (Murray 2017). Faster internet has been shown to increase employment rates, although the overall impact is modest (Hjort and Poulsen 2017).

BOX 4.1 Can industrial policy drive poverty reduction?

Driven by the rapidly expanding labor force in many African countries, and perhaps the less-than-expected employment effects of horizontal reforms, industrial policy has recently staged a comeback in some African countries. Industrial policy has largely been considered a bad idea in development thinking over the past decades, mainly on grounds that allocation of resources in an economy is too complex to be centralized and that the market will naturally identify sectors with an inherent competitive advantage (Hausmann and Rodrik 2006). In recent years, there has been a shift in thinking: more development thinkers and practitioners now argue that identifying and prioritizing certain sectors for large-scale government investments to make those sectors viable and competitive is an essential, or indeed indispensable, complement to generic business climate reforms. Special economic zones (SEZs) and industrial parks increasingly show up in countries' medium-term development plans, mainly to attract and accommodate international firms looking for cheap labor to manufacture labor-intensive, low-tech products—primarily textiles and garments and pharmaceuticals (Newman et al. 2016).

Regardless of the success of the new generation of industrial policies, it is unlikely to be sufficient to accommodate a bulging labor force driven by higher population growth. Among low-income African countries, Ethiopia has arguably the most active and ambitious industrial development strategy and has recently inaugurated Africa's biggest industrial park—in Hawassa, about 270 kilometers south of Addis Ababa. More parks are in the pipeline or currently being built. The investments in industrial parks are accompanied by massive investments in transport, energy, and infrastructure to link the production sites to international markets.

Initial developments have been encouraging, with major players in the global textiles and garments industry investing in Ethiopia (Mihretu and Llobet 2017). Yet despite the scale, ambition, and initial success of the industrialization agenda, the creation of an estimated 2 million manufacturing jobs in the next 10 years (EIC 2017) pales in comparison with labor force growth of 20 million over the same period. Even with an optimistic multiplier effect of, say, two, the employment generated, while encouraging and much needed, will not be nearly enough to accommodate a rapidly growing labor force.

The Formal Sector's Marginal Impact on Poverty Reduction

Formal wage employment is unlikely to absorb substantial numbers of African workers in the short-to-medium run, even when carefully targeted. Moreover, the formal wage sector will likely remain marginal in terms of poverty reduction specifically. Workers in the formal sector tend to come from relatively privileged backgrounds and are typically secondary- or postsecondary-educated (low-tech manufacturing being a notable exception, with the potential to provide employment to workers with only primary education).

Expanding the formal wage sector will reduce "official" unemployment among Africa's urban postsecondary graduates—a particularly vocal and politically influential group—but will not lead to noticeable dents in poverty.[9] As noted earlier, this does not mean governments should not invest in the infrastructure, skills, and policy reforms to enable a thriving formal sector and firm growth. But it does emphasize that in the short-to-medium run, a more balanced approach to generating off-farm employment, with due attention to the operating environment and productivity of household enterprises, will be needed to accelerate poverty reduction.[10]

The choice between the formal or informal sector, or between SMEs and large firms or household enterprises, or between manufacturing or services, is not entirely an either-or one. There is a general private sector agenda that would benefit the entire range of firms, from household enterprises to large firms (entailing macro fundamentals, the business environment, skills building of the population, infrastructure upgrading, and so on). Yet most African governments will face some trade-offs between the short-term and the long-term agendas in terms of policies and programs to help firms grow. These trade-offs cut across many areas, such as finance and prioritizing access to finance (do you give small grants to households or large grants to bigger firms, as in the YouWin program in Nigeria?); infrastructure (where to build roads?); and electricity (what is more needed: big grids for large firms or off-grid solar energy for household enterprises and micro, small, and medium enterprises [MSMEs]?).

Despite the importance of the household enterprises for employment and poverty reduction, particularly in the short-to-medium run, their potential should not be exaggerated. Though household enterprises create many jobs through entry, they rarely are a source of job creation through expansion or growth. Few household enterprises grow and add jobs, and those that do typically add only a single job (as further discussed in the next section). It is unclear whether an improved operating environment for household enterprises would lead to more of them expanding and adding jobs, given the high share of businesses started out of necessity rather than opportunity (box 4.2). Nor is it likely that household enterprises will provide the kind of high-productivity employment that can drive overall growth. Like others (such as Page and Söderbom [2015]), we caution against overselling the potential of household enterprises for employment creation (that is, as job creators, especially for good jobs). They can, however, provide a better alternative (or complement) to agriculture for relatively low-skilled workers seeking better lives and livelihoods.

BOX 4.2 Are household enterprises created of necessity or opportunity?

Household enterprises are often categorized into two distinct groups: opportunity enterprises and necessity enterprises. "Opportunity" entrepreneurship describes those businesses that are started to take advantage of an economic opportunity. These businesses could grow into the larger formal firms of tomorrow. They are also called "constrained gazelles," "transformational" enterprises, or "improvement-driven" businesses. On the other hand, small-scale informal enterprises may be driven by necessity as the lack of wage jobs and formal unemployment insurance push people to jump-start self-employment as a survival strategy.

Empirical research suggests that necessity entrepreneurship constitutes the bulk of household enterprises in low-income countries. Across seven West African countries, 56–71 percent of household enterprises are found to be "survivalist" or driven by necessity (Grimm, Knorringa, and Lay 2012). Necessity entrepreneurship accounts for more than half of self-employment in countries that are not within the Organisation for Economic Co-operation and Development (OECD), compared with 25 percent in the OECD (Poschke 2013b). The inability to find a wage job is frequently cited as a motivation to start a household enterprise.

Necessity entrepreneurship is not bad and may indeed be better than the alternative of subsistence agriculture. But irrespective of whether one is pushed or pulled into having a household enterprise, the sheer prevalence of necessity firms has implications for public policy. Necessity enterprises tend to be small and may have limited scope or ambition to ever grow and expand. Though they usually survive, they do not tend to create employment other than for the members of the household.

Although public policy aimed at facilitating entry into nonfarm enterprise activities can benefit both

(Box continues next page)

BOX 4.2 Are household enterprises created of necessity or opportunity? *(continued)*

necessity and opportunity entrepreneurs, interventions aimed at facilitating growth and job creation in household enterprises will likely be more effective when geared toward the opportunity entrepreneurs. Policies affecting high-ability entrepreneurs—who may have the potential to grow into small or medium-size firms—may indirectly affect the entry of low-ability entrepreneurs and thus the prevalence of microfirms (Poschke 2013a).

However, identifying high-potential and constrained enterprises and entrepreneurs is a challenge (see the discussion in Fafchamps and Woodruff [2016]), as is developing the right tools to raise their capacity. The average annual employment growth of 1.15 percent in Tanzania's MSMEs masks a large heterogeneity across firms: 88 percent of the sample did not grow at all, while the average annual employment growth among the 12 percent of the sample that did grow was an impressive 13 percent (Diao, Kweka, and McMillian 2017). And although the evidence on what works for the necessity-type activities is mixed, as discussed later in the chapter, efforts to raise the incomes from these activities is a critical need to tackle the region's poverty challenge.

Key Traits of Household Enterprises

Household enterprises are important income sources for the poor and nonpoor alike in both rural and urban areas. Many country-specific studies characterize household enterprises, usually drawing on household surveys with relevant content in the questionnaire about the nature of the enterprise. Firm surveys are less common as a source because many, by design, do not sample very small business activities (or businesses with no or very few hired workers). As such, they paint a very different picture of the landscape of employment regarding firm traits, especially in low- and medium-income countries (World Bank 2012). We use recent data from 10 African countries to look in detail at the characteristics of the household enterprises and specifically what sets the enterprises of the poor apart from those of wealthier households.[11]

Enterprise Size, Relation to Poverty, and Constraints Affecting Survival

In Africa, household enterprises largely equate to self-employment or owner-operated activities. More than 70 percent of household enterprises have only one worker, the owner (figure 4.2). Fewer than 20 percent of household enterprises engage some other family members, while about 10 percent hire outside labor for a wage. The enterprises of the poor are more likely than enterprises in the top consumption quintile to be one-person affairs: 77 percent of enterprises in the bottom quintile engage only one person (the owner), compared with 65 percent in the wealthiest quintile. Poor household enterprises are also less likely to employ hired labor (nonhousehold members), while the share of enterprises that engage any other family members is stable across quintiles.

Put differently, although household enterprises are small across the board, the poor's enterprises tend to be smaller still. The difference in size between poor and wealthier household enterprises stems from a higher prevalence of hired wage employees among the latter. Poor households rely almost uniquely on household members to work in their enterprises, while wealthier households rely a little bit more on hired labor.

That household enterprises are small suggests they do not create much employment. Indeed, the view of a household enterprise or poor entrepreneur getting credit and flying off into prosperity is romanticized and largely mistaken. Even if they survive, most household enterprises never expand employment (Fox and Sohneson 2012). However, household enterprises are also numerous. They have created and will mainly continue to create employment through entry more than through growth. Although this may not make them important vehicles for economic growth (lacking economies of scale), the ease of entry and exit does make them important vehicles for income diversification, including to cope with shocks ex post (as discussed in chapter 5) and to reduce poverty (box 4.3).

Household enterprises run by poorer households also tend to be younger, though the differences are small. A quarter of household enterprises in the bottom consumption quintile have been in operation for less than two years, compared with 21 percent in the top quintile. The higher share of young

FIGURE 4.2 The poor's household enterprises tend to be smaller than those of the nonpoor

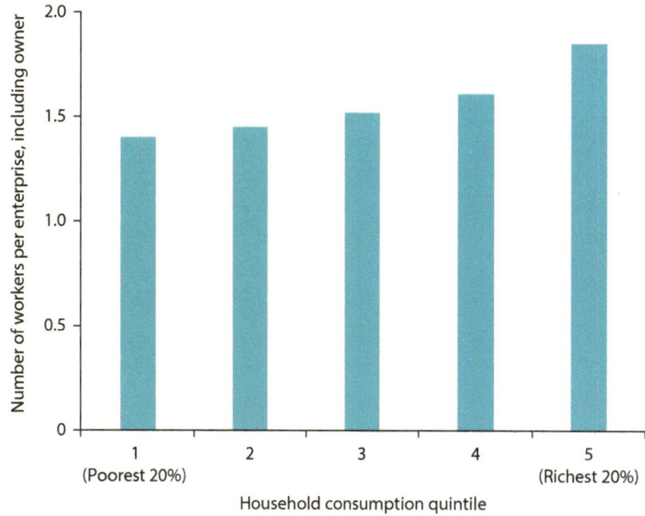

Source: Nagler 2017.

BOX 4.3 Job creation by nonfarm enterprises in Rwanda shows a high churn rate and the importance of location for market access

Informal nonfarm enterprises typically create jobs through entry and shed jobs through exit rather than by growing or scaling back the number of employees. This is nicely demonstrated by Rwanda's Establishment Censuses (ECs). Rwanda conducted its first EC in 2011, followed by another in 2014. In contrast to many other countries, Rwanda's EC also surveys informal microenterprises as long as they have a fixed establishment.

Comparison of the 2011 and 2014 ECs shows that between the census rounds, about 102,000 new informal microenterprises were started, creating 136,000 jobs (roughly 1.3 jobs per enterprise). Yet the total stock of informal microenterprises increased by only 27,000 and total employment in microenterprises by 46,000. These figures suggest a high degree of churning, with informal microfirms entering the market and creating jobs (though most often only for the owner) but exiting rapidly, destroying those same jobs. Indeed, survival rates for informal microfirms are fairly low: only about one-third of enterprises surveyed in 2011 still existed by 2014. Positive net job creation was mainly a result of firm entry outpacing firm exit.

Some nonfarm enterprises do, however, manage to grow. Matching surviving microenterprises across the 2011 and 2014 ECs, about 70 percent of enterprises that employed one person in 2011 still employed one person three years later. Of those that managed to expand, 80 percent added one single job. One-person household enterprises that managed to add jobs tended to be owned by a man with at least some secondary education, located in areas with higher market accessibility (defined as shorter travel time to a population center) or close to international borders.

The effects of location point to the importance of market demand: being closer to population centers or international borders presumably captures the size of the market and is associated with a higher likelihood of expansion. From a policy perspective, expanding access to secondary education, which remains highly unequal in many parts of Africa, and improving rural connectivity appears important to maximize the growth potential of microenterprises.

household enterprises and entrants among the bottom quintiles, at least in some countries,[12] may point to lower survival rates for poor enterprises.

Constraints to operating a household enterprise may be more binding for poor than for wealthier households, resulting in a higher degree of churning among poor households' enterprises. The lack of market access and demand is the main constraint for household enterprises in Ethiopia across the board (also found by Hardy and Kagy [2018] in the case of female garment makers in Ghana).

Other constraints differ across welfare levels. Access to finance is twice as important a constraint for the bottom 40 percent as for the top quintile. In contrast, enterprises in the top quintile are more constrained by utility-related barriers, in particular access to electricity. Still, a quarter of all nonfarm businesses in the bottom 40 percent have been in operation for more than 10 years. Of course, that households are still in the bottom 40 percent despite having an enterprise that survived for more than 10 years must mean that these household enterprises are not very profitable.

Potential for Employment Generation

That even older household enterprises are small confirms that household enterprises typically do not create much employment. The oldest household enterprises in the 10-country sample tend to be only marginally larger than those established only a year before the survey. In Uganda, household enterprises that have been in operation for more than 10 years have, on average, 2.0 workers (including the owner), compared with 1.6 workers for enterprises that were established only a year ago. In Malawi, Mali, and Tanzania, young and old enterprises have roughly the same number of workers.

Employment generation is further mainly confined to urban enterprises with educated owners, underscoring the role of market demand and skills. Urban household enterprises that have been in operation for 10 years or more have on average more than 2 workers, compared with 1.6 for newly established urban enterprises.[13] There is no such gradient for rural enterprises. Similarly, household enterprises with an educated owner (more than primary school) seem to add workers through time (from 1.7 for young enterprises to 2.4 for older ones), while there is no such pattern for enterprises with uneducated owners (figure 4.3). The larger size of older household enterprises in urban areas or with educated owners is entirely due to a higher number of wage employees (nonhousehold workers).

Though the magnitudes of job creation involved are still small, the ongoing secular developments in Africa—urbanization and rising education levels among the youth—would suggest cautious optimism on the job potential of household enterprises. In addition, given the sheer number of household enterprises in Africa, even limited job creation per household enterprise can still add up to many jobs.

Differences by Location, Seasonality, Gender, and Financial and Human Capital

Reflecting the geographic concentration of the poor, the enterprises of the poor are more likely to be rural. More than 80 percent of household enterprises in the bottom 40 percent are rural, while more than half of enterprises (56 percent) in the top quintile are urban.

Enterprises in the bottom 40 percent are also more likely to be seasonal: More than half the enterprises in the bottom quintile operate fewer than 12 months per year, and a quarter operate for less than half of the year. In contrast, close to 70 percent of enterprises in the top quintile are active throughout the year, and only 12 percent operate fewer than six months in any given year. There is considerable variation in seasonality across countries: 35 percent of household enterprises in the bottom 40 percent in Burkina Faso and Ethiopia operate fewer than six months

FIGURE 4.3 Urban household enterprises and those with better-educated owners tend to grow over time

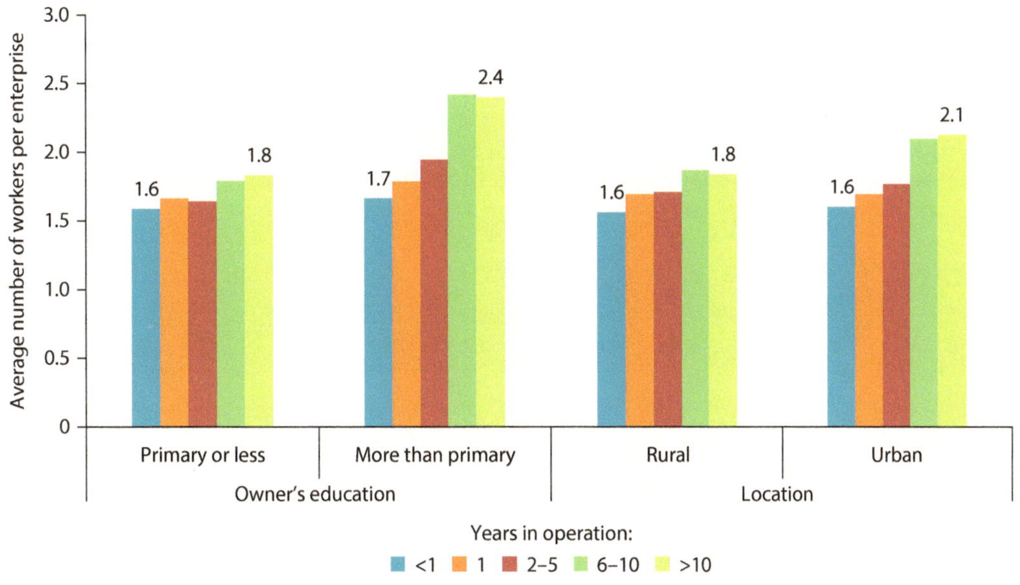

Source: Nagler 2017.

per year, while this applies to only about 10 percent of such enterprises in Ghana and Uganda.

The higher degree of seasonality among enterprises in the bottom 40 percent is linked to the agricultural cycle: Enterprises in the bottom 40 percent in Africa are predominantly rural, and the rural nonfarm economy has substantial supply-and-demand links with agriculture (box 4.4). In contrast, household enterprises in the top quintile, which are more likely to be urban, tend to operate year-round.

The local nonfarm economy also links back to agriculture. In rural Africa, where access to credit is generally constrained, income from nonfarm enterprises can help ease those constraints, enabling households to purchase farm inputs and invest in productivity-increasing technology (Adjognon, Liverpool-Tasie, and Reardon 2017). Through this mechanism, income from agriculture enables households to operate nonfarm enterprises, which in turn enable investments in farm inputs, potentially raising agricultural productivity.

The links between agriculture and rural nonfarm activity highlight the importance of agricultural productivity growth and support for infrastructure and services such as storage and basic processing. Having more agricultural produce that can be kept for longer periods can keep the rural nonfarm economy going even during the agricultural lean season.

The start-up capital for household enterprises mainly comes from the households' own income and savings. Depending on the country, between 45 percent (Mali) and more than 80 percent (Burkina Faso, Niger, and Uganda) of household enterprise start-ups are financed by the household's own resources. Better-off household enterprises are more often financed by gifts from family and friends, while poorer household enterprises are more likely to not require any capital at all (as a result of which these enterprises are often active in low-return activities without

BOX 4.4 The farm economy and nonfarm employment are strongly linked

The agricultural economy can influence the nonfarm economy through supply and demand links. On the supply side, the harvest season brings extra cash income to rural households, which can be used to invest in the operation of a household enterprise. In Ethiopia, for instance, agricultural income was the main or secondary source of start-up capital for household enterprises (Loening, Rijkers, and Söderbom 2008). On the demand side, higher agricultural income following the harvest increases local demand for nonfarm goods and services, stimulating the nonfarm economy, particularly the agro-food part of it.

These factors can result in household enterprise operations that align with agriculture, whereby activities peak in the immediate postharvest season rather than providing income throughout the lean season. Figure B4.4.1 illustrates this dynamic in Ethiopia.

FIGURE B4.4.1 In Ethiopia, rural nonfarm activity peaks soon after the main harvest

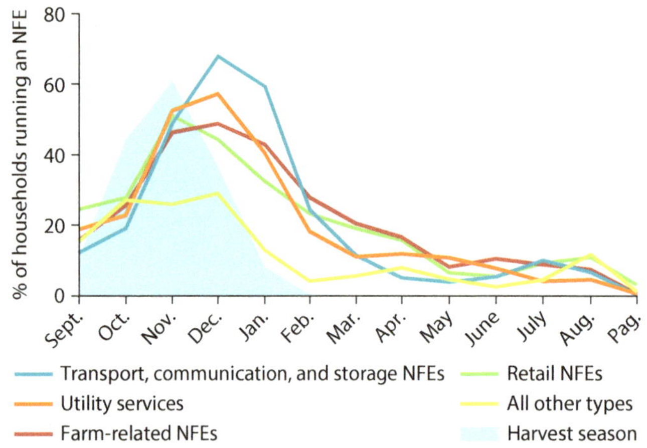

Source: World Bank 2015a.
Note: NFE = nonfarm enterprise; Pag. = *Pagumiene*, the 13th month in the Ethiopian calendar, typically a short month of either five or six days depending on whether it is a leap year. The shaded "harvest season" area depicts the temporal intensity of the harvest—starting in September, peaking in November, and continuing as late as January for some crops.

entry barriers). The numbers also point to the marginal role of financial institutions, including microfinance, in providing credit to the household enterprise sector: in the countries where data are available, fewer than 3 percent of household enterprises were started through a formal bank or microfinance loan, regardless of wealth quintile.

Country context seems to determine whether household enterprises are more likely to be owned by women or men. In Malawi, Mali, and Niger, household enterprises are more likely to be owned by men, and this holds across the wealth distribution. In Burkina Faso, Ghana, and Nigeria, household enterprises are more likely to be owned by women, and this holds for poor and wealthier households alike. In the top 20 percent of households, however, there is some dropping off in the share of household enterprises owned by women. In Ethiopia, women make up half of household enterprise owners in the first and fourth wealth quintiles but only 37 percent in the top quintile. In Burkina Faso, more than 60 percent of household enterprises in the bottom 80 percent are owned by women, but this drops to 55 percent in the top quintile. A similar pattern is observed in Ghana, Rwanda, and Tanzania. The opposite is observed in Malawi, a matriarchal society, where there are more female owners in the top quintile.

Generally, in Africa, female-owned household enterprises are often less profitable and less likely to grow, be they microenterprises or SMEs (Campos and Gassier 2017). Though the empirical evidence is limited, women in non-OECD countries tend to be overrepresented among the "necessity" entrepreneurs and expect their businesses to grow less (Poschke 2013b). Controlling for other factors, women-owned household enterprises in Rwanda were substantially less likely to expand than male-headed ones and tended to remain one-person firms even if they survived for a long time (World Bank 2016b).

In the six African countries in the World Bank's Living Standards Measurement Study-Integrated Surveys on Agriculture (LSMS-ISA), rural female-headed household enterprises have significantly lower productivity and profits (Nagler and Naudé 2017), possibly because of sorting by sector and size and lower factor intensity (Filmer and Fox 2014; Rijkers and Costa 2012). These gaps partly reflect differences in normative expectations regarding daily provision for the family, women's need to prioritize savings over investment, and maybe also a tendency to hide some income from husbands—each of which limits business growth for women's enterprises (Friedson-Ridenour and Pierotti 2018).

Household enterprises are mainly run by persons with at least some primary education (completed or not). This is the group of workers that tends to be excluded from wage income opportunities because of lack of education, and for whom household enterprises are a good alternative income choice (on average, better than agriculture or to help cope with shocks). The exceptions are a number of countries in West Africa (mainly Burkina Faso, Mali, and Niger), where the low education levels mean that enterprises are mainly run by people who never went to school. Overall, the share of household enterprises run by better-educated persons increases with wealth but remains low among tertiary-educated workers. The latter typically have access to regular well-paying jobs in the public and formal private sectors.

Potential for Income Generation

Given that the enterprises of the poor are smaller, more likely to be rural, and more likely to be run by less-educated people, it is no surprise their profits are also lower (hence the household remains poor). Across all countries, household enterprise profits increase with household welfare and then take a big jump between the fourth and fifth consumption quintiles, as in Burkina Faso, Rwanda, and Uganda (figure 4.4). The enterprises in the top quintile appear structurally different: they are somewhat bigger and are much more likely to employ paid nonhousehold members, be located in urban areas, have more-educated owners, and earn far higher profits.

Household enterprises can nevertheless make an important contribution to the incomes of the poor. The extent to which enterprises are important income generators depends a lot on the country context. For example, household enterprise income accounts for less than 10 percent of total household income in the bottom 40 percent in Ethiopia and Malawi, compared with more than 35 percent in Ghana and Nigeria (figure 4.5). Household enterprises tend to account for a larger share of total income among wealthier households, which are overrepresented in urban areas.

Drivers of Household Enterprise Creation and Shrinkage

Finally, while both push (necessity) and pull (opportunity) factors influence the creation of household enterprises, the

FIGURE 4.4 **Enterprise profits rise with household wealth and take a big jump in the top quintile**

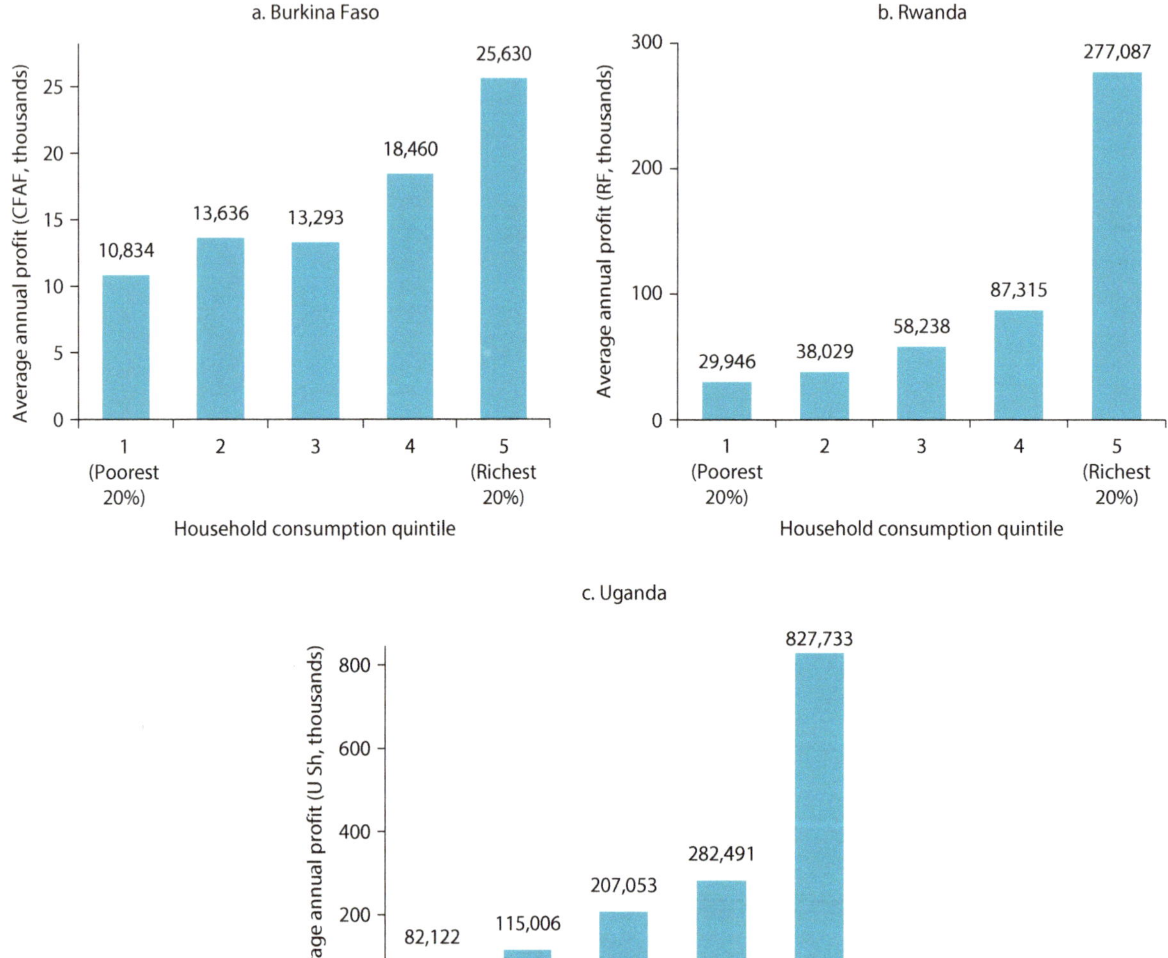

Source: Nagler 2017.

limited available evidence suggests that push factors dominate. Inability to find a waged or salaried job was cited as the main reason to start a household enterprise in the Republic of Congo and Tanzania (Fox and Sohnesen 2012). In Mozambique, more than half of household enterprise owners mentioned a push factor as the main reason to start the enterprise, mainly the inability of finding a wage job.[14]

Pull factors were, however, more important in rural than in urban areas, which may indicate that in rural areas, household enterprises may be more attractive than subsistence agriculture or may be an attractive complement to the agricultural labor calendar

FIGURE 4.5 The contribution of household enterprises to income is higher among wealthier households

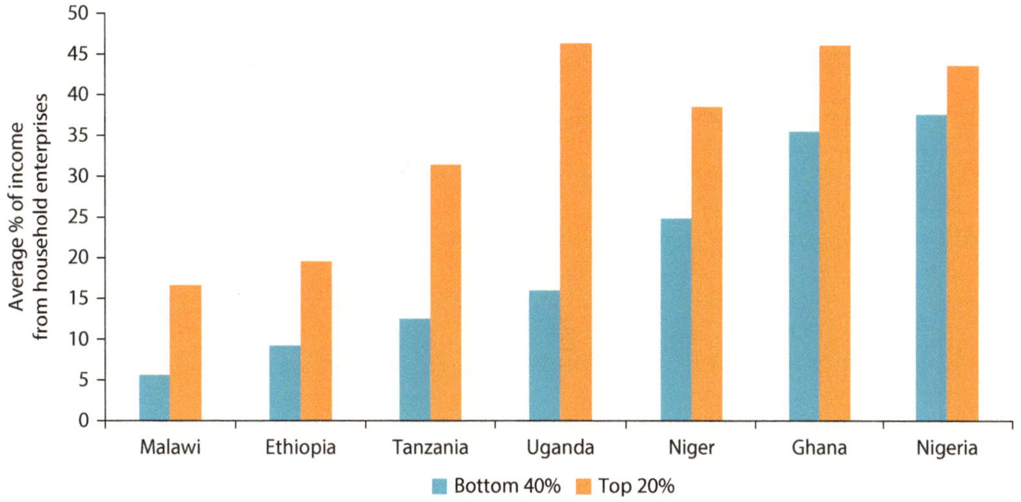

Source: Nagler 2017.

during the agricultural slack seasons. Better understanding the push and pull factors in establishing household enterprises—and the roles of agricultural seasonality, infrastructure, and the business environment in mediating those factors—is an area for further research.

As the pace of formal wage job creation in Africa picks up and more people access wage jobs, the household enterprise sector is likely to shrink. In Africa's food supply chains, this is already starting to happen; Reardon et al. (2015), for example, speak of this as a "quiet revolution." In other words, as urban food markets grow, the share of purchased foods increases rapidly (among both urban and rural households), and food processing moves from the farm to SMEs. Thousands of often informal MSMEs in trucking, wholesale, warehousing, cold storage, first- and second-stage processing, local fast food, and retail have emerged in response. Examples include the proliferation of SME mills-cum-retailers of teff in Ethiopia that now sell teff flour or enjera directly—increasingly replacing the common practice of buying teff as a grain and cleaning and processing it at home (Minten et al. 2013). In Tanzania, local supermarket chains, small-format supermarket independents, and new-format retail clusters are emerging, selling a proliferation of domestically processed and branded foods and generating wage employment.

This transition also stands to happen in other sectors, making these in-between SMEs that cater to the domestic markets and operate in conjunction with the larger-scale, export-oriented modern firms particularly important in the transition toward formal wage employment (Diao and McMillan 2018). Yet, as shown earlier, the low base of wage employment in Africa combined with a rapidly expanding labor force implies that the share of formal wage employment will remain low in the foreseeable future, even under highly optimistic scenarios. This means that even if household enterprises are mainly established because of push factors (the inability to find a wage job), marginally increasing their productivity and earnings has the potential to pull millions out of poverty. For this reason, the next section looks at the available evidence on how to facilitate earnings growth among household enterprises.

Better Household Enterprises for the Poor

Although household enterprises exhibit enormous heterogeneity in earnings and productivity, the median household enterprise is active in easy-to-enter sectors where the scope for earnings growth is limited. The growth potential of household enterprises is often constrained by the size of the local market, the skills and education of the owner, and indeed the owner's aspirations. Many household enterprises remain small even if they remain in business for almost a lifetime. In addition, household enterprises are usually run alongside other economic activities (agriculture, other enterprises, and so on) as part of a "portfolio of work" or diversified income, thus constraining the labor and capital investment that is devoted to the enterprise (sometimes especially for women).

Arguably, public policy has largely neglected the development of a vision and strategy for household enterprises in general, instead focusing on SMEs and large firms (Filmer and Fox 2014). Efforts to alleviate poverty in Africa cannot rely on spillovers from the modern wage sector only; they need to focus more directly on the large numbers of poor whose employment and incomes are not likely to be affected by such firms' growth in the near term.

What, then, works to raise the income and employment potential of the enterprises of the poor? The evidence base remains thin and context-specific. Most interventions and impact evaluations have focused on the supply side, examining the roles of access to credit and finance, technical and business skills training, soft or "life skills" training, and the like.

Interventions have aimed to facilitate both the entry of new enterprises and the growth of existing ones. "Capital-centric" programs have aimed to relax the capital constraints by offering cash or in-kind grants, subsidized loans, or connections with microfinance services. "Skills-centric" approaches have focused on providing technical and vocational skills, business skills, life and soft skills, and so on. More recently, programs have tended to bundle various interventions to tackle multiple constraints at the same time.

Insights from Capital-Centric Programs

Capital-centric programs assume that poor households are credit-constrained, preventing them from entering into relatively more lucrative nonfarm self-employment activities. Similarly, lack of access to capital can also constrain growth and expansion among already existing household enterprises. Alleviating the credit constraint—by providing either cash grants, in-kind capital or assets, or access to microfinance or financial services—can relax the credit constraint, enabling poor households to overcome the entry barriers to nonfarm self-employment or helping existing enterprises to invest and grow profits.

Impact of Cash or In-Kind Grants

Many studies review the existing evidence (Campos and Gassier 2017; Cho 2015; Cho and Honorati 2014; Cho, Robalino, and Watson 2016; Grimm and Paffhausen 2015; Karlan, Knight, and Udry 2012; Kluve et al. 2016; McKenzie and Woodruff 2014; Reeg 2015; Vermeire and Bruton 2016). There is substantial evidence that cash or in-kind grants of capital or assets can jump-start self-employment, increasing the creation of household enterprises.

The effect of cash or in-kind grants on entry into nonfarm self-employment has been documented by various evaluations in different countries and contexts: In northern Uganda, one-off cash grants of about US$370 to underemployed youth led to investments in business assets and vocational training, with substantial and persistent effects on earnings:[15] earnings of youth who had received the cash grants were 40–50 percent higher than those of the control group at two and four years following the grant (Blattman, Fiala, and Martinez 2014). Young women experienced particularly high returns on the cash grant, increasing earnings by more than 84 percent relative to the controls. However, after nine years, there were no differences between those with and without the grants in employment, earnings, and consumption (Blattman, Fiala, and Martinez 2018). In rural Kenya, beneficiaries of an unconditional cash transfer increased their revenues from business activities, though without a discernible impact on profits.[16]

In Ethiopia and Ghana, beneficiaries of the BRAC graduation model pioneered in Bangladesh—which consists of the transfer of a productive asset (usually livestock), combined with training and temporary consumption support—increased ownership of and income from microenterprises (Banerjee et al. 2015). Only in Ghana did the effect persist until three years after the start of the program. Still, in Uganda, poor women who were offered US$150 cash grants, together with business training and supervision, doubled their microenterprise ownership and incomes 16 months after the intervention.

Beneficiaries of a cash plus business training and mentoring intervention in rural Kenya shifted time from leisure and household activities to nonfarm enterprise activity, leading to a 34 percent increase in per capita income one year after the intervention. In addition, the intervention was comparatively cheap.[17] In Ethiopia, a US$300 grant and business training raised earnings by 33 percent; moreover, it outperformed industrial wage work, which did not raise employment or income after a year (Blattman and Dercon 2018).

Outside Africa, research has also found positive impacts of cash grants or asset transfers on entry into household enterprises (Banerjee et al. 2015; Gertler, Martinez, and Rubio-Codina 2012; Macours, Premand, and Vakis 2012). Taken together, these results suggest that poor households and individuals are indeed capital-constrained to start businesses and that alleviating these constraints through grants may lead to considerable returns in earnings and employment (without having the oft-assumed perverse effects). In remote rural settings, cash grants can also help households finance the temporary migration of one or more members to towns and cities to work in casual nonfarm self-employment, which has been shown to substantially increase consumption in Bangladesh (Bryan, Chowdhury, and Mobarak 2014).

The effects of infusing cash into existing microenterprises has been more mixed, particularly in Africa. In Ghana, providing US$133 cash grants to tailors did not have lasting impacts on profits. Capital, in the form of cash or in-kind grants, had limited effects in increasing the productivity of microenterprises, and only for male-headed ones, suggesting that capital alone is not enough to grow subsistence enterprises owned by women (Fafchamps et al. 2014). In Tanzania, a cash grant (of about US$90) combined with business training tailored to existing microenterprises led to a large increase in sales and profits among male entrepreneurs, although with no discernible effects on female-owned enterprises.[18] These findings are echoed in Uganda, where a combined subsidized loan plus training intervention led to increased business profits and employment in male-owned microenterprises, with no effects on women-owned ones.[19]

Outside Africa, cash grants of US$100–US$200 had strong effects on the short-term profits of small-business owners in Mexico and Sri Lanka (De Mel, McKenzie, and Woodruff 2008; McKenzie and Woodruff 2008). Mirroring the Africa results, male-owned microenterprises in Sri Lanka had high returns to capital, while women-owned ones experienced no gains in profits following the grant. Grants also had some long-lasting impacts on the survival and profitability of male-owned firms. Taken together, these results suggest that providing capital and, especially in Africa, combining it with business trainings can be effective in increasing the incomes and profits of existing household enterprises. The longer-term impacts of such interventions have not been examined, however, and these interventions tend not to work for female-owned businesses.[20]

Impact of Expanded Microfinance

Though the effectiveness of cash grants confirms the importance of credit constraints, the expansion of microfinance has not proven effective in relaxing these constraints. A review of the impact of microfinance in Africa suggests that impacts on business incomes have been mixed, with some studies documenting positive impacts (mainly on agricultural incomes) while others show no or even negative impacts (Van Rooyen, Stewart, and de Wet 2012).

A potential explanation for the failure of microfinance to live up to its promise in Africa is that it has yet to reach the household enterprise sector: as shown in the previous section, microfinance institutions are of marginal importance in providing start-up capital for household enterprises. And despite the rather high returns to capital documented in the impact evaluations, household enterprise owners—both those currently in business and those who have closed shop—tend to report lack of access to finance as a major business constraint (Nagler and Naudé 2017). Female-owned enterprises in the region face larger hurdles than male-owned enterprises in accessing finance (World Bank 2019).

However, lack of access to finance is only one of many constraints, and addressing it alone is unlikely to be sufficient. In Tanzania, the promotion and registration of a mobile savings account among women microentrepreneurs increased savings, and they obtained more microloans through the mobile account, but there were not significant impacts on firm sales and profits (Bastian et al. 2018). In Malawi and Uganda, savings accounts did not affect business investments (Dupas et al. 2018), though positive impacts were found in Kenya for women market vendors but not for men operating taxis (Dupas and Robinson 2013).

Insights from Skills-Building Interventions

While the capital-centric approaches summarized above are fairly new, skills-building interventions have long been the preferred instrument to promote microenterprises. In this logic, start-up of new microenterprises and growth of existing ones are constrained by a lack of skills, with skills broadly defined to include technical and vocational skills, business and entrepreneurial skills, financial literacy, life and soft skills, and so on. Investing in skills training can alleviate this constraint, enabling people to start new businesses or expand existing ones.

Despite the ubiquity of skills programs, the evidence on their effectiveness is thin. Nontechnical business skills trainings do not tend to lead to higher sales and profits, though in some contexts they lead to a higher rate of business start-ups, at least in the short term. Business trainings targeted at existing microfirms have resulted in a change of business practices, but they have rarely improved productivity or the microfirms' likelihood of survival.

In addition, these types of trainings, though typically offered free of charge, have suffered from low take-up rates, shedding doubt on their perceived usefulness (McKenzie and Woodruff 2014). Even tailored individualized training does not seem to spur firm growth: in Ghana, winners of a small-business plan competition received individualized training (but no cash), with no significant impacts on firm growth (Fafchamps and Woodruff 2016).

On the other hand, some targeted interventions to address specific causes of low profitability can make meaningful impacts. For example, in Kenya, household enterprises were losing approximately 5–8 percent of total profits because they did not have enough change on hand to break larger bills (Beaman, Magruder, and Robinson 2014). Interventions that raised awareness of the issue with firms significantly altered change management and reduced lost sales.

Next to training in general business skills, technical and vocational trainings have also been commonplace skills interventions. Observational studies—albeit without a valid comparison group in most cases—have documented a wide range of effects, from no significant returns in Rwanda and Tanzania to large returns in Ghana, with higher returns to vocational training among the little-educated (Fox and Sohnesen 2012). In contrast, a rigorous impact evaluation in Malawi finds no returns to apprenticeship training for the low-skilled (Cho et al. 2013).

Probably one of the more effective examples of vocational training comes from Liberia, where beneficiaries of the Adolescent Girls Initiative (AGI) received six months of technical and business skills training followed by six months of active placement support and supervision, leading to a significant increase in earnings relative to a control group (Adoho et al. 2014). The AGI intervention, however, was expensive (between US$1,200 and US$1,650 per woman), which lays bare the general issue with technical and vocational training interventions: They are often expensive, with program costs often ranging between US$1,000 and US$2,000 per person in low- and middle-income countries. Combined with their modest returns and the uncertain persistence of returns through time, it is hard to find a technical skills program that passes a simple cost-benefit test.

Potential Synergies from Integrated Approaches

As shown above, when combined with a cash intervention, business or technical skills trainings can be effective. Several of the studies mentioned earlier combined interventions to tackle capital and skills constraints simultaneously and found significant impacts on enterprise start-up and profits. In certain settings, the cash component was only effective if it was combined with business training.[21] However, given that training components typically add substantially to the overall cost of a program, cash transfers by themselves tend to be more cost-effective.

Some efforts effectively use cash as a means toward both training and start-up. In Uganda, the government's Youth Opportunities Program framed the US$382 cash grant as a vocational and enterprise start-up intervention, though the cash grant remained unconditional and unmonitored. Most of the youth invested in skills training and mainly in tools and materials, leading to a significant increase in nonfarm enterprise activity and earnings, with good cost-benefit results in the medium term, but these gains disappear after nine years (Blattman, Fiala, and Martinez 2014, 2018).

Recent research has highlighted another potential explanation for why household enterprises hardly ever grow and add workers. Although it is often implicitly assumed that household enterprises in poor countries face a frictionless market for workers and can hire and fire according to needs (given high unemployment and the lack of labor regulations in the informal sector), small firms may face high labor market search costs and, as a result, typically refrain from hiring. This hypothesis was tested in Ghana through a government-implemented worker screening and placement program where small enterprises that were randomly offered one or more workers chose to hire them and had increased revenue and profits (Hardy and McCasland 2017). In addition, the number of workers per enterprise and the total volume of hours worked increased after the intervention, meaning that there was no displacement effect on existing employment. Though similar research in other countries would be needed to examine whether these findings hold, the mere hypothesis that small enterprises in poor labor-surplus countries are in fact labor-constrained is thought-provoking and merits further investigation.

In sum, the most consistent finding from the recent literature has been the impact of cash grants on stimulating entry into nonfarm self-employment, with large increases in incomes from a low base, at least in the short run. Business skills programs can be effective in certain settings but typically only if they are combined with a cash grant component. On their own, skills trainings tend to have tepid effects and fail to pass a cost-effectiveness test. Although cash grants have been effective in increasing entry into nonfarm self-employment for both men and women, grants to existing household enterprises have had effects only on male-owned businesses.

Nonetheless, important gaps remain in our understanding of what works to make these income opportunities more lucrative for the poor and near poor. With some exceptions, most studies and impact evaluations refer to urban settings, while most of Africa's poor live in rural areas. We also know less about what works with respect to agriculture value chains—that is, how to grow the microbusinesses that link with smallholder farmers.

Finally, few studies focus specifically on poor or near-poor households, which may face different constraints than other types of entrepreneurs. An emerging and promising approach to reach the poorest and more vulnerable is to combine safety net interventions with packages of support (including skills, finance, advisory services, working space, and so on) to facilitate entry into self-employment and raise the labor earnings of social protection beneficiaries. These combined "protection and promotion" interventions, which seek to tap into latent local demand, are currently being implemented on a large scale in several African countries, with ongoing impact evaluations examining their effects. Yet, quite often, the most binding constraint is the lack of demand for the goods and services that the poor could produce and provide.

Fostering Demand: The Role of Towns and Regional Trading

The demand side of household enterprise growth has received far less attention, despite being at least as important, if not more so. Although supply-side interventions can help entry into self-employment and, to some extent, increase earnings, the survival and growth of these small enterprises is ultimately determined by the demand for the goods and services they provide. Employment for the poor off the farm is largely centered on locally derived demand—demand from neighbors and adjacent communities for goods and services of various kinds.

Increasing the demand for these goods and services produced by the poor and vulnerable is a critical aspect to raising their incomes, notwithstanding the broader "private sector" agenda outlined earlier in this chapter. However, the demand side lends itself less easily than the supply side to being evaluated (regarding the roles of market access, connectivity, and agglomeration), which partly explains the small evidence base. Five areas of policy attention to foster demand for the goods and services produced by the poor come to mind.

First, as highlighted in chapter 3, agriculture continues to form the basis of rural livelihoods, especially for the poor, despite the slow but steady move out of farming (Davis, Di Giuseppe, and Zezza 2017). Low agricultural productivity translates into low rural incomes, constraining local demand for nonagricultural goods and services provided by household enterprises. Boosting agricultural productivity from the current low levels will be an absolute prerequisite to increase rural incomes and expand rural nonfarm activity. Chapter 3 outlines a set of policy priorities to achieve this critical goal.

Second, improving rural connectivity and access to markets is another important aspect of the demand-side agenda. In remote rural areas, the size of the market is limited to the size of the village, with often very low purchasing power. Connecting rural areas with roads and population centers extends the market, offering more potential to household enterprises. The importance of connectivity comes out clearly in empirical research. In Uganda, for instance, productivity of household enterprises falls among the households farthest from a population center (Nagler and Naudé 2017). In Rwanda, one-person enterprises with higher domestic market accessibility or located closer to international borders are more likely to add employment (World Bank 2016b). And in Ethiopia, more than half of nonfarm enterprise owners mention lack of market access as the single main constraint to business growth, and rural enterprises in the highest connectivity quartile have substantially higher productivity levels, controlling for other influences (World Bank, forthcoming[a]).

Rural connectivity, however, remains limited across much of Africa. Using a new methodology that integrates high-resolution data on the spatial distribution of the population and geographic information system (GIS) data on the road network, the share of the rural population that lives within two kilometers of the nearest road in good condition is estimated to be 17 percent in Zambia; 20–30 percent in Ethiopia, Mozambique, and Tanzania; and just over 50 percent in Kenya and Uganda (World Bank 2016a). Scaling up investments in rural accessibility in a fiscally sustainable way, possibly through adoption of lower design standards for what will mostly be low-traffic roads, will be important to grow the rural nonfarm economy and increase the productivity of household enterprises.[22] Recent technology advances can also help overcome, or even leapfrog, traditional high-cost investments in infrastructure, as described in Fundamentals 3, "Leapfrogging with Technology (and Trade)."

Third, most off-farm employment opportunities will not be generated locally but rather in either nearby or distant urban centers. But not all urban development has equal poverty-reducing potential. Cross-country research suggests that, compared with agglomeration in megacities, it is especially migration out of agriculture into secondary towns and the rural nonfarm economy that results in more inclusive growth patterns and stronger poverty reduction (Christiaensen and Todo 2014).[23]

Case country evidence from India, Mexico, and Tanzania points in the same direction: for poverty reduction, growing towns matters more than growing cities (Gibson et al. 2017; Berdegué and Soloaga 2018; and Christiaensen, De Weerdt, and Kanbur 2018, respectively). Small towns in rural areas provide local centers of economic activity and demand and are more accessible to the poor because of proximity and the lower threshold for migration (Rondinelli and Ruddle 1983). This proximity facilitates especially the first move, which is often the most difficult (Ingelaere et al. 2018). The type of employment available in towns (unskilled and semiskilled) also tends to be more compatible with the skill sets of the poor. Public investments to make rural towns grow can increase demand for agricultural products produced in surrounding rural areas, increasing rural incomes, which in turn would increase demand for nonfarm goods and services produced by household enterprises.

Improving rural connectivity and infrastructure and strengthening towns will be especially important to capitalize on the ongoing dietary shifts in Africa. Urbanization and rising urban incomes mean that demand for food is increasing and diets are shifting to higher-value and processed products (Allen et al. 2016; Minde, Tschirley, and Haggblade 2012). This dietary revolution has the potential to create many new employment opportunities both on and off the farm, in activities such as processing, storage, transport and distribution, retailing, food services, and so on. For these jobs to materialize, governments will need to invest in market access and infrastructure that respond to the needs of higher-value crops (such as logistics, cold storage, and so on) as well as in skills and technologies required by higher-value and perishable foods. And governments need to take a strategic approach that considers the spatial patterns of investments aimed at bringing smallholders into the commercial agriculture value chain. (Agroterritorial development is discussed in detail in Nogales and Webber [2017].) Other town activities include mining and tourism, trading and administrative functions, and the provision of public and social services (education and health care).

Fourth, an action agenda to support secondary town and city development, and thus off-farm employment generation, is needed (Roberts 2014, 2016). With the capitals and cities drawing most of people's imagination and policy makers' attention, this agenda has so far been broadly neglected. Furthermore, in small towns and megacities alike, governments view household enterprises, which are mostly informal, more often than not as detrimental to urban spaces rather than as a critical source of income for the poor and many nonpoor. However, efforts to "sanitize" the city centers of such enterprises may well impoverish vulnerable workers who depend on dense foot traffic for their livelihoods.

Finding ways to leverage and integrate informal enterprises in the broader urban development plans, rather than harassing them, is another important agenda to assist the poor in making the most of household entrepreneurship (box 4.5). More recently, examples of "inclusive cities" are emerging, such as from Bhubaneswar, India; Durban,

BOX 4.5 How *not* to do it: Governments' approaches to household enterprises have ranged from wishing them away to outright harassment

Many governments around the world are not keen on seeing their informal economies flourish. Yet most people who work off the farm and in household enterprises are in the informal economy. Many of the motivations behind resistance to growing the informal economy are quite understandable: the informal economy contributes little or nothing in taxes, can undercut competition from the formal sector, can cause urban congestion, and so on.

Attempts to deal with the informal sector, particularly in urban areas, have included induced "formalization"; relocation to planned markets outside of the city center (as part of a "decongestion" agenda); and legal and extralegal harassment from local authorities, including confiscation of business inventory or demolition of the temporary business structure (and even violence). How governments interact with informal vending is political—influenced by party politics, decentralization frameworks, and electoral considerations. At best, aggressive and forced interventions are futile. At worst, they destroy livelihoods and further reduce incomes for already vulnerable households.

Evaluation of formalization attempts, mostly outside Africa, suggests that formalization policies result in only a modest increase in the number of firm registrations and that formalizing household enterprises contributes little to tax revenues. In addition, many informal firms appear not to benefit much from formalization. Relocation, often to less expensive peri-urban areas far from customers, does not fit the needs of informal businesses, which need premises with a lot of foot traffic in central business districts to survive. As a result, many informal businesses soon return to their former areas of operation, even if it comes with the risk of further harassment. Overall, these policies and approaches are counterproductive because they increase rather than reduce poverty and vulnerability and further constrain the already limited opportunities for employment in many African cities.

What, then, can governments do? It will be important to acknowledge that even if the formal sector keeps on growing fast, its low base will mean that the bulk of young people will end up in the informal sector in the foreseeable future. Rather than trying to suppress it, facilitating the operation of informal enterprises can improve employment opportunities for Africa's youth. Integrating household enterprises or the informal economy in general into urban or national development plans would be a start, because it would provide a framework for the government and the informal sector to start discussing the design of a supportive policy framework that facilitates the operation of household enterprises while still protecting the public interest. At the local level, cities can be more inclusive by including representatives of informal workers in participatory policy-making and rule-setting processes. Associations of household enterprises can be formed not only to advocate for their members and improve the voice of household enterprises, but also to hold their members to account if agreements are not respected. In the many secondary towns in Africa, which do not yet face intense service delivery pressures and high land values, an opportunity exists to properly plan for markets and household enterprise working space to accommodate and absorb informal workers as these towns grow and as the move out of agriculture persists.

Sources: Bruhn and McKenzie 2013; Chen and Beard 2018; Filmer and Fox 2014, 161–64, boxes 5.8 and 5.9; Resnick 2017; Resnick, forthcoming.

South Africa; and several from South America (Chen and Beard 2018).

And finally, a fifth area is supporting cross-border trade. The demand for one's goods and services often comes from just across the border, underscoring the importance of deepening Africa's regional integration. The importance of cross-border trade is vividly illustrated by the surprising concentration of agriprocessing enterprises along the eastern and northern borders of Zambia (as well as along the expected central-southern Lusaka–Lilongwe axis), catering to Lilongwe in Malawi and Lumbumbashi in the Democratic Republic of Congo, respectively (map 4.1).

Cross-border trade is often also an important driver of town development (the so-called border towns). The challenges for furthering Africa's regional integration priorities are reviewed in Brenton and Hoffmann (2016). They paint a cautiously optimistic picture, emphasizing flexibility and simplicity, active outreach to the private sector, and a focus on joint infrastructure.

Cutting across this agenda is digital technology, which holds great promise to connect the enterprises of the poor with expanding urban demand for goods and services.[24] More middle-class urbanites are ordering, through phone and informal networks, myriad services

MAP 4.1 Agriprocessing firms concentrate along the borders in Zambia

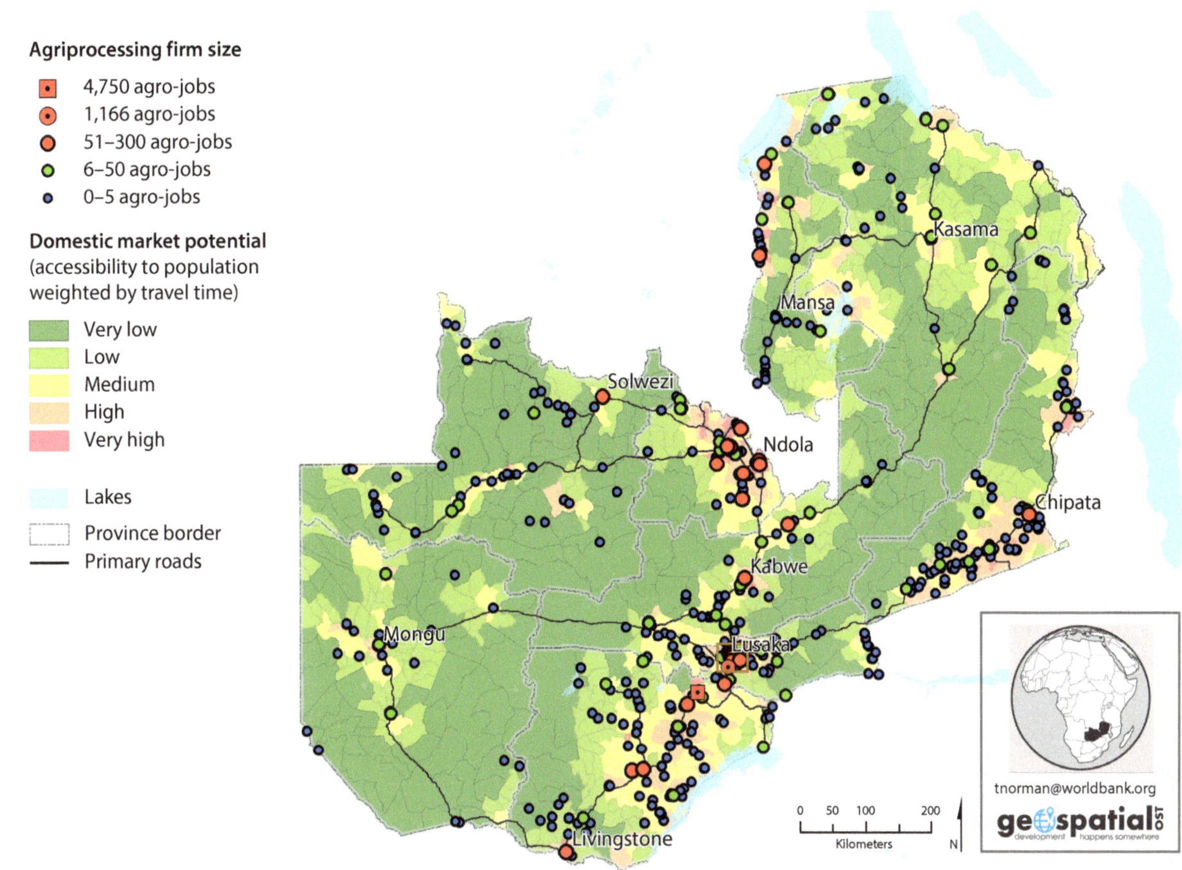

Source: Norman, Merotto, and Blankespoor 2018. Used with permission; further permission required for reuse.

to be performed in their homes, ranging from plumbing and electrical repair tasks, hairdressing, and curtain-fitting to satellite dish installation and gardening, among many more. Digital technology and platforms have the potential to dramatically expand market access for the self-employed or small enterprises that usually provide these task-based jobs ("gigs").

Though not the kind of regular formal employment that African governments strive for, the "gig economy" has the potential to increase earnings of the self-employed (Ng'weno and Porteous 2018) while also offering a gradual pathway to formalization by connecting digital platforms to social insurance schemes. Capitalizing on this trend will require equipping youth from poor households with at least basic education and digital skills while making internet connectivity affordable, reliable, and widely available. How technology can further help Africa leapfrog many of its infrastructural constraints needed for household enterprises and businesses to thrive and employment opportunities to grow, including for the poor, is explored in Fundamentals 3, "Leapfrogging with Technology (and Trade)."

Notes

1. Although agriculture still employs the bulk of Africa's working-age population (ages 15–65 years), its share of employment has been steadily decreasing (World Bank, forthcoming[b]; Yeboah and Jayne 2018). Projections put it at about 50 percent of employment by 2020, albeit with a higher share (60 percent) in low-income countries and a much higher share among the poor (Fox et al. 2013).
2. Among the various studies on rural nonfarm employment, see Barrett, Reardon, and Webb (2001); Gindling and Newhouse (2014); Haggblade, Hazell, and Reardon (2007); and Nagler and Naudé (2017).
3. These patterns draw on studies including Filmer and Fox (2014), World Bank (2012), and Yeboah and Jayne (2018).
4. Some work that appears to be self-employment could also be characterized as dependent self-employment (Eichhorst et al. 2013), where employment categories are blurred. This is the case of minibus drivers in urban areas who are paid (and taxed) as self-employed but who operate the minibus company owner's equipment and have to work the routes and schedules set by the owner (Rizzo, Kilama, and Wuyts 2015). A second example are street hawkers or similar urban retailers. They operate with little capital other than the goods they sell and with no employees, and sometimes in mobile locations. Labor surveys identify these people as self-employed, yet we lack data about how these retail goods are acquired and how they are repaid, to appropriately understand whether they are more appropriately thought of as informal wage workers who are akin to sales persons working on commission (Beegle and Gaddis 2017). Recently, there has been an effort to define this in survey efforts (ILO 2018).
5. There are important aspects to the bundled category of wage employment. First, wage employment includes public and private sector employment. Here, there is a marked distinction between resource-rich and non-resource-rich countries. Resource-rich countries have, on average, a much higher share of public sector employment in wage employment (about 70 percent) than do low-income and low-middle-income countries, which average around 30 percent (Filmer and Fox 2014). Second, owing to data limitations, we cannot make the distinction between informal, casual, or daily wage labor and more permanent forms of wage employment for a regional description. These two types of wage employment are very different, though, and it is likely that workers from poor households are engaged in casual employment, while workers from better-off households are overrepresented in permanent wage employment of "higher quality." For a discussion on casual wage labor and possible underestimation of the scope of this in Africa, see Mueller and Chan (2015) and Oya and Pontara (2015).
6. Yeboah and Jayne (2018) define the off-farm segments of the agro-food system as including all prefarm and postfarm value-addition activities within the agriculture value chains including assembly, trading, wholesaling, storage, processing, retailing, preparation of food for selling to others

outside the home, beverage manufacturing, farmer input distribution, and irrigation equipment operators.

7. Because of limitations in the available databases, we do not classify wage workers in the region (and in figure 4.1) by formal or informal or high-skilled versus low-skilled. But indirect evidence suggests that wage work among the poor is quite different from wage work among the rich. The evidence comes from using the occupation classification of wage workers based on the International Standard Classification of Occupations. Among nonagricultural wage workers in the data, there is a gradient in the occupation groupings. The share of those in higher-skilled occupations—managers, professionals, technicians and associate professionals, clerical support workers, craft and related trade workers, armed-forces occupations, plant and machine operators, and assemblers—increases with income. The share of those working in services and sales; skilled agricultural, forestry, and fishery workers; and elementary occupations (including street vendors and related sale and service workers, domestic workers, garbage collectors, cleaners, and transport laborers) declines with income. By the third consumption quintile (the 40th–60th percentile), there are more of the higher-skilled group than the lesser-skilled group among nonagricultural wage workers.
8. Premature deindustrialization refers to the modern-day phenomenon whereby "countries are running out of industrialization opportunities sooner and at much lower levels of income compared to the experience of early industrializers" (Rodrik 2016).
9. "Official" unemployment refers to the definition set forth by the International Labour Organization (ILO) statistical methods, which consider the unemployed to be persons who are not working but who are available to work and are actively seeking work. The ILO thus excludes people who have stopped actively searching. By this strict definition, then, the unemployment rate (the unemployed defined as a share of the labor market, employed and unemployed) in Africa is lower than the rate in high-income economies, as noted by World Bank (2012) and many others. Moreover, this official definition of unemployment is at odds with the popular discourse on the problem of unemployment. Several alternative approaches, some introduced by the ILO, are now more often being used in studies to more appropriately reflect labor conditions of concern, such as NEET (those who are not in employment, education, or training); the working poor; and the underemployed (using an hours threshold).
10. One area of focus, especially over the past decade or so, has been on improving the business climate in Africa to boost private sector development. Influenced by—or in some cases, mildly obsessed with—the World Bank Group's annual *Doing Business* rankings (http://www.doingbusiness.org/), countries have tended to focus on generic reforms that aim to ease the cost of doing business for all firms and sectors in an economy. These include, for instance, reducing the time to formally register a business, get electricity, and register property; the availability of finance; the ease of trading across borders; and so on. However, such reforms do not automatically translate into greater formal private sector activity and employment. Rwanda, for instance, has been a star performer in *Doing Business*—improving its rank from 139th in 2006 to 46th in 2015, putting it ahead of countries such as Italy and Luxembourg. Nonetheless, Rwanda's formal private sector remains very small in terms of employment. This is not an exception in Africa, where generic "enabling environment" efforts have generally not delivered on structural transformation and inclusive growth (Akileswaran et al. 2017). Besley (2015, 107) argues that "implicit within the *Doing Business* approach is the plausible belief that, in the end, it is likely to be the development of larger, formal sector firms that will be engines of employment creation and poverty reduction." The discussion here counsels caution and calls for a more balanced approach.
11. This section draws on the work in Nagler (2017). The findings are similar to the earlier findings in Fox and Sohnesen (2012) from eight countries (Burkina Faso, Cameroon, the Republic of Congo, Ghana, Mozambique, Rwanda, Tanzania, and Uganda, covering surveys from 2003 to 2009) as well as the description in Filmer and Fox (2014), although the profile here specifically focuses

on traits of enterprises operated by poor versus nonpoor households.

12. In Malawi and Tanzania, more than 20 percent of household enterprises in the bottom 40 percent were new entrants (less than one year old), while in Burkina Faso, Mali, and Uganda the share of poor households' enterprises that were new was below 5 percent. The share of household enterprises that are new declined with household wealth in Ghana, Niger, and Tanzania, but there was no relationship with wealth in Burkina Faso, Malawi, and Uganda.
13. More workers in older firms than in younger firms does not necessarily indicate that older firms have grown through time. They may just have started out with more workers. Without enterprise panel data, however, this cannot be disentangled.
14. Côte d'Ivoire appears to be a notable exception. Only 3 percent of household enterprise owners reported the inability of finding a wage job as the main motivation to go into self-employment. Rather, the expectation to earn more—a pull factor—was the main motivation (Christiaensen and Premand 2017).
15. Though the cash grants were framed as part of an enterprise start-up program, the grant remained unconditional.
16. The cash transfers did, however, lead to a large increase in household consumption. Grants were either US$404 (purchasing power parity [PPP]) or US$1,525 (PPP) and were paid either in monthly installments or as a lump sum. The monthly installments mainly improved food consumption, while the lump-sum payments tended to be invested in durables (Haushofer and Shapiro 2016).
17. At an estimated US$300 per beneficiary (about US$714 in PPP), the program in rural Kenya was cheaper than the BRAC model, which varied between US$1,538 and US$5,742 PPP (Banerjee et al. 2015; Gobin, Santos, and Toth 2016).
18. The combined intervention (cash plus training) was effective, at least for males, while the effect of either one of the two interventions was not (Berge, Bjorvatn, and Tungodden 2014).
19. Cash grants did not have any significant effects in this study (Fiala 2015).
20. Fafchamps et al. (2011) argue that many of the women drawn into subsistence self-employment operate at a low efficiency owing to scale, are in the nonfarm enterprise sector because of labor market imperfections, and are necessity entrepreneurs. For these kinds of businesses, support is unlikely to lead to large gains in outcomes. Berge, Bjorvatn, and Tungodden (2014) find, in their study on Tanzania, that domestic obligations and lack of influence over business decisions may to some extent explain the weak effects of these interventions on women-owned businesses.
21. This was the case for Uganda (Fiala 2015) and Tanzania (Berge, Bjorvatn, and Tungodden 2014).
22. Maintaining rural roads can also provide temporary off-farm employment for rural youth.
23. Similarly, other cross-country work, looking at the effect on economic growth instead of poverty reduction, shows that although city size and urban concentration have a positive effect on growth in high-income countries, there is no such effect on low- and middle-income countries. If anything, the effect is likely negative (Frick and Rodríguez-Pose 2016, 2018).
24. In *World Development Report 2013: Jobs*, see "E-links to jobs: New technologies open new frontiers" (World Bank 2012, 268).

References

Adjognon, Serge G., Lenis Saweda O. Liverpool-Tasie, and Thomas A. Reardon. 2017. "Agricultural Input Credit in Sub-Saharan Africa: Telling Myth from Facts." *Food Policy* 67: 93–105.

Adoho, Franck, Shubha Chakravarty, Dala T. Korkoyah, Mattias Lundberg, and Afia Tasneem. 2014. "The Impact of an Adolescent Girls Employment Program: The EPAG Project in Liberia." Policy Research Working Paper 6832, World Bank, Washington, DC.

Akileswaran, Kartik, Antoine Huss, Dan Hymowitz, and Jonathan Said. 2017. "The Jobs Gap: Making Inclusive Growth Work in Africa." Report, Tony Blair Institute for Global Change, London.

Allen, Andrea, Julie Howard, M. Kondo, Amy Jamison, Thomas Jayne, J. Snyder, David Tschirley, and Kwame Felix Yeboah. 2016. "Agrifood Youth Employment and Engagement Study." Study report, Michigan State University, East Lansing.

Allen, Thomas, Philip Heinrigs, and Inhoi Heo. 2018. "Agriculture, Food and Jobs in West Africa." West African Papers No. 14, Organisation for Economic Co-operation and Development, Paris.

Banerjee, Abhijit, Esther Duflo, Nathanael Goldberg, Dean Karlan, Robert Osei, William Parienté, Jeremy Shapiro, Bram Thuysbaert, and Christopher Udry. 2015. "A Multifaceted Program Causes Lasting Progress for the Very Poor: Evidence from Six Countries." *Science* 348 (6236): 773–89.

Barrett, Christopher, Thomas Reardon, and Patrick Webb. 2001. "Nonfarm Income Diversification and Household Livelihood Strategies in Rural Africa: Concepts, Dynamics, and Policy Implications." *Food Policy* 26 (4): 315–31.

Bastian, Gautam, Iacopo Bianchi, Markus Goldstein, and Joao Montalvao. 2018. "Short-Term Impacts of Improved Access to Mobile Savings, with and without Business Training: Experimental Evidence from Tanzania." CGD Working Paper 478, Center for Global Development, Washington, DC.

Beaman, Lori, Jeremy Magruder, and Jonathan Robinson. 2014. "Minding Small Change among Small Firms in Kenya." *Journal of Development Economics* 108: 69–86.

Beegle, Kathleen, and Isis Gaddis. 2017. "Informal Employment in Africa: What Do We Know and What Can We Do to Know More?" Paper presented at the International Statistical Institute (ISI) 2017 Conference, Marrakesh.

Berdegué, Julio, and Isidro Soloaga. 2018. "Small and Medium Cities and Development of Mexican Rural Areas." *World Development* 107: 277–88.

Berge, Lars Ivar Oppedal, Kjetil Bjorvatn, and Bertil Tungodden. 2014. "Human and Financial Capital for Microenterprise Development: Evidence from a Field and Lab Experiment." *Management Science* 61 (4): 707–22.

Besley, Timothy. 2015. "Law, Regulation, and the Business Climate: The Nature and Influence of the World Bank Doing Business Project." *Journal of Economic Perspectives* 29 (3): 99–120.

Bhorat, Haroon, Francois Steenkamp, and Christopher Rooney. 2016. "Africa's Manufacturing Malaise." UNDP-RBA/WPS 3/2016, United Nations Development Programme (UNDP), New York.

Blattman, Christopher, and Stefan Dercon. 2018. "The Impacts of Industrial and Entrepreneurial Work on Income and Health: Experimental Evidence from Ethiopia." *American Economic Journal: Applied Economics* 10 (3): 1–38.

Blattman, Christopher, Nathan Fiala, and Sebastian Martinez. 2014. "Generating Skilled Self-Employment in Developing Countries: Experimental Evidence from Uganda." *Quarterly Journal of Economics* 129 (2): 697–752.

———. 2018. "The Long Term Impacts of Grants on Poverty: 9-year Evidence from Uganda's Youth Opportunities Program." NBER Working Paper 24999, National Bureau of Economic Research, Cambridge, MA.

Brenton, Paul, and Barak Hoffmann, eds. 2016. "Political Economy of Regional Integration in Sub-Saharan Africa." Report No. 103324, World Bank, Washington, DC.

Bruhn, Miriam, and David McKenzie. 2013. "Using Administrative Data to Evaluate Municipal Reforms: An Evaluation of the Impact of Minas Fácil Expresso." *Journal of Development Effectiveness* 5 (3): 319–38.

Bryan, Gharad, Shyamal Chowdhury, and Ahmed Mushfiq Mobarak. 2014. "Underinvestment in a Profitable Technology: The Case of Seasonal Migration in Bangladesh." *Econometrica* 82 (5): 1671–748.

Campos, Francisco, and Marine Gassier. 2017. "Gender and Enterprise Development in Sub-Saharan Africa: A Review of Constraints and Effective Interventions." Policy Research Working Paper 8239, World Bank, Washington, DC.

Chen, Martha A., and Victoria A. Beard. 2018."Including the Excluded: Supporting Informal Workers for More Equal and Productive Cities in the Global South." Working paper, World Resources Institute, Washington, DC.

Cho, Yoonyoung. 2015. "Entrepreneurship for the Poor in Developing Countries." Article, IZA World of Labor online platform, Institute for the Study of Labor (IZA), Bonn. doi:10.15185/izawol.167.

Cho, Yoonyoung, and Maddalena Honorati. 2014. "Entrepreneurship Programs in Developing Countries: A Meta-Regression Approach." *Labour Economics* 28: 110–30.

Cho, Yoonyoung, Davie Kalomba, Ahmed Mushfiq Mobarak, and Victor Orozco. 2013. "Gender Differences in the Effects of Vocational Training." Policy Research Working Paper 6545, World Bank, Washington, DC.

Cho, Yoonyoung, David Robalino, and Samantha Watson. 2016. "Supporting Self-Employment and Small-Scale Entrepreneurship: Potential Programs to Improve Livelihoods for Vulnerable Workers." *IZA Journal of Labor Policy* 5 (7): 1–26.

Christiaensen, Luc, Joachim De Weerdt, and Ravi Kanbur. 2018. "Decomposing the Contribution of Migration to Poverty Reduction: Methodology and Application to Tanzania." *Applied Economics Letters* 26 (12): 978–82.

Christiaensen, Luc, and Patrick Premand, eds. 2017. "Jobs Diagnostic, Côte d'Ivoire: Employment, Productivity, and Inclusion for Poverty Reduction." Report No. AUS13233, World Bank, Washington DC.

Christiaensen, Luc, and Yasuyuki Todo. 2014. "Poverty Reduction during the Rural-Urban Transformation: The Role of the Missing Middle." *World Development* 63: 43–58.

Davis, Benjamin, Stefania Di Giuseppe, and Alberto Zezza. 2017. "Are African Households (Not) Leaving Agriculture? Patterns of Households' Income Sources in Rural Sub-Saharan Africa." *Food Policy* 67: 153–74.

De Mel, Suresh, David McKenzie, and Christopher Woodruff. 2008. "Returns to Capital in Microenterprises: Evidence from a Field Experiment." *Quarterly Journal of Economics* 123 (4): 1329–72.

Diao, Xinshen, Josaphat Kweka, and Margaret McMillan. 2017. "Economic Transformation in Africa from the Bottom up: Evidence from Tanzania." IFPRI Discussion Paper 1603, International Food Policy Research Institute, Washington, DC.

Diao, Xinshen, and Margaret McMillan. 2018. "Toward an Understanding of Economic Growth in Africa: A Reinterpretation of the Lewis Model." *World Development* 109: 511–22.

Dupas, Pascaline, Dean Karlan, Jonathan Robinson, and Diego Ubfal. 2018. "Banking the Unbanked? Evidence from Three Countries." *American Economic Journal: Applied Economics* 10 (2): 257–97.

Dupas, Pascaline, and Jonathan Robinson. 2013. "Savings Constraints and Microenterprise Development: Evidence from a Field Experiment in Kenya." *American Economic Journal: Applied Economics* 5 (1): 163–92.

EIC (Ethiopia Investment Commission). 2017. "Ethiopia: Export Trade Performance and FDI Inflows—Overview of Recent Developments and Projections." Report, EIC, Addis Ababa.

Eichhorst, Werner, Michela Braga, Ulrike Famira-Mühlberger, Maarten Gerard, Thomas Horvath, Martin Kahanec, Marta Kahancová, et al. 2013. "Social Protection Rights of Economically Dependent Self-Employed Workers." IZA Research Report No. 54, Institute for the Study of Labor (IZA), Bonn.

Fafchamps, Marcel, David McKenzie, Simon R. Quinn, and Christopher Woodruff. 2011. "When Is Capital Enough to Get Female Microenterprises Growing? Evidence from a Randomized Experiment in Ghana." NBER Working Paper 17207, National Bureau of Economic Research, Cambridge, MA.

———. 2014. "Microenterprise Growth and the Flypaper Effect: Evidence from a Randomized Experiment in Ghana." *Journal of Development Economics* 106: 211–26.

Fafchamps, Marcel, and Mans Söderbom. 2006. "Wages and Labor Management in African Manufacturing." *Journal of Human Resources* 41 (2): 356–79.

Fafchamps, Marcel, and Christopher Woodruff. 2016. "Identifying Gazelles: Expert Panels vs. Surveys as a Means to Identify Firms with Rapid Growth Potential." Policy Research Working Paper 7647, World Bank, Washington, DC.

Fiala, Nathan. 2015. "Economic Consequences of Forced Displacement." *Journal of Development Studies* 51 (10): 1275–93.

Filmer, Deon, and Louise Fox. 2014. *Youth Employment in Sub-Saharan Africa.* Washington, DC: World Bank.

Fox, Louise, C. Haines, J. Huerta Munoz, and A. Thomas. 2013. "Africa's Got Work to Do: Employment Prospects in the New Century." IMF Working Paper 13/201, International Monetary Fund (IMF), Washington, DC.

Fox, Louise, and Thomas Pave Sohnesen. 2012. "Household Enterprises in Sub-Saharan Africa: Why They Matter for Growth, Jobs, and Livelihoods." Policy Research Working Paper 6184, World Bank, Washington, DC.

Frick, Susanne, and Andrés Rodríguez-Pose. 2016. "Average City Size and Economic Growth." *Cambridge Journal of Regions, Economy and Society* 9 (2): 301–18.

———. 2018. "Change in Urban Concentration and Economic Growth." *World Development* 105: 156–70.

Friedson-Ridenour, Sophia, and Rachael S. Pierotti. 2018. "Intrahousehold Economic Resource Management and Women's Microenterprises: A Case Study from Urban Ghana." Unpublished study, World Bank, Washington, DC.

Gelb, Alan, Christian J. Meyer, Vijaya Ramachandran, and Divyanshi Wadhwa. 2017. "Can Africa Be a Manufacturing Destination? Labor Costs in Comparative Perspective." Working Paper 466, Center for Global Development, Washington, DC.

Gertler, Paul J., Sebastian W. Martinez, and Marta Rubio-Codina. 2012. "Investing Cash Transfers to Raise Long-Term Living Standards." *American Economic Journal: Applied Economics* 4 (1): 164–92.

Gibson, John, Gaurav Datt, Rinku Murgai, and Martin Ravallion. 2017. "For India's Rural Poor, Growing Towns Matter More than Growing Cities." *World Development* 98: 413–29.

Gindling, T. H., and David Newhouse. 2014. "Self-Employment in the Developing World." *World Development* 56: 313–31.

Gobin, Vilas J., Paulo Santos, and Russell Toth. 2016. "Poverty Graduation with Cash Transfers: A Randomized Evaluation." Monash Economics Working Papers 23-16, Department of Economics, Monash University, Victoria, Australia.

Golub, Stephen S., Janet Ceglowski, Ahmadou Aly Mbaye, and Varun Prasad. 2017. "Can Africa Compete with China in Manufacturing? The Role of Relative Unit Labour Costs." *World Economy* 41 (6): 1508–28.

Grimm, Michael, Peter Knorringa, and Jann Lay. 2012. "Constrained Gazelles: High Potentials in West Africa's Informal Economy." *World Development* 40 (7): 1352–68.

Grimm, Michael, and Anna Luisa Paffhausen. 2015. "Do Interventions Targeted at Micro-Entrepreneurs and Small and Medium-Sized Firms Create Jobs? A Systematic Review of the Evidence for Low and Middle Income Countries." *Labour Economics* 32: 67–85.

Haggblade, Steven, Peter Hazell, and Thomas Reardon, eds. 2007. *Transforming the Rural Nonfarm Economy*. Baltimore: Johns Hopkins University Press.

Hallward-Driemeier, Mary, and Gaurav Nayyar. 2018. *Trouble in the Making? The Future of Manufacturing-Led Development*. Washington, DC: World Bank.

Hardy, Morgan, and Gisella Kagy. 2018. "Mind The (Profit) Gap: Why Are Female Enterprise Owners Earning Less Than Men?" *AEA Papers and Proceedings* 108: 252–55.

Hardy, Morgan, and Jamie McCasland. 2017. "Are Small Firms Labor Constrained? Experimental Evidence from Ghana." Research paper, Private Enterprise Development in Low-Income Countries (PEDL) initiative, Centre for Economic Policy Research (CEPR), Washington, DC.

Haushofer, Johannes, and Jeremy Shapiro. 2016. "The Short-Term Impact of Unconditional Cash Transfers to the Poor: Experimental Evidence from Kenya." *Quarterly Journal of Economics* 131 (4): 1973–2042.

Hausmann, Ricardo, and Dani Rodrik. 2006. "Doomed to Choose: Industrial Policy as Predicament." Unpublished paper, Harvard Kennedy School of Government, Harvard University, Cambridge, MA.

Hjort, Jonas, and Jonas Poulsen. 2017. "The Arrival of Fast Internet and Employment in Africa." NBER Working Paper 23582, National Bureau of Economic Research, Cambridge, MA.

Honorati, Maddalena, and Sara Johansson de Silva. 2016. *Expanding Job Opportunities in Ghana*. Directions in Development Series. Washington, DC: World Bank.

ILO (International Labour Organization). 1993. "Resolution Concerning the International Classification of Status in Employment (ICSE), Adopted by the Fifteenth International Conference of Labour Statisticians." ILO, Geneva.

———. 2018. "20th International Conference on Labour Statisticians." Report of the Conference, ILO, Geneva.

Ingelaere, Bert, Luc Christiaensen, Joachim De Weerdt, and Ravi Kanbur. 2018. "Why Secondary Towns Can Be Important for Poverty Reduction: A Migrant Perspective." *World Development* 105: 273–82.

Karlan, Dean, Ryan Knight, and Christopher Udry. 2012. "Hoping to Win, Expected to

Lose: Theory and Lessons on Micro Enterprise Development." NBER Working Paper 18325, National Bureau of Economic Research, Cambridge, MA.

Kluve, Jochen, Susana Puerto, David Robalino, Jose Manuel Romero, Friederike Rother, Jonathan Stöterau, Felix Weidenkaff, and Marc Witte. 2016. "Do Youth Employment Programs Improve Labor Market Outcomes? A Systematic Review." IZA Discussion Paper No. 10263, Institute for the Study of Labor (IZA), Bonn.

La Porta, Rafael, and Andrei Shleifer. 2014. "Informality and Development." *Journal of Economic Perspectives* 28 (3): 109–26.

Lall, Somik Vinay, J. Vernon Henderson, and Anthony J. Venables. 2017. *Africa's Cities: Opening Doors to the World.* Washington, DC: World Bank.

Loening, Josef, Bob Rijkers, and Måns Söderbom. 2008. "Nonfarm Microenterprise Performance and the Investment Climate: Evidence from Rural Ethiopia." Policy Research Working Paper 4577, World Bank, Washington, DC.

Macours, Karen, Patrick Premand, and Renos Vakis. 2012. "Transfers, Diversification and Household Risk Strategies: Experimental Evidence with Lessons for Climate Change Adaptation." Policy Research Working Paper 6053, World Bank, Washington, DC.

McKenzie, David, and Christopher Woodruff. 2008. "Experimental Evidence on Returns to Capital and Access to Finance in Mexico." *World Bank Economic Review* 22 (3): 457–82.

———. 2014. "What Are We Learning from Business Training and Entrepreneurship Evaluations around the Developing World?" *World Bank Research Observer* 29 (1): 48–82.

McMillan, Margaret, Dani Rodrik, and Claudia Sepulveda. 2017. "Structural Change, Fundamentals, and Growth: A Framework and Country Studies." Policy Research Working Paper 8041, World Bank, Washington, DC.

Mihretu, Mamo, and Gabriela Llobet. 2017. "Looking beyond the Horizon: A Case Study of PVH's Commitment in Ethiopia's Hawassa Industrial Park." Report No. 117230, World Bank, Washington, DC.

Minde, Isaac, David Tschirley, and Stephen Haggblade. 2012. "Food System Dynamics in Africa: Anticipating and Adapting to Change." Working Paper 1, Modernizing African Food Systems, Michigan State University, East Lansing.

Minten, Bart, Seneshaw Tamru, Ermias Engida, and Tadesse Kuma. 2013. "Ethiopia's Value Chains on the Move: The Case of Teff." Ethiopia Strategy Support Program II Working Paper 52, International Food Policy Research Institute (IFPRI), Addis Ababa.

Mohammad, Amin, and Asif Islam. 2015. "Are Large Informal Firms More Productive than the Small Informal Firms? Evidence from Firm-Level Surveys in Africa." *World Development* 74: 374–85.

Mueller, Bernd, and Man-Kwun Chan. 2015. "Wage Labor, Agriculture-Based Economies, and Pathways out of Poverty: Taking Stock of Evidence." Leveraging Economic Opportunities (LEO) Report No. 15, U.S. Agency for International Development (USAID), Washington, DC.

Murray, Sally. 2017. "New Technologies Create Opportunities." Working Paper 2017/156, United Nations University World Institute for Development Economics Research (UNU-WIDER), Helsinki.

Nagler, Paula. 2017. "A Profile of Non-Farm Household Enterprises in Sub-Saharan Africa." MERIT Working Papers 048, United Nations University–Maastricht Economic and Social Research Institute on Innovation and Technology (MERIT), Maastricht University and Erasmus Research and Business Support, Erasmus University, Rotterdam.

Nagler, Paula, and Wim Naudé. 2017. "Non-Farm Entrepreneurship in Rural Sub-Saharan Africa: New Empirical Evidence." *Food Policy* 67: 175–91.

Newman, Carol, John Page, John Rand, Abebe Shimeles, Måns Söderbom, and Finn Tarp, eds. 2016. *Manufacturing Transformation: Comparative Studies of Industrial Development in Africa and Emerging Asia.* United Nations University World Institute for Development Economics Research (UNU-WIDER) Studies in Development Economics. Oxford, U.K. Oxford University Press.

Ng'weno, Amolo, and David Porteous. 2018. "Let's Be Real: The Informal Sector and the Gig Economy Are the Future, and the Present, of Work in Africa." CGD Note, October, Center for Global Development (CGD), Washington, DC.

Nogales, Eva Gálvez, and Martin Webber, eds. 2017. *Territorial Tools for Agro-Industry Development: A Sourcebook.* Rome: Food and Agriculture Organization of the United Nations (FAO).

Norman, Therese, Dino Merotto, and Brian Blankespoor. 2018. "It's All About the Processing: Spatial Analysis of Agro-Firm Location and Jobs Potential in Zambia." Unpublished manuscript, World Bank, Washington, DC.

Oya, Carlos, and Nicola Pontara, eds. 2015. *Rural Wage Employment in Developing Countries: Theory, Evidence and Policy*. London and New York: Routledge.

Page, John, and Måns Söderbom. 2015. "Is Small Beautiful? Small Enterprise, Aid and Employment in Africa." *African Development Review* 27 (S1): 44–55.

Poschke, Markus. 2013a. "The Decision to Become an Entrepreneur and the Firm Size Distribution: A Unifying Framework for Policy Analysis." IZA Discussion Paper No. 7757, Institute for the Study of Labor (IZA), Bonn.

———. 2013b. "Entrepreneurs Out of Necessity: A Snapshot." *Applied Economics Letters* 20 (7): 658–63.

Reardon, Thomas, David Tschirley, Bart Minten, Steven Haggblade, Lenis Saweda Liverpool-Tasie, Michael Dolislager, Jason Snyder, and Claire Ilumba. 2015. "Transformation of African Agrifood Systems in the New Era of Rapid Urbanization and the Emergence of a Middle Class." In *Beyond a Middle Income Africa: Transforming African Economies for Sustained Growth with Rising Employment and Incomes*, edited by Ousmane Badiane and Tsitsi Makombe, 62–74. ReSAKSS Annual Trends and Outlook Report 2014. Washington, DC: International Food Policy Research Institute (IFPRI).

Reeg, Caroline. 2015. "Micro and Small Enterprises as Drivers for Job Creation and Decent Work." Discussion Paper 10/2015, German Development Institute, Bonn.

Resnick, Danielle. 2017. "Governance: Informal Food Markets in Africa's Cities." In *IFPRI Global Food Policy Report 2017*, 50–57. Washington, DC: International Food Policy Research Institute (IFPRI).

———. Forthcoming. "The Politics of Crackdowns on Africa's Informal Vendors." *Journal of Comparative Politics*.

Rijkers, Bob, and Rita Costa. 2012. "Gender and Rural Non-Farm Entrepreneurship." *World Development* 40 (12): 2411–26.

Rizzo, Matteo, Blandina Kilama, and Marc Wuyts. 2015. "The Invisibility of Wage Employment in Statistics on the Informal Economy in Africa: Causes and Consequences." *Journal of Development Studies* 51 (2): 149–61.

Roberts, Brian H. 2014. *Managing Systems of Secondary Cities: Policy Responses in International Development*. Brussels: Cities Alliance.

———. 2016. "Rural Urbanization and Development of Small and Intermediate Towns." *Regional Development Dialogue* 35: 1–23.

Rodrik, Dani. 2016. "Premature Deindustrialization." *Journal of Economic Growth* 21 (1): 1–33.

Rondinelli, Dennis, and Kenneth Ruddle. 1983. *Urbanization and Rural Development: A Spatial Policy for Equitable Growth*. New York: Praeger Publishers.

Söderbom, Måns, and Francis Teal. 2004. "Size and Efficiency in African Manufacturing Firms: Evidence from Firm-Level Panel Data." *Journal of Development Economics* 73 (1): 369–94.

Söderbom, Måns, Francis Teal, and Anthony Wambugu. 2005. "Unobserved Heterogeneity and the Relation between Earnings and Firm Size: Evidence from Two Developing Countries." *Economics Letters* 87 (2): 153–59.

Van den Broeck, Goedele, and Miet Maertens. 2015. "Female Employment Reduces Fertility in Rural Senegal." *PLoS One* 10 (3): e0122086.

Van Rooyen, C., R. Stewart, and T. de Wet. 2012. "The Impact of Microfinance in Sub-Saharan Africa: A Systematic Review of the Evidence." *World Development* 40 (11): 2249–62.

Vermeire, Jacob A. L., and Garry D. Bruton. 2016. "Entrepreneurial Opportunities and Poverty in Sub-Saharan Africa: A Review and Agenda for the Future." *Africa Journal of Management* 2 (3): 258–80.

World Bank. 2012. *World Development Report 2013: Jobs*. Washington, DC: World Bank.

———. 2015a. "Ethiopia Poverty Assessment." Report No. 100631, World Bank, Washington, DC.

———. 2015b. "More, and More Productive, Jobs for Nigeria: A Profile of Work and Workers." Report No. 103937, World Bank, Washington, DC.

———. 2015c. "Rwanda Poverty Assessment." Report No. 100631, World Bank, Washington, DC.

———. 2016a. "Measuring Rural Access: Using New Technologies." Report No. 107996, World Bank, Washington, DC.

———. 2016b. "Rwanda at Work." Rwanda Economic Update 9, World Bank, Washington, DC.

———. 2019. "Profiting from Parity: Unlocking the Potential of Women's Businesses in Africa." Report of the Africa Region Gender Innovation Lab and the Finance, Competitiveness and Innovation Global Practice, World Bank, Washington, DC.

———. Forthcoming(a). *Ethiopia Employment and Jobs Study*. Washington, DC: World Bank.

———. Forthcoming(b). *Making Economic Transformation Work for the African Poor*. Washington, DC: World Bank.

Yeboah, Felix Kwame, and Thomas S. Jayne. 2018. "Africa's Evolving Employment Trends: Implications for Economic Transformation." *Journal of Development Studies* 54 (5): 803–32.

FUNDAMENTALS 3

LEAPFROGGING WITH TECHNOLOGY (AND TRADE)

Luc Christiaensen and Siddhartha Raja

Africa's infrastructure gap is huge. The challenge of servicing rural and remote areas, where the poor are concentrated, is even more pronounced. The existence of large economies of scale in infrastructure development induces monopolization, often in state-run entities, while limited demand today makes short-run cost recovery difficult. This favors a focus on more densely populated areas, with frequent mismanagement of state monopolies further raising the costs of infrastructure provision. As a result, most of the poor in rural areas (and to a lesser extent in urban areas) remain deprived of access to affordable and reliable information and communication infrastructure, energy, and transport services. Without these, it is hard to access markets and public services, increase productivity, and raise income in either farm or off-farm activities.

However, change is here: in recent years, technology has made huge advances (such as wireless connectivity, solar power, and drones) that can fill the infrastructure gaps to reach the poor—at least in theory. This Fundamental reviews what low- and middle-income countries might expect from these technological developments.

New technologies hold great promise to accelerate Africa's poverty reduction by enhancing the returns to the work people do. But they will only deliver on this promise when public policies facilitate three elements as part of a larger effort: (a) the removal of barriers to technologies' adaptation to local conditions and their deeper diffusion, (b) the establishment of a wider base of skills among consumers and producers of these technologies, and (c) the presence of an appropriate enabling ecosystem to take advantage of the new opportunities that technologies are bringing.

Trends, Challenges, and Leapfrogging Opportunities

Over the past decade, use of telecommunication services has become widespread in Africa, with 73 percent of Africa's population now having a cellular phone subscription (World Bank 2018a). However, as of 2018, still only about 25 percent of Africans were using the internet (figure F3.1); in rural areas internet use is virtually nonexistent (Raja 2017). And mobile phones have not spread in all countries to the same extent. In the Central African Republic, for example, fast internet and mobile-phone reception remain largely confined to the area in and around Bangui, the capital.

At 42 percent, Africa's household electrification rate is also the lowest in the world. In its rural areas, the electrification rate is 22 percent (among urban households, 71 percent). Aside from low access rates, households and firms often also endure several hours of unpredictable outages, constraining the utilization of electricity for productive use (World Bank 2018a). Physical connectivity also remains a challenge, especially for rural areas. The share of the rural population that lives within 2 kilometers of the nearest road in good condition is only 17 percent in Zambia; 20–30 percent in Ethiopia, Mozambique, and Tanzania; and just over 50 percent in Kenya and Uganda (World Bank 2016).

Possibilities for Mobile-Phone and Internet Expansion

Technological advances offer the opportunity to leapfrog these gaps in infrastructure access and use. The first taste of such leapfrogging possibilities has come with the spread of mobile phones. Three important

FIGURE F3.1 **Mobile internet is expanding throughout Africa**

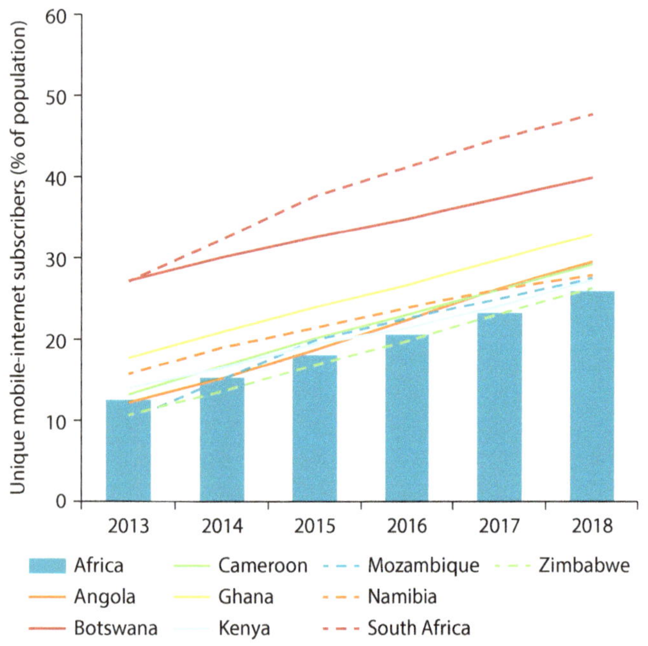

Source: Global System for Mobile Association (GSMA) Intelligence 2018 database, https://www.gsmaintelligence.com/.

features explain its success. First, wireless technology eliminated the need for landlines, dramatically reducing the fixed-cost investment and thus the economies of scale for service providers. Together with a liberalization of the telecommunication market, this enabled new firms to enter and bypass the monopolistic state-owned national enterprises that often lacked the financial resources (and incentives) to expand services (James 2016). As mobile phones were more widely adopted, mobile phones were further commodified, and the fixed costs for users declined rapidly as well.

Second, new pay-as-you-go business models, such as prepaid phone cards and mobile-phone kiosks, reduced the risk for nonpayment and enabled bite-size access to the services. This especially benefited the liquidity-constrained poor.

Third, the technology quickly made other leaps possible, such as the development of M-Pesa in Kenya ("M" for mobile, "pesa" for "money" in Swahili), a service that lets people store and send money through the phone, suddenly putting a rudimentary "bank account" in everyone's pocket. With mobile money transfers and payments now a possibility, and thus lower transaction costs, new applications are being developed. Hello Tractor in Nigeria, an app for renting tractors, reduces search and matching costs, bringing the economies of scale of high-productivity, lumpy capital goods within the reach of smallholders (Jones 2018). This in turn increases the value of cell phone possession and generates important network effects: more people having a cell phone means more people can subscribe and use the service, which enables more-efficient matching.

Reliable mobile-phone connections have not reached all areas yet, especially not rural and remote areas and Africa's lower-income countries. And internet penetration is only just starting. Technological advances, however, make further leapfrogging possible. First, over the past couple of years, there has been a huge increase in the number of undersea internet cables connecting Africa to the rest of the world, increasing bandwidth capacity and dramatically reducing the connection cost. Second, advanced wireless technologies help cover last-mile connectivity for internet services. Internet packages with unlimited downloads are now available in Kenya's slums for as little as 50 cents per day (*Economist* 2017a). This in turn paves the way for cheap or even free voice communication and other innovations.

Innovations for Electricity Access

Africa might similarly leapfrog straight to cheap renewable electricity provided by minigrids based on shared solar photovoltaic (PV) systems and direct current (DC) distribution lines. Modern energy services, especially electricity, are a critical component needed for economic growth (Modi et al. 2006; Parshall et al. 2017).

New approaches to electricity services such as rooftop solar-battery home systems or solar lamps are already proving to be impactful. Ugandan children who received solar lamps had better health, especially during their exam periods, than others who were exposed to indoor air pollution from their use of candles or kerosene lamps (Furukawa 2013). Rwandan households using pico solar lights[1] have a significant improvement in the quality of air within their homes, and children improved their quality of study (Grimm et al. 2017). However, these systems, at best, only power a couple of light-emitting diode (LED) bulbs, a radio or television, and a phone charger.

Minigrids especially hold promise for the many rural towns and villages that are hard to reach with the national grid, although when diesel-powered, they remain expensive to run. The development of inexpensive, compatible products (for example, refrigerators, solar pumps, and grain mills) is further enabling increased productive use of electricity. Greater aggregate demand from productive electricity use further improves the commercial viability of the minigrids. It also helps generate income-earning opportunities on and off the farm (as discussed in chapter 4), opening pathways out of poverty.

Through prepaid smart meters, electricity can be sold in small quantities, and problems with nonpayment can be further overcome. Customers pay in advance for a certain amount of electricity. When they run out of cash, the power is cut off until the account is reloaded, which, with mobile money, becomes easy. There have been several examples of successful minigrids of different types in South Asia and East Asia. So far, Tanzania is one of the few African countries to implement a larger minigrid electrification program, though several other countries (including Kenya, Nigeria, Rwanda, and Uganda) have started to review their policies to support minigrids. This is a dynamic space to watch (Banerjee et al. 2017; Tenenbaum et al. 2014).

Breakthroughs for Physical Connectivity

Leapfrogging the physical connectivity gap is more challenging. Drones may provide one solution. With today's technology, they can help deliver small, valuable items such as blood and medical supplies to remote areas. The widely touted partnership between drone start-up Zipline and the Rwandan Ministry of Health provides one example. It reduced the delivery time from four hours to less than 45 minutes and reduced dependence on reliable electricity to store medicines. By 2017, more than 20 percent of the blood supply outside of the capital, Kigali, was delivered by drones (World Bank 2018b). Orders can be placed on WhatsApp, and delivery is announced one minute before arrival. The company is now expanding its service in Tanzania (*Guardian* 2018).

However, this is not the only possibility to reduce transport costs. Other applications are being developed, such as the short message service (SMS)-based Moovr in Kenya—an Uber for cows. It connects truck drivers in Kenya with smallholder farmers in remote areas who want to get their cattle to market (*Economist* 2017c). It reduces search and matching costs, breaks transport monopolies, and helps farmers capture the economies of scale and services from a vehicle without having to own one, not unlike how mobile phones helped leapfrog fixed landlines.

Finally, following trade liberalization and increased South-South trade, especially with China and India, new forms of transport have come within the reach of small, informal sector businesses (as owners or leasing operators).[2] Motorcycles as well as motorized tricycles able to carry up to one ton of goods along Africa's rugged rural roads are widely seen today across rural Africa, though less so in southern Africa (Starkey 2016; Starkey and Hine 2014). In 10 years, the number of motorcycles in Tanzania increased from fewer than 10,000 to 800,000 (Starkey 2016). Although motorcycles and tricycles do not do away with the need to expand the rural road network or for bus and other vehicle services, they have been instrumental in opening up the rural hinterlands (Aikins and Akude 2015).

With motorcycle and tricycle taxi services now available and callable by mobile phone, the World Bank raised its estimated distance for an all-season road providing rural connectivity from 2 kilometers to at least 5 kilometers (depending on the terrain, paths, and bridges) in constructing its 2016 Rural Access Index.[3] These taxi services are also giving rise to new employment opportunities for unskilled workers (Mukhtar et al. 2015). At the same time, in the wake of this rapid expansion, road safety and regulatory compliance have become pressing concerns.

How Can the Poor Benefit from These Technological Advances?

The poor can benefit from these leapfrogging technologies directly, as adopters, or indirectly through the wider and cheaper availability of goods and services following adoption by others. They can benefit as producers and consumers through greater access to productivity-enhancing capital goods and better market access to buy and sell their goods and services. However, most of the benefits to the poor are likely indirect, at least in the medium term. This is because technological diffusion typically follows an S-curve, with the poor typically the latecomers in the process and the (richer) early adopters reducing the risks for technology providers and serving as the entry point for new markets. Put differently, the growth channel from technological leapfrogging is likely more important than the inequality-reducing one (Galperin and Viecens 2017).

The benefits from technological leapfrogging are typically also largest where the gaps are the greatest, with benefits often only emerging later given the important network effects, especially with digital technologies (Galperin and Viecens 2017; James 2016). To illustrate the potential (see also chapter 2, "Africa's Demography and Socioeconomic Structure"), between 2008 and 2014, access to M-Pesa services lifted almost 200,000 Kenyan households out of extreme poverty, or 2 percent of Kenyan households (Suri and Jack 2016).

Public interventions in three areas can help harness the potential from these leapfrogging technologies to accelerate poverty reduction in Africa:

- *Access:* More poor areas and people need access to the technologies to begin with. This requires public policy to remove market and regulatory failures that hold technology diffusion back (digital or otherwise). As far back as 2009, already only about 8 percent of the continent's population lived in areas that are commercially unviable for mobile cellular networks to serve, if appropriate policy and regulatory regimes were in place. Internet services needed greater public support (Williams, Mayer, and Minges 2011).
- *Skills:* Adequate skills to use the technology productively and even adapt it to the local circumstances are often missing.
- *Enabling business environment:* Many of the benefits of digital and other technologies come from the applications, products, and business models that develop on the backbone of information and communication technology (ICT) and solar networks. This requires an enabling business environment whereby the joint availability of the different technologies often are mutually reinforcing (for example, mobile payment, solar energy and power, and transport service platforms).

Policies to Expand Access

The liberalization of mobile-phone and internet services has been critical to Africa's mobile-phone success. At the same time, adequate regulations and a competition policy to prevent monopolistic behavior are key, including to ensure interoperability. With World Bank support, Kenya ruled, for example, that M-Pesa's mobile network provider Safaricom could not contract small stores on an exclusive basis (see Riley and Kulathunga [2017] for details). After implementation of the decree, small agents in rural areas raised their income by 49 percent.

Implementing efficient regulations for infrastructure sharing can also make internet access more affordable, by lowering fixed costs. In Indonesia, the government limited the construction of new telecommunications towers near existing ones to incentivize infrastructure sharing (ITU 2016).

Minigrids need, above all, clear legal frameworks to reduce regulatory risks for companies and their investors. Such frameworks would include tariff-setting rules, streamlined import procedures, standards and certification mechanisms for vendors and installers, dependable incentives for renewables and energy-efficient appliances, and education and awareness campaigns. Subsidization on a trial basis may also be needed to show proof of concept of adequate demand (including through generation of new activities) and thus commercial viability, which could then help attract the significant concessional and commercial finance needed (Carlin et al. 2017).

Finally, sector-specific taxes and fees on operators, consumers, and devices affect affordability and can inhibit the accessibility to the poor of ICT, energy, and transport services (GSMA 2016). In 2011, the tax share of handset costs was, for example, the highest in Africa (29 percent). In some countries, the tax system discourages the expansion of sorely needed mobile coverage (*Economist* 2017b). The need for greater domestic revenue mobilization (discussed in chapter 6, "Mobilizing Resources for the Poor") must be weighed against the potential for long-run growth, including by closing the digital divide.

Policies to Strengthen the Technology Skills Base

Beyond wide and reliable mobile and internet penetration, the multiple skills to take advantage of the new technologies are equally necessary. Countries need to improve the quantity and quality of education systems to tap the opportunities that technology brings (see also Fundamentals 1, "Africa's Human Development Trap"). Adequate skills provide the essential building blocks to benefit from the types of changes in the nature of employment in the coming decades—as automation and the "gig economy" (trading in tasks) take hold.

In countries where digital technologies are more widely diffused, skills development programs—whether part of formal or nonformal systems—should expand their offerings related to digital skills to include elements ranging from the basic skills needed to use these technologies (digital literacy) to more sophisticated training on occupation-specific tools and applications. Focused training programs could further help connect individuals to specific digital work opportunities. For example, Nigeria is developing a Smart Nigeria Digital Economy Project that aims to help up to 3 million Nigerians find and deliver digital work through various online platforms (Adewumi 2017).

More broadly, across countries, investment in advanced STEM (science, technology, engineering, and mathematics) graduates and skills to not only operate and maintain but also to adjust and develop technologies for local problems can pay off greatly. The benefits to the poor of these skill investments are likely mostly indirect, to the extent that such programs accelerate the technological leapfrogging of market failures and increase income sharing among the extended family when the children take advantage of the new digital employment opportunities.

Policies to Create an Enabling Business Environment

Finally, even with access to technology and the skills to use those technologies, the poor might not benefit if the enabling "ecosystem" is not in place. For example, the technology for mobile-money transfer services is easily replicable across mobile networks and hence countries. It is a simple enough service for the poor to use. However, if the appropriate regulatory frameworks are not in place—either to permit mobile telecommunications companies to handle money transfers or to place restrictions on their functioning—the result will be low adoption (box F3.1).

BOX F3.1 Rules matter for mobile money adoption

As of 2017, almost 22 percent of all adults across Sub-Saharan Africa had a mobile money account. However, there are clear regional divergences (map BF3.1.1).

Mobile money accounts have most widely penetrated in East Africa. With 73 percent of adults having a mobile money account, Kenya leads the way. Neighboring countries Uganda and Tanzania follow with, respectively, 51 percent and 39 percent of adults having a mobile money account. There is also a substantial uptake in Gabon, Namibia, and Zimbabwe, where the share of mobile money accounts among adults also amounts to about 50 percent. The importance of mobile money has further been on the rise in West Africa, especially in Burkina Faso, Côte d'Ivoire, Ghana, and Senegal, where more than 30 percent of adults now have a mobile-phone money account.

Within countries, adoption is further correlated with economic status. On average, across 30 countries in Africa for which data are available, the richest 60 percent of the population are more than twice as likely as the bottom 40 percent to have mobile money accounts.

What explains the variation across countries? Part of the reason is varying regulatory acceptance for mobile money. The Global System for Mobile Association (GSMA), the global mobile industry association, developed the Mobile Money Regulatory Index to capture the effectiveness of a country's

MAP BF3.1.1 Mobile money account penetration in Sub-Saharan Africa varies widely by country

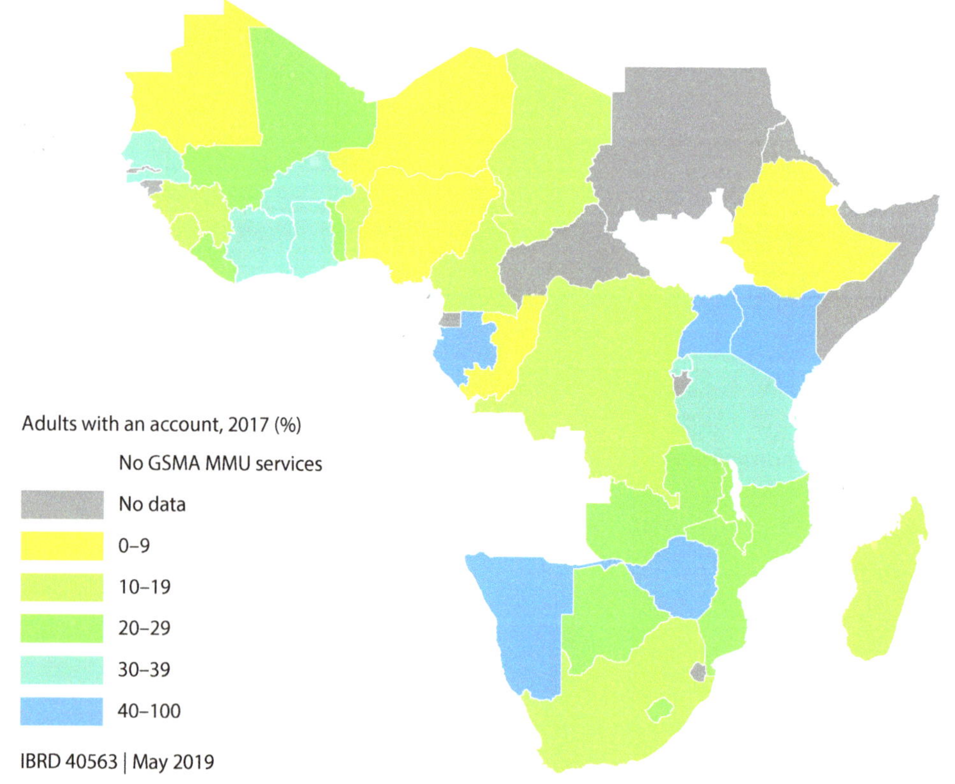

Source: Demirgüç-Kunt et al. 2018.
Note: "No GSMA MMU services" indicates the absence of mobile money account services included in the Global System for Mobile Association (GSMA) Mobile Money for the Unbanked (MMU) database.

(Box continues next page)

BOX F3.1 Rules matter for mobile money adoption *(continued)*

regulatory framework in creating an enabling environment to develop mobile money systems.[a] This single composite index ranges between 0 and 100, with higher scores indicating a more enabling regulatory framework. In Africa, a simple correlation analysis—controlling for a country's gross domestic product (GDP), population, share of population owning an account at a financial institution, and ranking in the World Bank's *Doing Business* index—shows that a 10-point increase in a country's regulatory index score increases the share of adults with a mobile-phone account by 6 percent.

Regulatory reforms to address barriers in market entry and uptake recently introduced in both Ethiopia and Nigeria are thus believed to be able to spark mobile money adoption. At less than 1 percent and 6 percent, respectively, mobile money account penetration in Ethiopia and Nigeria is still very low. They are Africa's sleeping mobile money giants (GSMA 2018). Together, they also account for 27 percent of Africa's poor.

Sources: Demirgüç-Kunt et al. 2015, 2018; GSMA 2018.
a. The GSMA Mobile Money Regulatory Index is an interactive tool available on the GSMA website: https://www.gsma.com/mobilemoneymetrics/#regulatory-index.

Similarly, if regulatory frameworks and institutions are not in place to enable competitive markets or investment in core infrastructures, the availability of technology might not have a significant effect. For example, absent well-functioning transport and logistics networks, e-commerce services alone cannot move physical goods across locations.

In sum, the new technologies hold great promise to accelerate Africa's poverty reduction, but they will deliver fully on their promise only when public policies facilitate three elements as part of a larger package: First, the removal of barriers to their adaptation to local conditions and their deeper diffusion. Second, a wider base of skills—including both the consumers as well as the technicians of these technologies. And third, the presence of an appropriate enabling ecosystem.

Until that time, technological advancement and adoption will continue at their own pace but with a smaller set of beneficiaries and the risk of deeper inequality as the "better connected"—in all senses of that term—will continue to benefit, while others, including the poorest, will lag in realizing those benefits and be held back from leapfrogging out of poverty.

Notes

1. Pico solar lights are lights powered by pico solar systems. These consist of much smaller and cheaper solar cells than traditional solar systems but provide enough energy to power low-power gadgets, portable devices, and LED lights. Their limited up-front cost makes them more readily accessible.
2. Until the 1990s, there were relatively few, mainly medium-size, Japanese "trail" motorcycles used by agricultural extension officers and nongovernmental organization personnel. Costs came down rapidly, however, when China, India, and some other Asian countries started mass producing and exporting medium-size motorcycles, ranging in cost from about US$2,000 for the Japanese motorcycles to perhaps US$600 for the Chinese and Indian ones. As a result, they also became affordable for some rural people, especially when the costs could be shared by families or through payments for rural transport services (motorcycle taxis).
3. The travel cost per kilometer by minibus is about 10–50 percent of the cost per kilometer traveled by motorcycle (US$0.05–US$0.10 per kilometer by minibus compared with US$0.13–US$0.34 by motorcycle). Yet motorcycles typically travel on the rough rural roads in the same area. They seldom "compete" on exactly the same routes as minibuses. Also, the motorcycle fares are

for one person traveling only. Costs may be 60 percent less if two people are traveling. From this perspective, motorcycles and tricycles are an important complement to, rather than a substitute for, minibus transport (Starkey 2016).

References

Adewumi, Bode. 2017. "Digital Economy Set to Create Over 3 Million Jobs in Nigeria." *Nigerian Tribune*, May 2.

Aikins, Kojo Atta, and Gilbert Senyo Akude. 2015. "The Impact of Motor Tricycles on Transportation of Agricultural Produce in the Pru District of Ghana." *Global Journal of Biology, Agriculture and Health Sciences* 4 (3): 22–26.

Banerjee, Sudeshna, Malik Kabir, Andrew Tipping, Juliette Besnard, and John Nash. 2017. "Double Dividend: Power and Agriculture Nexus in Sub-Saharan Africa." Report No. 114112, World Bank, Washington, DC.

Carlin, Kelly, Josh Agenbroad, Eric Wanless, Stephen Doig, and Claire Henly. 2017. "Energy within Reach: Growing the Minigrid Market in Sub-Saharan Africa." Report, Rocky Mountain Institute, Basalt, CO.

Demirgüç-Kunt, Asli, Leora Klapper, Dorothe Singer, and Peter Van Oudheusden. 2015. "The Global Findex Database 2014: Measuring Financial Inclusion around the World." Policy Research Working Paper 7255, World Bank, Washington, DC.

Demirgüç-Kunt, Asli, Leora Klapper, Dorothe Singer, Sariya Ansar, and Jake Hess. 2018. *The Global Findex Database 2017: Measuring Financial Inclusion and the Fintech Revolution*. Washington, DC: World Bank.

Economist. 2017a. "Beefing Up Mobile-Phone and Internet Penetration in Africa." *The Economist*, November 9.

———. 2017b. "How the Taxman Slows the Spread of Technology in Africa." *The Economist*, November 9.

———. 2017c. "The Sharing Economy, African Style." *The Economist*, November 9.

Furukawa, Chishio. 2013. "Do Solar Lamps Help Children Study? Contrary Evidence from a Pilot in Uganda." *Journal of Development Studies* 50 (2): 319–41.

Galperin, Hernan, and M. Fernanda Viecens. 2017. "Connected for Development? Theory and Evidence about the Impact of Internet Technologies on Poverty Alleviation." *Development Policy Review* 35 (3): 315–36.

Grimm, Michael, Anicet Munyehirwe, Jörg Peters, and Maximiliane Sievert. 2017. "A First Step up the Energy Ladder? Low Cost Solar Kits and Household's Welfare in Rural Rwanda." *World Bank Economic Review* 31 (3): 631–49.

GSMA (Global System for Mobile Association). 2016. "Digital Inclusion and Mobile Sector Taxation 2016: The Impacts of Sector-Specific Taxes and Fees on the Affordability of Mobile Services." Deloitte study commissioned by the Global System for Mobile Association (GSMA), London.

———. 2018. "2018 State of the Industry Report on Mobile Money." Annual trend and data report Global System for Mobile Association (GSMA), London.

Guardian. 2018. "'Uber for Blood': How Rwandan Delivery Robots Are Saving Lives." *The Guardian*, January 2. https://www.theguardian.com/global-development/2018/jan/02/rwanda-scheme-saving-blood-drone.

ITU (International Telecommunication Union). 2016. *Trends in Telecommunication Reform 2016: Regulatory Incentives to Achieve Digital Opportunities*. Geneva: ITU.

James, Jeffrey. 2016. "Mobile Phone Use in Africa: Implications for Equality and the Digital Divide." In *The Impact of Mobile Phones on Poverty and Inequality in Developing Countries*, 89–93. Cham, Switzerland: Springer.

Jones, Van. 2018. "How Hello Tractor's Digital Platform Is Enabling the Mechanization of African Farming." *AgFunder News*, July 4.

Modi, Vijay, Susan McDade, Dominique Lallement, and Jamal Saghir. 2006. *Energy and the Millennium Development Goals*. New York: World Bank and United Nations Development Programme (UNDP).

Mukhtar, A., M. Waziri, B. Abdulsalam, and I. M. Dankani. 2015. "Assessment of Tricycle as a Tool of Poverty Alleviation in Maiduguri, Borno State, Northeast Nigeria." *Journal of Humanities and Social Science* 20 (8): 14–18.

Parshall, Lily, Dana Pillai, Shashank Mohan, Aly Sanoh, and Vijay Modi. 2017. "National Electricity Planning in Settings with Low Pre-Existing Grid Coverage: Development of a Spatial Model and Case Study of Kenya." *Energy Policy* 37 (6): 2395–2410.

Raja, Siddhartha. 2017. "Technological Leapfrogging." Background note prepared for *Accelerating Poverty Reduction in Africa*, World Bank, Washington, DC.

Riley, Thyra A., and Anoma Kulathunga. 2017. *Bringing E-money to the Poor: Successes and Failures*. Washington, DC: World Bank.

Starkey, Paul. 2016. "The Benefits and Challenges of Increasing Motorcycle Use for Rural Access." Paper for the International Conference on Transport and Road Research, Mombasa, March 15–17.

Starkey, Paul, and John Hine. 2014. "Poverty and Sustainable Transport: How Transport Affects Poor People with Policy Implications for Poverty Reduction. A Literature Review." Technical report, Overseas Development Institute, London; UN-Habitat, Nairobi; and U.K. Department for International Development (DFID), London.

Suri, Tavneet, and William Jack. 2016. "The Long-Run Poverty and Gender Impacts of Mobile Money." *Science* 354 (6317): 1288–92.

Tenenbaum, Bernard W., Chris Greacen, Tilak Siyambalapitiya, and James Knuckles. 2014. *From the Bottom Up: How Small Power Producers and Mini-Grids Can Deliver Electrification and Renewable Energy in Africa*. Directions in Development Series. Washington, DC: World Bank.

Williams, Mark D. J., Rebecca Mayer, and Michael Minges. 2011. *Africa's ICT Infrastructure: Building on the Mobile Revolution*. Direction in Development Series. Washington, DC: World Bank.

World Bank. 2016. "Measuring Rural Access Using New Technologies." Report No. 107996, World Bank, Washington, DC.

———. 2018a. *Africa's Pulse: An Analysis of Issues Shaping Africa's Economic Future,* vol. 17 (April). Washington, DC: World Bank.

———. 2018b. "Business Unusual: Accelerating Progress towards Universal Health Coverage." Report No. 122036, World Bank, Washington, DC.

Managing Risks and Conflict 5

Ruth Hill (with contributions from Patrick Eozenou and Philip Verwimp)

Risk and conflict increase poverty and keep people poor. Shocks bring economic costs, but much of the economic impact of uninsured risk comes from the costly avoidance behavior it induces every year.

Risk and conflict are higher in Africa than in other regions for a number of reasons: Dominant livelihoods are much riskier. Health systems are weaker. Civil war is still a major issue in Africa. And many shocks are covariate, affecting entire communities more than a single household.

Addressing risk and conflict requires preventing shocks and managing them when they do occur. In many cases, the cost of prevention is lower than the cost of managing the event. Cost-effective strategies to reduce exposure exist but are not widely used (for example, development of markets for price risk and specific interventions for drought and health such as irrigation and insecticide-treated bed nets, respectively). There is some evidence that aid can reduce the probability of conflict at the margins, but more evidence is needed.

When prevention is not possible, a mix of safety nets, savings, and insurance instruments can help households manage in the aftermath of a shock. But preshock development of financial markets is weak, and safety net investments are too often made after the shock occurs. There is a continued reliance on ex post humanitarian aid to help households, which by its nature is neither timely nor predictable.

Addressing risk and conflict requires action before shocks occur. There is room for more technological innovation and better information systems, but fundamentally encouraging action before *shocks occur will require addressing the incentives that currently keep the action* after *shocks occur.*

For governments, this requires addressing the perverse political incentives that reward them for big postdisaster gestures rather than planning for a rainy day. In addition, coping with disasters using humanitarian aid is much cheaper (that is, free) than predisaster investments in prevention and preparedness.

For individuals, this will require inducing households to overcome mindsets that limit investment in risk reduction and management: a scarcity-induced focus on the present, an attitude of resignation, and an aversion to ambiguity.

The Urgency of Risk Management

Poverty reduction is not just about assets and effort; bad luck sets people back. Some households experience welfare gains in some years but setbacks in other years. And although many households are moving out of poverty, many are falling into poverty (figure 5.1). For example, Uganda experienced the second-fastest rate of poverty reduction of any country in Sub-Saharan Africa from 2006 to 2013, but analysis shows that for every three people who moved out of poverty during this period, two people fell back into poverty (Ssewanyana and Kasirye 2012).

FIGURE 5.1 The share of nonpoor in Africa who fall into poverty is about the same as the share of poor people who move out of poverty

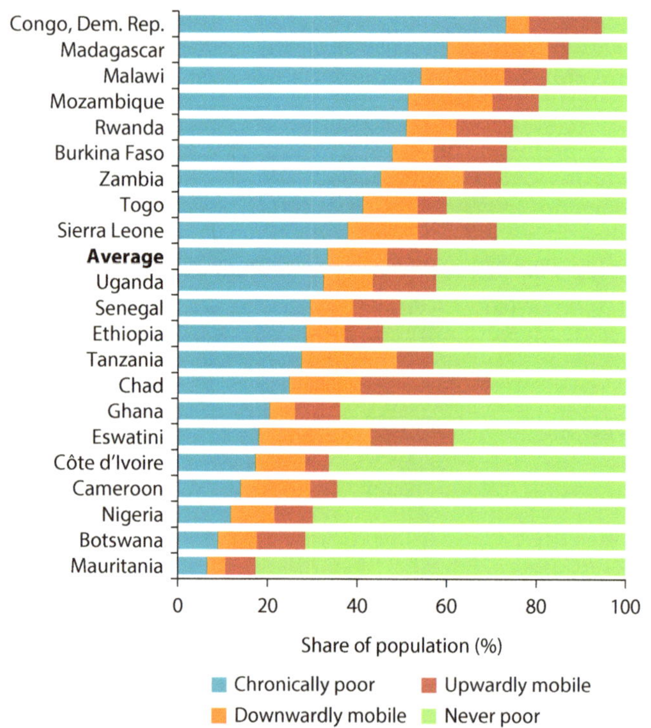

Source: Dang and Dabalen 2018.

Note: Poverty statistics refer to the latest household survey year for each country. The "chronically poor" category includes households that were poor in both periods of the analysis; "downwardly mobile" refers to households that fell into poverty in the second period; "upwardly mobile" includes those who were poor in the first period but not poor in the second period; and "never poor" includes households that were nonpoor in both periods.

Volatility and the shocks that often reverse gains and limit progress are critical factors in efforts to reduce poverty. As shown in the rest of this chapter, households in Africa are subject to frequent shocks and are ill-placed to manage them. This causes the shocks to increase poverty. Importantly, they also keep people poor, because households engage in costly behavior to avoid shocks.

The shocks that pose the largest risks to welfare in Africa—ill health, drought, price shocks, and conflict—primarily affect income rather than assets and are slow in onset rather than sudden. However, they vary in how many people are affected by them at once, the magnitude and breadth of their impact, and their persistence. Importantly, this has implications for the types of strategies that can be used to manage them.

How, then, to accelerate poverty reduction in this context? Addressing some of the overarching drivers of these shocks, such as climate change or the underlying drivers of violent conflict, is beyond the scope of this work. Rather, the focus is on interventions that help households either reduce their exposure to shocks (such as irrigation or bed nets) or better manage shocks that cannot be avoided or should be embraced given the opportunity they bring (such as financial market development and adaptive safety nets). Reducing and managing risk is expensive, and this chapter focuses on cost-effective interventions. In the case of conflict, the chapter features emerging lessons on the role of well-directed public programs to reduce conflict and how financial inclusion can help households manage in the face of an increased risk of violence.

Although there is still considerable room for innovation on policies and technologies to reduce and manage risk, in many cases solutions are available but not used. The private and public sectors have roles to play on both fronts and, crucially, both types of interventions require households and governments to act *before* shocks occur.

Why are these solutions not used? A variety of explanations exist: Behavioral and financial constraints limit households' investments in reducing exposure and increasing preparedness for shocks. Lack of trust, asymmetric information, and high fixed costs constrain the development of financial markets, including the supply of financial services and products for poor households. And political incentives that discourage saving for a rainy day and encourage big spending in the aftermath of a disaster, as well as limited fiscal and technical capacity, limit the degree to which governments invest to reduce risk and establish systems to provide timely support when shocks occur.

Risk and Conflict Increase Poverty and Keep People Poor

Health shocks, natural disasters, and conflict carry a large human cost in Africa. Every day, 550 women in Africa die in childbirth.[1] In 2011, the Horn of Africa drought resulted in about 100,000 deaths (Christian 2009; Hillier and Dempsey 2012). From 2014 to 2016, about 10,000 civilians died from conflict in Africa every year.[2]

These events also affect poverty. Drought in Malawi reduces consumption by a third, and a moderate drought that causes a 30 percent yield loss is predicted to reduce consumption by 15 percent and 9 percent in Uganda and Ethiopia, respectively (McCarthy, Brubaker, and de la Fuente 2016; World Bank 2015a, 2016a). Worsening real producer prices contributed to poverty increases in Madagascar from 2005 to 2010 (Thiebaud, Osborne, and Belghith 2016), and uneducated urban households in Ethiopia reduced their consumption by 10–13 percent because of higher food prices in urban markets at the end of 2010 (Hill and Porter 2016). Malaria alone reduces income by 10 percent when it goes undetected and untreated (Dillon, Friedman, and Serneels 2014). Poverty in African countries has increased by 2.5 percent on average because of out-of-pocket health payments alone (Eozenou and Mehta 2016). Shocks can matter even before one is born: in Mozambique, those exposed to drought in utero had fewer years of schooling (Baez and Caruso 2017).

Shocks cast a long shadow on welfare. Income shocks increase the probability of being infected by the human immunodeficiency virus (HIV) (Burke, Gong, and Jones 2015). When a child's household experiences a shock, investments in education and nutrition are reduced, and this increases the child's likelihood of being in poverty as an adult. The impact of nutritional and educational shocks on incomes earned as an adult is substantial—including a 3 percent reduction in annual earnings in Ethiopia, 20 percent lower wages in Burundi, and 14 percent lower lifetime earnings in Zimbabwe.

The shadow of conflict can be particularly long for three reasons. First, conflict begets conflict; hence current conflict increases the risk of future conflict. A relapse into conflict is most likely to occur in the first few years after the end of the previous conflict episode (Collier, Hoeffler, and Söderbom 2008). Postconflict peace is typically fragile: nearly half of all civil wars result from postconflict relapses.

Second, conflict affects trust and attitudes in a way that natural disasters do not. Exposure to violence has been found not only to reduce trust (Nunn and Wantchekon 2011) but also, more specifically, to increase within-group cohesion while simultaneously decreasing out-of-group trust and the sense of being constrained by societal norms and values (Cassar, Grosjean, and Whitt 2013; Nasir, Rockmore, and Tan 2016; Rohner, Thoenig, and Zilibotti 2013). Being exposed to violence can also change preferences. In Kenya, postelection violence sharply increased individual risk aversion (Jakiela and Ozier 2015b).

And third, conflict has far-reaching consequences, including forced displacement and the migration of those who can migrate. These effects have led some scholars to refer to civil war as "development in reverse" (Collier et al. 2003). In addition to loss of life and assets, conflict causes many people to migrate in a short period. The welfare of these households, forced to move, worsens. In Mali, among those displaced because of the 2012 coup d'état, employment rates fell from 70 percent to 26 percent, and food insecurity increased from 6 percent to 46 percent (box 5.1).

Wealth does not keep a household from being targeted; indeed, in some conflicts, it may even increase the probability of being targeted (Mercier, Ngenzebuke, and Verwimp 2016). During the Rwandan genocide, the educated, urban-dwelling, middle-aged male Tutsi landowners in rural areas were more likely to be killed (De Walque and Verwimp 2010; Verwimp 2003).

The most educated often choose to migrate when faced with conflict. Although they may not be part of the poor in Africa, they deliver services that are essential for poverty reduction such as access to information, knowledge and education, and health care, as well as the maintenance of the rule of law. Forced displacement, which affected 24 million Africans in 2018, is a type of poverty trap (box 5.2).

However, the subtler impact of volatility on welfare occurs not when disasters strike but in the costly behavior driven by the anticipation of shocks that households are ill placed to cope with (uninsured risk). The direct impact of a calamity on well-being is the visible, headline-grabbing way that conflict or poorly managed disasters set back progress. However, the persistent impact of uninsured risk on household behavior every year—regardless of whether the feared event occurs—is arguably the larger constraint to accelerating poverty reduction in Africa.[3] One study found that about two-thirds of the impact of risk was attributed to the ex ante

BOX 5.1 Displaced Malians suffered substantially but less than those staying behind

At the height of the crisis following the 2012 coup d'état in Mali, more than 500,000 people were displaced—almost half the population of the north, estimated at 1.2 million in 2009. In October 2014, there were 86,000 internally displaced persons (IDPs) and another 146,000 Malian refugees in other countries. The lack of data on the impact of such displacement often hinders the evidence base to make policy recommendations. A combination of baseline face-to-face survey data with follow-up interviews via mobile phone helped to shed some light on these impacts (Etang-Ndip, Hoogeveen, and Lendorfer 2015).

In Mali, the better-educated and wealthier households, many of them traders, were more likely to flee the crisis, and those who had returned by 2015 were less affected than those who remained displaced. Those displaced by the crisis experienced a dramatic decline in employment (from 70 percent to 26 percent), income, and food security: only 54 percent of the IDPs reported having three meals a day by June 2014, compared with 94 percent of them before the crisis.

Over time, the impact of the crisis diminished, and by February 2015, most children were going to school, and employment levels and number of meals consumed had returned to precrisis levels. Loss of wealth was especially significant, however, with IDPs and refugees losing at least 60 percent of their durables (in value) and 90 percent and 75 percent of their animals, respectively. Before the crisis, these households were estimated to have been in the third and fourth wealth quintiles of Mali's northern population. Loss in durables was 20 percent among returnees; estimates place them in the fourth wealth quintile precrisis.

However, welfare loss tells only part of the story. In June 2014, 52 percent of IDPs in Bamako felt insecure on the street at night (30 percent during the day). This rose to 85 percent among the returnees in Kidal and Gao. More important, 14 percent of IDPs reported having experienced death or physical violence in their households, compared with 4 percent of the returnees and 1 percent of refugees. Those who had stayed in northern Mali were even worse off.

BOX 5.2 Forced displacement is a poverty trap in Africa

The scale of the displacement crisis in Africa is large. As of mid-2018, the region hosted 35 percent of the global displaced population, accounting for approximately 24 million people, which is larger than the populations of 36 out of 48 African countries. Of the top 20 countries in the world in terms of displaced populations being hosted, 7 are in Africa.

View of the Landscape of Forced Displacement in Africa

Displacement in Africa is generated prevalently by conflict, concentrated around conflict areas and in a few countries. The main sources of conflict-related displacement in Africa are generated around three regions:

- *Lake Chad:* the war on Boko Haram, conflicts with other organized militant groups, and conflict in the Central African Republic
- *Great Lakes:* conflicts in Burundi, clashes in eastern Kivu (the Democratic Republic of Congo), and civil war in South Sudan
- *Horn of Africa:* conflicts in South Sudan, instability in Somalia, and authoritarianism in Eritrea.

The Democratic Republic of Congo, Nigeria, South Sudan, and Sudan are, by far, the countries with the largest numbers of displaced people (World Bank 2017a–f).[a]

Forced displacement in Africa has unique features. First, it is concentrated in a large geographical area, but the bulk of displaced persons live in a few countries.

Second, IDPs and refugees typically remain close to their places of origin. South Sudanese settle across the border in the poorest northern region of Uganda, Somalis settle across the border in the poorest northern regions of Kenya, Eritreans settle across the border in the poorest regions of Ethiopia, and the IDPs in northern Nigeria settle in poor nearby northern municipalities.

Third, these areas are as poor or poorer than the places of origin; they are marginalized places in many dimensions. They are also environmentally fragile areas that are vulnerable to major environmental disasters such as prolonged droughts.[b]

Fourth, they are often politically unstable areas, characterized by civil conflicts where terror groups of various natures roam freely across borders and manage lucrative illegal trades. In sum, these are areas often neglected by central governments, infrastructure is scarce, services are weak or nonexistent, and development assistance has been historically low. They are poor peripheries of poor countries.

Fifth, unlike their counterparts in middle-income countries in other regions, more than half of African refugees are hosted in camps (Devictor 2016). The largest refugee and IDP camps are in Africa. With more than 240,000 residents, the Dadaab refugee complex in Kenya is the largest in the world and represents the third-largest city in Kenya. The Mafa and Konduga IDP settlements in Nigeria have more than 100,000 residents each. Host governments regard the density of these settlements as a source of instability, and in recent years they have adopted policies increasingly leaning toward the camps' closure.

In terms of rights, the Convention Relating to the Status of Refugees (also known as the 1951 Refugee Convention and ratified by 44 of 48 countries in Africa) explicitly provides for work rights for those refugees who are legally staying in the country.[c] Yet despite such rights, de facto barriers exist such as encampment, high permit fees, and complex paperwork, along with other barriers like lack of knowledge of local language and cultural differences (Asylum Access 2014). And the laws of some countries may not align with the Convention to which the country is a party and thus exclude refugees from national labor markets.

Poverty and Well-Being of Displaced Populations

Evidence on the poverty and welfare of displaced populations in Africa is scarce[d] (Sarzin 2017; Verme 2016). However, even without ideal data and evidence, it is clear that poverty is higher among the displaced than in the general population.

Several features of this population make raising their well-being especially difficult. Displaced persons face weak labor demand in the places of destination. Destinations, as noted above, are not selected because of economic opportunities.

Displaced populations are also subject to multiple vulnerabilities beyond the monetary dimension. Many have been direct victims of violence or have witnessed violence, resulting in profound

(Box continues next page)

BOX 5.2 Forced displacement is a poverty trap in Africa *(continued)*

psychological distress. Once displaced, many children are unaccompanied and face the threat of exploitation. Many women fled gender-based violence and, once in a displaced situation, continue to face the same threat. Displaced populations typically have a higher share than regular populations of single parents (particularly mothers), children, unaccompanied children, and people with disabling psychological and physical disorders.

Access to services is problematic because it is more complex for displaced populations and generally limited to the services offered by the international community. Host countries have limited capacity to expand services for the newcomers.

Source: Verme 2017.
a. For further historical statistics on the forced displacement crisis in Africa, see Sarzin (2017) and Verwimp and Maystadt (2015).
b. For discussion of drylands and livelihoods, see Cervigni and Morris (2015).
c. For the various details and nuances regarding work rights, see the Convention (UNHCR 2010).
d. The impact of refugees and IDPs on host communities is also an important and somewhat controversial issue. Some studies have shown that they have the potential to create businesses and jobs in local communities (Asylum Access 2014; Sanghi, Onder, and Vemuru 2016; Verwimp and Maystadt 2015).

effect (that is, the behavioral response to risk) and one-third to the impact of disasters when they occur (Elbers, Gunning, and Kinsey 2007).

When the Ebola pandemic struck West Africa in 2014, the fear of infection carried a large economic cost. The impact of the pandemic on gross domestic product (GDP) in the three countries most affected—Guinea, Liberia, and Sierra Leone—arose largely because of the fear that the pandemic brought and the aversion behavior that resulted (World Bank 2014a). An estimated 80–90 percent of the economic costs of epidemics result from the aversion behavior they induce rather than the direct costs of health care and lost labor (Lee and McKibbin 2003).

The presence of risk often also indicates the presence of opportunity—a chance for things to turn out much better than expected and for households to get themselves on a path to higher income growth (World Bank 2014b). For example, when households cannot manage the risk in their environment, they may eschew investments and livelihood strategies (such as cultivation of high-risk, high-return crops) that offer great reward but leave them too exposed to the elements of nature, the economic ups and downs of a weak economy, or the uncertain behavior of others. When farm households have an opportunity to insure their crops, investment in agricultural inputs goes up: in Ghana, spending on inputs rose by 88 percent, from US$375 to US$705 (Karlan et al. 2014); in Mali, spending on inputs increased by 14 percent (Elabed and Carter 2015); and in Ethiopia, use of fertilizer rose by 13 percentage points (Berhane et al. 2012). The returns to these inputs vary in any given year given weather conditions and prices (Rosenzweig and Udry 2016), but even assuming a relatively low average return to input use, these increases amount to an average increase in income growth of 1–9 percent a year—enough to move many of these farmers out of poverty and to offset the losses associated with one-in-five-year events.

Similarly, in the face of potential violence from conflict, households may avoid the acquisition of visible assets such as houses, livestock, or motorbikes, at the cost of the income gains these investments can bring.

In the case of uninsured health risk, the lack of insurance encourages households to eschew investments that would reduce their long-run exposure to risk (such as prenatal care, preventive health care, and early treatment), which reduces health outcomes and earnings. Underinvestment in health treatment also poses significant public health risks: a 10 percentage point increase in the share of out-of-pocket health expenditures was associated with a 3.2 percentage point increase in bacterial isolates tested that showed antibiotic resistance (Alsan et al. 2015).[4]

So, how can poverty reduction be accelerated in this context of widespread uninsured risk? The following sections examine what we know about the most prevalent types of shocks, who is most affected, and what tools are available to reduce exposure to and manage the impact of shocks.

Prevalence of Shocks and Conflict in Africa

On nearly all aspects of risk, African households are more exposed to loss than households in other regions (figure 5.2). For example, a woman living in Africa is 30 percent more likely than a woman living anywhere else in the world to be trying to earn income during a large economic recession, 6 times more likely to experience an epidemic in her country, 8 times more likely to have her crops affected by drought, 9 times more likely to live in a fragile and conflict-affected country, and a staggering 29 times more likely to die giving childbirth. In household surveys, African households are more likely than those in other regions to report price, natural disaster, health, and crime shocks (Heltberg, Oviedo, and Talukdar 2015).

The most prevalent shocks to welfare concern prices, weather, health, and conflict. These shocks usually affect income but not assets, are slow in onset, and affect many households in one location at the same time. These features have implications for how shocks are managed. Rural life is arguably riskier than urban life, but the shocks that

FIGURE 5.2 Life in African countries is riskier than in other regions

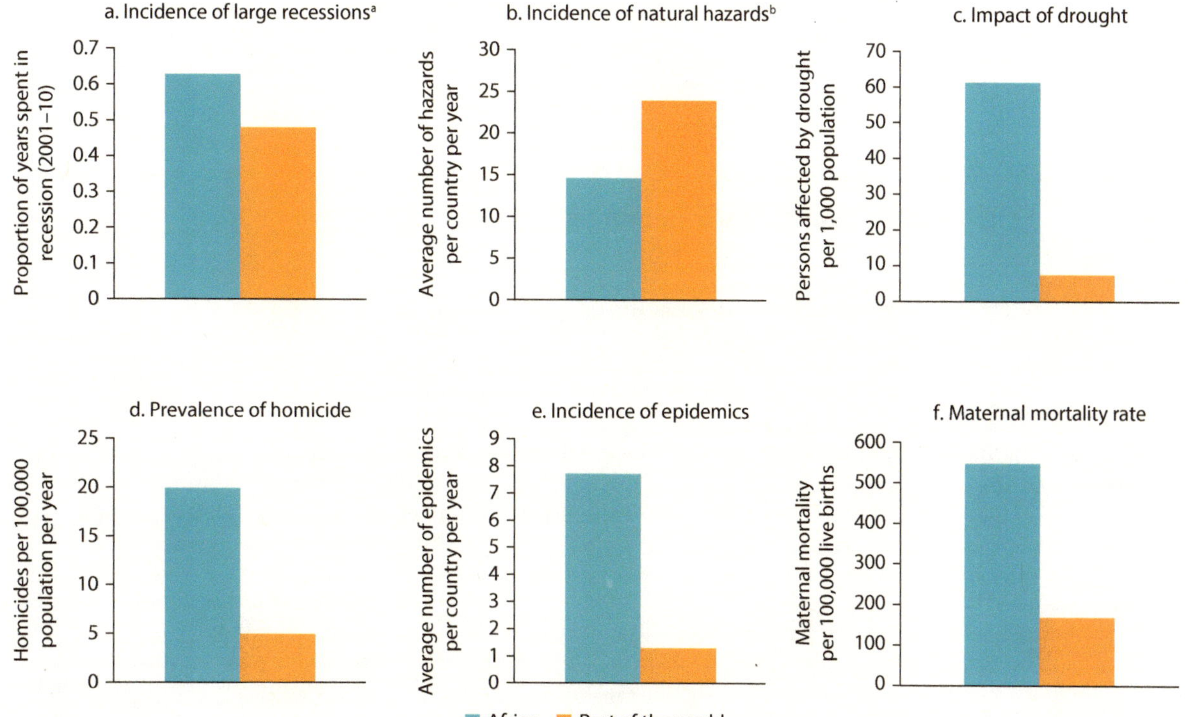

Source: World Bank 2014b.
Note: All graphs show the simple average across countries.
a. "Large recessions" are defined as a 5 percent decline in GDP per capita growth from peak to trough.
b. "Natural hazards" refer to the number of droughts, earthquakes, and floods per country per year.

affect urban life might have more severe consequences. In general, less is known about the vulnerability of urban life in Africa. Urbanization, progress in addressing communicable diseases, and climate change are changing the nature of risk in Africa.

The Nature of Shocks in Africa

Losses Primarily to Income

Shocks in Africa are primarily shocks to household income, not necessarily to household assets. Between 60 percent and 90 percent of poor households in Ethiopia, Malawi, Niger, Tanzania, and Uganda (households in the bottom 40 percent of the consumption distribution in their country) reported experiencing a shock that caused income losses in a specified period (from one year to five years) before the survey (Nikoloski, Christiaensen, and Hill 2016).[5] Income losses were just as prevalent for nonpoor households. Asset shocks were also widespread but not as frequent as shocks to income (box 5.3).

Prevalence of Various Risks

Climate and price shocks are the most frequently reported shocks, followed by serious illness and death (Nikoloski, Christiaensen, and Hill 2016).[6] In addition, 60 percent of households surveyed in 36 countries reported at least one member experiencing a serious illness or injury in the month before the survey (figure 5.3, panel a), and 47 percent of households reported an illness that resulted in lost labor (Eozenou and Mehta 2016).

Objective data on the prevalence of shocks also points to the importance of drought (figure 5.3, panel b) in relation to health risk. About a third of Africa's population have a 1-in-10 chance of experiencing drought and malaria—34.1 percent in the case of drought and 30.8 percent in the case of malaria. Conflict is also highly prevalent (figure 5.3, panel b): 19 percent of Africa's population has a 1-in-10 chance of living in an area affected by conflict.[7] Riverine flood risk is increasing and is higher than the risk of coastal flooding, but it is still relatively

BOX 5.3 In Africa, shocks affect income more often than assets

Shocks are often associated with the destruction or loss of physical assets, both public and private. Natural disasters, conflict, and theft can destroy bridges, roads, schools, factories, houses, and livestock. The loss of public assets carries both direct and indirect costs, as public services are interrupted and the activities of firms and households that rely on these services experience disruptions in their economic production (Hallegatte 2014).

It can take years for households to recover from asset losses (Dercon 2004; Lybbert et al. 2004). For a model calibrated using Zimbabwean data, shocks to household assets reduce aggregate growth by about 20 percent over a 20-year period (Elbers, Gunning, and Kinsey 2007). About half of that reduction (that is, 10 percent) is estimated to come directly from losses in assets.

Yet, in Africa, shocks are more often characterized by income losses, which are on average twice as prevalent as asset losses for households in Africa (figure B5.3.1).

Income losses are more prevalent, in part, because of the type of shocks most experienced in Africa. Drought is much more common than other natural disasters. Drought reduces the income of agricultural households and also causes the loss of animal assets. A contract loss or a sudden drop in output prices reduces the income flow for household businesses. International commodity prices affect the prices farmers receive, helping to reduce poverty when prices are good (Deininger and Okidi 2003) but increasing poverty when prices are low. A coffee farmer tending coffee trees at the beginning of the season in June 2011 would have seen a 14 percent

(Box continues next page)

BOX 5.3 In Africa, shocks affect income more often than assets *(continued)*

FIGURE B5.3.1 Income losses are twice as prevalent as asset losses in Africa

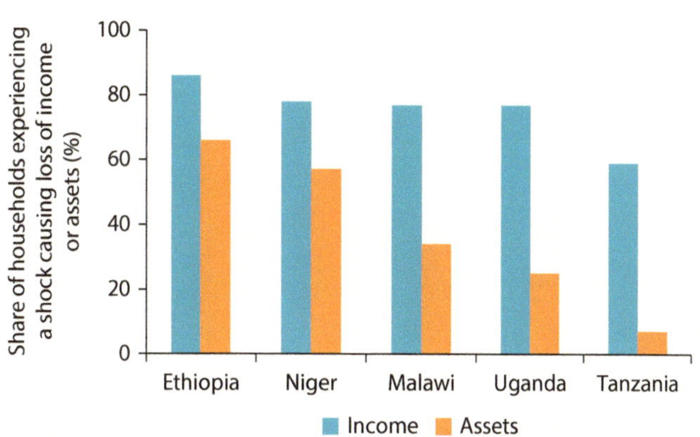

Source: Nikoloski, Christiaensen, and Hill 2016.
Note: This refers to shocks that occurred in the year (Ethiopia, Malawi, Niger, and Uganda) or five years (Tanzania) preceding the survey. Surveys are from 2008 to 2013.

reduction in the price by the time of the berry harvest at the end of the season and a 21 percent reduction in the price by the time new trees were ready to harvest years later. In contrast, high food prices can reduce income in urban Africa if wages are slow to respond (Headey et al. 2012).

Ill health also reduces a household's capacity to earn income. Survey data suggest that 76 percent of households that report illness stop their regular activity because of the illness or injury (Eozenou and Mehta 2016). Quantifying the impact is challenging, but an analysis of the impact of a malaria testing and treatment program in Nigeria provides some indication. Those who were offered testing and treatment earned 10 percent more, as a result of both increased labor supply and labor productivity, than those who were not offered the intervention (Dillon, Friedman, and Serneels 2014).

uncommon in Africa. In 2010, 13.6 million people had a 1 percent or higher chance of experiencing a coastal flood in Africa, and 56.4 million people were at risk of experiencing a riverine flood (Jongman, Ward, and Aerts 2012). Earthquake risk (not shown in figure 5.3) is low and present primarily in the Horn of Africa.

Many of the most frequently reported shocks are highly covariate—meaning they are experienced by many in the community and are not isolated incidents—particularly price and weather risk. Contrary to common expectation, price risk is by far the most covariate shock reported (that is, the shock most likely to affect multiple households in a geographic area), followed by climate shocks and crop disease (figure 5.3, panel c). The reason that climate risk is less covariate than price risk is likely a result of the heterogeneity of crops, planting times, and varieties that are present within villages when traditional agronomic practices predominate (Hill and Robles 2010). Illness, theft, death, and business and employment shocks are mostly idiosyncratic in nature.

Risks overlap, and some countries are particularly susceptible to multiple types of risk. The risk of different types of extreme weather events of drought and flood are correlated: floods are more likely to occur in drought-prone places. Some risks

FIGURE 5.3 The nature of risk in Africa varies by country, type of shock, and poverty level

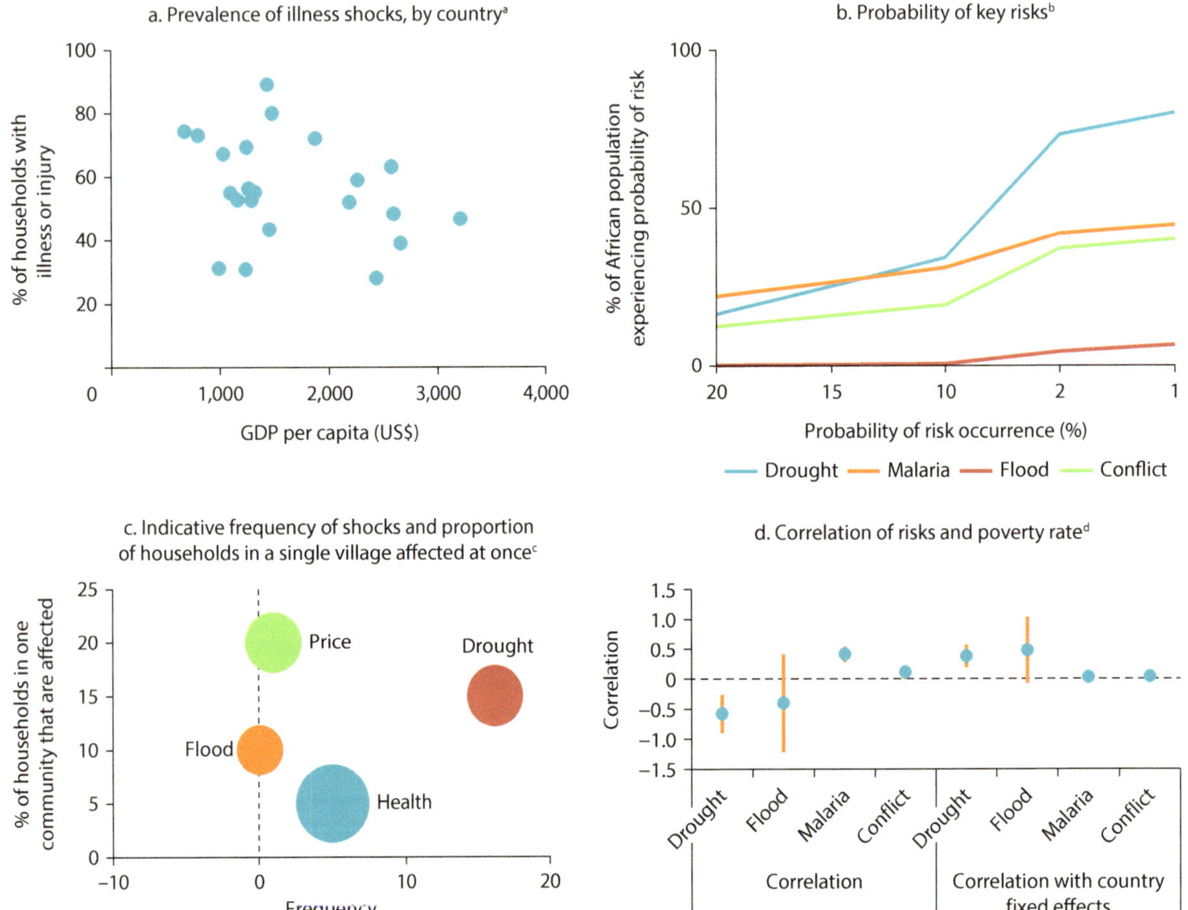

Sources: Panel a: Eozenou and Mehta 2016; panels b and d: Fisker and Hill 2018; panel c: World Bank Living Standards Measurement Study-Integrated Surveys on Agriculture (LSMS-ISA) survey data in Nikoloski, Christiaensen, and Hill 2016.

a. Data are from household surveys in 36 countries. Percentages are households in which at least one member reported experiencing a serious illness or injury in the month before the survey.

b. Figure shows the probability of risk to the African population as a ratio: for example, about a third of the population have a 1:10 (1-in-10) chance of experiencing either drought or malaria. The population's risk of conflict is determined by the percentage living within a 25-kilometer radius of 10 conflict-related fatalities in the previous year.

c. Bubble size is indicative of the relative impact on multiple-household welfare within a community. The figure is indicative based on findings reported in Nikoloski, Christiaensen, and Hill (2016) and does not reflect real data points.

d. Drought is rural only. Observations = 19.9 million pixels. Unconditional correlation using per-pixel population as weight. Standard errors clustered at the level of first administrative units (610 regions). All models include country fixed effects. The vertical orange lines indicate the standard-error range.

overlap because one type of shock, such as bad weather, can increase the risk of other shocks when mitigating action is not quickly forthcoming. For example, risk of disease is much higher in places where flood risk is high. Too little or too much rainfall can increase health risk (Hallegatte et al. 2016).

Weather shocks can also have other knock-on effects. For each 1 standard deviation increase in warmer temperatures or rainfall, the frequency of interpersonal violence rises by 4 percent and the frequency of intergroup conflict rises by 14 percent (median estimates; Hsiang, Burke, and Miguel 2013). Much price volatility in Africa is driven by local conditions not global price movements: the coefficient of variation of maize in domestic markets in Africa is 38 percent compared with the coefficient of variation of import parity of 18 percent (Minot 2011). In Ethiopia, a moderate drought induces a 3–4 percent increase in cereal prices (Hill and Fuje 2018).

The risk profile of countries varies across the continent. Countries along the north of Africa from east to west experience high drought and conflict risk (map 5.1). Malaria risk is particularly high in coastal western Africa and central Africa. Risk is in general lower in southern Africa, although drought risk is as high in western southern Africa as in the north of the continent.

Overlaying exposure to risk and poverty rates shows that poorer places are often riskier places (figure 5.3, panel d). Poverty is higher in places that are more conflict-prone and that have a higher health risk, as measured by malaria incidence. Poverty is not higher in places in the continent that are more prone to drought risk, but within a country, the more drought-prone places are poorer. There is no obvious relationship between flood risk and poverty, perhaps because flood risk is higher in coastal areas and this brings advantages, too.

MAP 5.1 Some parts of Africa are hit harder by risk

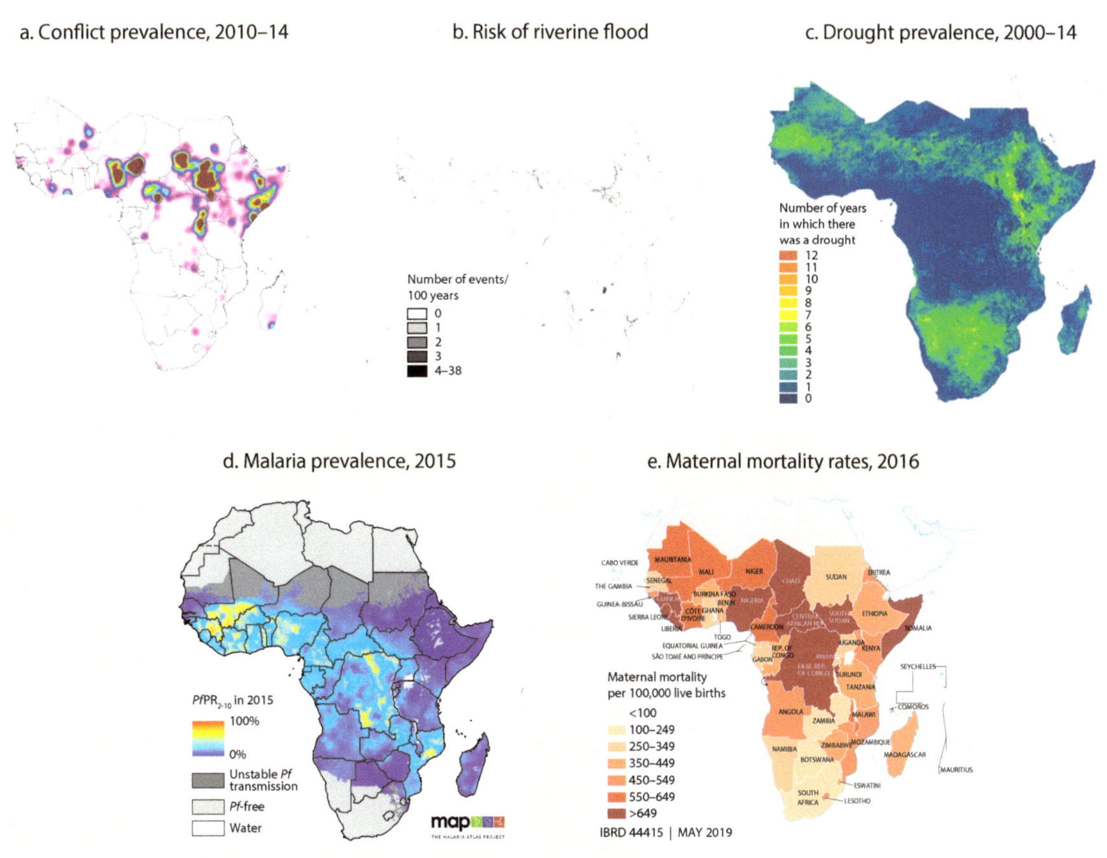

Sources: Panels a–c: Fisker and Hill 2018; panel d: the Malaria Atlas Project (https://map.ox.ac.uk/); panel e: World Development Indicators database, maternal mortality ratio.
Note: Panel c: A drought year is defined as a year in which at least half the growing period months are recorded to have a predicted greenness anomaly value below the 10th percentile of predicted greenness. Panel d: Each 5 km[2] pixel on the map shows the predicted *Plasmodium falciparum (Pf)* prevalence rate as a proportion of all children ages 2–10.

Risk Profiles by Wealth, Rural or Urban Location, and Gender

The risk of weather shocks, illness, and conflict is much higher for some households. Interestingly, although riskier places are poorer, at the household level, income shocks are reported by most households and are not much more commonly reported among poor households (figure 5.4).

However, rural life, where 80 percent of Africa's poor are, is in general more susceptible to risk than urban life (figure 5.5). This is largely because agriculture is a risky business, and rural Africans, on average, obtain most of their income from agriculture, much of it from rainfed agriculture (Davis, Di Giuseppe, and Zezza 2017). They are thus very much exposed to the vagaries of the weather.

This exposure is further compounded by crop and livestock disease and volatility in the price of inputs and crops. Not only do harvests vary significantly from year to year, so do returns from these harvests. As a result, the coefficient of variation in agricultural profits across time for a household employed in agriculture is found to be much higher (0.9 in Ghana and 1.5 in India) than the coefficient of variation in profits from nonfarm enterprises (0.5 in Sri Lanka) (Rosenzweig and Udry 2016).

Poorer access to water, sanitation, and health services in rural areas further increases the susceptibility of those households to

FIGURE 5.4 Unexpected income losses are reported by rich and poor alike

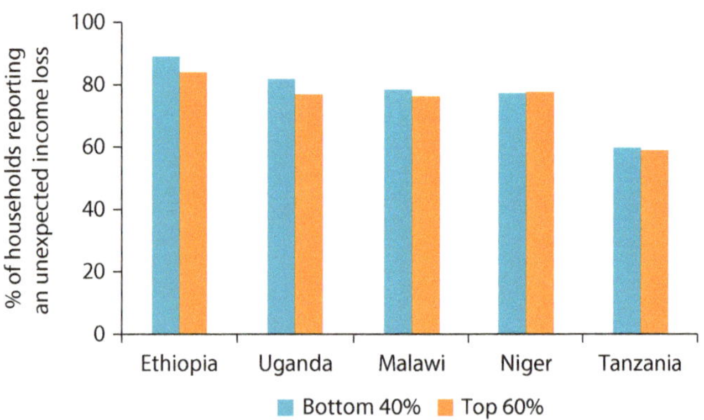

Source: World Bank Living Standards Measurement Study-Integrated Surveys on Agriculture (LSMS-ISA) reported in Nikoloski, Christiaensen, and Hill (2016).
Note: "Bottom 40%" and "Top 60%" represent household consumption levels.

FIGURE 5.5 Rural life is particularly risky in Africa

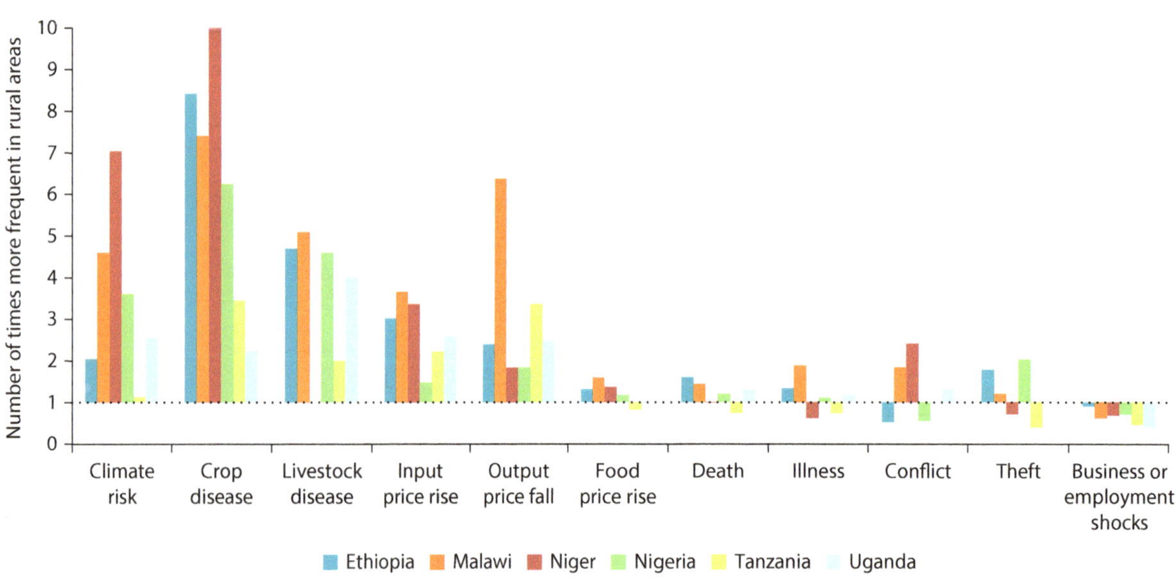

Source: World Bank Living Standards Measurement Study-Integrated Surveys on Agriculture (LSMS-ISA) in Nikoloski, Christiaensen, and Hill (2016).
Note: "Climate risk" refers to drought or flood.

serious illness shocks relative to urban households. Theft is just as likely to be a risk to rural households as to urban households. The urban poor are more susceptible to employment and business shocks as well as to flood risk (Hallegatte et al. 2016), and it is possible that although shocks are in general less frequent in urban areas, they are more devastating when they occur. For example, food price shocks have been shown to be particularly devastating to urban households (Hill and Porter 2016).

Households headed by women have a different risk profile than households headed by men. Death shocks are 1.5–2 times more prevalent among female-headed households (figure 5.6), highlighting that female headship is often synonymous with widowhood and loss of a male head. Marital dissolution often brings great hardship (Djuikom and van de Walle 2018) because it is common for widows and divorcées to inherit little or nothing and, in some settings, to be expropriated of all possessions and ejected from the marital home (Cooper 2008; HRW 2017; Izumi 2007).

Although female-headed households are less susceptible than others to agricultural price risk, they are more susceptible to food price risk. This is consistent with female-headed households farming less commercially than male-headed households. Further, the higher prevalence of food price shocks (in three out of five countries) indicates that female-headed households are more reliant on sources of income that do not adjust quickly when food prices increase.

Changing Exposure to Shocks and Conflict

The risks that characterize life in Africa are not static in nature; they are evolving. Although some shocks may become less prevalent, they may also become more challenging to manage, particularly for poor households. Health risk may fall, and weather may become a less important source of income variation, but conflict will likely remain high. In addition, health risk may become more challenging to manage as the risk of more repeated shocks increases. Although there

FIGURE 5.6 Female-headed households often face more risk

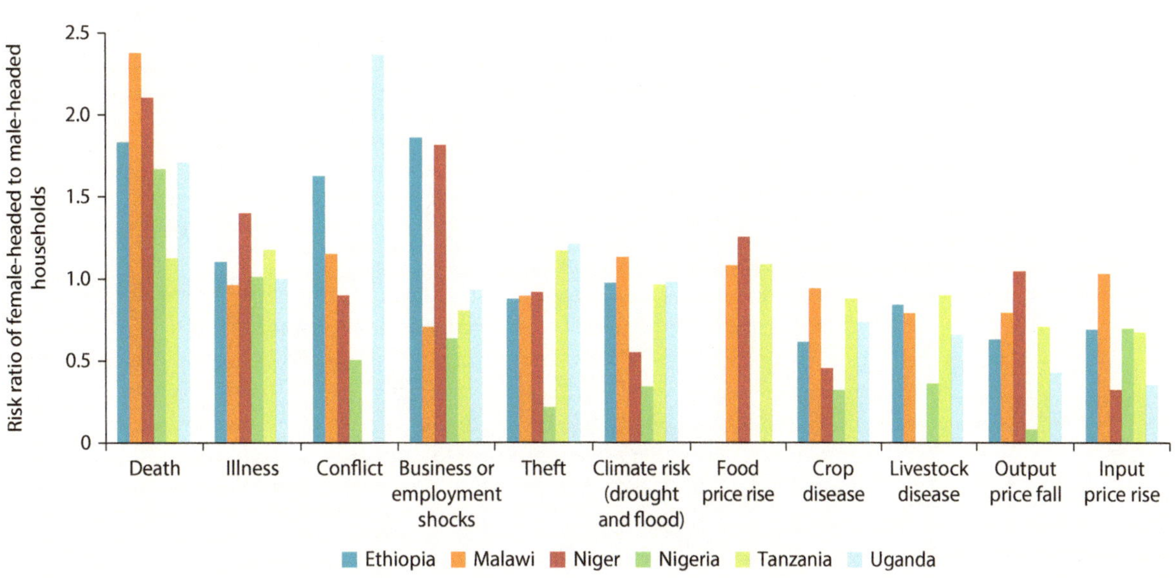

Source: World Bank Living Standards Measurement Study-Integrated Surveys on Agriculture (LSMS-ISA) in Nikoloski, Christiaensen, and Hill 2016.

is no clear evidence that price volatility will increase, urbanization will increase the share of the poor who experience welfare losses when food prices rise. As a result, food price volatility may become a larger threat to poverty reduction in future years.

Climate Change

Climate change will substantially change the incidence and severity of natural disasters, as well as increase the probability of conflict and health risks in some locations. In most African countries, climate change is predicted to reduce the income of the bottom 40 percent by more than 8 percent by 2030 (Hallegatte et al. 2016).

Changes in rainfall patterns are predicted to significantly increase exposure to flood (Hirabayashi et al. 2013; Jongman, Ward, and Aerts 2012). Globally, the number of people exposed to riverine floods could increase by 4–5 percent. Coastal flooding risk also increases rapidly as sea levels rise; while this affects cities in South Asia and Southeast Asia much more than in Africa, it also puts some African coastal cities, such as Abidjan, Côte d'Ivoire, at greater risk of flooding (Hallegatte et al. 2016). Working with static hazard maps of climate risk (maps that documented exposure to risk in 2015) and allowing for population growth and urbanization shows that the African population exposed to riverine flood risk will increase by 8 percent by 2050 (Fisker and Hill 2018).

When it comes to drought, the literature is not as conclusive. The Intergovernmental Panel on Climate Change (IPCC) forecasts that certain parts of Africa (for example, East Africa) will see more erratic rainfall, whereas the predicted effects on the Sahel belt are ambiguous; some researchers find a continuation of the present greening, while others expect prolonged drought periods (Boko et al. 2007). On average, yield decreases in Africa are predicted to be negligible for rice and wheat and relatively small (8 percent) for maize (Fischer, Byerlee, and Edmeades 2014). However, even though average yields may be marginally affected, the frequency and intensity of temperature and rainfall extremes would increase, increasing the number of droughts. East Africa, which currently experiences considerable water stress, is expected to see an improvement in water resources and a slight reduction in the number of drought days, while the rest of Africa will experience a 10–20 percent increase in the number of drought days (Prudhomme et al. 2014). Although climate change will be the driving force behind changes in drought risk, urbanization will cause the proportion of the population exposed to a one-in-five-year drought to decline by 2 percent by 2050 (Fisker and Hill 2018).

Health Risks

Turning to health, communicable diseases such as malaria that have been the main causes of death and disease in Africa are expected to become less important. The proportion of the population that had a one-in-five chance of being infected by malaria fell from over a third in 2000 to 22 percent in 2015. The risk of malaria infection is expected to continue to decline (Bhatt, Weiss, and Gething 2015), although climate change could slow this progress (Hallegatte et al. 2016).

Noncommunicable diseases (NCDs) are expected to become the leading cause of death by 2030 (Marquez and Farrington 2013). Urbanization, increased life expectancy (and the aging of the population that accompanies this), and changes in nutrition are some of the drivers behind the increasing health burden imposed by NCDs. In addition, road traffic injuries are an increasing cause of death in Africa, particularly among young men.

Although some diseases are being successfully tackled, pandemic risk is increasing in Africa. The spread of animal diseases has been increasing over the past 30 years, and an estimated 75 percent of pathogens capable of causing human diseases are now of animal origin, or "zoonotic" (Smith et al. 2014). Human and animal population dynamics may increase the risk of animal-to-human and human-to-human transmission of diseases in the future, increasing the risk of pandemics in the continent (Eozenou and Mehta 2016). Dense urban living facilitates the spread of infectious diseases, and countries experiencing rapid urbanization resulting in the multiplication of informal settlements become particularly vulnerable if commensurate improvements in access to health services are not made. The demand for livestock and poultry products is expected to increase substantially in Africa over the next 30 years, compounding the problem (Herrero et al. 2014).

Conflict-Related Risks

Unfortunately, conflict has become, or remains, a pressing threat to many Africans. Since 2010, the number of acts of violence against civilians as well as the number of protests and riots together with battles over territory have risen sharply (figure 5.7).

There has also been an increase in the number of fatalities. Two countries that mark the increased prevalence of conflict are Kenya and

FIGURE 5.7 The risk of conflict has been increasing

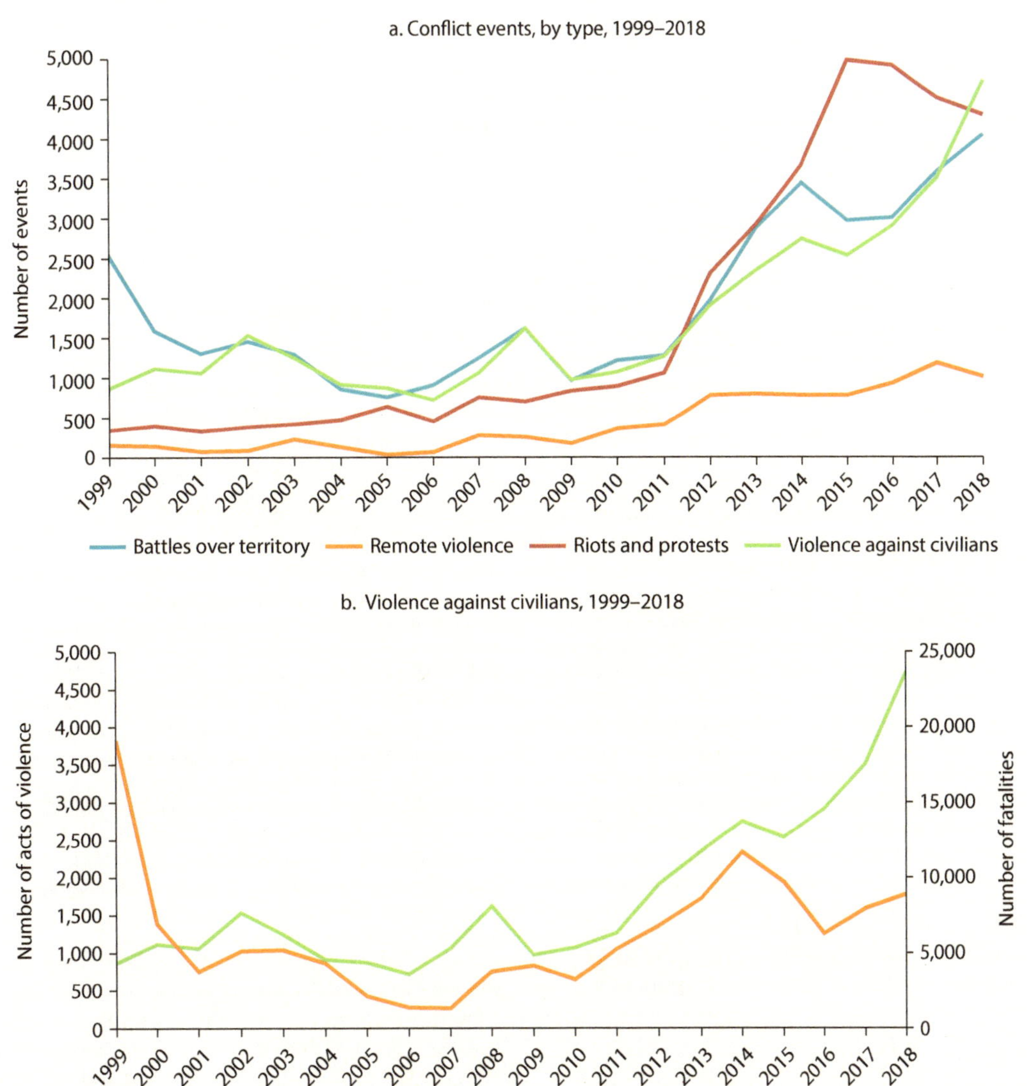

Source: Armed Conflict Location and Event Data Project (ACLED) database: https://www.acleddata.com/.

FIGURE 5.8 Conflict events have recently increased in Kenya and Nigeria

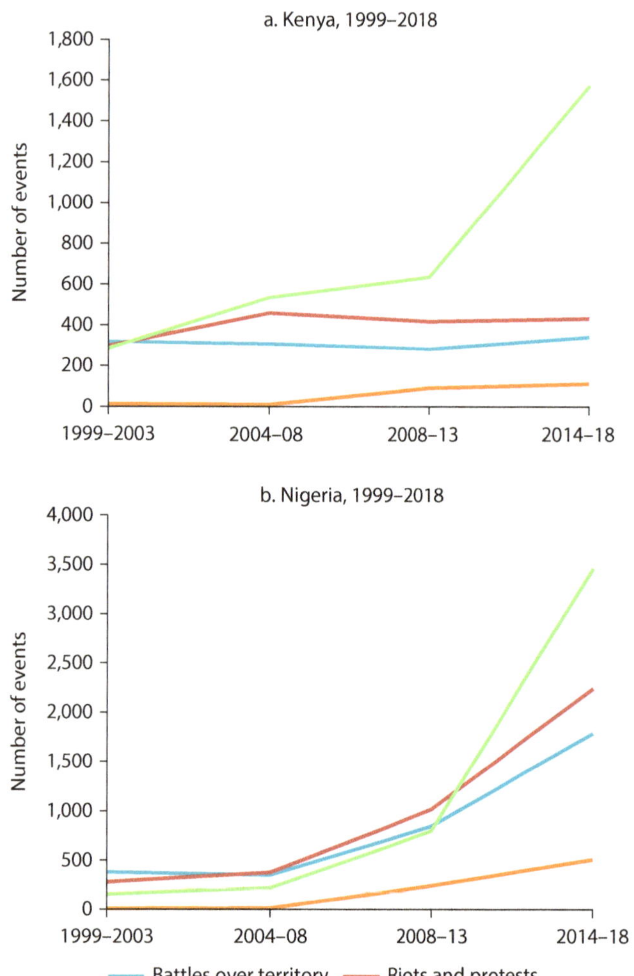

Source: Armed Conflict Location and Event Data Project (ACLED) database: https://www.acleddata.com/.

Nigeria. Kenya has seen a sharp increase in acts of violence against civilians (figure 5.8, panel a). This is the case for Nigeria, too, a country that is also embroiled in a rising number of battles for territory in the north as well as protests and riots (figure 5.8, panel b).

Violence against civilians has also increased sharply from 2010 onward in the Democratic Republic of Congo, Somalia, South Africa, South Sudan, Sudan, and to a lesser degree also in Burundi, Cameroon, the Central African Republic, Madagascar, Malawi, Mali, and Mozambique. It is not clear whether this is a blip or a trend.

Aggregate Volatility of Risk

These volatile factors interact with each other. Future climate shocks are predicted to increase conflict incidence in an average place and year from 17 percent during 1997–2011 to 24 percent during 2012–30 (Harari and La Ferrara 2018).

In addition to climate change, population concentration in urban areas, youth unemployment, the manipulation of elections, the disregard of constitutional term limits, and the discovery of more natural resources may spell new mass violence in Africa. For example, Sierra Leone chiefdoms with greater diamond wealth had more armed clashes than areas without these resources (Bellows and Miguel 2009).

Reducing Exposure to Shocks in Africa

The cost of reducing exposure to shocks through prevention is often much lower than the cost of managing a shock when it occurs. Perhaps the best example is the cost of pandemic prevention. The large costs of pandemics greatly exceed the cost of required investments to build well-functioning disease surveillance systems. The Ebola epidemic of 2014 cost an estimated US$10 billion. Functioning disease surveillance systems and better-equipped public health systems would have allowed such losses to be avoided. As a result, the returns from investing in disease surveillance systems are estimated to be 123 percent (World Bank 2012).

Economic development reduces exposure to risk. Investments in infrastructure and the development of markets that come with economic development reduce transaction costs and price volatility. With development comes a reduction in rainfed agriculture as a main source of income, which today leaves many farm households exposed to income shocks. Raising the productivity of poor farm households, as discussed in chapter 3 ("Earning More on the Farm"), will reduce this risk.

However, policy makers should not focus only on economic growth and raising agricultural productivity for smallholders. There are cost-effective strategies to reduce risk, particularly exposure to weather and health risks, but governments and individuals underinvest in these strategies. Underinvestment is particularly a problem for the poorest households—leaving the poor in Africa more exposed to risk that might be avoided through cost-effective policies and investments.

Risk Reduction through Development: The Example of Price Risk

Improvements in domestic crop markets in Africa would reduce price volatility. The high costs of transactions and of transporting food across countries in Africa cause local variations in supply and demand to be an additional, important source of food price volatility. Road investments and growth of urban centers increase market access for many farmers. The introduction of mobile phones also improves the efficiency of markets. Mobile-phone coverage reduces spatial price dispersion by 6 percent in Niger for semiperishable commodities (Aker and Fafchamps 2015). The impact of drought is lower for well-connected markets in Tanzania (Baffes, Kshirsagar, and Mitchell 2015). In Ethiopia, a moderate drought affected prices less in places that saw faster increases in market access (Hill and Fuje 2018).

Lower fuel prices will also help. The increase in fuel prices from 2007 to 2008 may have caused a 20–25 percent increase in food prices (Minot 2011). Analysis of livestock prices across Africa shows that price volatility can be even larger in livestock markets. In Burkina Faso, livestock prices fall by 0.3 percent for every 1 percent reduction in rainfall because of increased supply of livestock in local, poorly integrated livestock markets (Lang and Reimers 2015).

Good international trade policies and monetary policies are also needed to reduce price volatility. In Kenya, maize imports are impeded by a high tariff, and in West Africa, a 15 percent tariff on rice imports is present in 11 Economic Community of West African States (ECOWAS) countries. Tariffs increase the price band in which domestic harvest conditions influence prices, leading to high price volatility in places where aggregate production is dependent on weather conditions from year to year. When maize prices rose in 2007–08, Malawi, Tanzania, and Zambia banned the export of maize. In 2008, cereal prices in Ethiopia rose by 174 percent of the increase in international prices because of restrictions on foreign exchange (Minot 2011).

More sophisticated crop markets, such as forward contracts, would help insulate poor farmers from price volatility. Sudden price drops cause farmers to receive less for crop production than anticipated when crop investment decisions were made. Most farmers and traders in Africa sell produce in "spot markets," exchanging goods for cash in hand for a price determined at the point of sale (Fafchamps and Minten 2001). For traders this may present little price risk because changes in the price at which goods are sold are quickly passed on to the farmers from whom traders buy goods (Fafchamps and Hill 2008). But for farmers—the occupation of most of Africa's poor households—selling in spot markets means they face substantial price risk. Farmers invest in crops six months to three years in advance of their sale, when they plant and tend to crops in the field. Forward contracts would reduce price risk, but they are not used.

Prices matter not only for the poor farmers. For food buyers, sudden food price increases are not met by immediate increases in wages and income for those in nonagricultural sectors. In many African countries, the public sector is a main employer—one in five urban workers are in the public sector in Ghana, Rwanda, and Uganda—and the public sector often plays an important role in setting wages (World Bank 2016b). Appropriately indexing civil servant salaries, particularly for low-skilled occupations, could help reduce the cost of food price increases for households that are net buyers.

Targeted, Cost-Effective Interventions to Reduce Health and Weather Risks

Health Risk Interventions

Reducing health risk requires improvements in access to and the quality of water, sanitation, and health care services. Three investments in particular can dramatically reduce exposure to health risk in Africa: malaria prevention; water, sanitation, and hygiene (WASH); and mass immunization.

Malaria Prevention. The risk of malaria has fallen impressively in the region, but malaria is still the second-biggest killer in Africa (after human immunodeficiency virus and acquired immune deficiency syndrome [HIV/AIDS]) and the second-highest mortality risk for children. Malaria control through indoor residual spraying (IRS) and insecticide-treated bed nets (ITNs) has been highly effective. ITNs have been found to reduce child mortality by 20 percent in communitywide trials in Africa (Giardina et al. 2014).

Together, ITNs and other forms of malaria control such as IRS have had a significant impact on the spread of malaria where they are used (Giardina et al. 2014). The spread of ITNs over the past couple of decades has been impressive (Noor et al. 2009), as shown in map 5.2, panels a.1 and a.2. Still, one in four children in Africa live in a household with no ITN or IRS. There is considerable scope to tackle malaria through more ITNs and IRS.

Water, Sanitation, and Hygiene (WASH). Better investments in WASH can dramatically reduce the risk of ill health. Despite considerable progress, diarrhea is still the third-largest killer of children ages 1–59 months in Africa (Liu et al. 2016). This is largely preventable through improved sanitation and water services. It is estimated that 88 percent of diarrheal deaths are caused by unsafe water, inadequate sanitation, and insufficient hygiene (UNICEF 2006). In addition to being a leading cause of death in children, inadequate WASH can cause many other health and nutrition problems by limiting nutrient absorption (Prüss-Üstün et al. 2008). Estimates suggest that improving WASH conditions might reduce deaths by 6.3 percent globally and reduce the global burden of disease by 9.1 percent (measured in disability-adjusted life years).

Improving WASH outcomes requires continued investments in access to clean water and improved sanitation services. As more households in Africa get access to some form of WASH services, there needs to be an increased focus on providing access to *quality* services—for example, ensuring that households have access not only to piped water but also to water free from contaminants, and that not only is the practice of open defecation ended but the quality of sanitation facilities is improved.

Certain household investments and behaviors can reduce the incidence of diarrhea and other diseases tremendously, but these are not common. Water treatment can greatly reduce the incidence of diarrhea and improve health (Kremer et al. 2011), yet less than 10 percent of African households purchase water treatment (Ahuja, Kremer, and Zwane 2010). Handwashing can reduce the incidence of diarrhea and respiratory infections (Mbakaya, Lee, and Lee 2017).

Mass Immunization. Mass immunization is one of the most cost-effective ways of reducing health risk. African countries

MAP 5.2 Many cost-effective risk-reducing strategies are not well used

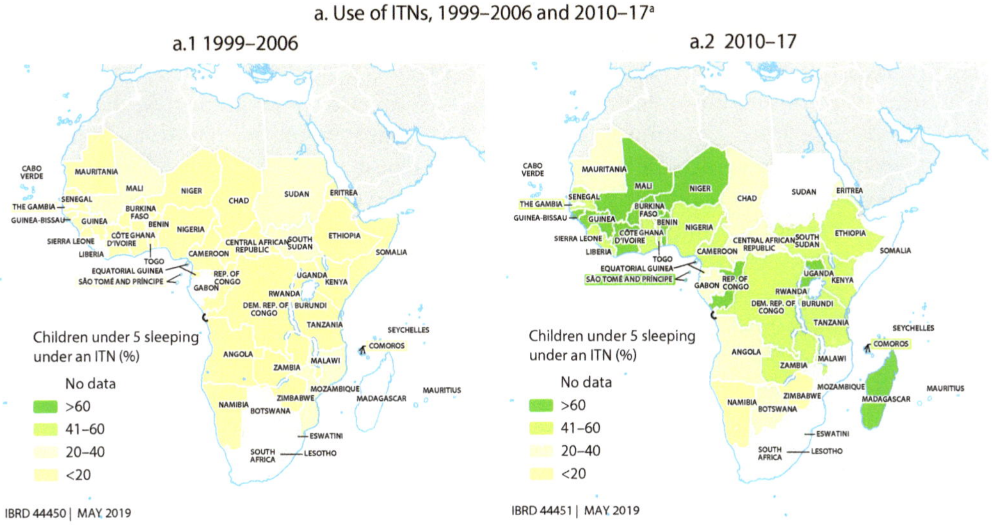

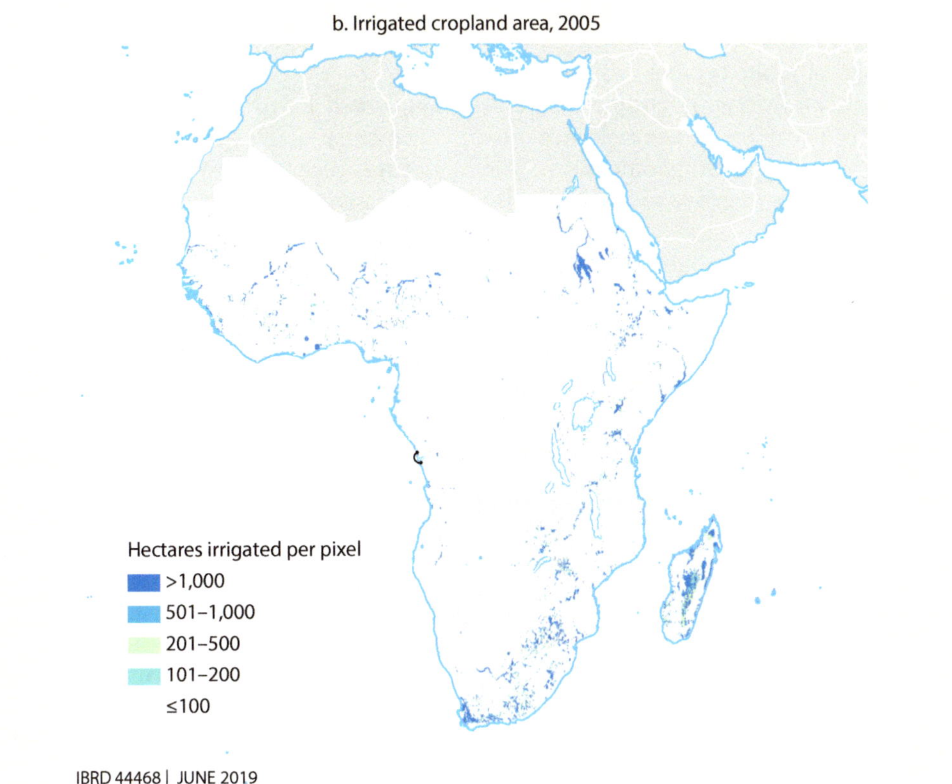

Sources: Panel a: Demographic and Health Survey data; panel b: HarvestChoice 2015 (http://www.harvestchoice.org/).
a. ITNs = insecticide-treated bed nets.

have increased the proportion of one-year-olds who have received three doses of the diphtheria-pertussis-tetanus vaccine (DPT3) from 38 percent in 1985 to 79 percent in 2017 (UNICEF data). However, a third of the world's unimmunized children live in Africa, and more must be done to ensure that other vaccines are provided, that the full vaccination schedule is properly adhered to, and that more of the funding for routine vaccines comes from domestic sources.

Weather Risk Interventions

Turning to weather risk, cost-effective strategies to reduce exposure to drought include irrigation, improved land management, and improved seeds.

Irrigation. Irrigation reduces the variation of crop yields and can increase average yields, but the cost of doing this varies by geography, the type of crops grown, and market conditions. For some farmers, irrigation is a way to reduce risk at negligible cost (or even at an income gain). For other farmers, it will prove too costly to be worthwhile.

The average cost of groundwater development is two to four times higher than surface water irrigation (Awulachew, Erkossa, and Namara 2010). Individual smallholder irrigation using low-cost pumps has been spreading fast in some regions, drawing water from both groundwater and surface sources (Cervigni and Morris 2015), but overall, a very small share of African land is currently irrigated (map 5.2, panel b).

With current technologies, there is significant unexploited potential, even in some of the driest parts of Africa. Africa's drylands have developed less than one-third of their technical irrigation potential, and more than one-fifth of the area that has been developed is not in use (Cervigni and Morris 2015). Making conservative assumptions about the costs and returns to investment capital, up to 3 million hectares of African dryland are suitable for small-scale irrigation development, and a further 1.5 million hectares could potentially be developed under large-scale irrigation given the large dams in existence or currently being planned and built (Xie et al. 2015).

Improved Land Management. Land management practices such as farmer-managed natural regeneration (FMNR) of trees and land is another approach to reduce weather risk. High rates of forest depletion drive land and water degradation and increase water stress. Where soil and water conservation have been improved, dramatic improvements have been seen (box 5.4). Although there has been a recent increase in FMNR

BOX 5.4 Farmer-managed natural regeneration of trees and land holds promise for reducing drought risk

Farmer-managed natural regeneration (FMNR) has gained popularity in many dryland areas in Africa as a way to reduce water stress (Cervigni and Morris 2015). In Niger, there are more than 5 million hectares of newly regenerated tree cover on croplands. The increasing tree cover can reduce exposure to droughts by reducing local temperatures; making more water available to nearby crops (a phenomenon known as hydraulic lift); reducing the sensitivity of yields to loss of rainfall given the better nutrient quality of soils that FMNR allows; and helping households manage risk better by ensuring that forest products can still be harvested during drought times.

If high-tree-density FMNR practices were used more widely, there would be an estimated 50 percent reduction in the number of drought-affected people in Africa's drylands (Cervigni and Morris 2015). In Ethiopia, soil and water conservation (terracing and bunds), community-scale watershed management, and expansion and protection of forest cover to generate more and cleaner water and diverse livelihoods has had an impact on yields, resulting in sizable increases in some places.

in Africa, there is still significant room for expansion. It only pays off in the long term and can be a risky investment as tree saplings are vulnerable to drought and disease in early years.

Improved Seeds. Finally, use of improved seeds that are more tolerant to drought and floods and more resistant to pests and disease can reduce risk. In the past, robust varieties have typically been associated with lower yields, but in recent years, varieties have been bred that provide the same or better yields that traditional varieties do and have increased resilience to climate stress.

The Drought Tolerant Maize for Africa project has produced such varieties for 13 countries in Africa, and in Nigeria and Zambia these seeds have become the most prevalent maize varieties grown. Adoption is not universally widespread, however, with adoption depending on the strength of local seed supply and extension systems. Poorer households are often less likely to be able to invest in new seeds and less likely to be engaged with extension systems.

Emerging Lessons on Reducing the Risk of Conflict

Given the damaging and persistent effects of conflict on welfare, preventing conflict is a priority. However, the causes of conflict are complex and often entrenched. Addressing the drivers of fragility will require different approaches in different contexts. Many factors contribute to conflict, and enumerating them is beyond the scope of this chapter.

Here we examine emerging lessons on the role of aid and well-directed public programs aimed at reducing conflict. There is some evidence that aid can reduce the probability of conflict at the margins. Foreign aid in general reduces the probability of violent conflict (Collier and Hoeffler 2002; De Ree and Nillesen 2009). Explicitly structuring this aid so that it increases when there are negative shocks to income (from weather, commodity price fluctuations, and so on) may help (Miguel 2007).

Jobs programs targeted to would-be combatants could also have marginal benefits in some contexts. Job creation for unemployed young men in a dissident region might be most effective in preventing armed conflicts from occurring in conflict-prone countries and regions. Yet it is possible that this will have only a marginal effect on violent conflict, and only in specific contexts where the conflict is in part economically motivated (Blattman and Ralston 2015).

Designing successful labor market programs in conflict-affected countries is challenging, and few countries have succeeded in generating additional employment. In one successful case, a program of agricultural training, capital inputs, and counseling for unemployed Liberian ex-fighters increased their farm employment and profits and shifted work hours away from illicit activities (Blattman and Annan 2016). The capital provided to these ex-combatants was crucial in this case. In the search for effective interventions in postconflict settings, the development community needs more such analyses (Blattman and Miguel 2010; Brück 2016).

Finally, disarmament, demobilization, and reintegration (DDR) programs for ex-combatants have also had some success. DDR programs have had welfare-increasing effects on the households of the former combatants as well as at the village level in Burundi (D'Aoust, Sterck, and Verwimp 2016). However, the effects disappear after a few years, pointing to the need for policies providing sustained economic development. Further evidence of the impact of these programs on keeping peace is also needed.

How Do Households Manage Shocks?

It is neither possible nor optimal to eliminate risk. Sometimes risk reflects the existence of a good opportunity for income growth that households can take advantage of. Households use a variety of approaches to manage negative shocks.

Types of Coping Mechanisms

Tapping into savings is the most widely used coping mechanism, even for poor households. Hypothetical questions in the Global Financial Inclusion Survey (Findex) on how households would finance emergencies showed that 20 percent of individuals (with little difference between men and women) would rely most on savings, second only to family and friends (Demirgüç-Kunt et al. 2015b). However, poor households (with less income to save) are much less able to use savings than rich households—on average, savings are used a third less often by households in the bottom 40 percent than households in the top 60 percent (Nikoloski, Christiaensen, and Hill 2016), as shown in figure 5.9. Although not suitable for adequate protection against large income losses, savings can help households manage small income shocks.

Households often choose to save in the form of physical assets such as small ruminants when access to banking is limited. Unfortunately, when shocks are community-wide, poor households may resort to selling assets such as livestock when prices are depressed. Much has been made of households' tendency to sell productive assets in the aftermath of a shock, reducing their ability to produce in the future. This does take place, and can be impoverishing when it does. However, a body of careful econometric evidence from several famines in different African countries shows that although livestock is sold during times of famine, this is a strategy of last resort, with a preference given to reducing consumption and liquidating nonproductive assets instead, particularly among poorer households (Dercon 2004; Hoddinott 2006; Kazianga and Udry 2006; Little et al. 2006; Lybbert et al. 2004).

FIGURE 5.9 Savings, family, and friends help households cope with shocks

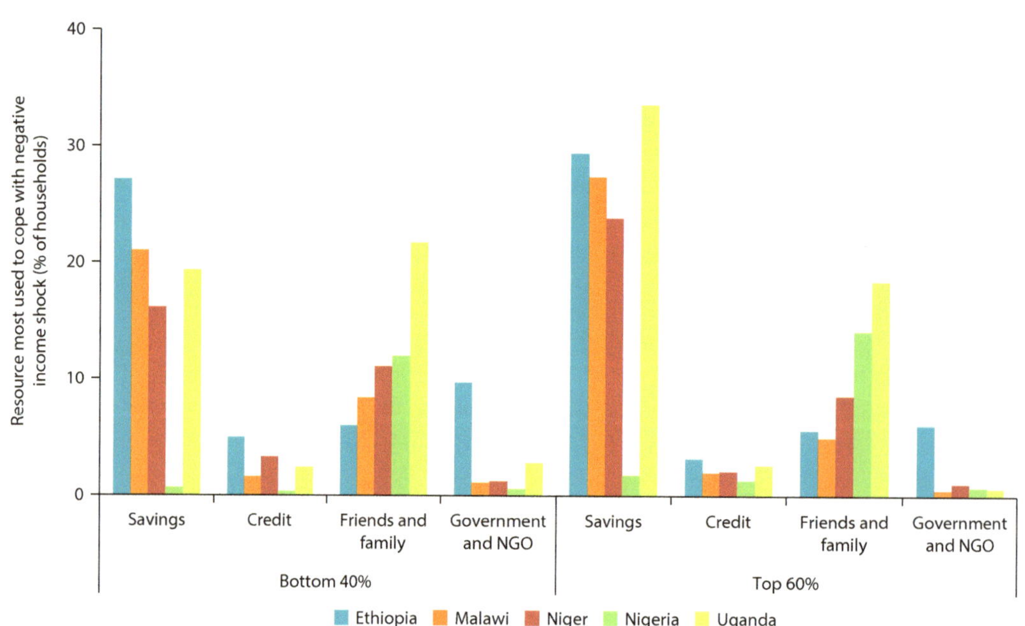

Source: Nikoloski, Christiaensen, and Hill 2016.
Note: NGO = nongovernmental organization. "Bottom 40%" and "Top 60%" represent household consumption levels.

Assistance from family and friends is the second most important means by which households manage shocks, but it is particularly important for the bottom 40 percent. This is also the most common way that households in Africa report they could finance an emergency (Demirgüç-Kunt et al. 2015b). The strength of informal safety nets such as these, in countries across Africa, has been well documented. However, friends and relatives may only be effectively relied upon to help manage relatively small risks, and risks that do not affect everyone in the informal network at the same time.

In addition, the strength of such informal networks in Africa carries costs of its own that can hinder poverty reduction. The expectation that better-off network members will support those less fortunate than themselves can encourage people to avoid investing in visible high-return activities and to engage in costly strategies to hide or tie up financial capital (Brune et al. 2016; Fafchamps and Hill 2015; Jakiela and Ozier 2015a). For example, in Cameroon, nearly 20 percent of members in a microfinance network took loans for the sole purpose of signaling that they had no cash (Baland, Gurkinger, and Mali 2011).

Borrowing is much less used. Few households can obtain credit to manage in the aftermath of shock. The third most reported source of emergency funds in the 2015 Global Findex Survey was taking a loan in advance of work to be paid (Demirgüç-Kunt et al. 2015b). For some households, this loan is taken against agricultural goods to be sold. Borrowing from other informal or formal lenders was negligible.

Increasing income from other sources by increasing the time spent on nonagricultural activities is another means by which households manage risks to agriculture. Sometimes this entails temporary migration. However, this type of diversification cannot manage all risks. Diversification can be helpful to manage risks that target one sector—such as diversifying out of agriculture when drought hits—but it is an ineffective tool to manage more widespread risks such as lower food prices in rural areas that affect income from nonagricultural sources of income, too (World Bank 2016a).

In addition, diversification can result in a household becoming a "jack of all trades and master of none." Diversification to cope with shocks can often result in small-scale, informal activities without the scale advantages that can come from specialization. This has been shown for Bangladesh and India (Skoufias and Bandyopadhyay 2013; Skoufias, Bandyopadhyay, and Olivieri 2016). Households with more diversified portfolios were not better able to withstand shocks in Burkina Faso, Ethiopia, Kenya, Mali, Niger, Somalia, and Zimbabwe (Boudreau 2013). This finding cautions against the premise that diversified livelihoods will be an effective means of increasing vulnerable households' resilience to adverse events.

Particular Impacts of Health Shocks

Health shocks often require unanticipated out-of-pocket payments for health care that, in the absence of health insurance, can impoverish. Out-of-pocket payments constituted almost 40 percent of health financing in Africa over 2008–13 (Eozenou and Mehta 2016). The impact of these payments on consumption and poverty can be assessed by examining what consumption would be if household spending on emergency health care payments were instead spent on food and basic essentials. About 1.2 percent of the population of Africa are pushed into poverty because of out-of-pocket payments for health care, and 36 percent of the population was already poor and pushed further into poverty by out-of-pocket payments in 2008–13 (Eozenou and Mehta 2016), as shown in figure 5.10.

However, many facing ill health choose to forgo care, often for financial reasons. On average, 16 percent of households do not seek care, and of those, 29 percent forgo care for financial reasons. This increases morbidity and reduces future income and consumption. These households not only forgo health care in the presence of shocks, as the earlier discussion highlighted, but

FIGURE 5.10 Out-of-pocket health care payments increase and deepen poverty in Africa

a. Share of population impoverished by out-of-pocket health costs, by country wealth level

% of people impoverished by out-of-pocket expenditures

4.5
4.0
3.5
3.0
2.5
2.0
1.5
1.0
0.5
0

0 2,000 4,000 6,000 8,000 10,000 12,000 14,000 16,000

GDP per capita (US$)

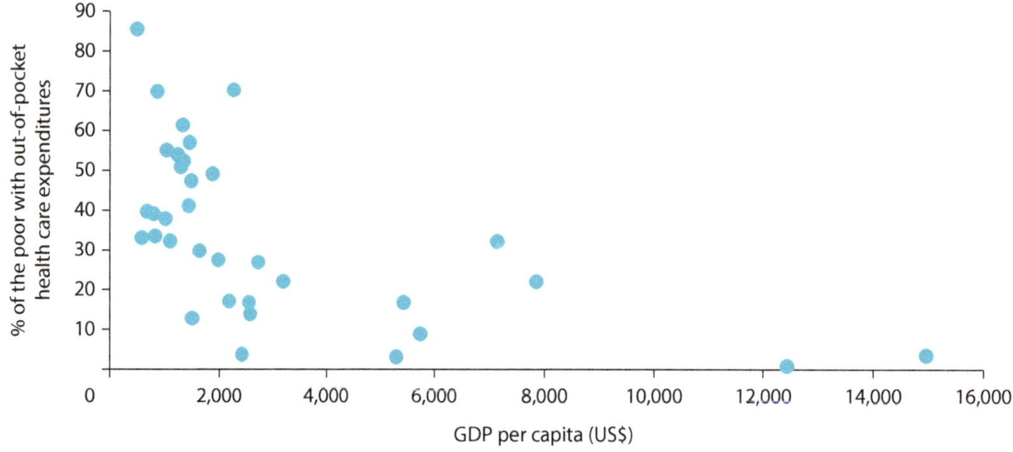

Source: Eozenou and Mehta 2016.
Note: Figure reflects data from household surveys in 26 countries, ranging from 2008 to 2013, by country.

also often reduce investments in schooling, even when school fees are not present, to save on the ancillary costs of sending children to school or so that school-age children can work to help the households meet their basic needs.

Better Insurance for the Poor

Notable for their limited use are the safety nets provided by governments or nongovernmental organizations (NGOs) as well as formal insurance mechanisms. Few households use either of those resources to manage the shocks they are most exposed to. Only about 5 percent of households report being able to rely on the government for help when a disaster hits (figure 5.9). The proportion of households using formal insurance is even lower. Poor households in Africa not only live in riskier environments but also lack access to formal insurance or reliable publicly financed assistance in the event of the common shocks they face.

When governments are ill prepared to respond to shocks, markets are weak, and households are poor and have little means to adapt, shocks hit harder, and uninsured risk is costlier. No one has died from drought in a high-income country in the past four decades, yet more people die from drought in Africa than from any other natural hazard (World Bank 2014b). Earlier financing to manage the Ebola outbreak would have allowed for a more comprehensive response during a period when insufficient response caused the number of Ebola cases to increase tenfold (Eozenou and Mehta 2016).

Households need a mix of tools to manage shocks. Small, frequent shocks such as moderate rainfall shortages or short-term illnesses are better managed with savings and transfers to households when they are too poor to save. Larger, less frequent shocks such as a drought or severe illness will require insurance and scalable safety nets for households that are too poor to purchase insurance. The appropriate mix of risk management tools will vary across households (see figure 5.11, which uses the examples of drought and health shocks). Investments in both financial markets and safety net systems are needed.

FIGURE 5.11 Managing health and weather shocks requires a mix of tools

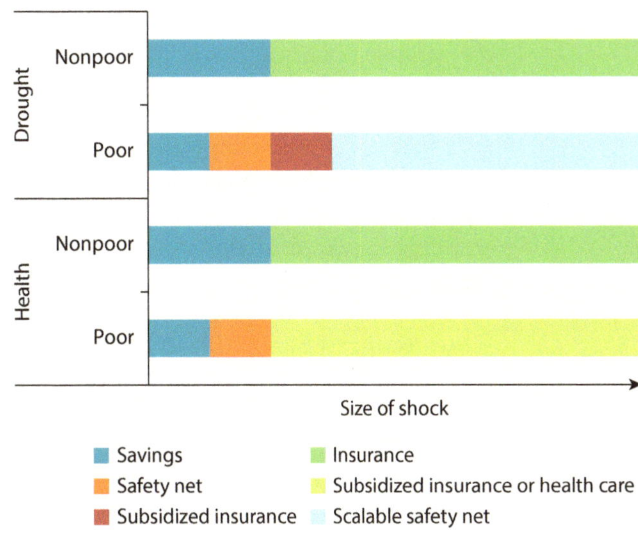

Note: Figure is indicative of findings regarding tools to manage shocks relative to household consumption level and does not reflect real data points.

Strengthening Financial Markets

Financial markets constitute a range of financial services that can help households manage risk. This section discusses the considerable potential to better develop financial markets to serve the needs of poor households.

Ways to Increase Savings

Savings are a household's first defense against an unexpected loss in income and can help households manage small, frequent shocks. Often these savings are informal and kept outside of the formal banking system: 60 percent of adults in Africa save money, but only 16 percent of these people use a financial institution to do so (Demirgüç-Kunt et al. 2015a). Others keep saved cash hidden in the home or use it to participate in informal savings clubs. (About 40 million unbanked women and 30 million unbanked men use informal groups to save.)

The limited use of formal savings accounts makes saved cash more susceptible to lose value, more subject to temptation for use for other purposes (sometimes because of requests from others), and sometimes less accessible for use in emergencies. Increased access to formal savings provides increased efficiency and security. For the poor, however, access to basic bank accounts will not necessarily increase savings (Dupas et al. 2018). When transaction costs are low enough, having a bank account can encourage increased savings (Demirgüç-Kunt, Klapper, and Singer 2017). And the poor, especially those who live in remote areas not well served by brick-and-mortar banks, will need different or simpler options than traditional bank accounts. The provision of a safe place to save money (a lockbox) was enough to increase health savings in Kenya by 66 percent (Dupas and Robinson 2013).

Systems for Mobile Money Transfers

Financial systems that enable easier, less costly sending of transfers can be a critical advantage when shocks occur. Remittances from family and friends are among the most common means of dealing with shocks. Digital payment systems allow payments to arrive much faster and without the cost of traveling to the nearest money transfer operator to receive it. Two-thirds of adults in Kenya reported a mobile money service as being the fastest and most convenient way to receive remittance transfers (Demirgüç-Kunt, Klapper, and Singer 2017). In Niger, when cash transfers using mobile money accounts were paid directly to women, it increased their power in intrahousehold decision making (Aker et al. 2016).

Africa is the region with the highest share of remittances being sent and received using accounts or over-the-counter money transactions, and many of these are made using mobile money services. However, there is scope to expand the use of mobile money: 42 percent of remittances are still received in cash (Demirgüç-Kunt et al. 2015a).

FIGURE 5.12 Formal health insurance coverage in Africa is low, and concentrated among the better-off

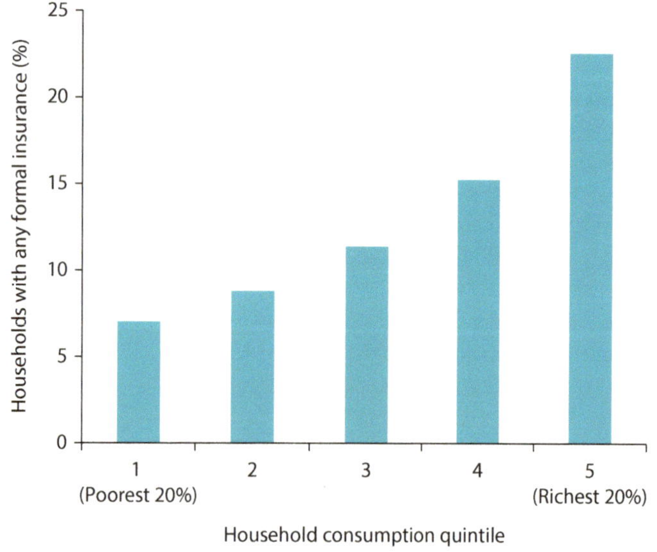

Source: Eozenou and Mehta 2016.

Help to Gain Insurance

Insurance or prepayment mechanisms are the appropriate financial tool for managing large, less frequent shocks that affect many people at once. However, few households in Africa, particularly poor households, have any type of insurance to manage health, climate, or price shocks.

A review of surveys in eight countries representing 30 percent of the African population shows that 17 percent of households in Africa have some form of health insurance (Eozenou and Mehta 2016). However, because surveys in countries with low rates of health insurance are less likely to include questions on health insurance, the Africa average is likely to be lower than this. Health insurance coverage is much lower for poorer households (7 percent in the poorest quintile) than for richer households (23 percent) (figure 5.12).

Except for Ghana's social health insurance program, there are few large social health insurance schemes in Africa, in contrast to other regions. For example, in India, 35 million households living in poverty have access to inpatient health care through a publicly subsidized insurance scheme, Rashtriya Swasthya Bima Yojana (RSBY, literally "National Health Insurance Program"). Many countries have some form of community-based health insurance, but low coverage is often a challenge except in Rwanda, where the scheme has almost achieved universal coverage. However, any form of health insurance is not always fully effective at overcoming the financial barriers to health care (Eozenou and Mehta 2016), and individuals formally covered by some form of health insurance scheme might still have to incur user fees or copayments at the point of service, which act as a deterrent for accessing needed care.

Yield insurance provides households with an insurance contract that guarantees payment when crop yields fall below a certain threshold because of an unexpected event such as poor weather or crop disease. Yield insurance struggles with the challenges of moral hazard, and in Africa nearly all yield insurance contracts are index-based.

However, given the paucity of area yield data in Africa, indexes are almost entirely dependent on data from satellites or weather stations rather than on the area yield indexes commonly used in other countries (for example, China, India, and the United States), and these are not always well correlated with yields on the ground.

Although there have been many pilot programs in Africa, large-scale adoption of standalone insurance products in Africa has not been observed, and when operated at a small scale, the costs of providing this insurance can be quite high. High take-up is only present for products that are linked to the purchase of other inputs such as seeds (for example, through the Syngenta Foundation's One Acre Fund for smallholders in Kenya) or that are highly subsidized and offered by trusted intermediaries. Substantial innovation in the quality and marketing of these products is needed for farmers to be able to use them to mitigate risk. However, as figure 5.11 shows, they can be an important part of the risk management solution for some households.

Another financial market tool to manage risk in agriculture is put options for agricultural commodities traded in global futures markets (such as coffee), which can provide financial protection against falls in prices that would reduce the income of farmers who produce these commodities. However, these options are traded for larger quantities than are sold by any one farmer, and Africa's farmers have no means by which to access this market, indicating another area where innovation in marketing is needed to increase the financial tools available to Africa's farmers.

Improving Safety Nets and Emergency Response

Safety nets, such as cash transfer programs or public works schemes, are becoming increasingly widespread in Africa (figure 5.13, panel a). Every African country has a safety net program of some description (Beegle, Honorati, and Monsalve 2018). However, many of these remain at a small scale and operate as pilots, failing to provide transfers to their entire target population of poor or vulnerable households in a permanent fashion (figure 5.13, panel b).

Safety nets can help households both build their resilience to shocks and offset losses from shocks. They can support households to save and invest in assets and human capital before shocks occur. The proportion of households in Africa that were saving was found to increase by 92 percent with the introduction of a safety net (Andrews, Hsiao, and Ralston 2018). When transfers are predictable and reliable, they provide households with a secure source of income that increases their resilience (Barca et al. 2015; Gilligan, Hoddinot, and Taffesse 2009).

Shock-Responsive Safety Net Programs

Safety nets can also expand at times when shocks hit—such as during a drought or price increase—to help offset income losses to poor households. Features of shock-responsive programs include expanding existing programs either vertically (temporarily adjusting transfer amounts or frequency) or horizontally (adding temporary beneficiaries); triggering new programs for a limited period (ideally building on the administrative systems of permanent programs); or modifying the program focus or target temporarily (see discussion in OPM 2017).

Important efficiency gains can be made by responding in a timelier manner with a predefined set of instruments and an adequate financing strategy. If households know they can rely on the state for a given amount of support in a given contingency, shock-responsive safety net programs could also have behavioral effects (in terms of increasing health and agricultural investment) similar to those brought about by insurance contracts.

There are few shock-responsive safety nets in place in the region. Many safety nets in Africa are established in the aftermath of disaster or conflict (Monchuk 2014), but few

FIGURE 5.13 The number of safety net programs in Africa is increasing, but their coverage is low

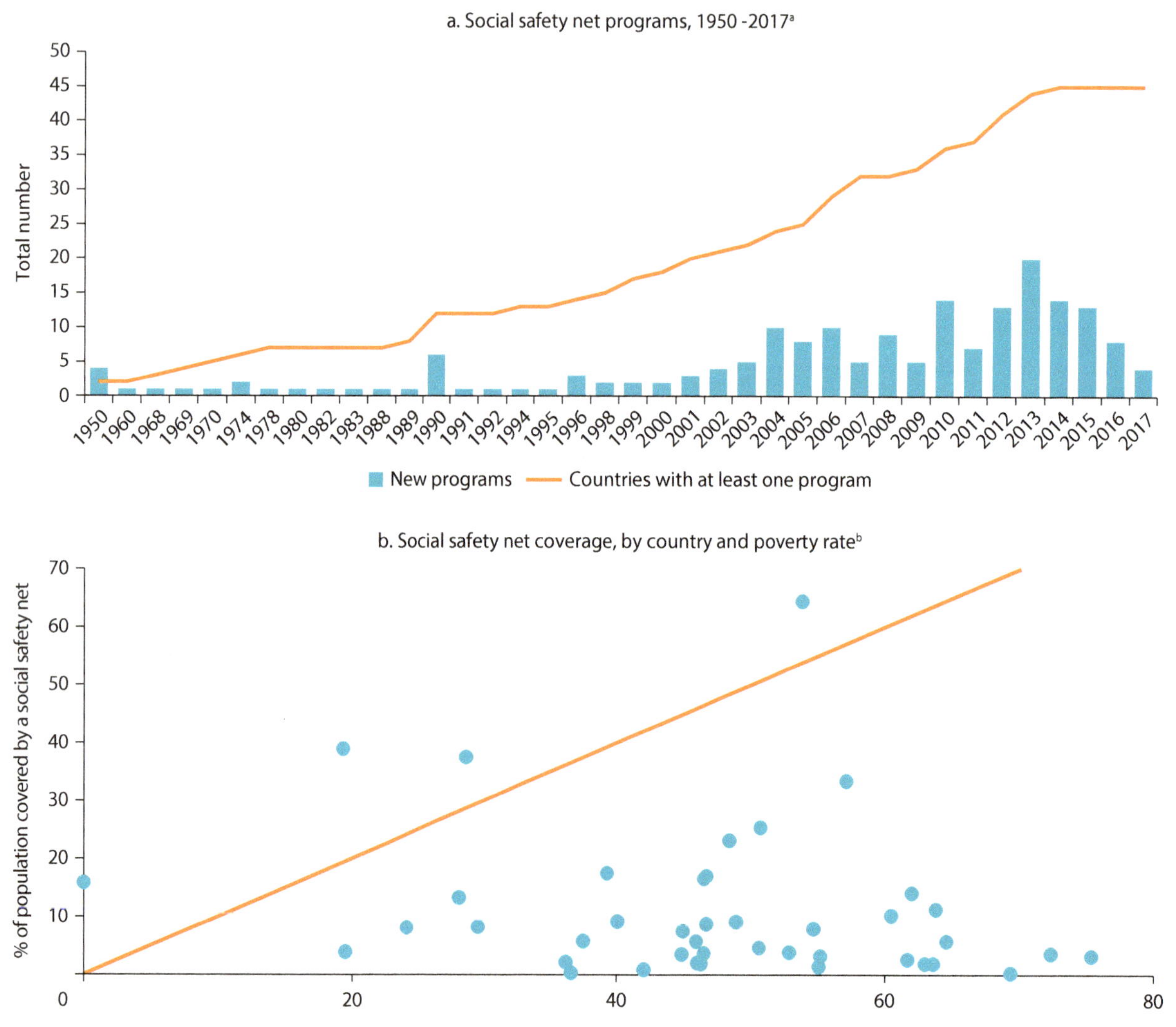

Source: Beegle, Honorati, and Monsalve 2018.

a. This figure considers regular programs (not emergency programs) that are still being implemented and for which information on the year of the launch is available.

b. Social safety net coverage rates are approximated by summing the number of direct and indirect beneficiaries of cash transfers, food-based transfers, and public works programs only. The beneficiaries of the other six program types (social pensions, school feeding, emergency programs, health care and education fee waivers, and other programs) are not included because their beneficiaries are more likely to overlap with those in other programs, which would result in overestimated coverage rates. The leftmost circle designates Mauritius, which records a poverty rate of less than 1 percent.

countries have safety net programs that can scale quickly to meet the additional needs of shocks. Programs are increasingly being designed with this idea in mind. In Ethiopia, the Productive Safety Net Program includes a 5 percent contingency financing that can be used to increase the scale of the program in the event of a drought or food price increase. Kenya's Hunger Safety Net Program in northern Kenya covers the poorest pastoralists in a scalable safety net: the poorest beneficiaries receive transfers every year, and the number of beneficiaries increases when rains are sparse and livestock pasture is inadequate. This program complements the Kenya Livestock Insurance Program, which provides insurance subsidies to the better-off but still vulnerable households (box 5.5). Such scalable safety net systems are still in a nascent stage in Africa.

Humanitarian Aid after Disasters

Many countries in Africa rely on humanitarian assistance to provide support to their citizens in the event of a disaster. Donors contribute US$1.6 billion a year to United Nations (UN) appeals for funding to respond to natural disasters.

However, humanitarian assistance is neither reliable nor timely. The process of securing humanitarian aid in the event of a slow-onset emergency, such as drought, takes, on average, one year from rain failure to food aid distribution—with many points when the resources are provided as the result of politics and negotiation rather than need. This is twice as long as the estimated speed of a shock-responsive safety net with financing (Clarke and Hill 2013).

The correlation between the cost of World Food Programme (WFP) food-related programs and total seasonal rainfall in Kenya is only –26 percent (Chantarat et al. 2007). Assessments of the correlation between rainfall-predicted assistance and actual assistance received for other countries indicate a wide range of correlation, from 39 percent to 82 percent (Clarke and Hill 2013). While this variation could indicate the paucity of rainfall indexes to identify need, it could also indicate the unreliability of food aid arriving to meet income shortfalls.

A second source of unreliability in providing emergency assistance to needy households is the challenge of correctly targeting emergency relief. Distribution is easiest and cheapest in areas where food aid has been previously distributed, leading to a bias in

BOX 5.5 Safety nets and subsidized insurance help protect pastoralists in Kenya

Pastoralism in Kenya's northern regions is highly susceptible to droughts. Herders have traditionally migrated to manage the spatiotemporal variation in forage and water availability, and although this provides considerable protection, it does not allow the risk to be fully managed. In these regions, the Kenyan government provides an unconditional cash transfer to the poor through the Hunger Safety Net Program (HSNP), which increases in scale to cover the other poor, vulnerable households when drought conditions are severe. It also provides insurance subsidies for index-based livestock insurance (the Kenya Livestock Insurance Program) to poor but better-off households that are not covered in the HSNP.

The coexistence of noncontingent transfers to the poor, state-contingent transfers to other poor, and insurance subsidies for the near-poor is unique and provides an opportunity to study the effects of different protection strategies and to simulate the welfare and fiscal gains of integration.

Comparing the estimated impact of each program can provide an assessment of the benefits for poverty reduction from an integrated approach to social protection that provides different programs for the poor and the vulnerable. Simulated welfare outcomes for the past five years under different types of programs in Kenya find little difference in the poverty rate between offering a larger transfer to the poor every year and having a smaller transfer to the poor but the ability to scale up to vulnerable households when drought conditions were severe (Jensen, Ikegami, and Mude 2017). This is because for the actual weather experienced in the past five years, these two effects cancelled out, and this may not hold true for other weather draws. There is also little difference in poverty between providing free insurance or subsidizing insurance purchases for vulnerable households.

This analysis highlights the need for further research on how best to design and integrate safety nets and insurance subsidies to determine which combination of policies will most cost-effectively protect households and reduce poverty.

locations selected for food aid distribution (Jayne et al. 2002). Within selected locations, beneficiaries have to be quickly identified, resulting in targeting errors. There is little recent data on the quality of food aid targeting. An old study indicates errors of inclusion of 42 percent and errors of exclusion at 40 percent (Jayne et al. 2001), suggesting that although targeting is progressive, it is not by much.

As a result, few households report being able to rely on government support when disaster strikes—around 1–1.5 percent in countries with comparable data (as indicated earlier in figure 5.9). The human cost of this is severe. In Somalia, aid was needed 4 months into the 2011 drought as death rates started to increase, but the major peak in funding occurred 10 months after the start of the disaster, with aid presumably reaching households with some delay after that. More than 100,000 people had died before financing increased (Talbot, Dercon, and Barder 2017). For those who do survive, the cost of a slow response in terms of lost future income from nutritional and asset losses is estimated at a total discounted current value of US$1,294 per household (Clarke and Hill 2013).

Despite the severe costs of reliance on humanitarian aid for financing public support in the aftermath of a disaster, it remains an attractive mode of crisis management for governments because the financing under these conditions is free and other sources of finance carry a cost. For example, although the World Bank's Catastrophe Deferred Drawdown Option (Cat DDO) would allow a country to have quick access to finance in the event of a disaster, this would be in the form of a loan and counted against a country's International Development Association (IDA) commitment, making it costlier than grants in the form of humanitarian aid. The international financial system thus incentivizes countries not to prepare in advance of a disaster, thus compounding the political and behavioral incentives that tend to result in underinvestment of risk reduction relative to disaster management (see the discussion below on political incentives and other constraints).

Reforming humanitarian financing so that it allows for reliable and quick disbursement as much as possible would allow countries to prepare in advance of emergencies and build systems, such as shock-responsive safety nets, that can respond nimbly in the event of disaster. Such reforms would require humanitarian aid to use decision rules as much as possible to determine when support will be provided and to ensure that financing is readily available when those decision criteria are met (Clarke and Dercon 2016). The decision rules could be data driven (for example, using a parametric index) or could include some discretion. Parametric triggers are desirable in that they automatically allow financing to be available. However well designed, though, parametric triggers cannot capture all the cases in which emergency funding is needed. And clear rules on how payments are made in these cases are also needed. The most cost-effective financing strategy will depend on the risk and circumstance but may include layering multiple sources of finance (Clarke et al. 2017).

In effect, this would require donors to shift their humanitarian contributions from ex post provision to ex ante funding of appropriate funds and instruments. Supporting risk pools, such as the Africa Risk Capacity (ARC), that provide payouts to African member countries in the event of a drought (by providing capital or by paying member countries' contributions) would be one way to do this.

Risk pools have been used in response to pandemics. In the aftermath of the Ebola epidemic, the World Bank's Pandemic Emergency Fund (PEF) was launched to provide fast financing to help countries in Africa and elsewhere to respond to future epidemics. The PEF combines insurance (disbursed when parametric triggers are met) and cash (disbursed more flexibly) to address a larger set of emerging pathogens that may not yet meet the activation criteria for the insurance window. Donors have paid the insurance premiums for the insurance window and contributed funding to the cash window. The World Bank Group estimates that if the PEF had existed in mid-2014 as the Ebola outbreak was spreading rapidly in West Africa, it could have mobilized an initial US$100 million as early as July to severely limit the spread and severity of the epidemic. Instead, money at that scale did not begin to flow until three months later. During that three-month period, the number of Ebola cases increased tenfold.

Reforming humanitarian financing is essential, but it will not improve support to households on the ground unless it is combined with improved planning. The ARC requires each member country to develop a contingency plan of how payouts would be used to support households in need. However, even when contingency plans have been in place, considerable work has had to be undertaken after the disaster to determine how to use the financing. At the most basic level, preparation *before* a crisis can involve better contingency planning that details how food aid will be delivered. This type of planning can identify constraints, such as lack of information or port capacity, that can be fixed before the disasters and ensure that government support is timelier and better targeted (Choularton 2007). More-advanced planning would involve the design of programs that provide targeted support in the event of a disaster, such as safety net systems that scale employment guarantee schemes or publicly subsidized insurance.

Finally, for displaced persons, the agenda goes beyond reforming the financing and coordination and includes a new approach to aiding displaced persons (box 5.6).

Addressing Constraints to Investment in Risk Prevention and Management

Although these tools to manage and respond to shocks exist, life in Africa is still very risky. Several dimensions constrain the use of more cost-effective means of reducing and managing risk in Africa, ranging from the behavioral, to political will and capacity, to tight fiscal space. And despite the emphasis here on these available tools, there is still scope for more innovation to ensure that better approaches to reduce and manage risk become available.

Behavioral Constraints that Limit Household Investment

Several tools are available to reduce and manage risk that households do not use. Some investments to reduce risk exposure can be costly for poor households to finance—such as investing in irrigation systems or buying health insurance. Credit is often not available to the poor for such investments. Lack of access to credit has been shown to limit investment in irrigation in India, particularly when these investments cannot be liquidated (for example, bore wells rather than pumps, as discussed in Fafchamps and Pender 1997).

Relatedly, the highly seasonal nature of the income of many African households means cash is in short supply for many months of the year, compounding this problem. When insurance is offered at a time when cash payments are made, take-up is higher, allowing households to benefit from greater coverage. Households provided with cash transfers in Tanzania were 36 percent more likely to enroll in the most prevalent type of health insurance, the Community Health Fund (Evans, Holtemeyer, and Kosec 2016).

Abstracting from the ability to finance actions that could reduce a household's risk, there are critical behavioral aspects to choosing these investments that can reduce risk exposure. First and fundamentally, using formal savings and insurance requires consumers to put their trust in such financial institutions. This can be particularly problematic regarding insurance: in an environment where regulation of insurance companies and products is weak, consumers may be correct to have low levels of trust in insurance companies (Clarke and Wren-Lewis 2016).

In addition, although these investments may help households reduce and manage

BOX 5.6 A new humanitarian-development paradigm emerges for managing long-term displacement crises

Looking ahead, a new paradigm for addressing the needs of displaced persons is emerging. The Syrian and European Union (EU) refugee crises of the past few years have brought the plight of the displaced populations to global attention. This renewed attention, in turn, has highlighted the shortcomings of the existing approach to address displacement crises, particularly if protracted, and these changes are important for Africa.

Historically, the approach to managing refugee and IDP crises has focused on the humanitarian side, where shelter and protection were the primary objectives in the expectation that crises would be temporary. At a later stage and with the extension of crises into the long term, the development community was called upon to intervene with development programs. Neither of these two approaches proved successful in addressing protracted situations, and the new push for solutions determined by recent events has fostered the creation of a new paradigm—one where the humanitarian and development communities engage in displacement crises together from the very beginning (Devictor 2016).

This new paradigm entails a shift from population-based policies (programs for refugees and IDPs) to area-based policies (programs for areas X and Y hosting refugees, IDPs, or both). This shift recognizes that the victims of displacement crises are not only the displaced but also the host communities and that both communities face a crisis that needs to be addressed first and foremost with economic means—in short, economic growth. This, in turn, has led to the creation of "compacts," policies that group a bundle of economic and social protection programs targeting a specific area. First piloted in the Middle East, "compacts" are now starting to be experimented in Africa, starting with Ethiopia. The new paradigm is therefore *very* new, but it has now reached Africa and is expected to be a real game changer for managing displacement crises.

By turning policies from being population-based to being area-based, the scope for development organizations' involvement changes. Organizations such as the World Bank have the knowledge and experience to design and implement growth policies. Regulatory business reforms, micro and macro credit policies, investment policies, public-private partnerships, labor market policies, and privatization and liberalization processes are the areas where the World Bank has a comparative advantage. What needs to be developed is the protocol for the implementation of these policies in fragile environments that require quick responses and frequent adaptations because of volatility and security considerations.

Forced displacement situations are volatile by nature, even when protracted, and sustainable development solutions are hard to implement. Food assistance programs may be urgently needed but may displace finance and human resources from other programs addressing forced displacement. This highlights the difficulty of the development planning process with these populations. On the one hand, the development community is needed to find sustainable development solutions for protracted displacement situations. On the other hand, forced displacement situations remain highly volatile, even when protracted.

As argued above, poverty reduction efforts in the context of forced displacement require joint humanitarian and development actions that are area-based, multidimensional, and growth oriented. However, none of these measures would be feasible in the absence of a secure environment. This is the responsibility of security organizations such as national or international military organizations that are typically operationally disconnected from development organizations and only broadly connected with humanitarian organizations. While the humanitarian-development new paradigm is in its infancy, a further leap forward toward cooperating with security organizations will be needed to ensure that humanitarian and development operations can operate in a secure environment long enough to become effective as tools for prevention of further conflict. In the absence of these preconditions, conflict, displacement, and poverty remain locked in a self-reproducing cycle.

Source: Verme 2017.

risk, they do not yield much of a return in the immediate future. Some may even be quite costly for several years before gains are realized. This is particularly true not only for investments in natural regeneration of trees and land but also for savings in environments where real interest rates are low and for purchases of insurance to cover extreme events. Poor households are more likely than richer households to focus more attention on the pressing demands of the present—a scarcity-induced focus on the present (Mullainathan and Shafir 2013; World Bank 2015b)—making prioritizing investments of this type particularly challenging for poor households. In addition, individuals often exhibit time-inconsistent behavior, behaving more impatiently in the present (choosing consumption over saving and investing) than they would want their future selves to behave.

Devices that help individuals commit to an action can help overcome this challenge (Dupas and Robinson 2013). For many in Africa, as discussed earlier, devices that help households save also help protect against demands on cash from family and friends.

Resignation to the uncertainty of life and low aspirations of poor households in Africa also play a role in explaining why some of the tools that are available to help manage risk are not used (also see box 2.2 in chapter 2). At lower income levels, individuals are more likely to agree that it is better to live day-to-day because of the uncertainty of the future (Haushofer and Fehr 2014; World Bank 2015b). This resignation may in part arise because of the high degree of uncertainty that poor individuals face. However, it limits the degree to which households take actions to control the risk in the world around them. Certain interventions—such as screening videos that document individuals succeeding in taking actions hitherto unimagined by the viewers—can alter individual aspirations (Bernard et al. 2014).

Relatedly, individuals often have little information available to them about the risks they face; they are not sure how likely bad events are and what losses they would experience were a bad event to occur. This is even more pronounced when the nature of the risk is changing, such as weather risk in the presence of climate change. This uncertainty is unpleasant; individuals have an inherent aversion to ambiguity. Ambiguity about the probability or nature of losses can cause households to choose to avoid risk and limit their exposure to the ambiguous, but it can also cause them to avoid the use of uncertain new tools that may help reduce exposure to risk (such as a water disinfectant) or to help manage risk (such as a new insurance product) (Bryan et al. 2016).

In the presence of credit constraints and factors such as present-time bias, resignation, and ambiguity, even small barriers to better risk prevention and management can cause inaction. Even small obstacles to investing in health care can cause individuals to forgo preventive health care. Thus, even very low prices can cause adoption of preventive health care practices to fall substantially (figure 5.14).

FIGURE 5.14 Take-up of preventive health care products drops precipitously in response to very small fees

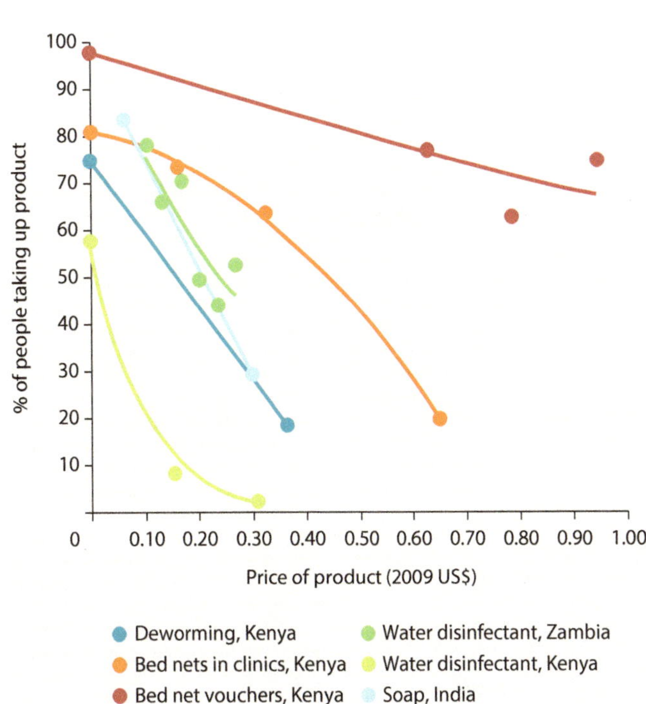

Source: World Bank 2015b, 150.

Behavioral factors mean that households' actions to reduce risk exposure do not depend only on their financial means or lack thereof. And these factors are arguably greater obstacles for the poor who have more to lose from risk. Offering products for free can encourage poor households to experiment with a product that they are unsure will benefit them, and it may also indicate a social norm that the product should be used by everyone.

When targeting is difficult or a large share of the population would need to be targeted, universal subsidies may prove more efficient. However, it is important that subsidies are designed to be "smart" and do not encourage households to overconsume risk. For insurance, this can mean providing information on the full price of the product and providing temporary vouchers; not going below the actuarially fair price; providing proportional subsidies, not premium caps; and ensuring a long-term government financing plan if the subsidies are likely to be in place for a long time (Hill et al. 2014). Strong outreach to encourage take-up can also help increase demand or investments to improve the efficiency with which markets provide products and services to reduce and manage risk.

Constraints to Development of Savings and Insurance Markets

Constraints to household investment limit the demand for products that aid risk prevention and management. Besides weak demand, other factors limit the supply of these products. Many insurance companies in Africa earn a large share of their income from covering nonpoor urban consumers, usually for vehicle or life insurance. The market remains underdeveloped for other products and for rural households.

Asymmetric information—where insurance companies lack information about the types of people they insure (adverse selection) and the types of behavior that insured individuals adopt (moral hazard)—impedes market growth and makes insurance costlier.

High fixed costs in insurance infrastructure and reinsurance can result in natural monopolies or monopsonistic competition. Insurance is a service good with relatively high design and infrastructure costs and relatively low marginal costs for issuing policies. As such, insurance markets are characterized by high fixed costs and low variable costs. Only large insurance companies might be able to afford the high fixed costs involved in reinsurance and establishing the necessary infrastructure for an effective insurance scheme, which could result in market concentration. More generally, many of the risks that affect households in Africa are strongly covariate across a geographic area. This requires a large risk pool (larger than the affected area) or large investments in capital, which in turn make insurance more expensive. Increasing the risk pool may be challenging in a small country or when insurance operations are just starting.

Clear regulation and public investment can help address these problems. It is important for public intervention to get as close as possible to addressing the root distortion that causes the market to fail or function poorly. This requires knowing the market, how it works, and where the imperfections are.

Investing in information systems can reduce asymmetric information. Index insurance provides a way of overcoming adverse selection and moral hazard in agricultural insurance markets, but the cost it introduces is basis risk (the difference between the index on which the insurance is based and the loss an individual experienced). Reducing basis risk requires high-quality indexes. Public investment in a network of tamper-resistant and reliable weather stations has increased the quality of the index and increased the demand for products. Halving the average distance between a farmer and the reference weather station increased demand by 18 percent (Hill et al. 2014), and reducing the distance between a farmer and the reference weather station by 1 kilometer increased demand by 6 percent (Mobarak and Rosenzweig 2013). However, insurance contracts based on area yield indexes do in general carry much lower basis risk (Carter, Galarza, and Boucher 2007; Mahul, Verma, and Clarke 2012). Typically, government statistical agencies capture this type of data annually for government statistical purposes. With additional investment and improvement in the speed and reliability of collection, these data can be used for insurance purposes also.

Investments in information systems to detect disasters can improve public safety nets, too. Early-warning systems that provide information on climate and price shocks and disease surveillance systems that provide information on pandemics provide early indications that disasters are unfolding and allow governments to plan their response.

Mandates and care of chronic conditions can help overcome adverse selection in health insurance. Enrollment in voluntary health insurance schemes is often more prevalent in households with chronically sick members, which is evidence of adverse selection (Wagstaff et al. 2009). Perhaps one of the most effective ways of addressing adverse selection in health insurance markets is to make insurance coverage mandatory. When it is mandatory, insurance premiums become cheaper as the riskiness of the insurance pool falls. However, it may be important for premium subsidies to be present to help households pay for mandatory coverage or to ensure political support for mandating. Mandates can also be challenging to enforce.

Care of chronic conditions can also help address adverse selection. For example, in Cambodia, the government provides free health care to all those who suffer from chronic health conditions, such as tuberculosis, allowing private insurance products to omit coverage for such conditions and be less subject to adverse selection (Levine, Polimeni, and Ramage 2016). Public provision of insurance for chronic conditions may become increasingly important for encouraging private health insurance markets to develop as the health burden of chronic diseases becomes higher in Africa.

Fixed costs may fall with better regulation and public investment. Providing a clear regulatory framework to reduce investment uncertainty and public provision of some of the fixed investments that need to be undertaken can help encourage market development. In particular, support to help design insurance policies may be needed in contexts where there is limited capacity within the private insurance market for innovation in product design.

Political Incentives and Other Constraints to Ex Ante Government Action

Government commitment and public financing has an important role to play in developing shock-responsive safety nets and in increasing the use of irrigation, bed nets, and other risk-prevention investments.

Yet public financing of programs to reduce volatility is limited. Public spending on irrigation has been a key driver of agricultural gains in Asia, yet irrigation receives less than 10 percent of agriculture public spending in all countries in Africa except Mozambique, where it receives about 15 percent (Goyal and Nash 2017). Cambodia, India, and Thailand were able to increase health insurance coverage through publicly funded health insurance schemes. China's agricultural microinsurance market grew to be the second-largest agricultural insurance market in the world by 2008 because of government support and subsidies, and in fact 63 percent of agricultural insurance markets in middle- and low-income countries receive premium subsidies. There are no state-sponsored agricultural insurance programs in Africa. As for health insurance, Ghana and Rwanda are notable as being the only countries to have increased health insurance coverage nationwide through important government revenue financing and (in the case of Rwanda) donor-funded support.

Safety net programs are also not at scale to serve the poor. On average, the region devotes 1.7 percent of GDP for social safety nets, but given the extent of poverty, around a quarter of the poor are covered by a social safety net intervention. In low-income countries, only 20 percent of the population received any social safety net assistance, while higher-income countries cover around 30 percent of the population (Beegle, Honorati, and Monsalve 2018).

Some African countries provide safety nets that do provide some protection to their citizens. Safety net coverage as a share of total population in southern Africa is almost four times that of central Africa and twice that of eastern and western Africa. South Africa spends 3.3 percent of GDP on social transfers (the child support grant and the old-age grant are the two largest programs), reducing poverty by 8.8 percentage points (Inchauste et al. 2016). Ethiopia spends 2 percent of GDP on social transfer programs (World Bank 2014b). However, to date, in many countries, humanitarian assistance is still the main source of funding for helping households manage health and climate risks.

Four key constraints to effective government action in this area can be articulated. First are the perverse political incentives. Investing resources to reduce risk and develop systems to respond to disasters in years when they do not occur can be hard to justify. Saving for a rainy day does not offer any visible benefits and may not even be used before the next election. Conversely, big spending in the wake of disasters suggests that governments know what they are doing (Clarke and Dercon 2016). Evidence from India, Mexico, and the United States shows that electorates reward government spending on disaster management but not spending on disaster preparedness (Boudreau 2016; Cole, Healy, and Werker 2012; Healy and Malhotra 2009).

Public advocacy that encourages electorates to be more supportive of disaster preparedness and less supportive of ad hoc spending on disaster response could help. However, this phenomenon is compounded in Africa by the international humanitarian financial system, which has been likened to begging bowls (Clarke and Dercon 2016) in which funding comes only after disasters occur and the same funding is not present to help governments reduce risk and develop systems to respond. In addition, the unreliability of humanitarian finance can make it difficult for governments to invest in systems that will commit support to citizens in the event of a disaster when the funding is not certain. Further action is needed to develop contingency plans and safety net systems and to assess how to bring together different sources of financing to support these plans.

Second, many countries in Africa realistically lack fiscal space to spend on such investments. Chapter 6 ("Mobilizing Resources for the Poor") further discusses issues with the limited fiscal space for spending that matters most to the poor. Policies that might be adopted and make fewer demands on public resources may be of limited benefit for the poor. Contributory insurance schemes (such as employment-related health insurance) have the problems of making labor more expensive, not covering the unemployed, and encouraging informal labor markets (Gill, Revenga, and Zeballos 2016). Donor funding can be used to sustainably cover costs (such as for health insurance in Cambodia), and schemes can be increasingly domestically financed over time as they become more proven (as in the case of Ethiopia's safety net or Ghana's national health insurance scheme, although the latter is running a serious deficit now).

Certainly, some spending could be realigned to more effectively reduce risk. For example, irrigation could become a higher priority in agriculture spending to increase both agricultural growth and the stability of agricultural incomes (Goyal and Nash 2017). Some expenditures put in place to protect the poor (for instance, some broad subsidies on food or some energy products) or other programs that fail to target the poorest can also be redirected to better-targeted safety net programs that build resilience and could be scaled up when disasters strike.

Third, countries face not only fiscal constraints but also capacity constraints. Many of the most promising strategies to reduce and manage risk require quite sophisticated technical expertise to put into action—for example, water engineers, agronomists, health care professionals, actuaries, and other insurance professionals. This technical expertise is not always readily available in each country in Africa.

Finally, tackling some aspects of risk and volatility requires coordination across national borders, because the risks are too large to be managed cost-effectively by one country alone. Drought risk can better be managed in a regional risk pool such as the ARC. Pandemic risk can better be managed collectively across countries. However, this requires considerable investment in coordinating across governments and agreement beforehand on who owns what risk and who will do what.

The Need for Innovation

Although many beneficial tools are available, cost-effective technologies to manage risk are still lacking in some cases. For example, although irrigation is beneficial in many places where it is underused, it is not beneficial everywhere. Even if the existing potential for irrigation were fully exploited in East and West Africa, it would only comprise at most 20 percent of cropland (Cervigni and Morris 2015). Cheaper technologies for irrigation are needed, particularly in places where groundwater is deep. In addition, better technologies are needed for harvesting and using rainwater where irrigation will remain having limited potential. There is also often little information available on the type of groundwater resources available, which determines the type and cost of irrigation to be used, and investments in the basic information base is also often needed. In recent years, drought-tolerant seeds that do not impose a cost of average yields have emerged, but seeds that provide this type of protection and do not put farmers out of pocket as a result of the cost of seed purchase or lower yields are not available in many places.

Financial innovation is also needed. There are still too few tools to help households manage the risk of lost income when drought occurs. Few index-insurance products have proven that the index on which they are based is of sufficient quality to make this a useful insurance product for many farmers in Africa (Morsink, Clarke, and Mapfumo 2016). Although many pilot crop index insurance schemes have been tested in Africa, few have achieved scale, in part because of the poor quality of the indexes but also because the products are costly and too complex for farmers to understand. Further innovation in agricultural insurance is needed to develop good indexes and products that benefit the poor. It may be the case that insuring groups of farmers is more realistic (with indexes that capture aggregate risk) than insuring individual farmers (Dercon et al. 2014).

Information and communication technologies can also help strengthen financial markets in Africa. Low rates of saving with formal institutions reflect low rates of formal account ownership. In 2014, 34 percent of the adult population in Africa had a bank account, and only 25 percent of the bottom 40 had one, compared with the global average of 62 percent. Although low, formal account ownership has increased by about 50 percent from 24 percent in 2011, largely because Africa now leads the world in the proportion of adults (12 percent) who have a mobile money account. If everyone who received private sector wages in cash received this in an account, 7 percent more people in Africa would be banked, and if everyone who received payment for sales of crops received this in an account, 36 percent more people in Africa would be banked (Demirgüç-Kunt et al. 2015a).

The most prevalent disasters in Africa are slow in onset, and improving information about shocks as they gradually unfold can improve the speed of the response and prevent the disasters from having such a large impact on welfare. Improving the speed and efficiency of data collection in early-warning systems can help—a good example being the WFP's mobile vulnerability monitoring, in which food security questions are collected monthly from households by mobile-phone interviews. This has been rolled out in multiple countries across Africa and has increased the quality of the information on food security available after a disaster.

Information on the nature of risk and its impact on welfare is also not always readily available. Household survey data are needed to inform who is poor, who is at risk of falling into poverty, and what shocks households report experiencing. Without such data, it is not possible to design and implement social assistance and social insurance programs (Gill, Revenga, and Zeballos 2016).

In addition to household surveys, risk modeling is required to provide information on the frequency and severity of risks that affect household livelihoods. Risk modeling is a widely used tool in risk management in high-income markets but is not often applied to the risks that are most common in Africa. Most modeling considers the impact of natural disasters on physical assets such as buildings and bridges, but in Africa the impact of natural disasters, such as drought, on livelihoods is the more pressing concern.

Notes

1. Maternal mortality data from the World Health Organization (WHO) Global Health Observatory (GHO) database: http://www.who.int/gho/maternal_health/mortality/maternal_mortality_text/en/.
2. Data from the Armed Conflict Location and Event Data Project (ACLED): https://www.acleddata.com/.
3. The term "uninsured risk" describes the risk of shocks to income that affect household consumption because households cannot use safety nets or financial assets and markets to manage them. Insurance here does not refer to the narrow definition of formal insurance contracts.
4. Environmental factors believed to be predictors of resistance (such as sanitation, animal husbandry, and poverty) and other structural components of the health sector were included as controls but were not significant.
5. Nikoloski, Christiaensen, and Hill (2016) use the same approach as Heltberg, Oviedo, and Talukdar (2015) but focus on data on self-reported shocks collected in World Bank Living Standards Measurement Study-Integrated Surveys on Agriculture (LSMS-ISA) in six Sub-Saharan African countries. This section draws substantially on Nikoloski, Christiaensen, and Hill (2016).
6. Self-reported health data may suffer from, or are often reported with, significant reporting bias, especially for poor households (see, for example, Das, Hammer, and Sánchez-Paramo 2012), but high levels of weather and health risk are also observed in objective data.
7. A household is in an area affected by conflict if a household is in a 25-kilometer radius of 10 conflict-related fatalities in the previous year. This definition is used because much of the cost of conflict comes not from direct exposure to violence but rather from the insecurity associated with conflict. The cost of insecurity can account for half the cost of the impact of conflict on household consumption (Rockmore 2017).

References

Ahuja, Amrita, Michael Kremer, and Alix Peterson Zwane. 2010. "Providing Safe Water: Evidence from Randomized Evaluations." *Annual Review of Economics* 2: 237–56.

Aker, Jenny C., Rachid Boumnijel, Amanda McClelland, and Niall Tierney. 2016. "Payment Mechanisms and Antipoverty Programs: Evidence from a Mobile Money Cash Transfer Experiment in Niger." *Economic Development and Cultural Change* 65 (1): 1–37.

Aker, Jenny C., and Marcel Fafchamps. 2015. "Mobile Phone Coverage and Producer Markets: Evidence from West Africa." *World Bank Economic Review* 29 (2): 262–92.

Alsan, Marcella, Lena Schoemaker, Karen Eggleston, Nagamani Kammili, Prasanthi Kolli, and Jay Bhattacharya. 2015. "Out-of-Pocket Health Expenditures and Antimicrobial Resistance in Low-Income and Middle-Income Countries: An Economic Analysis." *The Lancet Infectious Diseases* 15 (10): 1203–10.

Andrews, Colin, Allan Hsiao, and Laura Ralston. 2018. "The Impacts of Safety Nets in Africa: How Can They Contribute to Development Objectives?" In *Realizing the Full Potential of Social Safety Nets in Africa,* edited by Kathleen Beegle, Aline Coudouel, and Emma Monsalve, 87–137. Washington, DC: World Bank.

Asylum Access. 2014. *Global Refugee Work Rights Report 2014: Taking the Movement from Theory to Practice.* Report, Asylum Access, Oakland, CA.

Awulachew, Seleshi Bekele, Teklu Erkossa, and Regassa E. Namara. 2010. "Irrigation Potential in Ethiopia: Constraints and Opportunities for Enhancing the System." Report, International Water Management Institute (IWMI), Colombo, Sri Lanka.

Baez, Javier, and German Caruso. 2017. "Do Weather Shocks Influence Long-Term Household Well-Being in Mozambique?" Regional Quality of Education Study in Africa. Background paper, World Bank, Washington, DC.

Baffes, John, Varun Kshirsagar, and Donald Mitchell. 2015. "What Drives Local Food Prices? Evidence from the Tanzanian Maize Market." Policy Research Working Paper 7338, World Bank, Washington, DC.

Baland, Jean-Marie, Catherine Gurkinger, and Charlotte Mali. 2011. "Pretending to Be Poor: Borrowing to Escape Forced Solidarity in Cameroon." *Economic Development and Cultural Change* 60 (1): 1–16.

Barca, V., S. Brook, J. Holland, M. Otulana, and P. Pozarny. 2015. "Qualitative Research and Analyses of the Economic Impacts of Cash Transfer Programmes in Sub-Saharan Africa." Synthesis Report, Food and Agriculture Organization of the United Nations (FAO), Rome.

Beegle, Kathleen, Maddalena Honorati, and Emma Monsalve. 2018. "The Landscape of Poverty and Social Safety Nets in Africa." In *Realizing the Full Potential of Social Safety Nets in Africa*, edited by Kathleen Beegle, Aline Coudouel, and Emma Monsalve, 49–85. Washington, DC: World Bank.

Bellows, John, and Edward Miguel. 2009. "War and Local Collective Action in Sierra Leone." *Journal of Public Economics* 93 (11–12): 1144–57.

Berhane, Guush, Daniel Clarke, Stefan Dercon, Ruth Hill, and Alemayehu Seyoum Taffesse. 2012. "Financial Innovations for Social and Climate Resilience: Ethiopia Case Study." Unpublished research report, World Bank, Washington, DC.

Bernard, Tanguy, Stefan Dercon, Kate Orkin, and Alemayehu Seyoum Taffesse. 2014. "The Future in Mind: Aspirations and Forward-Looking Behavior in Rural Ethiopia." CSAE Working Paper 2014-16, Center for the Study of African Economies, University of Oxford.

Bhatt, S., D. J. Weiss, and P. W. Gething. 2015. "The Effect of Malaria Control on *Plasmodium falciparum* in Africa between 2000 and 2015." *Nature* 526 (7572): 201–11.

Blattman, Christopher, and Jeannie Annan. 2016. "Can Employment Reduce Lawlessness and Rebellion? A Field Experiment with High-Risk Men in a Fragile State." *American Political Science Review* 110 (1): 1–17.

Blattman, Christopher, and Edward Miguel. 2010. "Civil War." *Journal of Economic Literature* 48 (1): 3–57.

Blattman, Christopher, and Laura Ralston. 2015. "Generating Employment in Poor and Fragile States: Evidence from Labor Market and Entrepreneurship Programs." Unpublished paper, World Bank, Washington, DC.

Boko, Michel, Isabelle Niang, Anthony Nyong, Coleen Vogel, Andrew Githeko, Mahmoud Medany, Balgis Osman-Elasha, Ramadjita Tabo, and P. Z. Yanda. 2007. *Africa. Climate Change 2007: Impacts, Adaptation and Vulnerability.* Contribution of Working Group II to the Fourth Assessment Report of the Intergovernmental Panel on Climate Change (IPCC), edited by M. L. Parry, O. F. Canziani, J. P. Palutikof, P. J. van der Linden, and C. E. Hanson, 433–67. Cambridge, U.K.: Cambridge University Press.

Boudreau, Laura. 2016. "Disasters and Discipline: The Political Economy of Natural Disasters and of Sovereign Disaster Risk Financing and Insurance in Mexico." Background study for Disaster Risk Finance Impact Analytics Project, World Bank, Washington, DC.

Boudreau, Tanya. 2013. "Livelihoods at the Limit: Reducing the Risk of Disasters and Adapting to Climate Change." Report, Food Economy Group and Save the Children, London.

Brück, Tilman. 2016. "A Review of the Impact of Employment Programmes on Peace in Fragile and Conflict-Affected Countries." Unpublished paper, International Security and Development Center (ISDC), Berlin.

Brune, Lasse, Jessica Goldberg, Xavier Giné, and Dean Yang. 2016. "Facilitating Savings for Agriculture: Field Experimental Evidence from Malawi." *Economic Development and Cultural Change* 64 (2): 187–220.

Bryan, David, Philip Matthews, Eunsoo Shim, Spencer Dawkins, and Dean Willis. 2016. "Concepts and Terminology for Peer to Peer

SIP." Memo, Internet Engineering Task Force (IETF), Fremont, CA.

Burke, Marshall, Erick Gong, and Kelly Jones. 2015. "Income Shocks and HIV in Africa." *Economic Journal* 125 (585): 1157–89.

Carter, Michael R., Francisco Galarza, and Stephen Boucher. 2007. "Underwriting Area-Based Yield Insurance to Crowd-In Credit Supply and Demand." *Savings and Development* 31 (3): 335–62.

Cassar, Alessandra, Pauline Grosjean, and Sam Whitt. 2013. "Legacies of Violence: Trust and Market Development." *Journal of Economic Growth* 18 (3): 285–318.

Cervigni, Raffaello, and Michael Morris. 2015. *Confronting Drought in Africa's Drylands: Opportunities for Enhancing Resilience.* Africa Development Forum Series. Washington, DC: World Bank.

Chantarat, Sommarat, Christopher B. Barrett, Andrew G. Mude, and Calum G. Turvey. 2007. "Using Weather Index Insurance to Improve Drought Response for Famine Prevention." *American Journal of Agricultural Economics* 89 (5): 1262–68.

Choularton, Richard. 2007. "Contingency Planning and Humanitarian Action: A Review of Practice." Human Practice Network Paper 59, Overseas Development Institute (ODI), London.

Christian, Parul. 2009. "Impact of the Economic Crisis and Increase in Food Prices on Child Mortality: Exploring Nutritional Pathways." *Journal of Nutrition* 140 (1): 177S–181S.

Clarke, Daniel Jonathan, and Stefan Dercon. 2016. *Dull Disasters? How Planning Ahead Will Make a Difference.* Oxford, U.K.: Oxford University Press.

Clarke, Daniel Jonathan, and Ruth Hill. 2013. "Cost-Benefit Analysis of the African Risk Capacity Facility." IFPRI Discussion Paper 1290, International Food Policy Research Institute (IFPRI), Washington, DC.

Clarke, Daniel Jonathan, Olivier Mahul, Richard Andrew Poulter, and Tse-Ling Teh. 2017. "Evaluating Sovereign Disaster Risk Finance Strategies: A Framework." *Geneva Papers on Risk and Insurance: Issues and Practice* 42 (4): 565–84.

Clarke, Daniel Jonathan, and Liam Wren-Lewis. 2016. "Solving Commitment Problems in Disaster Risk Finance." Policy Research Working Paper 7720, World Bank, Washington, DC.

Cole, Shawn, Andrew Healy, and Eric Werker. 2012. "Do Voters Demand Responsive Governments? Evidence from Indian Disaster Relief." *Journal of Development Economics* 97: 167–81.

Collier, Paul, V. L. Elliott, H. Hegre, Anke Hoeffler, M. Reynal-Querol, and Nicholas Sambanis. 2003. *Breaking the Conflict Trap: Civil War and Development Policy.* Policy Research Report. Washington, DC: World Bank.

Collier, Paul, and Anke Hoeffler. 2002. "Aid, Policy and Peace: Reducing the Risks of Civil Conflict." *Defence and Peace Economics* 13 (6): 435–50.

Collier, Paul, Anke Hoeffler, and Måns Söderbom. 2008. "Post-Conflict Risks." *Journal of Peace Research* 45 (4): 461–78.

Cooper, Elizabeth. 2008. *Inheritance Practices and the Intergenerational Transmission of Poverty in Africa: A Literature Review and Annotated Bibliography.* London: Overseas Development Institute; Manchester: Chronic Poverty Research Centre.

D'Aoust, Olivia, Olivier Sterck, and Philip Verwimp. 2016. "Who Benefited from Burundi's Demobilization Program?" *World Bank Economic Review* 32 (2): 357–82.

Dang, Hai-Anh H., and Andrew L. Dabalen. 2018. "Is Poverty in Africa Mostly Chronic or Transient? Evidence from Synthetic Panel Data." *Journal of Development Studies* 55 (7): 1527–47.

Das, Jishnu, Jeffrey Hammer, and Carolina Sánchez-Paramo. 2012. "The Impact of Recall Periods on Reported Morbidity and Health Seeking Behavior." *Journal of Development Economics* 98 (1): 76–88.

Davis, Benjamin, Stefania Di Giuseppe, and Alberto Zezza. 2017. "Are African Households (Not) Leaving Agriculture? Patterns of Households' Income Sources in Rural Sub-Saharan Africa." *Food Policy* 67: 153–74.

De Ree, Joppe, and Eleonora Nillesen. 2009. "Aiding Violence or Peace? The Impact of Foreign Aid on the Risk of Civil Conflict in Sub-Saharan Africa." *Journal of Development Economics* 88 (2): 301–13.

De Walque, Damien, and Philip Verwimp. 2010. "The Demographic and Socio-Economic Distribution of Excess Mortality during the 1994 Genocide in Rwanda." *Journal of African Economies* 19 (2): 141–62.

Deininger, Klaus, and John Okidi. 2003. "Growth and Poverty Reduction in Uganda, 1992–2000:

Panel Data Evidence." *Development Policy Review* 21 (4): 481–509.

Demirgüç-Kunt, Asli, Leora Klapper, and Dorothe Singer. 2017. "Financial Inclusion and Inclusive Growth: A Review of Recent Empirical Evidence." Policy Research Working Paper 8040, World Bank, Washington, DC.

Demirgüç-Kunt, Asli, Leora Klapper, Dorothe Singer, Peter Van Oudheusden, Saniya Ansar, and Jake Hess. 2015a. "The Global Findex Database 2014: Financial Inclusion in Sub-Saharan Africa." Findex Notes #2014-8, World Bank, Washington, DC.

———. 2015b. "The Global Findex Database 2014: Measuring Financial Inclusion around the World." Policy Research Working Paper 7255, World Bank, Washington, DC.

Dercon, Stephan. 2004. "Growth and Shocks: Evidence from Rural Ethiopia." *Journal of Development Economics* 74 (2): 309–29.

Dercon, Stefan, Ruth Hill, Daniel Jonathan Clarke, Ingo Outes-Leon, and Alemayehu Seyoum Taffesse. 2014. "Offering Rainfall Insurance to Informal Insurance Groups: Evidence from a Field Experiment in Ethiopia." *Journal of Development Economics* 106: 132–43.

Devictor, Xavier. 2016. *Forcibly Displaced: Toward a Development Approach Supporting Refugees, the Internally Displaced, and Their Hosts.* Washington, DC: World Bank.

Dillon, Andrew, Jed Friedman, and Pieter M. Serneels. 2014. "Health Information, Treatment, and Worker Productivity: Experimental Evidence from Malaria Testing and Treatment among Nigerian Sugarcane Cutters." Policy Research Working Paper 7120, World Bank, Washington, DC.

Djuikom, Marie Albertine, and Dominique van de Walle. 2018. "Marital Shocks and Women's Welfare in Africa." Policy Research Working Paper 8306, World Bank, Washington, DC.

Dupas, Pascaline, Dean Karlan, Jonathan Robinson, and Diego Ubfal. 2018. "Banking the Unbanked? Evidence from Three Countries." *American Economic Journal: Applied Economics* 10 (2): 257–97.

Dupas, Pascaline, and Jonathan Robinson. 2013. "Why Don't the Poor Save More? Evidence from Health Savings Experiments." *American Economic Review* 103 (4): 1138–71.

Elabed, Ghada, and Michael R. Carter. 2015. "Ex-Ante Impacts of Agricultural Insurance: Evidence from a Field Experiment in Mali." Unpublished paper, University of California, Davis.

Elbers, Chris, Jan Willem Gunning, and Bill Kinsey. 2007. "Growth and Risk: Methodology and Micro Evidence." *World Bank Economic Review* 21 (1): 1–20.

Eozenou, Patrick Hoang-Vu, and Parendi Mehta. 2016. "Health Risk in Sub-Saharan Africa." Background paper for *Accelerating Poverty Reduction in Africa*, World Bank, Washington, DC.

Etang-Ndip, Alvin, Johannes G. Hoogeveen, and Julia Lendorfer. 2015. "Socioeconomic Impact of the Crisis in North Mali on Displaced People." Policy Research Working Paper 7253, World Bank, Washington, DC.

Evans, David, Brian Holtemeyer, and Katrina Kosec. 2016. "Cash Transfers and Health: Evidence from Tanzania." Policy Research Working Paper 7882, World Bank, Washington, DC.

Fafchamps, Marcel, and Ruth Hill. 2008. "Price Transmission and Trader Entry in Domestic Commodity Markets." *Economic Development and Cultural Change* 56 (4): 729–66.

———. 2015. "Redistribution and Group Participation: Comparative Experimental Evidence from Africa and the UK." NBER Working Paper 21127, National Bureau of Economic Research, Cambridge, MA.

Fafchamps, Marcel, and Bart Minten. 2001. "Property Rights in a Flea Market Economy." *Economic Development and Cultural Change* 49 (2): 229–67.

Fafchamps, Marcel, and John Pender. 1997. "Precautionary Saving, Credit Constraints, and Irreversible Investment: Theory and Evidence from Semiarid India." *Journal of Business and Economic Statistics* 15 (2): 180–94.

Fischer, Tony, Derek Byerlee, and Greg Edmeades. 2014. *Crop Yields and Global Food Security: Will Yield Increase Continue to Feed the World?* Canberra: Australian Centre for International Agricultural Research.

Fisker, Peter, and Ruth Hill. 2018. "Mapping the Nature of Risk in Sub-Saharan Africa." Background paper for *Accelerating Poverty Reduction in Africa*, World Bank, Washington, DC.

Giardina, Federica, Simon Kasasa, Ali Sié, Jürg Utzinger, Marcel Tanner, and Penelope Vounatsou. 2014. "Effects of Vector-Control

Interventions on Changes in Risk of Malaria Parasitaemia in Sub-Saharan Africa: A Spatial and Temporal Analysis." *The Lancet Global Health* 2 (10): e601– e615.

Gill, Indermit, Ana Revenga, and Christian Zeballos. 2016. "Grow, Invest, Insure: A Game Plan to End Extreme Poverty by 2030." Policy Research Working Paper 7892, World Bank, Washington, DC.

Gilligan, Daniel, John Hoddinot, and Alemayehu Seyoum Taffesse. 2009. "The Impact of Ethiopia's Productive Safety Net Programme and Its Linkages." *Journal of Development Studies* 45 (10): 1684–706.

Goyal, Aparajita, and John Nash. 2017. *Reaping Richer Returns: Public Spending Priorities for African Agriculture Productivity Growth.* Washington, DC: World Bank.

Hallegatte, Stephane. 2014. "The Indirect Cost of Natural Disasters and an Economic Definition of Macroeconomic Resilience." Policy Research Working Paper 7357, World Bank, Washington, DC.

Hallegatte, Stephane, Mook Bangalore, Laura Bonzanigo, Marianne Fay, Tamaro Kane, Ulf Narloch, Julie Rozenberg, David Treguer, and Adrien Vogt-Schilb. 2016. *Shock Waves: Managing the Impacts of Climate Change on Poverty.* Climate Change and Development Series. Washington, DC: World Bank.

Harari, Mariaflavia, and Eliana La Ferrara. 2018. "Conflict, Climate and Cells: A Disaggregated Analysis." *Review of Economics and Statistics* 100 (4): 594–608.

HarvestChoice. 2015. "Irrigated Cropland Area (ha, 2005)." International Food Policy Research Institute, Washington, DC, and University of Minnesota, St. Paul.

Haushofer, Johannes, and Ernst Fehr. 2014. "On the Psychology of Poverty." *Science* 344 (6186): 862–67.

Headey, Derek, Fantu Nisrane Bachewe, Ibrahim Worku, Mekdim Dereje, and Alemayehu Seyoum Taffesse. 2012. "Urban Wage Behavior and Food Price Inflation: The Case of Ethiopia." Ethiopia Strategy Support Programme II Working Paper 41, International Food Policy Research Institute (IFPRI), Washington, DC.

Healy, Andrew, and Neil Malhotra. 2009. "Myopic Voters and Natural Disaster Policy." *American Political Science Review* 103 (3): 387–406.

Heltberg, Rasmus, Ana María Oviedo, and Faiyaz Talukdar. 2015. "What Do Household Surveys Really Tell Us about Risk, Shocks, and Risk Management in the Developing World?" *Journal of Development Studies* 51 (3): 209–25.

Herrero, Mario, Petr Havlik, J. McIntire, Amanda Palazzo, and Hugo Valin. 2014. "African Livestock Futures: Realizing the Potential of Livestock for Food Security, Poverty Reduction and the Environment in Sub-Saharan Africa." Report produced by the Office of the Special Representative of the UN Secretary General for Food Security and Nutrition and the United Nations System Influenza Coordination (UNSIC), Geneva.

Hill, Ruth, and Habtamu Fuje. 2018. "What Is the Impact of Drought on Prices? Evidence from Ethiopia." Draft paper, Poverty and Equity Global Practice, World Bank, Washington, DC.

Hill, Ruth, Gissele Gajate-Garrido, Caroline Phily, and Aparna Dalal. 2014. "Using Subsidies for Inclusive Insurance: Lessons from Agriculture and Health." ILO Microinsurance Paper 29, International Labour Organization, Geneva.

Hill, Ruth, and Catherine Porter. 2016. "Vulnerability to Drought and Food Price Shocks: Evidence from Ethiopia." Policy Research Working Paper 7920, World Bank, Washington, DC.

Hill, Ruth, and Miguel Robles. 2010. "Flexible Insurance for Heterogeneous Farmers: Results from a Small Scale Pilot in Ethiopia." IFPRI Discussion Paper 01092, International Food Policy Research Institute, Washington, DC.

Hillier, Debbie, and Benedict Dempsey. 2012. *A Dangerous Delay: The Cost of Late Response to Early Warnings in the 2011 Drought in the Horn of Africa.* London: Save the Children and Oxfam.

Hirabayashi, Yukiko, Roobavannan Mahendran, Sujan Koirala, Lisako Konoshima, Dai Yamazaki, Satoshi Watanabe, Hyungjun Kim, and Shinjiro Kanae. 2013. "Global Flood Risk under Climate Change." *Nature Climate Change* 3 (9): 816–21.

Hoddinott, John. 2006. "Shocks and Their Consequences across and within Households in Rural Zimbabwe." *Journal of Development Studies* 42 (3): 301–21.

HRW (Human Rights Watch). 2017. "You Will Get Nothing: Violations of Property and

Inheritance Rights of Widows in Zimbabwe." Report, HRW, New York.

Hsiang, Solomon M., Marshall Burke, and Edward Miguel. 2013. "Quantifying the Influence of Climate on Human Conflict." *Science Express* 341 (6151): 1235367.

Inchauste, Gabriela, Nora Lustig, Mashekwa Maboshe, Catriona Purfield, and Ingrid Woolard. 2016. "The Distributional Impact of Fiscal Policy in South Africa." In *Distributional Impact of Taxes and Transfers: Evidence from Eight Developing Countries*, edited by Gabriela Inchauste and Nora Lustig, 233–66. Washington, DC: World Bank.

Izumi, Kaori. 2007. "Gender-Based Violence and Property Grabbing in Africa: A Denial of Women's Liberty and Security." *Gender and Development* 15 (1): 11–23.

Jakiela, Pamela, and Owen Ozier. 2015a. "Does Africa Need a Rotten Kin Theorem? Experimental Evidence from Village Economies." *Review of Economic Studies* 83 (1): 1–38.

———. 2015b. "The Impact of Violence on Individual Risk Preferences: Evidence from a Natural Experiment." Policy Research Working Paper 7440, World Bank, Washington, DC.

Jayne, Thomas, John Strauss, Takashi Yamano, and Daniel Molla. 2001. "Giving to the Poor? Targeting of Food Aid in Rural Ethiopia." *World Development* 29 (5): 887–910.

———. 2002. "Targeting of Food Aid in Rural Ethiopia: Chronic Need or Inertia?" *Journal of Development Economics* 68: 247–88.

Jensen, Nathaniel, Munenobu Ikegami, and Andrew Mude. 2017. "Integrating Social Protection Strategies for Improved Impact: A Comparative Evaluation of Cash Transfers and Index Insurance in Kenya." *Geneva Papers on Risk and Insurance: Issues and Practice* 42 (4): 675–707.

Jongman, Brenden, Philip J. Ward, and Jeroen C. J. H. Aerts. 2012. "Global Exposure to River and Coastal Flooding: Long Term Trends and Changes." *Global Environmental Change* 22 (4): 823–35.

Karlan, Dean, Robert Osei, Isaac Osei-Akoto, and Christopher Udry. 2014. "Agricultural Decisions after Relaxing Credit and Risk Constraints." *Quarterly Journal of Economics* 129 (2): 597–652.

Kazianga, Harounan, and Christopher Udry. 2006. "Consumption Smoothing? Livestock, Drought, and Insurance in Rural Burkina Faso." *Journal of Development Economics* 79 (2): 413–46.

Kremer, Michael, Jessica Leino, Edward Miguel, and Alix Peterson Zwane. 2011. "Spring Cleaning: Rural Water Impacts, Valuation, and Property Rights Institutions." *Quarterly Journal of Economics* 126 (1): 145–205.

Lang, Simon, and Malte Reimers. 2015. "Livestock as an Imperfect Buffer Stock in Poorly Integrated Markets." Global Food Discussion Paper 65, Göttingen University.

Lee, Jong-Wha, and Warwick J. McKibbin. 2003. "Globalization and Disease: The Case of SARS." Paper presented to the Asian Economic Panel Meeting, Tokyo, May 11–12.

Levine, David, Rachel Polimeni, and Ian Ramage. 2016. "Insuring Health or Insuring Wealth? An Experimental Evaluation of Health Insurance in Rural Cambodia." *Journal of Development Economics* 119: 1–15.

Little, Peter, M. Priscilla Stone, Tewodaj Mogues, A. Peter Castro, and Workneh Negatu. 2006. "'Moving in Place': Drought and Poverty Dynamics in South Wollo, Ethiopia." *Journal of Development Studies* 42 (2): 200–25.

Liu, Li, Shefali Oza, Dan Hogan, Yue Chu, Jamie Perin, Jun Zhu, Joy E. Lawn, Simon Cousens, Colin Mathers, and Robert E. Black. 2016. "Global, Regional, and National Causes of Under-5 Mortality in 2000–15: An Updated Systematic Analysis with Implications for the Sustainable Development Goals." *The Lancet* 388: 3027–35.

Lybbert, Travis J., Christopher B. Barrett, Solomon Desta, and D. Layne Coppock. 2004. "Stochastic Wealth Dynamics and Risk Management among a Poor Population." *Economic Journal* 114 (498): 750–77.

Mahul, Olivier, Niraj Verma, and Daniel Clarke. 2012. "Improving Farmers' Access to Agricultural Insurance in India." Policy Research Working Paper 5987, World Bank, Washington, DC.

Marquez, Patricio V., and Jill L. Farrington. 2013. "The Challenge of Non-Communicable Diseases and Road Traffic Injuries in Sub-Saharan Africa: An Overview." Report No. 79293, World Bank, Washington, DC.

Mbakaya, Balwani Chingatichifwe, Paul H. Lee, and Regina L. T. Lee. 2017. "Hand Hygiene Intervention Strategies to Reduce

Diarrhoea and Respiratory Infections among School Children in Developing Countries: A Systematic Review." *International Journal of Environmental Resources and Public Health* 14 (4): 371.

McCarthy, Nancy, Josh Brubaker, and Alejandro de la Fuente. 2016. "Vulnerability to Poverty in Rural Malawi." Policy Research Working Paper 7769, World Bank, Washington, DC.

Mercier, Marion, L. Rama Ngenzebuke, and Philip Verwimp. 2016. "The Long-Term Effect of Conflict on Welfare: Evidence from Burundi." Working Paper 198, Households in Conflict Network (HiCN), Institute of Development Studies, University of Sussex, Brighton, U.K.

Miguel, Edward. 2007. "Poverty and Violence: An Overview of Recent Research and Implications for Foreign Aid." In *Too Poor for Peace? Global Poverty, Conflict and Security in the 21st Century*, edited by Lael Brainard and Derek Chollet, 50–59. Washington, DC: Brookings Institution Press.

Minot, Nicholas. 2011. "Transmission of World Food Price Changes to Markets in Sub-Saharan Africa." IFPRI Discussion Paper 1059, International Food Policy Research Institute, Washington, DC.

Mobarak, Ahmed Mushfiq, and Mark R. Rosenzweig. 2013. "Informal Risk Sharing, Index Insurance, and Risk Taking in Developing Countries." *American Economic Review* 103 (3): 375–80.

Monchuk, Victoria. 2014. *Reducing Poverty and Investing in People: New Role of Safety Nets in Africa*. Directions in Development: Human Development Series. Washington, DC: World Bank.

Morsink, Karlijn, Daniel Clarke, and Shadreck Mapfumo. 2016. "How to Measure Whether Index Insurance Provides Reliable Protection." Policy Research Working Paper 7744, World Bank, Washington, DC.

Mullainathan, Sendhil, and Eldar Shafir. 2013. *Scarcity: Why Having Too Little Means So Much*. New York: Times Books.

Nasir, Muhhamad, Marc Rockmore, and Chih Ming Tan. 2016. "It's No Spring Break in Cancun: The Effects of Exposure to Violence on Risk Preferences, Pro-Social Behavior and Mental Health." Working Paper 207, Households in Conflict Network (HiCN), Institute of Development Studies, University of Sussex, Brighton, U.K.

Nikoloski, Zlatko, Luc Christiaensen, and Ruth Hill. 2016. "Coping with Shocks: Evidence from Six African Countries." Background paper for *Accelerating Poverty Reduction in Africa*, World Bank, Washington, DC.

Noor, Abdisalan M., Juliette J. Mutheu, Andrew J. Tatem, Simon I. Hay, and Robert W. Snow. 2009. "Insecticide-Treated Net Coverage in Africa: Mapping Progress in 2000–07." *The Lancet* 373 (9657): 58–67.

Nunn, Nathan, and Leonard Wantchekon. 2011. "The Slave Trade and the Origins of Mistrust in Africa." *American Economic Review* 101 (7): 3221–52.

OPM (Oxford Policy Management). 2017. "Shock-Responsive Social Protection Systems Research: Literature Review. 2nd ed." Project literature review, OPM, Oxford, U.K.

Prudhomme, Christel, Ignazio Giuntoli, Emma L. Robinson, Douglas B. Clark, Nigel W. Arnell, Rutger Dankers, Balázs M. Fekete, et al. 2014. "Hydrological Droughts in the 21st Century, Hotspots and Uncertainties from a Global Multimodel Ensemble Experiment." *Proceedings of the National Association of Sciences* 111 (9): 3262–67.

Prüss-Üstün, Annette, Robert Bos, Fiona Gore, and Jamie Bartram. 2008. *Safer Water, Better Health: Costs, Benefits and Sustainability of Interventions to Protect and Promote Health.* Geneva: World Health Organization.

Rockmore, Marc. 2017. "The Cost of Fear: The Welfare Effect of the Risk of Violence in Northern Uganda." *World Bank Economic Review* 31 (3): 650–69.

Rohner, Dominic, Mathias Thoenig, and Fabrizio Zilibotti. 2013. "Seeds of Distrust: Conflict in Uganda." *Journal of Economic Growth* 18 (3): 217–52.

Rosenzweig, Mark, and Christopher Udry. 2016. "External Validity in a Stochastic World." NBER Working Paper 22449, National Bureau of Economic Research, Cambridge, MA.

Sanghi, Apurva, Harun Onder, and Varalakshmi Vemuru. 2016. "'Yes' in My Backyard? The Economics of Refugees and Their Social Dynamics in Kakuma, Kenya." Report No. AUS14056, World Bank, Washington, DC.

Sarzin, Zara. 2017. "Stocktaking of Global Forced Displacement Data." Policy Research Working Paper 7985, World Bank, Washington, DC.

Skoufias, Emmanuel, and Sushenjit Bandyopadhyay. 2013. "Rainfall Variability, Occupational Choice, and Welfare in Rural

Bangladesh." Policy Research Working Paper 6134, World Bank, Washington, DC.

Skoufias, Emmanuel, Sushenjit Bandyopadhyay, and Sergio Olivieri. 2016. "Occupational Diversification as an Adaptation to Rainfall Variability in Rural India." *Agricultural Economics* 48 (1): 77–89.

Smith, Katherine F., Michael Goldberg, Samantha Rosenthal, Lynn Carlson, Jane Chen, Cici Chen, and Sohini Ramachandran. 2014. "Global Rise in Human Infectious Disease Outbreaks." *Journal of the Royal Society Interface* 11 (101): 20140950.

Ssewanyana, Sarah, and Ibrahim Kasirye. 2012. "Poverty and Inequality Dynamics in Uganda: Insights from the Uganda National Panel Surveys 2005/06 and 2009/10." EPRC Research Series 94, Economic Policy Research Centre (EPRC), Kampala.

Talbot, Theodore, Stefan Dercon, and Owen Barder. 2017. "Payouts for Perils: How Insurance Can Radically Improve Emergency Aid." Report, Center for Global Development, Washington, DC.

Thiebaud, Alessia, Theresa Osborne, and Nadia Belhaj Hassine Belghith. 2016. "Isolation, Crisis and Vulnerability: A Decomposition Analysis of Inequality and Deepening Poverty in Madagascar (2005–2010)." In "Shifting Fortunes and Enduring Poverty in Madagascar: Recent Findings," edited by Theresa Osborne and Nadia Belhaj Hassine Belghith, 39–84. Report of the Poverty Global Practice, Africa Region, World Bank, Washington, DC.

UNHCR (United Nations High Commissioner for Refugees). 2010. "Convention and Protocol Relating to the Status of Refugees." Text of the 1951 Convention Relating to the Status of Refugees, text of the 1967 Protocol Relating to the Status of Refugees, and Resolution 2198 (XXI) Adopted by the United Nations General Assembly, UNHCR, Geneva.

UNICEF (United Nations Children's Fund). 2006. *Progress for Children: A Report Card on Water and Sanitation. Number 5, September 2006*. New York: UNICEF.

Verme, Paolo. 2016. "The Economics of Forced Displacement: An Introduction." *Region and Development* 44: 141–63.

———. 2017. "Breaking the Poverty Trap Cycle during Protracted Forced Displacement Crises in Sub-Saharan Africa." Background note for *Accelerating Poverty Reduction in Africa*, World Bank, Washington, DC.

Verwimp, Philip. 2003. "Testing the Double Genocide Thesis for Central and Southern Rwanda." *Journal of Conflict Resolution* 47 (4): 423–42.

Verwimp, Philip, and Jean-Francois Maystadt. 2015. "Forced Displacement and Refugees in Sub-Saharan Africa." Policy Research Working Paper No. 7517, World Bank, Washington, DC.

Wagstaff, Adam, Magnus Lindelow, Jun Gao, Ling Xu, and Juncheng Qian. 2009. "Extending Health Insurance to the Rural Population: An Impact Evaluation of China's New Cooperative Medical Scheme." *Journal of Health Economics* 28 (1): 1–19.

World Bank. 2012. "People, Pathogens and Our Planet, Volume 2: The Economics of One Health." Economic and Sector Work, Report No. 69145-GLB, Agriculture and Rural Development, World Bank, Washington, DC.

———. 2014a. *The Economic Impact of the 2014 Ebola Epidemic: Short- and Medium-Term Estimates for West Africa*. Washington, DC: World Bank.

———. 2014b. *World Development Report 2014: Risk and Opportunity*. Washington, DC: World Bank.

———. 2015a. "Ethiopia Poverty Assessment 2014." Report No. AUS6744, World Bank, Washington, DC.

———. 2015b. *World Development Report 2015: Mind, Society, and Behavior*. Washington, DC: World Bank.

———. 2016a. "The Uganda Poverty Assessment Report 2016. Farms, Cities and Good Fortune: Assessing Poverty Reduction in Uganda from 2006 to 2013." Report No. ACS18391, World Bank, Washington, DC.

———. 2016b. "Why So Idle? Wages and Employment in a Crowded Labor Market. 5th Ethiopia Economic Update." Report No. 110730, World Bank, Washington, DC.

———. 2017a. "Cameroon Forced Displacements Note." Fragility, Conflict, and Violence Crosscutting Solutions Area. Unpublished report, World Bank, Washington, DC.

———. 2017b. "Chad Forced Displacements Note." Fragility, Conflict, and Violence Crosscutting Solutions Area. Unpublished report, World Bank, Washington, DC.

———. 2017c. "Djibouti Forced Displacements Note." Fragility, Conflict, and Violence Crosscutting Solutions Area. Unpublished report, World Bank, Washington, DC.

———. 2017d. "Ethiopia Forced Displacements Note." Fragility, Conflict, and Violence Crosscutting Solutions Area. Unpublished report, World Bank, Washington, DC.

———. 2017e. "Niger Forced Displacements Note." Fragility, Conflict, and Violence Crosscutting Solutions Area. Unpublished report, World Bank, Washington, DC.

———. 2017f. "Republic of Congo Forced Displacements Note." Fragility, Conflict, and Violence Crosscutting Solutions Area. Unpublished report, World Bank, Washington, DC.

Xie, Hua, Weston Anderson, Nikos Perez, Claudia Ringler, Liang You, and Nicola Cenacchi. 2015. "Agricultural Water Management for the African Drylands South of the Sahara." Background report for the Africa Drylands Study, International Food Policy Research Institute (IFPRI), Washington, DC.

FUNDAMENTALS 4

POLITICS AND PRO-POOR POLICIES

Kathleen Beegle

Governance—the process of designing and implementing policy—underlies every aspect of how countries develop and how their institutions function. Unfortunately, quite often, the governance process fails to deliver, especially for the poor: Governments may fail to adopt pro-poor policies or to shift toward progressive spending. Or when adopted, these policies may fail to achieve their intended goals or are distorted from them in implementation.

Putting governance front and center of the development agenda is essential for promoting sustained economic growth and encouraging more equitable and peaceful societies. It is then also a critical aspect of the poverty agenda in Africa because it drives the realization of the best technical work and policy formulation. There is a wealth of discussion and evidence on how governance, corruption, power structures, and the like impede poverty reduction. The purpose of this Fundamental is not to delve into the complex topic of governance but to highlight how politics in particular intersects with the poverty agenda. Overlaying persistent poverty in Africa is a story of political leadership—the incentives and will of elites at both the local and national levels to pursue pro-poor policies, broadly defined.

Varying Politics and Incentives, Varying Results

Adverse political incentives thwart efforts to pursue effective pro-poor policies. This is a challenge not just in countries with high levels of corruption and weak institutions (World Bank 2016). It has been argued that the variance in not only abilities but also motivations of African elites explains why some countries in Africa have inclusive growth while others struggle to accelerate poverty reduction despite growth (Mosley 2014).

Part of the challenge may be that government leaders and decision makers often live apart from the communities they tax or spend on, so their incentives to spend on public goods may be different from the incentives of their taxpayers. For such leaders, the primary consequences of poor roads or lack of security are poor public opinion of leadership by citizens or at worst an administrative sanction. The potential costs of poor education or of crime affecting lives and property may not be incorporated fully into public investment decisions when a leader does not live in an affected community or neighborhood and when there is little likelihood of criminal prosecution or other consequences for negligence in failing to provide or maintain a service.

Voting does not necessarily fix this problem. Competition in the market for votes, like other competition, might generally provide what the public wants—with a twist that arises when voters can observe inputs. But often those markets are imperfect, and instead decisions to spend and locate funds for infrastructure will turn to those who reward the incumbent government. In other words, if the very poor have little economic clout or political voice, their well-being may be ignored. And instead, policies that have tangible benefits and that are concentrated among groups of individuals with more clout are easier to carry out.

Public investments respond to political systems. The sharing mechanism for district funds in Ghana from the central government is significantly influenced by politics, with swing-voting districts receiving extra funds (Fumey and Egwaikhide 2018). In Kenya, districts that shared ethnicity with the president received twice as much expenditure on roads and had four times the length of paved roads built (Burgess et al. 2015). Electoral competition can reduce ethnicity-related policy distortions: patronage took place mostly during autocratic periods and not during the periods of multiparty political competition. Also in Kenya, a choice experiment in which 179 elected county councilors in rural Kenya chose among alternative water infrastructure projects revealed substantial favoritism to their home villages (Hoffmann et al. 2017). In Sierra Leone, chiefdoms with less political competition have significantly worse development outcomes (Acemoglu, Reed, and Robinson 2014). And in Africa, vote buying is associated with lower provision of broadly delivered pro-poor public services in health and education (Khemani 2015).

Channels for Change

Despite the sizable challenges, there are experiences where countries have political leadership that leads to improved rules, institutions, and processes that have helped them move closer to reaching their development goals. As outlined in *World Development Report 2017: Governance and the Law*, such change happens through three channels: (a) shifting incentives; (b) considering the interests of previously excluded participants, thereby increasing contestability; and (c) reshaping the preferences and beliefs of those in power (World Bank 2017).

Incentives are fundamental to enabling commitment in the policy arena, including policies that benefit the poor. The low quality of public services—especially schools and health services—may prompt the upper classes to use private services, which in turn weakens their willingness or incentive to fiscally support public services. But the right incentives can spur change: the first antipoverty programs in 19th-century England and Wales were pushed by the wealthy land gentry who were eager—against the backdrop of the Industrial Revolution, which was drawing labor to cities (as well as the threat of the neighboring French Revolution)—to keep labor in rural areas.

Contestability—concerning who is included or excluded from the policy arena—is determined by the relative power of the different actors and barriers to entry. When procedures for selecting and implementing policies are more contestable, those policies are perceived as fair and induce cooperation more effectively; that is, they are seen as more legitimate. Participation and ownership in the design of rules can also increase voluntary compliance. However, entrenched social norms may make it difficult for poor and disadvantaged groups to participate in policy discussions and formulation; participants in civic activities tend to be wealthier and better educated.

The preferences and beliefs of decision makers matter for shaping whether the outcome of the bargain will enhance welfare and whether the system will be responsive to the interests of those who have less influence. Changes in preferences can help jump-start coordination to work toward a better-for-all situation. Accumulating evidence about the effectiveness of pro-poor spending and policies can shift decision makers' beliefs toward such efforts. Shifting the leaders' beliefs through robust evidence and debunking the myth that lazy recipients misuse benefits was influential in scaling up social safety nets in Africa (see chapter 3 in Beegle, Coudouel, and Monsalve 2018).

In the political space, another approach is to recognize and invest in the critical role of citizen political engagement (the ability to select and sanction political leaders, be it through electoral institutions or other means) in conjunction with transparency (citizens' access to information about government actions) (Devarajan and Khemani 2016; World Bank 2016). Nonpolitical forms of citizen engagement—bypassing the political process—may have more limited benefits. Within Africa, resource-rich countries especially suffer from fraught accountability relationships, which partly explains their poor track record on human development, despite high national incomes (de la Brière et al. 2017).

References

Acemoglu, Daron, Tristan Reed, and James A. Robinson. 2014. "Chiefs: Economic Development and Elite Control of Civil Society in Sierra Leone." *Journal of Political Economy* 122 (2): 319–68.

Beegle, Kathleen, Aline Coudouel, and Emma Monsalve, eds. 2018. *Realizing the Full Potential of Social Safety Nets in Sub-Saharan Africa.* Washington, DC: World Bank.

Burgess, Robin, Remi Jedwab, Edward Miguel, Ameet Morjaria, and Gerard Padró i Miquel. 2015. "The Value of Democracy: Evidence from Road Building in Kenya." *American Economic Review* 105 (6): 1817–51.

de la Brière, Bénédicte, Deon Filmer, Dena Ringold, Dominic Rohner, Karelle Samuda, and Anastasiya Denisova. 2017. *From Mines and Wells to Well-Built Minds: Turning Sub-Saharan Africa's Natural Resource Wealth into Human Capital.* Directions in Development Series. Washington, DC: World Bank.

Devarajan, Shantayanan, and Stuti Khemani. 2016. "If Politics Is the Problem, How Can External Actors Be Part of the Solution?" Policy Research Working Paper 7761, World Bank, Washington, DC.

Fumey, Abel, and Festus O. Egwaikhide. 2018. "Redistributive Politics: The Case of Fiscal Transfers in Ghana." *International Journal of Social Economics* 46 (2): 213–25.

Hoffmann, Vivian, Pam Jakiela, Michael Kremer, and Ryan Sheely. 2017. "There Is No Place Like Home: Theory and Evidence on Decentralization and Politician Preferences." Working paper, Harvard University, Cambridge, MA.

Khemani, Stuti. 2015. "Buying Votes versus Supplying Public Services: Political Incentives to Under-Invest in Pro-Poor Policies." *Journal of Development Economics* 117: 84–93.

Mosley, Paul. 2014. "Two Africas? Why Africa's 'Growth Miracle' Is Barely Reducing Poverty." Brooks World Poverty Institute Working Paper No. 191, University of Manchester, U.K.

World Bank. 2016. *Making Politics Work for Development: Harnessing Transparency and Citizen Engagement.* Policy Research Report. Washington, DC: World Bank.

———. 2017. *World Development Report 2017: Governance and the Law.* Washington, DC: World Bank.

Mobilizing Resources for the Poor

6

Kathleen Beegle and Alejandro de la Fuente

The agenda to address poverty in Africa extends beyond shifting programs and policies. It also requires careful revisiting of a range of fiscal issues. Current levels of public spending that effectively reach and benefit the poor are not nearly sufficient and are often poorly spent. This chapter explores how poverty reduction can be accelerated by mobilizing more resources, domestically and internationally, and by spending more efficiently and with a greater focus on the needs of the poor in terms of both raising their income today and investing in the next generation.

What is the path to tackle these challenges? First, on the revenue side, countries need to mobilize more resources domestically. While mobilizing domestic revenues (with value added tax [VAT] expansion currently a favorite vehicle), countries need to make sure the poor are net receivers. Other promising avenues include improving tax compliance, with a larger focus on local large taxpayers, corporate taxes, and transfer (mis)pricing (which has a global agenda) as well as on excise and property tax collection. Yet, even with improvements in domestic resource mobilization, international development assistance will still be critical in the poorest and most fragile countries for both direct spending and to leverage private capital. Aid makes up more than 8 percent of gross national income (GNI) for half of Africa's low-income countries, but in recent years aid to countries in the region has been declining.

Second, spending patterns need to shift toward more pro-poor investments and improvement of the levels spent in critical sectors, the instrument or programs for a given investment, and the efficiency of implementation. The levels of spending on "pro-poor" sectors have a mixed track record, with some countries generally reaching international targets (as in education) but others falling short (in health; water, sanitation, and hygiene [WASH]; risk management; and agriculture and rural infrastructure). The choice of program design matters for given spending: untargeted programs can result in large shares of spending going to nonpoor households. One obvious area for attention are the currently high subsidy expenditures (in energy and fertilizer), which are often regressive and have little impact on poverty. Cash transfers seem more effective and efficient than subsidies where evidence exists, but more evidence is needed to compare their performance with public-good provision for the poor in agriculture and rural infrastructure, security, risk management, education, and health. Agricultural and rural spending should tilt more heavily toward investment in public goods.

And finally, significant inefficiencies in spending need to be addressed. It is not only low spending that explains the low quality of health and education services.

Africa's Large Poverty Financing Gap

Beyond shifting development priorities and policies, the agenda to accelerate poverty reduction in Africa requires the harnessing of more resources. The message about spending more and spending better to address the critical needs of the poor is at the core of the Addis Ababa Action Agenda that emerged from the Third International Conference on Financing for Development in 2015.[1]

Assessing a country's poverty financing gap requires a sense of the needs of the country's poor as well as of the country's capacity to mobilize the resources to meet those needs. This is challenging both conceptually and datawise. One metric regularly used to gauge needs is the aggregate poverty gap (APG): the monetary value of the gap between the income of the poor and the international poverty line, aggregated across the poor population. It gives an estimate of the amount necessary to mechanically lift all the poor out of poverty through redistribution. As such, it provides a first (and imperfect) benchmark.[2]

In 17 out of 45 countries with data, representing more than one-third of the poor in Africa, at least 10 percent of GDP (in 2016 prices) would be needed to fill the aggregate poverty gap. All but two (Lesotho and Zambia) of these are low-income countries. For Burundi, the Central African Republic, the Democratic Republic of Congo, Madagascar, Malawi, and Mozambique, closing the gap would require more than 50 percent of the country's GDP. By comparison, government tax revenues were only 9 percent on average in Africa's low-income countries.

Filling the poverty income gap would leave nothing for public-good provision, so clearly it is not a realistic option. Not surprisingly, the APG is 3 percent or less of GDP (in 2016) for most of Africa's middle-income countries (17 out of 20 countries), with Lesotho, Nigeria, and Zambia being exceptions. In most of the non-low-income countries, the challenge is not so much the amount of resources required by the poor to reach the poverty line but the decision and effort to redirect resources to the poor to raise incomes. Using a different but related metric, in 22 (mainly middle-income and resource-rich) countries, out of the 43 for which there are data, closing the gap would imply a rate of less than 10 percent on the income of the nonpoor above the poverty line (figure 6.1).[3]

Despite rapid growth in natural resource revenue, for most countries in Africa, it is also not sufficiently large to address the poverty gap, even in theory (figure 6.2). In only five African countries (Angola, Botswana, the Republic of Congo, Gabon, and Mauritania) would a direct transfer of 7 percent (or less) of resource revenues fill the poverty gap.

These numbers indicate that especially Africa's low-income countries are unlikely to have the financial capacity to overcome poverty and that the need for international financial assistance will continue. Other direct estimates of the cost to make certain core social services available or to finance achievement of the United Nations Sustainable Development Goals (SDGs)—which come with their own conceptual and measurement challenges—confirm the large gap between existing domestic resources (combined with overseas development assistance) and the cost of reaching global targets (DFI and Oxfam 2015; Greenhill et al. 2015; Schmidt-Traub 2015).

Fiscal Systems in Africa

Revenue and Spending Space

States get tax revenues directly (for example, from personal and corporate income taxes) and indirectly (for example, from VAT, excise taxes, and customs duties). Some governments obtain further revenues through grants from donors, international organizations, and natural resources, when available. These different revenue sources—as well as governments' ability to manage arrears, borrow, and attract private capital for public-private partnerships—determine the fiscal space for African governments to spend. There are huge challenges to both raising

FIGURE 6.1 High poverty levels imply high tax rates on the nonpoor to cover need

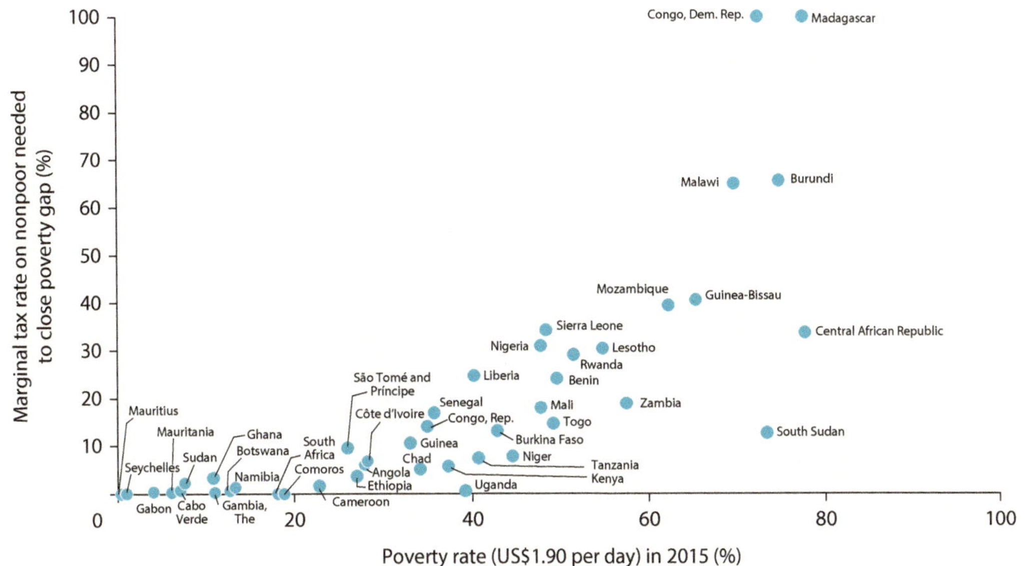

Source: World Bank calculations.
Note: In the figure, the marginal tax rate on the nonpoor is capped at 100 percent.

revenues domestically and increasing other sources of revenue, including from international aid (which is decreasing) or international financial markets, given rising debt levels.

Domestic Resources

In most of Africa's low-income countries, the domestic revenue imperative remains stark. Several have tax revenues (that is, revenues net of grants) of less than 13 percent of GDP —the "tipping point" below which executing basic state functions and sustaining development become problematic (Gaspar, Jaramillo, and Wingender 2016). Among Africa's low-income countries, the average 2013 tax revenue share of GDP was 14 percent (figure 6.3). It was slightly larger for lower-middle-income countries (19 percent). The Organisation for Economic Co-operation and Development (OECD) average in 2015 was 34.3 percent (OECD 2017).

However, a country's level of economic development does not fully predetermine its capacity to raise revenues. Government

FIGURE 6.2 Natural resource revenues are not sufficient to eliminate the poverty gap

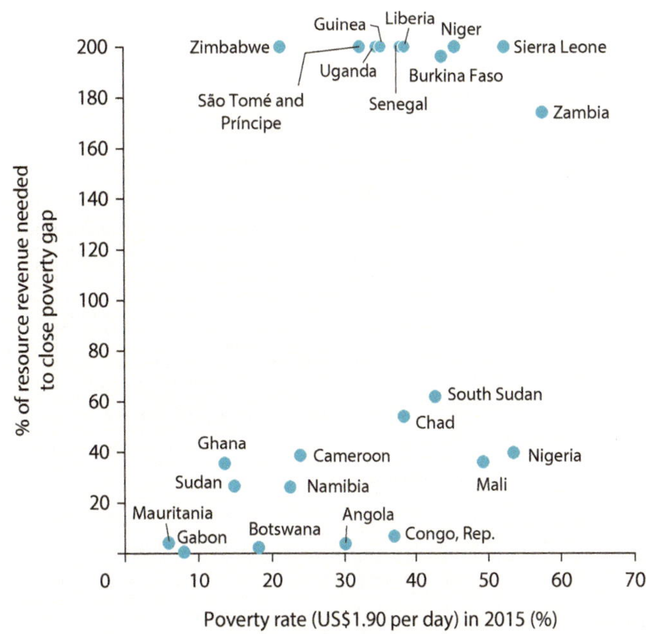

Source: World Bank elaboration.
Note: In the figure, the share of natural resource revenue is capped at 200 percent. Data are from 23 out of 48 African countries with natural resource revenues and nonmissing data on the level of resources.

FIGURE 6.3 Most African countries have a domestic revenue deficit

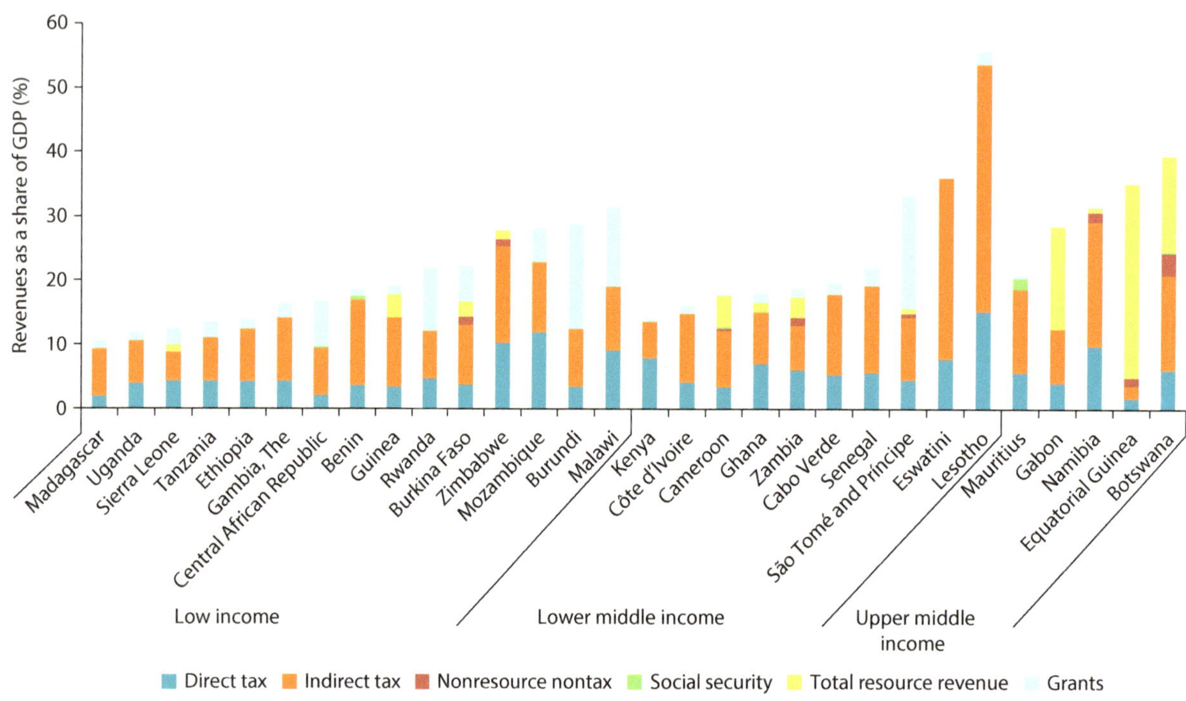

Source: World Bank calculations, based on the International Centre for Tax and Development (ICTD) and United Nations University World Institute for Development Economics Research (UNU-WIDER) Government Revenue Dataset: https://www.wider.unu.edu/project/government-revenue-dataset.
Note: Country data are from years ranging from 2011 to 2013. Countries without disaggregated data on direct and indirect taxes are excluded. Direct and indirect tax categories exclude taxes on natural resources. Total resource revenue includes tax and nontax revenue (for example, licensing fees, royalties) from natural resources.

revenue exceeded 20 percent of GDP in Mozambique and Zimbabwe, both low-income countries. Lately, domestic revenue collection has also improved across Africa. The region experienced the world's largest increase in tax revenue as a share of GDP since the turn of the century (IMF 2015). As noted, however, this is from a low level, and disconcertingly, the countries with the lowest domestic resource mobilization are also projected to grow these revenues at lower rates, further widening the gap (DI 2015).

Most African countries rely heavily on indirect taxes on the sale of goods and services. These include VAT, trade taxes paid at the port, and excise taxes (such as fuel taxes). VAT, in particular, has led the way to raise domestic revenues. Indirect taxes are often also invisible to consumers, and if kept simple, easier to administer. This makes them a preferred tax instrument in many lower-income countries, where administrative capacity is limited. In addition, informal businesses are widespread in low-income countries; they are generally cash-based and hard to tax. Therefore, lower-income countries rely more than middle-income countries on indirect taxes, but this has pernicious consequences on welfare, as the next section shows.

Direct taxes are the second main source of revenues for African countries. Yet total revenues from personal income taxes amount to only half of the revenues from indirect taxes. The main direct taxes are personal and corporate income taxes. Their contribution as a share of GDP has not been improving, either because governments have discouraged marginal increases in corporate and personal income taxes or because income earners have avoided complying. Property taxation contributes little (0.1–0.2 percent of GDP, for those countries where reliable information exists) (Moore and Prichard 2017).

Some countries in Africa also generate substantial revenues from natural resources. Out of 37 countries for which data are available, 22 are considered resource rich—from countries rich in oil (like Chad and the Republic of Congo) to those that mine diamonds (Botswana) and minerals (Mauritania and Niger). In these countries, revenues from natural resources make up 10–20 percent of GDP.

Tax revenues in low- and middle-income countries with substantial natural resources tend to be higher than in countries at the same income level that lack such resources. So, in principle, resource revenues can enhance spending on pro-poor sectors such as the social sectors (for example, health and education); agricultural and rural development; and social protection programs, including cash transfer schemes that strengthen the poor's risk management capacity. However, these revenues often go directly from the extracting companies to governments, without citizen involvement. This weakens citizens' ability to scrutinize government expenditures (as discussed in chapter 1). As a result, poverty reduction is slower and multiple human development indicators are worse in resource-rich countries in Africa than in other countries at the same income level (Beegle et al. 2016; de la Brière et al. 2017).

Taken together, the low base on which to tax, the limited capacity to tax more, and the political inability to channel national income from natural resources to pro-poor spending result in a large poverty financing gap. Low-income countries face the greatest needs, have the lowest taxable base, and are least efficient in mobilizing revenues. Financing from foreign donors or international organizations will remain a critical source of funding for many of the poorest African countries in the foreseeable future.

Foreign Assistance

While domestic resources are the largest resource available to African countries in aggregate, aid makes up more than 8 percent of gross national income (GNI) in half the low-income countries in Africa (figure 6.4).[4] It is often geared toward pro-poor sectors such as health, agriculture, and education. For example, aid finances three-quarters of public health spending in Rwanda (DI 2015), and donor funds finance 90 percent of public agriculture spending in Burundi (Pernechele, Balié, and Ghins 2018). The sectors of education, health, and financial support to the poorest through safety nets account for around a third of all donor aid.

Global official development assistance (ODA) to African countries has been increasing—reaching an all-time high of US$140 billion in 2016 (at current prices)—and increasing marginally in nominal terms from US$45.8 billion in 2013 to US$46.3 billion in 2017 (after a dip to $42.5 billion in 2016). Unfortunately, though, the region's population growth means that ODA has declined in per capita terms, from US$48.30 to US$42.60.[5]

ODA per capita to African countries has declined, at least in part, because donor countries were spending more in their own countries on refugees and asylum seekers. Such spending more than doubled in three years, from less than 4 percent of total donor spending before 2013 to 11 percent in 2016. Germany and Italy spent more on in-country costs than they gave in aid to Africa; Norway and Switzerland had increases in in-country refugee costs and decreases in aid flowing to low- and middle-income countries. Four OECD Development Assistance Committee (DAC) donors—Austria, Greece, Hungary, and Italy—allocated more than 50 percent of their bilateral assistance in 2016 to in-donor refugee costs. When in-donor refugee costs are excluded, only three countries—Luxembourg, Norway, and Sweden—out of the 29 DAC donor countries reached the United Nations (UN) target of 0.7 percent of ODA as a share of GNI in 2016 (ONE 2017).

The combined resources from domestic revenue and ODA at current levels do not suffice to reach the SDGs related to universal education, universal health, and scaled-up safety nets in low- and middle-income countries; billions more are needed (Greenhill et al. 2015; Manuel et al. 2018).

FIGURE 6.4 ODA is a large share of GNI in low-income countries

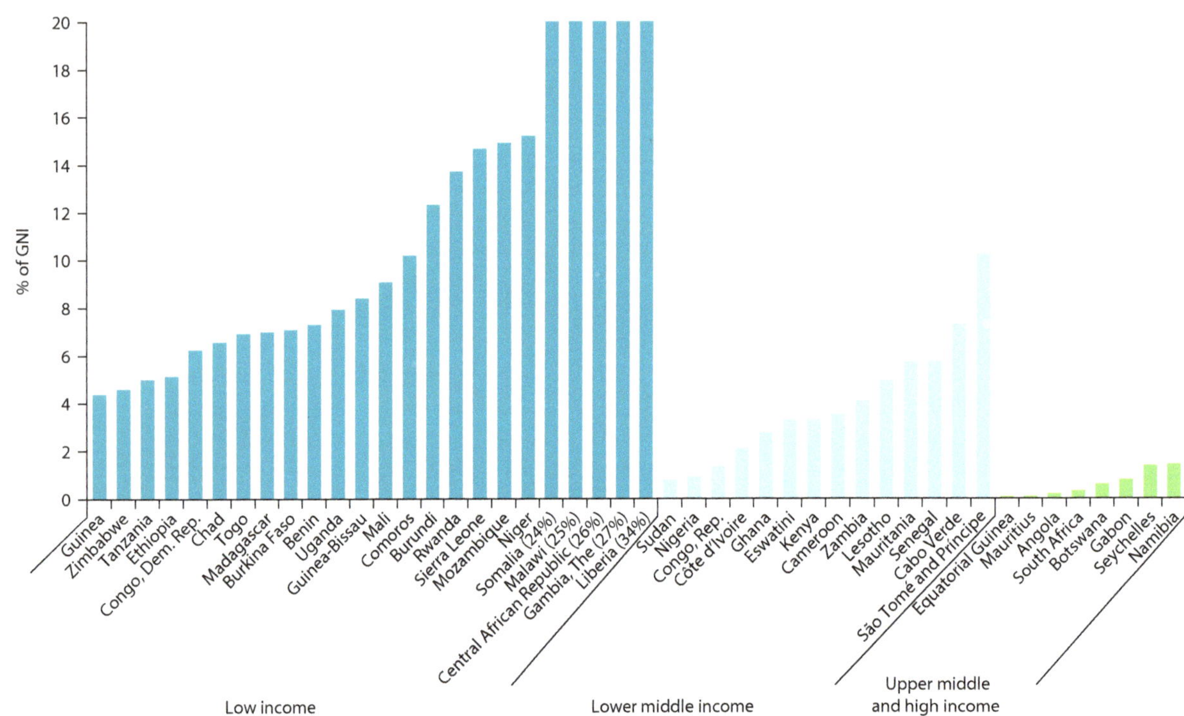

Source: Organisation for Economic Co-operation and Development (OECD) 2017 data, https://data.oecd.org/.
Note: GNI = gross national income; ODA = official development assistance. ODA data do not include aid inflows from international charities, international nongovernmental organizations, and private donations.

The costs to reach global targets in education, health, and financial support needed for the poorest in Sub-Saharan Africa total US$262 billion in 2017 prices (Manuel et al. 2018).

In light of Africa's revenue shortfalls, ODA is increasingly also being used to catalyze private sector investment in low- and middle-income countries, though the jobs and poverty impacts of blended finance need to be better understood (ONE 2017). Donors should recommit to the UN's original ODA target of spending 0.7 percent of their national income on development aid overseas and reverse the trend of a declining share of ODA to Africa. In 2015, DAC countries spent 0.3 percent of GNI on ODA globally and 0.1 percent in Africa. If donors met aid targets (0.7 percent of GNI), the financing gap in low-income and lower-middle-income countries would be met (Greenhill et al. 2015).

Debt and Other Fiscal Challenges

Governments could, in principle, also borrow domestically and internationally. Yet many will find it difficult. Lenders may be unfamiliar with small countries that do not normally borrow. Countries that do borrow may have large existing debts and may not be able to raise additional sums.[6] Since the start of 2017, Standard & Poor's has downgraded the credit rating of four African countries: the Republic of Congo, Gabon, Namibia, and South Africa. And for those with an International Monetary Fund (IMF) program, there may be additional restrictions related to taking on debt.[7] A few countries are facing repayment problems—for example, the Republic of Congo and Mozambique. And even those with low debts may find it difficult to borrow when they most need to, because of the normalization of monetary policy in high-income countries, a decrease in other sources of funding, and rising sovereign risks in the region.

Overall, although debt levels remain lower than in the late 1990s—when several international debt relief initiatives were implemented—debt has been rising more rapidly in Africa than in other regions since 2009. Median government debt is expected to be around 50 percent of GDP in 2017, more than 15 percentage points higher than in 2013.

Over the same period, fiscal space (as proxied by an increase in the number of tax years needed to repay the public debt burden) tightened for 36 of 44 countries in the region. In these 36 countries, the median number of tax years needed to repay the debt fully has increased by 1.1 years; in the Central African Republic, the Republic of Congo, The Gambia, and Mozambique, this indicator increased by more than 2.5 years (World Bank 2017). Country debt concerns are back on the radar, which, combined with insufficient revenues described earlier and lagging ODA commitments, magnify the sense that the scope for borrowing to finance the poverty financing gap is rapidly declining.

Finally, Africa's frequent exposure to natural disasters (as discussed in chapter 5, "Managing Risks and Conflict") poses specific fiscal challenges. These warrant special attention because they could be largely avoided through better ex ante planning, financing, and instrument design. Revenue collection can drop when disasters strike, while the need for public spending shoots up.[8]

Humanitarian aid has been the most common source of public support in the aftermath of a disaster. The financing provided under these conditions is free, while other sources of finance carry a cost (chapter 5). On average, at least US$1.6 billion is provided in humanitarian aid to African countries every year (Talbot, Dercon, and Barder 2017). That fundraising starts after an emergency means aid comes too late and is costly to deliver.

Supporting risk pools, such as the African Union's Africa Risk Capacity, which provides payouts to African member countries in the event of a drought, can help governments improve their fiscal resilience to disasters. As chapter 5 highlights, this has already been done for pandemics in the Pandemic Emergency Fund. The savings from the reduced ex post need for humanitarian aid could be used to finance such schemes ex ante.

A Mixed Record on Spending on Pro-Poor Sectors

Many measures to tackle poverty are embedded in the provision of basic services and direct transfers (for example, schools, clinics, or cash transfers that help to build human capital and manage risks) as well as in the sectoral allocation of public spending toward sectors more likely to benefit the poor, such as agriculture. As such, tracking pro-poor spending is usually sectorally focused, even though, importantly, within-sector spending choices can also have quite different effects on poverty (Owori 2017), as also discussed in chapter 3, "Earning More on the Farm."

Five key points emerge in this regard. First, although many African countries are close to meeting or exceeding global targets for pro-poor sectoral spending as a share of GDP or government expenditures, absolute (per capita) spending levels are very low. They often have room to expand pro-poor spending through reallocation, such as by reducing energy subsidies, discussed below. Second, within-sector spending is often ill targeted to the needs of the poor, and implementation is inefficient. Third, as a result of the first two factors, many poor people still pay for access to basic services critical for human development, have high out-of-pocket expenditures, or lack the public goods needed to increase their earnings (for example, agricultural innovation and rural infrastructure). Fourth, resource-rich countries spend less on education and health than other African countries of similar income level, and what *is* spent is spent less efficiently. And finally, in health and education as well as in agriculture and risk management (humanitarian aid), a large share of funding in many countries comes from donors, questioning government commitment and independence as well as the sustainability of pro-poor spending.[9]

Among the social sectors, African governments consistently spend more on education (4.3 percent of GDP on average across low- and middle-income countries in Africa), typically followed by health (1.8 percent of GDP) and social safety nets (1.4 percent of GDP) (figure 6.5). On average, spending is in the target range for education (4–6 percent of GDP per capita or at least 15–20 percent of public expenditure) under the Education for All (EFA) initiative. But health spending (about 4 percent of GDP per capita) is below the international target of the Abuja Declaration (15 percent of public expenditure).

Spending on social safety nets is the lowest of all the social sectors, but it is much lower than the regional average in most countries, given that there is a concentration of social safety net spending in southern Africa. The average 1.4 percent of GDP spent on social safety nets is also well below the share spent on energy subsidies (3.8 percent of GDP on average).

Agriculture spending is also 1.4 percent of GDP on average. As such, few countries reach the 2003 Maputo Declaration target of allocating 10 percent of public spending on agriculture (Goyal and Nash 2017). The average is 3 percent (as discussed in chapter 3).

Given the low levels of GDP per capita in Africa, the absolute levels of pro-poor spending per person can be strikingly low, especially in low-income countries. And there is important heterogeneity across country groupings and sectors. Resource-rich countries, for example, spend less on critical social services (education, health, and social safety nets) as a share of their GDP (that is, given their income level) than their non-resource-rich counterparts.

How governments should spend more on social sectors, WASH, and agriculture is not clear-cut. The alternatives include raising higher revenues and setting those increased funds aside for these sectors, to borrow, or to receive grants so that they have funds to spend. The choice between

FIGURE 6.5 African countries vary in spending by sector, but education spending dominates

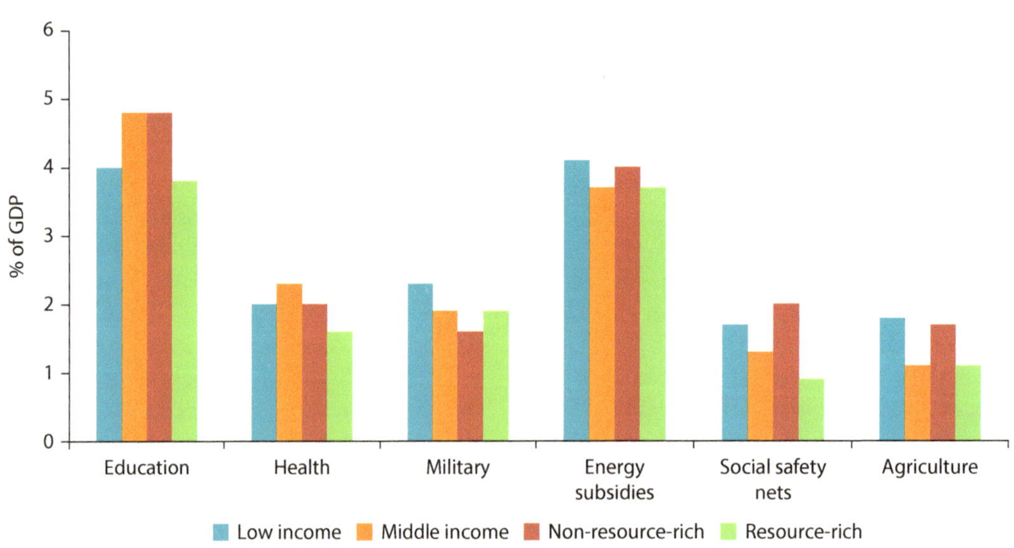

Sources: World Development Indicators database (education, health, and military); IMF 2015 (energy subsidies); Beegle, Coudouel, and Monsalve 2018 (social safety nets); International Food Policy Research Institute (IFPRI) Statistics on Public Expenditures for Economic Development (SPEED) database (agriculture).
Note: Figure shows country average spending as a percentage of GDP among low- and middle-income African countries.

borrowing, setting grant funds aside, or raising revenues depends on the country's circumstances.

As highlighted earlier, the window for debt financing is already rapidly narrowing in most African countries. Furthermore, debt servicing is a factor that crowds out spending in key areas for the poor (so-called Millennium Development Goal [MDG] sectors). Low debt servicing is associated with reaching MDG spending targets. Since 2012, spending on debt interest has been increasing again.

A budget-neutral solution would be to reallocate resources toward pro-poor sectors within the current spending envelope and spend more efficiently. One obvious candidate for expenditure shifting is energy subsidies, a topic covered in more depth later in the chapter.

FIGURE 6.6 Not all African countries are reaching spending targets in education

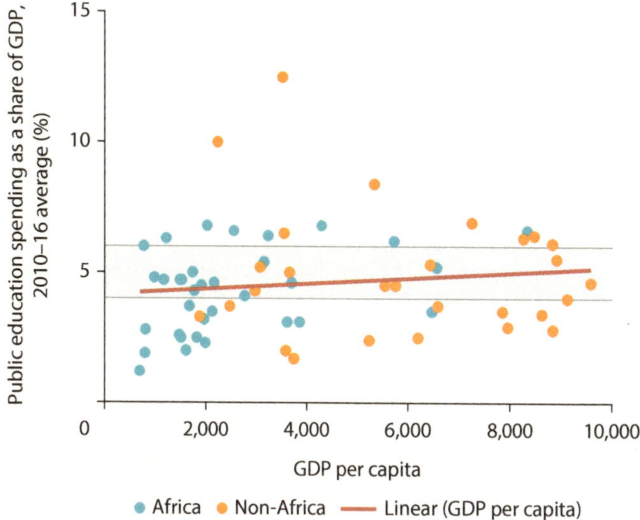

Source: United Nations Educational, Scientific, and Cultural Organization (UNESCO) 2010–16 mean spending.
Note: Highlighted horizontal section indicates the Education for All (EFA) target range of 4–6 percent.

Spending in Pro-Poor Sectors

Across Africa, there are substantial differences in how much governments spend on education. Although low-income countries are improving, they still mostly miss the EFA initiative target of 4–6 percent of GDP (UN 2015), as shown in figure 6.6. However, education spending as a share of total government expenditure is somewhat more positive than as a share of GDP—and, using this measure, it is higher in Africa than in any other low- and middle-income regions.

In health spending, African countries fall short of several targets. For example, achieving universal health coverage is estimated to cost US$86 per capita for low-income countries and 5 percent of GDP per capita for other countries (Greenhill et al. 2015). As noted earlier, African governments spend an average of 1.8 percent of GDP, or about 4 percent of GDP per capita, on health.

As for the share of government expenditure on health, the Abuja Declaration target is 15 percent. The region has moved toward this target, with increasing shares going to health. However, government spending per person on health for African countries is lowest in the world.

In addition, no African countries met their 2015 MDG targets for health spending, with average spending reaching about half of the target (DFI and Oxfam 2015). And households still finance much of their own health costs: out-of-pocket spending is 40 percent of total health expenditures, not unlike other regions. But such spending is associated with increases in poverty (Eozenou and Mehta 2016); see also the discussion on health shocks in chapter 5.

Within Africa's health spending, there are shortfalls in funds for modern contraception, leading to a large unmet need in some countries. The lowest-income countries are noted as lacking both the political will and financial resources for family planning programs. These governments often rely mainly on donor assistance (Speidel 2018) whose support can fluctuate with donor country politics. Globally, there is a widening funding gap in terms of meeting the current demand for contraception, limiting access to family planning for the poorest women in African countries who rely on public services (Reproductive Health Supplies Coalition 2018).

Funding for modern contraceptive services is a good investment in many ways. Among others, it reduces the costs of health programs because the cost of preventing an unintended pregnancy through modern contraception is far lower than the cost of health services for unintended pregnancies. Each additional dollar spent on contraception would reduce the cost of maternal and newborn health care in Africa by US$1.79 (Guttmacher Institute 2017).

Safety nets have been expanding in Africa, with all countries having at least one program and often several. However, their size remains small. Despite multiple positive impacts and a proven record of not creating dependency (Beegle, Coudouel, and Monsalve 2018), social safety nets in Africa provide low coverage and benefits relative to needs. Even if all existing social safety nets were perfectly targeted to the poor, not all needs would be met (see chapter 5, figure 5.13, panel b).

Safety net benefits in Africa are too low to move families out of poverty or reduce the poverty gap in a meaningful way: cash transfer programs targeted to the poor provide on average about US$35 a month, equivalent to about 10–15 percent of household consumption in the country. Both coverage and amounts are generally lower in low-income countries than in middle-income countries. But when predictable, they provide an important form of insurance.

The WASH subsector, equally critical for the poor, also suffers from limited investment in terms of finance and human resources in Africa. The global average government WASH budget per capita stands at US$19. Direct comparisons among regions are limited for lack of data; however, for a sample of 57 countries that provided WASH-specific budgets (WHO and UN-Water 2017), the data do suggest that African governments spend considerably less on WASH budgets per capita (US$3.88, excluding South Africa) than other regions, such as Latin America and the Caribbean (US$33.23) or Eastern and South-Eastern Asia (US$34.25). Only Central and Southern Asia, when India is included, fares lower (US$3.10).[10]

Low spending on WASH gets compounded by the large disparities across income groups and urban-rural areas within Africa. Rural and poor households are deeply affected by inadequate access to WASH in Africa. In 19 countries, children from the top wealth quintile are more than 30 percentage points more likely to have access to adequate WASH than children from the bottom wealth quintile (World Bank 2018a).

Finally, in terms of sector spending, agriculture leaders in Africa established the 2003 Maputo Declaration with a goal of allocating 10 percent of total national spending to agriculture, which was reaffirmed in the African Union's 2014 Malabo Declaration on Agriculture and Postharvest Losses. Most countries in the region have missed that target.

Africa lags other regions in public investments in agriculture in terms of both share of government budget and share of GDP. Agriculture spending per capita averages about US$19, about a third lower than in South Asia, which was the next lowest region (Goyal and Nash 2017).

Disparities and Outcomes in Social Sector Spending

Spending levels (overall or by sector) are not usually tracked subnationally, although one could make the case that this should be done for many sectors. Some evidence suggests that the poorest places are not getting equal, let alone greater, spending. Recent work using geotagged aid data and data sources as proxies for poverty (night lights, other remoteness measures, and health outcome estimates) finds that aid specifically is disproportionately going to richer areas (Briggs 2018).

Country-level studies often show disparities in public spending suggesting the same. Government health expenditures in the Democratic Republic of Congo were 1.8–3.5 times higher in Kinshasa than in provinces with higher poverty rates, and though not adjusted for price-level differences, this disparity is reflected in starkly unequal access to service and health outcomes (Barroy et al. 2014). In Ghana, government spending per pupil is higher in regions with lower poverty rates (Abdulai et al. 2018).

Even when spending data are not readily available, because the bulk of health and education spending goes toward salaries, disparities in staffing per capita between poor and less-poor areas (which is well documented in many studies) reflects, in large part, overall unequal spending. Unequal investments in social sectors partly explains why geography is one of the strongest predictors of within-country inequality (Beegle et al. 2016).

Of course, spending does not necessarily equate to improved learning or health outcomes (de la Brière et al. 2017; World Bank 2018c). However, there may be a threshold effect, where spending below a certain level (conditional on country income status) does improve learning outcomes (Vegas and Coffin 2015). How much governments spend on health is particularly salient for health outcomes of the poor (Gupta, Verhoeven, and Tiongson 2003). And notably, even when reaching targets on spending (as a share of GDP), even the poorest families often pay for some key services, such as primary school. This is partly because they choose to send their children to private schools (reflection of quality) and partly because they must pay nonfee costs at public schools.

Are Africa's Fiscal Systems Impoverishing?

Fiscal systems can have an impact on poverty and inequality, both through the government's overall fiscal situation and through the distributional implications of tax policy and public spending. Many policies can enhance equity. Governments can use taxes and transfers to redistribute income ex post, and they can use public spending—through the provision of public goods and services—to reshape the distribution of "opportunities" and foster mobility within and across generations (Bastagli 2016; Inchauste and Lustig 2017; Lustig 2018).

One tool for understanding which population segments bear the burdens and reap the benefits from various instruments for domestic resource mobilization and government spending is fiscal incidence analysis (FIA) (box 6.1). A summary and expansion of the FIA tool applied to 11 African countries through Commitment to Equity (CEQ) Assessments shows that many fiscal systems in the region

BOX 6.1 Fiscal incidence analysis offers a way to estimate the distributional impacts of taxes and transfers

Fiscal incidence analysis (FIA) is an increasingly used tool to assess who bears the burden and benefit from the different instruments upon which domestic resource mobilization and government spending depend (Lustig 2018; OECD 2017). It expands on earlier efforts, known as benefit incidence analysis, which focused only on the spending side, abstracting from how government spending was financed (Demery 2003). By demonstrating the extent to which individuals along the income distribution are either net payers or net beneficiaries from a system of taxes and transfers, FIA helps governments understand the overall impact of their fiscal policies on poverty and inequality.

Measuring the welfare impact of fiscal systems across countries requires a detailed grasp of each country's accounting and much effort and considerable judgment to identify categories of revenue and spending. The Commitment to Equity Institute[a] at Tulane University, along with various partners, has attempted this using a common methodology. The impact of the fiscal system on poverty can be analyzed creating "prefiscal" and "postfiscal" income measures. "Market income" is a prefiscal measure (income *before* any transfers or taxes of any kind have been added). "Consumable income" is a postfiscal income measure of how much individuals actually consume—that is, the net cash position

(Box continues next page)

BOX 6.1 Fiscal incidence analysis offers a way to estimate the distributional impacts of taxes and transfers *(continued)*

of households *after* the intervention of taxes and cash transfers. (Consumable income is calculated by adding the value of subsidies and direct transfers received to market income and then subtracting the value of direct and indirect taxes paid.)

A Commitment to Equity (CEQ) Assessment is a diagnostic tool providing a point-in-time economic analysis of the distribution (among a national population) of public, programmatic expenditures and the burdens created by public revenue collections (Lustig 2018). As such, it does not attempt to estimate the long-run benefit or investment value created by, for example, expenditures on health and education service delivery or infrastructure and "connectivity"-related spending. Many public expenditures have an inherent investment element, the inclusion of which would likely imply different conclusions about long-run inequality and poverty dynamics. A CEQ Assessment is restricted to the current impacts of public expenditures and revenue collections on poverty, inequality, and welfare more generally.

a. For more information, see the Commitment to Equity (CEQ) Institute website: http://www.ceqinstitute.org.

FIGURE 6.7 Fiscal policy in Africa frequently increases poverty

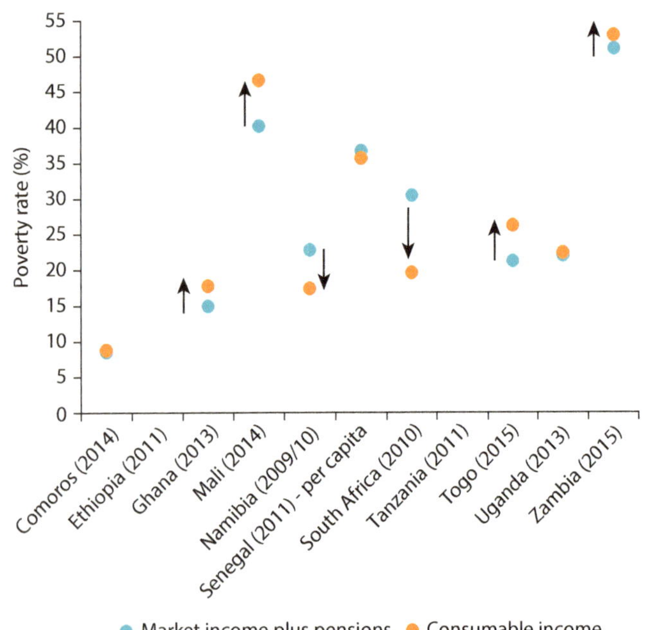

Source: de la Fuente, Jellema, and Lustig 2018.
Note: Figure shows the impact of taxes and transfers on poverty rates. "Market income" comprises pretax wages; salaries; income earned from capital assets (rent, interest, or dividends); and private transfers. "Consumable income" = market income + direct cash transfers and indirect subsidies – payment of direct taxes and indirect taxes (value added and excise taxes). Arrows indicate change in the poverty headcount rate, where poverty is defined as those below the $1.90 purchasing power parity (2011) poverty line. Year in parentheses after each country indicates the year of data.

are at best neutral in terms of poverty impacts or, at worst, sometimes, poverty increasing (de la Fuente, Jellema, and Lustig 2018). Namibia and South Africa are exceptions, because the fiscal systems of these two countries add significantly to household income through direct transfer spending (figure 6.7).

Yet even when the poverty rate is unchanged or has fallen, like in Namibia and South Africa, African fiscal systems may still create burdens for some poor and vulnerable households. That is, some poor and vulnerable individuals may end up paying more in taxes than they receive in transfers—a phenomenon known as "fiscal impoverishment" (FI) (Higgins and Lustig 2016).[11] The FI index summarizes the number of poor individuals who are estimated to have experienced net losses from fiscal policy (that is, they have paid more into the fiscal system in taxes than they are estimated to have received from it as benefits).[12]

The FI index is expressed as a rate among either the overall population or the poor population. When FI is stated in terms of the latter, it demonstrates how well the fiscal system protected poor and vulnerable households from losses. The proportion of poor households that are disadvantaged by the fiscal system can be very high (even exceeding 80 percent) in countries that deliver few cash benefits directly, like the Comoros, Ghana, Mali, Togo, Uganda, and Zambia (figure 6.8). These calculations do not correct, however, for the proportion of poor households that are net beneficiaries of the fiscal system and escape poverty as a result.

Underpinning these patterns are three proximate causes or drivers of this FI in Africa. There is a heavy reliance on consumption taxes like VAT to raise revenues and compensate for the low tax collection from other sources, including corporate, income, and property taxes. Governments also spend a lot on subsidies like energy subsidies (which fail to reach most poor households) and agricultural subsidies (which have low returns relative to other agricultural investments). And social protection systems provide only limited direct transfers targeting the poor, either because few households are covered, or transfer amounts are relatively low, or both. For these reasons, it is further anticipated that the group of poor people who escape poverty by virtue of being net fiscal receivers is also small.

Note also that the FI index and the discussion directly below refers to reductions in individuals' cash-based financial position or purchasing power. It does not include the effects of in-kind benefits like education, health, or infrastructure services because in-kind benefits cannot be "eaten"; that is, they neither increase nor decrease purchasing power over other goods and services.

Direct taxes create very small burdens for the bottom 40 percent, while indirect taxes paid by the bottom 40 percent often represent 10 percent or more of prefiscal income (figure 6.9). Subsidies—even when they are extensive—provide little benefit to poor and vulnerable households, which do not access the subsidized services (such as electricity and transport fuel) as much as the wealthy. Only in Namibia and South Africa do direct transfers provide compensation for the bottom 40 percent that are equal to or greater than the taxes paid.

In the aggregate, the total cash benefit transferred to the poorest 40 percent of the population through subsidies and direct transfer programs is smaller in absolute magnitude than the burden created (for the same population) by direct and indirect tax instruments. That is to say, most individuals in the bottom 40 percent—including most poor individuals—can expect to be net payers instead of net recipients.[13]

FIGURE 6.8 Fiscal systems in Africa create net losses for the poor even when the incidence of poverty is reduced

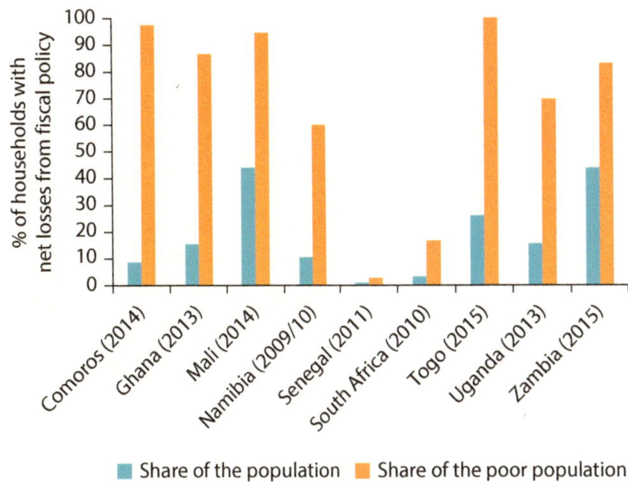

Source: de la Fuente, Jellema, and Lustig 2018.
Note: Poverty is defined as those below the $1.90 purchasing power parity (2011) poverty line. Year in parentheses after each country indicates the year of data.

Even if the fiscal system makes a portion of the poor net payers, arguably this would be fine if it is the only way to finance strongly progressive, extensive public expenditures on sectors that benefit the poor such as education and health. But is this the case for Africa? It is not clear that the poor benefit from in-kind spending in education and health as much as they could, given the problems with the quality of the services received, as discussed below.

Notably, a limitation of the FIAs reported here is that they do not account for infrastructure spending, which in some countries may improve quality of life or market access for the poor.

Mobilizing More (and Less-Harmful) Revenues

Addressing Heavy Reliance on Indirect Taxes and Unreliable Direct Taxes

As alluded to above, *how* taxes are raised matters to poverty as much as the *amount* raised, with the bottom 40 percent often significantly affected by indirect taxation.

FIGURE 6.9 Indirect taxes outweigh subsidy and transfer benefits for the bottom 40 percent of most African populations

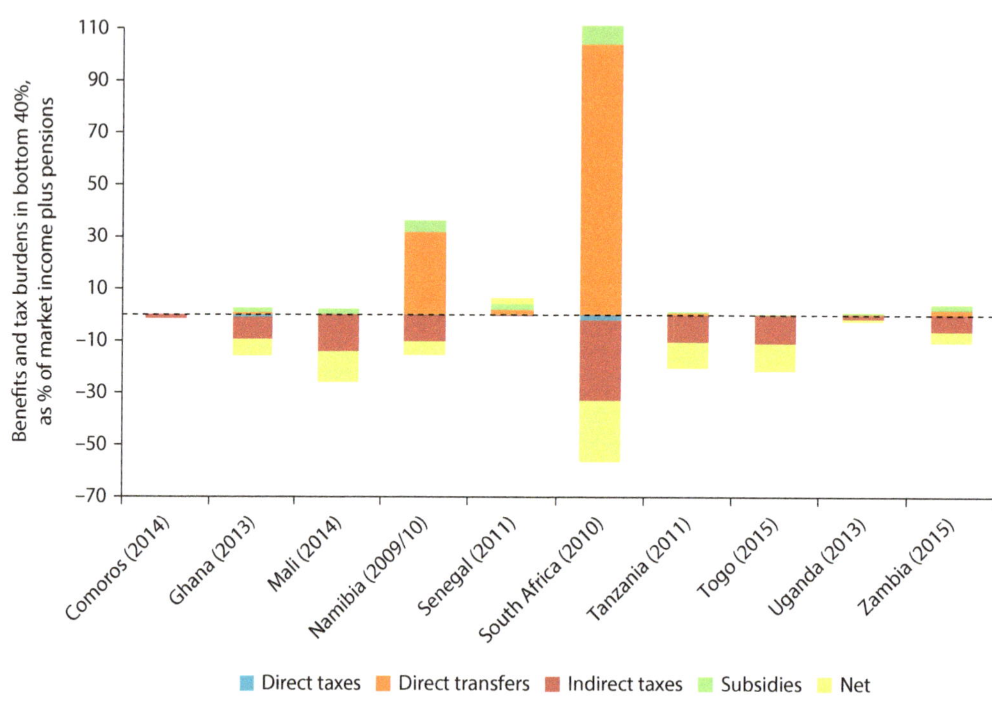

Source: de la Fuente, Jellema, and Lustig 2018.
Note: Direct transfers and subsidies represent 104 percent and 7 percent, respectively, of market income plus pensions in the bottom 40 percent of South Africans (in 2010). ("Market income" comprises pretax wages, salaries, income earned from capital assets, and private transfers.) Year in parentheses after each country indicates the year of data.

Many African governments indeed rely on indirect taxes such as VAT as the main channel to collect revenues, as mentioned before, especially in contexts where administrative capacity and tax collection are low.

The VAT Conundrum

To spare the poor, several goods and services—such as foodstuffs and kerosene—are further often granted preferential tax rates, because such expenditures typically take up a large proportion of poor households' total budget. Yet, although evidence from Ethiopia, Ghana, Senegal, and Zambia finds that preferential VAT rates help the poor, they are often not well targeted toward poor households in that many nonpoor households benefit from these exemptions (Harris et al. 2018). Often the goods and services exempted from VAT are also consumed in significant quantities by the nonpoor, implying important forgone tax revenues. Existing cash transfer schemes in these countries are better targeted, but given issues related to coverage, targeting, and the amounts transferred, they typically do not provide a suitable means of compensation to justify the cancellation of VAT exemptions.

This poses an important policy conundrum: VAT is a preferable taxation vehicle for efficiency and effectiveness, but it can hurt the poor. Tax exemptions on goods and services primarily consumed by the poor provide a way to mitigate the negative effects. Yet such goods and services are few and far between. VAT exemption thus often comes with significant tax revenue loss. Furthermore, the revenues raised through VAT and other indirect taxes will need to be properly channeled to the poor or vulnerable so that they become net receivers of the fiscal system.

Targeted cash transfers provide an alternative way to compensate the poor. But the resources dedicated to cash transfers are often insufficient (because of both insufficient coverage and low transfer amounts) and need to be weighed against other competing expenditure needs (spending on education, health, WASH, infrastructure, security, and so on).

Direct Taxation's Limited Potential

Direct taxes, on the other hand, tend to be progressive because richer people more often have formal jobs. Economists are quick to diagnose that direct taxes can affect efficiency and long-run growth—by disincentivizing investment, human capital acquisition, and innovation. Yet the evidence suggests that, for low-income countries, shifting away from consumption taxes such as VAT in favor of income taxes appears to have no negative effect on growth (McNabb and LeMay-Boucher 2014).

More important, the small formal sector in many African countries limits the scope for collecting more revenues through direct taxation. Personal income tax is generally limited in economies with large informal sectors because there are few formal employers. Nevertheless, there is room for direct taxation of a wider base of taxpayers, including from the informal sector. Inducing tax compliance also fosters good governance more widely; it comes along with a demand for state institutions that are more responsive, accountable, and competent.

Taxpayer noncompliance is a continual and growing global problem, but studies suggest that low- and middle-income countries, many of them in Africa, are the hardest hit (Cobham 2005; Fuest and Riedel 2009). Part of the reason is that it often does not seem to pay to pay taxes. If taxpayers perceive that they do not obtain corresponding benefits from their government, tax compliance decreases (Junquera-Varela et al. 2017), as several examples suggest. In Tanzania and Uganda, individuals who are more satisfied with the provision of basic health and educational services are more likely to have a tax-compliant attitude. In Kenya and South Africa, those satisfied with the provision of roads and electricity and the issuance of an identity card and obtaining police services, respectively, were more likely to have a tax-compliant attitude (Ali, Fjeldstad, and Sjursen 2014). And in Uganda, firms that suffer more frequent electricity outages (and thus experience drops in firm profitability) are more likely to evade taxes (Mawejje and Okumu 2016).

Options for Increasing Tax Revenue

Establishing better links between taxation and public spending performance is therefore crucial. Earmarking taxes or other domestic revenue (also called hypothecated taxes) is one approach to reassure citizens that domestic resources are not squandered. Some tax reforms might have proved difficult without earmarking. For example, Ghana raised the standard VAT rate from 10 percent to 15 percent in recent years by dedicating the additional revenue to financing the national health insurance program (Keen 2012). Cigarette taxes that raise revenue for health care is another example (box 6.2). These examples notwithstanding, however, fiscal experts usually do not favor earmarking because it reduces budgetary flexibility (Junquera-Varela et al. 2017).

Other ways have been explored to increase tax revenue without necessarily more enforcement. Direct participation in tax collection can also improve compliance. In Ghana, for example, the revenue authority invited informal sector associations (starting with transport, followed by 13 other sectors) to collect taxes from their members. In exchange, the associations were offered 2.5 percent of the revenue collected. Informal sector taxation represents only up to 5 percent of Ghana's Internal Revenue Service revenue, but broadening the revenue base is vital to building the social fiscal contract. A culture of taxpaying was created over time and encourages those in the informal sector to reengage constructively with the state (Joshi and Ayee 2009). Revenue

BOX 6.2 Tobacco taxes can provide a poverty win-win

African countries are experiencing the highest increase in the rate of tobacco use among low- and middle-income countries: the number of smokers in Africa is projected to increase by 148 percent by 2030, to 208 million smokers, or one-fifth of the total population. At the same time, in most African countries, tobacco remains relatively little taxed.

Higher tobacco taxes can boost government tax revenues and reduce the extent of smoking. Simulations from Senegal suggest that raising the ad valorem tax on tobacco to 60 percent (up from 45 percent currently) would reduce cigarette consumption by 17.1 percent. It would also more than double state tax revenues above those projected for 2018 under current tax rates (World Bank 2018b). In South Africa, cigarette sales declined by a third, and government revenue from tobacco taxes increased from R1 billion in 1993 to R9 billion in 2009. This is largely attributed to the country's aggressive tobacco tax policy, which raised the tobacco, excise, and VAT taxes combined from 32 percent of the retail price to 50 percent (Fuchs, Del Carmen, and Kechia Mukong 2018).

Such additional revenue could fund health-related programs or development investments, as in the following examples in WHO (2017):

- *In Côte d'Ivoire,* proceeds of an additional tobacco tax are directed to the acquired immune deficiency syndrome (AIDS) program and for tobacco control; proceeds of another additional tobacco tax are directed to sports.
- *In Mauritius,* a portion of tobacco tax revenues funds the treatment of health problems associated with cigarette consumption.
- *In Madagascar,* a portion of tax revenue from cigarettes is directed to finance the National Fund for the Promotion and Development of Youth, Sports and Recreation.

To be sure, tobacco taxes are usually regressive because low-income households allocate larger shares of their budget to tobacco than richer ones do. At the same time, although smokers are more prevalent among the poor, poorer households are also more responsive to cigarette price increases and are therefore more likely to benefit from reduced smoking in response to higher tobacco taxes (Marquez and Farrington 2013). Furthermore, when the indirect (health) effects are considered, poor people get the largest share of health and economic benefits from smoking cessation following a tax rate hike (Marquez and Moreno-Dodson 2017). The potential long-run benefits of nonsmoking through a reduction in medical expenditures and an increase in healthy life years can offset the costs associated with tobacco taxes among low-income groups and the overall population, as was found in South Africa (Fuchs, Del Carmen, and Mukong 2018).

authorities in Mozambique and Tanzania have also embraced the informal sectors, increasing the revenues obtained from them through simplified tax procedures for small and microenterprises, taxpayer education, and outreach programs using local languages (Fjeldstad and Heggstad 2012).

Technology can further help. In a low-income setting, with limited resources to support revenue administration, relatively cheap delivery methods like short message service (SMS) texts can be effective. In Rwanda, a combination of positive messages underlying the importance of taxes to finance public goods and personalized messages to taxpayers, sent via SMS, nudged people to comply (Mascagni, Nell, and Monkam 2017). These and other simple nudges increased tax compliance by about 20 percent.

Taxing the Rich

In many African countries, the numbers of wealthy are growing fast (McCluskey 2016), as are the prices of real estate—one of the major assets held by the rich. And yet many rich people pay relatively low taxes on their assets and incomes or enterprises. In Ghana, income tax revenue could have been higher by 22 percent (equivalent to 0.5 percent of GDP) if everyone who filed income tax in 2014 had paid full amounts of income tax due (Asiedu et al. 2017). Wealthy individuals often have significant investments in local land and property and underdeclare their income from such activities. Out of 71 high-ranking Ugandan government officials owning large domestic business assets (like hotels and schools), only one had ever paid personal income taxes between 2011 and 2016 (Kangave et al. 2016). Entrenched power structures and corruption are powerful obstacles to taxing the rich. Those with assets to tax are generally well connected politically, frustrating any reform efforts. In Uganda, many of the better-off who owned enormous assets were top-ranking government officials.

Some tax losses also reflect logistical difficulties in verifying the concealment of income placed offshore (Keen 2012). It is difficult to trace and estimate the income and wealth of rich people. The best such estimates suggest that at least 30 percent of all African financial wealth is held offshore (Zucman 2014). This is higher than in any global region other than the Russian Federation and the Gulf States (Moore and Prichard 2017). Taxing wealth held offshore could be straightforward if there was more effective international cooperation.

On the domestic front, setting up special units focusing on large taxpayers has been one approach to increase revenues in Uganda and Zambia (Kangave et al. 2016; Ortiz, Cummins, and Karunanethy 2017). Detaching revenue authorities from political interference (typically from Ministries of Finance) can also help overcome some of the political barriers to more effectively taxing the rich. As of 2014, there were 17 semiautonomous revenue authorities (SARAs) in Africa (Fjeldstad 2014). On average, SARAs have not improved revenue collection in the region (Dom 2017), but some have made advances, like in Malawi and South Africa (Sarr 2016) and to some extent in Mozambique and Rwanda. In Rwanda, the government increased tax revenue as a share of GDP by approximately 50 percent between 2001 and 2013 despite declining import duties. Other revenue authorities have seen either little progress, like in Sierra Leone, or progress followed by stagnation, like in Zambia (Keen 2012; Sarr 2016). Incidentally, the signaling of equitable and credible enforcement can spur more compliance. Taxpayers would be reassured that tax collection is carried out without political bias or corruption.

The barrier to collecting more property taxes may be largely political, but some technical measures can also widen the base for these taxes. Recent experiences in Sierra Leone point to at least three options for improvement (Jibao and Prichard 2016). These include (a) simplified valuation methods that rely primarily on observable features of properties (as opposed to sophisticated, often imported, information technology systems); (b) transferring the responsibility for valuation and property tax collection away from central tax agencies through hands-on and continuous training of local staff (instead of high-cost, short-term training programs); and (c) long-term partnership at the local level, including continuous support to and pressure on political leaders when they have inevitably confronted political resistance.

Relatedly, concentrating the responsibility for collecting property taxes on those with stronger incentives to collect revenue can yield great results. In Lagos, Nigeria, the local government overhauled governance and property taxation since the early 2000s with the determination of Lagos's leaders to realize their "mega-city ambitions," in part to attract increased investment (Goodfellow and Owen 2018).

Revenues Lost from Multinationals and Cross-Country Competition

Transfer Mispricing by Multinational Corporations

Without overlooking domestic policies and revenue sources, additional revenues could further be raised from multinationals. A large portion of the tax bill of multinationals is domestic (through levies, payroll taxes, and import taxes). However, multinational companies can minimize their

BOX 6.3 Three stories illustrate African countries' losses of corporate tax revenue

A Dubai Multinational's Tax Evasion on Kenyan Flower Exports

In 2011, the Kenya Revenue Authority (KRA) began investigating the flower sector amid suspicions of trade mispricing, based on differences between prices at which flowers were exported from Kenya and the average price at which they were imported into Europe (US$3.70 per kilogram versus US$8.08 per kilogram). This gap in Kenya might be as much as US$500 million a year on its flower exports (Christian Aid 2014).

In 2012, the KRA ruled that Karuturi Global Ltd., an India-based multinational and the world's biggest producer of cut roses, had evaded taxes. The direct owners of Karuturi Kenya are Karuturi Overseas LLC, Dubai (a holding company), and Flower Express FZE, Dubai (a marketing company). Dubai Flower Centre functions as a free zone that has zero tax on income and profits, offers confidentiality to business owners, and operates as an offshore environment. The KRA ruling stated that Karuturi had used transfer mispricing to avoid paying the Kenyan government nearly US$11 million in corporate income tax.

A Dutch Beer Company's Tax Haven in Mauritius

SABMiller, one of the world's largest beer companies, based in the Netherlands, is estimated to have deprived African governments of as much as US$20 million per year by routing profits to sister companies through tax havens as "management fees" and running procurement through a subsidiary based in Mauritius (ActionAid 2010). The company pays no tax at all in countries such as Ghana. It avoids doing so because the brands of beer sold in African countries, though invented locally, are owned by SABMiller in the Netherlands. The African breweries pay the Dutch company massive royalties, on which the latter pays very little tax owing to the tax regulations in the Netherlands.

Shifting Mining Profits from Zambia to Switzerland

Mopani Mines in Zambia, one of the biggest mines and exporters in the world, produces and sells copper and cobalt to the international market. It is owned primarily by Glencore PLC (a multinational commodity mining and trading company based in Switzerland) through a string of holding companies in tax havens.

A pilot audit in 2011, commissioned by the Zambian Revenue Authority (ZRA) suggested systematic tax evasion by the company. It accused Mopani of selling copper to Glencore in Switzerland at below-market prices, effectively shifting profits from Zambia to Switzerland. The report also found evidence of artificially increased shipping costs, with an inexplicable doubling in Mopani's operational costs from 2005 to 2007. The mine was loss-making, and Mopani had paid no corporation tax because it had purchased the mine from the government 10 years before.

Calculations by ActionAid based on figures in the audit suggest that it cost the Zambian government £76 million a year in lost corporation taxes (more than the £59 million in annual aid from the U.K. government to Zambia). In addition, the Zambian government has been losing out on dividend payments related to its 10 percent share in the company.

Source: Christian Aid 2014.

tax bill on profits through transfer mispricing. Simply put, this takes place when a company can appear to lose money—or to make very little profit—in the country it is operating in, while making money in secrecy jurisdictions (trading through a subsidiary) where there is no real production and sales activity going on and remarkably low (or no) tax applied.[14] Trading goods that are mispriced to avoid tariffs is not illegal, but there is widespread agreement that multinationals should refrain from this type of tax-minimizing behavior.

However, evidence shows that multinational companies do give into this temptation (box 6.3). A recent study using confidential tax return data finds that South African firms with connections to tax havens with no corporate tax report 47 percent lower profits and a 7 percent higher likelihood of reporting a loss than firms with no such connection (Reynolds and Wier 2016).

These responses are roughly twice as large as what have been observed in high-income countries. This finding supports the commonly held view that multinational firms operating in low- and middle-income countries are more aggressive in their tax planning.

Outside of South Africa, because of a lack of data, little is known of the region's corporate tax revenue losses. For low- and middle-income countries, ballpark estimates suggest that revenue losses from base erosion and profit shifting range from 0.3 percent to 2 percent of GDP, albeit with big variations across countries (Crivelli, de Mooij, and Keen 2016; Forstater 2018; Johannesen, Tørsløv, and Wier 2016; Johansson et al. 2017; UNCTAD 2015). Countries like Chad, the Comoros, Guinea, Namibia, and Zambia face losses of 3–7 percent of GDP (Cobham and Janský 2017).

Domestic revenues make up the bulk of revenues that a country could mobilize from forgone opportunities. Nonetheless, the potential additional revenue from more effectively tackling transfer mispricing is nontrivial. Support to conduct transfer pricing audits in Zambia and Tanzania resulted in returns of 10 to 1 and 100 to 1, respectively (Moore and Prichard 2017). Similarly, a joint program of technical assistance for price audits between the OECD and the African Tax Administration Forum (ATAF) between 2015 and 2017 yielded additional revenues of more than US$120 million. Corporate taxes constitute 30 percent of total tax revenue in Africa, which is almost three times the world average of 12 percent (UNCTAD 2015). Some African countries rely almost entirely on corporate taxation. Tanzania, for instance, collects 70 percent of all taxes from the 450 largest companies operating in the country.

A "Race to the Bottom" from Cross-Country Competition

Another important tax gap in African countries relates to tax incentives designed to attract foreign investors and curb profit shifting. Such measures have become more pervasive despite limited evidence of their effectiveness (OECD 2014; Van Parys and James 2010). The share of countries offering tax holidays in Africa (which may go from 5 years to 15 years) increased from 10 percent in 1980 to 80 percent in 2005 (Keen and Mansour 2010). Similarly, in 2005, 17 countries had free zones compared with 1 country in 1980. By one study, the value of tax exemptions in six African countries amounts to a third of the total taxes collected on average (Moore and Prichard 2017).

Profit shifting from multinationals enhances a harmful "race to the bottom" in corporate taxes between states, which results in lower tax revenues. This has been the case in most regions within Africa (figure 6.10). Such a race to the bottom is a global phenomenon, but it affects Africa the most given its heavier reliance on these types of taxes.

An Agenda for African Corporate Tax Revenues

When adding it all together—aggressive tax planning by multinationals, high reliance on corporate taxes, increasingly lower corporate tax rates, increased exposure to multinational activity, and increased complexity in multinational corporate activity—the future does look dire for African corporate tax revenues.

To tackle transfer pricing, fundamental reform of the system may be needed. One common proposal is the use of "formula apportionment" whereby a simple distribution key is used to allocate profit across countries. For example, if a multinational company has 10 percent of its sales and 10 percent of its employees in South Africa, then 10 percent of that multinational company's profits would be allocated to South Africa. This type of system would likely increase the corporate tax payments in Africa while ensuring a sustainable simplicity of the system (Cobham and Loretz 2014).

Another increasing trend is to devote more resources to challenging transfer mispricing. In 2000, only South Africa and Zambia had transfer pricing laws and regulations in place. By 2014, this number had increased to 14. Still, many low-income African countries

FIGURE 6.10 Corporate tax rates in Africa have declined

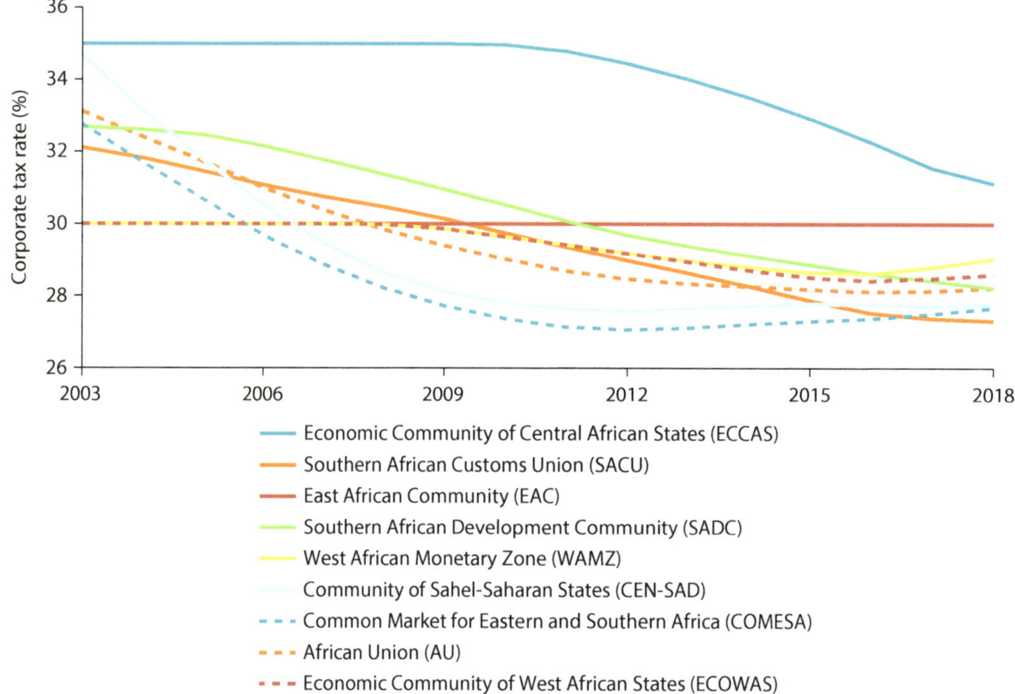

Source: World Bank estimations based on KPMG database.

have little knowledge, staff (lawyers and accountants), and resources to challenge the accounts of multinationals for transfer mispricing. Capacity still needs to be developed for auditing, enforcement, and dispute resolution.

Given that profit shifting by abusive transfer pricing happens among multinationals, a number of measures are needed at the global level to foster transparency among multinationals and to reform the current rules for their taxation. These measures include

- *A global system for effective automatic information exchange* among tax administrations like the Global Forum on Transparency and Exchange of Information for Tax Purposes;[15]
- *Public disclosure of beneficial owners* of companies, foundations, and trusts;
- *Enhanced transparency of multinational companies' tax practices* through worldwide combined tax reports and public country-by-country reporting; and
- *Full participation of African countries* in the OECD's ongoing Base Erosion and Profit Shifting (BEPS) project, which seeks to reform the rules for the taxation of multinational companies.[16]

Finally, rather than lowering their corporate tax rates to limit profit shifting, countries could focus on reducing other constraints that pose higher concerns for investors than tax levels. Such measures include the time required to start a business, register property, and improve the quality of infrastructure (Fjeldstad 2014; Moore and Prichard 2017). A poorly executed program of audits for potential transfer mispricing could also increase the unpredictability of the tax system.

Tapping Mining Income

For some countries, a major cause of revenue loss concerns revenues generated in extractive industries. Natural resources as a prominent source of government revenues remains relevant despite recent downturns, given the prospects of new mineral resource discoveries and the eventual bounce back of falling commodity prices (Roe and Dodd 2017). At the same time, there is now a consensus that government revenues from extractive industries are far too small.

The effective tax rate in mining is typically 45–65 percent of export value (IMF 2012). In 2010–11, Ghana, Sierra Leone, and Zambia received only 2–12 percent of the value of their mineral exports from natural resource taxation and royalties (Christian Aid 2014). Concession trading in copper and cobalt mining in the Democratic Republic of Congo lost an estimated US$1.36 billion, conservatively, in 2010–12 relative to the country's health and education budget of US$698 million (APP 2013).

The failure of African countries to capture income from the extractives sector is driven by a mix of factors, including overly generous tax incentives, tax dodging, weak tax revenue authorities, and the corruption of elites. In some cases, governments give generous tax concessions to extractive companies—undercutting their own revenue codes—and the governments lack the capacity or will to properly track what the industries should be paying. (See, for example, the discussion on Liberia in SDI [2014].)

African state companies in the extractive sector also lack transparency, and the problem is compounded by the "global governance deficit" in some international extractive companies that are major investors in Africa (APP 2013). Levying appropriate royalty payments and corporate taxes from private companies have recently helped countries like Ghana and Zambia to raise more revenues.[17]

Further, governments must do more to ensure that natural resource revenues are not squandered. This does not always require more and higher taxes, but it does require more transparency and disclosure. The Extractive Industries Transparency Initiative (EITI) allows citizens to track how their country's natural resources are being managed and how much revenue they are generating (for example, how much in royalties and taxes are paid to their governments). EITI emphasizes the principle of "publish what you pay," and so information has to be published on each element of the chain, including licensing, contracting, production, taxation, and royalty payments, as well as the way revenues flow to the treasury.

Equally crucial for effective EITI implementation is the support of a coalition of government, companies, and civil society. Transparency can lead to accountability only if there is public understanding of what the figures mean and public debate about how the country's resource wealth should be managed. Therefore, the EITI standard requires reports to be published regularly, to be comprehensible, and to promote and contribute actively to public debate.

Several African countries are EITI-compliant—including Ghana, Mali, and Nigeria—but others, such as Angola, Botswana, Namibia, South Africa, and Zimbabwe, are not. Although EITI seems to have achieved its institutional goals, some operational goals appear to be unmet, including a relative failure in empowering the public to hold governments and companies accountable (Rustad, Le Billon, and Lujalac 2017).

This work finds that the fiscal policies in place matter for the public revenue effects of increased foreign direct investment (FDI) from EITI. It also finds that the main cause of low natural resource revenue may be not so much corruption as unfavorable contractual terms regarding taxation.

Toward Better Spending for the Poor

The fiscal agenda to reduce poverty in Africa is not only about greater revenues and higher expenditures. It is equally critical to improve the efficiency and equity of that spending to be more impactful for poor and vulnerable households—in other words, not only getting more for each dollar spent but also spending more in the sectors and subsectors as well as the places that improve the lives of the poor more effectively within the given budget.[18]

Overspending on Subsidies

Consumer price subsidies are one way to "repay" consumers some of their taxes. They are almost always regressive: those with assets or services to subsidize are generally better off than the poorer segments that often pay indirect taxes that pay for the subsidies. For instance, the bottom 20 percent receives less than 15 percent of the region's subsidies for kerosene—the fuel type most used by the poor. In the case of liquefied petroleum gas and gasoline, only 3 percent of the value of the subsidy goes to the bottom 20 percent because they consume so little of these fuels. For African countries, on average, for every US$1 in untargeted gasoline subsidies going to the poorest 40 percent of households, US$23 goes to the top 60 percent of households (Coady, Flamini, and Sears 2015). Two-thirds of global poverty in 2012 (based on US$2.50 per day) would have been covered with redistribution of national fossil fuel subsidies to the poor (Sumner 2016).

Subsidies are, hence, a very inefficient way of increasing the consumption of the poorest households (box 6.4). Replacing energy subsidies with a basic income guarantee could both save money and have health and environmental benefits (Coady et al. 2017; IMF 2017).

Within agriculture, farm input subsidies were almost phased out in the 1990s, during a period of structural adjustment in Africa, but they have made a strong comeback owing partly to residual support for subsidies among African leaders and partly to the uncertainties about food supply during the 2007–08 global food and fertilizer price instability. Ten African governments spend roughly US$1.2 billion annually on input subsidies alone, primarily on fertilizers (Goyal and Nash 2017). In principle, farm input subsidies could make a dent in poverty by making key inputs available to a large population of poor farmers to potentially raise their productivity,[19] thereby promoting household and national food security and enhancing rural incomes. But have farming input subsidies delivered?

The existing body of research shows only a modest impact of fertilizer subsidy programs on yields and overall production, which in turn attenuates the subsidy programs' contribution toward reduction of either retail food prices or poverty. (Regarding the impact of farm input subsidy programs on poverty, see Ricker-Gilbert [2016] for Malawi; Mason and Smale [2013] and Mason and Tembo [2015] for Zambia; and Jayne et al. [2016] for Africa in general.)

The input subsidies' lack of impact on productivity and poverty gets magnified because African countries do not spend much on agriculture. Farm input subsidy programs have crowded out other complementary public investments that have proven to be more efficient drivers of agricultural productivity growth (box 6.4), as discussed in chapter 3. Take the cases of Malawi and Zambia, two of the largest spenders on agriculture in the region: in 2014, both countries' budget allocations to fertilizer and seed subsidies exceeded 40 percent of the total budget to the Ministry of Agriculture (Goyal and Nash 2017).

Removing subsidies and shifting that spending to public goods and services could improve efficiency and possibly equity. Such reform creates winners and losers and thus places political pressures on the government. Vested interests and populist pressures exist in all countries. Transport leaders, mining companies, and politically connected firms will want to hold on to energy subsidies, for example, to keep the preferential treatment in their business as well as to raise barriers to entry for newcomers.

The political economy of agricultural subsidies is no less real. Political influence concentration is associated with more subsidies (figure 6.11). Nonetheless, some countries have managed to remove subsidies (Inchauste and Victor 2017). To address the politics of reform, first, it may be necessary to compensate affected groups to preempt opposition. Such compensations may not be cost-efficient, but failing to compensate them (for instance, in the Dominican Republic, transporters and middle classes

BOX 6.4 Farm input subsidies are less effective than alternative policies in reducing poverty

The CEQ Institute developed impact and spending effectiveness indicators to facilitate comparisons between fiscal expenditures and their impacts on social indicators like the poverty gap or inequality (Enami 2018). The Impact Effectiveness Indicator provides a single number indicating how close a program is to achieving its maximum potential impact (given the magnitude of spending on the program). For example, a program that provides a transfer equal to 10 percent of median per capita income to the poorest 10 percent of households will have a larger impact on poverty gap reduction than a program that provides the same-size transfer to the poorest 5 percent of households and the richest 5 percent of households. The Impact Effectiveness Indicator would give the first program a higher score than the second.

FIGURE B6.4.1 Direct transfers have greater poverty impact than subsidies

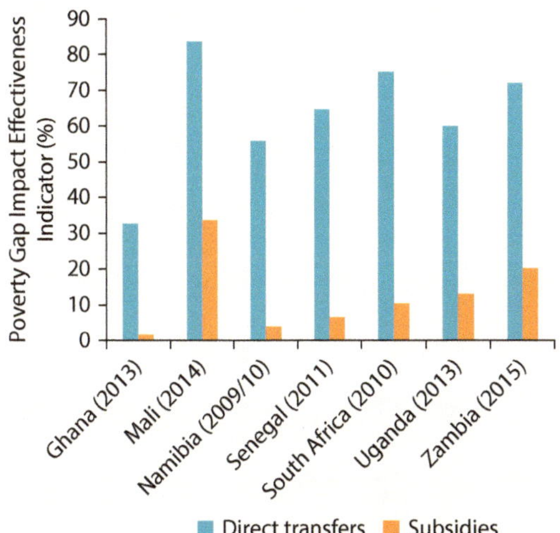

Source: de la Fuente, Jellema, and Lustig 2018.
Note: The Poverty Gap Impact Effectiveness Indicator is (basically) the actual amount of poverty gap reduction achieved by the item in question (in the numerator) relative to the theoretical maximum poverty gap reduction achievable by the same instrument at the same level of expenditure (in the denominator). In other words, for example, in Mali direct transfers achieve over 80 percent of their theoretical maximum poverty gap reduction while in Ghana direct transfers achieve just over 30 percent of their theoretical maximum poverty gap reduction. Year in parentheses after each country indicates the year of data.

Subsidy expenditures are a particularly expensive way to protect poor households. When targeted, direct transfer (social safety net) spending achieves 50 percent or more of its maximum poverty gap reduction potential, but subsidies often achieve less than 10 percent of their maximum poverty gap reduction potential (figure B6.4.1). In other words, both instruments have the potential to reduce poverty, but subsidies are far less effective and therefore more expensive (de la Fuente, Jellema, and Lustig 2018).

Cost-benefit analysis is another useful tool when comparing several competing proposals. An investment whose benefits exceed the costs should be undertaken; among competing proposals, the one with the highest benefit-cost ratio should be preferred.

The benefit-cost estimates of subsidy programs suggest modest returns of these instruments at best. In Kenya, Malawi, and Zambia, subsidized fertilizer between 2005 and 2010 had an estimated ratio of benefits to cost of generally less than 1—indicating that costs were higher than benefits (Goyal and Nash 2017). In Malawi, the national benefit-to-cost ratio for improved seeds was estimated to be 2.48 (Lunduka and Ricker-Gilbert 2016). In contrast, the cost of subsidized fertilizer far exceeded the benefits to farmers across the board, with a benefit-cost ratio for subsidized fertilizer of 0.42. By comparison, spending on public goods such as agricultural research and development (R&D), improved connectivity of rural areas, modernized and smart extension systems, and irrigation are associated with high returns (Dabalen et al. 2017; Fuglie and Rada 2013).

for removing the fuel and electricity subsidies) could have stopped the reform from passing altogether.

Second, consumers need to see what they get in exchange for rising prices if the process is to be sustained. Strong communication on the need for price liberalization and trust in the ability of government to handle competing interests is important to sustain price increases.

When, and if, subsidies are scaled back, it needs to happen along with a scaling-up of social protection systems. Redistribution has been shown to significantly increase the odds that reforms will succeed. A review of reforms in the Middle East and

FIGURE 6.11 Greater concentration of political influence can result in more subsidies

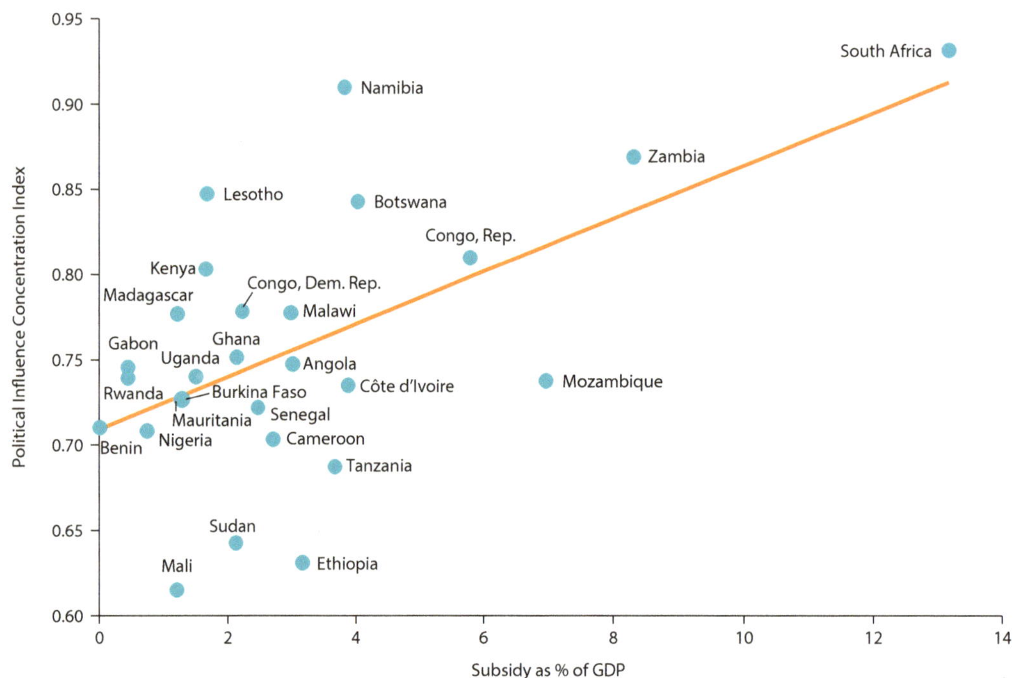

Source: Bolch, Ceriani, and López-Calva 2017.
Note: The Political Influence Concentration Index is measured by how many individuals at the bottom of the income distribution (the potential winners from more-redistributive policies starting from the poorest) would need to come together to outweigh the opposition from the top of the income distribution by accounting for the wealth owned by those individuals.

North Africa classifies all reforms that are combined with cash and in-kind transfers as successful, as opposed to only 17 percent of those without such transfers (Sdralevich et al. 2014).

However, greater revenues for government do not automatically lead to higher allocations for safety net programs, because Ministries of Finance come under many competing demands to reallocate the savings. Concerted efforts from civil society or from external financiers to ensure that, as part of the subsidy reform, safety nets are funded adequately are vital. In recent years, the IMF has suggested introducing or expanding social protection programs to compensate vulnerable households during price subsidy reforms (Feltenstein 2017). Equally useful, politicians could earmark part of those savings to build credible commitments to carry out the reform as intended.

How Inefficiencies in Fertilizer Subsidies Hinder Their Pro-Poor Agenda

Why are fertilizer subsidy programs in Africa often not efficient? The reasons for the limited success of fertilizer subsidy programs that come with high costs are relatively well understood and reflect technical, market, and political failures.

Causes of Subsidy Inefficiency

To start with, fertilizer use is not always and everywhere profitable. Nitrogen application on carbon-deficient soils (with low soil organic matter) has been shown to be inefficient and economically unprofitable (Marenya and Barrett 2009). A study in Zambia showed limited maize yield response to basal fertilizer application on highly acidic soils—which represent most of the farms in Zambia (Burke, Jayne, and Black 2012).

Other technical factors affecting why fertilizer may not reach its potential are the late application of fertilizer, inadequate weeding, and limited use of crop rotation and intercropping. Smallholders need complementary inputs such as land, labor, and some level of soil fertility and management ability to make use of inputs. These complementary inputs are likely to be in short supply among poorer smallholders.

Administrative deficiencies in program implementation compound the low returns. For instance, in Malawi, an inefficient tonnage allocation formula (small quantities provided to many contractors) raises average purchase costs, and an inefficient fertilizer delivery mechanism has increased logistical costs, compounded in recent years by the depreciation of the Malawi kwacha.

Corruption and elite capture are also widespread political factors that create inefficiencies. Elite capture—whereby those with social connections and resources obtain a disproportionate share of the benefits—is sometimes present in the community-based targeting schemes that many of these programs employ.[20] Diversion (measured as the difference between what was supposed to be allocated and what was received by the targeted population) is estimated to be around 38 percent in Zambia (Mason and Jayne 2013). The leaked subsidies primarily end up being sold on commercial markets. Because the targeted groups of these transfers are small-scale farmers, this level of corruption has a huge impact on aggregate pro-poor spending.

The conventional wisdom is that scaling back in-kind subsidies is damaging politically; the flip side of this is the belief that establishing or scaling up such subsidies is politically beneficial. Evidence from Malawi suggests that the Farm Input Subsidy Program substantially increased support for Bingu wa Mutharika and his Democratic Progressive Party (DPP) in the 2009 election (Dionne and Horowitz 2016). In Zambia, the quantity of subsidized fertilizer received by constituencies increased with the ruling party's margin of victory in that constituency (Jayne et al. 2016). However, in Ghana and Kenya, such programs seemed to disproportionately go to areas with more opposition supporters in the last presidential election (Jayne et al. 2016).

When designed to target productivity, these programs may end up excluding poor farmers. Village chiefs in Malawi and Tanzania target households that have demonstrated higher returns to farm inputs, resulting in an allocation that is more productively efficient but less pro-poor (Basurto, Dupas, and Robinson 2017; Giné et al. 2017).

Widespread anecdotal reports suggest that governments and fertilizer import companies may collude to overbill the cost of delivering fertilizer to designated supply points. The price differential between the retail fertilizer price and the world market price (the fertilizer retail-import price gap) is negatively correlated with measures of government effectiveness (Shimeles, Gurara, and Birhanu Tessema 2015). Average retail prices of urea (the largest volume fertilizer product) in Malawi, Tanzania, and Zambia reveal a substantial gap compared with the free-on-board price (box 6.5).

Reforms to Increase Subsidy Efficiency

Given the politics of farm input subsidies and the laudable objectives of farm productivity and food security, it is plausible to assume that African governments will continue to run input subsidy programs for some time to come. Still, these programs can be made more efficient through a number of steps. Some are simply a matter of continuing current actions in certain countries, while others entail larger changes that require some piloting before full implementation could occur.

Regarding market factors, to start with, the public sector needs to make fertilizer use more profitable for farmers and thereby raise effective commercial demand. This would involve identifying how to streamline costs and reduce risks in fertilizer supply chains to reduce the farmgate price of fertilizer (as discussed, for example, in Jayne, Wanzala, and Demeke [2003]). Curbing the anticompetitive conduct of global and regional fertilizer suppliers that keep prices high is also a priority

BOX 6.5 Fertilizer markets are often not competitive

In more than half the African countries, one fertilizer supplier holds more than 50 percent of the market. The fertilizer industry is conducive to cartelization because the essential mined inputs—potassium and phosphorus—come from only a few countries and are supplied by few companies (World Bank Group and ACF 2016).

Take the case of southern and eastern African countries: only a few large firms, led by Yara, dominate fertilizer supply in the region. Explicit collusive arrangements between these suppliers and higher levels of concentration lead to higher fertilizer prices. This in turn contributes to making fertilizer unprofitable (Harou et al. 2017) and results in higher food prices. Nearly 50 percent of the rise in food prices during the 2007–08 food crisis was due to the overcharge in the fertilizer markets caused by fertilizer cartels (Gnutzmann and Spiewanowski 2016).

The potential impact of the fertilizer cartels has been detected in Malawi, Tanzania, and Zambia (the region's three biggest spenders on fertilizer), where fertilizer costs substantially exceed world prices. Although world prices (free-on-board basis in the Arab Gulf states) started dropping in November 2011, the prices in these African countries did not decline until later (figure B6.5.1).

On the technical side, fertilizer subsidies have crowded out other public investments that have proved more cost-effective. Scaling back subsidy programs to redirect more resources into other agricultural interventions is worth considering. Investments in irrigation and improved seeds to boost yields have proved more cost-effective than subsidies for raising smallholder crop productivity—and may raise the efficiency of fertilizer use. Farmer training and education programs to promote better management and soil fertility improvement practices could also improve the efficiency of fertilizer use.

In Zambia, for instance, the Competition and Consumer Protection Commission uncovered the collusive agreement between two firms before 2013. Prices started to come down in 2014 and 2015 only after a new firm entered and changes were made in the procurement processes that had undermined new entrants' ability to bid to supply the government's farmer support program. Tackling collusion in Zambia has already led to savings of US$21 million per year. Removing regulatory restrictions that inhibit entry, competitive public procurement, market intelligence to detect competition issues, and global antitrust enforcement in the fertilizer industry are critical to curb export cartels.

FIGURE B6.5.1 African and world urea prices show a large gap

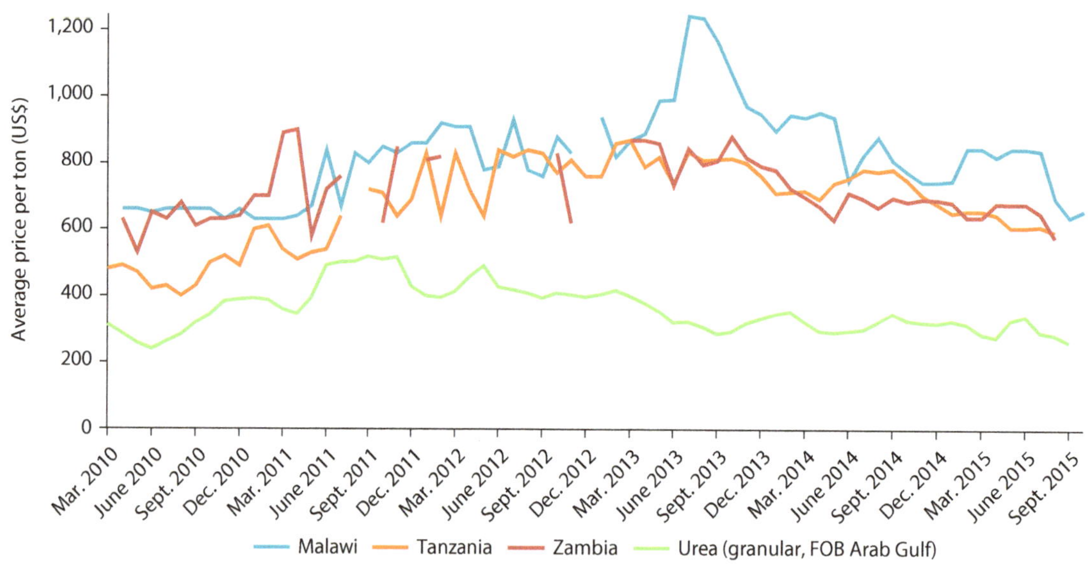

Source: Roberts 2017.
Note: FOB = free on board.

(box 6.5). High fertilizer prices undermine agricultural production and are one explanation for high food prices in African cities. Effective regional institutions are required to discipline market power. Cartels that operate across countries are not necessarily evident to individual governments. For example, market sharing arrangements for sales across a group of countries will only be readily apparent if data on sales and marketing strategies are obtained for the countries together.

Another way to reduce costs is to increase private sector participation in fertilizer retail. Shifting some of the administrative burdens of running these programs (such as the storage, bagging, inland transport, and retail distribution) from the government to the private sector may bring important cost savings. Private sector participation could be encouraged by providing flexible input vouchers (FIVs) redeemable at any private retail store. An example would be an FIV program to enable beneficiaries to redeem their subsidies for the input mix that best meets their needs instead of for a predefined package of inputs (Ricker-Gilbert 2016). Another variant would be an e-voucher such as the ones that already exist in Nigeria or have been recently piloted in Malawi and Zambia. Use of an e-voucher with FIVs could help ensure accountability and swift repayment for products from the government to private sector retailers.

Governments also need to confront and tackle the problem of diversion of subsidy program fertilizer by authorities. Many subsidy programs in Africa seem to suffer from underreporting or hiding of program costs. Some governments do not publish the fiscal costs of their farm subsidy programs. Others report the budgeted costs but not ex post expenditures, which have been found to be substantially higher in some cases.

Transparency and reduced elite capture will critically depend on how beneficiaries are selected. Serious challenges are associated with identifying the beneficiaries to be targeted by fertilizer subsidy programs using various means of targeting (Ricker-Gilbert 2016). When village voucher committees targeted recipients in Tanzania, for example, the distribution of vouchers was not better than what uniform or random allocation of vouchers would have yielded (or even worse in some respects) despite the substantial efforts and costs involved compared with random targeting (Pan and Christiaensen 2012).

Ghana's input subsidy program moved in 2010 from a targeted voucher program, similar to Malawi's Farm Input Subsidy Program (FISP), to a universal input subsidy program. Under Ghana's current "waybill system," any smallholder who registers with a private input supplier is eligible to receive a subsidy for fertilizer and seed. This system moves the administrative burden of the program from the government to the private sector. The government's role in Ghana's subsidy program is only to approve the transfer and reimburse the private sector (Resnick and Mather 2016). Though there are still issues with corruption under the waybill, the administrative costs of any universal subsidy program may be lower than under a targeted program because the costs of identifying "eligible" beneficiaries are eliminated. At the same time, however, nonpoor households will be benefiting.

In terms of form, there are good reasons to have an in-kind subsidy in agriculture instead of cash, whether delivered through an e-voucher or in-kind paper. For some countries, whose input markets are yet to be well developed, an in-kind voucher system (or, equivalently, an e-voucher) could provide private input suppliers with predictable demand every year. In theory, welfare gains for the rural poor in Malawi would be larger if the subsidy were distributed in cash rather than in kind (Dabalen et al. 2017). Another approach is to combine fertilizer programs with cash transfers to exploit potential complementarities, as found in Malawi (Pace et al. 2018).

Boosting Pro-Poor Spending within Sectors

Certainly, increased government spending on sectors that are critical for the poor—such as agriculture, WASH, education, health, and safety net systems—is part of the solution. However, at the same time, current spending could be made more impactful for the poor. The spending in these sectors underperforms for the poor in two dimensions: within-sector allocations and productivity of spending.

Within-Sector Spending

Within-sector spending is not neutral regarding the poor and nonpoor. In agriculture, chapter 3 highlighted the importance of staple crop productivity and the important remaining role for public spending on public goods (in agriculture and rural infrastructure) to raise it.

In education, inequality in public sector spending in Africa is common and means that children from wealthier households benefit more from public resources allocated to education. This results from two channels: First, children from poor households are less likely to attend postprimary schools for which per pupil spending is higher (Darvas et al. 2017). Second, within school levels, more public resources go to schools in wealthier, often urban, areas (Bashir et al. 2018). This is, in some cases, because of horizontal imbalances in funding resulting from decentralization of service delivery. Partly this reflects the fact that teacher salaries are by far the largest category of public expenditures on schooling. The distribution of teachers, especially trained and experienced ones, is biased toward urban schools, leaving rural schools with higher pupil-teacher ratios. Also, urban public schools have better infrastructure and learning materials.

In health, government expenditures are skewed toward tertiary services. In the Democratic Republic of Congo, 87 percent of government health expenditure was focused on hospitals, used disproportionately by the wealthy (Barroy et al. 2014). The unequitable spending relates to both staffing and nonstaff costs. Again, in the Democratic Republic of Congo, the modest operating budget almost entirely goes to hospitals. Though hospitals can presumably help people avoid large health costs and income shocks, evidence suggests this spending is off-target from a poverty perspective.

Capital investments in both education and health services need to be rebalanced toward primary education and care, which are usually more cost-effective. Public investments in curative care are especially regressive, driven by the lower use of such services by the poor (Castro-Leal et al. 2000). Lower usage is attributed to several factors, including the perceptions of poor households about illness as well as low access and quality of services for poor households.

Productivity of Spending

Spending more on services that are needed and used more by the poor does not necessarily imply the spending is effective. The effectiveness of spending is as important as its magnitude, but the quality of public schooling, health care, and other service provision is generally low, even when adjusted for spending levels.

One measure of efficiency of spending (broadly) is evidence of an early-grade bulge. This is swollen enrollments, particularly in grade one, with much smaller enrollments in the upper-primary grades. It is attributed to the enrollment of overage and underage children in grade one, high official repetition rates, and high dropout rates between grades one and two. The bottom-left quadrant of figure 6.12 shows those countries that have a current high level of this bulge and it has gotten worse. Beyond primary education, there are large inefficiencies in secondary education spending in Africa—the largest being in low-income countries where the consequences are arguably greatest in terms of poverty reduction (Grigoli 2015). Globally, health care systems in Africa are the least efficient, and this is also the region with the neediest people (Sun et al. 2017).

In agriculture, ample evidence shows that rebalancing the composition of public agriculture spending in Africa could reap massive payoffs for reducing poverty and increasing agricultural productivity. Although studies often show low returns to spending in the sector, specific types of spending (such as investments in core public goods related to R&D,

FIGURE 6.12 Inefficiency in the primary years of education remains a challenge for many African countries

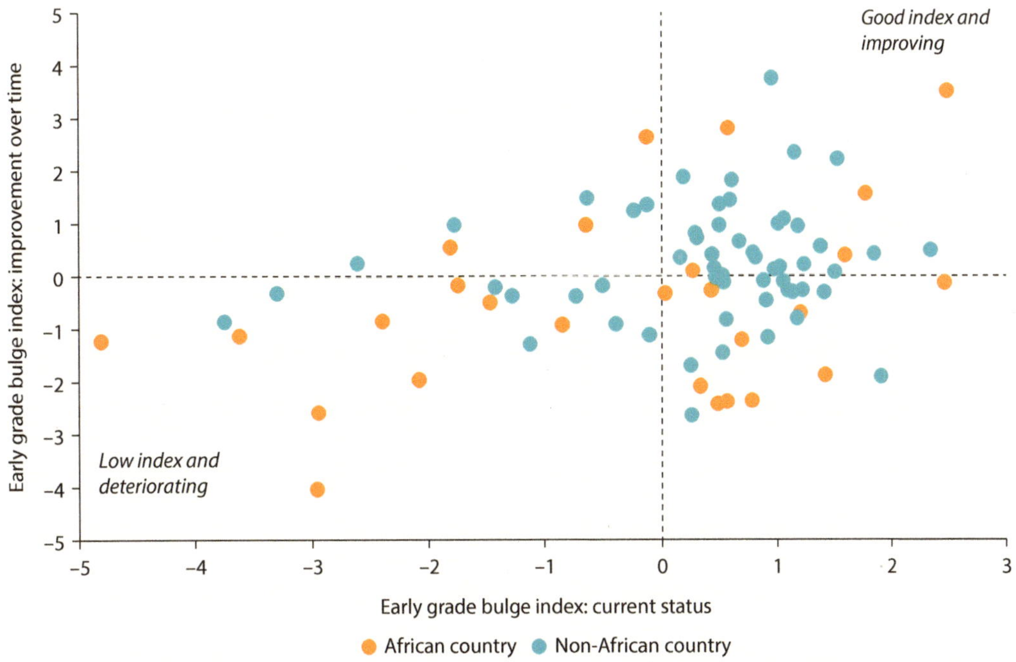

Source: Bashir et al. 2018.
Note: The value of the index is the standardized predicted score estimated after applying factor analysis to four indicators: the gross intake ratio in grade one, the enrollment ratio in grade one, the ratio of grade two to grade one enrollment, and the gross enrollment ratio in preprimary education. Values over zero indicate better progression, and values under zero indicate lower progression, respectively, in the early grades. Figure shows improvement over a 35-year period.

technology generation and diffusion, and market links) yield high returns for productivity. The inevitable conclusion is that choices about how to allocate public agriculture spending matter significantly (see the detailed discussion in Goyal and Nash [2017]).

Inefficient spending on services manifests in several ways. When public teachers and doctors shirk and do not show up for work, children learn less and get sick more often (Duflo, Dupas, and Kremer 2015). Absenteeism is rife among teachers in public primary schools in Africa (much less so in private schools). Over 40 percent of the teachers were not in the classroom teaching during random unannounced spot checks in Kenya, Mozambique, Tanzania, and Uganda (table 6.1). Similar problems plague public health services. Clinicians in Senegal spend an average of 39 minutes per day counseling patients, while in Tanzania the number is even lower, at just half an hour (World Bank 2013a, 2013b).

TABLE 6.1 Service providers are often absent at schools and health clinics in Africa
Percent

Country and year of data	Classroom teacher absence rate	Health worker absence rate
Kenya (2012)	42	29
Madagascar (2016)	38	27
Mozambique (2014)	56	—
Niger (2015)	27	33
Nigeria (2013)	19	—
Senegal (2012)	29	20
Tanzania (2014)	47	14
Togo (2013)	34	—
Uganda (2013)	52	—

Source: World Bank Service Delivery Indicators country reports, http://www.sdindicators.org.
Note: — = not available.

Wage disparities between the public and private sectors may also suggest less value for a given level of spending. Public sector teachers in Kenya earn 50 percent more than their private sector counterparts at the same level of skills and experience (Barton, Bold, and Sandefur 2017). The misallocation of teachers and health workers can exacerbate inefficient spending. When teachers or health workers are not deployed effectively, some schools or health clinics are overstaffed when others are understaffed.

Poor quality of services is not just about absenteeism and the deployment of staff. Public health staff may either lack the knowledge and skills necessary to provide quality public services or fail to apply them when required. In Tanzania, 28 percent of doctors perform no physical examination of the average patient, and only just over half of health providers could correctly diagnose malaria—despite malaria being endemic. Similarly, more than two-thirds of Senegalese and Tanzanian clinicians could not correctly diagnose diarrhea with severe dehydration. Surveys of civil servants in Ethiopia, Ghana, and Nigeria (among other countries) show that officers have limited access to infrastructure to aid them in their daily duties (Rogger 2017).

And, of course, services require more than human resources. However, spending money on more inputs does not necessarily solve the problem. For example, in Sierra Leone, buying more textbooks did not have an impact on learning; many schools stored the books instead of distributing them (Sabarwal, Evans, and Marshak 2014). Primary health clinics need basic equipment and infrastructure to be impactful. In rural Uganda, teachers reported through scorecards that lack of staff housing was the root cause of their absenteeism. Monitoring teachers' housing (which at the time was monitored by only 17 percent of schools) as opposed to teacher absenteeism shifted a co-responsible dynamic (Barr et al. 2012).

Approaches to Improve Spending Allocation and Productivity

There is no single solution to mistargeted resources and the poor quality of services, but several approaches can be identified. Improved financial accountability is one avenue in health (CMI 2008) and in education (Hubbard 2007). Other avenues to improve pro-poor investments include better financial management, results-based financing approaches, private provision, decentralization, better inputs and support to civil servants, and information and social accountability. Many of these have been detailed in other reports (for example, see the discussion in de la Brière et al. [2017]). Technology also can serve an important role (see Fundamentals 3, "Leapfrogging with Technology (and Trade)").

There is a role for providing information to the poor to improve service delivery (known as a client empowerment approach or social accountability).[21] How exactly information should be disseminated to improve politicians' actions is less evident, but some commonalities are informing the public how services perform in their community relative to others and enabling and incentivizing citizens to actively monitor service providers. Regarding the latter, higher-tier officers could signal, for example, that such inputs from local citizens would be taken seriously to hold frontline officials accountable for service delivery at the last mile.

Despite enthusiasm among some that bottom-up pressure can significantly contribute to address these problems, others are doubtful and stress the need for top-down solutions (Booth 2012). Public information and additional transparency in some circumstances might even induce stronger patronage systems and worse service delivery than private information sharing with leaders (Hoogeveen 2013).

Several civic education and information experiments and campaigns have shown results. In western Kenya, some primary schools randomly obtained funds to hire an additional contract teacher, and parents (school management committees) received information on how to hire and monitor the teacher (Duflo, Dupas, and Kremer 2015). In those schools that received both an additional teacher and school-based management training, teachers were less absent, and children displayed higher test scores.

In Uganda, families received report cards containing baseline information on the quality of health services in their communities. Those cards were used at subsequent meetings between the community and the health care providers to design an action plan to monitor and improve service quality (Björkman and Svensson 2009). This combination of relevant information and local monitoring improved the performance of health workers and was highly successful in reducing child mortality.

In Mali, civic education about budget size and mandated responsibilities of government officials along with additional information on the local government's performance relative to neighboring governments led to more citizen participation at community meetings (Gottlieb 2016).

Although successful community accountability efforts may be driven by social sanctions by community members toward local civil servants (Bold, Molina, and Safir 2017), there may be other mechanisms at play. In Uganda, an information campaign on capitation grants served as a signal from higher-tier ministries to lower-level officials that they were being monitored and would be held accountable for leakages.

Local involvement or greater access to information alone may not suffice. Greater community participation did not suffice without the score reports in Uganda, nor did hiring a teacher occur in the Kenya experiment without the school-based management training information. In Benin, schools in villages with greater radio access enjoyed neither greater government inputs (such as teachers or books), nor more-responsive service providers (lower teacher absenteeism), nor more active parent-teacher associations (Keefer and Khemani 2014).

And vested interests can thwart reforms. In the teacher-hiring experiment in Kenya, efforts by the government to implement the contract teacher program could not be effectively implemented through the public sector, partly because of the political power of the teachers' unions in thwarting program implementation. How best to improve efficiency in spending remains an exigent space for further experimentation and learning.

Notes

1. See also the World Bank and International Monetary Fund Development Committee document, "From Billions to Trillions: Transforming Development Finance" (World Bank and IMF 2015).
2. On the downside, the APG does not provide a direct estimate of the amount of public investments and support needed to strengthen the earnings capacity of the poor today and thus of their children in the future (through human capital investment today), nor of the amount needed to prevent those close to the poverty line from falling back. Still, it is a frequent starting point for considering a country's poverty financing needs and whether it has, in principle, the domestic means to meet them. For applications of this method, see, for example, Chandy, Noe, and Zhang (2016); Olinto et al. (2013); Ravallion (2009); and Sumner (2012).
3. Another approach is to estimate the impact from redistributing the income from a country's billionaires to the poor, which is found to have a modest impact on the rate of poverty for countries in the region (Chandy, Noe, and Zhang 2016).
4. We lack estimates of aid inflows from international charities, international nongovernmental organizations, and private donations.
5. ODA data from the OECD Development Assistance Committee (DAC) database.
6. Between 2010 and 2017, seven countries accounted for more than three-fourths of the total African bond debt issued: Angola, Côte d'Ivoire, Ghana, Kenya, Nigeria, South Africa, and Zambia (World Bank 2017).
7. Seventeen countries have an IMF Extended Credit Facility and/or Extended Fund Facility (Benin, Burkina Faso, Cameroon, the Central African Republic, Chad, Côte d'Ivoire, Gabon, Ghana, Guinea, Guinea-Bissau, Madagascar, Mali, Mauritania, Niger, São Tomé and Príncipe, Sierra Leone, and Togo). Two countries have IMF Stand-By Agreement and/or Stand-By Credit Facility (Kenya and Rwanda).
8. However, governments do not increase spending as much as is needed in the aftermath of a disaster (see chapter 5).
9. For a discussion about how, when, and why poverty can be a priority in the national budget, see Foster et al. (2003), which summarizes five relevant African country case studies.

10. Regions are UN SDG regions: https://unstats.un.org/sdgs/indicators/regional-groups/.
11. Note that the FI calculation holds in the aggregate; those who benefit and those who pay may not be the same poor or vulnerable individuals.
12. The FI index estimates the net losses experienced by those who are "postfiscal" poor, or those who would be classified as poor given their CEQ consumable income levels. The "fiscal gains to the poor" (FGP) index, meanwhile, estimates the net gains experienced by those who are "prefiscal" poor, or those who would be classified as poor given their CEQ market income levels.
13. To repeat: we refer here to individuals' cash-based financial position in terms of purchasing power, and we are not including the value of in-kind benefits like education, health, or infrastructure services.
14. First, a corporation working in a low- or middle-income country sets up a subsidiary in a tax haven. Second, it sells its product at an artificially low price to this subsidiary—enabling it to declare minimal profits and consequently pay very little tax to the government of the low- or middle-income country. Third, its subsidiary in the tax haven sells the product at the market price—for comparatively huge profits coupled with a low tax rate (or none at all). In other words, corporations are manipulating prices to pay minimal taxes, which, among other things, causes low- to middle-income countries to annually lose three times more revenue to tax havens than they receive in foreign aid (Mosselmans 2014).
15. See "Global Forum on Transparency and Exchange of Information for Tax Purposes," Tax Topics, OECD: https://www.oecd.org/tax/transparency/.
16. See "Base Erosion and Profit Shifting," Tax Topics, OECD: https://www.oecd.org/tax/beps/.
17. For a set of principles and policy options on taxation of and revenue collection from natural resources, see NRGI (2014).
18. Better spending for the poor also relates to finding the right sources of financing—including "crowding in" private sector finance and public-private partnerships (often in infrastructure)—to enable governments to allocate more resources to pro-poor investments.
19. Farm input subsidies, particularly on inorganic fertilizer, have been justified on the basis that soil nutrients, particularly nitrogen, are essential for maize production and that most smallholders lack the cash resources or access to credit that would enable them to purchase inorganic fertilizer at commercial market prices.
20. Studies on the impact of elite capture include programs in Tanzania by Pan and Christiaensen (2012); in Malawi by Kilic, Whitney, and Winters (2015); and in Nigeria by Liverpool-Tasie (2014).
21. The Global Partnership for Social Accountability program identifies the following as the key social accountability activities or approaches: budget literacy campaigns, citizen charters, citizen report cards, community contracting, community management or contracting, community oversight, community scorecards, grievance redress mechanisms, independent budget analysis, and participatory budgeting, among others. Devarajan and Khemani (2018) discuss the role of civil society in overcoming government failures such as the ones described here.

References

Abdulai, Abdul-Gafaru, Imran Aziz, Catherine Blampied, Soumya Chattopadhyay, Christine Ellison, Romilly Greenhill, Adam Salifu, and Rachel Thompson. 2018. "Leaving No One Behind in the Health and Education Sectors: An SDG Stock Take in Ghana." Research report, Overseas Development Institute (ODI), London.

ActionAid. 2010. "Calling Time: Why SABMiller Should Stop Dodging Taxes in Africa." Report, ActionAid UK, London.

Ali, Merima, Odd-Helge Fjeldstad, and Ingrid Hoem Sjursen. 2014. "To Pay or Not to Pay? Citizens' Attitudes toward Taxation in Kenya, Tanzania, Uganda, and South Africa." *World Development* 64: 828–42.

APP (Africa Progress Panel). 2013. *Africa Progress Report 2013. Equity in Extractives: Stewarding Africa's Natural Resources for All.* Geneva: APP.

Asiedu, Edward, Chuqiao Bi, Dan Pavelesku, Ryoko Sato, and Tomomi Tanaka. 2017. "Income Tax Collection and Noncompliance in Ghana." Ghana Policy Brief, World Bank, Washington, DC.

Barr, Abigail, Lawrence Bategeka, Madina Guloba, Ibrahim Kasirye, Frederick Mugisha, Pieter Serneels, and Andrew Zeitlin. 2012. "Management and Motivation in Ugandan Primary Schools: An Impact Evaluation Report." Working Papers PIERI 2012-14, Policy Impact Evaluation Research Initiative, Partnership for Economic Policy, Nairobi, Kenya.

Barroy, Helene, Francoise Andre, Serge Mayaka, and Hadia Samaha. 2014. "Investing in Universal Health Coverage: Opportunities and Challenges for Health Financing in the Democratic Republic of Congo." 2014 Health Expenditure Review, Report No. 103444, World Bank, Washington, DC.

Barton, Nicholas, Tessa Bold, and Justin Sandefur. 2017. "The Public-Private Sector Wage Gap: Evidence from Kenyan Teachers." Paper presented at the Centre for the Study of African Economies (CSAE) Conference 2017, "Economic Development in Africa," University of Oxford, March 19–21.

Bashir, Sajitha, Marlaine Lockheed, Elizabeth Ninan, and Jee-Peng Tan. 2018. *Facing Forward: Schooling for Learning in Africa*. Africa Development Forum Series. Washington, DC: World Bank.

Bastagli, Francesca. 2016. "Bringing Taxation into Social Protection Analysis and Planning." Guidance Note, Overseas Development Institute (ODI), London.

Basurto, Pia M., Pascaline Dupas, and Jonathan Robinson. 2017. "Decentralization and Efficiency of Subsidy Targeting: Evidence from Chiefs in Rural Malawi." NBER Working Paper 23383, National Bureau of Economic Research, Cambridge, MA.

Beegle, Kathleen, Luc Christiaensen, Andrew Dabalen, and Isis Gaddis. 2016. *Poverty in a Rising Africa*. Washington, DC: World Bank.

Beegle, Kathleen, Aline Coudouel, and Emma Monsalve, eds. 2018. *Realizing the Full Potential of Social Safety Nets in Sub-Saharan Africa*. Washington, DC: World Bank.

Björkman, Martina, and Jakob Svensson. 2009. "Power to the People: Evidence from a Randomized Field Experiment on Community-Based Monitoring in Uganda." *Quarterly Journal of Economics* 124 (2): 735–69.

Bolch, Kimberly Blair, Lidia Ceriani, and Luis Felipe López-Calva. 2017. "Arithmetics and Politics of Domestic Resource Mobilization." Policy Research Working Paper 8029, World Bank, Washington, DC.

Bold, Tessa, Ezequiel Molina, and Abla Safir. 2017. "Clientelism in the Public Sector: Why Public Service Reforms May Not Succeed and What to Do About It." Background paper for *World Development Report 2017: Governance and the Law*, World Bank, Washington, DC.

Booth, David. 2012. "Working with the Grain and Swimming against the Tide: Barriers to Uptake of Research Findings on Governance and Public Services in Low-Income Africa." *Public Management Review* 14 (2): 163–80.

Briggs, Ryan C. 2018. "Poor Targeting: A Gridded Spatial Analysis of the Degree to Which Aid Reaches the Poor in Africa." *World Development* 103: 133–48.

Burke, William J., T. S. Jayne, and Roy Black. 2012. "Getting More 'Bang for the Buck': Diversifying Subsidies Beyond Fertilizer and Policy Beyond Subsidies." Food Security Research Project Policy Synthesis No. 52, Michigan State University, East Lansing.

Castro-Leal, Florencia, Julia Dayton, Lionel Demery, and Kalpana Mehra. 2000. "Public Spending on Health Care in Africa: Do the Poor Benefit?" *Bulletin of the World Health Organization* 78 (1): 66–74.

Chandy, Laurence, Lorenz Noe, and Christine Zhang. 2016. "The Global Poverty Gap Is Falling. Billionaires Could Help Close It." *Up Front* (blog), Brookings Institution, January 20. https://www.brookings.edu/blog/up-front/2016/01/20/the-global-poverty-gap-is-falling-billionaires-could-help-close-it/.

Christian Aid. 2014. "Africa Rising? Inequalities and the Essential Role of Fair Taxation." Report, Christian Aid, London; Tax Justice Network Africa, Nairobi.

CMI (Chr. Michelsen Institute). 2008. "Corruption in the Health Sector." U4 Issue 2008:10, U4 Anti-Corruption Resource Centre, CMI, Bergen, Norway.

Coady, David P., Valentina Flamini, and Louis Sears. 2015. "The Unequal Benefits of Fuel Subsidies Revisited: Evidence for Developing Countries." IMF Working Paper 15/20, International Monetary Fund.

Coady, David, I. Parry, Louis Sears, and B. Shang. 2017. "How Large Are Global Fossil Fuel Subsidies?" *World Development* 91: 11–27.

Cobham, Alex. 2005. "Tax Evasion, Tax Avoidance and Development Finance." Queen Elizabeth House Working Papers QEHWPS129, Oxford Department of International Development, University of Oxford.

Cobham, Alex, and Petr Janský. 2017. "Global Distribution of Revenue Loss from Tax Avoidance." United Nations University World Institute for Development Economics Research (UNU-WIDER) Working Paper 2017/55, UNU-WIDER, Helsinki, Finland.

Cobham, Alex, and Simon Loretz. 2014. "International Distribution of the Corporate Tax Base: Implications of Different Apportionment Factors Under Unitary Taxation." ICTD Working Paper 27, International Centre for Tax and Development, Brighton, U.K.

Crivelli, Ernesto, Ruud de Mooij, and Michael Keen. 2016. "Base Erosion, Profit Shifting and Developing Countries." *FinanzArchiv: Public Finance Analysis* 72 (3): 268–301.

Dabalen, Andrew, Alejandro de la Fuente, Aparajita Goyal, Wendy Karamba, Nga Thi Viet Nguyen, and Tomomi Tanaka. 2017. *Pathways to Prosperity in Rural Malawi.* Directions in Development Series. Washington, DC: World Bank.

Darvas, Peter, Shang Gao, Yijun Shen, and Bilal Bawany. 2017. *Sharing Higher Education's Promise beyond the Few in Sub-Saharan Africa.* Directions in Development Series. Washington, DC: World Bank.

de la Brière, Bénédicte, Deon Filmer, Dena Ringold, Dominic Rohner, Karelle Samuda, and Anastasiya Denisova. 2017. *From Mines and Wells to Well-Built Minds: Turning Sub-Saharan Africa's Natural Resource Wealth into Human Capital.* Directions in Development Series. Washington, DC: World Bank.

de la Fuente, Alejandro, Jon Jellema, and Nora Lustig. 2018. "Fiscal Policy in Africa: Welfare Impacts and Policy Effectiveness." Background paper for *Accelerating Poverty Reduction in Africa*, World Bank, Washington, DC.

Demery, Lionel. 2003. "Analyzing the Incidence of Public Spending." In *The Impact of Economic Policies on Poverty and Income Distribution: Evaluation Techniques and Tools*, edited by Bourguignon François and Luis A. Pereira da Silva, 41–68. Washington, DC: World Bank.

Devarajan, Shantayanan, and Stuti Khemani. 2018. "If Politics Is the Problem, How Can External Actors Be Part of the Solution?" In *Institutions, Governance and the Control of Corruption*, edited by Kaushik Basu and Tito Cordella, 209–51. Cham, Switzerland: Palgrave Macmillan.

DFI (Development Finance International) and Oxfam. 2015. "Financing the Sustainable Development Goals: Lessons from Government Spending on the MDGs." Government Spending Watch 2015 Report, DFI and Oxfam, London.

DI (Development Initiatives). 2015. "Investments to End Poverty 2015: Meeting the Challenge: Reducing Poverty to Zero." Report of the Investments to End Poverty program, DFI, Bristol, U.K.

Dionne, Kim Yi, and Jeremy Horowitz. 2016. "The Political Effects of Agricultural Subsidies in Africa: Evidence from Malawi." *World Development* 87: 215–26.

Dom, Roel. 2017. "Semi-Autonomous Revenue Authorities in Sub-Saharan Africa: Silver Bullet or White Elephant?" CREDIT Research Paper 17/01, Centre for Research in Economic Development and International Trade, University of Nottingham, U.K.

Duflo, Esther, Pascaline Dupas, and Michael Kremer. 2015. "School Governance, Teacher Incentives, and Pupil-Teacher Ratios: Experimental Evidence from Kenyan Primary Schools." *Journal of Public Economics* 123: 92–110.

Enami, Ali. 2018. "Measuring the Effectiveness of Taxes and Transfers in Fighting Inequality and Poverty." In *Commitment to Equity Handbook: Estimating the Impact of Fiscal Policy on Inequality and Poverty*, edited by Nora Lustig, 207–18. Washington, DC: Brookings Institution Press and the Commitment to Equity (CEQ) Institute at Tulane University.

Eozenou, Patrick Hoang-Vu, and Parendi Mehta. 2016. "Health Risk in Sub-Saharan Africa." Background paper for *Accelerating Poverty Reduction in Africa*, World Bank, Washington, DC.

Feltenstein, Andrew. 2017. "Subsidy Reforms and Implications for Social Protection: An Analysis of IMF Advice on Food and Fuel Subsidies." Background paper BP/17-01/02, Independent Evaluation Office of the International Monetary Fund, Washington, DC.

Fjeldstad, Odd-Helge. 2014. "Tax and Development: Donor Support to Strengthen

Tax Systems in Developing Countries." *Public Administration and Development* 34 (3): 182–93.

Fjeldstad, Odd-Helge, and Kari Heggstad. 2012. *Building Taxpayer Culture in Mozambique, Tanzania and Zambia: Achievements, Challenges and Policy Recommendations*. CMI Report R 2012:1. Bergen, Norway: Chr. Michelsen Institute.

Forstater, Maya. 2018. "Tax and Development: New Frontiers of Research and Action." CGD Policy Paper 118, Center for Global Development, Washington, DC.

Foster, Mick, Adrian Fozzard, Felix Naschold, and Tim Conway. 2003. "How, When and Why Does Poverty Get Budget Priority: Poverty Reduction Strategy and Public Expenditure in Five African Countries, Synthesis Paper." ODI Working Paper 168, Overseas Development Institute, London.

Fuchs, A., Giselle Del Carmen, and Alfred Kechia Mukong. 2018. "Long-Run Impacts of Increasing Tobacco Taxes: Evidence from South Africa." Policy Research Working Paper 8369, World Bank, Washington, DC.

Fuest, Clemens, and Nadine Riedel. 2009. "Tax Evasion, Tax Avoidance and Tax Expenditures in Developing Countries: A Review of the Literature." Report prepared for the U.K. Department for International Development (DFID), Oxford University Centre for Business and Taxation, Oxford, U.K.

Fuglie, Keith, and Nicholas Rada. 2013. "Resources, Policies, and Agricultural Productivity in Sub-Saharan Africa." Economic Research Report No. 145, Economic Research Service, U.S. Department of Agriculture, Washington, DC.

Gaspar, Vitor, Laura Jaramillo, and Philippe Wingender. 2016. "Tax Capacity and Growth: Is There a Tipping Point?" IMF Working Paper WP/16/234, International Monetary Fund, Washington, DC.

Giné, Xavier, Shreena Patel, Bernardo Ribeiro, and Ildrim Valley. 2017. "Targeting Inputs: Experimental Evidence from Tanzania." Unpublished working paper, World Bank, Washington, DC.

Gnutzmann, Hinnerk, and Piotr Spiewanowski. 2016. "Fertilizer Fuels Food Prices: Identification through the Oil-Gas Spread." Unpublished working paper, Leibniz Universität Hannover, Germany.

Goodfellow, Tom, and Olly Owen. 2018. "Taxation, Property Rights and the Social Contract in Lagos." ICTD working paper, International Centre for Tax and Development, Brighton, U.K.

Gottlieb, Jessica. 2016. "Greater Expectations? A Field Experiment to Improve Accountability in Mali." *American Journal of Political Science* 60 (1): 143–57.

Goyal, Aparajita, and John Nash. 2017. *Reaping Richer Returns: Public Spending for African Agriculture Productivity Growth*. Africa Development Forum Series. Washington, DC: World Bank.

Greenhill, Romilly, Paddy Carter, Chris Hoy, and Marcus Manuel. 2015. "Financing the Future: How International Public Finance Should Fund a Global Social Compact to Eradicate Poverty." Development Progress Report, Centre for Aid and Public Expenditure, Overseas Development Institute (ODI), London.

Grigoli, Francesco. 2015. "A Hybrid Approach to Estimating the Efficiency of Public Spending on Education in Emerging and Developing Economies." *Applied Economics and Finance* 2 (1): 19–32.

Gupta, Sanjeev, Marjin Verhoeven, and Erwin R. Tiongson. 2003. "Public Spending on Health Care and the Poor." *Health Economics* 12 (8): 685–96.

Guttmacher Institute. 2017. "Adding It Up: Investing in Contraception and Maternal and Newborn Health 2017." Fact sheet, Guttmacher Institute, New York.

Harou, Aurélie P., Yanyan Liu, Christopher B. Barrett, and Liangzhi You. 2017. "Variable Returns to Fertiliser Use and the Geography of Poverty: Experimental and Simulation Evidence from Malawi." *Journal of African Economies* 26 (3): 342–71.

Harris, Tom, David Phillips, Ross Warwick, Maya Goldman, Jon Jellema, Karolina Goraus, and Gabriela Inchauste. 2018. "Redistribution via VAT and Cash Transfers: An Assessment in Four Low and Middle-Income Countries." Working Paper W18/11, Institute for Fiscal Studies, London.

Higgins, Sean, and Nora Lustig. 2016. "Can a Poverty-Reducing and Progressive Tax and Transfer System Hurt the Poor?" *Journal of Development Economics* 122 (September): 63–75.

Hoogeveen, Johannes. 2013. "Will Public Access to Information Really Lead to Better Public Services in Developing Countries?"

Unpublished paper, World Bank, Washington, DC.

Hubbard, Paul. 2007. "Putting the Power of Transparency in Context: Information's Role in Reducing Corruption in Uganda's Education Sector." CGD Working Paper 136, Center for Global Development, Washington, DC.

IMF (International Monetary Fund). 2012. "Fiscal Regimes for Extractive Industries: Design and Implementation." Policy paper, IMF, Washington, DC.

———. 2015. *Regional Economic Outlook: Sub-Saharan Africa. Dealing with the Gathering Clouds*. Washington, DC: IMF.

———. 2017. *Fiscal Monitor: Tackling Inequality*. Washington, DC: IMF.

Inchauste, Gabriela, and Nora Lustig, eds. 2017. *The Distributional Impact of Taxes and Transfers: Evidence from Eight Low- and Middle-Income Countries*. Washington, DC: World Bank.

Inchauste, Gabriela, and David G. Victor, eds. 2017. *The Political Economy of Energy Subsidy Reform*. Directions in Development Series. Washington, DC: World Bank.

Jayne, J. Govereh, M. Wanzala, and M. Demeke. 2003. "Fertilizer Market Development: A Comparative Analysis of Ethiopia, Kenya, and Zambia." *Agricultural, Food, and Resource Economics* 28 (4): 293–316.

Jayne, Thomas S., Nicole M. Mason, William J. Burke, and Joshua Ariga. 2016. "Agricultural Input Subsidy Programs in Africa: An Assessment of Recent Evidence." Feed the Future Innovation Lab for Food Security Policy Research Paper No. 29, Department of Agricultural, Food, and Resource Economics, Michigan State University, East Lansing.

Jibao, Samuel, and Wilson Prichard. 2016. "Rebuilding Local Government Finances After Conflict: Lessons from a Property Tax Reform Programme in Post-Conflict Sierra Leone." *Journal of Development Studies* 52 (12): 1759–75.

Johannesen, Niels, Thomas Tørsløv, and Ludvig Wier. 2016. "Are Less Developed Countries More Exposed to Multinational Tax Avoidance? Method and Evidence from Micro-Data." United Nations University World Institute for Development Economics Research (UNU-WIDER) Working Paper 2016/10, UNU-WIDER, Helsinki, Finland.

Johansson, Åsa, Øystein Bieltvedt Skeie, Stéphane Sorbe, and Carlo Menon. 2017. "Tax Planning by Multinational Firms." Organisation for Economic Co-operation and Development (OECD) Economics Working Paper No. 1355, OECD Publishing, Paris.

Joshi, Anuradha, and Joseph Ayee. 2009. "Autonomy or Organization? Reforms in the Ghanaian Internal Revenue Service." *Public Administration and Development* 29 (4): 289–302.

Junquera-Varela, Raul Felix, Marijn Verhoeven, Gangadhar P. Shukla, Bernard Haven, Rajul Awasthi, and Blanca Moreno-Dodson. 2017. *Strengthening Domestic Resource Mobilization: Moving from Theory to Practice in Low- and Middle-Income Countries*. Directions in Development Series. Washington, DC: World Bank.

Kangave, Jalia, Suzan Nakato, Ronald Waiswa, and Patrick Lumala Zzimbe. 2016. "Boosting Revenue Collection through Taxing High Net Worth Individuals: The Case of Uganda." ICTD Working Paper 45, International Centre for Tax and Development, Brighton, U.K.

Keefer, Philip, and Stuti Khemani. 2014. "Mass Media and Public Education: The Effects of Access to Community Radio in Benin." *Journal of Development Economics* 109: 57–72.

Keen, Michael. 2012. "Taxation and Development—Again." IMF Working Paper WP/12/220, International Monetary Fund, Washington, DC.

Keen, Michael, and Mario Mansour. 2010. "Revenue Mobilisation in Sub-Saharan Africa: Challenges from Globalisation II—Corporate Taxation." *Development Policy Review* 28 (September): 573–96.

Kilic, Talip, Edward Whitney, and Paul Winters. 2015. "Decentralized Beneficiary Targeting in Large-Scale Development Programs: Insights from the Malawi Farm Input Subsidy Program." *Journal of African Economies* 24 (1): 26–56.

Liverpool-Tasie, Lenis Saweda O. 2014. "Farmer Groups and Input Access: When Membership Is Not Enough." *Food Policy* 46: 37–49.

Lunduka, Rodney W., and Jacob Ricker-Gilbert. 2016. "The Contribution of Alternative Investments to the Subsidy Fertilizer to the Value of Agricultural Revenue in Smallholder Rural Farmers in Malawi." Technical report, World Bank, Washington, DC.

Lustig, Nora, ed. 2018. *Commitment to Equity Handbook: Estimating the Impact of Fiscal*

Policy on Inequality and Poverty. Washington, DC: Brookings Institution Press and the Commitment to Equity (CEQ) Institute at Tulane University.

Manuel, Marcus, Harsh Desai, Emma Samman, and Martin Evans. 2018. "Financing the End of Extreme Poverty." Research report, Overseas Development Institute (ODI), London.

Marenya, Paswel P., and Christopher B. Barrett. 2009. "State-Conditional Fertilizer Yield Response on Western Kenyan Farms." *American Journal of Agricultural Economics* 91 (4): 991–1006.

Marquez, Patricio V., and Jill L. Farrington. 2013. "The Challenge of Non-Communicable Diseases and Road Traffic Injuries in Sub-Saharan Africa." Report No. 79293, World Bank, Washington, DC.

Marquez, Patricio V., and Blanca Moreno-Dodson, eds. 2017. "Tobacco Tax Reform at the Crossroads of Health and Development: A Multisectoral Perspective." Report No. 12026, World Bank, Washington, DC.

Mascagni, Giulia, Christopher Nell, and Nara Monkam. 2017. "One Size Does Not Fit All: A Field Experiment on the Drivers of Tax Compliance and Delivery Methods in Rwanda." ICTD Working Paper 58, International Centre for Tax and Development, Brighton, U.K.

Mason, Nicole M., and T. S. Jayne. 2013. "Fertiliser Subsidies and Smallholder Commercial Fertiliser Purchases: Crowding Out, Leakage, and Policy Implications for Zambia." *Agricultural Economics* 64 (3): 558–82.

Mason, Nicole M., and Melinda Smale. 2013. "Impacts of Subsidized Hybrid Seed on Indicators of Economic Well-Being among Smallholder Maize Growers in Zambia." *Agricultural Economics* 44 (6): 659–70.

Mason, Nicole M., and Solomon T. Tembo. 2015. "Do Input Subsidy Programs Raise Incomes and Reduce Poverty among Smallholder Farm Households? Evidence from Zambia." Working Paper 92, Indaba Agricultural Policy Research Institute (IAPRI), Lusaka, Zambia.

Mawejje, Joseph, and Ibrahim Mike Okumu. 2016. "Tax Evasion and the Business Environment in Uganda." *South African Journal of Economics* 84 (3): 440–60.

McCluskey, R. 2016. "African Governments Aren't Taxing the Rich. Why They Should." *The Conversation* (blog), April 3. https://theconversation.com/african-governments-arent-taxing-the-rich-why-they-should-57162.

McNabb, Kyle, and Philippe LeMay-Boucher. 2014. "Tax Structures, Economic Growth and Development." International Centre for Tax and Development (ICTD) Working Paper 22, Institute of Development Studies, Brighton, U.K.

Moore, Mick, and Wilson Prichard. 2017. "How Can Governments of Low-Income Countries Collect More Tax Revenue?" Working Paper 70, International Centre for Tax and Development (ICTD), Brighton, U.K.

Mosselmans, Isabella. 2014. "Tax Evasion: The Main Cause of Global Poverty." *Africa at LSE* (blog), March 7. http://blogs.lse.ac.uk/africaatlse/2014/03/07/tax-evasion-the-main-cause-of-global-poverty/.

NRGI (Natural Resource Governance Institute). 2014. "Natural Resource Charter. 2nd ed." NRGI, New York.

OECD (Organisation for Economic Co-operation and Development). 2014. "Fragile States 2014: Domestic Revenue Mobilisation in Fragile States." Report, OECD, Paris.

———. 2017. *Revenue Statistics in Africa 1990–2015.* Paris: OECD.

Olinto, Pedro, Kathleen Beegle, Carlos Sobrado, and Hiroki Uematsu. 2013. "The State of the Poor: Where Are the Poor, Where Is Extreme Poverty Harder to End, and What Is the Current Profile of the World's Poor?" *Economic Premise* No. 125 (October), World Bank, Washington, DC.

ONE. 2017. *The 2017 DATA Report: Financing for the African Century.* Annual statistical report, The ONE Campaign, Washington, DC.

Ortiz, Isabel, Matthew Cummins, and Kalaivani Karunanethy. 2017. "Fiscal Space for Social Protection and the SDGs: Options to Expand Social Investments in 187 Countries." Extension of Social Security Working Paper 48, International Labour Office, Geneva.

Owori, Moses. 2017. "Pro-Poor Orientation of the 2017/18 Uganda Budget: What Will the 'Industrialisation' Focus Mean for the Poorest and Most Vulnerable People?" Report, Development Initiatives, Bristol, U.K.

Pace, Noemi, Silvio Daidone, Benjamin Davis, Sudhanshu Handa, Marco Knowles, and Robert Pickmans. 2018. "One Plus One Can Be Greater than Two: Evaluating Synergies of

Development Programmes in Malawi." *Journal of Development Studies* 54 (11): 2023–60.

Pan, Lei, and Luc Christiaensen. 2012. "Who Is Vouching for the Input Voucher? Decentralized Targeting and Elite Capture in Tanzania." *World Development* 40 (8): 1619–33.

Pernechele, Valentina, Jean Balié, and Léopold Ghins. 2018. *Agricultural Policy Incentives in Sub-Saharan Africa in the Last Decade (2005–2016).* Rome: Food and Agriculture Organization of the United Nations (FAO).

Ravallion, Martin. 2009. "Do Poorer Countries Have Less Capacity for Redistribution?" Policy Research Working Paper 5046, World Bank, Washington, DC.

Reproductive Health Supplies Coalition. 2018. "Global Contraceptive Commodity Gap Analysis 2018." Report, Reproductive Health Supplies Coalition, Brussels.

Resnick, Danielle, and David Mather. 2016. "Agricultural Input Policy under Uncertainty: Applying the Kaleidoscope Model to Ghana's Fertilizer Subsidy Program (2008–2015)." IFPRI Discussion Paper 01551, International Food Policy Research Institute, Washington, DC.

Reynolds, Hayley, and Ludvig Wier. 2016. "Estimating Profit Shifting in South Africa Using Firm-Level Tax Returns." United Nations University World Institute for Development Economics Research (UNU-WIDER) Working Paper 128, UNU-WIDER, Helsinki, Finland.

Ricker-Gilbert, Jacob. 2016. "Review of Malawi's Farm Input Subsidy Program in 2016 and Direction for Re-design." Report prepared for the Poverty and Social Impact Analysis of the Malawi Farm Input Subsidy Program, World Bank, Washington, DC.

Roberts, Simon. 2017. "(Re)shaping Markets for Inclusive Economic Activity: Competition and Industrial Policies Relating to Food Production in Southern Africa." CCRED Working Paper 12/2017, Centre for Competition, Regulation and Economic Development, Johannesburg, South Africa.

Roe, Alan, and Samantha Dodd. 2017. "Dependence on Extractive Industries in Lower-Income Countries: The Statistical Tendencies." United Nations University World Institute for Development Economics Research (UNU-WIDER) Working Paper 98, UNU-WIDER, Helsinki, Finland.

Rogger, Daniel. 2017. "Who Serves the Poor? Surveying Civil Servants in the Developing World." Policy Research Working Paper 8051, World Bank, Washington, DC.

Rustad, Siri Aas, Philippe Le Billon, and Päivi Lujalac. 2017. "Has the Extractive Industries Transparency Initiative Been a Success? Identifying and Evaluating EITI Goals." *Resources Policy* 51: 151–62.

Sabarwal, Shwetlena, David K. Evans, and Anastasia Marshak. 2014. "The Permanent Input Hypothesis: The Case of Textbooks and (No) Student Learning in Sierra Leone." Policy Research Working Paper 7021, World Bank, Washington, DC.

Sarr, Babacar. 2016. "Assessing Revenue Authority Performance in Developing Countries: A Synthetic Control Approach." *International Journal of Public Administration* 39 (2): 146–56.

Schmidt-Traub, Guido. 2015. "Investment Needs to Achieve the Sustainable Development Goals: Understanding the Billions and Trillions." SDSN Working Paper, Sustainable Development Solutions Network, United Nations, New York.

SDI (Sustainable Development Institute). 2014. "Liberia: Poverty in the Midst of Plenty—How Post-War Iron Ore Mining Is Failing to Meet Local People's Expectations." Report, SDI, Monrovia, Liberia.

Sdralevich, Carlo, Randa Sab, Younes Zouhar, and Giorgia Albertin. 2014. "Subsidy Reform in the Middle East and North Africa: Recent Progress and Challenges Ahead." Departmental Paper No. 14/08, International Monetary Fund, Washington, DC.

Shimeles, Abebe, Daniel Zerfu Gurara, and Dawit Birhanu Tessema. 2015. "Market Distortions and Political Rent: The Case of Fertilizer Price Divergence in Africa." IZA Discussion Paper 8998, Institute for the Study of Labor (IZA), Bonn.

Speidel, Joseph. 2018. "Africa's Population Challenge." Unpublished report, Bixby Center for Global Reproductive Health, University of California, San Francisco.

Sumner, Andy. 2012. "From Deprivation to Distribution: Is Global Poverty Becoming a Matter of National Inequality?" IDS Working Paper 394, Institute of Development Studies, Brighton, U.K.

———. 2016. *Global Poverty: Deprivation, Distribution, and Development Since the Cold War.* Oxford, U.K.: Oxford University Press.

Sun, Daxin, Haksoon Ahn, Tomas Lievens, and Wu Zeng. 2017. "Evaluation of the Performance of National Health Systems in

2004–2011: An Analysis of 173 Countries." *PLoS One* 12 (3): e0173346.

Talbot, Theodore, Stefan Dercon, and Owen Barder. 2017. "Payouts for Perils: How Insurance Can Radically Improve Emergency Aid." Report, Center for Global Development, Washington, DC.

UN (United Nations). 2015. "Addis Ababa Action Agenda of the Third International Conference on Financing for Development." Resolution (A/Res/69/313) adopted by the General Assembly on July 27, UN.

UNCTAD (United Nations Conference on Trade and Development). 2015. *World Investment Report 2015*. Geneva: UNCTAD.

Van Parys, Stefan, and Sebastian James. 2010. "Why Lower Tax Rates May Be Ineffective to Encourage Investment: The Role of the Investment Climate." Working Paper 10/676, Faculty of Economics and Business Administration, Ghent University, Belgium.

Vegas, Emiliana, and Chelsea Coffin. 2015. "When Education Expenditure Matters: An Empirical Analysis of Recent International Data." *Comparative Education Review* 59 (2): 289–304.

WHO (World Health Organization). 2017. *Global Tobacco Epidemic, 2017: Monitoring Tobacco Use and Prevention Policies*. Geneva: WHO.

WHO and UN-Water (World Health Organization and United Nations Water). 2017. *Financing Universal Water, Sanitation and Hygiene under the Sustainable Development Goals: UN-Water Global Analysis and Assessment of Sanitation and Drinking-Water (GLAAS) 2017 Report*. Geneva: WHO.

World Bank. 2013a. "Service Delivery Indicators: Senegal, April 2012." Report No. 90372, World Bank, Washington, DC.

———. 2013b. "Service Delivery Indicators: Tanzania, April 2012." Report No. 90373, Washington, DC: World Bank.

———. 2017. *Africa's Pulse: An Analysis of Issues Shaping Africa's Economic Future*, vol. 16 (October). Washington, DC: World Bank.

———. 2018a. "All Hands on Deck: Reducing Stunting through a Multisectoral Approach in Sub-Saharan Africa." Report, World Bank, Washington, DC.

———. 2018b. "2014 Tax Increase on Tobacco and Results of Modelling the Impact of Additional Tobacco Tax Policy Adjustments." Report of the Global Tobacco Control Program, World Bank, Washington, DC.

———. 2018c. *World Development Report 2018: Learning to Realize Education's Promise*. Washington, DC: World Bank.

World Bank Group and ACF (African Competition Forum). 2016. "Breaking Down Barriers: Unlocking Africa's Potential through Vigorous Competition Policy." Report No. 106717, World Bank, Nairobi, Kenya.

World Bank and IMF (International Monetary Fund). 2015. "From Billions to Trillions: Transforming Development Finance. Post-2015 Financing for Development: Multilateral Development Finance." Statement by the heads of the African Development Bank, Asian Development Bank, European Bank for Reconstruction and Development, European Investment Bank, Inter-American Development Bank, World Bank Group, and IMF. Document DC2015-0002 of the Development Committee, World Bank and IMF, Washington, DC.

Zucman, G. 2014. "Taxing across Borders: Tracking Personal Wealth and Corporate Profits." *Journal of Economic Perspectives* 28 (4): 121–48.

www.ingramcontent.com/pod-product-compliance
Lightning Source LLC
Chambersburg PA
CBHW050900210326
41597CB00002B/31

* 9 7 8 1 4 6 4 8 1 2 3 2 3 *